PARLIAMENTARY SOVEREIGNTY IN THE UK CONSTITUTION

The status of the doctrine of parliamentary sovereignty in the contemporary UK constitution is much contested. Changes in the architecture of the UK constitution, diminishing academic reverence for the doctrine, and a more expansive vision of the judicial role all present challenges to the relevance, coherence and desirability of this constitutional fundamental.

At a time when the future of the sovereignty of Parliament may look less than assured, this book develops an account of the continuing significance of the doctrine. It argues that a rejuvenation of the manner and form theory is required to understand the present status of parliamentary sovereignty. Addressing the critical challenges to the doctrine, it contends that this conception of legally unlimited legislative power provides the best explanation of contemporary developments in UK constitutional practice, while also possessing a normative appeal that has previously been unrecognised. This modern shift to the manner and form theory is located in an account of the democratic virtue of parliamentary sovereignty, with the book seeking to demonstrate the potential that exists for Parliament—through legislating about the legislative process—to revitalise the UK's political constitution.

Volume 4 in the series Hart Studies in Constitutional Law

Parliamentary Sovereignty in the UK Constitution

Process, Politics and Democracy

Michael Gordon

·H A R T·
PUBLISHING
OXFORD AND PORTLAND, OREGON
2015

Published in the United Kingdom by Hart Publishing Ltd
16C Worcester Place, Oxford, OX1 2JW
Telephone: +44 (0)1865 517530
Fax: +44 (0)1865 510710
E-mail: mail@hartpub.co.uk
Website: http://www.hartpub.co.uk

Published in North America (US and Canada) by
Hart Publishing
c/o International Specialized Book Services
920 NE 58th Avenue, Suite 300
Portland, OR 97213-3786
USA
Tel: +1 503 287 3093 or toll-free: (1) 800 944 6190
Fax: +1 503 280 8832
E-mail: orders@isbs.com
Website: http://www.isbs.com

British Library Cataloguing in Publication Data
Data Available

ISBN: 978-1-84946-465-9

Typeset by Compuscript Ltd, Shannon
Printed and bound in Great Britain by
CPI Group (UK) Ltd, Croydon CR0 4YY

For my Mum

Acknowledgements

This book explores a subject which I have been grappling with over a number of years. I have accrued a great many personal debts during this time, and owe thanks to a lot of people.

The argument presented here develops and expands on claims originally defended as part of my PhD thesis, completed at the University of Manchester in 2011. I could not have asked for a better supervisor than Rodney Brazier, who was an immense source of advice and encouragement during my time in Manchester, and gave generous comments and feedback which were invaluable to the development of my thesis. I was also fortunate to benefit from the insights of Joseph Jaconelli and Anthony Bradley, who, as my examiners, gave me much to think about when beginning the process of expanding my thesis into this monograph.

I'm also grateful to those who have provided me with opportunities to present papers on various aspects of this work over the last few years—in particular, Roger Masterman, Keith Ewing, and successive convenors of the SLS Public Law stream: Javier Garcia Oliva, Ann Lyon and John Stanton. The comments and questions I received from participants at these seminars were of great help when refining and developing my arguments about parliamentary sovereignty, and I've tried to respond to many of the (very useful) challenges posed to my initial claims in this book.

Whether at these seminars or elsewhere, I'm grateful to all those colleagues who have taken the time to discuss the ideas I defend here over the last few years—there are too many to name individually, but the (hopefully ongoing) conversations I've been able to benefit from have considerably improved the overall argument I make in this book.

The School of Law and Social Justice at the University of Liverpool has provided an ideal setting in which to pursue my research, and I'd like to thank all of my colleagues there for contributing to the cultivation of a stimulating, highly supportive, and good humoured academic environment. I also thank the School for providing me with a period of research leave in semester 2 of 2013/14 to complete this work, and successive cohorts of undergraduate Law students for asking many and varied questions about parliamentary sovereignty in general, and the manner and form theory in particular.

There are a number of friends and colleagues who deserve special thanks, for engaging in discussions which prompted me to sharpen my ideas and reasoning, while also offering more general feedback and support at various times while I have been working on this research; in particular, Eleanor Drywood, John Fanning, Michelle Farrell, Matt Gibson, Myles Harrison, Thomas Horsley, Majida Ismael, James Organ, John Picton, Stephanie Reynolds, Helen Stalford,

Brian Thompson and Adam Tucker. I'm especially grateful to Michael Dougan, with whom I collaborated on early work on the European Union Act 2011. The arguments I make relating to this crucial statute here (for which I alone accept responsibility) have doubtlessly been enhanced by this initial joint research, and the comments Michael offered on the sections of this text he kindly read in draft form also certainly helped to improve the final book.

At Hart Publishing, I'm grateful to Richard Hart, for his enthusiasm about my initial proposal, Rachel Turner, for managing the process up to submission so efficiently, and Mel Hamill and the production team, for turning my manuscript into a polished final product.

Finally, I thank my family, for their constant support and inspiration. Will, Beth and Ady; my Dad, Andrew; and Grandma, Teresa, have encouraged and motivated me throughout, without which I would not have been able to complete this long-running project. Most of all, I'm incredibly grateful to my Mum, Ann, for everything she has done for me along the way, and it is to her that this book is dedicated.

Mike Gordon
Nov 2014

Summary Table of Contents

Detailed Table of Contents

Parliamentary Sovereignty in the UK Constitution: Process, Politics and Democracy

Introduction

THE SUPREMACY OF Parliament *is* the Constitution'. So wrote Sir Ivor Jennings in *The Law and the Constitution*, a claim repeated as late as 1959.[1] Such bold rhetoric might today appear rather antiquated. For in the contemporary UK constitution, this fundamental legal doctrine is increasing challenged in stark terms: it is archaic,[2] infelicitous,[3] immature,[4] outdated,[5] austere,[6] a spectre,[7] a puzzle,[8] a shadow,[9] a myth,[10] a pretence,[11] a prison,[12] a relic,[13] a straitjacket,[14] even an impossibility.[15] Changes in the constitutional architecture of the UK, from membership of the European Union to devolution,

---

[1] WI Jennings, *The Law and the Constitution*, 5th edn (London, University of London Press, 1959) 314.

[2] G Letsas, 'Lord Sumption's Attack on Strasbourg: More Than Political Rhetoric?', *UK Constitutional Law Association Blog* (9 December 2013): www.ukconstitutionallaw.org.

[3] TRS Allan, *The Sovereignty of Law: Freedom, Constitution, and Common Law* (Oxford, Oxford University Press, 2013) 133.

[4] See M Elliott, 'Embracing "Constitutional" Legislation: Towards Fundamental Law?' (2003) 54 *Northern Ireland Law Quarterly* 25, 40, describing the decision in *Thoburn v Sunderland City Council* [2002] EWHC 195, [2003] QB 151—which poses a potentially profound challenge to the doctrine of parliamentary sovereignty—as the 'the UK constitution's coming of age'.

[5] J Laws, 'Law and Democracy' [1995] *PL* 72, 82.

[6] A Lester, 'The Utility of the Human Rights Act: a reply to Keith Ewing' [2005] *PL* 249, 252.

[7] NW Barber, 'The Afterlife of Parliamentary Sovereignty' (2011) 9 *International Journal of Constitutional Law* 144.

[8] ibid 148.

[9] J Mitchell, *Devolution in the UK* (Manchester, Manchester University Press, 2009) 221.

[10] ibid 219.

[11] I Leigh and R Masterman, *Making Rights Real: The Human Rights Act in its First Decade* (Oxford, Hart Publishing, 2008) 130.

[12] V Bogdanor, 'Imprisoned by a Doctrine: The Modern Defence of Parliamentary Sovereignty' (2012) 32 *OJLS* 179.

[13] See Lord Steyn in *R (on the application of Jackson) v Attorney General* [2005] UKHL 56, [2006] 1 AC 262, [102]: '[t]he classic account given by Dicey of the doctrine of the supremacy of Parliament, pure and absolute as it was, can now be seen to be out of place in the modern United Kingdom'. For praise of this 'modern hypothesis of constitutionalism', see J Jowell, 'Parliamentary Sovereignty Under the New Constitutional Hypothesis' [2006] *PL* 562, 570.

[14] AW Bradley, 'The Sovereignty of Parliament—Form or Substance?' in J Jowell and D Oliver (eds), *The Changing Constitution*, 7th edn (Oxford, Oxford University Press, 2011) 68.

[15] See the analysis of A Tucker, 'Uncertainty in the Rule of Recognition and in the Doctrine of Parliamentary Sovereignty' (2011) 31 *OJLS* 61; discussed chapter 3 of this volume, n 136.

have prompted reassessment of the Westminster Parliament's claim to possess a legislative authority which is unlimited by law. Academic reverence for the doctrine is certainly diminished, with many scholars increasingly convinced that the rule of law and basic human rights are too valuable to remain subject to the will of an elected legislature. Doubtlessly influenced by these trends, some of the UK's most senior judges have attempted to craft a more expansive vision of the judicial role, which could ultimately provoke a direct confrontation between the courts and Parliament.[16] Against this backdrop, we might wonder not whether the doctrine of the legislative sovereignty of Parliament *is* the constitution, but whether it is even still *in* the constitution.

At a time when the future of parliamentary sovereignty may look less than assured, this book argues that the doctrine remains a fundamental part of the contemporary UK constitution. Despite the constitutional change which has been experienced in the modern era, and despite the challenges which have been developed from the perspective of political or moral principle, the UK Parliament continues to possess legally unlimited legislative authority. Yet to be able to sustain this claim, we must reassess what it means to possess sovereign legislative power. In this respect, we must return to Jennings, and his understanding of the implications of legally unlimited legislative authority. For AV Dicey, recognised as the most authoritative exponent of this legal doctrine, while Parliament could enact law on any substantive matter whatever, there was one limit on its sovereign power: Parliament could not bind its successors.[17] This claim was crucially challenged by Jennings, whose manner and form theory of legally unlimited legislative power offered to Parliament an expanded law-making authority. Parliament's legally unlimited power was to be understood not only to allow the creation of law relating to any subject-matter, but also to permit the lawful enactment of legislation which altered the legislative process itself. For, as Jennings argued, so long as legislation was enacted in accordance with the 'manner and form' prescribed by law at a particular time—the legal rules establishing how legislative power was lawfully to be exercised—an Act of Parliament which changed the future 'manner and form' would itself be recognised as legally valid.

Jennings' manner and form theory has been much debated since it was first advanced in 1933.[18] Yet such debates have had a speculative air, in that Parliament has generally refrained from using its legislative power in such a way as to put these ideas to the test, while the Diceyan proposition that a sovereign legislature cannot bind its successors has retained the status of constitutional orthodoxy. In the contemporary UK constitution, however, these debates have moved rapidly

---

[16] See especially *R (on the application of Jackson) v Attorney General* [2005] UKHL 56, [2006] 1 AC 262 [107].

[17] See AV Dicey, *Introduction to the Study of the Law of the Constitution*, 8th edn (London, Macmillan, 1915).

[18] See WI Jennings, *The Law and the Constitution*, 1st edn (London, University of London Press, 1933).

from being academic to active. A series of recent developments prompt us to re-engage with the manner and form theory: first, ongoing attempts to understand the constitutional basis of the UK's membership of the European Union (EU); secondly, the decision of the House of Lords in *Jackson* as to the status of the Parliament Act 1949, and the state of the doctrine of parliamentary sovereignty more generally; and thirdly, the enactment, in the European Union Act 2011, of a scheme of statutory 'referendum locks' applicable to future legislative attempts to authorise the transfer of power or competence from the UK to the EU.

These developments pose critical challenges to the orthodox understanding of parliamentary sovereignty. Indeed, I will suggest that they demonstrate that the Diceyan conception of legislative sovereignty can no longer be maintained. Instead, Jennings' manner and form theory provides us with by far the best explanation of contemporary constitutional practice in the UK. And, as such, I will argue that a modern shift has occurred to the manner and form theory of parliamentary sovereignty: it must now be understood to represent the new constitutional orthodoxy in the UK.

Yet this book does not simply seek to defend the empirical claim that the manner and form theory has now been embraced in the UK constitution, and that the doctrine of parliamentary sovereignty persists, but in this shape. In light of the range of challenges to which the doctrine has been subjected in recent years, discussion of the sovereignty of Parliament has become increasingly defensive. It is has been enough, it often seems, to try to sustain the doctrine in the face of potent objections that it is no more. Much less attention, in contrast, has been given to consideration of the value or purpose of parliamentary sovereignty in a constitutional order. While necessarily engaging in defensive discussion of the continuing existence of parliamentary sovereignty, this book attempts at least to ensure that a more positive case for the doctrine is also explored from the very outset. It is all too easy to foresee the possibility that parliamentary sovereignty may be gradually eroded by future constitutional progress; in setting out clearly the function and virtue of the doctrine, at least what is at stake may more readily be appreciated.

This is of particular importance in relation to the manner and form theory, in light of its contemporary constitutional salience. To many, it will be less than obvious how the manner and form theory's status as the new constitutional orthodoxy should be received. This conception of parliamentary sovereignty may be thought to lack any clear normative justification. This is in part because Jennings failed to develop such an account, but also because subsequent manner and form scholars have generally viewed the theory as a way of tempering the absolutism of legally unlimited legislative authority.[19] As such, this book develops a new normative justification for the manner and form theory; one which is rooted in the democratic virtue of parliamentary sovereignty itself.

---

[19] See especially RFV Heuston, *Essays In Constitutional Law*, 2nd edn (London, Stevens and Sons, 1964) ch 1.

This democratic justification of the manner and form theory explains why it is appropriate to allocate to Parliament the legislative power to alter the future legislative process; using the theory of political constitutionalism as a framework, I argue that while legally unlimited, this power can, and will, be strongly conditioned by democratic politics. While it may appear that Parliament has the capability to abuse the power to alter the future legislative process—and bind its successors in the way that Dicey's orthodoxy sought to prevent—we should not, on this basis, feel compelled to withhold such power as a matter of law. Instead, concerns about the misuse of power—in this context, just as in relation to the substantive legislative authority of Parliament—can be comprehensively addressed at the level of political justification, rather than prohibited entirely as a matter of legal validity. Moreover, this democratic justification does not only serve to illustrate why the modern shift to the manner and form theory need not be a matter for regret, but also provides a basis on which that power might positively be used in the future. In an age of democratic disillusionment, the potential utility of the manner and form theory will be explored, and the possibilities it opens up for constitutional reform considered. In providing a number of ways in which citizens could be more directly engaged in the law-making process, I argue that the manner and form theory offers Parliament the potential—through legislating to alter the legislative process—to reinvigorate the democratic foundations of the UK's political constitution.

In developing this argument as to the contemporary constitutional authority of the manner and form theory, and a democratic justification for this conception of legally unlimited legislative power, I engage critically with a range of different accounts of the present status of parliamentary sovereignty, from common law constitutionalist claims that the doctrine is now subject to the overarching constraint of judicially articulated principle,[20] to attempts to sustain a more orthodox model of continuing sovereignty.[21] Most significant to the argument developed in this book, however, is the seminal work of Jeffrey Goldsworthy. For while the manner and form theory has received relatively little attention in recent years, and what it has received has been sporadic rather than systematic, Goldsworthy's work provides a powerful exception. Goldsworthy's procedure and form conception of parliamentary sovereignty bears similarity in many respect to the manner and form theory, in that it holds that Parliament's legislative authority extends to permit the lawful enactment of some legislation which alters the future 'procedure and form' for valid law-making.[22] Yet Goldsworthy does not accept in full the implications of the manner and form theory, instead seeking to preclude, as

---

[20] See especially Allan, *The Sovereignty of Law* (2013) n 3 above.
[21] See especially AL Young, *Parliamentary Sovereignty and the Human Rights Act* (Oxford, Hart Publishing, 2009).
[22] See J Goldsworthy, *Parliamentary Sovereignty: Contemporary Debates* (Cambridge, Cambridge University Press, 2010), expanding lines of argument initially established in J Goldsworthy, *The Sovereignty of Parliament: History and Philosophy* (Oxford, Oxford University Press, 1999).

a matter of law, the enactment of legislation making procedural changes which would diminish the substantive power of Parliament in future to legislate.

In seeking to reassert the manner and form theory, this book necessarily engages at length with the alternative 'procedure and form' model of parliamentary sovereignty, departing from the conclusions reached by Goldsworthy in a number of respects. First, I critique Goldsworthy's attempt to limit the scope of the procedural change which the manner and form theory lawfully permits, and argue instead that the concerns which prompt the development of this limitation—that Parliament might too readily restrict its future legislative capability—should be dealt at the level of (democratic) political justification, rather than legal validity. Secondly, I challenge the reliance of Goldsworthy (among others) on Hart's rule of recognition[23] as a practical explanatory tool to rationalise change to Parliament's legislative authority, rejecting as both unnecessary and undesirable the argument that we can characterise the change which has occurred to the doctrine of parliamentary sovereignty as change to the UK's rule of recognition. Thirdly, these differences in approach combine with respect to the crucial issue of statutory referendum requirements—of great contemporary significance in light of their inclusion in the European Union Act 2011—where I draw an alternative conclusion to that suggested by Goldsworthy's procedure and form model, in defending the legal permissibility of such legislative change to the future law-making process. As such, while there is a great deal to recommend Goldsworthy's important work on the doctrine of parliamentary sovereignty, my argument suggests that, in these respects, the manner and form theory, rather than the modified procedure and form model, provides a stronger account of the legislative authority of the UK Parliament.

My argument as to the present position of the doctrine of parliamentary sovereignty in the UK constitution develops in three parts. Throughout, I favour the terminology of the legislative 'sovereignty', rather than 'supremacy', of Parliament. While these terms can, in effect, be understood to be interchangeable, the language of sovereignty is preferred because it clearly indicates that the legislative power of Parliament is legally *unlimited*, rather than simply *ultimate*. As Hart noted, '[i]t is plain that the notions of a superior and a supreme criterion merely refer to a *relative* place on a scale and do not import any notion of legally *unlimited* legislative power'.[24] As such, the language of legislative sovereignty is more specific and establishes clearly the proper legal scope of the UK Parliament's law-making authority. While some—perhaps most notably Jennings[25]—have criticised the language of sovereignty as misleading, if we keep in mind that this is a legal concept rather than a claim to omnipotence, any such difficulties are avoided.

In Part I of the book, the nature and implications of the doctrine of parliamentary sovereignty are considered in detail. In Chapter one, the function and

---

[23] See HLA Hart, *The Concept of Law*, 2nd edn (Oxford, Oxford University Press, 1994).
[24] ibid 106.
[25] See Jennings, *The Law and the Constitution*, 5th edn (1959) n 1 above, 147.

virtue of the doctrine of parliamentary sovereignty in general are explored, developing a positive case for a constitutional order based on legally unlimited legislative authority. The manner in which the doctrine can be challenged is first examined, and the importance of separating claims about whether Parliament *is* sovereign from claims about whether Parliament *ought to be* sovereign—with respect to legal validity, as opposed to political justification—established. With respect to function(s), I suggest that the doctrine of parliamentary sovereignty is the central organising principle of the UK constitution, while also operating as a constitutional focal point—an overarching principle which serves as an access point to citizens for obtaining an understanding of constitutional rules, while also transmitting a symbolic (and contestable) message as to the potential legitimacy of the political system. The core virtue of parliamentary sovereignty, I argue, is that it ensures the constitutional primacy of (majoritarian) democratic decision-making, a claim which is then defended against a range of potential challenges, both practical and principled in nature.

In Chapter two, the manner and form theory of parliamentary sovereignty in particular becomes our focus. Jennings' account of the manner and form theory is discussed, and a number of minor difficulties with it are resolved, to establish a definition of this reconfigured understanding of legally unlimited legislative power. This account of the manner and form theory is then tested against four key objections. Two classic challenges, informed crucially by the work of Wade,[26] are initially assessed: first, that the manner and form theory is conceptually incoherent; and secondly, that the theory is unsupported by classic authority. Two modern challenges are then explored: first, that it is inappropriate to conflate considerations of manner *and* form in a common theory; and secondly, that the distinction between (lawful) procedural conditions and (unlawful) substantive limits on which the manner and form theory depends is unsustainable. These objections are rejected in turn, to establish that the manner and form theory provides a coherent potential account of the legally unlimited legislative power possessed by the UK Parliament.

The potential coherence of the manner and form theory having been demonstrated, in Part II we move on to consider the modern challenges posed to the doctrine of parliamentary sovereignty by contemporary constitutional developments in the UK. In Chapter three, a range of non-critical challenges, which do not serve to displace the doctrine of parliamentary sovereignty, are explored. The challenges posed by devolution and the enactment of the Human Rights Act 1998 are considered, and I argue that these significant constitutional developments are compatible with the doctrine. The challenge posed by common law constitutionalist theory is then addressed; I reject this as an unsustainable interpretation of the foundations of the UK constitution, which is both empirically unsound, and—because it is undemocratic and imprecise—normatively unattractive. While

---

[26] See especially HWR Wade, 'The Basis of Legal Sovereignty' (1955) 13 *CLJ* 172.

I argue on this basis that common law constitutionalism cannot serve to limit or qualify the legally unlimited legislative authority of Parliament, the possibility of the theory nevertheless obtaining further traction is acknowledged, with this issue providing a theme which runs throughout the remainder of Part II.

The three critical contemporary challenges to parliamentary sovereignty are then considered. In Chapter four, the constitutional challenge posed by the UK's membership of the EU is assessed. A number of potential explanations of the domestic constitutional basis of EU law are evaluated, and I argue that a manner and form reading of the European Communities Act 1972 provides the best account of the reconciliation which has been achieved between the sovereignty of Parliament and the supremacy of EU law. The starting point that Parliament has, in effect, created a new manner and form for the enactment of valid legislation which is substantively incompatible with EU law is taken further in Chapter five. Here, the legal status of the Parliament Acts 1911 and 1949, as examined by the House of Lords in the leading modern case of *Jackson*,[27] is addressed. In rejecting a common law constitutionalist analysis of *Jackson*, and attempts to reconcile the decision with the orthodox Diceyan understanding of parliamentary sovereignty, I suggest that we find further evidence here of the contemporary salience of the manner and form theory. For in *Jackson* we have confirmation from the Law Lords that Parliament has explicitly altered the manner and form required to produce valid future legislation, albeit in a way which creates an alternative law-making process, rather than modifies the traditional legislative formula.

In Chapter six, the culmination of this constitutional pattern is identified and explored: the explicit enactment by Parliament, in the European Union Act 2011, of a scheme of statutory 'referendum requirements' which explicitly purports to alter the future manner and form by supplementing the traditional legislative process. The legal effectiveness of these statutory referendum requirements is assessed, and I argue that a manner and form analysis of the 2011 Act provides the most convincing explanation of the constitutional change which has occurred. I defend this conclusion against a number of objections—in particular, I argue that such referendum requirements must be considered *procedural* conditions, and thus legally valid (unless or until repealed), notwithstanding the impact they may have on the practical power of Parliament in future to legislate. On the basis of the arguments developed in Part II, I therefore conclude overall that a modern shift to the manner and form theory has occurred in the UK constitution: this conception of parliamentary sovereignty provides the best explanation of the contemporary change which has occurred, and must now be recognised as the new orthodoxy in relation to the legislative power of Parliament.

Finally, in Part III, the implications of this modern shift in constitutional understanding are explored; in particular, the virtue and function of the manner and form theory are evaluated. In Chapter seven, I develop a new normative

---

[27] *R (on the application of Jackson) v Attorney General* [2005] UKHL 56, [2006] 1 AC 262.

justification for the manner and form theory of legally unlimited legislative authority. Rooted in a framework provided by political constitutionalist theory, this democratic justification for the manner and form theory demonstrates that, while Parliament's power to alter the future legislative process is unlimited as matter of law, it is structured and conditioned by the operation of the democratic political system. On this basis, I argue that potential concerns as to the use of the legislative power to alter the future manner and form can—and should—be dealt with as matters of political justification, rather than questions of legal validity. I then outline the normative (democratic political) framework in which these issues fall to be considered, suggesting in particular that the notion 'Parliament cannot bind its successors'—although fundamentally flawed as a statement of the legal scope of parliamentary legislative authority—can be usefully re-purposed as a strong political injunction (or perhaps even a binding constitutional convention).

The book concludes, in Chapter eight, by examining the potential utility of the manner and form theory. I argue that the democratic justification set out in Chapter seven not only demonstrates that the modern shift to this conception of parliamentary sovereignty in the UK is a welcome development, but also provides a substantive guide to the future potential use of the expanded legislative power which must now be recognised. I outline and explain the condition of use which obtains for the exercise of this power to be politically justified: that Parliament's legislative power to alter the future legislative process will be used to achieve democratic ends. A number of potential ways in which this power could be used are then sketched, including democratic reform of the existing legislative institutions, the existing legislative process, and the possibility of achieving structural change to the UK constitution itself. In light of the democratic disillusionment of citizens with the contemporary state of the UK's political constitution, I argue that change to the legislative process might be considered as part of a broader strategy to address this fundamental democratic, political and constitutional challenge. While I do not set out to demonstrate definitively the desirability of any particular change to the legislative process—such as statutory referendum requirements or standing citizens' assemblies—which might have the effect of more fully engaging citizens in the operation of the political system, that acceptance of the manner and form theory opens up a range of such possibilities to legitimate consideration is suggested to be a core part of the virtue of this conception of legislative authority. I finally reflect on the broader possibility that, if used extensively, the manner and form theory may provoke a challenge to the doctrine of *parliamentary* sovereignty. While this (very distant) prospect cannot be dismissed, I suggest that the disaggregation of sovereign law-making power from its present parliamentary location would prompt us to think carefully and creatively about how we might design future institutional arrangements which can accommodate the democratically desirable notion of legally unlimited legislative authority. Parliamentary sovereignty remains an important part of the UK's foreseeable constitutional future, but were it eventually to be displaced, the concept which underpins the doctrine—that legislative power should be legally unlimited in a democratic political system—could, and should, I argue, be retained.

The argument across this book therefore seeks to explore, in the context of the doctrine of parliamentary sovereignty in the UK constitution, the interaction between ideas of process, politics and democracy. This is not intended to be a laudatory account of UK constitutional exceptionalism—on the contrary, there are many real deficiencies with our present arrangements. Yet the manner and form theory of parliamentary sovereignty—which makes available the possibility of lawful and democratic change to the legislative process, rather than condemns this prospect as constitutionally forbidden—should be seen as part of the solution, rather than the problem. The challenge of thinking about how this power might justifiably be used is one which we need not evade. Instead, we might freely consider how legislating to change the legislative process might help to revitalise the democratic foundations of the UK's political constitution.

Part I

What is the Sovereignty of Parliament?

1

The Function and the Virtue
of Parliamentary Sovereignty

I. INTRODUCTION

WHAT IS THE sovereignty of Parliament? When seeking to establish a working understanding of this fundamental constitutional doctrine, it is customary, and indeed necessary, to begin with Dicey. For while the sovereignty of Parliament was conclusively established in the events and aftermath of the English Civil War,[1] around two centuries before the publication of the first edition of AV Dicey's seminal text *An Introduction to the Study of the Law of the Constitution* in 1885, the account of the doctrine developed therein still constitutes the framework within which modern debate about the legislative power of Parliament occurs. In Dicey's famous formulation:

> The principle of Parliamentary sovereignty means neither more nor less than this, namely, that Parliament thus defined has, under the English constitution, the right to make or unmake any law whatever; and, further, that no person or body is recognised by the law of England as having a right to override or set aside the legislation of Parliament.[2]

Two critical, related points can be discerned in this. First is the 'positive' notion that Parliament may 'make or unmake any law whatever', in accordance with which the UK's legislature is entitled to enact legislation relating to any substantive subject-matter. Secondly, and the 'negative' corollary of the first point, no other institution is empowered to reject legislation duly enacted by Parliament.[3]

---

[1] See J Goldsworthy, *The Sovereignty of Parliament: History and Philosophy* (Oxford, Oxford University Press, 1999). Goldsworthy argues that the supremacy of Parliament was recognised in the sixteenth century, and that the King in Parliament was 'in practice, fully sovereign' from the 1530s onwards (at 58, 229–30). But it was not until the English Civil War in the seventeenth century that it was confirmed that sovereignty was vested in the King in Parliament as a 'composite institution' comprising the Crown, House of Commons and House of Lords acting together in exercise of a shared power, with the competing notion that this authority had been afforded to the Crown alone, to be exercised with parliamentary consent, ultimately rejected (at 124–25, 230–31). See generally, C Hill, *The Century of Revolution: 1603–1714* (London, Thomas Nelson and Sons, 1961); C Hill, *Intellectual Origins of the English Revolution* (Oxford, Oxford University Press, 1965).
[2] AV Dicey, *Introduction to the Study of the Law of the Constitution*, 8th edn (London, Macmillan, 1915) 37–38.
[3] ibid 38.

Yet it must be clearly established what kind of unlimited power the doctrine of parliamentary sovereignty affords to Parliament, given the multiple meanings the notion of 'sovereignty' can be understood to bear.[4] According to Dicey, the legal sovereignty of Parliament was crucially distinct from political sovereignty; it was 'a merely legal conception, and means simply the power of law-making unrestricted by any legal limit'.[5] Political sovereignty, in contrast, was held by 'that body ... in a state the will of which is ultimately obeyed by the citizens of the state'.[6] In a democratic state—even the palpably imperfect, barely democratic state of Dicey's time[7]—the electorate would therefore be politically sovereign.[8] As a result, the doctrine of parliamentary sovereignty does not ascribe to Parliament the power of an 'omnipotent body'.[9] Instead, for Dicey, the purpose of the doctrine of parliamentary sovereignty was to give Parliament the freedom to 'legally legislate on any topic whatever which, in the judgment of Parliament, is a fit subject for legislation'.[10] The result of all this is not that there are no limits on the content of an Act of Parliament. The legislative power of any sovereign was, according to Dicey, subject to an external limit, 'the possibility of popular resistance',[11] and an internal limit, the fact that the sovereign 'exercises his powers in accordance with his character, which is itself moulded by the circumstances under which he lives, including under that head the moral feelings of the time and the society to which he belongs'.[12] Where sovereign power is vested in a representative assembly, it should 'produce a coincidence, or at any rate diminish the divergence, between the external and the internal limitations on the exercise of sovereign power'.[13] For Dicey, then, the doctrine of parliamentary sovereignty was consistent with the fact that there are limits on the substance of an Act of Parliament. They could not, however, be legal limits.

Parliament may therefore be subject to a range of political, moral or practical limits at any moment, but this does not endanger its claim to possess legislative sovereignty. For the notion of legal sovereignty is simply a claim about legal

---

[4] See, eg M Loughlin, *The Idea of Public Law* (Oxford, Oxford University Press, 2003) 72: 'Sovereignty has been given such a variety of ambiguous and confused meanings that many have suggested, in the interests of precision and rigour, the concept should be altogether abandoned'. Loughlin rejects this argument: see generally ch 5 for his particular 'relational' conception of sovereignty, which is described as 'the foundational concept underpinning public law', 93.

[5] Dicey, *Law of the Constitution* (1915) n 2 above, 70.

[6] ibid 70.

[7] At the time Dicey wrote the first edition of *Law of the Constitution*, despite the recent passing of the Representation of the People Act 1884 (the Third Reform Act), which created a uniform franchise between counties and boroughs, the right to vote was still only extended to men who satisfied a property qualification. As a result, approximately 58% of men were eligible to vote, but due to the total exclusion of women, only about 17% of the population in total: see generally P Foot, *The Vote: How It Was Won, and How It Was Undermined* (London, Bookmarks, 2012) 162–70.

[8] Dicey, *Law of the Constitution* (1915) n 2 above, 71.

[9] ibid 74.

[10] ibid 67–68.

[11] ibid 76.

[12] ibid 77.

[13] ibid 80.

power, and in particular, that the institution in which such sovereignty is vested has a power to make law which cannot be limited by law. Parliamentary sovereignty, as captured in Dicey's account, is thus a doctrine which affords what can be conveniently characterised as legally unlimited legislative authority to the UK Parliament.

In one sense, this is an alluringly straightforward notion. Yet what it means to possess legally unlimited legislative authority is a contested matter. The crucial point of dispute, which will be central to the argument developed in this book, is whether a legally sovereign legislature can use its legislative authority to limit itself, or its successors. Viewed from one perspective this would seem to be impossible, at least if claims as to the possession of legal sovereignty are to persist. For a legally sovereign legislature cannot be subject to any legal limits whatsoever, even those of its own creation. However, if this were the case, would it not constitute a limit on the power of that sovereign legislature, in so far as it would be prevented from enacting a particular kind of legislation—legislation which limited the legislature, or its successors? If so, we seem to reach an unsatisfactory, and somewhat bewildering, impasse: whether a parliament can or cannot limit itself, it is not legally sovereign.

This fundamental problem will be considered in detail in Chapter two. Dicey's attempt to resolve this difficulty, by arguing bluntly that a sovereign Parliament could not bind it successors, will be rejected in favour of the 'manner and form' theory pioneered by Ivor Jennings.[14] The contemporary salience of this manner and form approach, which admits of the possibility of a legally sovereign Parliament exploiting its legislative authority to enact certain kinds of 'limits' which would 'bind' itself and its successors, will then become the focus of the remainder of the book. Yet to adopt such a focus is not to engage in arid debate about the true nature and implications of unlimited power (whether legal or otherwise), for I will argue that this can no longer be viewed simply as an academic dispute, if indeed it ever was. Instead, I will suggest that both the continuing place of parliamentary sovereignty in the UK constitution, and the potential to reinvigorate the political foundations of the constitution, depend significantly upon our ability to accept a manner and form understanding of the doctrine.

But what is most important for present purposes is that the manner and form theory which will be defended in this book is a conception of parliamentary sovereignty, and not a challenge to, or rejection of, this doctrine. As such, before turning our attention to debates as to how the notion of legally unlimited legislative authority should be interpreted, and what its practical implications are, this chapter considers the idea of parliamentary sovereignty in itself. That is, it is concerned with the two propositions identified above which together provide the basis of either the orthodox Diceyan account of the sovereignty of Parliament,

---

[14] See generally WI Jennings, *The Law and the Constitution*, 5th edn (London, University of London Press, 1959).

or the competing manner and form understanding: first, that Parliament may make or unmake any law whatever; and secondly, that nobody may override or set aside its legislation. Initially, the manner in which these propositions can (and have) been challenged will be considered, in order to establish how the defence of parliamentary sovereignty contained in this book will proceed. Two further issues will then be examined, to set out the context in which this defence of parliamentary sovereignty will develop. These issues are the function and the virtue of the sovereignty of Parliament.

II. CHALLENGING THE SOVEREIGNTY OF PARLIAMENT

The challenges made to the essential core of the notion of the legislative sovereignty of Parliament have broadly taken two forms. First, the idea of legally unlimited legislative authority may be contested empirically, by attempting to demonstrate that the UK Parliament does not possess the kind of sovereign power attributed to it by Dicey. Such a challenge is invited by Dicey's approach to public law, by which the role of an academic constitutional lawyer was 'to state what are the laws which form part of the constitution, to arrange them in their order, to explain their meaning, and to exhibit where possible their logical connection'.[15] Applying this methodology, Dicey presented his account of parliamentary sovereignty as 'an undoubted legal fact', but if the existence of legal limits on Parliament's legislative power can be identified, this factual basis for the doctrine would dissolve.[16] Analysing contemporary constitutional developments to determine whether legal limits to Parliament's legislative power have emerged is therefore a potent means to challenge the doctrine of parliamentary sovereignty. The key challenges which are arguably presented by modern developments in constitutional practice in the UK will be considered in depth in Part II of this book.

The second form of challenge is one less obviously anticipated in Dicey's work. While Dicey attempted to 'perform the part neither of a critic nor of an apologist, nor of an eulogist, but simply of an expounder' with a duty 'neither to attack nor to defend the constitution, but simply to explain its laws',[17] as Martin Loughlin has argued, 'his theory of public law was also influenced by a particular outlook or political ideology'.[18] The nature of Dicey's political ideology, and how it may have influenced his explication of the sovereignty of Parliament, will be discussed shortly.[19] For now, however, it is sufficient to note that despite Dicey's intentions, an account of the sovereignty of Parliament cannot be treated as a neutral statement about the constitution as it is, or, some would argue, as it was. Descriptive

---

[15] Dicey, *Law of the Constitution* (1915) n 2 above, 31.
[16] ibid 66–67.
[17] ibid 3–4.
[18] M Loughlin, *Public Law and Political Theory* (Oxford, Clarendon Press, 1992) 141.
[19] See text at nn 126–40, pp 42–44. See also chapter 2 of this volume, pp 59–63.

claims about the status of parliamentary sovereignty within the UK constitution must be informed by an understanding of the normative scheme underpinning the doctrine. If the underlying normative framework lacks appeal, and if our acceptance of parliamentary sovereignty is thus no longer justified, it can be argued that the doctrine must give way to a more desirable conception of legislative authority within the constitution. As such, the doctrine may also therefore be challenged by reassessing the justification for parliamentary sovereignty, drawing on moral and/or political philosophy to contend that the notion of legally unlimited legislative authority ought not to be accepted as a constitutional fundamental.

The two forms of challenge outlined above are not, however, necessarily to be considered to be discrete from one another. Indeed, as will subsequently be seen, many of those who challenge the sovereignty of Parliament do so on both descriptive and normative grounds, engaging in something like a Dworkinian process of constructive interpretation to evaluate concurrently the 'fit' and 'appeal' of the doctrine.[20] The relationship between the descriptive and normative elements of public law scholarship lies at the heart of elementary debates about the nature of the subject, and the philosophy of law more generally.[21] That constitutional discourse must move beyond the purported objectivism of Dicey seems clear, but there is nevertheless danger in adopting the Dworkinian method if the result is, as Richard Ekins argues, that on this approach 'persuasive moral and political theory is legally effective'.[22] For even if we accept that developing an account of a constitutional concept, principle, or practice will be in some sense an interpretive exercise,[23] there may be good reasons for endeavouring to separate what the law is and what it ought to be at the level of practical decision-making. Such a position, following Jeremy Waldron, can be characterised as 'normative legal positivism',[24] and distinguished from the descriptive legal positivism of HLA Hart.[25] Rather than argue that there is no inherent connection between law and morality on purely analytical or conceptual grounds—the position defended by Hart—normative positivism contends that a legal system may best operate if 'it is set up in a way that enables people, by and large, to determine what the law is on a given subject without having to exercise moral judgment'.[26] There may be a

---

[20] See R Dworkin, *Law's Empire* (Oxford, Hart Publishing, 1998), esp chs 2 and 3.

[21] See, eg the debate between Cane, Craig and Loughlin as to the role of theory and values in public law: P Cane, 'Theory and Values in Public Law' in P Craig and R Rawlings (eds), *Law and Administration in Europe: Essays in Honour of Carol Harlow* (Oxford, Oxford University Press, 2003); P Craig, 'Theory and Values in Public Law: A Response' in *Law and Administration in Europe* (ibid); M Loughlin, 'Theory and Values in Public Law: An Interpretation' [2005] *PL* 48; P Craig, 'Theory, "Pure Theory" and Values in Public Law' [2005] *PL* 440.

[22] R Ekins, 'Judicial Supremacy and the Rule of Law' (2003) 119 *LQR* 127, 131.

[23] See, eg N Barber, *The Constitutional State* (Oxford, Oxford University Press, 2010) ch 1; Loughlin, *Public Law and Political Theory* (1992) n 18 above; Loughlin, 'Theory and Values' [2005] n 21 above, 61–65.

[24] J Waldron, 'Normative (or Ethical) Positivism' in J Coleman (ed), *Hart's Postscript: Essays on the Postscript to the Concept of Law* (Oxford, Oxford University Press, 2001).

[25] See HLA Hart, *The Concept of Law*, 2nd edn (Oxford, Oxford University Press, 1994).

[26] Waldron, 'Normative (or Ethical) Positivism' (2001) n 24 above, 30.

range of reasons why law can be said to function best if this separation is effected, but prime among them is the desirability of ensuring the clarity and accessibility of legal rules. For in circumstances of widespread disagreement about justice, to make legal validity contingent on moral acceptability is to introduce potentially significant uncertainty into debates about the meaning of rules, while also granting priority to the beliefs of the judiciary, who will be called on to resolve these disputes.[27]

On the basis that there is value in seeking to separate judgements about what the law is from what the law ought to be, the defence of parliamentary sovereignty advanced in this monograph is premised on this notion: the question 'is Parliament sovereign?' does not simply collapse into the question 'is it justified that Parliament is sovereign?'. It is nevertheless essential that both questions are addressed for reasons both pragmatic and principled. From a pragmatic perspective, I make explicit the normative framework underpinning my account of the sovereignty of Parliament—both with respect to the sovereignty of Parliament as a general concept, and the particular species of this concept which will be ultimately defended—so that those who disagree that there is space between the 'is' and the 'ought' are free to attempt to evaluate the extent to which my claims about the latter might have influenced my claims about the former. Much more important, however, is the principled reason that a purely descriptive account of the sovereignty of Parliament would be inadequate. While I do not accept that the descriptive claim 'Parliament is sovereign' is simply a function of the normative claim 'it is justified that Parliament is sovereign', direct engagement with this latter claim is still a vital part of public law scholarship in and of itself.

A principled basis as to the importance of engaging with the political foundations of public law can be found in the work of Loughlin, who has sought to re-cast the subject as 'an exercise in political jurisprudence'.[28] Loughlin contends that modern public law scholarship has been unduly focused on the identification and analysis of the valid legal rules within a constitutional system, and, as a result, has paid insufficient attention to the role of law in generating and sustaining the public authority required to produce those rules.[29] Public law cannot be detached from such political considerations, but nor can it become an untethered 'science of political right', which seeks to distil and impose a 'mode of right-ordering of public life that free and equal individuals would rationally adopt'.[30] Instead, for Loughlin, the task of public law 'is to negotiate between the various conflicting accounts of political right that form part of its evolving discourse'.[31] And it is conceived as an exercise in political jurisprudence because this task is necessarily both

---

[27] See, eg J Waldron, *Law and Disagreement* (Oxford, Clarendon Press, 1999); M Tushnet, *Taking the Constitution Away from the Courts* (Princeton NJ, Princeton University Press, 1999).
[28] M Loughlin, *Foundations of Public Law* (Oxford, Oxford University Press, 2010) 11.
[29] ibid 10.
[30] ibid 159.
[31] ibid 164.

political and juristic—both law and politics are together exploited by a public law which is an 'immanent practice that conditions and sustains the activity of governing'.[32]

Loughlin's work thus provides a vital corrective to accounts of constitutionalism which presume that law is an instrument which is employed only to limit political authority and activity, a deficiency which is particularly evident in the common law constitutionalist challenge to parliamentary sovereignty. The challenge posed by the common law constitutionalist analysis, according to which the legislative power of Parliament takes effect subject to, and is thus limited by, a range of fundamental, judicially articulated common law principles, will be considered further—and ultimately rejected as both empirically and normatively unsustainable—in Part II.[33] But beyond this specific context, Loughlin's work also poses more fundamental questions about the way in which debates about parliamentary sovereignty should proceed. Loughlin argues that 'lawyers sometimes forget' that the 'institutional authority' which the doctrine of legal sovereignty establishes 'is built on a political relationship'.[34] As a result, 'the question of how, when, and why this basic fact might alter' is ousted 'beyond juristic concern'.[35] Yet if, as Loughlin urges, public law is understood as an exercise in political jurisprudence, this must be reversed; claims about the sovereignty of Parliament must be 'rooted in an appreciation of the nature of the contemporary political condition'.[36] We must not only analyse the rules of positive law, but also their political underpinnings, in 'the search for constitutional understanding'.[37]

It is this approach which will be followed in this book: the legal rule which establishes the doctrine of parliamentary sovereignty, and the legal rules which might present challenges to this doctrine, will be assessed, but not in the abstract. Instead, the function and virtue of the sovereignty of Parliament will first be considered, to make clear the constitutional context in which the legal debates, discussed in depth in Part II, occur. Then, in Part III, the virtue and function of the manner and form conception of parliamentary sovereignty in particular— which, it will be argued, emerges from these legal debates as the best explanation of contemporary constitutional practice—will itself be evaluated.

For some, however, there might be a contradiction in the adoption of a method which is both positivist (following Waldron) and political (following Loughlin). Loughlin in particular would reject the distinction between description and justification outlined above. For Loughlin, it is the positivist method which has played a critical role in the subjugation of questions of authority to questions of validity in public law scholarship.[38] Moreover, Loughlin's account of the methodology

---

[32] Loughlin, *Idea of Public Law* (2003) n 4 above, 163.
[33] See chapter 3, pp 126–49.
[34] Loughlin, *Idea of Public Law* (2003) n 4 above, 159.
[35] Loughlin, *Foundations of Public Law* (2010) n 28 above, 271.
[36] ibid 272.
[37] ibid 272.
[38] See, eg ibid 10.

of public law is explicitly anti-positivist. Loughlin's approach is, in contrast, interpretive, and he maintains that such a theory of public law must 'fuse description and evaluation in a way that positivists are unwilling to recognise'.[39] Yet while it could well be true that a focus on legal validity has contributed to questions relating to the origin and nature of constitutional authority being overlooked by many UK public lawyers, with Dicey identified by Loughlin as a notable and influential example,[40] it is much less clear that this is a necessary consequence of adopting a legal positivist methodology. This is especially the case with respect to the normative variant of legal positivism outlined above, which explicitly seeks to establish a rough separation of law and morality at what Waldron calls the 'retail level'—that of practical decision-making about the meaning of specific legal rules—in an account of the purpose of law as a social institution (the 'wholesale level').[41] If this rough separation is constructed to prevent legal judgements about the existence and content of constitutional rules from simply collapsing into moral-political judgements about what they ought to be, it is done in the context of deeper understanding of the purpose, nature and values of public law. Questions of legal validity may thus be detached from questions of the authority and legitimacy of those rules, yet this will only be a conditional separation, effected to preserve overarching values upon which a specific constitutional system is based, which may include certainty, accessibility and democracy. Of course, if we are to obtain anything more than a partial understanding of the constitutional rule, doctrine or system under consideration, validity cannot be the entirety of our inquiry, as Loughlin's work makes palpably clear. But this can be done, and the political underpinnings of public law acknowledged and understood, without reducing the validity of constitutional rules to a function of their attractiveness.[42]

This is just as applicable to consideration of a fundamental constitutional norm like the doctrine of parliamentary sovereignty as it is to any other legal rule. Indeed, perhaps it is more important given the constitutional centrality of this doctrine, and its role in promoting some of the values which the deployment of a positivistic approach to legal decision-making might serve to sustain (prime among them democracy). Before we turn to discuss this central place of parliamentary sovereignty in the UK constitution, and the constitutional values which it reflects, one final point must be noted. When an explanation is developed of the virtue of, first, the doctrine of parliamentary sovereignty in general, and secondly, the manner and form conception of the doctrine in particular, this still cannot be an exercise in abstract and unrestrained moral or political reflection. It is here that Loughlin's notion of public law as political jurisprudence becomes of particular significance, for it emphasises that the aspects of political right which

---

[39] Loughlin, 'Theory and Values' [2005] n 21 above, 62.
[40] Loughlin, *Foundations of Public Law* (2010) n 28 above, 4.
[41] Waldron, 'Normative (or Ethical) Positivism' (2001) n 24 above, 415.
[42] For further discussion of this point, see M Gordon, 'A Basis for Positivist and Political Public Law: Reconciling Loughlin's Public Law with (Normative) Legal Positivism' *Jurisprudence* (forthcoming).

are of relevance to this assessment are those immanent in the practice of a specific constitutional order, rather than an ideal scheme which is imposed as the result of abstract normative contemplation. It may not always be clear precisely what political principles or values are embedded in the constitutional practice of an existing polity, and even those principles or values which are found to be present may clash, as Loughlin demonstrates when allocating to public law a role in managing these conflicts between competing notions. But the rationale for any particular constitutional rule or doctrine must be drawn from the practice of the system of which it is a part. For when this is done, it provides an authentic basis for the evaluation of both the adequacy of this rationale, and the extent to which the constitutional rule it supports can be understood to be normatively justified, or in need of reassessment and, potentially, revision. It is from this positivist and political perspective that the challenges to parliamentary sovereignty will be addressed, rather than one which views all constitutional doctrine as malleable, and, if found to be unappealing, susceptible to being interpreted away. The political underpinning of the doctrine must be explored for parliamentary sovereignty to be both understood and (potentially) justified, but the absence of a compelling normative justification could not be taken, in itself, to undermine the legal authority of this fundamental constitutional norm.

With the approach—and rationale for the approach—which will be adopted in this book now established, we turn to examine the legal doctrine of parliamentary sovereignty in its constitutional context. Shortly, the virtue of the doctrine will be explored, but first we consider the function(s) of parliamentary sovereignty in the UK constitution.

III. THE FUNCTION OF PARLIAMENTARY SOVEREIGNTY

A constitution has a number of critical functions to perform. It must constitute public authority, and create the institutions and processes by which that authority can be exercised. It must also condition that authority, and create mechanisms by which those who exercise public power can be held to account.[43] Indeed, both of these functions—establishing and conditioning the exercise of public authority—will inherently be fulfilled in the very act of creating a constitution. A further, related function that a constitution must perform is to make claims as to the legitimacy of the power it constitutes, and mechanisms of accountability it establishes.[44] This is not to say that a constitution must or will be legitimate, only that it must seek to establish its legitimacy in some way. This could be done through claims of popular authorship, or of benevolent purposes, or the reflection of

---

[43] See, eg A Tomkins, *Public Law* (Oxford, Oxford University Press, 2003) 18.
[44] See, eg D Feldman, 'None, One or Several? Perspectives on the UK Constitution(s)' (2005) 64 *CLJ* 329, 335.

fundamental principles of political morality in a constitution's rules.[45] Whether or not a constitution is successful in establishing its legitimacy will be a matter for much debate, yet it is an essential function of a constitution to attempt to do so. In the absence of a codified constitutional instrument in the UK, these crucial functions are fulfilled to a significant extent by the doctrine of parliamentary sovereignty. In particular, the sovereignty of Parliament is both the central organising principle, and the focal point, of the UK constitution.

It may, however, be argued that this is an incomplete account of the core functions of a constitution. In addition to ascribing to constitutions the three functions identified above—which are described as the 'institutionalisation', restraining, and 'legitimating' of the power established—a fourth is suggested by David Feldman. This is 'flexibility'; Feldman argues that a constitution must be sufficiently elastic so as 'to allow adaptation to the pressures that arise naturally from the dynamic development of an organic state structure'.[46] While flexibility is no doubt a desirable, and common, feature to be found in a constitution, I am not sure that it is an essential function which is equivalent to those of constituting, conditioning, and legitimating power. While unlikely to be found in practice, a set of completely fixed constitutional rules is possible to imagine, whereas a constitution which did not constitute, condition, or attempt to legitimate power is not. Yet, even if it were thought that the provision of flexibility was an essential constitutional function, as opposed to something which is simply desirable and frequently exhibited by constitutions, this is also a function which the doctrine of parliamentary sovereignty could be understood to fulfil in the UK. For in allocating to Parliament the power to make or unmake any law whatever, the doctrine clearly provides huge scope for constitutional change to be effected. Indeed, as will be evident when the modern challenges to parliamentary sovereignty are considered in Part II of the book, it has primarily been Parliament's own use of its extensive legislative power to alter the UK constitution which has prompted questions as to whether that law-making authority has now been limited. Nevertheless, even if flexibility were to be considered an essential constitutional function, there could be little doubt that this is something which is ensured in large part by the

---

[45] Perhaps the most famous example of this is the preamble to the US Constitution of 1789: 'We the People of the United States, in Order to form a more perfect Union, establish Justice, insure domestic Tranquility, provide for the common defence, promote the general Welfare, and secure the Blessings of Liberty to ourselves and our Posterity, do ordain and establish this Constitution for the United States of America'. A more modern example may be found in the 2005 Constitution of Iraq, the preamble to which is considerably longer (the English translation is around 550 words), but concludes: 'We, the people of Iraq, of all components and across the spectrum, have taken upon ourselves to decide freely and by choice to unite our future, to take lessons from yesterday for tomorrow, and to enact this permanent Constitution, through the values and ideals of the heavenly messages and the findings of science and man's civilization. The adherence to this Constitution preserves for Iraq its free union of people, of land, and of sovereignty'.

[46] Feldman, 'None, One or Several?' (2005) n 44 above, 336.

existence of the doctrine of parliamentary sovereignty.[47] While the discussion of the function of parliamentary sovereignty which follows could arguably therefore be extended, the focus instead falls on the two constitutional roles discharged by the doctrine which are of greatest significance, and often fail to be appreciated.

A. A Central Organising Principle

The doctrine of parliamentary sovereignty serves as the central organising principle of the UK constitution. The legislative power which the doctrine attributes to Parliament is a key source of legal authority in the UK, but it is not the only source. The common law, as interpreted by the courts, is an independent locus of authority, as is the royal prerogative, which vests certain specified powers in the Crown, almost all of which are exercised on ministerial advice.[48] Yet while not all of the legal powers exercised by the institutions of the state flow from an allocation of capacity by Parliament (although many such powers do in fact flow from statutory authorisation), the legislative power of Parliament is hierarchically superior to all other constitutional authority. Legislation enacted by Parliament takes effect over and above any inconsistent rules of common law or prerogative powers, and can limit and modify both.[49] The supremacy of statute, which is derived from the doctrine of parliamentary sovereignty, means that all other constitutional rules and principles operate subject to the possibility that they may be altered, augmented or abolished by Parliament, even those rules and principles which do not derive their legal authority from Parliament. But it is not just the formal structure of constitutional norms which is organised by reference to the

---

[47] The role of constitutional conventions in ensuring flexibility would also need to be acknowledged, although many conventions may nonetheless be highly resistant to change: see R Wilson, 'The Robustness of Conventions in a Time of Modernisation and Change' [2004] *PL* 407.

[48] A notable exception could be a decision to appoint a Prime Minister after a general election which produces a hung Parliament, if a choice had to be made between a minority government formed by the party with the largest share of the vote, or a coalition of other parties which might command a majority in the House of Commons. *The Cabinet Manual: A Guide to Laws, Conventions and Rules on the Operation of Government*, 1st edn (October 2011) para 2.9 indicates that in such circumstances 'it is the responsibility of those involved in the political process, and in particular the parties represented in Parliament, to seek to determine and communicate clearly to the Sovereign who is best placed to be able to command the confidence of the House of Commons', although this does not exclude the *possibility* of the monarch having to exercise personal discretion as to who should be appointed Prime Minister.

[49] On the superiority of legislation over common law see, eg War Damages Act 1965 (reversing the decision of the House of Lords in *Burmah Oil Co v Lord Advocate* [1965] AC 75); Compensation Act 2006, s 3 (reversing the decision of the House of Lords in *Barker v Corus Steel* [2006] UKHL 20, [2006] 2 AC 572); Jobseekers (Back to Work Schemes) Act 2013 (reversing the decision of the Court of Appeal in *R (on the application of Reilly) v Secretary of State for Work and Pensions* [2013] EWCA Civ 66, [2013] 1 WLR 2239). On the superiority of legislation over the royal prerogative see, eg Bill of Rights 1689 (limiting or abolishing a range of 'pretended' powers claimed by the monarch prior to the English Civil War); Regency Act 1937 (providing for a regent to exercise certain royal functions while the monarch is under 18 or incapacitated); Fixed-term Parliaments Act 2011 (replacing the prerogative power to dissolve Parliament with a fixed statutory legislative term).

sovereignty of Parliament. The operation of the other branches of the state is also organised to a significant extent by reference to the relationship between these institutions and the sovereign Parliament.

The constitutional supremacy which is afforded to Parliament by its sovereign legislative authority plays an important role in controlling and structuring the activity of the executive. In order to obtain new legal powers, or to alter or supplement its existing powers, the government must gain Parliament's approval through the enactment of legislation.[50] When carrying out their allocated functions, ministers and officials must administer the law as it has been created by Parliament.[51] Ministers are also responsible to Parliament for the execution of their lawful functions, and the government must retain the confidence of the House of Commons (the chamber which has primacy within Parliament) to remain in office.[52] Similar considerations apply to the judiciary; the constitutional role of the courts is defined by their position relative to Parliament. The courts do not have the power to question the validity of Acts of Parliament,[53] although by statute they may be given specific powers to review the contents of primary legislation in some circumstances.[54] When courts seek to interpret legislation, they must do so in a way which gives effect to the intention of Parliament as expressed in the language used in the statute.[55] When reviewing the legality of action taken by public authorities in accordance with their statutory powers, the courts are ensuring that the executive is not exceeding the authority allocated to it by the sovereign Parliament.[56] The structure and composition of the courts—which may have a significant impact on their constitutional role—are also subject to legislative control,[57] and individual judges hold office provided that they are of good behaviour, subject to the possibility of removal on an address to both Houses of Parliament.[58]

---

[50] Novel executive powers cannot be obtained under the royal prerogative: *BBC v Johns* [1965] Ch 62.

[51] See, eg *Associated Provincial Picture Houses Ltd v Wednesbury Corporation* [1948] 1 KB 223.

[52] See *The Cabinet Manual*, 1st edn (2011) n 48 above, para 2.7; Fixed-term Parliaments Act 2011, s 2(3).

[53] *Edinburgh & Dalkeith Railway Co v Wauchope* (1842) 8 Cl & F 710; *British Railways Board v Pickin* [1974] AC 765. Arguments that this statement is no longer an accurate characterisation of constitutional principle will be considered in detail in chapter 3 of this volume.

[54] European Communities Act 1972, s 2(4); Human Rights Act 1998, s 4. The extent to which such statutory jurisdiction creates a challenge to parliamentary sovereignty will be considered in chapter 4 of this volume (with respect to membership of the European Union) and chapter 3 (with respect to the enactment of the Human Rights Act).

[55] See, eg *R v Gul (Mohammed)* [2013] UKSC 64, [2013] 3 WLR 1207, [38]–[40], [61]–[62].

[56] See, eg *R v Tower Hamlets London Borough Council, ex parte Chetnik Developments Ltd* [1988] AC 858, 872; *Porter v Magill* [2001] UKHL 67, [2002] 2 AC 357, [19].

[57] See, eg Constitutional Reform Act 2005, Part 3 (establishing a new Supreme Court for the UK).

[58] See, eg Senior Courts Act 1981, s 11(3); Constitutional Reform Act 2005, s 33. These modern statutes reiterate a legal position in relation to the tenure of the senior judiciary established by the Act of Settlement 1700. In practice, however, this power is simply not used: the only judge removed on an address to both Houses of Parliament was Sir Jonah Barrington in 1830: SA de Smith and R Brazier, *Constitutional and Administrative Law*, 8th edn (Harmondsworth, Penguin, 1998) 381.

The status of the doctrine of parliamentary sovereignty as the central organising principle of the UK constitution is therefore clear from two perspectives: it establishes the hierarchy of constitutional authority within which all legal rules and principles operate, while also providing a constant by reference to which the roles and activities of the executive and judiciary can be defined.

In some ways we can see its operation as a central organising principle to be a very formal role, clearly establishing the extent to which certain types of legal rule are valid, and the precise scope of the power of the other institutions of government. But in other ways the doctrine of parliamentary sovereignty is functioning in a much more subtle way when recognised as the central organising principle of the constitution. It operates as a crucial background condition, influencing and informing constitutional action even when considerations of legal power or validity are not directly in issue. That Parliament possesses legally unlimited legislative power does not inherently require a government to retain the confidence of the primary chamber of the legislature to persist in office. Nor does the language of parliamentary intention need to feature so prominently in judicial attempts to frame the process of statutory construction.[59] But Parliament's constitutional supremacy, an appreciation of which underpins both of these examples, is a consequence of its legal sovereignty. And if the doctrine of parliamentary sovereignty can therefore be seen to play a key role in organising the interactions between UK constitutional actors in a range of ways, it can be recognised to function both as a legal norm, and more than a legal norm, simultaneously.

But to understand the doctrine of parliamentary sovereignty as the central organising principle of the UK constitution does not give a complete account of its constitutional function, even when its dual role—in determining both precise questions of legal authority, and conditioning inter-institutional relationships—is understood. For to view parliamentary sovereignty to be a central organising principle is to observe the constitution from the inside, adopting the perspective of an internal constitutional actor familiar with the considerable intricacies of the UK's system of government. Yet the doctrine of parliamentary sovereignty also has an outward-facing function—that of a constitutional focal point—which can be understood instead from the perspective of the citizen.

B. A Constitutional Focal Point

The doctrine of parliamentary sovereignty can be understood to function as the focal point of the UK constitution. Whereas for constitutional actors—whether

---

[59] As Lord Griffiths noted in *Pepper v Hart* [1993] AC 593, 617, the courts have moved beyond a 'strict constructionist view of interpretation' based on the 'literal meaning of the language' to a 'purposive approach which seeks to give effect to the true purpose of legislation'. But these different approaches had a common aim: '[t]he object of the court in interpreting legislation is to give effect so far as the language permits to the intention of the legislature'.

ministers, parliamentarians, judges, or officials—the rules and practices of the UK constitution, and the roles of the institutions within it, will be a largely known quantity, this is much less likely to be the case for citizens. It may be easy to overstate the differences between codified and uncodified constitutions, which are united in their pursuit of the three functions identified above. Further, both codified and uncodified constitutions will be inherently incomplete, subject to contested interpretation, and susceptible to being modified by practice, conventions or understandings.[60] Yet where a constitution has been codified, it will at least have a tangible existence, and be available to citizens to locate, whether the text considered in the abstract makes much sense or not. In the UK, where no formal constitutional instrument is available, the notion of the sovereignty of Parliament provides an alternative focal point. This will admittedly offer a far less developed account of constitutional fundamentals than that provided by a codified text, yet this is not what conceiving of the doctrine as a focal point purports to offer. Instead, it is to view the doctrine of parliamentary sovereignty simply as a starting point for constitutional discovery.

The notion of the sovereignty of Parliament functioning as a constitutional focal point in the UK is important in two ways. First, it provides an access point for inquiries as to either the substance or structure of the UK constitution. As discussed above, when examining the doctrine's function as a central organising principle, parliamentary sovereignty plays a decisive role both in establishing the hierarchy in which the various rules of the constitution operate, while also conditioning the roles of the key institutions of central government. Queries as to either the status of particular constitutional norms or the manner in which particular branches of the state operate can therefore usefully proceed from an understanding of Parliament's legislative authority, for it is this sovereign law-making power which establishes the constitutional context in which the answers to such questions are found. But it is not the mere fact that an understanding of the doctrine of parliamentary sovereignty is essential to be able to resolve basic constitutional inquiries which makes it the focal point of the UK constitution. It is also the fact that the doctrine is both relatively visible and relatively comprehensible which makes it an appropriate constitutional focal point. For in a constitution beset by arcane offices, institutions and practices, Parliament (and in particular, the House of Commons within it) is a reasonably clear hub at the centre of UK political life. Further, while the notion of sovereignty is perhaps itself open to criticism for being esoteric, the broad terms of the idea as it applies to the UK Parliament can be captured quite concisely, without a slew of qualifications, when understood as legally unlimited legislative power. This is not to suggest that the sovereignty of Parliament is a perfectly accessible doctrine from which all search for constitutional understanding will seamlessly proceed and straightforwardly be resolved;

---

[60] See, eg M Foley, *The Silence of Constitutions: Gaps, 'Abeyances' and Political Temperament in the Maintenance of Government* (London, Routledge, 1989).

there is much complexity both within and stemming from this notion. Yet a focal point which is to some extent imperfect remains worthwhile, for its purpose is not to obscure uncertainty or offer easy answers. Instead, to understand parliamentary sovereignty to be the focal point of the UK constitution is to see it as simply providing a basic premise from which attempts to explore the operation of the constitution—an authentic account of which must include recognition of its contested, ambiguous or even contradictory elements—can begin.

The second sense in which this constitutional focal point is important veers away from the practical, and towards the symbolic. For in addition to providing citizens with an access point to understand the constitution, the doctrine of parliamentary sovereignty transmits a prominent message about the principled foundation on which the UK's system of government is based. It is a well-known notion that a constitution may have symbolic meaning, representing something (or some things) significant about the political life of the community which it constitutes.[61] There are a number of difficulties with this idea, for it is only in the act of constitution that the polity which is constituted becomes defined, inherently limiting the extent to which the values of a community may be represented in a foundational constitutional instrument.[62] Further, it has been suggested that many constitutions do not in fact reflect the values actually held by their citizens, again limiting the extent to which grand claims about the symbolic meaning of constitutional instruments, or norms, can be made.[63] And in the context of the UK in particular, some reject entirely the notion that the constitution even has a normative foundation, due to its lack of a formal constitutional text.[64] However, while the limitations of the constitution as a symbol must be recognised, such difficulties are no more acute in the context of an uncodified, as compared to a codified, constitution. While an uncodified constitution such as that of the UK may suffer from an inability to make sweeping declaratory statements of constitutional benevolence, it is just as capable of communicating claims about the political values of a community as a formal constitutional instrument. The key constitutional message given symbolic representation in the doctrine of parliamentary sovereignty is that of the primacy of democracy.

What is precisely meant by the primacy of democracy will be discussed in more detail below; for establishing this is, I will argue, the central virtue of parliamentary sovereignty. In essence, this central virtue of the doctrine is that it ensures,

---

[61] This notion has featured prominently in literature exploring attitudes to the US Constitution: see, eg ES Corwin, 'The Constitution as Instrument and as Symbol' (1936) 30 *American Political Science Review* 1071; M Lerner, 'Constitution and Court as Symbols' (1937) 46 *Yale Law Review* 1290; S Levinson, *Constitutional Faith* (Princeton NJ, Princeton University Press, 1988).

[62] See H Lindahl, 'Constituent Power and Reflexive Identity: Towards an Ontology of Collective Selfhood' in M Loughlin and N Walker (eds), *The Paradox of Constitutionalism* (Oxford, Oxford University Press, 2007) 19.

[63] See M Versteeg, 'Unpopular Constitutionalism' (2014) 89 *Indiana Law Journal* 1133.

[64] See, eg FF Ridley, 'There is No British Constitution: A Dangerous Case of the Emperor's Clothes' (1988) 41 *Parliamentary Affairs* 340, 359.

by allocating sovereign legislative power to Parliament, that the institution of UK central government which is democratically elected, representative and account-able has the final authority to determine the legal rules of the state. For present purposes, however, we are less concerned with how the doctrine of the sovereignty of Parliament ensures democratic government in the UK, than with the signals it transmits to this effect. For, when considering the function of the doctrine as a constitutional focal point, the substance of the message is less important than the fact that a message is being broadcast at all. Here the sovereignty of Parliament, understood as symbolically representative of the fundamental constitutional value of democracy, operates to fulfil the legitimating function of the UK consti-tution which was considered above. To discharge this legitimating function, it will be recalled, a constitution does not have to establish definitively the legitimacy of the system of government it creates, but to communicate claims as to a potential basis for such legitimacy. For the mere transmission of such claims opens up the constitution to scrutiny: in making legitimacy claims, the constitution invites those claims to be examined. In this sense, simply engaging in a discourse of legitimation is sufficient to expose the constitution, its principled foundations and normative basis, to critical assessment.

Once this matter is recognised, it serves to diminish the concerns identified above as to the deficiencies of the constitution as a symbol, for what is represented can be understood as subject to contestation, rather than imposing an absolute constitutional vision. Yet a constitution must still offer a premise around which debates about constitutional values and legitimacy can develop. As the focal point of the UK constitution, the doctrine of parliamentary sovereignty is positioned so as to provide this premise. The notion of parliamentary sovereignty represents the democratic foundation of the system of government it organises. In so doing, the doctrine communicates outwards to citizens a message as to the potential legiti-macy of the UK constitution. And this is a significant constitutional function in so far as it means that the manner in which power is constituted and conditioned is revealed as eligible for, or indeed demanding of, ongoing evaluation.

C. Significance of the Function of Parliamentary Sovereignty

The function of parliamentary sovereignty can therefore be understood when its operation as both the central organising principle and the focal point of the UK constitution are recognised. When these two roles are appreciated, we can see that the doctrine of parliamentary sovereignty fulfils in the UK a number of essential functions which any constitution must perform: constituting, conditioning, and legitimating power. Understood as a central organising principle, the sovereignty of Parliament structures to a significant extent the operation of the UK constitution—the powers which have been established, the conditions under which these pow-ers are exercised, and the interaction of the institutions which employ them. This role is further enhanced when parliamentary sovereignty is conceived as a constitutional focal point, for it provides citizens too with a route to access an understanding of the operation of the constitution, rather than being exclusively orientated towards informed constitutional actors. And when considered as a focal point, we further see the legitimating function of parliamentary sovereignty: it transmits outwards a claim as to the legitimacy of the constitutional order established, as a symbol of the primacy of a representative democratic institution and process. Indeed, when the function of parliamentary sovereignty is fully understood, it provides us with scope to understand Jennings' claim that the doctrine '*is* the Constitution' as being more than mere rhetoric, and possessing genuine substance.[65]

This account of the function of parliamentary sovereignty is not designed to eulogise a basic constitutional norm, or to try to blur the fact that the doctrine fundamentally remains a legal concept. Instead, it is to try to understand this legal rule in its constitutional and political context, to demonstrate the centrality and significance of the doctrine of parliamentary sovereignty in the contemporary UK constitution. This does not mean, however, that the doctrine of parliamentary sovereignty 'is never anything more than shorthand for—that is to say, an abbreviation that stands in place of a careful account of—the complex, contingent, and possibly changing relationships between Parliament, legislation, and the courts'.[66] Indeed, in advancing the claim that public law must focus on the 'practices of constitutional actors', Gee and Webber have argued:

> Within this frame, the very idea of ultimate sovereignty is misplaced; claims about ultimate sovereignty in a customary constitution seem too certain for the ambiguous and changing relationships between constitutional actors that Dicey attempted to summarize and simplify in his definition of parliamentary sovereignty.[67]

Yet to eliminate the doctrine of parliamentary sovereignty from public law discourse in the name of enhancing our understanding of constitutional practice would actually have the opposite effect. For parliamentary sovereignty is not simply a term which reflects and captures constitutional practice; it is a doctrine which, I have argued, crucially shapes and organises that practice. The doctrine cannot be stripped away to reveal 'true' constitutional practice, for such practice is, to a significant extent, a function of the recognition by constitutional actors and institutions of the sovereignty of Parliament. As such, were discussion of constitutional practice to become disengaged from the doctrine of parliamentary

---

[65] Jennings, *Law and the Constitution* (1959) n 14 above, 314.

[66] G Gee and G Webber, 'A Grammar of Public Law' (2013) 14 *German Law Journal* 2137, 2148.

[67] ibid 2150. For a similar objection, from a different perspective, see NW Barber, 'The Afterlife of Parliamentary Sovereignty' (2011) *International Journal of Constitutional Law* 144, 154: 'it would probably be best if constitutional scholars ceased discussing sovereignty as an ongoing rule of the Constitution, however interpreted or reinterpreted. Attention could more profitably be directed to the questions that often hide behind such discussion, questions relating to the position and vitality of Parliament within the Constitution, the United Kingdom's relationship with Europe, the future of devolution, and so on'. See also V Bogdanor, 'Imprisoned by a Doctrine: The Modern Defence of Parliamentary Sovereignty' (2012) 32 *OJLS* 179, 194.

sovereignty, the result would be, in the short term, to produce an inauthentic account of the operation of the constitution. And in the longer term, shorn of the terminology of parliamentary sovereignty, the ordering of, and relationships between, UK constitutional actors would be susceptible to changing from their present state. Such change may, for some, be a good thing, and it is certainly the case that it cannot be absolutely prevented by continuing to understand the constitution as founded on the doctrine of parliamentary sovereignty. Yet if the doctrine is to be dispensed with, it must be done transparently, and justified, rather than cast off in pursuit of a better understanding of 'real' constitutional practice. For the operation of the constitution cannot be comprehended apart from the doctrine; and the nature of constitutional practice is revealed, rather than distorted, when parliamentary sovereignty, and its function, are understood.

It is of course the case, however, that the doctrine of parliamentary sovereignty is not the only way that the constitutional functions identified above could be fulfilled. Indeed, there is no doubt that, despite its central constitutional role, the doctrine could be replaced, whether by the adoption of a codified constitution or acceptance of some other fundamental doctrine or principle. But at a time when scepticism about the continuing constitutional relevance of parliamentary sovereignty abounds, we must at least appreciate what is at stake when we encounter casual calls for it to be abandoned. Such claims are often founded on the idea that the rule of law or principle of legality has replaced the doctrine of parliamentary sovereignty at the apex of the constitution.[68] Indeed, this notion has even been articulated judicially, most clearly by Lord Hope in *R (Jackson) v Attorney General*: 'The rule of law enforced by the courts is the ultimate controlling factor on which our constitution is based'.[69] In Chapter five it will be argued that the legal force of such a claim is limited, and in Chapter three the philosophical difficulties with the notion that the rule of law could become the ultimate principle of the UK constitution will be explored. But there is also a conceptual difficulty with this notion, which becomes evident when the function of the doctrine of parliamentary sovereignty is understood.

The rule of law cannot replace the sovereignty of Parliament as the fundamental norm of the UK constitution because it is incapable of performing the functions that this would necessitate. The rule of law is a principle of accountability, not of power. There is much dispute about how the principle of the rule of law is to be understood,[70] but perhaps at the very least it stands for the idea

---

[68] See, eg J Laws, 'Law and Democracy' [1995] *PL* 72; TRS Allan, *Constitutional Justice: A Liberal Theory of the Rule of Law* (Oxford, Oxford University Press, 2001); J Jowell, 'Parliamentary Sovereignty Under the New Constitutional Hypothesis' [2006] *PL* 562; S Lakin, 'Debunking the Idea of Parliamentary Sovereignty: the Controlling Factor of Legality in the British Constitution' (2008) 28 *OJLS* 1.

[69] *R (Jackson) v Attorney General* [2005] UKHL 56, [2006] 1 AC 262 [107].

[70] For an overview of the key lines of dispute, see P Craig, 'Formal and Substantive Conceptions of the Rule of Law: An Analytical Framework' [1997] *PL* 467; B Tamanaha, *On the Rule of Law* (Cambridge, Cambridge University Press, 2004).

that power should be exercised in accordance with the law. Yet the rule of law can have nothing to say about where that power should lie; instead, it simply recognises power which is vested elsewhere. It therefore cannot fulfil the dual role of constituting and conditioning power, unlike the doctrine of parliamentary sovereignty, and it cannot function as a central organising principle of a constitution. For it is a principle which, in these respects, is essentially empty; the rule of law simply refers an institution, actor or citizen seeking to understand the operation of the constitution to the powers which have been established by law. A substantive norm, or set of norms, is still thus required to determine the nature of the constitutional settlement—the actual powers which have, by legal means, been established—upon which the notion of the rule of law will be parasitic, and as to the content of which, the rule of law will be silent. Similarly, the rule of law is also incapable of serving as a constitutional focal point. For the fact that it makes reference to power, rather than establishes it, means that it can make no claims as to the legitimacy of the system of government which has been constituted. Instead, it simply indicates that the power ought to be lawful, which begs all of the important questions.[71]

It might be objected that a more substantive account of the rule of law could embed the principle with the kind of values necessary to allow it to fulfil these functions. Yet it is arguable that such a step—whether treating the rule of law as grounded in liberty,[72] equality,[73] or some other combination of values[74]—simply distorts the very nature of the rule of law. As Raz has argued, for example, on such an approach the rule of law effectively becomes 'the rule of the good law', and 'to explain its nature is to propound a complete social philosophy'.[75] Privileging a particular conception of the good by incorporating it into the rule of law may thus be objectionable in itself, but even aside from this, such an approach does not enable the objection outlined above to be evaded. For even on a substantive account of the rule of law, it remains a principle about power, not a principle of power. The rule of law may be understood to prescribe how power ought to be exercised by taking a more elaborate view of what legality constitutes, and perhaps even offer a principled marker against which an allocation of power can be assessed. But reference to this principle cannot tell us how power in a constitutional system is arranged and organised. Nor could even a value-laded account of the rule of law fulfil the legitimating function of a constitution. For even if there is some form of legitimacy bestowed on a constitution by virtue of its legal nature, whatever value is contended to be inherent in a substantive account of the rule of law will be lent to *any* system of government established by law. As a result,

---

[71] See, eg D Beetham, *The Legitimation of Power* (London, Macmillan, 1991) 17: 'On its own, legal validity is insufficient to secure legitimacy, since the rules through which power is acquired and exercised themselves stand in need of justification'.

[72] See, eg Allan, *Constitutional Justice* (2001) n 68 above.

[73] See, eg S Sedley, 'Human Rights: A Twenty-First Century Agenda' [1995] *PL* 386.

[74] See, eg T Bingham, *The Rule of Law* (London, Penguin, 2011).

[75] J Raz, 'The Rule of Law and its Virtue' (1977) 93 *LQR* 195, 195.

any claim to legitimacy which derives from the rule of law will be generic rather than specific, and does not represent the kind of *claim* of legitimacy that is made by a constitution with respect to the particular ordering of power which it has instituted. It will not therefore transmit a message as to the value of that particular constitutional system to citizens which can be scrutinised in a meaningful way, providing a starting point for analysis of the legitimacy of authority. For taking the rule of law to be the ultimate constitutional principle would tell us nothing about whether the system constituted was any more or less legitimate than any other governmental structure which could be established by law.

The rule of law cannot therefore operate as the ultimate constitutional foundation of any particular system of government. When the constitutional function of the doctrine of parliamentary sovereignty is understood, the need for a sceptical attitude to be taken to suggestions it could be replaced by the rule of law becomes clear. For while the potential exists for these two fundamental constitutional principles to clash—as was perhaps most obviously evident in Dicey's ultimately unsuccessful efforts to reconcile them[76]—this does not mean they are equivalent, such that one could displace the other. Parliamentary sovereignty is not inherently eternal, and could be superseded but, given the functions fulfilled by the doctrine, not by the rule of law. As such, attempts to maintain that the rule of law has achieved constitutional ascendancy must be rejected; while of real significance, the principle is incapable of providing the basis of a constitution.

With the function of parliamentary sovereignty now established, we can turn to the matter of whether this is an appealing doctrine to adopt to fulfil these essential constitutional functions.

IV. THE VIRTUE OF PARLIAMENTARY SOVEREIGNTY

The central virtue of the doctrine of parliamentary sovereignty is that it ensures the primacy of democracy in the UK constitution. This claim was introduced in outline above, when considering the doctrine's function in offering a legitimating claim as to the public authority constituted in the UK. Yet here, however, we are not simply interested in acknowledging the fact that such a claim is made by the doctrine of parliamentary sovereignty. Instead, the substance of this claim must be understood and assessed, to establish whether it is a credible basis on which a legitimate constitutional order can be founded. The substance of the claim is this: the legal norm which establishes Parliament's legislative sovereignty in the UK ensures the constitutional primacy of a representative democratic institution, and the democratic process of which that institution is a result.

That ensuring the primacy of democracy is the central virtue of the doctrine of parliamentary sovereignty, and will be the focus of the remainder of this chapter,

---

[76] Dicey, *Law of the Constitution* (1915) n 2 above, 402–9.

does not exclude the possibility that there could be others. Yet it is the relationship between parliamentary sovereignty and democracy which is of greatest significance, for it provides the central justification for the present and ongoing allocation to Parliament of legally unlimited legislative power. The democratic basis of the doctrine must therefore be understood, for it will be the necessary core of any account of the virtue of parliamentary sovereignty. Further, to the extent that other virtues might be identified, they seem to be derivative of the democratic nature of parliamentary sovereignty.

To argue, for example, that parliamentary sovereignty has virtue because it gives priority to decision-making which is political, or deliberative, or by a representative body, might seem to engage ideas of political constitutionalism—a theory which is concerned with establishing and analysing the key constitutional function(s) of politics. Whether this constitutional philosophy, most influentially articulated by John Griffith,[77] is a descriptive account of the relationship between law and politics as it is—'law is not and cannot be a substitute for politics'[78]—or a normative vision of what ought to be—'political decisions should be taken by politicians … this means by people who are removable'[79]—there is significant scope to develop an account of the political constitution which affords a prominent place to a notion of legislative authority which is limited by any means other than law. The potential synergy between parliamentary sovereignty and political constitutionalism, pivoting on the significance of accountability through politics, can be acknowledged here, but will become of greater importance in Part III of this book. For there I will argue that it is when a manner and form conception of parliamentary sovereignty is adopted that this relationship becomes most relevant. This is because there is not simply the possibility of using political constitutionalism to expound a democratic justification for this conception of parliamentary sovereignty, but also the potential to exploit the manner and form theory to reinvigorate the foundations of the UK's political constitution.[80] For present purposes, however, the priority which the doctrine affords to political limits cannot be considered to represent a free-standing virtue of parliamentary sovereignty, even if the desirability of political constitutionalist thinking were to be accepted. Even if thought to provide the most (or only) effective form of accountability, the value of political constitutionalism must be contingent upon whether the politics to which priority is afforded is democratic. And, as such, it is in the democratic foundation of parliamentary sovereignty that the virtue of the doctrine must be located. This

---

[77] J Griffith, 'The Political Constitution' (1979) 42 *MLR* 1.

[78] ibid 16.

[79] ibid 16. See T Poole, 'Tilting at Windmills? Truth and Illusion in "The Political Constitution"' (2007) 70 *MLR* 250, on the 'polemical' nature of Griffith's work. Poole rejects the claims of Adam Tomkins, made in *Our Republican Constitution* (Oxford, Hart Publishing, 2005) 37, 39, that Griffith's work was entirely descriptive: 253. See further G Gee, 'The Political Constitutionalism of JAG Griffith' (2008) 28 *Legal Studies* 20; G Gee and G Webber, 'What Is a Political Constitution?' (2010) 30 *OJLS* 273.

[80] See chapter 7, pp 293–301.

requires two issues to be considered. First, what should we understand democracy to mean and to require? Secondly, what is the relation between this understanding of democracy and parliamentary sovereignty?

A. Democracy: Majoritarian or 'Constitutional'?

As John Dunn has noted, democracy is 'today the overwhelmingly dominant, and increasingly the well-nigh exclusive, claimant to set the standard for legitimate political authority'.[81] Yet while it is almost beyond doubt that public power should be democratic to be legitimate, there is much scope for argument about what democracy means, and what it requires in practice. For Dunn, the idea is a 'very simple' one: 'that in human political communities it ought to be ordinary people (the adult citizens) and not extra-ordinary people who rule'.[82] From this basic idea of self-government by the people, we may discern a number of components of democracy. One such component would be the notion of popular sovereignty, by which, according to Tom Paine, 'a Nation has at all times an inherent indefeasible right to abolish any form of Government it finds inconvenient, and establish such as accords with its interest, disposition, and happiness'.[83] This is an extra-constitutional democratic notion, establishing the right of a community, at least conceptually, to constitute a system of government of their choice. Complementing the principle that the people may choose for themselves the means by which they are to be governed, is the idea of democracy as 'a method of group decision making characterized by a kind of equality among the participants at an essential stage of the collective decision making'.[84] In addition to identifying and justifying an extra-constitutional right to constitute a chosen political system, the democratic idea of self-government also therefore animates the intra-constitutional matter of how collective decisions are to be taken. And underpinning both the idea that the people should be able to choose and constitute a form of government, and participate on equal terms in collective decision-making within their community, is some notion of the political equality of members of the polity.[85] It is this notion of the political equality of citizens which gives force to, and is manifested by, the extra-constitutional and intra-constitutional aspects of democracy.

This basic democratic ideal is, however, very abstract, and both subject to interpretation, and the need to be translated for implementation in practice. The direct, participatory democracy of the ancient Athenian Assembly, dating from the end of the sixth century BC, offered to citizens quite different opportunities

---

[81] J Dunn, 'Conclusion' in J Dunn (ed), *Democracy: The Unfinished Journey 508 BC to AD 1993* (Oxford, Oxford University Press, 1992) 239.

[82] J Dunn, 'Preface' in Dunn (ed), *Democracy: The Unfinished Journey* (1992) v.

[83] T Paine, *Rights of Man* (Mineola NY, Dover Publications, 1999) 92.

[84] T Christiano, 'Democracy', *The Stanford Encyclopaedia of Philosophy* (2006): plato.stanford.edu/entries/democracy/

[85] See, eg R Dahl, *On Political Equality* (New Haven CT, Yale University Press, 2006) 2.

to engage in the political life of their community to those available in modern representative democratic states.[86] And alongside differences in institutions, participation and processes, differences in how the citizenry or electorate has been defined must also be recognised in order to understand the changing nature of democratic practice from the time of the ancient Greeks to the acceptance of the universal franchise.[87] Yet even if the modern representative variant of democracy is focused upon giving citizens the authority to select, remove, influence and call to account those who exercise political power in nation states, rather than literally to govern themselves, a range of contested issues remain. One such issue is the extent to which democratic processes can, or should, be limited. Is the outcome of a decision-making process which is democratic in nature necessarily to be respected? Or is the legitimacy of any particular decision dependent upon its substantive quality, rather than the manner in which it was taken? These key questions as to how democratic political systems ought to be designed reveal a fundamental tension in the modern understanding of democracy. This is between majoritarian and 'constitutional' conceptions of democracy.

A majoritarian conception of democracy can be found in the work of Jeremy Waldron. As Waldron has observed, '[t]here are many of us, and we disagree about justice'.[88] Waldron argues that this pervasive social disagreement 'means that a results-driven approach is ... unavailable to us as a political community' if the state is to be structured on the basis of democratic principles.[89] The essence of democracy, Waldron maintains, is the right of all people to participate in the making of political decisions. When participatory rights are claimed, the people who do so 'want to be among those who determine the social goals and conceptions of the common good relative to which political management and political instrumentality will be defined'.[90] Consequently, Waldron argues, if

> we resolve to treat each other's views with respect, if we do not seek to hide the fact of our differences or to suppress dissent, then we have no choice but to adopt procedures for settling political disagreements which do not themselves specify what the outcome is to be.[91]

Waldron argues that making political decisions by majority vote respects the citizens in a community in two ways. First, 'it respects their differences of opinion about justice and the common good: it does not require anyone's sincerely held view to be played down or hushed up because of the fancied importance

---

[86] J Dunn, *Setting the People Free: The Story of Democracy* (London, Atlantic, 2006) 18; R Dahl, *Democracy and Its Critics* (New Haven CT, Yale University Press, 1989) 14, 18–19. On ancient Athenian democracy, see generally S Hornblower, 'Creation and Development of Democratic Institutions in Ancient Greece' in Dunn (ed), *Democracy: The Unfinished Journey* (1992) n 81 above.

[87] On the gradual extension of the franchise see Foot, *The Vote* (2012) n 7 above, Part I.

[88] J Waldron, *Law and Disagreement* (Oxford, Clarendon Press, 1999) 1.

[89] ibid 300.

[90] ibid 243.

[91] ibid 304.

of consensus'.[92] Secondly, majoritarian decision-making is respectful because it 'involves a commitment to give *equal* weight to each person's view in the process by which one view is selected as the group's'.[93] As such, a demand for democratic political equality can be satisfied by affording to citizens an 'equal voice and equal decisional authority' within their community.[94]

Majoritarian democracy is rejected by Ronald Dworkin, in favour of what he calls the 'constitutional conception of democracy'.[95] Such a conception of democracy does not seek to produce decisions which are acceptable to a simple majority of citizens, on the basis that this affords equal weight and respect to their differing views about the requirements of justice. Instead, the constitutional conception of democracy has the contrasting aim that 'collective decisions be made by political institutions whose structure, composition, and practices treat all members of the community, as individuals, with equal concern and respect'.[96] As a result of this, for Dworkin, '[d]emocracy means government subject to conditions ... of equal status for all citizens'.[97] The majoritarian process may still be regularly used for the resolution of nearly all political matters. However:

> [T]he constitutional conception requires these majoritarian procedures out of a concern for the equal status of citizens, and not out of any commitment to the goals of majority rule. So it offers no reason why some nonmajoritarian procedure should not be employed on special occasions when this would better protect or enhance the equal status that it declares to be the essence of democracy, and it does not accept that these exceptions are a cause of moral regret.[98]

This is an explicitly 'result-driven' approach to democracy.[99] The process used to make a decision is of secondary importance to whether that decision itself is democratic, at least in terms of Dworkin's own constitutional conception of democracy. As such, the democratic process may be limited if to do so substantively 'improves democracy'.[100] For Dworkin, the limitation of the democratic process is demanded by a commitment to democracy itself, and to the underlying equality of citizens to which it is designed to give effect. And this is a 'constitutional' conception of democracy because it is in a state's constitution that such limits must be established and defined, and subject ultimately to being enforced in the courts.

---

[92] ibid 109.
[93] ibid 114.
[94] J Waldron, 'The Core of the Case Against Judicial Review' (2006) 115 *Yale Law Journal* 1346, 1389.
[95] R Dworkin, *Freedom's Law: The Moral Reading of the American Constitution* (Oxford, Oxford University Press, 1996) 17.
[96] ibid 17.
[97] ibid 17.
[98] ibid 17.
[99] ibid 34.
[100] ibid 32.

Dworkin's 'constitutional' conception of democracy is not without appeal, especially in so far as it indicates that there are constitutive conditions of majoritarian decision-making—which, for example, we may take to include the universal franchise, free and fair elections, freedom of political expression and association, and access to official information—which must be sufficiently respected for this process to be considered democratic.[101] Yet there are fundamental problems with what Dworkin considers this understanding of democracy to provide: a democratic justification for the judicial enforcement of legal limitations on majoritarian decision-making. While we may readily accept that democracy must be about more than majoritarian decision-making,[102] it should not be about less than majoritarian decision-making. This may mean that, in Waldron's words, 'everything *is* up for grabs in a democracy, including the rights associated with democracy itself', rather than prioritising certain political values under the guise that they are the basic tenets which underpin a democratic system.[103] But to insulate by law particular values or rights from being considered, altered or augmented through regular political mechanisms simply because they are deemed to be fundamental to democracy is problematic in two related ways.

The first problem is the lack of any agreed account of what the necessary preconditions to democratic decision-making are, and, more importantly, what practical provision must be made to ensure any such preconditions are respected. Dworkin's claim that concern for the equal status of all citizens in a community is the foundation of democracy is far from accepted by all,[104] and is remarkably vague. If, as Dworkin suggests, the state can be seen to lack the authority to take action which undermines the fundamental prerequisites of democracy, and is constitutionally prevented from doing so, a specific conception of justice—that which is thought to provide the basis of democracy—will inherently be elevated

---

[101] This does not, however, mean that these conditions should necessarily be understood as conceptually prior to, or above, the democratic process. Instead, rather than viewing democracy as being the result of these conditions obtaining, we might see it as the source of such necessary, and valuable, precepts: see Dahl, *Democracy and Its Critics* (1989) n 86 above, 175: 'the democratic process endows citizens with an extensive array of rights, liberties, and resources sufficient to permit them to participate fully, as equal citizens, in the making of collective decisions by which they are bound ... Seen in this light, the democratic process is not only essential to one of the most important of political goods—the right of the people to govern themselves—but is itself a rich bundle of substantive goods'.

[102] This is evident in the broad-ranging criteria which it has been argued should be taken into account when attempting to audit the extent to which a state is democratic: see D Beetham, 'Key Principles and Indices for a Democratic Audit' in D Beetham (ed), *Defining and Measuring Democracy* (London, Sage, 1994). The most recent audit of democracy in the UK considered 15 separate topics, across four main areas: Citizenship, Law and Rights; Representative and Accountable Government; Civil Society and Popular Participation; and Democracy Beyond the State: see S Wilks-Heeg, A Blick and S Crone, *How Democratic is the UK? The 2012 Audit* (Liverpool, Democratic Audit, 2012).

[103] Waldron, *Law and Disagreement* (1999) n 88 above, 303.

[104] For example, for an argument for democracy premised on a reconciliation between individual freedom and equality, see C Gould, *Rethinking Democracy: Freedom and Social Co-operation in Politics, Economy and Society* (Cambridge, Cambridge University Press, 1988). Or for an account of democracy which emphasises the significance of social and participatory aspects, see C Pateman, *Participation and Democratic Theory* (Cambridge, Cambridge University Press, 1974).

above, and protected by law against, the claims of all others. But precisely what conception of justice this will be—Equality? Liberty? Fraternity? Equal concern and respect? Autonomy? Some combination?—and how far the protection of it would extend, will depend on the view of the courts tasked with enforcing constitutional limits on the democratic process as to what the essential preconditions of democracy are. It is far from clear that developing abstract premises about the essential nature of democracy into concrete propositions about what should be beyond the reach of the democratic process is a task which courts are equipped to fulfil. Recent decisions of the US Supreme Court and European Court of Human Rights in relation to limiting the financing and broadcasting of political advertising—each case, incidentally, being decided by bare majorities—demonstrate clearly the extent to which judicial attempts to define the appropriate limits of the democratic process may diverge, and are highly contentious.[105] When the scope for disagreement about even the fundamental structuring of the democratic process is obvious, to privilege a judicially formulated understanding of democracy by constitutional means is to risk the imposition of unanticipated limits on collective decision-making which cannot be removed, and might appear unjustifiable to many.[106]

The second problem is even more profound. To preclude certain categories of decision from being taken on a majoritarian basis is to disregard the respect which is accorded to citizens as a result of their very engagement in a democratic process. As Waldron persuasively argues, if a decision-making 'process is non-democratic, it inherently and necessarily does an injustice, in its operation, to the participatory aspirations of the ordinary citizen'.[107] And this applies equally to decision-making about how a democratic process should be constituted and structured as much

---

[105] In the US Supreme Court, see *Citizens United v Federal Elections Commission* 558 US 310 (2010), rejecting as unconstitutional, by a 5–4 majority, legislation which sought to prevent corporations from funding political advertising in the period immediately prior to an election. In the European Court of Human Rights, see *Animal Defenders International v United Kingdom* (App No 48876/08) [2013] EMLR 28, upholding a ban on paid political advertising on broadcast media in the UK, by a 9–8 majority, as it was not a disproportionate interference with the Art 10 right to freedom of expression. See also in the US Supreme Court, *Shelby County v Holder* 570 US __ (2013), striking down by a 5–4 majority key parts of the Voting Rights Act 1965, which was designed to prevent changes in state electoral regulations which had a disproportionate impact on minority ethnic voters; and *McCutcheon v Federal Elections Commission* 572 US __ (2014) in which, again by a 5–4 majority, the overall cap on political donations by individuals to federal candidates in a two year electoral cycle was struck down as unconstitutional.

[106] The decision of the US Supreme Court in *Citizens United* drew criticism from President Obama in his subsequent State of the Union address on 27 January 2010: 'With all due deference to separation of powers, last week the Supreme Court reversed a century of law that I believe will open the floodgates for special interests—including foreign corporations—to spend without limit in our elections': www. whitehouse.gov/the-press-office/remarks-president-state-union-address. The decision also drew strong criticism from Dworkin himself, who condemned it in 'The Decision That Threatens Democracy', *The New York Review of Books* (13 May 2010). Yet while Dworkin rejected the substantive result reached in *Citizens United*, the phenomenon of courts establishing the parameters of democratic activity is precisely the one demanded by his constitutional conception of democracy.

[107] J Waldron, 'A Right-Based Critique of Constitutional Rights' (1993) 13 *OJLS* 18, 50.

as any other matter requiring collective action. Even if the 'right decision' about what democracy entails is reached by non-democratic means, 'then—sure—there is something democratic to set against that loss; but that is not the same as there being no loss in the first place'.[108] Therefore, while Dworkin's defence of a constitutional conception of democracy is premised on the idea that it serves to protect fundamental democratic rights and values from the will of a potentially fickle majority, the adoption of such a conception in fact actually harms democracy in a quite significant way. Since it precludes the people in a society from defining for themselves the conditions under which governance will be optimally democratic—allocating this task instead to the courts—such an approach can be seen as 'a rather insulting form of disenfranchisement'.[109] For if disagreements about justice must be settled by democratic means, disagreements about *how* disagreements about justice are to be settled—essentially, disagreements about democracy—must be matters that a political community is entitled to resolve for itself.

There nevertheless remains a range of objections to the majoritarian conception of democracy. It can be argued that it understates the capacity of courts to resolve sensitive, and divisive, political questions.[110] Or that it overstates the capacity of democratic institutions and processes to function in a way which reflects the views of the autonomous citizens they ought to represent.[111] It may produce a 'tyranny of the majority'.[112] It may be subject to capture by elite groups.[113] It may foreclose the possibility of political participation by other means, with judicial review argued to be one such avenue by which citizens (and perhaps especially those in minority groups) might engage with communal decision-making processes.[114] Or that disagreement about the meaning of the right to participation,[115] or the collective decision-making procedures through which it is given effect,[116] may undermine its claim to provide a legitimate means of bypassing disagreement about substantive justice.

There may be force to many of these objections, although there are responses to them too. Surely, for example, the tyranny of a minority should be recognised as a qualitatively greater evil than a tyranny of the majority. Indeed, as Waldron has argued, 'the majoritarian aspect actually mitigates the tyranny, because it indicates that there was at least one non-tyrannical thing about the decision: It was

---

[108] Waldron, *Law and Disagreement* (1999) n 88 above, 293.

[109] Waldron, 'The Core of the Case Against Judicial Review' (2006) n 94 above, 1406.

[110] The classic account of judicial decision-making as a principled, Herculean endeavour is Dworkin's 'law as integrity': R Dworkin, *Law's Empire* (Oxford, Hart Publishing, 1986).

[111] See, eg RP Woolf, *In Defence of Anarchism* (New York, Harper & Row, 1976) 38–58.

[112] The phrase was first used by Alexis de Tocqueville in 1835: see A de Tocqueville (GE Bevan trans), *Democracy in America* (London, Penguin, 2003 [1835]) 292.

[113] See, eg R Michels (E and C Paul trans), *Political Parties: A Sociological Study of the Oligarchical Tendencies of Modern Democracy* (London, Jarrold, 1915).

[114] See, eg A Kavanagh, 'Participation and Judicial Review: A Reply to Jeremy Waldron' (2003) 22 *Law and Philosophy* 451; A Lever, 'Is Judicial Review Undemocratic?' [2007] *PL* 280.

[115] See, eg J Raz, 'Disagreement in Politics' (1998) 43 *American Journal of Jurisprudence* 25, 47.

[116] See, eg T Christiano, 'Waldron on Law and Disagreement' (2000) 19 *Law and Philosophy* 513, 520.

not made in a way that tyrannically excluded certain people from participation as equals'.[117] Further, the extent to which a 'decisional majority' is actually likely to be a coalition of interests in which 'minority groups' might have real political influence must also be recognised.[118] Similarly, to view judicial review as providing a route to political participation might be thought to overlook a great many difficulties both with obtaining access to the courts, and the form of argument and reasoning which will be exhibited there if admission is gained.[119] And while there may be disagreement about how democratic decision-making procedures should be structured, such disagreements will have a less explicit moral character, and as such, are likely to be easier to resolve one way or the other than disagreements about the substantive requirements of justice. Strategically, if disagreement must be bypassed somewhere, then it will be less contentious to do so at the procedural level than at the level of political morality, in order to provide a foundation on which decisions about collective action can be based.[120]

Ultimately, however, acceptance of a majoritarian conception of democracy must be assured from the perspective of fundamental philosophical principle. Debates about what democracy requires, and in particular whether the results of a democratic process should or should not be limited, can be seen to depend, perhaps decisively, on 'how one sees the world'.[121] If this is the case, such debates may be simply 'irresoluble on rational grounds'.[122] Yet if we accept that the people in a community have the right, or indeed responsibility, to govern themselves—or at least to choose and hold to account those who do—a majoritarian conception of democracy must be, in principle, the correct basis on which to constitute a legitimate system of government. The prospect of achieving more democratic results by non-democratic means is likely to be illusory, since the criteria for determining what democracy does or does not require cannot be objectively and exhaustively identified from a position which is above or outside the democratic process.[123] Instead, a majoritarian decision-making process internalises debate and disagreement about even the nature of democracy itself. In this sense, any particular majoritarian democratic decision-making process cannot be considered perfect, and as Waldron has argued, all political actors, whether politicians

---

[117] Waldron, 'The Core of the Case' (2006) n 94 above, 1396.

[118] See, eg M Tushnet, *Taking the Constitution Away from the Courts* (Princeton NJ, Princeton University Press, 1999) 159; R Bellamy, *Political Constitutionalism: A Republican Defence of the Constitutionality of Democracy* (Cambridge, Cambridge University Press, 2007) 238, 255. The phrase 'decisional majorities' comes from Waldron, 'Core of the Case' (2006) n 94 above, 1397.

[119] See, eg A Tomkins, *Our Republican Constitution* (Oxford, Hart Publishing, 2005) 26; T Poole, 'Questioning Common Law Constitutionalism' (2005) 25 *Legal Studies* 142, 157–63.

[120] See, eg DA Strauss, 'Constitutions, Written and Otherwise' (2000) 19 *Law and Philosophy* 451, 461.

[121] M Tushnet, 'How Different are Waldron's and Fallon's Core Cases For and Against Judicial Review?' (2010) 30 *OJLS* 49, 69.

[122] ibid 70.

[123] See, eg AC Hutchinson, 'A "Hard Core" Case Against Judicial Review' (2008) 121 *Harvard Law Review Forum* 57, 58–60.

or members of the electorate, should keep a system 'under review' to ensure that it can be improved where possible.[124] But in ensuring that disagreements about democratic procedures are not settled and then never revisited, the majoritarian internalisation of debate about the fundamental tenets of the democratic process facilitates a dynamic process of constitutional change in place of the procession to a pre-determined, yet inevitably disputed, destination offered by a results-driven conception of democracy. Indeed, we may be led to conclude that an outcome-orientated understanding of democracy is not really democratic at all. And consequently, the contention that the judicial protection of whatever set of fundamental rights and values are said to constitute and sustain democracy is itself democratic, must be rejected.

With a majoritarian understanding of the nature of democracy now established, we turn to explore the relationship between this conception of democratic decision-making and parliamentary sovereignty. The link between the two is crucial if the virtue associated with majoritarian democratic decision-making can also attach to the doctrine of parliamentary sovereignty. But it is also important even for those who do not accept the argument in favour of majoritarian democracy advanced above, and, by extension, are therefore inclined to reject parliamentary sovereignty. For demonstrating the existence of a link between the two places a burden on the critic to make clear the understanding of democracy on which their rejection of parliamentary sovereignty is based. Where a normative foundation for rejection of the sovereignty of Parliament is not made explicit, this will require underlying motivations to be exposed and evaluated. Where, in contrast, parliamentary sovereignty is rejected overtly on the basis that a majoritarian conception of decision-making is lacking in appeal, the implications for democracy will need to be addressed. In particular, if, as I have suggested above, the 'constitutional' conception is a deficient understanding of what democracy requires, those who reject parliamentary sovereignty must confront the questions of whether they are advocating a departure from democratic government in itself, how this can be justified, and the extent to which it is legitimate. The continuing legal validity of the doctrine of parliamentary sovereignty may not depend on whether it has virtue as a fundamental constitutional norm, but those who argue that it has been displaced must still be obliged to explain what could provide the democratic foundation of the UK constitution (assuming one is thought necessary) in its absence.

B. Parliamentary Sovereignty and Democracy

I have argued above that the best understanding of democracy requires decisions about collective action in a political community to be taken on a majoritarian

---

[124] Waldron, 'The Core of the Case' (2006) n 94 above, 1389.

basis, and that there should not, as a result, be a limitation on the outcomes than can be reached via a democratic process. From this perspective, there is a clear affinity between majoritarian democratic decision-making and the notion of legally unlimited legislative power: what democracy can be said to require is given effect by this constitutional principle. Yet even this alignment of democratic and constitutional principle remains abstract. The precise nature of the democratic institutions and processes which are to be used for the exercise of legally unlimited legislative power is not prescribed by the bare acceptance of a majoritarian conception of democracy. A range of different institutional and procedural arrangements for the democratic exercise of legislative power can, and have, been imagined. Variations, for example, may exist as between presidential and parliamentary systems of government, federal and unitary states, bicameral and unicameral legislatures, or even the extent to which democratic decision-making is direct or representative.[125] While a majoritarian model of democratic decision-making may therefore be understood to recommend that legislative authority be legally unlimited, it does not inherently recommend a constitutional order founded on parliamentary sovereignty.

Nevertheless, the sovereign UK Parliament as presently constituted does provide a forum for democratic decision-making, although this has not always been the case. We saw above that while Dicey attributed legal sovereignty to Parliament, he believed political sovereignty rested with the electorate. This, Dicey argued, meant that 'the arrangements of the constitution are now such as to ensure that the will of the electors shall by regular and constitutional means always in the end assert itself as the predominant influence in the country'.[126] As such, Paul Craig has argued that Dicey's formulation of the doctrine of parliamentary sovereignty was 'firmly embedded within a conception of self-correcting majoritarian democracy'.[127] There are, however, reasons to doubt Craig's claim that Dicey's conception of parliamentary sovereignty was the result of a 'perfect union' between '"black letter" precedent and political principle'.[128] Certainly, as noted above, it is difficult to conceive of the electorate of Dicey's era as being democratic by modern standards, for it was not until six years after Dicey's death in 1922 that equal voting rights were extended to women and men over

---

[125] It might be thought that underlying the specific institutional variations that may be identified is a broader distinction between 'consensual' and 'Westminster' democracies: see A Lijphart, *Democracies: Patterns of Majoritarian and Consensus Government in Twenty-One Countries* (London, Yale University Press, 1984). Lijphart also uses the terminology of 'majoritarian' democracy, but it is important to note that for him it denotes a type of democratic system which is equivalent to the 'Westminster' model. This distinguishes Lijphart's usage of majoritarian democracy from the narrower meaning attributed to it in this book, where, following Waldron, a majoritarian understanding of democracy refers to a particular conception of *decision-making*, rather than the nature of the (power concentrating) political *system* which tends to form around such an approach to decision-making.

[126] Dicey, *Law of the Constitution* (1915) n 2 above, 71.

[127] P Craig, 'Dicey: Unitary, Self-Correcting Democracy and Public Law' (1990) 106 *LQR* 105, 108.

[128] ibid 108.

the age of 21.[129] Furthermore, Dicey's own view of the relationship between parliamentary sovereignty and democracy was less than straightforward.

Dicey was initially unconcerned about the extension of the franchise. This was not, however, the result of any great faith in the democratic ideal, but because the impact of democracy had been 'tempered by snobbishness'.[130] Dicey believed that '[d]emocracy in England has to a great extent inherited the traditions of the aristocratic government, of which it is the heir'.[131] Consequently, as John McEldowney has noted, 'at the heart of Dicey's faith in parliamentary sovereignty was his belief that English gentlemen would only pass morally acceptable laws'.[132] Dicey was therefore content to explicate a legal doctrine which vested total legislative authority in the political elite because he trusted that Members of Parliament would exercise this power wisely. That Dicey's belief in the sovereignty of Parliament was underpinned by his confidence in the English establishment, rather than any inherent merits of representative democracy, is apparent in his eventual willingness to subvert his own doctrine to prevent Home Rule in Ireland. When it became clear that the political establishment could not be trusted to continue to support the Union between Great Britain and Ireland, Dicey argued that that a referendum should be held before legislation implementing Irish Home Rule could be legitimately passed by Parliament.[133]

This was not, however, as Weill has argued, because he was 'an ardent supporter of popular sovereignty'.[134] Instead, Dicey could not accept the elected Parliament's proposed solution to the Irish question, a topic with which he was fixated throughout his life, and sought to do whatever he could to impede Home Rule. As Weill notes, Dicey also considered other measures which could prolong the Union, including 'for the King to dissolve Parliament and cause an election on Home Rule' or 'for the Crown to withhold Royal Assent after Home Rule passed the Commons'.[135] Most extreme was Dicey's willingness 'to declare Home Rule unconstitutional if it did not receive the People's consent'.[136] These further proposals should be seen as Dicey's desperate final attempts to maintain the Union after his faith in the establishment had been destroyed, rather than a principled

---

[129] Representation of the People (Equal Franchise) Act 1928. Indeed, Dicey personally edited eight editions of *An Introduction to the Study of the Law of the Constitution*, the final iteration being published in 1915. Women were not entitled to vote at any time during the life of Dicey's text, for it was not until the Representation of the People Act 1918 that the franchise was extended to women aged 30 and over, and who satisfied a property qualification (while removing the property qualification for all men, who were entitled to vote from the age of 21).

[130] AV Dicey, *Lectures on the Relation between Law and Public Opinion in England during the Nineteenth Century* (London, Macmillan, 1905) 57.

[131] ibid 58.

[132] JF McEldowney, 'Dicey in Historical Perspective—A Review Essay' in P McAuslan and JF McEldowney (eds), *Law, Legitimacy and the Constitution* (London, Sweet & Maxwell, 1985) 59.

[133] See AV Dicey, *A Leap in the Dark; or Our New Constitution* (London, John Murray, 1893) 197–201.

[134] R Weill, 'Dicey was not Diceyan' (2003) 62 *CLJ* 474, 493.

[135] ibid 491.

[136] ibid 491.

attempt to vindicate the sovereignty of the people.[137] Indeed, when it is further considered that Dicey's despair at the prospect of Home Rule meant he 'came close to urging armed resistance on the part of the northern counties of Ireland', such a conclusion seems unavoidable.[138]

Dicey was ultimately unconvinced of the value of democratic governance, arguing that 'a modern democracy, while it protects the people from unpopular laws, gives inadequate security for the passing of laws which are in themselves wise and good'.[139] Instead, Dicey saw parliamentary sovereignty as concentrating power in a ruling elite who could use it to maintain the status quo. But as his faith in the ruling class waned, so did Dicey's faith in the sovereignty of Parliament. Parliamentary sovereignty was not, for Dicey, the result of a 'perfect union' between precedent and democracy, nor was it designed to guarantee that the democratic will of the electorate would be vindicated. Indeed, Dicey's equivocal attitude to the relationship between this constitutional doctrine and democratic principle, which fluctuated over the course of his life,[140] demonstrates clearly that a relationship between parliamentary sovereignty and democracy cannot be presumed. Yet while Dicey's work shows us that parliamentary sovereignty is not an inherently democratic constitutional principle—which he defended, and then abandoned, for complex, but not democratic, reasons—the contemporary foundation of the doctrine is such that it reveals a contingent, yet stable, connection between democracy and the legally unlimited legislative authority of Parliament. For it is a doctrine which has the virtue of ensuring the primacy of democracy in the UK constitution.

Parliamentary sovereignty ensures the primacy of democracy in the UK constitution because it is to a democratic institution that the doctrine allocates legally unlimited legislative authority. This institution is, in technical terms, the Queen-in-Parliament: for the House of Commons, House of Lords and the monarch must all assent for legislation to be validly enacted. While neither the monarch nor the House of Lords is in any way democratic—the identity of the monarch being determined on a hereditary basis, and members of even a reformed House of Lords selected, rather than popularly elected[141]—members of the House of

---

[137] See further M Qvortrup, *A Comparative Study of Referendums: Government by the People*, 2nd edn (Manchester, Manchester University Press, 2005) for discussion of Dicey's views on the utility of referendums more generally. While Qvortrup's account is relatively sympathetic to Dicey, the point that he was not a democratic idealist is clearly made: 58–60.

[138] Lord Bingham, 'Dicey Revisited' [2002] PL 39, 43. See AV Dicey, *A Fool's Paradise: Being a Constitutionalist's Criticism on the Home Rule Bill of 1912* (London, John Murray, 1913).

[139] AV Dicey, *Lectures on the Relation between Law and Public Opinion in England during the Nineteenth Century*, 2nd edn (London, Macmillan, 1914) lxxii.

[140] See further I McLean and A McMillan, 'Professor Dicey's Contradictions' [2007] PL 435. In response, Bogdanor has argued that Dicey's 'polemical works on Irish Home Rule are not works of law', and thus he did not abandon the legal doctrine of parliamentary sovereignty: V Bogdanor, 'The Consistency of Dicey: A Reply to McLean and McMillan' [2008] PL 19.

[141] There are three means by which members of the House of Lords are selected: (i) appointment as a life peer, by the Queen on the advice of the Prime Minister, under the Life Peerages Act 1958; (ii) by virtue of holding office as one of the 26 most senior bishops of the Church of England; (iii) by

Commons are democratically elected, accountable, and removable.[142] And the democratic legitimacy of the House of Commons in particular can be seen to extend to legislation produced by the Queen-in-Parliament in general. For the House of Commons is the primary chamber in Parliament, both as a matter of law[143] and constitutional convention.[144] Further, the role of the monarch in granting royal assent to legislation is entirely formal, and exercised by convention on ministerial advice.[145] Moreover, the House of Commons is the only directly elected institution in the UK's system of central government. The democratic legitimacy of the government is derived from that of the House of Commons, for it is the person able to control a majority in this chamber who will be appointed Prime Minister, and asked to form a government.[146] The House of Commons therefore has no competitor in terms of democratic legitimacy among the institutions within the UK's central constitutional architecture.[147]

'election' from one of a number of closed classes of peers holding hereditary titles, in accordance with the House of Lords Reform Act 1999, s 2. When a seat becomes vacant as a result of the death of the previous incumbent, a poll to choose a replacement will be conducted either among those hereditary title holders eligible to be selected for the relevant seat, or the members of the House as a whole, by House of Lords Standing Order 10. 92 such hereditary peers are in this way exempted from the general disqualification which the 1999 Act created. There remain some judicial life peers appointed under the terms of the Appellate Jurisdiction Act 1876 as Lords of Appeal in Ordinary, although this legislation has now been repealed, and any peers are disqualified from sitting in the Upper Chamber while holding judicial office: Constitutional Reform Act 2005, s 137(3).

[142] Representation of the People Act 1983. There has traditionally been no formal recall power to allow members of a parliamentary constituency to attempt to remove their elected representative in between elections, although a commitment to legislate to create such a power was made by the coalition government upon taking office: The Coalition, *Our Programme for Government* (2010) 27. A draft Recall Bill was published in 2011, but was criticised heavily by the House of Commons Political and Constitutional Reform Committee: *Recall of MPs* (HC 373, 28 June 2012). The Recall of MPs Bill 2014–15 was subsequently introduced in the House of Commons on 11 September 2014, and would make provision for a recall petition to be triggered in limited circumstances: (i) if an MP is convicted of an offence, and sentenced to 12 months or less in prison; or (ii) an MP is suspended from the House of Commons for at least 21 sitting days. If at least 10% of registered electors in a constituency sign a recall petition, a by-election would be held.

[143] Parliament Acts 1911 and 1949.

[144] The subordinate status of the non-elected House of Lords is evident from a range of conventions, including the Salisbury convention, which prescribes that the Upper Chamber will not oppose the enactment of legislation intended to implement commitments contained in the government's manifesto, and the convention that the Lords considers government business in reasonable time. The nature of these conventions, among others, was considered by a Joint Committee on Conventions, *Conventions of the UK Parliament* (HL Paper 265-I, HC 1212-I, 3 November 2006). The Joint Committee also endorsed the general primacy of the House of Commons: [57].

[145] Royal assent has not been refused since 1707, when Queen Anne refused to assent to the Scottish Militia Bill. On the process generally, see R Brazier, 'Royal Assent to Legislation' (2013) 129 *LQR* 184.

[146] This principle is assured as a matter of constitutional convention, and is also now recognised in *The Cabinet Manual*, 1st edn (2011) n 48 above, paras 2.7–2.8.

[147] Following the devolution of legislative power to Scotland, Wales and Northern Ireland, there may now be competitors to the House of Commons in terms of democratic legitimacy in three of the constituent nations of the UK. Any challenge posed to parliamentary sovereignty by devolution will be considered in Chapter 3 of this volume, but it is important to note here that the democratic legitimacy that the Scottish Parliament, National Assembly for Wales, and Northern Ireland Assembly each undoubtedly possess cannot extend to the UK as a whole.

There are therefore two elements to the democratic nature of parliamentary sovereignty: both the 'parliamentary' and the 'sovereignty' tell us something distinctive about the relationship between the doctrine and democracy. It is both the composition of Parliament as a legislative institution, and the fact that the law-making power it exercises is unlimited by law, which together establish the fundamentally democratic nature of the doctrine of parliamentary sovereignty. But it is also important to understand the implications of this in terms of the virtue of parliamentary sovereignty, for it is when these two democratic elements are understood in combination that the nature of this claim becomes clear. This, I have suggested, is that the doctrine ensures the primacy of democracy in the UK constitution.

Parliamentary sovereignty, as it is manifested in the contemporary UK constitution, may be a fundamentally democratic constitutional foundation, but it must be understood to ensure the *primacy* of democracy, rather than democracy per se. As should be clearly evident from the discussion of the relationship between the doctrine and democratic principle in Dicey's era above, the existence of parliamentary sovereignty does not establish or guarantee democracy; that legally unlimited legislative power is allocated to a parliament is neither a necessary or sufficient condition for the emergence of a politics which can be considered democratic. Further, as considered above, it must be recognised that democracy is about more than just majoritarian political decision-making.[148] The existence of a democratic culture in a community is also vital, with citizens willing and able to engage in the political life of their society, and official governmental actors adopting an attitude which is responsive to public opinion, concerns, and criticism.[149] The substantive legal regulatory environment will play a key, yet far from definitive, role in fostering (or inhibiting) the kind of political culture in which democracy can function. In addition to making provision for the franchise to be universally distributed to citizens, legal norms which make possible (or at least do not interfere with) classic civil liberties like freedom of political speech and association, and provide access to official information, will certainly be a bare minimum for democratic self-government of a community to be considered credibly established. But building on this, regulation of political finance will also be required, to ensure disparities in wealth and other economic resources cannot unduly distort the operation of the democratic process. Even on a skeletal account of the arrangements which must underpin an effective democratic politics, the

---

[148] See text at nn 96–97.

[149] On the requirement that democracy be 'contestatory', enabling citizens to challenge decisions made by those in authority, see P Pettit, *Republicanism: A Theory of Freedom and Government* (Oxford, Oxford University Press, 1997) 183–203. Pettit argues that (republican) democratic institutions should be structured so that decision-making is deliberative, inclusive, and responsive. Adopting a similar approach, but rejecting Pettit's arguments against majoritarianism, see Bellamy, *Political Constitutionalism* (2007) n 118 above, 218–21. For a critique of republicanism from a popular democratic perspective, see J McCormick, *Machiavellian Democracy* (Cambridge, Cambridge University Press, 2011) 141–69.

funding of political parties and campaigns, ownership of media outlets, and lobbying, among other things, will therefore need to be monitored, and likely controlled by legal rules.[150]

Yet while the recognition of a legal doctrine of parliamentary sovereignty cannot, in and of itself, ensure optimal democratic practice in a community, it is an important part of the overall picture. For the doctrine of parliamentary sovereignty can guarantee that decisions which are the outcome of a democratic process have ultimate legal authority, and are resistant to reversal or subversion by non-democratic means or institutions. It is in this sense that the sovereignty of Parliament establishes the primacy of democracy: by affording constitutional priority to the outcomes of a democratic decision-making process. On a majoritarian understanding of democracy—which rejects the substantive limits imposed by the 'constitutional' conception—this is significant in itself for the democratic life of a political community. Yet it is true that this cannot eliminate the possibility of outcomes which some might believe to be insufficiently democratic, or even undemocratic, in substance; such outcomes would have constitutional primacy, and be legally unchallengeable, whatever they may be. Any such results would, however, be in principle entirely open to being revisited through the democratic process, as part of an ongoing collective commitment to articulate a basis for the ordering of the political life of the community that could attract and retain the support of at least a majority of citizens, or their representatives. Acceptance of the doctrine of parliamentary sovereignty may not therefore control the precise detail of the kind of democratic political system which a community will develop; it obviously does not stipulate, for example, how political parties should be funded, or political associations regulated. But it is through the democratic process that the ideal of democracy must be further defined and given effect in political practice. In the contemporary UK constitution, it is the attribution of legally unlimited legislative authority to the democratic Parliament which provides the process by which what democracy requires—as any other matter which necessitates collective action—can be democratically delineated. In ensuring the primacy of democracy as a matter of constitutional law, the doctrine of parliamentary sovereignty therefore establishes one of the basic conditions of democratic political life—a democratic process for the making of communal decisions—while also creating the means by which a more elaborate understanding of democratic practice can be freely pursued without legal inhibitions. In this sense, the role of parliamentary sovereignty in ensuring the primacy of democracy is a key part of the democratic architecture of the UK constitution, even if it is just one element

---

[150] See, eg KD Ewing, *The Funding of Political Parties in Britain* (Cambridge, Cambridge University Press, 1987); KD Ewing, *The Cost of Democracy: Party Funding in Modern British Politics* (Oxford, Hart Publishing, 2007); J Rowbottom, *Democracy Distorted: Wealth, Influence and Democratic Politics* (Cambridge, Cambridge University Press, 2010); S Wilks-Heeg, 'Tackling the Power Gap: A New Constitutional Reform Agenda' in G Lodge and G Gottfried (eds), *Democracy in Britain: Essays in Honour of James Cornford* (London, Institute for Public Policy Research, 2014).

among a number which identify a political system as being based on the idea of self-government by the people.[151]

C. Parliamentary Sovereignty and Democracy: Two Challenges

There are two challenges which may be levelled against the argument as to the democratic virtue of parliamentary sovereignty which has been developed above. One of these challenges is conceptual, and the other is practical. First, it might be claimed that a doctrine which allocates sovereignty to a Parliament is incapable of being truly democratic. For it might be thought that the democratic commitment to self-government must recommend a constitutional order founded on the idea of popular sovereignty—the sovereignty of the people—rather than that of a Parliament. If popular and parliamentary sovereignty are therefore cast as competing principles, we might be led to conclude that parliamentary sovereignty is conceptually incapable of being democratic. Or if this is too strong, at the very least we might need to reconsider whether a doctrine of parliamentary sovereignty can exhibit the kind of constitutional virtue I have sought to attribute to this fundamental norm above. This is a potentially potent challenge, for an understanding of parliamentary sovereignty which presents the doctrine as being opposed to, or competing with, popular sovereignty is one which can be found in a number of sources. Such an approach, for example, underpins the work of Weill,[152] is evident in some of the concerns about the UK constitution raised in 2012 by Democratic Audit,[153] and, as we have already seen, was a source of significant tension for Dicey when he sought to argue against Home Rule for Ireland.[154]

This first challenge, however, must be rejected. For to view parliamentary sovereignty and popular sovereignty as competing principles or theories is to mischaracterise their essential nature. If we recall the basic components of the democratic idea of self-government by the people which were identified above, we can distinguish between the extra-constitutional and the intra-constitutional

---

[151] We can therefore reject, on this basis, Oliver's claim that to recognise the democratic virtue of parliamentary sovereignty commits us to question the democratic credentials of states with constitutional limits on majoritarian decision-making: see D Oliver, 'Parliament and the Courts: A Pragmatic (or Principled) Defence of the Sovereignty of Parliament' in A Horne, G Drewry and D Oliver (eds), *Parliament and the Law* (Oxford, Hart Publishing, 2013) 311. This is clearly not the case; we can suggest that a doctrine of legally unlimited legislative authority is optimally democratic, in principle, without this argument entailing that any state which does not possess such a constitutional norm cannot be a democracy. Indeed, as Oliver herself notes, '[d]emocracy is not an all or nothing thing'.

[152] R Weill, 'Centennial to the Parliament Act 1911: The Manner and Form Fallacy' [2012] *PL* 105, developing an argument premised on the notion that parliamentary sovereignty and popular sovereignty are two of three 'conflicting constitutional theories' (the third being the manner and form theory).

[153] S Wilks-Heeg, A Blick and S Crone, *How Democratic is the UK? The 2012 Audit* (Liverpool, Democratic Audit, 2012) 10: 'in the UK, parliament ... rather than the people, is regarded as sovereign'.

[154] See text at nn 133–138.

aspects of democracy.[155] On an extra-constitutional plane, the people are democratically entitled to establish (and abolish) whatever form of government they see fit, and this political right is in principle unlimited by law, although it may, of course, be very difficult to exercise effectively in practice. But in exercising this constituent power, and forming a system of government, the sovereignty of the people must be translated into institutional form.[156] This does not extinguish the extra-constitutional aspect of democracy; it simply means that the democratic instinct at its root must *also* be given effect intra-constitutionally. In so doing, the idea of democracy as a means of making collective decisions in a group composed of political equals becomes of primary relevance. Exactly what institutions and processes will be constituted for the making of collective democratic decisions will vary from community to community, but in large, complex nation states, it is practically inevitable that this will involve representative government of some kind. To allocate legally unlimited legislative authority to such a representative institution as a matter of constitutional law—as does the doctrine of the legislative sovereignty of Parliament in the UK—must not be understood to create an institution which competes with the people for sovereignty. Instead, it is to give the extra-constitutional notion of popular sovereignty expression at an intra-constitutional level. Both popular and parliamentary sovereignty are manifestations of the idea of democracy, but simply operating in different contexts, on different planes. That the UK constitution was not explicitly 'authored' by 'We the People' does not undermine its democratic credentials, for there can be no doubt that the present constitution could be popularly, legitimately displaced. It is this fact which demonstrates that, from an extra-constitutional perspective, the UK constitution is founded on an acceptance of popular sovereignty, which, on an intra-constitutional level, must be developed into institutions and processes which ensure that collective decision-making is democratic. The doctrine of parliamentary sovereignty is the constitutional norm which achieves this, and is not therefore a principle which competes with popular sovereignty, either conceptually or in practice. Instead, parliamentary and popular sovereignty share a common democratic basis.[157]

The second challenge concerns the practical claim that Parliament is a democratic body which legislates for the UK. As I have argued above, what makes the doctrine of parliamentary sovereignty able to ensure the primacy of democracy is that it combines two elements: (i) legally unlimited legislative authority, which is (ii) vested in a democratic institution. If the institution which exercises legally unlimited legislative power is not democratic, then it will also be the case that the doctrine of parliamentary sovereignty is not democratic. The argument developed above rests on the fact that Parliament—and in particular, the House

---

[155] See text at nn 81–85.
[156] See Loughlin, *Idea of Public Law* (2003) n 4 above, 113.
[157] See KD Ewing, 'The Human Rights Act and Parliamentary Democracy' (1999) 62 *MLR* 79, 98–99.

of Commons which is primary within it—is democratic because it is an elected institution. Yet it may be argued that to consider this point in isolation is artificial. In particular, whether Parliament is democratic may be irrelevant, if the reality of actual constitutional practice is considered. For the House of Commons may well be the only directly elected institution in UK central government, but it, and its vast legislative power, is controlled by the indirectly elected Prime Minister and his or her government. This is the spectre of the 'elective dictatorship' objected to (selectively, when out of government) by Lord Hailsham: a government which can command a majority in the House of Commons will in effect have the sovereign power of Parliament at its disposal.[158] It is not Parliament, on this analysis, that actually possesses sovereign legislative authority, but the government and the constitutionally dominant Prime Minister, who will ultimately make, and be able to enforce—relying on a combination of the payroll vote, coercion by the whips and party patronage—decisions about the legislation which is to be enacted. A government may, of course, be replaced by the electorate at a general election, but given that a government is chosen indirectly, with the House of Commons serving as a form of 'electoral college',[159] the process by which such a rejection can be effected will not necessarily be straightforward. In any event, in the period between general elections the government will be able to ensure that its Bills are enacted by Parliament. According to this objection, then, Parliament is not sovereign, but subservient, and neither a government nor a Prime Minister can boast the democratic credentials necessary to justify their legislative hegemony. The doctrine of parliamentary sovereignty is not therefore democratic; instead it serves to bolster the already powerful UK executive.

There is, of course, some truth in this objection, in that the government certainly has a profound influence on the activity of the House of Commons and the House of Lords. Nevertheless, a number of counterpoints can be made to the 'elective dictatorship' challenge. The legislative power of Parliament may well be controlled in practice by the government, but this does not mean that Parliament has become entirely submissive. Indeed, in contrast, there is much recent evidence to suggest that Parliament is both willing and able to assert itself against the government. A detailed case study of the passage of the Legislative and Regulatory Reform Act 2006 by Peter Davis, for example, demonstrates the crucial role that the parliamentary scrutiny of proposed legislation can play in preventing the government from enacting constitutionally undesirable statutes. The Bill that would become the Legislative and Regulatory Reform Act 2006 as initially drafted would have provided the government with a potentially wide-ranging power to legislate without the approval of Parliament, yet 'became instead a demonstration of how

---

[158] See Lord Hailsham, *The Dilemma of Democracy: Diagnosis and Prescription* (London, Collins, 1978).
[159] R Brazier, *Constitutional Reform: Reshaping the British Political System*, 3rd edn (Oxford, Oxford University Press, 2008) 43.

parliamentary scrutiny can work well'.[160] This may be but one example but, as Davis notes, it is of 'particular interest' for this Act 'started as a potentially comprehensive bypassing of [parliamentary scrutiny] procedures, yet the application of those procedures themselves resulted in its scope being significantly narrowed before enactment'.[161] More recent examples of the effectiveness of parliamentary scrutiny of legislation have also been identified by Adam Tomkins, who highlights, among other things, the significant fact that '[s]elect committees of both Houses produce an ever-increasing volume of very high-quality work, which informs and enriches debates both within and beyond Parliament'.[162] It is also a conclusion which is supported by the Democratic Audit of the UK published in 2012, which identified an overall improvement in the 'democratic effectiveness of Parliament' since 2002.[163] In particular, the use of pre- and post-legislative scrutiny and the introduction of Public Bill committees are highlighted by the Democratic Audit as having contributed to a 'strengthening of parliament, particularly the House of Commons'.[164]

Further, if the quality and effectiveness of parliamentary scrutiny is understated by the 'elective dictatorship' challenge, then, as Philip Cowley and Mark Stuart have shown, it can also not be assumed that a government can readily control its backbench MPs, and rely on them to support the legislation it promotes. Rather, after assessing the frequency and scale of backbench rebellions during Tony Blair's reign as Prime Minister, Cowley and Stuart conclude that 'there is plenty of evidence that MPs today are more independent-minded and willing to defy their whips now than they used to be'.[165] While even regular rebellions will not necessarily cause a government to be defeated frequently, this provides a necessary corrective to the view that Parliament has become institutionally subdued. And this trend has continued, indeed becoming more pronounced, in the present era of coalition government, as backbench rebellions have been occurring even more frequently, at a potentially unprecedented rate when compared to all post-war parliaments.[166]

Indeed, as Matthew Flinders and Alexandra Kelso have argued, the 'parliamentary decline thesis'—which undoubtedly underpins the 'elective dictatorship' challenge we are considering here—is 'deeply flawed', and the 'perpetuation [of

---

[160] P Davis, 'The Significance of Parliamentary Procedures in Control of the Executive: A Case Study—the Passage of Part 1 of the Legislative and Regulatory Reform Act 2006' [2007] *PL* 677, 700.

[161] ibid 678.

[162] A Tomkins, 'What's Left of the Political Constitution?' (2013) 14 *German Law Journal* 2275, 2277.

[163] S Wilks-Heeg, A Blick and S Crone, *How Democratic is the UK? The 2012 Audit* (Liverpool, Democratic Audit, 2012) Introduction, p 5.

[164] ibid 5, 232–33.

[165] P Cowley and M Stuart, 'A Rebellious Decade: Backbench Rebellions under Tony Blair, 1997–2007' in M Beech and S Lee (eds), *Ten Years of New Labour* (Basingstoke, Palgrave Macmillan, 2008) 117.

[166] See P Cowley and M Stuart, 'A Coalition with Two Wobbly Wings: Backbench Dissent in the House of Commons' (2012) 3 *Political Insight* 8, 9.

this narrative] represents an extreme example of lazy thinking and the failure of scholars collectively ... to reflect on dominant disciplinary assumptions'.[167] Further, often overlooked considerations highlighted by Flinders and Kelso, in addition to those already considered, are 'the role of intra-party machinery and processes as critical but generally unobserved control mechanisms', and the insights provided by political diaries and memoirs, which paint 'a consistent picture of an executive–legislative relationship that is more balanced, or at the very least respectful', than the critics assume.[168] For Flinders and Kelso, a shift in the balance of power from the legislature to the executive has occurred, based on differences in 'institutional resources and capacity', but the parliamentary decline thesis has:

> *over-stated* the extent of this shift in the constitutional balance of power, it has failed to acknowledge that parliamentary democracy was founded on the principle of 'strong government' and did not therefore include a proactive or assertive role for the legislature, and it has largely overlooked the existence of informal, but no less important, executive control mechanisms.[169]

The notion that Parliament is an ineffectual body is therefore largely a caricature. The evidence of Parliament's capacity to scrutinise legislation, the independence of many MPs, and the existence of informal mechanisms by which relationships between ministers and parliamentarians are conditioned, indicates that the 'elective dictatorship' objection should be rejected. The government does not have the unfettered ability to enact whatever legislation it chooses, and Parliament is not merely a ratifying chamber. While it is a core feature of the UK's parliamentary system, and indeed not inappropriate, that government legislation will generally be enacted, rather than some unintended modern aberration,[170] it is Parliament that legislates, both in principle and in practice. To suggest otherwise is to distort the relationship between the legislature and the executive in the UK.

However, even looking beyond the evidence which indicates that Parliament's effectiveness and independence is often misrepresented, it is not clear that

---

[167] M Flinders and A Kelso, 'Mind the Gap: Political Analysis, Public Expectations and the Parliamentary Decline Thesis' (2011) 13 *British Journal of Politics and International Relations* 249, 249–50.

[168] ibid 257–58. Flinders and Kelso cite A King, 'Modes of Executive–Legislative Relations: Great Britain, France and West Germany' (1976) 1 *Legislative Studies Quarterly* 11, as to the importance of considering intra-party control mechanisms among the range of modes of executive-legislative relations. Also cited is the analysis of David Blunkett's memoirs contained in D Richards and H Mathers, 'Political Memoirs and New Labour: Interpretations of Power and the "Club Rules"' (2010) 12 *British Journal of Politics and International Relations* 498, and C Mullin, *A View From the Foothills* (London, Profile, 2010), as providing evidence of the role that intra-party and intra-parliamentary mechanisms can play in conditioning relations between government ministers and parliamentarians.

[169] ibid 251.

[170] See, eg the classic acknowledgment by Bagehot in 1867 that '[t]he efficient secret of the English Constitution may be described as the close union, the nearly complete fusion, of the executive and legislative powers ... The connecting link is *the cabinet*' (emphasis added): W Bagehot, *The English Constitution* (Oxford, Oxford University Press, 2001) 11.

this line of challenge is coherent in principle. While there is no doubt that the authority of Parliament, and its ability to scrutinise government legislation, could be enhanced,[171] the fact remains that it is a democratic institution, even if an imperfect one. But the virtue of parliamentary sovereignty is not premised on the perfection of the democratic decision-making process to which the doctrine affords legal priority.[172] Indeed, the fact that a democratic process will internalise disagreement about the propriety of the operation of that process itself clearly shows that the possibility of improvement is inherently embedded in a majoritarian conception of democracy. From one perspective, this might be viewed as a failing of democracy, and of a legal doctrine which permits the contours of democratic decision-making to be a matter subject to ongoing negotiation and revision among participants. From an alternative perspective, however, these same characteristics are part of the virtue of such an approach. For what from one perspective is intolerable imperfection, can instead be seen as a commitment to avoid complacency about the functioning of the political system, and a willingness to explore new ways in which a system of government can be improved. It may therefore be the case that this 'elective dictatorship' objection is less practical than it first appears, and instead simply reproduces the dispute between majoritarian and constitutional conceptions of democracy already encountered above.

Yet even remaining at a practical level, if it were the case that this line of challenge was correct, and that parliamentary sovereignty is an elaborate and undemocratic smoke-screen which further entrenches the power of the executive, what would follow? Is the legal limitation of legislative power a necessary consequence of accepting the 'elective dictatorship' objection? This was certainly the view advanced by Lord Hailsham, who proposed the adoption of an entrenched Bill

---

[171] See, eg the now partially implemented report of the Select Committee on Reform of the House of Commons, *Rebuilding the House* (HC 1117, 24 November 2009). A number of the 'Wright' committee's recommendations, including the election of select committee chairs and the establishment of a Backbench Business Committee, have been implemented, but other key proposals—such as the creation of a House Business Committee—are yet to be acted upon: see Select Committee on Reform of the House of Commons, *Rebuilding the House: Implementation* (HC 372, 15 March 2010); House of Commons Political and Constitutional Reform Committee, *Revisiting Rebuilding the House: The Impact of the Wright Reforms* (HC 82, 18 July 2013); House of Commons Political and Constitutional Reform Committee, *Revisiting Rebuilding the House: The Impact of the Wright Reforms—Government Response* (HC 910, 9 December 2013).

[172] It is for this reason that more general democratic objections to representative parliamentary democracy, which lack the easy rhetorical flair of the 'elective dictatorship' challenge, also fail to undermine the democratic virtue of the doctrine of the sovereignty of Parliament. In particular, we are right to be concerned about a number of important practical problems with the UK's democratic political system, such as the adequacy of the first-past-the-post voting system, or the potentially arbitrary basis on which constituency boundaries may be drawn and redrawn: see, eg G Lodge and G Gottfried, *Worst of Both Worlds: Why First Past the Post No Longer Works* (London, IPPR, 2011); 'Boundary Changes Battle: Lib Dems Could Be Biggest Losers', *The Guardian* (5 June 2011), citing research conducted by the Democratic Audit as to the effect of the (ultimately unimplemented) proposed review by the Boundary Commission. Yet these are exactly the kinds of problems which need to be confronted through the democratic process, rather than taken as a reason to place substantive legal limitations, enforced by the courts, on the power of the legislature.

of Rights,[173] and as we shall see in Chapter three, this underlying idea has gained contemporary traction (even if manifested differently in institutional terms) in the form of 'common law constitutionalism'. It would also seem to be the result recommended by the constitutional conception of democracy, if indeed this theory, or something like it, does underpin the challenge we are considering here. Yet to suggest that legislative power in the UK is not exercised by a sufficiently democratic body does not, in itself, demonstrate that the doctrine of parliamentary sovereignty is without virtue. The argument as to the democratic virtue of parliamentary sovereignty which I have developed in this chapter is dependent on a combination of two factors: the essential claim is that (i) a democratic institution (ii) should possess legally unlimited legislative power. The majoritarian democratic argument in favour of the constitutional provision of legally unlimited legislative power in principle is thus free-standing, and not logically dependent upon whether any particular institution or set of arrangements is deemed to be democratic to a sufficient extent. As a result, even if the UK Parliament was thought to be insufficiently democratic, this would not mean that parliamentary sovereignty, as a legal doctrine, should be entirely rejected. Instead, the 'parliamentary' limb of the doctrine would need to be reconceptualised—with the constitutional recipient of legally unlimited law-making authority either reformed or replaced—but the underlying notion of legislative sovereignty vested in a democratic institution could, and should, endure.

The argument that Parliament does not in practice operate in a sufficiently democratic manner does not, therefore, undermine the argument that parliamentary sovereignty is a legal doctrine which has democratic virtue. If accepted, the 'elective dictatorship' objection would call for re-examination of the suitability of the conditional recipient of legally unlimited law-making authority, rather than total rejection of the notion of legislative sovereignty. Any argument as to the democratic necessity of the limitation of legislative power must therefore be justified in its own terms, rather than being grounded in the perceived shortcomings of existing practice. From a conceptual perspective, however, a number of deficiencies have already been identified in the constitutional understanding of democracy, which, in my view, render unlikely the prospect of a positive democratic case for the limitation of legislative power being developed.[174] And in any event, if the practical performance of Parliament is to be critiqued as part of such attempts to dispose of the doctrine of parliamentary sovereignty, a dose of realism about the effectiveness of judicial restraints on legislative power might also be required. For if the courts are to be relied on to circumscribe the law-making authority of the legislature in the name of democracy, significant concerns about their composition, accountability, procedures, and the results they have reached would also need to be dispelled. Alternatively, however, it may be concluded that the clear democratic

---

[173] Hailsham, *The Dilemma of Democracy* (1978) n 158 above.

[174] These issues are considered further in the context of the challenge posed by common law constitutionalism to the doctrine of parliamentary sovereignty: see chapter 3 of this volume, pp 126–49.

virtue of the doctrine of parliamentary sovereignty makes such endeavours unnecessary. For acceptance of the legislative sovereignty of Parliament ensures in principle the primacy of democracy in the UK constitution, and even benevolent judicial intervention to limit this power would violate the best understanding of what it means to live in a community in which the people govern themselves.

V. CONCLUSION

An answer to the question 'what is parliamentary sovereignty?' must provide us with an account of the content of this fundamental legal doctrine. As we will see in Part II, the traditional account of the content of the doctrine is increasingly subject to challenge, sometimes to the point of rejecting that parliamentary sovereignty has any continuing legal force at all. Yet its nature as a legal norm means that the different ways in which parliamentary sovereignty can (and has) been challenged should not be confused. The current and continuing legal validity of the doctrine of parliamentary sovereignty does not depend upon it being a desirable constitutional principle. This does not, however, mean that the legal validity of the doctrine of parliamentary sovereignty is all with which constitutional lawyers should be concerned. Instead, the political context in which this fundamental constitutional rule exists and operates must be examined if we are to obtain anything like a full understanding of the sovereignty of Parliament, and the constitution of which is it an essential part. It is from this perspective that the function and virtue of parliamentary sovereignty have been considered in this chapter. For while there can be no doubt that the doctrine of parliamentary sovereignty could be displaced as the fundamental norm of the UK constitution, we must appreciate fully what is at stake when such a course of action is considered. The importance of the doctrine from a functional perspective—as a central organising principle and constitutional focal point—and the virtue of the doctrine from a normative perspective—in ensuring the primacy of democracy—means that a significant challenge is posed to those who would seek to eliminate parliamentary sovereignty from the UK's constitutional architecture. Casual suggestions that parliamentary sovereignty has been limited, distorted or dissolved will not suffice. Critics of the doctrine must ensure that any vision of the constitution post-parliamentary sovereignty anticipates how questions of constitutional function and virtue would be confronted.

Yet this is not to say the orthodox conception of the doctrine of parliamentary sovereignty advanced by Dicey should be accepted without further consideration, simply on the basis of the functions it fulfils and the virtue it possesses. Rather, key questions internal to the doctrine of parliamentary sovereignty require attention. In particular, as noted above, is the matter of what the contours of legally unlimited legislative power actually are. Can a legally sovereign Parliament limit itself or its successors? To answer this fundamental question about the scope of legally unlimited law-making power, the manner and form theory of legislative authority must now be considered.

2

The Manner and Form Theory of Parliamentary Sovereignty

I. INTRODUCTION

THE DOCTRINE OF parliamentary sovereignty is a legal norm which allocates legally unlimited legislative power to the UK Parliament. In the previous chapter, however, a potential difficulty with this notion was discerned. Can sovereign legislative power be exercised in such a way as to limit sovereign legislative power? As Gray argued, this is a philosophical conundrum which has parallels with debates about omnipotence:

> 'Can God create for Himself an impossible task?' If He can do so, so it is reasoned, then the impossibility of that task must mean that God is not therefore omnipotent; if He cannot create such a task, there is something which He is unable to do and He is not therefore omnipotent. Therefore God is not omnipotent. Likewise if Parliament is sovereign, there is nothing it cannot do by legislation; if there is nothing Parliament cannot do by legislation, it may bind itself hand and foot by legislation; if Parliament so binds itself by legislation there are things which it cannot do by legislation; and if there are such things Parliament is not sovereign.[1]

The conundrum is one which does not seem open to logical resolution: if a sovereign Parliament cannot limit itself or its successors, it is not sovereign; if a sovereign Parliament can limit itself or its successors, it is not sovereign. From either perspective, the notion that Parliament possesses legislative sovereignty might seem to collapse into incoherence. Or, less dramatically, if a practical way forward is sought, there is little here to grasp for insight as to which of these stark alternative interpretations of the implications of legislative sovereignty ought to be preferred.

As we saw in the previous chapter, Dicey's solution to this problem was to endorse a third principle as being a consequence of the sovereignty of Parliament, in addition to the two core ideas that, first, Parliament could make or unmake any law whatever, and secondly, that nobody was empowered to override the

---

[1] HR Gray, 'The Sovereignty of Parliament Today' (1953) 10 *University of Toronto Law Journal* 54, 54. See also HLA Hart, *The Concept of Law*, 2nd edn (Oxford, Oxford University Press, 1994) 149–50.

legislation of Parliament.[2] This third principle was that a sovereign Parliament cannot 'bind its successors'.[3] For Dicey, 'a sovereign power cannot, while retaining its sovereign character, restrict its own powers by any particular enactment'.[4] The alternative—which Dicey described as 'Limited Sovereignty'—was dismissed as 'a contradiction in terms', although he did recognise the possibility of the complete abdication of sovereignty.[5] And from Dicey's determination that parliamentary sovereignty could not be understood to empower the enactment of legislation which limited the power of any future Parliament, the notion that Parliament cannot bind its successors became constitutional orthodoxy, widely accepted as a necessary concomitant of the doctrine of legally unlimited legislative power.[6]

Yet Dicey assumed too much in asserting that Parliament was incapable of binding its successors without sacrificing its sovereignty. As the philosophical conundrum set out above indicates, this solution, while straightforward and superficially attractive, is an interpretation of sovereignty which is far from unproblematic. That Dicey recognised the possibility of the abdication of sovereign power demonstrates that philosophical preconceptions as to the nature of omnipotence cannot disguise the fact that political authority is not eternal and unchanging. But such a disposition to shifts in the locus of sovereignty should also inform our attempts to understand the internal characteristics of legally unlimited legislative power, rather than allowing sweeping exclusions to sideline fuller reflection on this complex point. Reiteration of the orthodox mantra that 'Parliament cannot bind its successors' only serves to distort the debate about the proper extent of sovereign law-making authority, with the breadth of this claim obscuring what is the crucial issue: what *kind* of limits might a sovereign Parliament seek to place on itself and its successors? Of most significance is whether a distinction needs to be acknowledged as between a Parliament seeking to limit its successors absolutely as to substance, and a Parliament seeking to place procedural conditions upon how legislative power is in future to be exercised.

---

[2] AV Dicey, *Introduction to the Study of the Law of the Constitution*, 8th edn (London, Macmillan, 1915) 37–38.

[3] ibid 65, citing A Todd, *Parliamentary Government in the British Colonies* (London, Longmans & Co, 1880) 192.

[4] ibid 66, fn 3.

[5] ibid 66, fn 3.

[6] See, eg *Ellen Street Estates v Minister of Health* [1934] 1 KB 590, 597 (Maugham LJ). The explanation of parliamentary sovereignty offered on the UK Parliament website also includes the claim that 'no Parliament can pass laws that future Parliaments cannot change': www.parliament.uk/about/how/sovereignty/. And this proposition is also frequently referred to by political actors: see, eg the debate on the (then) EU Bill at second reading in *Hansard*, HC Deb, Vol 520 col 191 (7 December 2010). Public debate about the lawfulness of a private members bill designed to guarantee an 'In-Out' referendum on membership of the European Union—the EU (Referendum) Bill, promoted by James Wharton MP in the 2013–14 session of Parliament—also took this notion for granted, on both sides of the argument: see, eg 'Editorial—EU Referendum: Gesture Politics', *The Guardian* (4 July 2013): 'As a constitutional position it is a nonsense, because no parliament can bind its successors'; 'Cameron In Coalition Clash Over Referendum', *Reuters* (1 July 2013): '"We've never made any secret of the fact that parliament can't bind its successor", Wharton told a news conference. "A future parliament could repeal it".'

As we shall see, the orthodox dogma that Parliament cannot bind its successors has been interpreted to forbid both substantive limits and procedural conditions entirely. But, as a result, this orthodoxy has been stretched beyond its proper scope. For whether Parliament has the authority to legislate to alter the legislative process may, *but also may not*, raise the issue of Parliament or its successors being bound. A re-orientation in perspective may therefore provide us with a better way to understand the nature and, crucially, the extent of legally unlimited legislative power. Such an alternative approach is provided by the 'manner and form theory' of parliamentary sovereignty, pioneered by Sir Ivor Jennings. The development and definition of the manner and form theory will first be considered, before dealing with four main objections to this approach to parliamentary sovereignty. The understanding of the manner and form theory established and defended in this chapter will then provide a basis for addressing the modern challenges to the doctrine of parliamentary sovereignty in Part II of this book.

II. DEVELOPMENT AND DEFINITION OF THE MANNER AND FORM THEORY

Sir Ivor Jennings was the most important and influential of all of Dicey's critics. Before we turn to the detail of Jennings manner and form conception of parliamentary sovereignty, the background to its development needs to be understood. In successive editions of *The Law and the Constitution*—the title immediately marking a difference in approach to Dicey's study of *The Law of the Constitution*, with Jennings keen to emphasise the connection between, rather than the distinctiveness of, their common two subjects—Jennings pursued a dispute with Dicey which spanned the entire spectrum of constitutional law. Moreover, their debates were underpinned by fundamental differences in legal and political philosophy. As Jennings noted, Dicey saw the constitution 'through Whig spectacles'.[7] This political perspective, Jennings argued, led Dicey to 'postulate individualism as a fundamental doctrine'.[8] As a result, 'the Constitution was for him an instrument for protecting the fundamental rights of the citizen, and not an instrument for enabling the community to provide services for the benefit of its citizens'.[9] Jennings, however, was sympathetic to collectivist politics.[10] This disposition is evident in Jennings' description of the constitution as 'only an organisation of men and women',[11] which he believed should operate as a 'lubricant rather than a barrier to social, economic and political change'.[12] So whereas Dicey saw the role of the constitution as being to protect individual rights against encroachment by

---

[7] WI Jennings, 'In Praise of Dicey 1885–1935' (1935) 13 *Public Administration* 123, 128.

[8] ibid 132.

[9] ibid 132.

[10] See, eg AW Bradley, 'Sir William Ivor Jennings: A Centennial Paper' (2004) 67 *MLR* 716, 724.

[11] WI Jennings, *The Law and the Constitution*, 1st edn (London, University of London Press, 1933) viii.

[12] KD Ewing, 'The Law and the Constitution: Manifesto of the Progressive Party' (2004) 67 *MLR* 734, 735.

an over-zealous state, for Jennings its function was to facilitate state action in the name of the common good.

The fundamental nature of the difference in outlook between Dicey and Jennings can be seen in two examples. First, their understandings of the nature of public law scholarship diverged markedly. For Dicey, the role of the constitutional lawyer was 'to state what are the laws which form part of the constitution, to arrange them in their order, to explain their meaning, and to exhibit where possible their logical connection'.[13] Constitutional history was 'simple antiquarianism' to a lawyer,[14] and inquiries into political theory 'too high' and 'speculative' for the legal mind.[15] Knowledge of such disciplines was, according to Dicey, unnecessary to understand the law of the constitution. Dicey's separation of law from its historical and political context was, however, directly challenged by Jennings. Referring to Dicey's conception of the function of the constitutional lawyer, Jennings argued:

> That this is the whole duty of a professor of public law is not a doctrine which the present writer is prepared to admit. The boundaries between law and political science cannot be drawn so fine. Public law is not all contained in the 'rules recognised by the Courts.' The rules themselves cannot be understood save in their ideological context. The constitution produced by consideration of the rules only is a travesty of the truth.[16]

To fully understand the operation of the constitution required 'an examination of the social and political forces which make for changes in the ideas and desires and habits of the population and its various social strata'.[17] Ultimately, Jennings maintained, 'all public law is applied politics'.[18] And that their disparate scholarly approaches were a function of deep philosophical disagreement as to the very role and nature of law is further apparent from Loughlin's classification of Dicey and Jennings in his influential study of 'styles of public law thought'.[19] For Loughlin, Dicey was a normativist of the conservative variety.[20] This was the 'dominant tradition of public law thought',[21] which Dicey 'played a major role in shaping'.[22] Jennings, in contrast, was part of the functionalist 'dissenting tradition'.[23] Whereas

---

[13] Dicey, *Law of the Constitution* (1915) n 2 above, 31.

[14] ibid 14.

[15] ibid 20.

[16] Jennings, 'In Praise of Dicey' (1935) n 7 above, 128.

[17] Jennings, *Law and the Constitution*, 1st edn (1933) n 11 above, viii.

[18] WI Jennings, 'The Institutional Theory' in *Modern Theories of Law* (London, Wildy & Sons, 1963) 77.

[19] M Loughlin, *Public Law and Political Theory* (Oxford, Clarendon Press, 1992) 58. On the intellectual foundations of normativism and functionalism, see chs 5 and 6 respectively, and M Loughlin, 'The Functionalist Style in Public Law' (2005) 55 *University of Toronto Law Journal* 361.

[20] The normativist style is sub-divided by Loughlin into conservative normativists and liberal normativists. On liberal normativism see Loughlin, *Public Law and Political Theory* (1992) 206–10 and ch 9.

[21] Loughlin, *Public Law and Political Theory* (1992) n 19 above, 139.

[22] ibid 159.

[23] Loughlin, 'The Functionalist Style' (2005) n 19 above, 398.

normativism 'essentially reflects an ideal of the autonomy of law' and seeks to 'subordinate government to law', functionalism 'views law as part of the apparatus of government' which can be used to enable state action to further social ends.[24] The contrast between the opposing perspectives of Dicey and Jennings is thus stark.

The comprehensive differences between Dicey and Jennings as to the nature and purpose of public law are manifested in the second example of their dis-agreement, which concerned the nature of the rule of law. For Dicey, the 'rule or supremacy of law' had three aspects.[25] First, governmental action could only be carried out in accordance with strict legal rules, rather than on the basis of arbi-trary discretion. Secondly, the law applied equally to all people, whether citizens or government officials, and was to be administered in the ordinary courts rather than in special tribunals. Thirdly, the fundamental principles of the constitution had been established and developed in the ordinary courts by judicial decisions vindicating the rights of the private individual against the state. Jennings, who compared the notion of the rule of law to 'an unruly horse',[26] challenged each of these three elements. Regarding the first aspect of the rule of law, Jennings argued that Dicey had failed to consider 'that public authorities do in fact possess wide discretionary powers'.[27] Such powers are still 'derived from the law',[28] and so the 'sinister connotation' which Dicey attached to them was unwarranted.[29] Secondly, Jennings argued that Dicey's rejection of the French notion of administrative law failed to appreciate fully that the purpose of such *droit administratif* was 'not to exclude public officers from liability for wrongful acts, but to determine the powers and duties of public authorities and to prevent them from exceeding or abusing their powers'.[30] Whether the courts carrying out this important task are called administrative courts or not is immaterial; for Jennings, '[w]hat matters is their independence of administrative influence and control'.[31] Thirdly, Jennings claimed that Dicey's belief in the constitutional prominence of common law prin-ciple was based on a 'very partial presentation of the facts'.[32] The legal rules pro-tecting the rights of individuals against governmental interference formed only one part of the constitution: Dicey, Jennings argued, had failed to acknowledge that 'the principles governing constitutional relationships have been established primarily through the growth of practice, insisted upon, in some cases, through

---

[24] Loughlin, *Public Law and Political Theory* (1992) n 19 above, 60.
[25] Dicey, *Law of the Constitution* (1915) n 2 above, 179.
[26] WI Jennings, *The Law and the Constitution*, 5th edn (London, University of London Press, 1959) 60.
[27] ibid 55.
[28] ibid 307.
[29] ibid 306.
[30] ibid 313.
[31] ibid 313.
[32] ibid 39.

victory in arms; though in the more recent period legislation has been the chief instrument of development'.[33]

Jennings' challenge to Dicey's idea of the rule of law therefore offers clear evidence of the near absolute ideological rift between them. Dicey's account of the rule of law had been warped, Jennings argued, by his particular conception of the constitution, which was 'dominated by the doctrine of *laissez-faire*' and held that the purpose of government 'was to protect the individual against internal and external aggression'.[34] Jennings, in contrast, contended that the principle of democracy was of far greater value to our system of government than the 'imprecise' theory of the rule of law.[35] Jennings criticised those making claims about the existence of the rule of law who used it as shorthand 'for distinguishing democratic or constitutional government from dictatorship'.[36] Ultimately, Jennings argued,

> democracy rests not upon any particular form of executive government, nor upon the limitation of the powers of the legislature, nor upon anything implicit in the character of its penal laws, but on the fact that political power rests in the last analysis on free elections, carried out in a State where criticism of the Government is not only permissible but a positive merit, and where parties based on competing policies or interests are not only allowed but encouraged.[37]

The 'atmosphere of freedom which is more easily felt than analysed' which exists in such a democratic society could not, Jennings maintained, be appropriately represented by 'a formal concept dignified by such a name as the rule of law'.[38]

It is against this backdrop of comprehensive disagreement—about the nature of the constitution and the role of law, as manifested in their specific disputes about public law scholarship and the rule of law—that we must explore Jennings' challenge to Dicey's understanding of parliamentary sovereignty. When this background is considered, what is most striking is a significant difference in tone. For Jennings' challenge to the orthodox understanding of the doctrine is seemingly devoid of the underlying political and philosophical conflict which characterised their disagreement about almost everything else of constitutional importance. Instead, Jennings' challenge is presented as being based on logic and legal authority, with any political or principled rationale underpinning his alternative conception of parliamentary sovereignty not made explicit. This point will be of real significance when a potential normative justification for the manner and form theory is developed in Chapter seven, for the failure to address this issue by its leading proponent means that we lack a clear starting point from which such an account can be developed. But it is also significant for present purposes, because

---

[33] ibid 38.
[34] ibid 55.
[35] ibid 60.
[36] ibid 60.
[37] ibid 60.
[38] ibid 61–62. See further chapter 7 of this volume, pp 290–293.

the style of Jennings' challenge will necessarily frame the discussion of the manner and form theory which is contained in this chapter. Jennings' critique of the Diceyan orthodoxy, and subsequent development of the manner and form theory, are founded on arguments from logic and authority, and as such, it will be objections from these perspectives which will be addressed here. This will be done in order to establish a definitive understanding of this conception of parliamentary sovereignty, which will then be explored further in Part II and Part III. First, however, Jennings' seminal understanding of the manner and form theory will be outlined.

A. Jennings' Account of the Manner and Form Theory

Jennings accepted, with Dicey, that the doctrine of parliamentary sovereignty was the 'dominant characteristic' of the UK constitution.[39] He was broadly content to recognise the truth of the two classic Diceyan propositions that Parliament can make or unmake any law whatever, and that no court can override an Act of Parliament.[40] This much is clear from Jennings' famous example of the extraordinary scope of Parliament's legislative authority, which extended to 'all persons and all places': if Parliament 'enacts that smoking in the streets of Paris is an offence, then it *is* an offence'.[41] Instead, Jennings sought to develop an alternative understanding of these core propositions, and in particular, to challenge the Diceyan assumption that Parliament cannot bind its successors. The manner and form theory is not, therefore, a challenge to the sovereignty of Parliament; rather, it is a reconfiguration of the notion, and implications, of legally unlimited legislative authority.

The logical element of Jennings' challenge to Dicey developed from a difference in terminology. In particular, Jennings was critical of the idea that Parliament could be understood to possess 'sovereignty'. For Jennings the 'quasi-theological origin' of the notion of sovereignty, which was 'a doctrine developed at the close of the Middle Ages to advance the cause of the secular State against the claims of the Church', made it an inappropriate concept by which to characterise the legislative power of Parliament.[42] Adopting Bodin's definition of sovereignty as 'supreme power',[43] Jennings noted that there were in fact 'many things ... which

---

[39] ibid 144.

[40] One potential difference with Dicey is that Jennings noted that 'the fact that the *courts* do not regard themselves as competent to restrict exercise of the legislative power is not in itself conclusive of the extent of that power'. Instead, a constitution could recognise 'the old principle that excess of legislative authority is a matter between the legislature and the electors', although this is not an argument Jennings sought to pursue in relation to the UK constitution: ibid 145.

[41] ibid 170.

[42] ibid 147. For a similar view from one of Jennings' contemporaries, see HJ Laski, *A Grammar of Politics*, 4th edn (London, George Allen & Unwin Ltd, 1960) 45–46.

[43] ibid 147. See J Bodin (MJ Tooley trans), *Six Books of the Commonwealth* (Oxford, Basil Blackwell, 1967) chs VIII and X.

Parliament cannot do'.[44] Prime among these limits was the need for Members of Parliament to seek re-election, and to be mindful of what 'general opinion about them may be'.[45] Dicey too recognised that Parliament was subject to a range of political and moral limits on its power, but his attempt to account for the non-omnipotence of the legislature—drawing a distinction between legal sovereignty, located in Parliament, and political sovereignty, enjoyed by the electorate—was crucially rejected by Jennings:

> [L]egal sovereignty is not sovereignty at all. It is not supreme power. It is a legal concept, a form of expression which lawyers use to express the relations between Parliament and the courts. It means that the courts will always recognise as law the rules which Parliament makes by legislation; that is, rules made in the customary manner and expressed in the customary form.[46]

The legislative power of Parliament was thus 'derived from the law',[47] and specifically, from the 'common law'.[48]

This error on the part of Dicey was crucial, and, according to Jennings, led him to the flawed conclusion that Parliament could not bind its successors. By characterising Parliament as legally sovereign, rather than possessing legislative power derived from the law, Dicey converted inapt conceptual precepts into fundamental constitutional orthodoxy. Jennings did not doubt that a sovereign truly possessing supreme power could never be bound by their own acts, for a true sovereign could do anything at any time. Even if such a sovereign did purport to limit the scope of their potential future action, for instance, by 'binding himself not to make laws except with the consent of an elected legislature', they would still remain ultimately free to avoid any such self-imposed restrictions. When considered in terms of the example offered by Jennings, a sovereign genuinely in possession of supreme power could 'abolish the legislature without its consent and … continue legislating by his personal decree'.[49] The UK Parliament was not, however, sovereign in this sense. Its power was not absolutely supreme, but dependent on certain conditions having been satisfied for a valid statute to be lawfully enacted: its legislative authority could only be exercised in the manner and form prescribed by law. When this was acknowledged, Jennings argued, 'the courts have no concern with sovereignty, but only with the established law'.[50] Parliament

---

[44] ibid 148.

[45] ibid 148.

[46] ibid 149.

[47] ibid 150.

[48] ibid 156. While Jennings classified the principle of the supremacy of Parliament as a rule of common law, it is important to note that he understood that it 'was not established by judicial decisions, however; it was settled by armed conflict and the Bill of Rights and the Act of Settlement. The judges did no more than acquiesce in a simple fact of political authority, though they have never been called upon precisely to say so': ibid 39. As will be seen in chapter 3 of this volume, this acknowledgment of the true origin of the doctrine has been overlooked by many common law constitutionalists when seeking to analyse the legislative power of Parliament.

[49] ibid 152.

[50] ibid 152.

'has for the time being power to make laws of any kind in the manner required by the law'.[51] If Parliament adheres to the procedure required by law to produce valid legislation, this 'will be recognised by the courts, *including a rule which alters this law itself*.[52] Parliament, therefore, was capable of doing what Dicey thought was impossible—legally limiting itself and binding its successors—'because its power to change the law includes the power to change the law affecting itself'.[53]

Jennings' logical contention that Parliament may impose legal limitations on itself and its successors was supported with an argument from authority. How would the courts react if the legislature attempted to follow such a course of action? Jennings relied on the Australian case of *Trethowan*[54] and the South African case *Harris*[55] to illustrate the point that a legislature can only produce valid legal enactments if it adheres to the manner and form required by the established law of the day. In both cases, it was held that where an alternative manner and form was laid down in law, it had to be followed for legislation to be validly enacted, with the Privy Council ruling in *Trethowan* that a referendum was required to enact legislation abolishing the Legislative Council of New South Wales,[56] and the Supreme Court of South Africa deciding in *Harris* that even a sovereign legislature could not disregard the requirement that legislation removing franchise rights from citizens on racial grounds had to be passed by a two-thirds majority in Parliament.[57] These cases are clearly not determinative of the scope of Parliament's power under the UK constitution. Having been decided outside of the UK, they can only offer a persuasive indication of how the courts have dealt with similar questions of legislative competence in other jurisdictions.[58] While cases in circumstances such as these are inevitably contentious, being

---

[51]   ibid 153.
[52]   ibid 153.
[53]   ibid 153.
[54]   *Attorney-General for New South Wales v Trethowan* [1932] AC 526. For more detailed discussion of this case, see generally J Goldsworthy, *Parliamentary Sovereignty: Contemporary Debates* (Cambridge, Cambridge University Press, 2010) ch 6.
[55]   *Harris v Minister of the Interior* 1952 (2) SA 428. For more detailed discussion of this case, see generally DV Cowen, 'Legislature and Judiciary—Reflections on the Constitutional Issues in South Africa: Part I' (1952) 15 *MLR* 282; I Loveland, *By Due Process of Law?: Racial Discrimination and the Right to Vote in South Africa 1855–1960* (Oxford, Hart Publishing, 1999) ch 8.
[56]   In accordance with the Constitution Act 1902 (as amended in 1929) s 7A.
[57]   In accordance with the South Africa Act 1909 ss 35, 152. The Nationalist South African government did not, however, accept this outcome. Initially, through the High Court of Parliament Bill, which was introduced in 1952 following the Appellate Division's judgment in *Harris (No 1)*, the government attempted to turn Parliament itself into a court with superior appellate jurisdiction. This was unanimously rejected by the Appellate Division in *Minister of the Interior v Harris (No 2)* 1952 (4) SA 769. Subsequently, the government increased the size of the panel of judges required to hear such cases from five to eleven by the Appellate Division Quorum Act 1955, and altered, by the Senate Act 1955, the composition of the Senate so as to give it the necessary two-thirds majority to enact the South Africa Act Amendment Act 1956, which overruled the decision in *Harris (No 1)*. The legality of this was accepted by the restructured Appellate Division in *Collins v Minister of the Interior* 1957 (1) SA 552. See Loveland, *By Due Process of Law?* (1999) n 55 above, chs 9 and 10.
[58]   See also *Bribery Commissioner v Ranasinghe* [1965] AC 172 for a similar decision by the Privy Council, pertaining to the Ceylon Parliament, discussed further below.

underpinned by complex constitutional questions as to the proper distribution of public power, Jennings maintained that the precise scope of the legislative power of the UK Parliament was even more difficult to establish. This was due to the peculiar nature of the UK's uncodified constitution, where 'our laws and our institutions have grown together' rather than being deliberately designed and delineated in a written document.[59] Jennings claimed that 'our constitutional law is the product of the alliance between the common lawyers and the Parliament men in the reign of Charles I' which ultimately resulted in the subjugation of the Crown,[60] but 'the one question which was not settled was the relation between Acts of Parliament and the common law'.[61] This was

> not settled because the judges, as sensible men, acquiesced in the assumption of power by the Long Parliament, the restoration of Charles II, the accession of William and Mary under the Bill of Rights, and the accession of the Hanoverians under the Act of Settlement.[62]

While on strictly legal grounds, Jennings contended, all of these developments could have been subjected to significant challenges, in the name of political expediency such questions were left unasked. This deference of the judiciary to the legislature in constitutional matters has endured, and as a result Jennings argued that 'given the tradition of the last hundred years ... that Parliament could do as it pleased, the courts would not be anxious to read limitations into the power of Parliament'.[63]

Such a judicial attitude could be seen, Jennings claimed, in the case of *Ellen Street Estates v Minister of Health*,[64] where the Court of Appeal held that the Acquisition of Land (Assessment of Compensation) Act 1919 had been impliedly repealed by the Housing Act 1925, to the extent that the two were inconsistent. In particular, the Court held that the provision in section 7 of the 1919 Act—which stated that other Acts authorising the acquisition of land shall 'have effect subject to this Act, and so far as inconsistent with this Act those provisions shall cease to have or shall not have effect'—should be disregarded. In the course of his judgment, Maugham LJ provided an influential exposition of the doctrine of implied repeal, asserting that:

> The Legislature cannot, according to our constitution, bind itself as to the form of subsequent legislation, and it is impossible for Parliament to enact that in a subsequent statute dealing with the same subject-matter there can be no implied repeal. If in a subsequent Act Parliament chooses to make it plain that the earlier statute is being to some extent repealed, effect must be given to that intention just because it is the will of the Legislature.[65]

---

[59] Jennings, *Law and the Constitution*, 5th edn (1959) n 26 above, 157.
[60] ibid 157–58.
[61] ibid 159.
[62] ibid 159.
[63] ibid 162.
[64] *Ellen Street Estates v Minister of Health* [1934] 1 KB 590. See also *Vauxhall Estates v Liverpool Corporation* [1932] 1 KB 733.
[65] [1934] 1 KB 590, 597.

However, while Jennings accepted that the case was correctly decided, because '[t]he implication that the Act of 1919 was *pro tanto* to be repealed was so evident that it was almost an explicit repeal',[66] he considered the famous remarks of Maugham LJ to be 'obiter dictum, because Parliament had not purported in the Act of 1919 to deprive itself of the power of repealing the Act of 1919'.[67] As a result, for Jennings, *Ellen Street Estates* was 'not an authority for saying that Parliament cannot deprive itself of that power'.[68] While Jennings was therefore unable to point to any binding decision of a UK court which endorsed the manner and form theory of parliamentary sovereignty, he instead sought to demonstrate that there was no such decision which definitively prevented such an understanding of legally unlimited legislative power from being credibly advanced.

Further, Jennings argued that the past legislative precedents which Dicey invoked to support the orthodox understanding of parliamentary sovereignty did not definitively undermine a manner and form approach. In particular, the fact that provisions which professed to be everlasting in the Union with Scotland Act 1706 and the Union with Ireland Act 1800 had been subsequently repealed did not prove that Parliament cannot bind its successors.[69] Jennings offered two ways in which the repeal of provisions which purported to be eternal could be rationalised:

> At best they show what Parliament thought of its own powers, and not what the courts thought those powers were. At worst they were unlawful exercises of power, like many such exercises between 1641 and 1689, acquiesced in by everybody because they were sensible.[70]

Ultimately, however, Jennings concluded that such precedents could be 'explained away' by looking beyond the legal formality to constitutional reality.[71] Upon doing so, '[w]hat Parliament really did' in relation to the Acts of Union with Scotland and Ireland 'was to ratify two treaties whereby its own power was extended to neighbouring territories'.[72] As a result, these treaties were open to future amendment by Act of Parliament in accordance with the public international law principle of *rebus sic stantibus*—a fundamental change of circumstances had rendered the apparently 'everlasting' provisions inapplicable, with the consequence that they were not binding upon the Parliaments enacting subsequent amending legislation. The parliamentary precedents, as with the judicial precedents, did not then, for Jennings, provide conclusive evidence that a Parliament could never

---

[66] Jennings, *Law and the Constitution*, 5th edn (1959) n 26 above, 162.
[67] ibid 163.
[68] ibid 163.
[69] The examples famously cited by Dicey of legislation which was validly enacted in contravention of the terms of the Acts of Union with Scotland and Ireland respectively were the Universities (Scotland) Act 1853 and the Irish Church Act 1869; Dicey, *Law of the Constitution* (1915) n 2 above, 63–64.
[70] ibid 169.
[71] ibid 169.
[72] ibid 170.

bind its successors as to the manner and form for future legislation. Instead, they simply indicated that circumstances in which such a course of action could occur had not yet transpired in the UK.

B. The Manner and Form Theory: Difficulties and a Definition

The work of Jennings was critical in the development of a manner and form understanding of parliamentary sovereignty. For while Jennings has been followed by many others who were sympathetic to this (or a very similar) conception of legislative authority, it is remarkable how complete an account of the manner and form theory he established at the outset. This is not to say that the core of the manner and form approach outlined by Jennings has not been supplemented, often significantly, by subsequent theorists. Of particular influence in this respect were Heuston[73]—who might be seen as a highly effective 'codifier' of the manner and form theory[74]—and Latham[75]—who, as Oliver has argued, provided a 'theoretical grounding for Jennings' ideas',[76] in recognising that the identity of the sovereign, and conditions in which legislative power could be exercised, must be established in 'logically prior' rules of law.[77] But the idea which provides the very essence of the manner and form approach to parliamentary sovereignty—that legally unlimited legislative power can be used to alter even the legal rules which condition the law-making process—can be seen to emerge in Jennings' articulation of the theory. In developing this insight, it was Jennings who laid the ground for all future attempts to explain, defend or employ the basic scheme of the manner and form theory.[78]

A change in perspective was central to Jennings' ability to craft this new understanding of parliamentary sovereignty. Jennings crucially shifted the debate away from conceptual rumination on meaning and implications of sovereignty, and in so doing, sought to bypass the abstract circularity that such an approach could engender. Instead, Jennings focused on trying to reason about a specific legal doctrine, that which creates and allocates legally unlimited legislative authority,

---

[73] See RFV Heuston, *Essays In Constitutional Law*, 2nd edn (London, Stevens and Sons, 1964) ch 1.

[74] I owe this description of Heuston's contribution to Rodney Brazier.

[75] See RTE Latham, 'What is an Act of Parliament?' [1939] *King's Counsel* 152; RTE Latham, *The Law and the Commonwealth* (London, Oxford University Press, 1949).

[76] P Oliver, 'Law, Politics, the Commonwealth and the Constitution: Remembering R.T.E. Latham, 1909–43' (2000) 11 *King's College Law Journal* 153, 154.

[77] Latham, *Law and the Commonwealth* (1949) n 75 above, 523.

[78] For further work which is sympathetic, in one sense or another, to the manner and form approach of Jennings see, eg HR Gray, 'The Sovereignty of Parliament and the Entrenchment of Legislative Process' (1964) 27 *MLR* 705; JDB Mitchell, *Constitutional Law*, 2nd edn (Edinburgh, W Green & Son Ltd, 1968); G Marshall, *Constitutional Theory* (Oxford, Clarendon Press, 1971); G Winterton, 'The British Grundnorm: Parliamentary Supremacy Re-examined' (1976) 92 *LQR* 591; SA de Smith and R Brazier, *Constitutional and Administrative Law*, 8th edn (Harmondsworth, Penguin, 1998); AW Bradley, 'The Sovereignty of Parliament—Form or Substance?' in J Jowell and D Oliver (eds), *The Changing Constitution*, 7th edn (Oxford, Oxford University Press, 2011), continued

and its implications within a legal system. Yet we may recognise the value of this re-orientation of the debate about the scope of legally unlimited legislative power without necessarily endorsing the specific device which Jennings used to structure his argument. This device is the distinction he developed between 'sovereignty' and 'supremacy', with the former, in Jennings' view, being an inappropriate descriptor to adopt to characterise Parliament's law-making power.[79] As I have argued, however, there are actually reasons to prefer the terminology of 'sovereignty' when seeking to describe the legislative power of Parliament, for it indicates clearly that such power is unlimited, rather than simply ultimate.[80] But the argument underlying Jennings' account of the manner and form theory is compatible with use of the language of sovereignty, so long as it is understood that it is the legal concept of legislative sovereignty which is the subject of discussion. That parliamentary sovereignty is a legal doctrine which allocates legally unlimited law-making authority, rather than absolute power, to Parliament, is the key insight from which the manner and form theory can develop. And it is possible—indeed even preferable—to take this lesson from the work of Jennings without jettisoning the language of sovereignty.

Nor do we need entirely to accept the particular reasoning of Jennings as to the authority for the manner and form theory. We will return to the issue of the precedential support for (or at least, not against) the manner and form understanding of parliamentary sovereignty below, but difficulties with two specific points can be addressed here. First, acceptance of the manner and form theory is not contingent upon acceptance of Jennings' analysis of the susceptibility to repeal of the purportedly unalterable Acts of Union. We are not required to accept, and indeed should not accept, the argument that the courts' view of Parliament's sovereign legislative power would have been of greater significance than the view the legislature took of its own power to legislate in contravention of the Acts of Union, had such a judicial view been offered. As we shall see in Chapter three, while there has been some obiter speculation about the status of the Acts of Union, it has still not

---

[79] It was in developing his arguments against the use of the terminology of sovereignty that Jennings came closest to turning this challenge to the orthodoxy into one informed by the political and philosophical disagreement which pervaded nearly all of his other disputes with Dicey: see text at nn 42–50. Yet, although Jennings at one stage denounced the idea that Parliament was 'sovereign' as 'a political doctrine imported by the political philosophers and the academic lawyers', he did not clearly spell out what he believed to be the rationale for, or implications of, this assertion. If at its root was Jennings' dissatisfaction with a style of argument which he condemned as 'tortuous, not to say metaphysical', and which produced a theory which was 'an academic formulation which does not fit the law of England', then it is not clear that anything is added by claims that this was 'political': see Jennings, *Law and the Constitution*, 5th edn (1959) n 26 above, 160, 167. Jennings may simply have meant that questions as to sovereignty belong in the realm of politics rather than in that of law. Yet even if this is not the case, and the objection made here was to the substantive political character of the notion of sovereignty, as the point is not fully developed, it seems largely rhetorical, rather than an essential part of his argument against Dicey. Certainly, Jennings' objections to Dicey's conception of Parliament's legislative power do not draw on political ideas in anything like the same way as his challenge to Dicey's understanding of the rule of law: see text at nn 7–38.

[80] See Introduction, p 5.

been necessary for a definitive position as to whether the eternal provisions contained therein bind UK Parliaments to be judicially established.[81] Yet even had it been, there is no reason that the view of the courts as to the scope of Parliament's power ought to be preferred to the view of the sovereign legislature itself. Indeed, this issue will be discussed further in Chapter seven, when it will be argued that while the manner and form theory does not prohibit the courts from seeking to enforce, as a matter of law, the procedural conditions which Parliament may legislate to create, neither does it necessarily require these conditions to be judicially enforced. And ultimately, it may in fact be preferable if statutory changes to the future manner and form for the enactment of valid legislation are not subject to judicial enforcement. What is clear, however, is that to imagine that the courts, rather than the sovereign Parliament itself, can or should provide definitive answers to complex questions about the scope of legally unlimited legislative power, may actually be seen to jar with the underlying logic of the manner and form theory.

We are also not required to accept Jennings' alternative rationalisation of the fact that the Acts of Union have been contravened, which was that such developments simply might have been pragmatically tolerated because it was sensible to do so. His attempt to sidestep the problem by focusing on the Acts of Union as treaties, by which Parliament could not be bound, rather than viewing them as legislation, by which perhaps it could, is similarly unconvincing. That Jennings seemed forced to ground both of these possible explanations in appeals to reality over formality does not mean that an argument from the principles which underpin the manner and form theory is unavailable. If the binding force of such seemingly unalterable clauses is to be dismissed, they could, for example, instead be characterised as rhetoric, designed to bolster the newly effected political unions between nations and ensure the longevity of these novel constitutional settlements. For, as Mitchell noted, '[t]oo much cannot be built upon such phrases as "in all time coming" or "for ever," which were of common occurrence in the Acts of Parliament of Scotland'.[82]

Yet perhaps the most compelling reason that statutes which deviated from the initial terms of the Acts of Union were nevertheless subsequently accepted as valid can be discerned from Jennings' own assertion that '[o]ne would not like to see Parliament limiting its own power too lightly'.[83] The substantive restrictions on the scope of Parliament's legislative power seemingly contained in both Acts of Union, if given effect, would have prevented absolutely future legislation on specified subject matters. It may well be, as Mitchell argued, that '[t]he real objection ...

[81] See chapter three of this volume, n 27.
[82] Mitchell, *Constitutional Law* (1968) n 78 above, 70. See generally 69–74 for Mitchell's argument that the Acts of Union 1707 were constituent Acts, which 'hypothetically ... could have imposed limitations upon the Union Parliament', but that these 'limitations are, however, few and imposed in such a way that any infringement of them is improbable': 73.
[83] Jennings, *Law and the Constitution*, 5th edn (1959) n 26 above, 169–70.

is to the total renunciation of legislative competence in any field in a manner which leaves a vacuum'.[84] The eternal substantive limits ostensibly included in the Acts of Union may then have been disregarded because it would be constitutionally undesirable for Parliament to restrict permanently and absolutely its future legislative capacity. But formal changes to the legislative procedure cannot be objected to on this basis, as a statutory alteration of the manner and form would not prevent Parliament from enacting legislation in future on a specified topic. Instead, such legislative changes to manner and form merely modify the process which must be followed for a valid Act of Parliament to be created. It is by drawing on this distinction between substantive limitations, which are absolute in their restrictive effect, and procedural conditions, which are not—a distinction which is at the very heart of the manner and form theory—that we are able to explain most convincingly why the enactment of legislation which appears to contravene the terms of the Acts of Union is not prohibited. The manner and form theory can dispose of Dicey's argument on this point as to the impossibility of Parliament binding its successors, notwithstanding the weakness of Jennings' analysis here.[85] And indeed, in so doing, the crucial distinction upon which this understanding of legally unlimited legislative authority rests is more explicitly exposed.

The second problem presented in Jennings' understanding of the authority for the manner and form theory threatens to call into question whether this is truly an understanding of parliamentary sovereignty at all. For although Jennings broadly accepted the two Diceyan propositions which together establish the legally unlimited legislative power of Parliament—that the legislature may make or unmake any law whatever, and that no other body may override its statutes—in his later work there is some evidence of uncertainty as to whether the latter proposition can be supported. The passage entitled 'The Supremacy of Parliament Comes from the Law' is much extended in the fifth edition of *The Law and the Constitution*,[86] and considers the relationship between the common law and Acts of Parliament. Jennings here argued that, due to the absence of decided cases on the point, it was 'virtually impossible to prove that there are no principles of the common law which Parliament cannot repeal'.[87] This uncertainty was a reflection of the tentative settlement reached between the courts and the legislature following the restoration of monarchy in 1688, but also due to the fact that

---

[84] Mitchell, *Constitutional Law* (1968) n 78 above, 77. For a similar view, see SA de Smith and R Brazier, *Constitutional and Administrative Law*, 8th edn (Harmondsworth, Penguin, 1998) 96–7.

[85] In earlier editions of Jennings' text, he did consider the possibility that the difficulties posed by the Acts of Union might be dismissed because 'these provisions relate to the subject-matter and not to the method of legislation'. But surprisingly, in light of the centrality of the distinction between substance and process to the manner and form theory, this line of argument was rejected by Jennings as an explanation based on 'a desire rather to make the facts fit the rule than to draw the rule from the facts': WI Jennings, *The Law and the Constitution*, 2nd edn (London, University of London Press, 1938) 147–48.

[86] Compare, eg Jennings, *Law and the Constitution*, 2nd edn (1938) n 85 above, 144–45, where the equivalent passage spans less than one full page of text.

[87] Jennings, *Law and the Constitution*, 5th edn (1959) n 26 above, 160.

'[w]e have not had the extreme cases because Parliament has not been extreme'.[88] Yet while Jennings felt able to conclude that the 'modern trend is towards admitting the supremacy of Parliament over the common law', a proviso was added: '[i]n accepting this principle for the time being, however, we should be grateful for Coke's dictum that if the occasion arose, a judge would do what a judge should do'.[89] Keith Ewing has argued that in making this assertion, Jennings is now telling us that 'the defenders of the constitution are the judges, not the people'.[90] As we shall see in Chapter seven, this could therefore mark a significant shift in Jennings' constitutional philosophy, and perhaps, at least in part, help to explain the difficulty in establishing a clear normative justification for the manner and form theory in his work. It also seems to be a shift in perspective which is at odds with the vast legislative power obviously attributed to Parliament by Jennings' persistent claims as to the potential lawfulness of a Parisian smoking ban being enacted. Does the eventual inclusion of these potentially inconsistent comments signal that Jennings' acceptance of the doctrine of legislative sovereignty was qualified because of an absence of authority? And if so, could this have implications for our understanding of the manner and form theory, based as it was on Jennings' conception of Parliament's legislative power?

The departure in Jennings' later work from what had earlier appeared to be a clear acceptance of parliamentary sovereignty is certainly tentative and limited. As we have seen above, Jennings accepted in general the supremacy of Parliament over the common law, for it was the possibility of such legal rules being altered by legislation that enabled his manner and form theory to take shape. Perhaps, however, as Ewing suggests, 'Jennings initially had doubts which were now nagging more persistently, so that by the fifth edition he was looking for the possibility of safeguards against the abuse of constitutional power'.[91] Indeed, when discussing the 'dangers in the system',[92] Jennings showed concern about the possibility that a government could be elected on a wave of 'mass hysteria' and use the supreme power of Parliament to either play 'fast and loose with public policy' or even subvert the democratic constitution by abolishing general elections.[93] Although he argued that this 'problem must not be exaggerated', there is evidence here of a degree of trepidation on Jennings' part about the potential implications of relying on democracy as the primary means of controlling legislative action.[94]

Here, then, Jennings might best be seen to be speculating about the potential reaction of the judiciary to legislation in extremely grave circumstances. That it was in 'exceptional times' that 'the supremacy of Parliament is a very great danger'

---

[88] ibid 160.
[89] ibid 160.
[90] Ewing, 'The Law and the Constitution: Manifesto of the Progressive Party' (2004) n 12 above, 743.
[91] ibid 743.
[92] Jennings, *Law and the Constitution*, 5th edn (1959) n 26 above, 187.
[93] ibid 192.
[94] ibid 192.

can be seen from the hypothetical examples of iniquitous legislation that Jennings cites prior to acknowledging the possibility that the courts might discover a common law power to confront a nefarious regime.[95] It was the authoritarian legislation of a Parliament which

> sought to extinguish itself, or to prolong its own life indefinitely, or to expropriate all land without compensation, or to dissolve all trade unions, or to introduce slavery, or to forbid all public meetings except by the Government party, or to censor all newspapers so as to prevent the case for the Opposition being heard

to which Jennings postulated a judicial challenge.[96] The notion that the judges could be capable of striking down Acts of Parliament which were held to be in violation of fundamental tenets of the common law was therefore far from the core of Jennings' conception of legislative power. Rather, it was conjecture regarding a judicial rejoinder of last resort in remarkable, and unprecedented, circumstances. Yet whether this should be understood as an aberration, or a genuine shift in Jennings' thinking about the power of the legislature—and despite being tentative and limited—such comments may still ultimately amount to a denial of parliamentary sovereignty. Before reaching such a conclusion, however, we might hesitate to note that Jennings' observation about the role of a judge faced with iniquitous legislation is without doubt underdeveloped, and does not specify whether to disregard such a statute would be in exercise of a legal power, or acting upon a (non-legal) moral obligation. If the latter, while other questions would still remain, it is possible that Jennings' comments could be reconciled with recognition of the legislative sovereignty of Parliament.

Yet even if Jennings' acceptance of parliamentary sovereignty may eventually have become qualified, the manner and form theory must be seen to remain a reconfiguration of the notion of legally unlimited legislative power. Jennings' argument that Parliament can lawfully alter the future law-making process by legislation developed from an understanding of legislative power which was legally unlimited. That the architect of the manner and form theory subsequently sought to claim that the potential may have existed for Parliament's legislative power to be circumscribed by the courts, in exceptional circumstances, does not deprive this initial finding of its force. Even if Jennings ultimately came to doubt whether Parliament possessed legislative authority which was completely unlimited, this was not because he conceived of the manner and form theory as something which limited Parliament's law-making power. Instead, the power to make statutory changes to the manner and form for future legislation was based on an expanded understanding of the scope of Parliament's law-making authority; for Jennings, 'as the law now stands, Parliament can enact anything: but this of course means that Parliament can change the law which now stands'.[97] It is crucial that Jennings' late

---

[95] ibid 265.
[96] ibid 160.
[97] ibid 160–61.

doubts about the scope of Parliament's legislative power are seen as distinct from his argument in support of the manner and form theory. These doubts must not obscure the fact that the manner and form theory is itself an understanding of, and not a rejection of, or a challenge to, parliamentary sovereignty. For this status of the manner and form theory—as a reconfiguration of the doctrine of parliamentary sovereignty—will be of great significance to the arguments developed in the remainder of this book in two ways. First, in Part II, when it will be argued that the key modern challenges to parliamentary sovereignty are both explicable, and can be reconciled with the doctrine, when a manner and form understanding of legally unlimited legislative power is adopted. And secondly, in Part III, when a normative account of the virtue, and potential functionality, of the manner and form theory is developed, for this will build on the arguments presented in Chapter one as to the virtue of the doctrine of parliamentary sovereignty in general. For present purposes, however, it is sufficient to note that the coherence or stability of the manner and form theory in principle is not undermined by particular difficulties which are presented in Jennings' original account, whether they be related to the argument(s) employed to dispose of the problem seemingly posed by the Acts of Union, or uncertainty about the possibility of common law limits on Parliament's legislative power.

Instead, these difficulties can be stripped away, allowing the fundamental nature of the manner and form theory, essentially derived from the work of Jennings, to be explained and defined in the following terms: The UK Parliament has legally unlimited legislative authority; it can make or unmake any law whatever, and nobody may strike down or override its enactments. This legislative power is allocated to Parliament by a legal doctrine. Parliament may exercise its legally unlimited legislative power to alter the legal rules which determine how this legislative power is to be used, which may alternatively be described as changing the 'manner and form' prescribed by law for the valid enactment of statutes. Parliament is therefore lawfully entitled to legislate to alter the future legislative process. This may, in effect, create procedural conditions with which, as a matter of law, successor Parliaments are bound to comply in order to enact valid legislation. But such 'binding of successors' may only be as to the future legislative procedure; the manner and form theory does not recognise the possibility that absolute substantive limits could be created. For this would be to undermine the existence of the very legally unlimited legislative authority of which the manner and form theory is itself a consequence. And, further, procedural conditions which do not have the effect of 'binding' successors may also be introduced in exercise of this legislative authority; such legislative change may include the creation of alternative legislative procedures, or procedural conditions which, though valid, may ultimately be avoided or repealed. As such, the manner and form theory is a reconfiguration of the idea of parliamentary sovereignty which understands it to be permissible, as a matter of law, for legally unlimited legislative authority to be exercised in such a way as to create procedural conditions with which future legislation must comply to be validly enacted, but does not recognise absolute substantive limitations on successor Parliaments to be lawful.

It is this understanding of the manner and form theory of parliamentary sovereignty which will be discussed throughout the rest of this book. There are, however, a number of objections which can made to this understanding of the sovereignty of Parliament. The four most significant will be addressed in the remainder of this chapter.

III. OBJECTIONS TO THE MANNER AND FORM THEORY

With a definition of the manner and form theory now established—derived in essence from the work of Jennings, subject to the clarifications offered above— we turn to consider the four main objections to this understanding of legally unlimited legislative authority. The first objection to be considered is that the manner and form theory is conceptually incoherent, and cannot be accepted as a true interpretation of the notion of parliamentary sovereignty. The second objection is that there is an absence of authority which would be required to justify claims that this theory can offer a viable understanding of the legislative power of Parliament as a matter of UK constitutional law. The third challenge queries why this theory of legislative authority is one which considers the possibility of legislative alteration of the future manner and the future form of valid lawmaking together: why, in other words, is the theory one which encompasses (and thus permits) changes to both manner *and* form? The fourth challenge concerns the possibility of cultivating a sufficiently clear distinction between matters of process and of substance—the difficulty in drawing lines between these categories being potentially problematic in so far as it would prevent a determination as to whether a purported change to manner and form was a (permissible) procedural condition, or an (impermissible) absolute limitation. While these four broad lines of challenge do pose difficulties for those who wish to defend a manner and form understanding of parliamentary sovereignty, I will argue that the theory can nevertheless withstand them all. But responding to these lines of argument also presents an opportunity: to explore and illuminate further the fundamental nature of the manner and form theory before it is considered in contemporary UK constitutional context in Part II.

A. Conceptually Incoherent

The most influential challenge to the coherence of the manner and form theory of parliamentary sovereignty was developed by Sir William Wade. In a significant 1955 article 'The Basis of Legal Sovereignty', Wade sought to challenge the manner and form theory of Jennings, while reasserting the orthodox Diceyan understanding of Parliament's legislative authority.[98] Wade's challenge had two elements: it rejected the manner and form theory on both precedential and conceptual grounds. Wade's challenge to the manner and form theory from authority will be considered in the next section, but it is his theoretical argument which is of present, and perhaps greatest, importance. For Wade sought to demonstrate that the manner and form theory was, on conceptual grounds, an inherently incoherent interpretation of the notion of parliamentary sovereignty.

Wade argued that the doctrine of parliamentary sovereignty depended on a 'rule of common law which says that the courts will enforce statutes'.[99] But this was more than a simple common law rule: it was also 'the ultimate *political* fact upon which the whole system of legislation hangs'.[100] This special political status meant that the 'rule was above and beyond the reach of statute ... because it is itself the authority of statute'.[101] As such, Wade argued, 'if no statute can establish the rule that the courts obey Acts of Parliament, similarly no statute can alter or abolish that rule'.[102] Jennings' manner and form theory was thus based on a 'fallacy', for the doctrine of parliamentary sovereignty rested on a rule of 'judicial obedience' to statute which was 'unique in being unchangeable by Parliament'.[103] Yet while Wade's account of the doctrine of parliamentary sovereignty as the ultimate political fact in the legal system led him to conclude that it was impossible for Parliament to enact legislation altering the law-making process, he did not reject entirely the possibility that this rule could be changed. While Parliament was legally incapable of altering the manner and form according to which future legislation would be validly enacted, the rule could be changed by 'revolution', and institutional responsibility for determining such changes in this rule 'lies in the keeping of the courts, and no Act of Parliament can take it from them'.[104] Ultimately, Wade maintained,

> it is always for the courts, in the last resort, to say what is a valid Act of Parliament; and that the decision of this question is not determined by any rule of law which can be laid down or altered by any authority outside the courts.[105]

There seems to be an instinctively persuasive symmetry at the core of Wade's attempt to provide simultaneously a theoretical foundation for Dicey's understanding of the sovereignty of Parliament, and a dismissal of the very possibility of a manner and form conception of legally unlimited legislative authority. The rule of judicial obedience to statute is a political fact, so can only be altered by (political) revolution. It confers legal authority on statute, so cannot be modified

---

[98]   HWR Wade, 'The Basis of Legal Sovereignty' (1955) 13 *CLJ* 172.
[99]   ibid 186.
[100] ibid 189.
[101] ibid 188.
[102] ibid 188.
[103] ibid 189.
[104] ibid 189.
[105] ibid 189.

by (legal) statutory means. There are, however, four key problems with Wade's analysis.[106] First, despite the exceptional means of its creation, as compared to other legal rules, the doctrine of parliamentary sovereignty is, within the UK constitution, a legal rule. Wade is surely right to say, that the doctrine of Parliament's legislative sovereignty has a foundation in political fact, this legal norm emerging definitively in the aftermath of the English Civil War. But this is something that Jennings too recognised—what is crucial is not the manner of the doctrine's creation, but its status within an existing legal system. The rules of a particular constitutional system, once established, may prohibit the legal alteration of foundational norms, but, as I will argue in Part II, the rules of the UK constitution do not. Instead, they permit legislation to be enacted on any topic, amending any constitutional rule of any variety, whether legal—as with the common law, or the royal prerogative—or non-legal—as with constitutional conventions. Despite its extraordinary, and extra-legal, origins, the doctrine of parliamentary sovereignty takes effect in the UK constitution as a legal rule which is, like all others, subject to amendment in accordance with the rules of the system. Neither the origins of this fundamental constitutional norm, nor the fact that it—like any constitutional doctrine—must be susceptible to change by revolutionary means, can be used to sanctify the rules relating to the legislative process, removing absolutely the very possibility that they may be subject to revision by lawful means in accordance with the terms of the legal system of which they are a part.[107]

Secondly, Wade's analysis of the manner in which the doctrine of parliamentary sovereignty may change is based on a counter-intuitive notion. This notion is that all change to fundamental constitutional norms—those which Wade would understand to be based on political facts—must necessarily be revolutionary, or extra-legal. There is no doubt at all that such fundamental constitutional norms will inevitably be subject to the prospect of revolutionary change; any legal norm which sought to preclude such a possibility would, inherently, be ineffective at precisely the revolutionary moment which it was designed to condition. But Wade's argument seems to commit him to the view that all change to fundamental constitution norms must be revolutionary, which is at odds with our experience of how constitutions operate in practice.[108] A codified constitution—which may derive its authority from nothing more than political fact—may prescribe

---

[106] See, generally M Gordon, 'The Conceptual Foundations of Parliamentary Sovereignty: Reconsidering Jennings and Wade' [2009] *PL* 519.

[107] See ibid 532–33. See also Bradley, 'The Sovereignty of Parliament—Form or Substance?' (2011) n 78 above, 48–52; M Elliott and R Thomas, *Public Law*, 2nd edn (Oxford, Oxford University Press, 2014) 216.

[108] Indeed, Wade seemed subsequently to acknowledge the potential force of this criticism, and somewhat qualified his original position in accepting the possibility of incremental change to fundamental constitutional norms: '[e]ven without such discontinuity there might be a shift of judicial loyalty if we take into account the dimension of time': HWR Wade, *Constitutional Fundamentals* (London, Stevens & Sons, 1989) 37. Yet in the main, his original analysis was reaffirmed in this later work: 'a revolution of some kind, in the sense of a break in legal continuity, seems to be lurking in any situation where there is a shift of the seat or the forms of sovereign legislative power': 46.

a legal process to be followed for its amendment, and we have no conceptual, or practical, difficulty in accepting that the modification of constitutional rules executed in accordance with such processes is both lawful and legitimate. There is no reason that the same cannot be true of an uncodified constitution organised around a doctrine of parliamentary sovereignty, if the legally unlimited law-making authority that doctrine allocates to Parliament is understood to permit the use of legislative power to alter the future legislative process.[109]

Thirdly, Wade's account of the process of constitutional change is extremely, and unduly, court-centric. If all change to fundamental constitutional norms is necessarily revolutionary, and thus extra-legal, it seems paradoxical for such a critical role in ascertaining and legitimising change to a constitution to be afforded to the courts. Yet the courts are absolutely central to Wade's scheme of constitutional change. They have, at least conceptually, near unfettered authority—in Wade's words, 'a perfectly free choice'[110]—to determine what they will, and will not, recognise as law. This may be objected to on the grounds that it is a highly artificial theory which is far removed from the reality of revolutionary change, in which multiple constitutional and political actors will be engaged in, and influence, a complex process of reshaping or reconstituting a community's system of government. To use but the most relevant example, following the restoration of the English monarchy in 1688, the courts did not freely determine and then impose a rule as to the sovereign legislative power of the Crown in Parliament. Instead, as Jennings clearly understood, they acquiesced in the face of overwhelming political power.[111] The courts were not 'sovereign' in this matter; indeed, as de Smith noted, decisions taken to recognise the sovereignty of Parliament were

> actuated in some instances, no doubt, by a keen sense of self-preservation; the decision by the House of Commons in 1689 to commit two judges of the King's Bench to prison for having controverted the privileges of the House doubtless accelerated the process of self-examination.[112]

Yet Wade's account of the role of the courts in relation to fundamental constitutional change not only fails to characterise aptly the much more contingent, marginal role that the judiciary will be likely to play in such a process—while discounting the inevitable contributions of other actors—it is also objectionable in principle. For to ascribe to unelected, unrepresentative and unaccountable judges the definitive role in establishing the legality of fundamental change which—on Wade's own account—constitutes a revolutionary break with the

---

[109] See Gordon, 'The Conceptual Foundations of Parliamentary Sovereignty' [2009] n 106 above, 533–34.

[110] Wade, 'Basis of Legal Sovereignty' (1955) n 98 above, 192. Indeed, in his subsequent Hamlyn Lectures, Wade seemed, if anything, to go even further, describing the judges as 'sovereign' with respect to the determination of changes to fundamental constitutional rules: see Wade, *Constitutional Fundamentals* (1989) n 108 above, 33.

[111] See Jennings, *Law and the Constitution*, 5th edn (1959) n 26 above, 39. A similar point is made by SA de Smith, *Constitutional and Administrative Law* (Harmondsworth, Penguin, 1971) 71.

[112] de Smith, *Constitutional and Administrative Law* (1971) 71.

previous constitutional order seems near impossible to defend from a democratic perspective. And if, as I have argued in Chapter one, the virtue of parliamentary sovereignty is that it can ensure the primacy of democratic decision-making in the UK constitution, the fact that Wade's understanding of the doctrine leads to the adoption of such a role for the courts seems to indicate that this theory may unsettle, rather than preserve, the instinct and logic which underpins recognition of Parliament's legally unlimited legislative authority.[113]

Fourthly, Wade's analysis of the process of constitutional change threatens to institutionalise a conservative approach to foundational political reform. For in characterising all such constitutional change as revolutionary, Wade's work prevents absolutely the possibility of legal change to the doctrine of parliamentary sovereignty. Instead, any such change to the legislative process, or the institutions engaged in it, must follow an (admittedly artificial) break in constitutional continuity, and even then, can only be accepted upon endorsement by the judiciary. As John Allison has argued, this places Wade's theory at odds with 'the common-law's evolutionary case-law character',[114] and also with the flexibility conventionally associated with the UK's uncodified constitution, best captured in Griffith's famous observation that '[t]he constitution of the United Kingdom lives on, changing from day to day for the constitution is no more and no less than what happens'.[115] Yet the adoption of a theory which views constitutional change as something which occurs 'in the last resort', as Wade argued,[116] may be problematic for reasons which go beyond descriptive inaccuracy. For the lack of openness to constitutional change embedded in Wade's theory of parliamentary sovereignty may unjustifiably entrench in the wider political culture a sense that fundamental constitutional reform need not be seriously considered, because it is—at least in accordance with the rules of the existing system—impossible lawfully to effect. To make such crucial rules as those relating to the exercise of legislative authority immune from lawful alteration—and potentially, therefore, enhanced scrutiny—could serve to engender a sense of constitutional complacency which may be unwarranted, and is certainly undesirable. An understanding of parliamentary sovereignty which commits us, on conceptual grounds, to adopt—or at the very least, forces us to work against—such an attitude is one which must be treated with great scepticism.[117]

For these reasons, Wade's attempt to exclude on conceptual grounds the very possibility of a manner and form understanding of parliamentary sovereignty

---

[113] See Gordon, 'The Conceptual Foundations of Parliamentary Sovereignty' [2009] n 106 above, 534–38.

[114] JWF Allison, 'Parliamentary Sovereignty, Europe and the Economy of the Common Law' in M Andenas (ed), *Liber Amicorum in Honour of Lord Slynn of Hadley: Judicial Review in International Perspective* (London, Kluwer Law International, 2000) 189.

[115] JAG Griffith, 'The Political Constitution' (1979) 42 *MLR* 1, 19.

[116] HWR Wade, 'Sovereignty—Revolution or Evolution?' (1996) 112 *LQR* 568, 575.

[117] See Gordon, 'The Conceptual Foundations of Parliamentary Sovereignty' [2009] n 106 above, 538–43.

must be rejected. Wade's argument that this fundamental constitutional norm could not be altered by legal means is flawed, and his alternative account of the manner in which such rules could change presents a range of problems. Given the enduring influence of Wade's challenge to the manner and form theory, it is important that the difficulties which pervade his particular conceptual argument against this understanding of parliamentary sovereignty are clearly understood. Yet it may be objected that a similar, although more sophisticated, version of Wade's essential argument would not suffer from the range of problems identified above. Such an approach might be offered by Hart's theory of the rule of recognition. For Hart, the rule of recognition was a fundamental part of any legal system, and contained the criteria of legal validity against which all other legal norms were to be tested.[118] Yet being the ultimate criterion of legal validity, Hart's rule of recognition could be neither valid nor invalid.[119] Instead, the content of the rule of recognition would be determined by the beliefs and patterns of behaviour of the 'officials' within that legal system.[120] At its most basic, the attitude and practice of officials become broadly self-fulfilling; the rules which these actors (and also, ideally, citizens) within a legal system collectively accept as law, would be law.

There are clear similarities with Wade's discussion of parliamentary sovereignty as an ultimate political fact in Hart's later, and more fully developed, account.[121] In particular, Hart emphasises that the content or validity of a system's rule of recognition cannot be established by legal tests, but is instead dependent on extra-legal, or political, facts.[122] Further, in Hart's theory, officials are ascribed a definitive role in determining the content of the rule of recognition, but it is often made clear in *The Concept of Law* that, as for Wade, judicial figures would feature very prominently in this process.[123] Yet despite these similarities, Hart's conceptual architecture did not lead him to the singular conclusion adopted by Wade; that the rule affording legally unlimited legislative power to Parliament could not be altered by legislation. Instead, for Hart, to characterise the doctrine of parliamentary sovereignty as constituting a significant part of the UK legal system's rule of recognition left open the question of whether Parliament could, or could not, bind its successors. This was, Hart argued, a key example of the ambiguity

---

[118] HLA Hart, *The Concept of Law*, 2nd edn (Oxford, Oxford University Press, 1994) ch 6.

[119] ibid 109.

[120] ibid 114–17.

[121] See Allison, 'Parliamentary Sovereignty' (2000) n 114 above, 186–89 for discussion of the similarities between Wade's work, that of Hart, and also Kelsen's theory of the 'Grundnorm', a legal positivist pre-cursor—though different in significant respects—to the rule of recognition. For Hart's rejection of the assumed validity which the Grundnorm postulates, see *Concept of Law* (1994) 108–9.

[122] Hart, *Concept of Law* (1994) n 118 above, 109.

[123] See, eg ibid 152–54, for Hart's discussion of the role of courts in settling disputes as to uncertainty about some aspect of the content of the rule of recognition. Hart recognises that it may be problematic to assume that courts have the authority to determine such questions, and offers what is an essentially pragmatic argument in an attempt to justify this: 'The truth may be that, when courts settle previously unenvisaged questions concerning the most fundamental constitutional rules, they *get* their authority to decide them accepted after questions have arisen and the decision has been given. Here all that succeeds is success'.

which could exist at the edges of the rule of recognition—in the penumbra of uncertainty, which lay outside the core of settled meaning of a norm—and which was a necessary consequence of the open texture of law.[124] Hart thus identified two potential, and competing, understandings of sovereign power, either of which it would be legally permissible for a particular system to adopt. These alternative understandings of 'legal omnipotence' were 'a *continuing* omnipotence in all matters not affecting the legislative competence of successive parliaments, and an unrestricted *self-embracing* omnipotence the exercise of which can only be enjoyed once'.[125]

Hart's analysis of the doctrine of parliamentary sovereignty as constituting part of a rule of recognition thus avoids imposing an understanding of legally unlimited legislative power according to which the rules that establish and regulate the law-making process are inherently immune from statutory modification. Instead, this was an 'empirical question' which was open to resolution in different ways in any particular legal system.[126] Yet the conceptual framework provided by Hart for the analysis of legislative sovereignty is potentially problematic in another respect. For while Hart recognised that the question of whether Parliament could exercise its legally unlimited legislative authority to alter the future law-making process—as opposed to limiting substantively successor Parliaments—could not be disposed of simply by invoking the distinction between continuing and self-embracing sovereignty,[127] others have failed to follow this example. Instead, the particular questions raised by the manner and form theory have sometimes been considered *within* a framework which posits just two possible interpretations of legislative sovereignty—adopting Hart's terminology, one continuing and the other self-embracing—rather than being treated as issues which stand outside any such dichotomy.[128] To assume that the manner and form theory is simply a variant of self-embracing sovereignty,[129] a conception of legally unlimited legislative authority by which Parliament may limit its successors, is to misunderstand and misrepresent the essential nature of this approach. Jennings' manner and form theory was developed as a consequence of a deliberate attempt to move away from a starting point which postulated the existence of two extremes of sovereignty, from which one must be selected. And this is evident in the substance of the theory, which is compatible with neither a continuing nor a self-embracing conception of legal omnipotence. The manner and form theory does not enable

---

[124] ibid 127–29.
[125] ibid 149.
[126] ibid 150.
[127] See Hart's separate discussion of this issue, ibid 150–52.
[128] See, eg AL Young, 'Hunting Sovereignty: *Jackson v Her Majesty's Attorney-General*' [2006] *PL* 187; AL Young, *Parliamentary Sovereignty and the Human Rights Act* (Oxford, Hart Publishing, 2009); I McLean and A McMillan, 'Professor Dicey's Contradictions' [2007] *PL* 435; P Oliver, *The Constitution of Independence: The Development of Constitutional Theory in Australia, Canada and New Zealand* (Oxford, Oxford University Press, 2005).
[129] See, eg G Winterton, 'The British Grundnorm: Parliamentary Supremacy Re-examined' (1976) 92 *LQR* 591, 593.

the legislative competence of successor Parliaments to be limited absolutely—contrary to the self-embracing conception—yet it *does* permit the process by which such competence is to be exercised to be altered by legislation—contrary to the continuing conception. The manner and form theory will inevitably be distorted by consideration of it within a continuing–self-embracing duality, and attempts to frame the debate about the nature and scope of parliamentary sovereignty around these conceptions—and only these conceptions—must consequently be rejected.[130]

It is therefore problematic to adopt Hart's terminology if it is taken to exhaust the potential ways in which parliamentary sovereignty may be understood. Yet the idea that parliamentary sovereignty may be an aspect of the UK's rule of recognition does not commit us to adopting the distinction between continuing and self-embracing sovereignty. Instead, if the problematic use of this terminology is avoided, to analyse the doctrine of parliamentary sovereignty from a rule of recognition perspective can further demonstrate the deficiency of Wade's argument that the manner and form theory was a conceptually incoherent interpretation of legally unlimited legislative power. For the special status of a fundamental constitutional rule like that of the sovereignty of Parliament does not, as Hart showed, preclude any particular legal system from adopting an understanding of legislative power which permits the lawful alteration of the law-making process—on the contrary, this a matter which is open to be determined by the rules adopted in that particular legal system. Yet, despite the clear utility of the rule of recognition in providing a conceptual scheme which demonstrates the possibility of a manner and form understanding of parliamentary sovereignty, we should be cautious about attempts to engage it as a practical analytical tool. As we shall see in Part II, attempts to analyse change to the doctrine of parliamentary sovereignty as change to the rule of recognition are increasingly popular,[131] and have been employed in the context of a number of the different modern challenges to the legally unlimited legislative power of the UK Parliament.[132] However, attempts to explain contemporary constitutional developments as constituting changes to the rule of recognition in the UK raise a number of difficulties, both descriptive and normative in character, which will be explored fully as those specific arguments arise. For present purposes, it is sufficient to note that endorsement of Hart's theory of the rule of recognition in general, at a conceptual level, does not mean that it can, or should, usefully be exploited to dispose of the particular contemporary challenges posed to the doctrine of parliamentary sovereignty in the UK constitution.

---

[130] Gordon, 'The Conceptual Foundations of Parliamentary Sovereignty' [2009] n 106 above, 527–31. See also NW Barber, 'The Afterlife of Parliamentary Sovereignty' (2011) 9 *International Journal of Constitutional Law* 144, 147, fn 19.

[131] Although not an exclusively contemporary phenomenon; see, eg JDB Mitchell, 'What Happened to the Constitution on 1st January 1973?' (1980) 11 *Cambrian Law Review* 69, analysing the constitutional change brought about by UK membership of the EU.

[132] See chapter 4 of this volume, pp 179–82; chapter 5 of this volume, pp 218–22; chapter 6 of this volume, pp 273–75.

Indeed, I will suggest in Part II that the rule of recognition should not be used as a jurisprudential 'get out of jail free card', which can be used to bypass even the most seemingly insurmountable challenge to parliamentary sovereignty, on the extremely flexible basis that what the officials in the UK accept as law has simply changed. Instead, I will argue that characterising change to the doctrine of parliamentary sovereignty as change to the rule of recognition must be avoided wherever possible, and attempts to understand and explain such change within the existing legal parameters of the UK constitution—where available—are to be preferred. What is clear at present, however, is that Wade's attempt to demonstrate that the manner and form theory is conceptually incapable of offering such an explanation must be rejected.

B. Absence of Authority

Just as Wade sought to reject the manner and form theory on logical grounds, he also objected to Jennings' analysis of the precedents which were claimed to offer support for this alternative understanding of the doctrine of parliamentary sovereignty. Wade's challenge from authority had two main aspects; he sought to distinguish the precedents relied upon by Jennings, while reasserting those which had been dismissed. First, Wade argued that the decisions of the respective courts in the cases of *Trethowan*[133] and *Harris*[134] could not be seen as indicative of the legal position of Parliament in the UK constitution. For Wade, *Trethowan* 'in no way raised any question of the validity of acts of a sovereign legislature, but was rather concerned with subordinate, or delegated, legislative power', in this case that of the New South Wales Parliament, which had been created by, and was subject to, the Imperial Parliament at Westminster.[135] Wade argued that the decision in *Trethowan* was thus merely an example of a delegate illegitimately exceeding the scope of its authority, which offered no guidance about the possibility of a sovereign legislature binding its successors as to the manner and form required to produce valid legislation. Further, *Harris* was not, according to Wade, an example of a sovereign legislature being bound as to the future legislative process by a predecessor. The super-majority clause at issue in this case did not derive from a statute passed by the sovereign South African Parliament, but from an Act of the Westminster Parliament dating from an era when the latter legislature was legally supreme. When determining whether the South African Parliament's acquisition of sovereignty rendered this clause a constitutional relic, Wade maintained that 'the issue before the South African courts was fundamentally different from any other ordinary legal issue'.[136] In fact, on a true reading of the case, Wade argued

---

[133] *Attorney-General for New South Wales v Trethowan* [1932] AC 526.
[134] *Harris v Minister of the Interior* 1952 (2) SA 428.
[135] Wade, 'Basis of Legal Sovereignty' (1955) n 98 above, 173.
[136] ibid 173.

'that the courts were really called upon for a political or legislative decision, having no "law" to guide them, but having to create new law in a situation which should strictly be called revolutionary'.[137] The judiciary in *Harris* were therefore in precisely the conceptually revolutionary situation which has been considered above, and as such, the courts

> have to decide for themselves—*for no legislation can direct them*—what they will recognise as the proper expression of the new sovereign legal power. In this they have a perfectly free choice, for legally the question is ultimate (emphasis added).[138]

In such circumstances, the manner and form with which a sovereign legislature would have to comply to produce valid legal enactments was not determined by legislation enacted by a sovereign predecessor, but by a decision of the courts. The court in *Harris* upheld the requirement that an alternative legislative process was to be followed, but, for Wade, this was not because a sovereign Parliament had been, or could be, bound as to the future manner and form for law-making by statute.

Secondly, Wade contended that the case of *Ellen Street Estates*[139] did constitute sufficient proof that the traditional understanding of the doctrine of parliamentary sovereignty continued to be an accurate representation of UK constitutional practice. Indeed, Wade met claims that *Ellen Street Estates* alone was not adequate authority to sustain a Diceyan view of parliamentary sovereignty with a degree of exasperation, enquiring, '[w]hat more could be asked? It is not every day that the validity of Acts of Parliament is challenged in English courts, and one could hardly expect a long line of decisions'.[140] The crucial observations of Maugham LJ, discussed above, were not obiter, Wade maintained, but 'a necessary part' of the decision of the Court of Appeal.[141] It had been argued by counsel in *Ellen Street Estates* that section 7(1), which provided that inconsistent legislation 'shall not have effect', could be read as an attempt to alter the manner and form for future legislation, with the Act of 1919 yielding to an express repeal only. For Wade, therefore, 'the question of form' was 'squarely before the court' and the insistence of Maugham LJ that Parliament could not bind its successors as to manner and form was legally definitive.[142]

Wade's challenge from authority, however, is not persuasive. Wade's analysis of *Trethowan* is ultimately dependent on the pertinence of the distinction drawn between sovereign and subordinate legislatures. Following Jennings, Heuston argued that it was 'hard to see why' scholars such as Wade 'should attach so much importance to the formal source of the complex set of rules identifying the

---

[137] ibid 173.
[138] ibid 192.
[139] *Ellen Street Estates v Minister of Health* [1934] 1 KB 590.
[140] Wade, 'Basis of Legal Sovereignty' (1955) n 98 above, 184.
[141] ibid 184.
[142] ibid 176.

location and composition of the sovereign'.[143] Supposedly subordinate legislatures such as that of New South Wales in the *Trethowan* case were 'expressly given full powers to legislate for the peace, order and good government of the colony', and since it had 'long been settled that these are words which confer the widest amplitude of power', Heuston contended that such a legislature could thus be said to be in 'exactly the position of the United Kingdom Parliament'.[144] It is immaterial, with respect to the extent of their authority, whether the legal rules which prescribe how legislative power is to be exercised are found in a constitution, a statute or customary law. Instead, the universal point which can be seen to have been established in *Trethowan* was that a legislature must derive its power from the law, and this power can only be validly exercised in accordance with the procedures prescribed by law. If the legislative procedure set out in law—whatever the formal source of these rules—is legitimately altered, then the modified rules must be adhered to by a legislature if valid legislation is to be lawfully enacted. Indeed, as Heuston noted, the contrary view seems to be based on an implicit assumption that a legislature which owed its origin to statute was 'in some (never very clearly stated) way inferior to the Parliament of the United Kingdom'.[145]

Further, Wade's attempt to re-frame the decision in *Harris* in accordance with his theory of judge-led revolutionary constitutional change must also be seen to fail. The conceptual difficulties with this account of change to fundamental constitutional norms, discussed above, make Wade's reading of *Harris* hard to accept; in particular, to characterise the courts in this case as having a free choice as to which ultimate legal principles to 'invent ... to fill a vacuum'[146] feels both artificial and inaccurate.[147] Ultimately, despite Wade's attempt to portray it as a political decision, *Harris* demonstrates a fundamental legal principle: even a sovereign legislature—as was the Parliament of South Africa at the time the case was decided—is subject to the requirement that legally valid legislation be enacted in accordance with the manner and form established by law.

Moving from the persuasive to the domestic precedents, Wade's argument that *Ellen Street Estates* was authority for the proposition that Parliament cannot bind its successors as to manner and form is also difficult to sustain. The sheer fact that it was put to the court in *Ellen Street Estates* that section 7(1) should be read as purporting to control the form of subsequent legislation surely cannot contrive

---

[143] Heuston, *Essays In Constitutional Law* (1964) n 73 above, 26.
[144] ibid 26.
[145] ibid 25.
[146] Wade, 'Basis of Legal Sovereignty' (1955) n 98 above, 192.
[147] See, eg I Loveland, *By Due Process of Law?* (1999) n 55 above, 410: 'Harris No. 1 ... was an intensely conservative decision which was firmly rooted in South(ern) African constitutional law and tradition and buttressed by copious legal authority from other Commonwealth jurisdictions. In simple terms, the Appellate Division did not hold that there was a "new" constitution at all; rather it concluded that, contrary to the beliefs of the Malan government and its own per incuriam decision in Ndlwana, the "old" constitution was still very much in existence'. The reference is to *Ndlwana v Hofmeyr* [1937] AD 229, in which the court had previously indicated that the special legislative procedures set out in the South Africa Act 1909 were 'at the mercy of Parliament like everything else': 238.

to make Maugham LJ's comments anything more than obiter dictum. It is far from clear that this provision should be interpreted as an attempt to bind future Parliaments at all; the marginal note accompanying section 7—'Effect of Act on existing enactments'—gives no indication that the 1919 Act was intended to be applicable over future legislation, and hence bind successor Parliaments, yet this could not be taken into account by the court in *Ellen Street Estates*. Further, had the Parliament of 1919 intended to bind its successors by section 7(1), it would be reasonable to expect such a constitutionally significant move to have been debated as the Bill passed through Parliament. That this possibility was neither discussed in the House of Commons nor the House of Lords seems to confirm that Parliament did not intend to bind its successors. Indeed, at the second reading of the Bill in the Commons, the Attorney-General observed, 'I do not think that I need enter into the details of the proposals dealing with the effect that the new Act is to have upon existing enactments'.[148] It seems clear from this that section 7 was viewed as an uncontroversial provision which was not intended to restrict the legislative freedom of future Parliaments.

Yet even if section 7(1) is to be read as attempting to bind future Parliaments, its words must be taken literally, with the provision being seen as an absolute substantive limitation, rather than a procedural requirement that Parliament uses express words to deviate from the 1919 Act. Since the 1919 Act, as Joseph Jaconelli has argued, 'in no way purported to lay down that its terms could only be repealed in a certain manner and form', to the extent that *Ellen Street Estates* is authoritative, it is 'on the issue of entrenchment as to subject-matter only'.[149] The dictum of Maugham LJ in *Ellen Street Estates* should thus be viewed as an incidental reiteration of traditional thinking in a case where the issue of form was not before the Court of Appeal, rather than seen as an authoritative statement of constitutional law. Contrary to Wade's suggestion, *Ellen Street Estates* does not decisively demonstrate that Parliament cannot alter the legislative process by statute.

Wade may therefore be seen to dismiss the significance of *Trethowan* and *Harris* too readily, while making more of Maugham LJ's overreaching obiter dictum in *Ellen Street Estates* than the case warrants. Yet, while I have argued that Wade failed to rebut Jennings' claims as to the authority of the manner and form theory, this still may not take us very far. This is due to the necessarily speculative nature of Jennings' argument as to the precedential support for a manner and form understanding of parliamentary sovereignty. For at the time Jennings' vision of the manner and form theory was first outlined, and in the subsequent period when it was defended, there was no clear domestic judicial decision which could be said to demonstrate definitive support for this conception of parliamentary sovereignty. Instead, the most that Jennings could show was that it was an interpretation of legislative authority that it would be plausible for a UK court

---

[148] Sir Gordon Hewart MP, *Hansard*, HC Deb, Vol 114 col 2280 (10 April 1919).
[149] J Jaconelli, *Enacting a Bill of Rights: The Legal Problems* (Oxford, Clarendon Press, 1980) 165, fn 41.

to adopt, on the basis of the persuasive Commonwealth precedents, and which was not precluded by existing binding statements of legal principle. In this sense, while the particular arguments which Wade advanced against Jennings should be seen to fail, this does not mean that the manner and form theory could be seen to succeed. Rather, at this stage, the matter remained open, with the manner and form theory of parliamentary sovereignty neither excluded from nor included in the UK constitution.

The difficulty for Jennings and Wade in reaching any definitive conclusion as to the applicability of the manner and form conception of parliamentary sovereignty to the UK constitution is perhaps most apparent in relation to the comments of Lord Sankey in *British Coal Corporation v The King*.[150] The Statute of Westminster 1931—which was enacted to recognise as a matter of law the legislative independence of Australia, Canada, the Irish Free State, Newfoundland, New Zealand and South Africa—provided, by section 4, that no Act of the UK Parliament would extend to one of the Dominions 'unless it is expressly declared in that Act that that Dominion has requested, and consented to, the enactment thereof'. Jennings suggested that this should be viewed as an alteration of the future manner and form for legislation, and noted that the formula had been 'strictly followed in His Majesty's Declaration of Abdication Act, 1936' and other subsequent legislation applicable to the Dominions.[151] Yet, in a case heard before the Judicial Committee of the Privy Council as to the legality of Canadian legislation which prohibited the making of appeals to the King in Council in criminal matters, Lord Sankey addressed the possibility of repeal by the UK Parliament of section 4 of the Statute of Westminster 1931:

> It is doubtless true that the power of the Imperial Parliament to pass on its own initiative any legislation that it thought fit extending to Canada remains in theory unimpaired: indeed, the Imperial Parliament could, as a matter of abstract law, repeal or disregard s. 4 of the Statute. But that is theory and has no relation to realities.[152]

For Wade, Lord Sankey's observation was clear evidence that Jennings was wrong, and that purported changes to the manner and form for future legislation would not be recognised by the UK courts. A subsequent statute which did not contain a declaration of consent from the relevant Dominion would, according to Wade, nevertheless be given effect, and the Statute of Westminster repealed to the extent of any inconsistency with the later legislation.[153]

Of course, one of the key difficulties of drawing on a provision such as section 4 of the Statute of Westminster to find support either for or against a manner and form understanding of parliamentary sovereignty is that this example does not *only* raise questions as to the lawfulness of statutory changes to the

---

[150] *British Coal Corporation v The King* [1935] AC 500.
[151] Jennings, *Law and the Constitution*, 5th edn (1959) n 26 above, 163.
[152] *British Coal Corporation v The King* [1935] AC 500, 520.
[153] Wade, 'Basis of Legal Sovereignty' (1955) n 98 above, 177.

future law-making process. Instead, conceptual issues relating to the conferral of independence and the abdication of power must be at the heart of any attempt to understand the effect of this specific legislation. And in particular—as both Jennings and Wade recognised[154]—considerations of perspective therefore become critical. Whether the UK courts will continue to recognise that the UK Parliament has legally unlimited legislative power, and what conception of that power they will adopt, is one issue to be assessed. But when dealing with the distribution of power between constitutional orders established in different territories, the approach taken by those competing institutions must also be taken into account. In such circumstances, considerations of political fidelity will inevitably take priority, and the legislative, executive and judicial institutions of newly independent states will almost certainly disregard any attempt by a foreign 'sovereign' Parliament to reassert an expired legislative jurisdiction.[155] Yet even aside from the added complexity which is generated in this context, which can be bypassed to a reasonable extent by accepting that the perspective given is only that of a UK court, there is still ambiguity in the observation of Lord Sankey. This is most obvious with respect to the contrast drawn between 'theory' and 'realities': is the theory of parliamentary sovereignty something which has been, or could be, displaced by reality? Or does such theory continue to possess authority, with the reference to reality simply indicating that legislative power is extremely unlikely to be used in this way?[156]

However, of equal importance—if much less apparent—is Lord Sankey's potential conflation of the possibility of Parliament repealing or disregarding section 4. Contrary to their portrayal in *British Coal Corporation*, these are not equivalent alternatives, either of which might be options for Parliament to pursue 'as a matter of abstract law' (a phrase which, incidentally, reflects the same ambiguity generated by the dissonance Lord Sankey postulated between theory and reality—is 'abstract' law any less enforceable than other legal norms?). Instead, these two possibilities are logically opposed: if Parliament is able to disregard section 4, there is no need to repeal it; if section 4 is repealed, it is necessarily not

---

[154] See, eg Jennings, *Law and the Constitution*, 5th edn (1959) n 26 above, 166–68; Wade, 'Basis of Legal Sovereignty' (1955) n 98 above, 196–97.

[155] Such circumstances may in fact constitute a genuine example of the kind of revolution which was discussed by Wade, although his account of the role of the courts in such a process remains, in my view, open to real criticism. It is important to note, however, that in such situations attempts to follow existing legal processes are generally still seen as necessary, despite the fact that the very authority of these processes must be extinguished by the founding of a 'new' constitutional order; this paradox is considered at length in Oliver, *The Constitution of Independence* (2005) n 128 above.

[156] See further Lord Denning in *Blackburn v Attorney General* [1971] 1 WLR 1037, 1040: 'Take the Acts which have granted independence to the Dominions and territories overseas. Can anyone imagine that Parliament could or would reverse those laws and take away their independence? Most clearly not. Freedom once given cannot be taken away. Legal theory must give way to practical politics'. A similar ambiguity to that discussed above is evident in Lord Denning's comments, and from the response which they drew from Sir Robert Megarry VC in *Manuel v Attorney General* [1983] Ch 77, 89: 'I think that it is clear from the context that Lord Denning was using the word "could" in the sense of "could effectively"; I cannot read it as meaning "could as a matter of abstract law"'.

being disregarded, but engaged with as a provision which would be legally valid unless rescinded. Once this is recognised, we can see that the implications of Lord Sankey's observations as to the ability of Parliament to avoid the legal effect of section 4 of the Statute of Westminster are unclear. If Parliament can disregard the provision entirely, this would lend support to the orthodox Diceyan understanding of legislative sovereignty, whereby statutory attempts to bind successors are simply void.[157] If, in contrast, Parliament must repeal section 4 to avoid its effects—legislative action which the Statute of Westminster itself does not explicitly seek to prohibit—this would lend support to the manner and form theory, for it would indicate that compliance with the procedural condition that Dominion consent be declared would otherwise legally have been required. As it is, neither conclusion can be definitely supported on the basis of the obiter dictum of Lord Sankey.

That the debate between Jennings and Wade was ultimately inconclusive as to the support from authority for the manner and form theory was in essence a consequence of the paucity of the available precedents. The absence of a binding domestic decision directly confronting the issue of whether statutory changes to manner and form were legally valid led to argument being structured around a limited number of cases, many of which were not binding on UK courts or contained only fleeting, underdeveloped, or indirectly relevant judicial remarks. Even in the years following the debate between Jennings and Wade, argument as to the status of the manner and form conception of parliamentary sovereignty in the UK constitution retained a speculative air, even in the light of developments which were, in principle, potentially significant. The decision of the Judicial Committee of the Privy Council in *Bribery Commissioner v Ranasinghe* was the most notable development in this respect.[158] In this case, the Judicial Committee of the Privy Council held that the (then) Ceylon Parliament could not legislate for the appointment of Bribery Commissioners by ordinary legislation; instead, in accordance with the terms of the Ceylon (Constitution) Order 1946, a special legislative process, which required the speaker of the House of Representatives to certify that at least two-thirds of its members had voted in favour of the measure, needed to be followed for this legislation to be validly enacted. The general

---

[157] Wade sought to reject the argument that a purported manner and form provision in an Act of Parliament would be 'void' if it was not legally effective. Wade contended that the 'infirmity' of such manner and form provisions was 'no more than the common infirmity which is shared by all the Acts ever passed, viz., the possibility of being repealed'. Yet this is difficult to accept, for if the manner and form theory were rejected, such provisions would be different in that they would be intrinsically incapable of ever being legally effective. Wade did accept that such provisions would be 'legally futile', but there seems to be no substantive difference between this formulation and the language of voidness to which he objected: Wade, 'Basis of Legal Sovereignty' (1955) n 98 above, 186. Nor is there much difference between this and the view of Jennings, who argued that, if the manner and form theory were rejected, such provisions would be 'inoperative as law': Jennings, *Law and the Constitution*, 5th edn (1959) n 26 above, 163–64.

[158] *The Bribery Commissioner v Ranasinghe* [1965] AC 172.

principle which led to this conclusion was set out by Lord Pearce, giving the judgment of the Board:

> A legislature has no power to ignore the conditions of law-making that are imposed by the instrument which itself regulates its power to make law. This restriction exists independently of the question whether the legislature is sovereign, as is the legislature of Ceylon.[159]

The decision in *Ranasinghe* thus endorsed the principle established in *Trethowan*, and confirmed, following *Harris*, its applicability to both sovereign and non-sovereign legislatures alike. Perhaps of greatest importance, then, is the fact that this case was decided by the Privy Council, the judicial members of which were the Law Lords—now-a-days, of course, Justices of the Supreme Court[160]— who would hear an equivalent UK case. For, although the decision in *Trethowan* was also one of the Privy Council, the position of a sovereign legislature was not there considered by the Board. As such, and although still not a decision which would directly bind UK courts, Gray nevertheless argued that this case was 'a recognition by a British court of a principle that the powers of a sovereign legislature may be legally limited by "manner and form" requirements'.[161]

While this is no doubt correct, the decision of the Privy Council in *Ranasinghe* did not herald any general acceptance in the UK of the manner and form theory of parliamentary sovereignty. As Lord Pearce noted in *Ranasinghe*, 'in the Constitution of the United Kingdom there is no governing instrument which prescribes the law-making powers and the forms which are essential to those powers'.[162] Although I have argued in this chapter that such a difference should be immaterial to the question of whether a manner and form understanding of legally unlimited legislative power should be accepted, for defenders of Dicey's orthodoxy this variation would justify an alternative conclusion. And as we saw above, the Diceyan maxim that 'Parliament cannot bind its successors' is one which continues to feature prominently in mainstream constitutional discourse about the extent of legislative power in the UK.[163] Yet that this blunt mantra is oft-repeated does not mean that it is legally correct.[164] Indeed, that the debate between Jennings and Wade as to the support from authority for the manner and form theory cannot be shown to reach a definitive conclusion either way means

---

[159] *The Bribery Commissioner v Ranasinghe* [1965] AC 172, 197.

[160] Constitutional Reform Act 2005 s 138.

[161] HR Gray, 'The Sovereignty of Parliament and the Entrenchment of Legislative Process' (1964) 27 *MLR* 705, 705. See also Marshall, *Constitutional Theory* (1971) n 78 above, 53–57, especially at 57: 'the Privy Council [in *Ranasinghe*] at least seems to be edging a little in the direction of "self-embracing sovereignty"'.

[162] *The Bribery Commissioner v Ranasinghe* [1965] AC 172, 195.

[163] See text at n 6 above.

[164] See Bradley, 'The Sovereignty of Parliament—Form or Substance?' (2011) n 78 above, 68, suggesting that debate 'about ways in which the political process, the conduct of government, and the law's contribution to social order can be improved' will be 'stunted if it proceeds from the starting point that "Parliament is unable to bind its successors"'.

that there is no firm disinclination towards this conception of the doctrine of parliamentary sovereignty in the pertinent precedents. Instead, rather than being discounted, the question of the status of the manner and form theory in the UK constitution remains open to potential resolution in the light of modern developments. This task will be taken up in Part II, after two final objections to the manner and form theory have been considered.

C. Why 'Manner and Form'?

Why is the manner and form theory an understanding of legally unlimited legislative power which seeks to analyse statutory changes to the *manner* of future law-making and to the *form* of future law-making together? The manner in which legislation is to be enacted can be seen to refer to the action that must be taken by specified institutions or office-holders, in what particular sequence and in what particular time-scale, in order for measures recognisable as legally valid to be produced. The form in which legislation is to be enacted, in contrast, can be seen to refer to the particular language (if any) which must be used to express effectively the ends which a specific legal measure is created to achieve. Is it therefore inappropriate for a theory to adopt a common position in relation to the legality of changes to the rules which set out the manner and form for legislation, if these two categories are distinct? Rather than a theory of manner *and* form, do we instead require a theory of manner *and* a theory of form?

Such an objection to the manner and form theory can be found in the work of Fenwick and Phillipson. Fenwick and Phillipson have distinguished between requirements of manner and those of form, categorising both separately, alongside content-based limits, in a tripartite scheme of potential 'restrictions' on legislative power.[165] Criticising the tendency of manner and form theorists to treat these 'two types of restrictions' as if they 'may readily be lumped together', Fenwick and Phillipson argue that these considerations are actually 'very distinct'.[166] The key reason given is that

> a restriction based merely on form—that is, a requirement that a future statute must use express words in order to undo a previous statute—amounts to no real restriction upon the freedom of action of a future Parliament. It is a moment's work for a draftsman to insert such words into a statute ... By contrast, a requirement, say, that a two-thirds majority must be used to overturn a previous statute amounts to a very real fettering of future Parliaments, and thus a very real entrenchment of the provision in question.[167]

---

[165] H Fenwick and G Phillipson, *Text, Cases and Materials on Public Law and Human Rights*, 3rd edn (Abingdon, Routledge, 2011) 194.
[166] ibid 208.
[167] ibid 208.

That requirements of form can be readily satisfied whereas requirements of manner, depending on the precise nature of the condition specified, may not, is of importance for Fenwick and Phillipson, because if Parliament can too readily limit its successors, this would interfere with 'the democratic rights of future majorities to reverse the decisions of previous ones'.[168] Requirements as to manner, we might then infer, should be treated with much greater caution than those of form, and to conclude that because Parliament has the power to change the latter, it also necessarily has the power to alter the former, may be mistaken.

This is a significant objection, especially when the argument as to the virtue of the doctrine of parliamentary sovereignty, advanced in Chapter one, is recalled. For if, as I argued, this virtue is that the doctrine ensures the primacy of majoritarian democratic decision-making in the UK constitution, it might be thought that the potential for manner restrictions to limit this necessitates, at the very least, a cautious approach to be taken to the alteration of such procedural conditions. And that is if this possibility does not in fact suggest the existence of an outright contradiction between the manner and form theory in particular, and the account of parliamentary sovereignty in general, defended in this book. Perhaps, therefore, the incentive of avoiding these potential difficulties should be seen to encourage an approach to legally unlimited legislative authority which severs consideration of manner from consideration of form. Yet this objection is also significant because it raises an even more fundamental issue which is commonly overlooked: *why* is this theory one which takes manner and form together, and is it sustainable to do so?

The historical answer to this question is relatively clear. The phrase 'manner and form' from which the theory takes its name derives from the Colonial Laws Validity Act 1865. In particular, section 5 of the Act confirmed the power of colonial legislatures to enact a broad range of legislation,

> provided that such Laws shall have been passed in such Manner and Form as may from Time to Time be required by any Act of Parliament, Letters Patent, Order in Council, or Colonial Law for the Time being in force in the said Colony.

This provision was discussed in detail in *Trethowan*, for it was applicable to the legislature of New South Wales when the legality of the referendum requirement at issue in that case fell to be determined.[169] And given the importance of this decision for the development of Jennings' alternative conception of the doctrine of parliamentary sovereignty—both in terms of providing a basis for the reasoning which underpinned, and a persuasive precedent which supported, the manner and form theory—it is unsurprising that the language in which *Trethowan* was necessarily framed would become attached to the school

---

[168] ibid 202.
[169] The Colonial Laws Validity Act 1865 was subsequently made inapplicable to the Dominions by the Statute of Westminster 1931, s 2, as part of the recognition of the legislative independence of Dominion Parliaments.

of thought which it played a decisive role in prompting. As a result, the theory is one of manner *and* form because such requirements were considered in unison in the formative sources, both legislative and judicial, around which the theory originally developed.

Yet that manner and form have traditionally been considered together does not mean that they ought to be. There is also a logical reason that Jennings' theory was one which dealt with manner and form collectively. Jennings' argument in favour of the manner and form theory proceeded from the idea that Parliament could alter any legal rule, including those which conditioned the legislative process itself. It was therefore an extremely expansive interpretation of legally unlimited legislative sovereignty: whatever was not prohibited, in terms of law-making, would necessarily be permitted. While substantive limitations must obviously be excluded from this perspective, the adoption of such a starting point means that consideration of the potential differences between requirements as to manner and requirements as to form would never have been necessary to explore. For such differences, or any reasons that manner and form should be treated distinctly, would simply be irrelevant to the question of whether manner or form could be changed by statute; both kinds of change would be possible, because any change to the rules concerning the law-making process would be possible.

While this provides us with a logical reason for considering manner and form together, it does not address the objection advanced by Fenwick and Phillipson. This is the argument that requirements of manner and form should be seen as distinct, and the permissibility of their statutory alteration assessed separately, because of the disparate extent to which they impact on the ability of Parliament to legislate. And from this perspective, while requirements of form might be tolerable, we ought to be sceptical about accepting legislative changes to requirements of manner in particular, because the potentially profound limiting effect that such restrictions could have on Parliament may be seen as undemocratic. There are, however, two difficulties with this line of challenge. First, such a position assumes that legislative changes to the legislative process—and especially those relating to manner—will inherently be intended to limit or restrict the capacity of Parliament to legislate. Yet this is not the case; such change to the manner in which future legislation is to be enacted can be, but is not necessarily, concerned with the procedural limitation of Parliament. Instead, change to manner may make legislating less difficult (for example, by removing existing procedural requirements), or be entirely neutral as to whether law-making becomes more or less challenging (for example, by replacing existing institutions engaged in the legislative process with alternative institutions). When there is such variation in the potential effects that change to the requirements of manner may have, it is problematic to distinguish them from requirements of form on the basis that the former impose conditions which are more difficult to satisfy than the latter. For, there is no consistent difference between the ease with which conditions as to manner, and those as to form, may be satisfied by Parliament. And, moreover, this basic premise is itself flawed, for to assess changes to manner against the ease of their satisfaction is to discount the possibility that they may remove entirely procedural conditions which were previously in existence, rather than impose a more demanding process on the legislature.

Secondly, to focus on the ease or difficulty with which manner and form 'restrictions' can be satisfied overlooks the true purpose of such procedural changes. What is critical—and which reveals the common underlying characteristic which justifies the collective treatment of manner and form—is the effect such conditions are designed to have. Legislative alterations to either manner or form are intended to change the procedure by which law is enacted. This is obviously the case in relation to changes to manner, which will concern, and seek to alter, the nature, sequencing or time-scale of action which is required to be taken by institutions engaged in the legislative process for a valid measure to be created. But it is also, crucially, the case in relation to changes to form, something which is obscured when attention is principally given to whether such conditions can be readily complied with.

The reason for requiring a particular form of language to be used in order for legislation to be enacted will almost inevitably be to require Parliament to be completely clear, beyond any reasonable doubt, about what end it seeks to effect. The paradigm example of a change to form—the requirement that express language be used by the legislature to achieve a specified outcome—aims at precisely this. To view the satisfaction of an express language requirement as something which is simply to be disposed of in a moment by a draftsman fails to acknowledge the impact such provisions are designed to have on the legislature itself. For the purpose of such requirements is to force Parliament to confront explicitly and directly the consequences of the change in the law it intends to make, rather than bury controversial change in obscure or ambiguous language, and thus prompt clear attempts to justify such action as part of the legislative process. While relating to what is in effect a judicially cultivated condition as to form, rather than one imposed by legislation, the comments of Lord Hoffman as to the purpose of the interpretative 'principle of legality'[170] are equally applicable to any express language requirement:

> But the principle of legality means that Parliament must squarely confront what it is doing and accept the political cost. Fundamental rights cannot be overridden by general or ambiguous words. This is because there is too great a risk that the full implications of their unqualified meaning may have passed unnoticed in the democratic process. In the absence of express language or necessary implication to the contrary, the courts therefore presume that even the most general words were intended to be subject to the basic rights of the individual.[171]

The requirement that express language be used as part of the process of legislating is therefore designed to change that very process. Such conditions mark out

---

[170] See chapter 5 of this volume, pp 206–17.
[171] *R v Secretary of State for the Home Department, ex parte Simms* [2000] 2 AC 115, 131.

particular policy choices as being of a level of significance so as to deserve full parliamentary consideration, while seeking to ensure that legislative decisions which may be controversial are readily apparent, and can thus be subjected to sufficient scrutiny. Alterations to requirements of form thus share a common purpose with alterations to requirements of manner: both are designed to change the process by which law is made. It is this fact which justifies a common theory of manner and form.

The argument that legislative changes to manner and to form must be understood to be distinct, and their legal permissibility thus treated as unconnected rather than comparable, can therefore be rejected. Yet one important insight offered by this challenge is more difficult to dismiss. For while the underlying common purpose of statutory changes to manner and form must be appreciated—a purpose which is about more than simply the limitation of Parliament's legislative capacity—it nonetheless remains possible for restrictions which could be viewed as anti-majoritarian or undemocratic to be lawfully adopted in accordance with the manner and form theory. This possibility poses a fundamental challenge to any defender of the manner and form conception of parliamentary sovereignty, and is especially challenging to an account which is premised on the democratic virtue of the doctrine. Nevertheless, how this potential problem can be confronted, and how the possibility of such restrictions is to be accommodated in a framework reflecting the normative (democratic) virtue of the manner and form theory, will be discussed in detail in Chapter seven. The potential for anti-majoritarian procedural limits to be incorporated into the legislative process should not, however, be understood to amount to an argument that the manner and form theory of parliamentary sovereignty should be dismissed outright. Instead, a conception of legally unlimited law-making authority which takes a common approach to statutory conditions as to manner and those as to form—and understands the legislative alteration of both to be equally permissible as a matter of law—is in principle coherent, albeit not complete. For the common *permissibility* of legislative changes to manner and to form leaves open the question of what kind of change will be *justifiable*. It is when this latter issue is addressed that the problem posed by anti-majoritarian or undemocratic procedural limits falls to be considered, rather than being taken as of relevance to the viability of the manner and form theory itself.

With this argument as to the appropriateness of a theory which encompasses both manner *and* form in mind, a final point concerning terminology can be established. There is little doubt that an understanding of parliamentary sovereignty called 'the manner and form theory' has the potential to sound archaic and inaccessible (although this is unsurprising, given the origins of the phrase in nineteenth-century legislation concerning the powers of British colonial legislatures[172]). As such, the alternative terminology of 'procedure and form' favoured by

---

[172] See text at n 169 above.

Jeffrey Goldsworthy, the leading modern defender of parliamentary sovereignty, might be thought to be preferable, on the basis that it is intuitively more straight-forward.[173] However, there are two reasons that I do not follow Goldsworthy in adopting the language of procedure and form, despite the advantages that it may present. First, Goldsworthy explicitly adopts the terminology of procedure and form to emphasise the differences between his understanding of Parliament's legislative authority and those of other manner and form theorists, including Jennings.[174] These differences will be fully explored in the next section, but in essence, Goldsworthy accepts that certain requirements as to procedure or form will be 'consistent with parliamentary sovereignty', but seeks to exclude those which would 'make it so difficult for Parliament to legislate that its power to do so is diminished'.[175] It is the additional caveat that Parliament's power to legislate must not be diminished by procedural conditions which are difficult to satisfy that distinguishes Goldsworthy's conception of parliamentary sovereignty from that defended by Jennings. As such, in this book, I adopt the usage of 'the man-ner and form theory' in part to reinforce the fact that it is Jennings' conception of legally unlimited legislative authority, rather than the narrower formulation of Goldsworthy, which is defended.

The second reason that I follow the use of the terminology of manner and form is that Goldsworthy's alternative creates the impression that issues of form are distinct from those of 'procedure'. While Goldsworthy does not adhere to the argument rejected in this section, which maintains that conditions as to manner (or procedure) and those as to form should be subject to disparate legal treatment on the basis of their differences, to distinguish issues of 'procedure' from those of form is problematic. As has been argued above, the common characteristic which unites legislative changes to manner and to form is their shared purpose: to alter the process by which law is made. From this perspective, the legislative procedure is in part, although not exclusively, a function of the manner and form which must be adhered to for the enactment of valid legislation. If requirements as to the manner and form in which legislation must be enacted are two parts of an overall procedure for the creation of valid statutes, issues as to procedure and form are not in fact distinct. Instead, the form in which legislation is enacted is one aspect of an overall procedure.[176] It is this perspective which enables us to view manner and form as component parts of a legislative process, and demonstrates why a theory of manner *and* form is coherent. As such, the replacement of the language

---

[173] Goldsworthy, *Parliamentary Sovereignty: Contemporary Debates* (2010) n 54 above, ch 7.
[174] ibid 175.
[175] ibid 174.
[176] This will be the case even if there are no special requirements as to form at issue, such as an express language requirement in relation to a specified legislative purpose. For there must surely be some standard requirements of form with which Parliament must comply to produce valid legisla-tion, even if these standards are unstated and unlikely ever to be breached. For example, legislative provisions enacted in some kind of code—even if intelligible to those in possession of the relevant key—would presumably be invalid.

of manner with that of procedure has the potential to interfere with our ability to explain a core feature of this conception of legislative power. Therefore, even if the adoption of this admittedly more accessible terminology were possible—although to do so would risk blurring the differences in substance between Goldsworthy's position and that which I defend—it would risk the meaning of the manner and form theory becoming subtly warped. As a result, it is a theory of 'manner and form' which is the understanding of parliamentary sovereignty examined in this book.

D. Process and Substance

The final objection to parliamentary sovereignty to be considered in this chapter concerns the sustainability of a distinction between matters of process and matters of substance. The distinction between legislation which seeks to alter the future process that must be followed for the enactment of valid statutes, and legislation which seeks to limit absolutely the possibility of a particular subject-matter being the topic of valid statutes, is crucial to the manner and form theory. For if, in accordance with this understanding of parliamentary sovereignty, legislative change to the legislative process is permitted, but substantive statutory limitation of that process is not, we must be able to draw a line between these two different categories if the theory is to have any coherence or salience. In particular, the difference between procedural conditions—whether requirements as to manner or as to form—and substantive limitations must both be understood in principle, and capable of application in practice for the assessment of the legality validity of any purported legislative provisions.

Yet while the distinction between statutory modification of the legislative process and statutory limitation of the substantive extent of Parliament's legislative authority is easily appreciated in principle, how this translates into practice may be less clear cut. As Hart, for example, acknowledged, when discussing this issue as indicative of the uncertainty in fundamental constitutional rules: '[f]or though, indeed, the difference between circumscribing the area over which Parliament can legislate, and merely changing the manner and form of legislation, is clear enough in some cases, in effect these categories shade into each other'.[177] It may be clear that the requirement that express language be used to effect a certain legislative outcome is one of form. It may further be clear that requirements that a two-thirds majority vote in one House of Parliament be achieved, or that a certain time period between votes elapses, or that a referendum be held, to approve a particular legislative decision, are those of manner. And, as changes to the legislative process, such statutory provisions may therefore be viewed as legally valid in accordance with the manner and form theory of parliamentary sovereignty. Similarly, it may

---

[177] Hart, *Concept of Law* (1994) n 118 above, 151.

also be clear that a provision which prohibited the enactment of future legislation relating to any specific subject-matter—no matter how broad (for example, that which contravened human rights) or narrow (for example, the compensation payable for compulsory purchase of private land)—would be a substantive limit, and thus unlawful.

However, a number of less obvious examples, which are much more difficult to classify as either procedural conditions or substantive limitations, can also be imagined. Would, for example, the requirement that legislation on a particular topic be approved only by a 90 per cent majority in the House of Commons be a procedural condition or a substantive limit on law-making authority? The same question would be presented by a statutory requirement that 10 years elapse between votes in the two Houses of Parliament, or that legislation must be approved by 75 per cent of the total electorate voting in a referendum. These are obviously extreme, even absurd, examples. But they demonstrate an important principle: a statutory requirement may be in form a procedural condition, yet, depending on its precise terms, have an effect which is tantamount to that of an absolute substantive limitation. And this may be seen to reveal a significant contradiction at the heart of the manner and form theory of parliamentary sovereignty. For in permitting the statutory modification of the legislative process, on the basis of an expansive interpretation of the notion of legally unlimited law-making authority, the manner and form theory may incidentally create the possibility of such power being limited by law.

Does the existence of this potential contradiction definitively undermine the ability of the manner and form theory to offer a viable conception of parliamentary sovereignty? Or can the difficulties created by the ostensible overlap between procedural conditions and substantive limitations be transcended? The most promising way in which this problem might be circumvented is to seek to redraw the line between what can be considered procedural (and therefore permissible), and substantive (and therefore impermissible). We might in particular seek to avoid the contradiction which the manner and form theory otherwise appears to present by qualifying what can be considered to be 'procedural' in nature. For if we adopt a narrower understanding of the kind of statutory conditions which count as being genuinely concerned with procedure, there will be a consequent, but inevitable, expansion of what must be considered as 'substantive' limits on legislative power. And, as a result, the problematic borderline cases which are formally procedural, yet seem to have substantive effects, can be disposed of, because the enactment of such provisions will become beyond the legislative competence of Parliament.

A powerful attempt to craft such a solution to this contradiction has been provided by Goldsworthy. While Goldsworthy's work bears similarity to some aspects of the manner and form analysis of parliamentary sovereignty, his work also departs from the classic account of this theory in a number of respects. One example of this departure, as noted above, is the terminology Goldsworthy adopts, preferring to describe his conception of Parliament's legislative sovereignty as one which extends to incorporate the enactment of conditions of 'procedure and form'.[178] Yet this difference in language from the manner and form theory is not simply stylistic; instead, it is intended to illustrate a substantive difference between Goldsworthy and traditional manner and form theorists as to the extent to which legislative change to the legislative process will be legally permissible. Goldsworthy accepts the possibility that sovereign legislative power can be used to make statutory change to the legislative process. But he goes beyond the classic manner and form approach in seeking to constrain the kind of changes to legislative procedure which Parliament can lawfully effect:

> [l]egally binding and judicially enforceable requirements as to procedure or form are consistent with parliamentary sovereignty, provided that they do not control or restrict the substantive content of legislation, or make it so difficult for Parliament to legislate that its power to do so is diminished.[179]

Goldsworthy thus introduces an additional qualifying clause into the classic manner and form formula: the conditions of procedure or form which it will be 'legally unproblematic' for the legislature to enact are those which 'do not diminish Parliament's continuing substantive power to legislate'.[180] Whether Parliament's legislative power would be diminished by a particular procedural or formal condition is to be assessed by reference to the increased difficulty of law-making if it were to be conducted in accordance with the modified process. The ostensibly procedural conditions which are in fact inconsistent with legislative sovereignty are those which 'diminish parliament's substantive power, because they make it considerably more difficult for it to legislate'.[181] This limit is, for Goldsworthy, one which should be 'strictly construed',[182] and as such, it will be only 'very mild procedural requirements'[183] which it will be lawful for a sovereign Parliament to enact.

Goldsworthy's 'procedure and form' account of parliamentary sovereignty thus provides a means by which the contradiction provoked by the manner and form theory could potentially be circumvented. There are, however, a number of difficulties with this approach. Goldsworthy's account is one which departs from the logic underlying the manner and form theory, with the argument offered by Jennings—that Parliament's power to change the law, being legally unlimited, must include the power to change the legislative process—one which is explicitly

---

[178] See text at n 170 above.

[179] Goldsworthy, *Parliamentary Sovereignty: Contemporary Debates* (2010) n 54 above, 174.

[180] ibid 194. See also the similar formulation of this caveat in Goldsworthy's earlier work: J Goldsworthy, *The Sovereignty of Parliament: History and Philosophy* (Oxford, Oxford University Press, 1999) 16: A legislature's 'sovereign power is a continuing one even if it includes power to change the norms that govern its own composition, procedure, and form of legislation, provided that it cannot use that power to unduly impair its ability to change the substance of the law however and whenever it chooses'.

[181] ibid 198.

[182] ibid 198.

[183] ibid 182.

rejected.[184] This does not, of course, in itself mean that Goldsworthy's procedure and form model will not be persuasive. Yet it is important to note the reasoning behind Goldsworthy's rejection of Jennings, for it reflects to some extent the argument advanced by Wade, which I have challenged above.[185] For Goldsworthy, the fundamental objection to Jennings' analysis 'is essentially the same as the objection to common law constitutionalism'.[186] Jennings' key error, Goldsworthy argues, was to characterise the doctrine of parliamentary sovereignty as a norm of common law, which was therefore susceptible, like all rules of common law, to legislative alteration. But, as will be considered further in Chapter three, and as Goldsworthy's work has played a leading role in demonstrating, the sovereignty of Parliament is not a rule of common law.[187] Yet while this conclusion is fatal to the claims of common law constitutionalism—because it demonstrates definitively that the courts' power to develop the common law does not provide them with the authority to redefine or qualify the doctrine of parliamentary sovereignty— the same is not true in relation to the manner and form theory. Although it is certainly correct that Jennings characterised the sovereignty of Parliament as a rule of common law in key parts of his analysis, elsewhere he also used the term 'accepted law' to describe the doctrine.[188] It this latter usage, however—or, alternatively, the terminology of 'customary law' favoured by Mitchell[189]—which better reflects Jennings' understanding of the nature of parliamentary sovereignty.[190] For Jennings clearly recognised—in stark contrast with the common law constitutionalists, for whom this is an essential, indeed foundational, idea—that parliamentary sovereignty was not a legal norm which had been established by the courts.[191]

Moreover, even if it were not accepted that the language of the common law could be readily substituted out of Jennings' account in particular, the claim that parliamentary sovereignty is such a rule would still not be an essential part of the manner and form theory in general. It is irrelevant to the manner and form understanding of parliamentary sovereignty what variety of legal rules govern the legislative process. Instead, what is crucial is the acknowledgment that the legally unlimited legislative power possessed by Parliament extends to permit the alteration of these legal rules, regardless of whether they belong to the subset

---

[184]   ibid 175.
[185]   See text at nn 99–105.
[186]   Goldsworthy, *Parliamentary Sovereignty: Contemporary Debates* (2010) n 54 above, 115.
[187]   See chapter 3 of this volume.
[188]   Jennings, *Law and the Constitution*, 5th edn (1959) n 26 above, 156.
[189]   Mitchell, *Constitutional Law* (1968) n 78 above, 79.
[190]   See Gordon, 'The Conceptual Foundations of Parliamentary Sovereignty' [2009] n 106 above, 541.
[191]   See text at n 48 above. Elsewhere in *Parliamentary Sovereignty: Contemporary Debates* (2010) n 54 above, Goldsworthy does in fact recognise the sophistication of Jennings' understanding of the doctrine of parliamentary sovereignty as a rule of 'common law': see 44–45: 'Jennings was too subtle a thinker to suggest that, in this regard, the common law was judge-made law'. Yet this insight is not carried over to Goldsworthy's later analysis of Jennings' work.

of legal norms which we categorise as those of common law. That they are not rules of common law does not exhaust the possibility of their being legal rules. And it is in relation to this point that Goldsworthy makes the same error as Wade, albeit adopting the more sophisticated conceptual scheme of Hart. For Goldsworthy argues that the doctrine of parliamentary sovereignty 'was not made by Parliament: it was not, and could not have been, prescribed by statute, since any such statute would beg the question of Parliament's authority to enact it'.[192] As a result, for Goldsworthy, '[s]ince it is the source of Parliament's authority, it is prima facie superior to Parliament, and the notion that Parliament can alter it at will is therefore implausible'.[193] Instead, employing the work of Hart to enhance reasoning otherwise reminiscent of Wade, Goldsworthy maintains that the doctrine is part of the rule of recognition, which 'can be changed only if the consensus that constitutes it changes'.[194]

Goldsworthy's rejection of the manner and form theory is therefore subject to some of the same criticisms which were explored above in relation to Wade. Of greatest significance is that Goldsworthy's account, as did Wade's, seems to exclude the very possibility of a manner and form understanding of parliamentary sovereignty, by affording the legal rules regarding the legislative procedure a special status which necessarily elevates them beyond the reach of statute. Yet there is no reason that a particular legal system should not be able to permit the lawful alteration of the rules which govern the legislative process, regardless of how they originally come into being, if these rules are understood to be legal in nature.[195] And, as such, it is not inherently the case that the legitimate adoption of manner (or 'procedure') and form conditions by a legally sovereign Parliament must be contingent upon a broad shift in the official consensus underlying that system's rule of recognition. Instead, if the manner and form theory is understood to be a coherent interpretation of the doctrine of parliamentary sovereignty— about which there already exists the kind of official consensus necessary to constitute a rule of recognition—it is possible to understand change to the legislative process as being simply a consequence of Parliament's statutory action. Indeed, as I will argue in Part II, when considering whether some of the modern challenges to parliamentary sovereignty can best be characterised as changes in the UK's rule of recognition, it may be descriptively and normatively preferable to adopt a manner and form explanation of the relevant contemporary developments, rather than to rely on contentions about shifts in consensus which will be difficult to evaluate, and occur outside a constitutionally established process of democratic decision-making.[196]

---

[192] Goldsworthy, *Parliamentary Sovereignty: Contemporary Debates* (2010) n 54 above, 115.
[193] ibid 115.
[194] Ibid 115.
[195] See text at nn 106–7.
[196] See chapter 4 of this volume, pp 179–82; chapter 5 of this volume, pp 218–22; chapter 6 of this volume, pp 273–75.

Nevertheless, while Goldsworthy's rejection of the manner and form theory is arguably therefore flawed, his alternative procedure and form model may still be attractive, if it offers a compelling solution to the problem posed by statutory conditions which are procedural in form, but potentially substantive in effect. There are, however, also difficulties with Goldsworthy's account in this respect. For the crucial additional limit contained in Goldsworthy's model—which purports to solve this difficulty by preventing the enactment of procedural conditions which diminish the substantive power of Parliament—may actually be incompatible with two key ideas intrinsically associated with the doctrine of parliamentary sovereignty.

First, Goldsworthy's additional limit is problematic because it rests crucially on an assessment of how difficult a purported procedural alteration would make it for Parliament to legislate in future. Yet the doctrine of parliamentary sovereignty, whether understood from an orthodox or a manner and form perspective, is not concerned with the ease with which Parliament may enact legislation. Instead, the core claim of the doctrine of parliamentary sovereignty—that Parliament is vested with legally unlimited legislative authority—is one about potential capacity, rather than actual capability. The actual power of Parliament to enact legislation will unavoidably be limited by a range of non-legal limits, including those which are political, moral, and practical in nature. Indeed, the inevitable existence of these limits is a fundamental reason why a doctrine of legislative sovereignty can be accepted, for they serve critically to condition law-making power which, as a matter of law, is unlimited. This aspect of parliamentary sovereignty is something which is fully appreciated by Goldsworthy, who recognises that the doctrine 'does not purport to describe the scope of Parliament's likely desire and ability to enact statutes as a matter of practical politics'.[197] Yet in relation to the legal validity of statutes which seek to modify the legislative process, Goldsworthy's theory seems to conflate capacity and capability, making Parliament's lawful authority to enact legislation contingent upon such action not unduly affecting Parliament's practical power to enact legislation.

This conflation of capacity and capability is manifested in Goldsworthy's claim that a procedural condition which makes it more difficult for Parliament to legislate in future is something which diminishes its substantive legislative power. Yet much depends on what is meant here by 'substantive', and there is an elision in Goldsworthy's account of two different meanings of the term. On one hand, substantive may be understood to mean 'regarding substance', and be opposed to 'procedural', understood to mean 'regarding procedure'. On the other hand, however, substantive may be understood to mean 'something which is quantifiable, actual or real', and be opposed to 'something which is potential, hypothetical or artificial'. The tension between these two alternative understandings sometimes surfaces in Goldsworthy's account. At one stage, for example, the limit on Parliament's power

---

[197] Goldsworthy, *Parliamentary Sovereignty: Contemporary Debates* (2010) n 54 above, 303.

to enact procedure and form provisions is described as one 'which invalidates any requirement that in substance diminishes or destroys the Parliament's continuing plenary power'.[198] Yet this can be compared with the idea that procedural conditions will be valid if 'they do not diminish Parliament's continuing substantive power to legislate'.[199] In the former quote the usage of 'in substance diminishes' seem to cohere best with the understanding of substantive as something actual. In contrast, in the latter quote, 'substantive power' appears to reflect the alternative understanding that this is power regarding matters of substance.

The elision of these two different meanings of substantive is significant, because whether a link can be said to exist between difficulty in legislating and the diminishing of substantive power depends on which understanding is adopted. And this link is important to Goldsworthy's analysis, for it is the identification of an impact on substantive power which justifies the legal invalidity of what are, at least in formal terms, procedural conditions, based on a parallel with the doctrine of parliamentary sovereignty's general proscription of absolute limits on legislative authority. If we take substantive power to mean power in substance, or actual power, it seems quite clear that this could be diminished by difficulty in enacting legislation. Yet if substantive power is taken to mean power regarding substance—power concerning specified substantive matters—then it seems equally clear that this would *not* be diminished by difficulty in enacting legislation. For if power in this sense exists in relation to specified substantive matters, it exists aside from the circumstances in which, or the ease with which, it may be exercised. Crucially, it is this second kind of claim about substantive power which is made by the doctrine of parliamentary sovereignty; a claim relating to the capacity, rather than the capability, of Parliament to legislate. As a result, that it becomes more difficult, even if considerably so, for Parliament to legislate about a specific topic, whether because of a particular procedural condition or otherwise, does not mean we can say its substantive legislative power—understood as a claim about the scope of its authority in relation to particular matters of substance—has been diminished. Instead, the extent of that substantive power remains unchanged. The power to legislate about those substantive matters within legal competence—and in relation to a legally sovereignty Parliament, this will, of course, be all substantive matters— still exists; it just cannot be exercised as readily as was previously possible.

Goldsworthy's limit is thus not required by, and nor can be it justified by reference to, the doctrine of parliamentary sovereignty. While in one sense, substantive power can be understood to be diminished by difficulty associated with its exercise, it is not this kind of substantive power which is relevant to the doctrine of parliamentary sovereignty. An increased 'difficulty' in legislating is not something which can be understood to have an impact on the kind of substantive power which is implicated in the claims made by the doctrine of parliamentary

---

[198] ibid 193.
[199] ibid 194.

sovereignty. Yet we cannot, on this basis, dismiss entirely the manner and form contradiction, to which Goldsworthy's work might be understood to offer a solution. For to argue that *difficulty* in legislating does not diminish substantive power, in a sense which is relevant to the doctrine of parliamentary sovereignty, does not entail a commitment to the wider notion that conditions which are procedural in form are never capable of having substantive effects. Instead, Goldsworthy's limit cannot be justified essentially because it attempts to set the bar too low. In relation to the kind of substantive power with which the doctrine of parliamentary sovereignty is directly concerned, only those procedural conditions which make future legislation on a particular subject matter effectively impossible, as opposed to simply more difficult, can be understood to have an impact which takes them beyond the procedural. For, it is in circumstances when legislating becomes effectively impossible that an impact on Parliament's capacity, rather than capability, can be discerned. Goldsworthy certainly acknowledges the possibility of such ostensibly procedural conditions, which he characterises as those which would 'destroy' substantive legislative power.[200] But this element of his procedure and form model is rendered essentially irrelevant by its co-existence with a much lower invalidity threshold; that of power being diminished by a difficulty in legislating. It is, however, *only* a limit based on the effective impossibility of legislating, and the consequent destructive effect of this in relation to substantive legislative power, which an account of the scope of Parliament's legislative authority to enact conditions of procedure and form should accommodate. For to do otherwise, and set lower than is necessary the limit on the kind of change to the legislative process which Parliament can implement, will infringe upon, rather than preserve, the legislature's legal authority to legislate on any substantive matter.

Secondly, the practical application of Goldsworthy's proposed limit on legislative power to change the procedure or form could be problematic. This is in part because the test against which the validity of ostensibly procedural conditions would need to be determined—whether they had increased the difficulty in legislating to an extent to diminish Parliament's power—is a relatively vague one.[201] As noted above, Goldsworthy argues that this test should be applied strictly, and this is reflected in his treatment of super-majority requirements, such as that of a two-thirds majority vote for legislation to be enacted, which he suggests would be legally invalid. This is because such provisions 'should not be regarded as purely procedural', on the basis that '[i]n effect, they give a minority of members the power to veto legislation'.[202] Yet others might easily take a different view, and in particular, regardless of whether such super-majority requirements are desirable or not, find it difficult to accept that intra-parliamentary voting requirements

---

[200] ibid 194.
[201] The same point is made in AL Young, 'Parliamentary Sovereignty Re-defined' in R Rawlings, P Leyland and AL Young (eds), *Sovereignty and the Law: Domestic, European, and International Perspectives* (Oxford, Oxford University Press, 2013) 73.
[202] Goldsworthy, *Parliamentary Sovereignty: Contemporary Debates* (2010) n 54 above, 198.

are anything more than a procedural device. The key concepts of 'difficulty' and 'diminishing' are open-ended and relative, and disputes about the extent of inter-ference required to violate Goldsworthy's limit would be not be especially easy to settle by reference to these criteria alone.

Perhaps more significant, however, is the identity of the institution tasked with making such judgements. For, given we are dealing here with questions of the legal validity of statutory provisions, it is the courts who Goldsworthy accepts will have responsibility for ultimately determining whether particular procedural condi-tions are or are not within the legislative competence of Parliament. Of course, it may be suggested that this is not a feature which is unique to Goldsworthy's procedure and form model; the classic manner and form theory may also neces-sitate a role for the courts in establishing the legality of purported changes to the legislative process. Yet as I will argue in Chapter seven, while this may be a consequence of the adoption of the manner and form theory of parliamentary sovereignty, it will not inevitably be the case. And in any event, the defence of the manner and form theory advanced in Chapter seven will be one which leaves very little space at all for active judicial involvement in the process of ascertain-ing the proper limits of Parliament's power to legislate to change the legislative process. In Goldsworthy's account, however, this is not the case. For in elaborat-ing a limit which prevents Parliament from creating procedural conditions that make it more difficult to legislate in future, Goldsworthy severs the connection between permissibility and procedure on one hand, and impermissibility and substance on the other. Once we move away from this binary framework, judge-ments about what is and is not legally permissible in terms of statutory change to the legislative process inevitably become more complex, a matter which is intensi-fied by the relatively vague notions of 'difficulty' and 'diminished' around which Goldsworthy's particular test is organised. As a result, the test which the courts will need to apply on the procedure and form model of Parliament's legislative power is one which moves us away from making factual judgements on a more or less objective basis—is this statutory condition procedural or substantive, and therefore permissible or impermissible?—into much more contentious and subjective territory—does this increase the difficulty with which Parliament can legislate such that it diminishes its power?

When one of the classic propositions on which parliamentary sovereignty depends is that the courts have no authority to challenge an Act of Parliament,[203] to expect courts to resolve such disputes about whether an ostensibly procedural statutory change to the legislative process diminishes its sovereign power might be seen, in itself, to diminish that very power. Moreover, given the seminal role which Goldsworthy's work has played in defending the doctrine of parliamentary sovereignty from the judicial encroachment envisaged by the theory of common

---

[203] See, eg *Edinburgh and Dalkeith Railway Co v Wauchope* (1842) 8 Cl & F 710; *Lee v Bude and Torrington Junction Railway Co* (1871) LR 6 CP 576; *Pickin v British Railways Board* [1974] AC 765; *Manuel v Attorney General* [1983] Ch 77.

law constitutionalism, his explanation of the courts' role in this context seems somewhat surprising. For Goldsworthy argues that 'in each case, the judges would also have to be guided by their own assessment of constitutional principles, such as democracy and the rule of law, in deciding whether or not they should endorse any attempted entrenchment by Parliament'.[204] Although Goldsworthy is here referring to a particularly demanding kind of limit on legislative power—and one which may not be compatible with the defence of the manner and form theory I set out in Chapter seven—it seems reasonable to believe that this observation would be generally applicable to any judicial assessment of the legal validity of a procedural condition. Taken as such, it is a strikingly expansive conception of the judicial role in ascertaining the validity of legislative action, seemingly encouraging wide-ranging engagement by the courts with political and constitutional principles which are intrinsically contestable, with the judges' interpretation(s) of such principles to assume a prominent position in the justification of their decisions. And although the purpose of allocating such a role to the judges is to ensure that 'only the most important constitutional rules or principles, which enjoy wide-spread, non-partisan support, may be entrenched, and only in ways that are consistent with democratic principle',[205] it is far from clear that the courts are an appropriate organ to achieve this, both from a practical and a principled perspective.[206] It might thus be difficult to reconcile this idea of the courts' function with the prohibition on the judicial review of legislation established by the doctrine of parliamentary sovereignty.

Overall, given the potential significance of the problem posed by the possibility of statutory changes to the legislative process which are procedural in form, but substantive in effect, Goldsworthy's attempt to recalibrate the manner and form theory in such a way as to avoid this contradiction deserves serious attention. But while the 'procedure and form' model may in principle provide a means by which legality can be denied to such provisions, the very mechanism by which this is achieved—the additional limit which prohibits the enactment of procedural conditions which diminish Parliament's substantive power by increasing the difficulty in legislation—is not consistent with key elements of the doctrine of parliamentary sovereignty. For Goldsworthy's revised model conflates considerations of capacity and capability to set an inappropriately low threshold for the invalidity of statutory procedural conditions, while also creating space for significant judicial involvement in establishing the meaning and extent of this limit on legislative

---

[204] Goldsworthy, *Parliamentary Sovereignty: Contemporary Debates* (2010) n 54 above, 140.

[205] ibid 140.

[206] Elsewhere, Goldsworthy displays considerable sympathy for the 'old democratic ideal of government by ordinary people, elected to represent the opinions and interests of ordinary people', and some scepticism towards the 'aristocratic' tendencies of the judicial review of legislation on fundamental rights grounds: ibid 9–13. Although there is clearly a difference between such qualitative 'rights review' and assessing whether legislation is formally within parliamentary competence, Goldsworthy's views on the democratic propriety of increasing judicial scrutiny of the outcomes of the political process seem difficult to reconcile with the position he adopts here.

authority. When it is further recalled that Goldsworthy's rejection of the manner and form theory itself suffered from a number flaws discussed earlier in this chapter in relation to Wade, it seems that, ultimately, there is no compelling reason to embrace the procedure and form understanding of parliamentary sovereignty.

The potential contradiction which the manner and form theory may be seen to create is real enough, yet we do not need to abandon or excessively qualify this conception of legally unlimited legislative authority to address this problem. Rather than attempting to redefine what kind of statutory conditions can genuinely count as being procedural, and excluding any legislative change to the legislative process which has an impact on the ease with which Parliament can enact law, we should retain the account of the relationship between procedure and substance contained in the manner and form theory. While there may be difficulties, at the margins, in distinguishing between lawful procedural conditions and unlawful substantive limits, this provides an instinctively straightforward framework, developed from the logic of what it means to possess legally unlimited legislative power, which will be serviceable in all but the most complex cases. Yet to resolve questions of the legality of statutory change to the legislative process on the comparatively basic grounds of whether such change is essentially procedural or substantive in nature does not mean that the manner and form theory, properly understood, is incapable of preventing the effective limitation of Parliament. Instead, we can resolve the potential contradiction which the manner and form theory might appear to generate as part of an account of the normative virtue of this conception of parliamentary sovereignty. For such an account will seek broadly to establish how the manner and form theory can be justified in general, but also to structure, on this basis, how Parliament's power to legislate about the legislative process can legitimately be exercised. The problem posed by procedural conditions which are substantive in effect can thus be confronted as part of a wider scheme of *political* limits which condition the exercise of Parliament's *legal* authority, rather than by seeking to reorganise the claims made about the lawful scope of sovereign legislative power made by the manner and form theory. This normative account of the virtue, and potential functions of, the manner and form theory will be developed fully in Chapter seven. There I will argue that to rely on political limits to condition the exercise of Parliament's legislative authority in relation to the future law-making process is actually more consistent with the ideas underlying the doctrine of parliamentary sovereignty than to seek to restrict, as a matter of law, the scope of that power. And it is for this fundamental reason that Goldsworthy's procedure and form model, which adopts the alternative approach, should not be preferred to the manner and form theory which has been defended in this chapter.

IV. CONCLUSION

The manner and form theory of parliamentary sovereignty can be seen as a coherent interpretation of the idea of legally unlimited legislative authority. Since its emergence, most significantly in the work of Jennings, this conception of legislative power has been subjected to a considerable range of criticism. Yet while even Jennings' own account of the manner and form theory is unsatisfactory in some respects, and requires clarification and, to an extent, supplementation, this understanding of parliamentary sovereignty is one which can be defended against the objections which have been made to it. A Parliament which possesses legally unlimited legislative authority can be understood to have the power to enact legislation which changes the future process according to which law must be produced. This possibility cannot be dismissed by conceiving of the rules relating to the legislative process as being inherently immune from alteration by statute on the basis of their having some non- or extra-legal special status. Instead, it remains open to constitutional actors to adopt the manner and form understanding of parliamentary sovereignty, something which has not been precluded by any classic legal precedent as to the power of Parliament.

Nor should more modern objections to the manner and form theory be seen to succeed. In particular, it is coherent to consider together the possibility of changes to both manner and form, which are united by their procedural nature. Further, although the distinction between procedure and substance may give rise to a potential contradiction—in that what is procedural in form may limit substantively in effect—to seek to resolve this by recalibrating the legal claims made by the manner and form theory generates inconsistencies with the very notion of parliamentary sovereignty. The possibility that procedural conditions which are anti-majoritarian or substantive in effect may be enacted must certainly be taken seriously. Yet to prohibit, as a matter of law, such forms of legislative action may seem arbitrary and inconsistent with the notion of legally unlimited law-making power. Instead, the prospect of such difficulties may be more readily dealt with by exploring the justification for the manner and form theory, and, consequently, seeking to establish the circumstances in which the power to legislate to alter the legislative process may, and may not, be legitimately exercised. A complete account of the manner and form theory of parliamentary sovereignty will therefore need to recognise the importance of, and exploit, the framework of political limits which structure the use of this power. This will be considered in more detail in Chapter seven, when a normative justification of the manner and form theory will be developed, in light of which the core legal claims made by this conception of parliamentary sovereignty, set out in this chapter, must be understood.

Prior to this, however, with the essential legal nature of the manner and form theory now established and defended, we turn to the question which will be the focus of discussion in Part II: Is the manner and form theory an understanding of the doctrine of parliamentary sovereignty which is manifested in the law and practice of the contemporary UK constitution?

Part II

Understanding Modern Challenges to the Sovereignty of Parliament

3

The Non-Critical Challenges: Devolution, the Human Rights Act and Common Law Constitutionalism

I. INTRODUCTION

IN PART I, the nature of parliamentary sovereignty, and the manner and form understanding of this legal doctrine in particular, were considered. In Part II of this book, we turn to address the modern challenges posed to the sovereignty of Parliament with two key questions in mind. First, is the UK Parliament still legally sovereign in the contemporary constitution? Secondly, if so, what understanding of Parliament's legally unlimited legislative power must be adopted to best explain the modern constitutional developments which might appear to challenge the doctrine of parliamentary sovereignty?

Since the election to power of the first New Labour government in 1997, the UK constitution has experienced an era of reform.[1] The pace and scale of change has been dramatic: among other things, new institutions have been created to exercise legislative and executive powers in Scotland, Wales and Northern Ireland;[2] basic individual rights have been made directly actionable in domestic courts;[3] the composition of the House of Lords has been (partially) reformed;[4] a freedom of information scheme has been established;[5] a Supreme Court has been created to replace the Appellate Committee of the House of Lords, alongside reform to judicial leadership and appointments.[6] And while the government of Gordon Brown

---

[1] See, eg R Brazier, *Constitutional Reform: Reshaping the British Political System*, 3rd edn (Oxford, Oxford University Press, 2008); D Oliver, *Constitutional Reform in the UK* (Oxford, Oxford University Press, 2003); M Flinders, *Democratic Drift: Majoritarian Modification and Democratic Anomie in the United Kingdom* (Oxford, Oxford University Press, 2009); V Bogdanor, *The New British Constitution* (Oxford, Hart Publishing, 2009); A King, *The British Constitution* (Oxford, Oxford University Press, 2010).

[2] Initially by the Scotland Act 1998, Northern Ireland Act 1998, and Government of Wales Act 1998. The devolution legislation has now been amended by, among others, the Government of Wales Act 2006, the Northern Ireland Act 2009, and Scotland Act 2012.

[3] Human Rights Act 1998.

[4] House of Lords Reform Act 1999.

[5] Freedom of Information Act 2000.

[6] Constitutional Reform Act 2005.

flirted only fleetingly with something yet more profound—the eventual adoption of a written constitution[7]—the New Labour methodology of reform, by which there is plenty of reform but seemingly no methodology, was also adopted by the Conservative-Liberal Democrat coalition upon coming to office in 2010.[8] We have since seen the length of parliamentary terms fixed at five years;[9] the alternative voting system for elections to the House of Commons rejected at a national referendum;[10] restructuring of the process by which change occurs to the UK's relationship with the European Union;[11] change to the rules relating to succession to the Crown;[12] further modification of the judicial appointment process;[13] and, after a failed attempt to complete reform of the House of Lords,[14] relatively minor changes to some of the rules governing membership of the Upper Chamber.[15]

Debate is ongoing as to the overarching effect (if any) of this array of change to the UK constitution. Are we left with a constitution which is coherent or confused?[16] Has it been rationalised, or robbed of an underlying rationale?[17] Has formal institutional and structural reform distracted us from changes in governmental practice of greater significance?[18] Are we left with something new, or, whether essentially unchanged or slowly evolving, do many of the same core principles still lie beneath?[19] Resolving such questions is, of course, beyond the scope of this book. Nevertheless, this constitutional atmosphere—one of persistent, potentially sweeping change, of as yet uncertain cumulative effects—provides a crucial backdrop against which the modern challenges to the sovereignty of Parliament must be assessed. When so much seems to be changing, it is easy to assume that even the most fundamental constitutional doctrines, and perhaps especially one as ostensibly archaic as that of the 'sovereignty of Parliament', might also be unable to endure in the light of irresistible progress.

However, while changing constitutional circumstances may make the status of the doctrine ripe for reconsideration, we should be careful not to anticipate the inevitability of its displacement. The doctrine of parliamentary sovereignty may

---

[7] *The Governance of Britain*, (Cm 7170, 2007) [211]–[215].

[8] See, eg V Bogdanor, *The Coalition and the Constitution* (Oxford, Hart Publishing, 2011).

[9] Fixed-term Parliaments Act 2011.

[10] Parliamentary Voting System and Constituencies Act 2011.

[11] European Union Act 2011.

[12] Succession to the Crown Act 2013.

[13] Crown and Courts Act 2013.

[14] The House of Lords Reform Bill 2012–13 was withdrawn by the government in August 2012. See, eg P Wintour, 'Grand Plan for Lords Reform Meanders into Age of Tit-for-Tat', *The Guardian* (6 August 2012).

[15] House of Lords Reform Act 2014.

[16] See, eg King, *The British Constitution* (2010) n 1 above.

[17] See, eg Flinders, *Democratic Drift* (2009) n 1 above.

[18] See, eg C Foster, *British Government in Crisis, or The Third English Revolution* (Oxford, Hart Publishing, 2005).

[19] See, eg Bogdanor, *The New British Constitution* (2009) n 1 above; JWF Allison, *The English Historical Constitution: Continuity, Change and European Effects* (Cambridge, Cambridge University Press, 2007).

be challenged by contemporary constitutional developments in the UK—not all of which, it should be noted, originate in the era of reform described here—but the argument developed in this book is that it has not been disposed of. Instead, although Dicey's orthodox account of the sovereignty of Parliament may now be difficult to defend, I will suggest that developments in UK constitutional practice demonstrate that a manner and form conception of the doctrine has now been embraced. Further, and crucially, it is this adoption of the manner and form theory of legally unlimited legislative authority which enables the doctrine of parliamentary sovereignty to accommodate what would otherwise appear to be challenges to its continuing constitutional existence. As such, although our understanding of the implications of the notion of parliamentary sovereignty may need to change, we should not accept, even in an era of reform, that the doctrine is only now part of the UK's constitutional past.

To make this argument, the critical modern challenges to the doctrine of parliamentary sovereignty must be identified. Three are of great significance: the challenge posed to the sovereignty of Parliament by membership of the European Union,[20] the decision of the House of Lords as to the status of the Parliament Act 1949 in *Jackson*,[21] and the referendum locks created by the European Union Act 2011.[22] Each of these matters will be considered in detail in due course. Prior to this, however, three other topics must be considered, for they are developments which are also sometimes thought to present challenges to the doctrine of parliamentary sovereignty. These topics are the enactment of the Human Rights Act 1998, the creation of the devolution settlement, and a contemporary resurgence in common law constitutionalist theories of the UK constitution. I do not accept this analysis, however, and will explain in this chapter why each of these three developments does not challenge the sovereignty of Parliament, properly understood. As such, they are described in this chapter as 'non-critical challenges'. My argument should not, however, be mistaken for one of constitutional insignificance; each of the three non-critical challenges to be discussed here is, albeit in varying ways, constitutionally consequential, notwithstanding the fact that each can be reconciled with the doctrine of parliamentary sovereignty. These developments are therefore non-critical as challenges to the sovereignty of Parliament, not non-critical in terms of their broader constitutional impact.

While these three distinct issues are discussed together in this chapter, the reasons that they do not challenge the sovereignty of Parliament vary. In broad terms, two different reasons that the doctrine of parliamentary sovereignty is not challenged here can be identified. First, in relation to devolution and the Human Rights Act, these developments are best understood as placing political limits on Parliament's law-making capability, while leaving its legal power to legislate on

---

[20] See chapter 4 of this volume.
[21] *R (on the application of Jackson) v Attorney General* [2005] UKHL 56, [2006] 1 AC 262. See chapter 5 of this volume.
[22] See chapter 6 of this volume.

any matter intact. Secondly, and in relation to common law constitutionalism, in contrast, this challenge fails because it derives from an unsustainable interpretation of UK constitutional arrangements. Yet despite these differences as to why parliamentary sovereignty is not challenged, there is a common theme which justifies consideration of these three issues together. For these developments—devolution, the statutory protection of human rights and a resurgence in common law constitutionalist thinking—have all contributed to the construction of a more expansive constitutional role for the judiciary in the UK. The devolution legislation and Human Rights Act have done this by changing actual constitutional practice, through granting to the courts new powers to review the substantive contents of primary legislation enacted in the UK, or in one of its constituent nations. The theorising of common law constitutionalists has, in contrast, made a rhetorical contribution to this process, elucidating a conception of the judicial role which portrays the judges as increasingly prominent and significant constitutional actors. That this common law constitutionalist account of the proper role of the courts is, in my view, flawed, does not undermine the function it has served in offering a richer narrative in which the actual changes to the judicial role which have occurred can be located, and thus, suggested to add up to more than just the sum of their parts. The possibility that such a composite challenge could be developed, which fuses together a range of overlapping issues, and takes this as a basis for a rejection of parliamentary sovereignty, is something to which we must be sensitive when examining the three non-critical challenges at issue in this chapter. Nevertheless, by explaining in turn why each of these three separate issues does not present a challenge to parliamentary sovereignty, it will become clear that a basis on which a composite challenge to the doctrine could be developed simply does not exist.

II. DEVOLUTION

The devolution of legislative and executive power to new democratic institutions of government in Scotland, Wales and Northern Ireland is perhaps the most fundamental change to the UK constitution which has occurred in the modern era of reform. The current and future state of the devolution settlement raises questions of vast constitutional importance. Is it still appropriate to conceive of the UK as a unitary, rather than some variety of quasi-federal, state, and if not, what are the implications of this?[23] Is the asymmetry of the devolution settlement justified—both as between the nations with devolved institutions and powers, and in relation to the omission of England from this scheme?[24] For how long, and to what extent, will the devolution settlement continue to be dynamic, given that

---

[23] See, eg N Walker, 'Beyond the Unitary Conception of the UK Constitution?' [2000] *PL* 384.
[24] See, eg B Hadfield, 'Devolution, Westminster and the English Question' [2005] *PL* 286. See the proposals of the McKay Commission for the most recent attempt to conjure possible solutions to

discussion of the devolution of further powers persists in Scotland, Wales and Northern Ireland?[25] Will devolution ever be sufficient to satiate calls for independence from the UK among some in its constituent nations?[26] Nevertheless, despite its constitutional significance, the devolution settlement does not challenge the legislative sovereignty of the UK Parliament.[27]

The devolution settlement was created by legislation of the UK Parliament, and as a matter of legal principle, could be unmade by Act of Parliament. Indeed, all of the implementing legislation applicable to Northern Ireland, Scotland and Wales explicitly preserves the UK Parliament's legislative authority.[28] Parliament retains the ultimate lawful power to repeal unilaterally the devolution statutes. Further, even while operating within the parameters of the devolution settlement as presently constituted, Parliament is also still capable of enacting legislation with reference to any specific subject, which will have legal effect regardless of whether the statute relates to a matter for which competence has been devolved to Scotland, Northern Ireland or Wales. Of course, by convention the UK government will not usually seek to legislate in Parliament in Westminster on devolved matters without first obtaining the consent of the relevant devolved legislature.[29] However, the

the 'English Question': *Report of the Commission on the Consequences of Devolution for the House of Commons* (March 2013).

[25] Extension of fiscal powers provides the most interesting example of devolution as a dynamic settlement, and of the 'levelling up' which can occur on the basis of comparisons drawn between the three asymmetrical regimes. In Scotland, the Scotland Act 2012 made provision for an extension of devolved fiscal power following the report of the Calman Commission, *Serving Scotland Better: Scotland and the United Kingdom in the 21st Century* (June 2009). In Wales, the Silk Commission subsequently called for a similar extension of fiscal powers in *Empowerment and Responsibility: Financial Powers to Strengthen Wales* (November 2012). This call has been largely accepted by the UK government, and a Wales Bill to give effect to these changes was introduced to Parliament in March 2014. In Northern Ireland, a review of the Calman and Silk Commissions conducted by the Department of Finance and Personnel will make recommendations to the Northern Ireland executive and the UK government in autumn 2014: *Building a Prosperous and United Community* (June 2013). Responsibility for Air Passenger Duty has already been devolved to Northern Ireland by the Finance Act 2012.

[26] The referendum on Scottish independence held in September 2014 did not give voters the option to indicate a preference for further devolution of power—'devo-max'—as an alternative to independence, although the three main UK political parties together pledged during the campaign that further power would be devolved if Scotland remained in the union: 'Scotland Promised Extra Tax and Legal Powers For Referendum No Vote', *The Guardian* (5 August 2014).

[27] It has been argued that the doctrine of parliamentary sovereignty is not, in any event, recognised as a principle of Scottish—as opposed to English—constitutional law: see especially Lord President Cooper in *MacCormick v Lord Advocate* 1953 SC 396, 411: 'The principle of the unlimited sovereignty of Parliament is a distinctively English principle which has no counterpart in Scottish constitutional law'. I leave aside these claims here because, as Goldsworthy has shown, they are historically questionable: see J Goldsworthy, *The Sovereignty of Parliament: History and Philosophy* (Oxford, Oxford University Press, 1999) 166–69. Moreover, even if this were not the case, today it is generally accepted among Scottish lawyers that 'the dominant, and to all intents and purposes, settled position is the traditional Diceyan one': see N Walker, '*Scottish Self-Government and the Unitary Constitution*' in L Farmer and S Veitch (eds), *The State of Scots Law* (London, Butterworths, 2001) 99, cited in A Tomkins, 'Scotland's Choice, Britain's Future' (2014) 130 *LQR* 215, 220.

[28] Scotland Act 1998 s 28(7); Northern Ireland Act 1998 s 5(6); Government of Wales Act 2006 s 107(5).

[29] *Devolution: Memorandum of Understanding and Supplementary Agreements*, (Cm 5240, 2001) 8.

existence of the 'Sewel' convention merely shows that Parliament is not politically omnipotent, a fact which has never been in dispute. While the devolution of legislative power to Scotland, Wales and Northern Ireland has had a vast impact on the way in which the UK's system of government functions, and has undoubtedly, perhaps even irreversibly, limited the actual scope of Parliament's legislative power in practice, these are ultimately political limits. This does not mean they are trivial; indeed, such limits are crucial in enabling the devolution settlement to function effectively, and to ensure in particular that the devolved legislatures are treated with a level of respect which allows them to exercise powers to which they are entitled. Yet this also does not infringe the legislative sovereignty of the UK Parliament. The legislative authority of the UK Parliament remains legally unlimited notwithstanding the creation by statute of the devolution settlement, and therefore the central claim made by the doctrine of parliamentary sovereignty is not challenged by this aspect of the New Labour government's reform programme.

However, is this analysis too superficial? Is this account of the formal continuation of the sovereignty of the UK Parliament in the post-devolution era insensitive to more nuanced objections that might be advanced? Two particular such objections might develop in the following ways. First, in accordance with the devolution statutes, UK courts will now be required to hear challenges to the validity of domestic primary legislation. The substantive content of devolved legislation will be subject to judicial review on substantive grounds to ensure it is within the lawful competence of the enacting legislature,[30] both post-enactment and, potentially, prior to enactment on a reference.[31] Is there any scope for the courts to expand this statutory jurisdiction upwards, to develop a comparable jurisdiction to review Acts of the UK Parliament? This possibility might be seen in the comments of Lord Hope in *Axa General Insurance v Lord Advocate*,[32] which concerned the prospect of devolved legislation being susceptible to judicial review on grounds not explicitly detailed in the provisions establishing legislative competence contained in the devolution statutes. The notion of 'exceptional circumstances' review, discussed by Lord Hope in *Axa*, will be considered in detail in Chapter five, but may also be of relevance here. For although Lord Hope recognised that the question of whether the sovereignty of Parliament could be 'subject to limitation in exceptional circumstances' was not at issue in *Axa*, he also considered this matter to be 'still under discussion'.[33] Further, the fact that the democratic legitimacy of the Scottish Parliament was expressly acknowledged by Lord Hope, but yet not taken to be sufficient to exempt devolved primary legislation from the possibility of extra-statutory review in exceptional

---

[30]   Scotland Act 1998 s 29; Northern Ireland Act 1998 s 6; Government of Wales Act 2006 s 108.
[31]   Scotland Act 1998 s 33; Northern Ireland Act 1998 s 11; Government of Wales Act 2006 s 112.
[32]   *Axa General Insurance v Lord Advocate* [2011] UKSC 46, [2012] 1 AC 868.
[33]   ibid [50].

circumstances,[34] might be thought to indicate that the democratic virtue which I have suggested underpins the doctrine of parliamentary sovereignty could similarly be insufficient to exempt Acts of the UK Parliament from such judicial oversight.

But while the possibility that the courts might seek to establish a comparable power to review the substantive content of an Act of the UK Parliament—even if only in exceptional circumstances—would be a direct denial of the doctrine of parliamentary sovereignty, this challenge is not a necessary consequence of devolution. While the comments of Lord Hope in *Axa* arose in the context of devolution, they are essentially an echo, if not indeed a direct iteration, of common law constitutionalist theory. Any challenge that such comments thus pose to the sovereignty of Parliament therefore derives not from the fact that the courts must now, as part of the contemporary devolution settlement, exercise powers of judicial review in relation to some primary legislation—that of the devolved legislatures—but from a contestable, and controversial, conception of the nature of the UK constitution. Whether such a challenge to parliamentary sovereignty should be accepted will be discussed below. But that the UK Parliament has, in enacting the devolution statutes, obliged the courts to exercise powers of judicial review in relation to devolved primary legislation does not provide a basis for a challenge to parliamentary sovereignty; instead, such review is a consequence of the exercise of Parliament's legally unlimited legislative authority.

A second, yet much more potent, objection can also be imagined to the claim that devolution has not challenged the doctrine of parliamentary sovereignty. This is a consequence of the very democratic equivalence of the UK Parliament and the devolved legislatures which has been encountered above. Indeed, it may even be argued that to identify a democratic equivalence between these legislatures may not go far enough, for the voting systems used for elections to the Scottish Parliament, National Assembly for Wales, and Northern Ireland Assembly may easily be described as capable of producing more proportionate and representative institutions than is possible under the first-past-the-post voting system used for elections to the House of Commons.[35] Further, that devolution was also popularly established, having been approved at referendums in Scotland, Northern Ireland and Wales,[36] may also suggest it is a constitutional

---

[34] ibid [46], [49], [51].

[35] The additional member system is used in relation to Scotland and Wales; the single transferable vote system in relation to Northern Ireland. For an overview of the key differences, and comparison with first-past-the-post, see, eg Brazier, *Constitutional Reform* (2008) n 1 above, ch 4; *The Governance of Britain—Review of Voting Systems: The Experience of New Voting Systems in the United Kingdom Since 1997*, (Cm 7304, 2008).

[36] Devolution to Scotland was approved by 74.3% of those voting, on a 60.4% turnout, in 1997. A power to vary the income tax rate for Scotland was also approved by 63.5% in the same poll. In Wales, devolution was initially approved by a much narrower margin: 50.3% were in favour, on a 50.1% turnout. A subsequent referendum, held to approve the extension of the legislative power of the National Assembly for Wales in 2011, in accordance with the Government of Wales Act 2006 s 103, showed an increase in support of those voting—63.5% were in favour—although on a lower turnout

settlement with superior democratic legitimacy to that of the UK constitution founded on the sovereignty of Parliament. The fact that, at the very least, the UK Parliament now has democratic competitor institutions in three of the Union's constituent nations might be taken to suggest that the democratic virtue which I attributed to the doctrine of parliamentary sovereignty in Chapter one can no longer be assured. For the sovereignty of Parliament might, on this basis, be seen to subjugate democratic decision-making, rather than elevate it to a position of constitutional primacy. And, from this perspective, it may therefore be argued that the legislative sovereignty of the UK Parliament is no longer an appropriate foundation for the evolved UK constitution.

Such an objection, however, goes to the appeal of the doctrine of parliamentary sovereignty, rather than its legal force. The legal status of the doctrine is not contingent upon its desirability, and it cannot therefore be said to have dissipated simply because the advent of devolution raises questions about the appropriateness of parliamentary sovereignty as a constitutional fundamental.[37] Yet, while the immediate legal force of the sovereignty of Parliament is not challenged by uncertainty as to its continuing democratic virtue, this is a difficulty which must not be lightly dismissed. For if there is tension between the legal architecture of the UK constitution and the democratic ideals to which it purports to give effect, this has the potential to distort, and perhaps even destabilise, the operation of the political system which is constituted by the former, and animated by the latter. We are therefore compelled to consider whether the sovereignty of the UK Parliament is a constitutional doctrine which can continue to be defended in a changing democratic landscape.

It is, however, not clear how a post-devolution UK constitution would look if the notion of the legislative sovereignty of Parliament were displaced. Would this also amount to the abandonment of the notion of legally unlimited legislative power? The present legislative competence of the devolved legislatures is legally limited and subject to judicial oversight, an arrangement which can be objected to from a democratic perspective.[38] For the UK Parliament to lose its legislative sovereignty might therefore represent a profound shift, depriving democratic politics of the primacy which it has long been constitutionally afforded in the UK. Even if some principle of shared or 'divided' sovereignty were to become recognised,[39] and understood to establish for the devolved legislatures a sphere

of 35.2%. In Northern Ireland, devolution was approved as part of the referendum on the Good Friday Agreement held in 1998: 71.1% voted in favour, on an 81.1% turnout. For more detailed breakdowns of these referendum results, see 'Referendums in the United Kingdom': www.en.wikipedia.org/wiki/Referendums_in_the_United_Kingdom.

[37] For discussion of such issues as they relate to Scotland in particular, see G Little, 'Scotland and Parliamentary Sovereignty' (2004) 24 *Legal Studies* 540.
[38] See chapter 1 of this volume, pp 34–41.
[39] For the notion of 'divided sovereignty' in this context, see, eg Lord Steyn in *R (on the application of Jackson) v Attorney General* [2005] UKHL 56, [2006] 1 AC 262, [102]. See also J Mitchell, *Devolution in the UK* (Manchester, Manchester University Press, 2009) 222, discussing 'the prospect of a clash of sovereignties' as representing a potential challenge to the future of the UK.

of influence in which the UK Parliament was not lawfully entitled to interfere, it is difficult to conceive of a scheme by which clashes between national and Union level democratic institutions could be resolved without increasing the role of the courts. But, moreover, even the idea of shared sovereignty is a problematic one in the context of the existing asymmetrical devolution settlement. When there is no set of English institutions available to absorb some share of legislative sovereignty, this would lead to disparity of treatment between the constituent nations. For example, while the Scottish Parliament, hypothetically, might be free to legislate in any way in relation to matters within its competence without the prospect of interference by the UK Parliament, English matters would still lie to be settled by a body representing UK-wide interests. Whether the democratic institutions in constituent nations of a union state ought even to be entitled to the absolute protection of their competence that some conception of shared sovereignty might be seen to offer, at least while continuing to remain members of that larger union state, is open to debate.[40] But such arrangements would surely need to be capable of universal application to be justifiable, and this is something that the current devolution system could not offer. The adoption of a new formal codified UK constitution, with a federal-esque division of powers, could, of course, be a solution to this problem, but returns us to the initial difficulty: would the notion of legally unlimited legislative authority be abandoned, and if so, would this leave us with a constitution which is, as a consequence, less democratic than our present arrangements?[41]

It may therefore be that experiments with shared sovereignty, however this principle itself might be conceived, do not offer a promising path to a more democratic form of governance than that which is offered by a constitution founded on the sovereignty of Parliament. But when, in actual constitutional practice, a sphere of legislative freedom for the devolved legislatures can successfully be created by a series of political limits and understandings—which are crucially underpinned by an appreciation of the democratic credentials of these devolved institutions—is the notion that the UK Parliament retains legislative sovereignty really something which needs to be objected to? Instead, perhaps this creation of an effective system of devolved law-making competence within the UK might be seen to reflect the malleability of a constitution founded on legally unlimited legislative authority—a feature which has been exploited to establish, and not to impede, new sites of democratic activity. Nevertheless, the questions which are prompted by the existence of domestic democratic competitors to the UK Parliament, even if posing difficulties which are ultimately surmountable in the context of devolution at present, raise an important issue of principle: if

[40] This is certainly not to reject the fundamental political right to collective self-determination that each constituent nation should be understood to possess. Instead, it is to recognise that unless or until a right to secede from the UK is exercised, it is arguable that membership of the union requires an acceptance that ultimate legislative authority should lie with union institutions, rather than (in part) resting in constituent nations.

[41] See chapter 8 of this volume, pp 352–56.

the Westminster Parliament were no longer to be the optimal democratic vessel for legally unlimited legislative authority in the UK, could other institutional arrangements for the exercise of such power be developed? Devolution may not, therefore, challenge directly the doctrine of parliamentary sovereignty. It does, however, prompt us to think carefully about the relationship between the doctrine and its democratic virtue, both at present and in the future. We will return to this important theme in Chapter eight, when the potential utility of the manner and form theory will be explored, paying particular regard to the possibilities for further reform to the UK constitution that the adoption of this conception of parliamentary sovereignty may open up.

III. THE HUMAN RIGHTS ACT

The Human Rights Act 1998 (HRA) makes specified basic rights contained in the European Convention on Human Rights (ECHR) directly actionable in UK courts.[42] In addition to making it unlawful for public authorities to violate the relevant convention rights,[43] the HRA makes provision as to the compatibility of primary legislation with the ECHR. Section 3 imposes on courts a duty to interpret legislation 'so far as it is possible to do so' in a way which is compatible with convention rights. If an ECHR-compliant interpretation cannot be achieved, the courts are empowered to issue a declaration of incompatibility with respect to the legislation, in accordance with section 4. Crucially, such a declaration, by the terms of the HRA itself, 'does not affect the validity, continuing operation or enforcement of the provision in respect of which it is given'.[44] The protection of rights offered by the HRA is thus not absolute; Parliament may enact valid legislation which contravenes the ECHR, and the courts do not, as might be expected in relation to a traditional 'Bill of Rights', have the power to strike down offending statutes.[45] The HRA provides statutory protection of convention rights, but in a way which is entirely compatible with the doctrine of parliamentary sovereignty. Parliament enacted the HRA; it could repeal the HRA;[46] and the powers afforded

---

[42]   Human Rights Act 1998 s 1.

[43]   ibid s 6.

[44]   ibid s 4(6)(a).

[45]   In this sense, the HRA may be seen as one of a number of 'New Commonwealth' models of rights protection, which seek to map a 'third way' between legislative and judicial supremacy, instigating schemes of judicial review of legislation which nevertheless leave the final decision as to legal validity to political actors: see S Gardbaum, *The New Commonwealth Model of Constitutionalism: Theory and Practice* (Cambridge, Cambridge University Press, 2013).

[46]   The coalition government established a Commission on a Bill of Rights to consider whether the HRA ought to be replaced with an alternative form of rights protection, although due to political disagreement between the Conservatives and Liberal Democrats, it is unlikely that its report—which, by a 7 to 2 majority, concluded that there was an argument in favour of a UK Bill of Rights—will have any direct consequences: see The Commission on a Bill of Rights, *A UK Bill of Rights?—The Choice Before Us* (December 2012). The repeal of the HRA is to be the subject of a Conservative Party manifesto

to the courts by the HRA do not permit them to override primary legislation. The HRA cannot, therefore, be seen as a challenge to parliamentary sovereignty.

Yet, as we also queried in relation to devolution, is this initial conclusion insufficiently nuanced? Two issues which require further consideration relate to the manner in which the courts have applied the interpretative obligation imposed by section 3, and the manner in which Parliament has responded to declarations of incompatibility issued under section 4. First, when seeking to read legislation in such a way as to ensure compatibility with convention rights, is it possible for the courts to be excessively creative in their interpretive endeavours? If section 3 extends to permit the effective re-writing of Parliament's legislation, this might be seen as a challenge to its legislative sovereignty. The duty established in section 3 includes the limiting clause 'so far as it is possible to do so', which, taken alongside the fact that section 4 makes express provision for situations in which an ECHR-compliant construction of contested legislation cannot be achieved, indicates that the interpretive power given to the courts is to some extent constrained. Yet this statutory constraint is unhelpfully circular, with interpretation limited to what is 'possible', without what is 'possible' being delineated. In filling this void, the courts have taken section 3 to permit departure 'from the unambiguous meaning the legislation would otherwise bear'.[47] This is a remarkably broad understanding of section 3—which even allows 'a court to read in words which change the meaning of the enacted legislation'[48]—and seems to extend the judicial function under the HRA beyond that of simply interpreting legislation, and into the realm of legislating itself.

Yet, the fact that the courts have understood section 3 to permit legislation to be, in effect, re-written, in a number of controversial cases,[49] does not mean that the HRA is necessarily a challenge to the sovereignty of Parliament. For Parliament retains the power to reverse what it considers to be a flawed judicial decision in a human rights case, as much as in any other context.[50] As Crawford's survey of the use of the section 3 power indicates, there has as yet been no example of the UK Parliament taking direct action to adjust an interpretation with

---

commitment in the 2015 general election: 'Conservatives Promise to Scrap Human Rights Act After Next Election', *The Guardian* (30 September 2013).

   [47] *Ghaidan v Godin-Mendoza* [2004] UKHL 30, [2004] 2 AC 557, [30].

   [48] ibid [32].

   [49] See, eg *R v A (No 2)* [2001] UKHL 25, [2002] 1 AC 45; *Ghaidan v Godin-Mendoza* [2004] UKHL 30, [2004] 2 AC 557; *R (on the application of Hammond) v Secretary of State for the Home Department* [2005] UKHL 69, [2006] 1 AC 603; *Secretary of State for the Home Department v MB, Secretary of State for the Home Department v AF* [2007] UKHL 46, [2008] 1 AC 440; *R (Veolia ES Nottinghamshire Ltd) v Nottinghamshire County Council* [2010] EWCA Civ 1214, [2012] PTSR 185. For a comprehensive review of cases in which the section 3 power has been used by the courts, see C Crawford, 'Dialogue and Rights-Compatible Interpretations under Section 3 of the Human Rights Act 1998' (2014) 25 *King's Law Journal* 34.

   [50] See, eg Health and Social Care Act 2008, s 145(1); reversing the decision in *YL v Birmingham City Council* [2007] UKHL 27, [2008] 1 AC 95, in which the House of Lords had held that a company providing social care and accommodation under a contract with a local authority was not exercising a public function within s 6(3)(b) of the HRA.

which it disagrees.[51] This does not, however, mean that the expansive approach to interpretation adopted by the courts using section 3 is legitimate; indeed, it is arguable that in the most problematic cases, in which the courts appear to have strayed from the interpretation to the amendment of statutes, decisions have been wrongly reached even on the courts' own generous understanding of what is permitted by section 3. When the courts have held that 'a meaning which departs substantially from a fundamental feature of an Act of Parliament is likely to have crossed the boundary between interpretation and amendment',[52] it is difficult, for example, to justify the conclusion reached in *R v A*.[53] The legislative decision taken by Parliament at issue in this case—that in rape cases, evidence of a complainant's sexual history with the accused would be inadmissible in relation to a belief in consent, other than in narrowly drawn exceptional instances—was fundamentally altered by the House of Lords' ruling that such evidence would be admissible where deemed necessary to protect the defendant's right to a fair trial under Article 6 ECHR.[54] Yet such cases have been relatively few in number, and none, it would appear, have been sufficiently egregious to provoke a confrontation between Parliament and the courts.[55]

In any event, it should not be thought that creative judicial interpretation of legislation is a novel problem exclusively associated with the form of rights protection introduced by the HRA. Cases which long pre-date the enactment of the HRA can be identified where the courts have used interpretive techniques to bypass, rather than implement, the legislative intentions of Parliament— famously, for example, in *Anisminic v Foreign Compensation Commission*.[56] But such judgments can essentially be regarded as aberrations, and certainly do not amount to a denial of the sovereignty of Parliament. Similarly, the over-zealous use, on occasion, of the section 3 interpretive power, which was intended to offer the courts more scope for manoeuvre than did the traditional canons of statutory

---

[51] Crawford, 'Dialogue and Rights-Compatible Interpretations under Section 3 of the Human Rights Act 1998' (2014) n 49 above, 40. The only example identified by Crawford of the enactment of legislation which seems implicitly to reject an interpretation reached in accordance with section 3 relates to the Scottish Parliament: the Children's Hearings (Scotland) Act 2011 appears to reverse the effect of the decision in *M, Appellant* 2010 Fam LR 152 (Sh Ct).

[52] *Re S (Minors) (Care Order: Implementation of Care Plan)* [2002] UKHL 10, [2002] 2 AC 291, [40].

[53] *R v A (No 2)* [2001] UKHL 25, [2002] 1 AC 45.

[54] See, eg D Nicol, 'Law and Politics after the Human Rights Act' [2006] *PL* 722, 739 for critical discussion of *R v A*. See further the dissenting judgment of Lord Millett in *Ghaidan v Godin-Mendoza* [2004] UKHL 30, [2004] 2 AC 557 for a critique of the approach to interpretation taken by the majority in that case; [57], [70]–[72], [94]–[100]. And for a powerful challenge to the decision in *R (Hammond) v Secretary of State for the Home Department* [2005] UKHL 69, [2006] 1 AC 603, see D Mead, 'Talking About Dialogue', *UK Constitutional Law Association Blog* (15 September 2012).

[55] In the context of human rights law, it may simply be that the attention of Parliament is elsewhere; see, eg the Immigration Act 2014 s 19, which seeks to define a number of public interest factors to which the courts must have regard when determining whether an immigration status decision would violate a person's Article 8 ECHR right to a private and family life. The enactment of such legislation indicates that Parliament is willing to intervene when disagreements arise with the judiciary as to the requirements of the ECHR in particular circumstances.

[56] *Anisminic v Foreign Compensation Commission* [1969] 2 AC 147.

construction,[57] may be regarded as judicial overreaching. But it does not represent an incursion into the legislature's legal sovereignty, for whether Parliament opts to reverse such decisions or not, it has the legal authority to do so. Indeed, the ongoing acceptance by the courts of the sovereignty of Parliament, even in cases where their fidelity to the legislature's particular statutory intentions might be in question,[58] provides further evidence of the way in which the doctrine operates as a central organising principle of the UK constitution.[59] That such judicial recognition of the doctrine is not simply an elaborate 'pretence',[60] but can have a substantive conditioning effect on the use of section 3, is apparent from those cases in which the courts have held that a convention compatible interpretation of legislation cannot be achieved without trespassing into Parliament's territory.[61] Therefore, although the decisions reached in some cases may not fully respect the proper 'constitutional boundary'[62] between the legitimate activity of Parliament and the courts, this does not mean that this boundary has dissolved. Instead, the constitutional boundary still exists, and is one which, ultimately, it is for Parliament to define.

Secondly, can it be argued that, in practice, a declaration of incompatibility issued under section 4 has the effect of curtailing Parliament's legislative authority to such an extent that the notion of parliamentary sovereignty becomes superfluous, if not positively misleading? As the government acknowledged as the Human Rights Bill passed through the House of Commons, a judicial declaration of incompatibility is likely to be accepted by Parliament in 'the overwhelming majority of cases'.[63] And this is essentially what has transpired: government data which records responses to declarations of incompatibility demonstrates that, in the 19 cases where a declaration has become final, in only one instance has remedial action of some kind not (as yet) been taken.[64] Nevertheless, while in nearly all cases legislation which has been the subject of a declaration of incompatibility has been amended—although not always producing results which were compatible

[57] See, eg Lord Irvine, 'The Impact of the Human Rights Act: Parliament, the Courts and the Executive' [2003] *PL* 308, 319: '[Section 3] is a new and powerful tool of interpretation and that is exactly what it was intended to be'. For a critique of the idea that the HRA necessitates a new approach to statutory interpretation, see G Marshall, 'The Lynchpin of Parliamentary Intention: Lost, Stolen or Strained?' [2003] *PL* 236.

[58] See, eg *Ghaidan v Godin-Mendoza* [2004] UKHL 30, [2004] 2 AC 557, [112], [120]. See also *R (on the application of Sheldrake) v Director of Public Prosecutions* [2004] UKHL 43, [2005] 1 AC 264, [53] for Lord Bingham justifying use of the section 3 power to 'read down' legislation which was incompatible with Article 6 ECHR in terms of the intention of the Parliament which enacted the HRA in 1998.

[59] See chapter 1 of this volume, pp 23–25.

[60] I Leigh and R Masterman, *Making Rights Real: The Human Rights Act in its First Decade* (Oxford, Hart Publishing, 2008) 130.

[61] See, eg *Bellinger v Bellinger* [2003] UKHL 21, [2003] 2 AC 467, [37]; *R (on the application of Anderson) v Secretary of State for the Home Department* [2002] UKHL 46, [2003] 1 AC 837, [30], [58]; *Re S (Minors) (Care Order: Implementation of Care Plan)* [2002] UKHL 10, [2002] 2 AC 291, [39].

[62] *Re S (Minors) (Care Order: Implementation of Care Plan)* [2002] UKHL 10, [2002] 2 AC 291, [39].

[63] Jack Straw MP, *Hansard*, HC Deb Vol 317, col 1301 (21 October 1998).

[64] Ministry of Justice, *Responding to Human Rights Judgments: Report to the Joint Committee on Human Rights on the Government Response to Human Rights Judgments 2012–13*, (Cm 8727, 2013) 43.

with the ECHR[65]—Parliament retains the right not to accept the view of courts as to whether policy change is required.

This is clearly evident in light of the (ongoing) disagreement over the right of prisoners to vote. The domestic courts have issued a declaration of incompatibility in relation to section 3 of the Representation of the People Act 1983[66]—which excludes convicted offenders from voting while detained in prison—on the basis of a series of judgments of the European Court of Human Rights which have held this 'blanket ban' to be in violation of the right to vote, set out in Article 3 of Protocol 1 to the ECHR.[67] The options which Parliament is considering in response include simply maintaining the status quo,[68] and even if a compromise option, such as enfranchising only those serving shorter sentences, is eventually chosen, it is clearly within the legislature's power to refuse to take action to rectify this incompatibility. Indeed, it is perhaps notable that it is the prospect of being in violation of a decision of the Council of Europe, as a matter of international law, which seems most likely to compel Parliament to take action, if action is eventually taken.[69] Moreover, that the UK Supreme Court declined to exercise its discretion to grant a further declaration of incompatibility when the nature of the violation of the ECHR is already well established, and the range of possible responses being assessed by Parliament,[70] is indicative of the limitations of this judicial tool. For, while the making of a declaration will announce the existence of legislation which is incompatible with the ECHR, that there is no point in issuing further such declarations once the parameters of a dispute over rights are apparent simply emphasises the fact that these orders do not oblige Parliament

---

[65] See, eg the response to the declaration of incompatibility issued in *A and others v Secretary of State for the Home Department* [2004] UKHL 56, [2005] 2 AC 68. A scheme of indefinite detention of foreign nationals certified as suspected terrorists, pending their deportation was replaced, by the Prevention of Terrorism Act 2005, with a system of 'control orders', the particular use of which was held to violate, in a number of ways, the convention rights of controlees: *Secretary of State for the Home Department v JJ and others* [2007] UKHL 45, [2008] 1 AC 385; *Secretary of State for the Home Department v MB, Secretary of State for the Home Department v AF* [2007] UKHL 46, [2008] 1 AC 440; *Secretary of State for the Home Department v AF (No 3)* [2009] UKHL 28, [2010] 2 AC 269.

[66] *Smith v Scott* [2007] CSIH 9, 2007 SC 345.

[67] *Hirst v United Kingdom (No 2)* (2005) 42 EHRR 849; *Greens and MT v United Kingdom* (2010) 53 EHRR 710; *Scoppola v Italy (No 3)* (2012) 56 EHRR 663.

[68] The draft Voting Eligibility (Prisoners) Bill was published by the government in 2012, and was subject to scrutiny by a Joint Committee of both Houses of Parliament, which concluded in December 2013. While accepting the sovereignty of Parliament, the Joint Committee did not consider this, in itself, to constitute a reason not to give effect to the judgment of the European Court of Human Rights; Joint Committee on the Draft Voting Eligibility (Prisoners) Bill, *Draft Voting Eligibility (Prisoners) Bill: Report*, HL Paper 103, HC 924 (18 December 2013) [111]–[112]. The recommendation of the Joint Committee was for modest legislative action, permitting prisoners serving sentences of 12 months or less to vote. For the broader background to this dispute, and more detailed consideration of Parliament's earlier responses to the European Court of Human Rights' judgments, see J Hiebert, 'The Human Rights Act: Ambiguity about Parliamentary Sovereignty' (2013) 14 *German Law Journal* 2253, 2256–66; D Nicol, 'Legitimacy of the Commons Debate on Prisoner Voting' [2011] *PL* 681.

[69] See, eg the consideration given to this by the Joint Committee scrutinising the legislative solutions proposed by the government: ibid [77]–[113].

[70] *R (on the application of Chester) v Secretary of State for Justice* [2013] UKSC 63, [2014] AC 271, [39].

to act. At the very least, then, the saga of prisoners' voting rights provides us with an answer to the query posed by Ewing at the inception of the HRA: it appears that 'a wounded Act of Parliament' can 'survive a declaration of incompatibility to which the government and Parliament refuse to respond' for quite some time.[71]

Some may nevertheless object that to dismiss such arguments about the use of both section 3 and 4 in practice is to emphasise form over substance. Kavanagh, for example, has argued that parliamentary sovereignty seems to have been 'compromised' by the HRA: 'the HRA only preserves the doctrine of parliamentary sovereignty in formal terms, but limits the legislative power of Parliament in substance'.[72] The second part of Kavanagh's claim is without question true; Parliament's freedom to legislate is now constrained by mechanisms which it has created to try to ensure that its legislation is compatible with the ECHR. Yet this does not mean parliamentary sovereignty is merely a formal doctrine. It is a doctrine which establishes the scope of Parliament's legislative capacity as a matter of law. It does not claim that Parliament has unlimited legislative capability; indeed, the fact that Parliament's legislative power is limited, structured, conditioned and constrained by a variety of non-legal factors is critical in justifying the constitutional allocation of legal sovereignty to the legislature. Limits on the legislative power of Parliament in substance are not only, then, entirely compatible with the doctrine of parliamentary sovereignty; they are positively demanded by it. The fact that the mechanisms which have been used to create political constraints on Parliament's power are statutory does not transform them into absolute legal limits of the kind which would be incommensurable with the doctrine of parliamentary sovereignty. There may be scope for debate about whether the courts have adopted the most appropriate understanding of this statutory scheme. Perhaps in particular, there are legitimate questions as to whether there has been excessive recourse by the courts to creative interpretation under section 3 (if indeed this has always been interpretation), and the consequent relegation of section 4 declarations of incompatibility to a remedy of 'last resort'.[73] For this may have the effect of providing Parliament with fewer formal opportunities actively to determine how the incompatibility of legislation with the ECHR should be addressed. Yet even if the balance which has been found between section 3 and section 4 is such as to empower the courts to a greater extent than might originally have been imagined,[74] it was always clear that the HRA, however understood, would provide the judiciary with significant additional power.[75] While the magnitude of the power now exercised by the courts may be relevant to an assessment of whether the UK constitution is in transition from being one which is primarily 'political' to

---

[71] KD Ewing, 'The Human Rights Act and Parliamentary Democracy' (1999) 62 *MLR* 79, 99.

[72] A Kavanagh, *Constitutional Review under the UK Human Rights Act* (Cambridge, Cambridge University Press, 2009) 325, 336.

[73] *Ghaidan v Godin-Mendoza* [2004] UKHL 30, [2004] 2 AC 557, [39].

[74] See, eg C Gearty, *Principles of Human Rights Adjudication* (Oxford, Oxford University Press, 2004) 49–54.

[75] See, eg Ewing, 'The Human Rights Act and Parliamentary Democracy' (1999) n 71 above, 98–99.

one which is primarily 'legal',[76] it does not critically challenge the legally unlimited legislative authority of Parliament. For such judicial power is exercised within a system of statutory rights adjudication which is both compatible with, and subject to, the doctrine of parliamentary sovereignty.

IV. COMMON LAW CONSTITUTIONALISM

The final non-critical challenge to be considered in this chapter is that posed by the theory of common law constitutionalism. Although there may be an overlap between the challenge to parliamentary sovereignty said to emerge from the enactment of the Human Rights Act and that which is inherent in common law constitutionalism,[77] the difficulties that this constitutional theory poses are fundamentally quite different from those already considered in this chapter. Rather than being based on specific legislative events and their consequences—as were devolution and the Human Rights Act—the challenge posed by common law constitutionalism is conceptual. Common law constitutionalism is an interpretation of the nature of the UK constitution in which there is simply no place for a doctrine of legislative sovereignty. Yet while common law constitutionalism is not, therefore, an intrinsic consequence of an identifiable trigger event, it does not stand apart from constitutional practice. Instead, this way of thinking about the UK constitution, and the place of the common law within it, has regained popularity—and salience—largely as a result of the broader shifts in UK constitutional law associated with the era of reform discussed at the outset of this chapter. In particular, common law constitutionalism draws strength from the increasing modern empowerment of the judiciary which has been one result of the era of reform. The additional duties afforded to the courts as part of the devolution settlement and the introduction of the Human Rights Act have, of course, been crucial elements in this process. Yet other developments have been of at least equivalent significance—in particular, the powers exercised by the courts in relation to domestic legislation which contravenes EU law, in accordance with the terms of the UK's membership of the European Union,[78] and the creation of a Supreme Court, establishing an ultimate appellate forum which is visibly, as

---

[76] For a challenge to the view that the UK's political constitution is under pressure as a result of the enactment of the HRA, see eg R Bellamy, 'Political Constitutionalism and the Human Rights Act' (2011) 9 *International Journal of Constitutional Law* 86. See further chapter 7 of this volume, pp 300–01.

[77] One leading proponent of common law constitutionalism has, for example, argued that section 3 of the HRA 'is largely an affirmation, or reinvigoration, of the ordinary common law': TRS Allan, *The Sovereignty of Law: Freedom, Constitution, and Common Law* (Oxford, Oxford University Press, 2013) 168. Conversely, challenges which start from an assessment of the impact of the Human Rights Act may ultimately collapse into common law constitutionalism. Jeffrey Goldsworthy has suggested as much in relation to the work of Aileen Kavanagh: see J Goldsworthy, *Parliamentary Sovereignty: Contemporary Debates* (Cambridge, Cambridge University Press, 2010) 304.

[78] See chapter 4 of this volume.

well as functionally, independent from Parliament.[79] The modern re-emergence of common law constitutionalism must therefore be understood in this context, even though the claims made by this school of thought are not directly contingent upon any such developments having occurred. Consequently, as a theory which is based on a particular understanding of the inherent nature of the UK constitution, common law constitutionalism ultimately falls to be assessed in terms of the coherence, and attractiveness, of its core conceptual claims. Prior to this, however, we must first explore the nature of this theory, and its implications for the doctrine of parliamentary sovereignty.

A. A Rejection of Parliamentary Sovereignty?

Common law constitutionalism aims to affirm the primacy of the common law within the UK constitution. According to Poole, it is based on a conception of the common law as 'both the foundation-stone and the lodestar of the political community: that is, it both constitutes the political community and contains the fundamental principles that ought to guide its political and legal decision-making'.[80] The common law is thus 'reinvigorated ... as a burgeoning site of normativity'[81] and becomes the fulcrum of constitutional activity and discourse, operating to control and condition the entire panoply of state action. This is evidently an expansive project, one which has gripped UK public law in recent years. There are numerous contemporary constitutional scholars whose work can be seen to fall within the broad ambit of common law constitutionalism, and this interpretation of the constitution has also found favour with some members of the senior judiciary. The central task for a common law constitutionalist must be to establish the singular pre-eminence of the common law within a political community. Yet, at first glance, this might seem to be at odds with two of the dominant trends in UK public law over the past century: the expansion of the administrative arm of the state which so riled Lord Hewart,[82] and the emergence of statutory legislation as a primary source of constitutional rules, which has led Bogdanor to suggest the existence of 'an incipient codified constitution'.[83] Nevertheless, the development and defence of common law constitutionalist theories has been pursued with gusto, and in a range of different ways. However, as Poole maintains, while '[s]ubstantial differences certainly separate the theorists grouped together ... as common law constitutionalists', these differences 'are far outweighed by the

---

[79] See, eg R Masterman, *The Separation of Powers in the Contemporary Constitution: Judicial Competence and Independence in the United Kingdom* (Cambridge, Cambridge University Press, 2010) 225–27.

[80] T Poole, 'Back to the Future? Unearthing the Theory of Common Law Constitutionalism' (2003) 23 *OJLS* 435, 453.

[81] ibid 454.

[82] See Lord Hewart, *The New Despotism* (London, Ernest Benn, 1929).

[83] V Bogdanor, 'Our New Constitution' (2004) 120 *LQR* 242, 259.

striking deep-lying affinities which connect the theorists in question and which lend to their work a certain kinship'.[84] One key unifying characteristic of the contemporary body of work associated with common law constitutionalism is a rejection of the doctrine of parliamentary sovereignty.

That the possession by Parliament of legislative sovereignty could be challenged by a flourishing conception of the common law is apparent in the formative sources of this constitutional theory. Indeed, this is most clearly evident in the dictum of Coke CJ in *Dr Bonham's case*, which is often cited with approval by modern common law constitutionalists: 'when an Act of Parliament is against common right and reason, or repugnant, or impossible to be performed, the common law will controul it, and adjudge such Act to be void'.[85] However, this claim dates back to the early seventeenth century, and, had it even been correct at the time,[86] it would certainly be of questionable authority in the post-Civil War constitution. Nonetheless, while to some extent inspired by such historical notions, the contemporary strain of common law constitutionalism principally relies on a conceptual architecture to establish the subordination, rather than the sovereignty, of Parliament's legislative authority. The essential claim of modern common law constitutionalism is that there exists a higher plane of legal principle, given concrete meaning and effect in the common law, which serves to place inherent limits on the legislative power of Parliament. Parliament is legally incapable of violating these basic values, and, moreover, is also unable to alter or augment this body of fundamental law, the content of which is illuminated through judicial revelation. The sovereignty of Parliament is thus eliminated and replaced by the supremacy of the common law.

This essential position can be given substance, and thus justified, in a number of ways. For Trevor Allan it is the rule of law which requires common law supremacy: '[i]f there are inherent limits to what can properly count as "law", according to a proper understanding of the rule of law, there are limits to legislative supremacy that can be enforced at common law'.[87] The rule of law must be understood as 'a theory of legitimate government'[88] which rejects 'any assertion of arbitrary power', and thus secures for citizens 'an equal liberty, consonant with a basic equality of citizenship'.[89] It is through the development of the common law that these aspirations are 'most fully realized',[90] for 'any determination of the content of law ...

---

[84]   T Poole, 'Questioning Common Law Constitutionalism' (2005) 25 *Legal Studies* 142, 145.

[85]   *Dr Bonham's case* (1609) 8 Co Rep 107, 118a. This quotation is used, for example, by Allan as a prelude to his book *Constitutional Justice* (n 87 below).

[86]   See J Goldsworthy, *The Sovereignty of Parliament: History and Philosophy* (Oxford, Oxford University Press, 1999) 111–12, for discussion of the competing historical interpretations of Coke's intentions. Goldsworthy notes that 'even if in *Dr Bonham's* case Coke did advocate something like a power of judicial review, he later changed his mind': 112.

[87]   TRS Allan, *Constitutional Justice: A Liberal Theory of the Rule of Law* (Oxford, Oxford University Press, 2001) 240.

[88]   Allan, *The Sovereignty of Law* (2013) n 77 above, 119.

[89]   ibid 93.

[90]   ibid 121.

must reflect the moral or political values implicit in the presiding ideal of the rule of law'.[91] The 'scope and limits of parliamentary authority … are themselves elements of the *legal order*, whose nature and implications are worked out, case by case, in the evolution and development of the common law',[92] and, consequently, the courts can insist that legislative power 'must be employed in the service of the sovereignty of law and liberty'.[93] Indeed, from this perspective, parliamentary sovereignty is an impossible notion, because the rule of law renders the idea of legally unlimited power a contradiction in terms: 'all good lawyers know that absolute rules of any kind are repugnant to the common law'.[94]

For Sir John Laws, it is the 'logical priority of basic rights over democratic institutions'[95]—with the innate primacy of such rights stemming from 'man's essential moral nature … as an autonomous moral being'[96]—which necessitates the development of the 'higher-order' common law constitution to which Parliament is subject.[97] And for Jeffrey Jowell the constitutional pre-eminence of the common law is, appropriately, in light of the common law's 'underlying philosophy of pragmatism',[98] a state of affairs which has steadily evolved over time. For, while the courts were enhancing the common law standards of fair and just governance imposed through judicial review over the last half century, '[a]t the same time, consciously or unconsciously, they were chipping away at the rock of parliamentary supremacy by making it increasingly difficult for Parliament to authorise the infringement of the rule of law and … fundamental rights'.[99] Parliamentary sovereignty may therefore be assailed by analogy:

> [i]f executive power may not be unfettered, or free from judicial review, what principle permits the legislature to be unbounded, or untroubled by any judicial oversight? The notion that no power may be unconstrained is compelling as a general democratic principle.[100]

A 'changed hypothesis of constitutional democracy' has thus emerged, with the judges firmly ensconced as the 'guardians of constitutional propriety',[101] leaving exposed a constitution which 'contains nothing, in law or logic, to prevent the courts interpreting some rights, upon which democracy depends, as inviolable'.[102]

The influence, however, of common law constitutionalism extends well beyond the body of work which constitutes its central and most explicit examples.

---

[91] ibid 122.
[92] ibid 121.
[93] ibid 92.
[94] ibid 143.
[95] J Laws, 'Judicial Remedies and the Constitution' (1994) 57 *MLR* 213, 226.
[96] J Laws, 'The Constitution: Morals and Rights' [1996] *PL* 622, 623.
[97] J Laws, 'Law and Democracy' [1995] *PL* 72, 84.
[98] Lord Goff, 'The Future of the Common Law' (1997) 46 *International and Comparative Law Quarterly* 745, 760.
[99] J Jowell, 'Parliamentary Sovereignty Under the New Constitutional Hypothesis' [2006] *PL* 562, 575.
[100] ibid 578.
[101] ibid 577.
[102] J Jowell, 'Immigration Wars', *The Guardian* (2 March 2004).

Lord Woolf has, for example, embraced the outcome of the common law constitutionalist demolition of parliamentary sovereignty in arguing that 'ultimately there are even limits on the supremacy of Parliament which it is the courts' inalienable responsibility to identify and uphold'.[103] Lord Steyn has also maintained that the courts now possess the power to strike down a malevolent Act of Parliament; for example, a statute which extended the life of Parliament beyond five years or changed the role of the courts: 'We have now arrived at a position where a fundamental "disturbance of the building blocks of our constitution" would not be permitted ... In such exceptional cases the rule of law may trump parliamentary supremacy'.[104]

There are similarities, too, with the scheme of the bi-polar sovereignty defended by Sir Stephen Sedley, according to which the courts obtain a share of Parliament's sovereign power, which, in effect, serves to obfuscate the location of final law-making authority in the UK constitution.[105] For if both the courts and Parliament possess sovereign power, it is unclear which institution is entitled to have the final say about the validity of legal norms, eliciting the genuine possibility of irresolvable political and constitutional disputes. Sedley may accept that 'judicial sovereignty is a dangerous blueprint for the future',[106] yet to view the courts as sovereign within their own sphere, if it is to mean anything, necessarily limits the legislative supremacy of Parliament. As a result, as Allison has argued, bi-polar sovereignty 'might readily be dismissed as mere rhetoric in service of a polemical challenge to the traditional conception of sovereignty'.[107] And if so, such conceptual camouflage may therefore ultimately collapse into common law constitutionalism, especially on the formulation of Knight, whose re-invigorated interpretation of bi-polar sovereignty actively encourages the judicial repudiation of statutes.[108]

When such work is considered in sum, alongside other alternative theoretical accounts of the nature of the UK constitution with thematic preoccupations and methodological assumptions which are very similar to those of common law constitutionalism,[109] it might be seen to present a potent challenge to the doctrine of parliamentary sovereignty. However, while in principle modern common law constitutionalist theory presents a vision of political order in which legislative

---

[103] Lord Woolf, 'Droit Public—English Style' [1995] *PL* 57, 69.

[104] Lord Steyn, 'Democracy, the Rule of Law and the Role of Judges' [2006] 3 *European Human Rights Law Review* 243, 252–53, borrowing a phrase from the speech of Lord Carswell in *R (on the application of Jackson) v Attorney General* [2005] UKHL 56, [2006] 1 AC 262, [178].

[105] S Sedley, 'Human Rights: A Twenty-First Century Agenda' [1995] *PL* 386, 389.

[106] S Sedley, 'Governments, Constitutions and Judges' in G Richardson and H Glenn (eds), *Administrative Law and Government Action: The Courts and Alternative Mechanisms of Review* (Oxford, Clarendon Press, 1994) 36.

[107] Allison, *The English Historical Constitution* (2007) n 19 above, 218.

[108] See CJS Knight, 'Bi-polar Sovereignty Restated' (2009) 68 *CLJ* 361, 382.

[109] See, eg S Lakin, 'Debunking the Idea of Parliamentary Sovereignty: the Controlling Factor of Legality in the British Constitution' (2008) 28 *OJLS* 1; J McGarry, 'The Principle of Parliamentary Sovereignty' (2012) 32 *Legal Studies* 577, 592.

sovereignty can have no place—for all law-making authority exists subject to the reason of the common law—we must be convinced that this represents a sustainable interpretation of the UK constitution. In my view, it does not, for two reasons. First, it is not an empirically plausible account of UK constitutional practice; and secondly, it is an unattractive conception of constitutional order.

B. The Flaws of Common Law Constitutionalism: Empirical Problems

The first key flaw of common law constitutionalism is that it is an empirically dubious understanding of the nature of the UK constitution. This claim can be broken down into two further elements. First, as the seminal work of Goldsworthy has demonstrated, from a historical perspective, the idea that the UK has a common law constitution is largely a 'myth'.[110] There 'never was' a 'golden age of constitutionalism, in which the judiciary enforced limits to the authority of Parliament imposed by common law or natural law'.[111] The notion that the common law provided the framework of the UK constitution, within which all other norms originated and continue to operate, is thus a fiction. The common law, understood as the body of rules which it is within the jurisdiction of the judiciary to enunciate and develop, is, of course, part of the constitution.[112] But the doctrine of parliamentary sovereignty is not part of this body of rules. It was not established by judicial decision—as Goldsworthy has shown, this claim is 'plainly false'[113]—but recognised as the legal basis of the constitution by a broader range of actors in the political circumstances of the seventeenth century.[114] Nor is it open to the courts to seek to develop the common law in such a way as to assimilate the doctrine, simply because it is a legal rule which may be raised in cases argued before them. While the common law has extended its reach in the modern era—in particular, to control the exercise of royal prerogative powers[115]—this does not mean its expansion is irresistible. As Goldsworthy notes, 'the common law's subjugation of other sites of legal authority does not entail that, by some kind of immanent logic, it is entitled and destined to sweep the field'.[116] For once the true historical basis of the constitution is recognised, it becomes clear that the proper relationship between the common law and the sovereignty of Parliament is the inverse of that suggested by common law

---

[110] Goldsworthy, *Parliamentary Sovereignty: Contemporary Debates* (2010) n 77 above, ch 2.

[111] Goldsworthy, *The Sovereignty of Parliament: History and Philosophy* (1999) n 27 above, 235.

[112] For cases in which important common law principles have been established or developed, see, eg *Entick v Carrington* (1765) 2 Wils KB 275, *M v Home Office* [1994] 1 AC 377; *Al Rawi v The Security Services* [2011] UKSC 34, [2012] 1 AC 531.

[113] Goldsworthy, *Parliamentary Sovereignty: Contemporary Debates* (2010) n 77 above, 50.

[114] See chapter 2 of this volume, pp 64, 66, 78.

[115] See, eg *Council of Civil Service Unions v Minister for the Civil Service* [1985] AC 374; *R (on the application of Bancoult) v Secretary of State for Foreign and Commonwealth Affairs (No 2)* [2008] UKHL 61, [2009] 1 AC 453.

[116] Goldsworthy, *Parliamentary Sovereignty: Contemporary Debates* (2010) n 77 above, 47.

constitutionalism. The doctrine of parliamentary sovereignty is a fundamental constitutional norm in the UK because it was accepted as such by officials, with this acceptance reflected in official practice.[117] And the content of the doctrine, in allocating legally unlimited legislative authority to Parliament, means that it takes effect as the central organising principle of the UK constitution. It is the doctrine of parliamentary sovereignty, then, which establishes a framework in which all other norms function—including those of common law—because the power of Parliament to make or unmake any law creates a hierarchy of rules which reflects the constitutional supremacy of statute.[118] The common law is not the basic fabric of the UK constitution, and its place within the larger constitutional hierarchy is such that the authority of even the most fundamental norms expounded by the judiciary cannot be absolute.

Secondly, the traditional judicial perspective as to the legal status of the doctrine of parliamentary sovereignty, and the extent of Parliament's legislative authority as a matter of law, is reflective of the historical position. A long line of authoritative case law recognises the existence of Parliament's legislative sovereignty, and affirms, as a necessary consequence, the subordination of common law to statute. In *Edinburgh and Dalkeith Railway Co v Wauchope*,[119] in which it was claimed that a private Act of Parliament would not be applicable to those who had not received notice of its effects, Lord Campbell addressed this issue of principle directly:

> I cannot but express my surprise that such a notion should ever have prevailed. There is no foundation whatever for it. All that a Court of Justice can do is to look to the Parliamentary roll: if from that it should appear that a bill has passed both Houses and received the Royal assent, no Court of Justice can inquire into the mode in which it was introduced into Parliament, nor into what was done previous to its introduction, or what passed in Parliament during its progress in its various stages through both Houses. I trust, therefore, that no such inquiry will again be entered upon in any Court in Scotland, but that due effect will be given to every Act of Parliament, private as well as public, upon what appears to be the proper construction of its existing provisions.[120]

---

[117] In this sense, the process by which the doctrine of parliamentary sovereignty *obtained* legal authority is aptly characterised by Hart's theory of the formation of a legal system's rule of recognition: see chapter 2 of this volume, pp 79–83.

[118] Some common law constitutionalists will reject this idea of a historically grounded hierarchy of constitutional norms altogether: see, eg Allan, *The Sovereignty of Law* (2013) n 77 above, 171: 'The law is constructed … from the building blocks provided by both statute and precedent, interpreted in a mutually supportive way. Only reason itself is truly sovereign, making law dependent on deliberation and debate'. But such a denial of hierarchy is illusory, for it in truth establishes the sovereignty of *judicial* reasoning, with the court the forum, and judicial interpretation the means, by which legal synthesis is achieved.

[119] *Edinburgh and Dalkeith Railway Co v Wauchope* (1842) 8 Cl & F 710.

[120] ibid 723.

In *Lee v Bude and Torrington Junction Railway Co*,[121] in which it was alleged that an Act of Parliament has been fraudulently obtained by false recitals, Willes J observed:

> We sit here as servants of the Queen and the legislature. Are we to act as regents over what is done by parliament with the consent of the Queen, lords, and commons? I deny that any such authority exists. If an Act of Parliament has been obtained improperly, it is for the legislature to correct it by repealing it: but, so long as it exists as law, the Courts are bound to obey it. The proceedings here are judicial, not autocratic, which they would be if we could make laws instead of administering them.[122]

And in *Mortensen v Peters*,[123] a case concerning the compatibility of an Act of Parliament with the rules of international law, the Lord Justice General, Lord Dunedin maintained, '[f]or us an Act of Parliament duly passed by Lords and Commons and assented to by the King, is supreme, and we are bound to give effect to its terms'.[124]

The stark tone of these classic judgments, dismissing any suggestion that the terms of an Act of Parliament might be open to judicial challenge, is continued in precedents from the second half of the twentieth century. In *Cheney v Conn*,[125] in which the payment of income tax, in accordance with the Finance Act 1964, was challenged on the grounds that it would be used in part to fund the construction of nuclear weapons, in violation of international law, Ungoed-Thomas J held:

> What the statute itself enacts cannot be unlawful, because what the statute says and provides is itself the law, and the highest form of law that is known to this country. It is the law which prevails over every other form of law, and it is not for the court to say that a parliamentary enactment, the highest law in this country, is illegal.[126]

In the leading modern case of *British Railways Board v Pickin*,[127] a challenge to the validity of a private Act of Parliament—brought on the grounds that the legislature had been fraudulently misled into enacting the statute by a false recital in the preamble—was rejected in the House of Lords. Lord Reid endorsed the dictum of Lord Campbell in *Edinburgh and Dalkeith Railway Co* as representing 'a correct statement of the constitutional position', and went on to observe:

> The function of the court is to construe and apply the enactments of Parliament. The court has no concern with the manner in which Parliament or its officers carrying out its Standing Orders perform these functions ... For a century or more both Parliament and the courts have been careful not to act so as to cause conflict between them. Any such investigations as the respondent seeks could easily lead to such a conflict, and I would only support

---

[121] *Lee v Bude and Torrington Junction Railway Co* (1871) LR 6 CP 576.
[122] ibid 582.
[123] *Mortensen v Peters* (1906) 8 F (J) 93.
[124] ibid 100–101.
[125] *Cheney v Conn* [1968] 1 WLR 242.
[126] ibid 247.
[127] *British Railways Board v Pickin* [1974] AC 765.

it if compelled to do so by clear authority. But it appears to me that the whole trend of authority for over a century is clearly against permitting any such investigation.[128]

The judgment of Lord Morris was even more robust, in recognition of the fact that '[c]lear pronouncements on the law are to be found in a stream of authorities in the 19th century':

> The question of fundamental importance which arises is whether the court should entertain the proposition that an Act of Parliament can so be assailed in the courts that matters should proceed as though the Act or some part of it had never been passed. I consider that such doctrine would be dangerous and impermissible. It is the function of the courts to administer the laws which Parliament has enacted. In the processes of Parliament there will be much consideration whether a Bill should or should not in one form or another become an enactment. When an enactment is passed there is finality unless and until it is amended or repealed by Parliament. In the courts there may be argument as to the correct interpretation of the enactment: there must be none as to whether it should be on the Statute Book at all.[129]

Similarly, for Lord Wilberforce:

> The idea ... that an Act of Parliament, public or private, or provision in an Act of Parliament could be declared invalid or ineffective in the courts on account of some irregularity in Parliamentary procedure, or on the ground that Parliament in passing it was misled, or on the ground that it was obtained by deception or fraud, has been decisively repudiated by authorities of the highest standing from 1842 onwards.[130]

And these sentiments were echoed by Lord Simon, for whom 'the sovereignty of Parliament' meant that 'the courts in this country have no power to declare enacted law to be invalid'.[131]

Finally, in *Manuel v Attorney General*,[132] a challenge was made to the Canada Act 1982—legislation of the UK Parliament which brought into effect the Canadian Constitution Act 1982, and extinguished the possibility of UK involvement in amendment of the Canadian constitution in future—on the grounds that it had not been consented to by Canadian aboriginal groups. In the High Court, Sir Robert Megarry VC noted that 'a contention that an Act of Parliament is ultra vires is bold in the extreme', for it was 'contrary to one of the fundamentals of the British Constitution'.[133] Striking out this claim, Sir Robert Megarry VC held:

> I am bound to say that from first to last I have heard nothing in this case to make me doubt the simple rule that the duty of the court is to obey and apply every Act of

---

[128]   ibid 787–88.
[129]   ibid 790, 788–89. The 'settled and sustained line of authority' considered by Lord Morris, in addition to those cases cited above, included *Waterford, Wexford, Wicklow and Dublin Railway Co v Logan* (1850) 14 QB 672; *Earl of Shrewsbury v Scott* (1859) 6 CBNS 1; *Labrador Co v The Queen* [1893] AC 104; and *Hoani Te Heuheu Tukino v Aotea District Maori Land Board* [1941] AC 308 (PC).
[130]   ibid 792–93.
[131]   ibid 798. Lord Cross, the final member of the court, agreed with the other Law Lords as to the general applicability of the rule established in *Edinburgh and Dalkeith Railway Co*: 801.
[132]   *Manuel v Attorney General* [1983] Ch 77.
[133]   ibid 84.

Parliament, and that the court cannot hold any such Act to be ultra vires. Of course there may be questions about what the Act means, and of course there is power to hold statutory instruments and other subordinate legislation ultra vires. But once an instrument is recognised as being an Act of Parliament, no English court can refuse to obey it or question its validity ... There has been no suggestion that the copy [of the Canada Act 1982] before me is not a true copy of the Act itself, or that it was not passed by the House of Commons and the House of Lords, or did not receive the Royal Assent. The Act is therefore an Act of Parliament and the court cannot hold it to be invalid.[134]

This judgment was upheld in the Court of Appeal, with Slade LJ confirming that a judge sitting in a UK court 'would on any footing be bound to follow and apply the House of Lords decision in *Pickin v. British Railways Board* [1974] AC 765 and accordingly to reject the attack on the validity of [the Canada Act 1982]'.[135]

The common law constitutionalist interpretation of the UK constitution is therefore clearly contrary to all established precedent. These are not tentative, ambivalent, or qualified judgments, but a strong and clear line of authority which spans the nineteenth and twentieth centuries. They establish a clear, general proposition, familiar from the Diceyan formulation of the doctrine of parliamentary sovereignty: the validity of an Act of Parliament cannot be challenged by the courts.[136] The fact that the more specific contention of common law constitutionalism—that primary legislation takes effect subject to fundamental common law norms, and is invalid to the extent of any such contradiction—is not explicitly dealt with in these cases is due to the strength of the general proposition with which this claim is clearly incompatible.[137] In such circumstances, challenges to Acts of Parliament on common law grounds have not been argued

---

[134] ibid 86–87.

[135] ibid 109–10.

[136] This conclusion is challenged by the analysis in A Tucker, 'Uncertainty in the Rule of Recognition and in the Doctrine of Parliamentary Sovereignty' (2011) 31 *OJLS* 61. Tucker argues that the rule of recognition is 'indeterminate' which 'means that we simply cannot say there are no limits on parliamentary power. Rather, the imposition (or not) of such limits will depend on the judiciary's understanding of the point of allocating law-making power to Parliament and their stance on whether this point requires that power to be limited or not': 88. Yet this claim relies on treating every authority where the courts reject the opportunity to strike down an Act of Parliament as being specific to its particular 'marginal' circumstances (see especially the treatment of *Pickin*: 83) rather than being capable of sustaining the broader overarching doctrine which the judges in these cases certainly understood themselves to be bound by (and moreover, on the basis of which they acted). Further, this analysis serves to frustrate the possibility that a doctrine of legally unlimited legislative power could ever be achieved in practice; a rule of recognition would always be 'indeterminate'—and the legislative power of Parliament therefore not unlimited—until the courts decided that it was not. Given the argument is rooted in legal positivist theory, it is surprising that, in this respect, a restriction is suggested to exist which conceptually prevents a constitutional order founded on legally unlimited legislative authority from *ever* being socially constructed by law.

[137] Indeed, that judicial decisions can be directly reversed by statute shows the vulnerability of the common law in the face of a legislative intervention by Parliament: see, eg the War Damages Act 1965 s 1, reversing the decision in *Burmah Oil Co v Lord Advocate* [1965] AC 75, in which the House of Lords had held that the Crown had a duty at common law to pay compensation for property destroyed in lawful exercise of war time prerogative powers.

before the courts because, frankly, the notion of such a challenge would be legally absurd. The sheer weight of judicial authority in support of the doctrine of parliamentary sovereignty, and the derivative proposition that the validity of an Act of Parliament cannot be subject to judicial challenge, demonstrates that the courts—the very guardians of the common law which this constitutionalist theory seeks to empower—have adopted a position which decisively rejects common law constitutionalism.

On the methodology of public law which is employed in this book, the existence of this first flaw is sufficient to dispose of the challenge to parliamentary sovereignty posed by common law constitutionalism. For while I have argued that we must seek to assess parliamentary sovereignty in its constitutional and political context to understand the nature of, and potential justification(s) for, the doctrine, the legal authority of this fundamental norm does not depend upon its desirability.[138] The essential legal force of the doctrine of parliamentary sovereignty can therefore be adequately established by empirical argument. And on this approach, the combination of both the historical and long-standing judicial perspectives, outlined above, is more than sufficient to demonstrate the legal authority of the doctrine of parliamentary sovereignty, and its necessary corollary—the exclusion of common law constitutionalism.

This empirical argument is, however, unlikely to be accepted by proponents of common law constitutionalism. For, as we saw when considering the nature of this constitutional theory, common law constitutionalism does not exploit purely empirical claims to challenge the doctrine of parliamentary sovereignty. Instead, common law constitutionalism fuses arguments about legal force with those of moral or political authority. Allan, for example, has developed the most conceptually sophisticated account of common law constitutionalism, and is explicit about engaging such an approach to constitutional reasoning:

> We cannot identify the content of law with a merely descriptive account of judicial practice, viewed as a matter of empirical fact: it is a product of normative *judgement*, in which we attempt to make good moral sense of an array of such familiar legal 'sources' as Acts of Parliament, judicial precedent and influential dicta. An account of English law on any specific subject is always a *theory* of how best to read the relevant legal materials, guided by notions of justice and coherence.[139]

When this general method is employed in the context of debates about the sovereignty of Parliament, we see that the question of the legal authority of the doctrine is collapsed into the question of the political legitimacy of the doctrine. The doctrine must not only have a 'moral foundation', but this moral foundation will be taken to impose intrinsic limits on the legal scope of Parliament's

---

[138] See chapter 1 of this volume, pp 16–21.
[139] Allan, *The Sovereignty of Law* (2013) n 77 above, 5. Allan's methodology is strongly influenced by Dworkin's interpretive approach to legal theory and reasoning: see R Dworkin, *Law's Empire* (Oxford, Hart Publishing, 1998).

law-making power; exercises of legislative authority which are not justified, will not be lawful.[140]

In explaining the methodology which underpins the argument developed in this book, I have indicated that I believe the general approach adopted by common law constitutionalist theorists to be a problematic basis for legal reasoning: it introduces potentially significant uncertainty into debates about the content and validity of norms, while affording priority to judicial understandings of highly contested moral and political concepts.[141] Yet if it is supposed, for present purposes, that in line with the common law constitutionalist understanding of the nature of legal argument, constitutional doctrine must be morally attractive to be legally authoritative, we must also assess the substantive claims of common law constitutionalism against this criterion. In other words, the common law constitutionalist rejection of parliamentary sovereignty—in accordance with the theory's own methodology—must be normatively justifiable to be a viable interpretation of UK constitutional law. When common law constitutionalism is evaluated from this perspective, the second flaw of the theory becomes evident, for, in my view, it is not an attractive conception of constitutional practice. There are two reasons for this: first, the common law constitutionalist elevation of the judiciary is undemocratic; and secondly, the theory is irredeemably imprecise. And in this sense, the particular reasons that common law constitutionalism is unattractive, as a specific conception of UK constitutional order, are largely a function of the general problems created by the methodology of legal reasoning on the basis of which the theory has been developed. As a result, in exploring the normative deficiency of common law constitutionalism, we can also further illuminate the reasons why any methodology which fails to distinguish the question 'is Parliament sovereign?' from the question 'is it justified that Parliament is sovereign?' is fundamentally problematic.

C. The Flaws of Common Law Constitutionalism: Normative Problems

The second critical flaw of common law constitutionalism is that it presents a normatively unattractive conception of UK constitutional practice. First, the theory should be rejected because, in elevating the judiciary to a position of constitutional supremacy, it is profoundly undemocratic. I have defended a majoritarian conception of democracy in Chapter one of this book,[142] and it is from this perspective that the role afforded to the courts by common law constitutionalist theory must be assessed. Judges in the UK are unelected, unrepresentative and (politically or popularly) unaccountable. They are appointed by the Queen on

---

[140] ibid 134.
[141] See chapter 1 of this volume, pp 16–21.
[142] See chapter 1 of this volume, pp 34–41.

ministerial advice.[143] Following the enactment of the Constitutional Reform Act 2005, which created a Judicial Appointments Commission (JAC),[144] this process has become much more transparent than the secretive, informal 'tap on the shoulder' selection procedure which was in operation prior to April 2006. Yet while the JAC is responsible for the entire selection process in relation to judges of the High Court and below,[145] different selection procedures, to which the JAC only contributes, operate in relation to appointment to more senior positions. There is still a considerable degree of judicial involvement in appointment to these senior posts,[146] and while the Lord Chancellor has powers to reject or require reconsideration of any person selected for appointment,[147] these powers have barely been used.[148] Yet there is no public element to the selection process, and while the formal responsibility of the government for making recommendations provides some limited democratic accountability, there is no parliamentary involvement in judicial appointments.[149]

This revamped appointment process has failed to alleviate the lack of diversity in the higher judiciary. Griffith's famous claim that the judges are 'homogeneous', '[t]ypically coming from middle-class professional families, independent schools, Oxford or Cambridge, they spend twenty to twenty-five years in successful practice at the Bar, mostly in London, earning very considerable incomes by the time

---

[143] In relation to the senior judiciary, Justices of the Supreme Court are appointed on the recommendation of the Prime Minister: Constitutional Reform Act 2005 s 26(2). The Lord Chief Justice, other Heads of Division, Lord and Lady Justices of Appeal and High Court judges are appointed on the recommendation of the Lord Chancellor: Constitutional Reform Act 2005 ss 67, 77, 86.

[144] Constitutional Reform Act 2005 s 61.

[145] Constitutional Reform Act 2005 ss 87–88.

[146] Two of the five members of a selection panel for appointments to the Supreme Court will be senior judges: Supreme Court (Judicial Appointments) Regulations (SI 2013/2193) regs 5, 11. For appointment of the Lord Chief Justice, Heads of Division and Lord and Lady Justices of Appeal, at least two members of a five-person selection panel will be senior judges: Judicial Appointments Regulations (SI 2013/2192) regs 5, 11, 23.

[147] Constitutional Reform Act 2005 ss 27, 94C; Supreme Court (Judicial Appointments) Regulations (SI 2013/2193) regs 20–22; Judicial Appointments Regulations (SI 2013/2192) regs 8–10, 14–16, 26–28, 32–36.

[148] Between 2006 and 2013, only five selections out of approximately 3,500 were subject to rejection or reconsideration: G Gee, R Hazell, K Malleson and P O'Brien, *Consultation Response to Ministry of Justice—Judicial Appointments Commission: Triennial Review 2014* (April 2014) 2: www.ucl.ac.uk/constitution-unit/research/judicial-independence/jac-review-submission.

[149] This contrasts, for example, with the position in the USA, where nominees for the Supreme Court must be approved by the Senate following open confirmation hearings: US Constitution, Article II s 2. The New Labour government of Gordon Brown tentatively questioned whether there might be a role for Parliament to play in the confirmation of nominees for judicial office: *The Governance of Britain: Judicial Appointments*, (Cm 7210, 2007), 37–41. This was strongly resisted by the judiciary, who were 'completely opposed to any confirmation hearing': *Judicial Office: Response to Consultation Paper on behalf of the Judicial Executive Board and the Judges' Council* (10 April 2008) 1. The New Labour government decided not to proceed with parliamentary confirmation hearings for the judiciary, and the idea has not found favour with official actors since: see, eg the rejection of either pre- or post-appointment hearings in the House of Lords Select Committee on the Constitution, *Judicial Appointments*, HL Paper 272 (28 March 2008) [46], [48].

they reach their forties', is hardly less relevant today.[150] The unrepresentative nature of the judiciary is especially acute among the senior judges, where controversial common law challenges to Acts of Parliament would ultimately fall to be settled. The senior judiciary is still overwhelmingly male and white. As of April 2014,[151] only one of the 12 Justices of the Supreme Court was female, and all were white. All five Heads of Division were male, and none was from a black or minority ethnic (BME) group. Of the Lord Justices of Appeal, 18.4 per cent were female (seven out of 38 judges),[152] and none were from a BME group. In the High Court, 17.9 per cent of judges were female (19 out of 106),[153] and only three were from a BME group (3.3 per cent).[154] The Lord Chancellor and Lord Chief Justice have a statutory duty to take steps to encourage judicial diversity,[155] and the JAC and any selection panel convened for the purpose of making judicial appointments are under an obligation to 'have regard to the need to encourage diversity in the range of persons available for selection for appointments'.[156] However, considerations of judicial diversity are expressly subject to the overarching requirement that 'selection must be solely on merit'.[157] Changes made to the Constitutional Reform Act 2005 by the Crime and Courts Act 2013 have introduced 'tie-breaker' provisions into the judicial appointments process, which permit selection panels to give preference to candidates who improve the diversity of the judiciary.[158] Yet, while welcome, these provisions are very modest in ambition, applying only where candidates are of 'equal merit', and thus unlikely significantly to affect the judges' diversity deficit. They also leave untouched the core problem: the failure to recognise that 'the notion of merit is not an objective standard neutrally applied, but is socially constructed to the advantage of a narrow group of white, male lawyers',[159] and the consequent, yet unjustified, rejection of positive action

---

[150] JAG Griffith, *The Politics of the Judiciary*, 5th edn (London, Fontana Press, 1997) 7, 338. For example, research by the Sutton Trust in 2007 found that 70% of UK-educated senior judges attended independent fee-paying schools, and 78% of senior judges who went to university in the UK attended Cambridge or Oxford: see *The Educational Backgrounds of Leading Lawyers, Journalists, Vice Chancellors, Politicians, Medics and Chief Executives* (March 2009) 5, 8 www.suttontrust.com/our-work/research/download/54/.

[151] See *2014 Judicial Diversity Statistics* (1 April 2014): http://www.judiciary.gov.uk/publications/judicial-diversity-statistics-2014/.

[152] This has increased from 11.4% as of April 2013, when four out of 35 Lord Justices of Appeal were female; see *2013 Judicial Diversity Statistics* (1 April 2013): www.judiciary.gov.uk/publications/diversity-statistics-and-general-overview-2013/.

[153] This has increased from 16.7% as of April 2013, when 18 out of 108 High Court judges were female; ibid.

[154] This has decreased from 4.6% as of April 2013, when five out of 108 High Court judges were from a BME group; ibid.

[155] Constitutional Reform Act 2005 s 137A.

[156] Constitutional Reform Act 2005 s 64(1).

[157] Constitutional Reform Act 2005, s 63(2). 'Merit' is also the criterion on which Supreme Court Justices are to be appointed: s 27(5).

[158] Constitutional Reform Act 2005 s 27(5A), s 63(4).

[159] K Malleson, 'Diversity in the Judiciary: The Case For Positive Action' (2009) 36 *Journal of Law and Society* 376, 381. See also K Malleson, 'Rethinking the Merit Principle in Judicial Selection' (2006) 33 *Journal of Law and Society* 126.

as something which would lower standards, or devalue the achievements of the female and BME lawyers who were subsequently promoted to the bench.[160]

Further, once appointed, it is almost impossible for senior judges to be removed from office. They hold office 'during good behaviour', and can only be removed by the Queen 'on the address of both Houses of Parliament'.[161] Despite the fact that, as Bradley and Ewing maintain, '[t]he wording of the provision in the Act of Settlement from which these rules derived, suggests that the intention of Parliament was that ... Parliament itself should enjoy an unqualified power of removal',[162] this power has only been used once.[163] In practice, an extremely high level of misconduct would be required for a senior judge to be dismissed via this process. The effective requirement of behaviour in severely bad faith before a judicial dismissal will occur means that judges are held to a very different standard to politicians, who can be legitimately removed from office by the electorate for decisions taken in good faith, if those decisions are thought to be wrong. That the judges cannot be similarly held to account for their decisions is due to the need to maintain judicial independence, a principle now enshrined in statute,[164] and which conceptually limits the availability of the power to remove judges from office. Yet while it is vital that the courts are not subject to undue interference (or the prospect of undue interference) from the government, so that their impartiality is not in question when hearing challenges to the legality of the exercise of public power, we might see the ideas of judicial accountability[165] and judicial independence as complementary rather than contradictory.[166] This does not mean that the judges ought to be removable to the same extent as politicians, but establishing mechanisms of judicial accountability beyond the mere prospect of a judgment being appealed—something which is irrelevant in any event in relation

---

[160] While rejecting any introduction of quotas, the House of Lords Constitution Committee suggested that non-mandatory targets might be considered by the government if there has been 'no significant increase' in judicial diversity in the five years following the publication of its report: *Judicial Appointments*, HL Paper 272 (28 March 2008) [102], [105]. While it seems extremely unlikely that such improvement will occur in that timescale, this recommendation has been rejected by the government, a conclusion which was in line with that reached in 2010 by the Advisory Panel on Judicial Diversity: *The Government Response to the House of Lords Constitution Committee's Report: Judicial Appointments*, (Cm 8358, May 2012) 6–7.

[161] The tenure of Justices of the Supreme Court is governed by the Constitutional Reform Act 2005 s 33, and that of all other senior judges by the Senior Courts Act 1981 s 11(3).

[162] AW Bradley and KD Ewing, *Constitutional and Administrative Law*, 15th edn (Harlow, Pearson, 2010) 371.

[163] The only judge removed on an address to both Houses of Parliament was Sir Jonah Barrington in 1830: SA de Smith and R Brazier, *Constitutional and Administrative Law*, 8th edn (Harmondsworth, Penguin, 1998) 381.

[164] Constitutional Reform Act 2005 s 3.

[165] See generally A Sengupta, 'Judicial Accountability: A Taxonomy' [2014] *PL* 245.

[166] See, eg KD Ewing, 'A Theory of Democratic Adjudication: Towards a Representative, Accountable and Independent Judiciary' (2000) 38 *Alberta Law Review* 708, 726: 'far from undermining the independence of the judiciary ... robust accountability procedures would serve only to promote and protect it'.

to decisions of the Supreme Court—is nevertheless significant.[167] A recent positive development in this regard is the practice, since 2006, of senior judges appearing before, and submitting evidence to, a range of parliamentary select committees in the House of Commons and the House of Lords.[168] Yet while such committees provide in principle a useful public forum in which 'dialogue' can occur between the judiciary and Parliament,[169] offering to the judges an opportunity to air their views on matters of relevance to the justice system is at best an (understandably) limited and gentle form of accountability. It is certainly questionable whether this would be a sufficiently robust—or indeed wide ranging, given the limits on the substantive legal issues which can be discussed—channel of accountability if the judges were to obtain the kind of ultimate constitutional power envisaged by common law constitutionalism. Moreover, even more demanding mechanisms of judicial accountability would not change the fact that, from a common law constitutionalist perspective, the judges would not technically be responsible for the decisions they reached. Instead, on this theory, the judges are not decision-makers exercising political power, but simply vessels through which the evolving sentiment of the common law is expressed.

To highlight the unelected, unrepresentative, and (politically and popularly) unaccountable nature of the judiciary is not to portray judicial decision-making as either illegitimate or insignificant. Nor is it to suggest that judges ought to be elected in the UK, and therefore more readily removable from their positions, or that the security of judicial tenure should be otherwise diminished. Equally, to draw a 'distinction ... between democratic institutions and the courts' is not, as Lord Bingham famously feared, 'to stigmatise judicial decision-making as in some way undemocratic'.[170] It is of course true that 'the function of independent judges charged to interpret and apply the law is universally recognised as a cardinal feature of the modern democratic state',[171] but this does not mean that judicial decision-making is a democratic process. There is not a binary choice between democratic and undemocratic decision-making processes, with the judicial process necessarily either one or the other. Instead, judicial decision-making might be characterised as non-democratic—neither democratic nor inherently undemocratic in nature. Yet the non-democratic nature of judicial decision-making should be acknowledged rather than overlooked, for it is a crucial feature to consider when determining the proper scope of the judicial role, with the limits on the functions courts can be expected to perform being settled accordingly.

---

[167] See, eg A Le Sueur, 'Developing Mechanisms for Judicial Accountability in the UK' (2004) 24 *Legal Studies* 73.

[168] See, eg A Le Sueur and J Simson Caird, 'The House of Lords Select Committee on the Constitution' in A Horne, G Drewry and D Oliver (eds), *Parliament and the Law* (Oxford, Hart Publishing, 2013) 304–6; R Kelly, 'Select Committees: Powers and Functions', ibid; G Drewry, 'Parliamentary Accountability for the Administration of Justice', ibid.

[169] Le Sueur and Simson Caird, 'The House of Lords Select Committee on the Constitution', ibid, 304.

[170] *A and others v Secretary of State for the Home Department* [2004] UKHL 56, [2005] 2 AC 68, [42].

[171] ibid [42].

It is in expanding the boundaries of what is appropriate for judicial resolution to include highly-contested moral, political and social issues, and giving the courts the final word as to how such contentious problems can be confronted, that common law constitutionalism prompts us to embrace an undemocratic state of affairs. It is undemocratic for unelected, unrepresentative and (politically and popularly) unaccountable institutions to be empowered to make constitutionally definitive decisions about matters of significant political and moral importance. While we will consider below what might be the scope of the power of judicial override attributed to the courts by common law constitutionalism, at least initially, it could well be relatively limited.[172] And, of course, the courts will always have to make decisions in cases which require them to consider complex or contentious, sometimes even delicate, political issues. This is unavoidable. Nonetheless, in elevating the judges to the position of final arbiters of constitutionality, common law constitutionalism entitles the judiciary ultimately to control and condition the nature and extent of the action that can lawfully be taken by the state. Even if this power were not frequently exercised in practice, it is the sheer finality of judicial judgment as to whether the use of public power is constitutionally permissible which is, in principle, objectionable. For ultimately, the judges' conception of what represents 'good law'—established through the medium of what the common law deems acceptable—would be decisive, and not possible to challenge through the operation of the political process. No matter how representative and accountable the judges may become, because they are not elected and readily removable, ultimately their decisions should always be subject to revision by those who are; the non-democratic decision-making process made subject to the democratic decision-making process. In the UK, the doctrine of parliamentary sovereignty ensures that this is so, and the common law constitutionalist rejection of it can therefore be seen as fundamentally undemocratic in nature.

The second normative problem with common law constitutionalism is the imprecision of the theory.[173] Common law constitutionalism is imprecise because the rights, values and principles which it aims to prioritise and protect are not clearly stated, or even ascertainable, in advance of their judicial discovery. Prior

---

[172] As the power to strike down legislation attributed to the courts by common law constitutionalism is a potentially boundless one, however, there can be no guarantee that this power will be used sparingly. Indeed, as Goldsworthy has argued, even if it were to be accepted that the courts could refuse to apply only the most truly egregious statutes, the 'judges are almost certain to interpret such an authority too broadly'. As a result of the precedential reasoning process employed by the common law courts, although '[e]ach decision may extend the judges' authority only slightly ... the eventual cumulative effect is a massive expansion far beyond what was originally intended': Goldsworthy, *The Sovereignty of Parliament: History and Philosophy* (1999) n 27 above, 270. The same point is made by Tushnet, who maintains that 'judges will not sit around waiting for [extreme cases of oppression]. They will instead exercise the power of judicial review routinely': M Tushnet, *Taking the Constitution Away from the Courts* (Princeton, Princeton University Press, 1999) 162.

[173] The language of imprecision here echoes that in WI Jennings, *The Law and the Constitution*, 5th edn (London, University of London Press, 1959) 60: 'the rule of law is apt to be rather an unruly horse ... the idea includes notions which are essentially imprecise'.

to their articulation by the courts, all a citizen, or constitutional theorist, can do is speculate about what rights, values and principles will be deemed sacrosanct by the judges. Yet even this is something that the key common law constitutionalists are not prepared to attempt to do in detail; an attempt at constructing a comprehensive account of the essential principles upon which the theory is based is conspicuous by its absence. As Knight has noted, '[i]t is clear, and unsurprising, that the main theorists are unwilling to pin themselves down to a definitive list of situations in which the courts may be able to declare an Act of Parliament void'.[174] While this is certainly regrettable, it is not unexpected because the imprecision of common law constitutionalism is one of the theory's main attractions. The common law, according to Allan, must be understood as 'a steadily evolving order of justice, rooted in historical experience but open to changing ideas and perceptions'.[175] Thus, it is capable of providing 'a constantly evolving blend of traditional wisdom and fresh moral insight'.[176] Yet the flexibility required to facilitate the reconciliation of law and contemporary morality is purchased at the cost of certainty. The common law can never be permanently committed to a fixed set of values because the moral ideals of the future cannot be anticipated with any degree of accuracy. Consequently, the judges will only be able to elucidate the content of even any fundamental common law rights gradually, on a case-by-case basis. As Allan observes, their '"full implications" will become apparent only in the light of unfolding events', in the 'illuminating particularity' of 'specific instances'.[177] The 'content and scope' of such fundamental rights 'will reflect the context in which they operate'.[178] Common law norms can therefore only ever be provisionally recognised, as they are always vulnerable to being altered to meet a new set of moral circumstances. Thus, the values of the common law constitution will necessarily be imprecise to ensure that the theory's precious amenability is maintained.

However, the imprecision at the core of common law constitutionalism should be seen as a vice, rather than a virtue. To demonstrate this, we must think about the conceptual framework of common law constitutionalism, and in particular, the notions of fundamental rights and the rule of law which are drawn on to provide the substance of the theory.[179] First, consider a common law constitutionalist account of fundamental rights, in which terms the individualistic values of the common law will tend to be given concrete judicial effect.[180] Given the

---

[174] Knight, 'Bi-polar Sovereignty Restated' (2009) 383. Knight has, however, offered an attempt to fill this void: see CJS Knight, 'Striking Down Legislation under Bi-polar Sovereignty' [2011] *PL* 90.

[175] TRS Allan, 'Text, Context, and Constitution: The Common Law as Public Reason' in DE Edlin (ed), *Common Law Theory* (Cambridge, Cambridge University Press, 2007) 200.

[176] ibid 203.

[177] ibid 195.

[178] ibid 196.

[179] See text at nn 87–102.

[180] The common law constitutionalists are, of course, not alone in preferring to frame their moral and political claims in terms of rights. As Loughlin notes, '[i]t is beyond question that the rhetoric of rights has evolved very rapidly over the last two hundred or so years and now colonizes broad swathes of political discourse': M Loughlin, *Sword and Scales: An Examination of the Relationship between Law*

imprecision of common law values, it will be difficult for citizens to have a clear idea of the common law rights that they possess, or access to any straightforward means by which they can attempt to identify these rights. How can the members of a society seek to have their rights judicially vindicated if they are essentially unaware of the rights that they have? Should citizens be expected to bring speculative litigation to establish whether they have a right to housing, education or employment? Given that one of the central goals of common law constitutionalist theory is to protect individuals against the arbitrary misuse of public power, this seems a peculiarly inefficient approach to take.[181] It might be suggested that the common law constitutionalist position could be defended by invoking some notion of 'community morality'. When deciding what rights the common law will defend, a judge, according to Dworkin, must look to what is required by 'community morality'—the moral values 'presupposed by the laws and institutions of the community'—rather than to what is appropriate according to his or her own political preferences.[182] On this basis, it may be that the rights which the common law will protect from legislative interference are those are which are deeply embedded in a community's constitutional arrangements, and thus implicitly accepted by the people as being morally or politically fundamental, even if particular citizens may not be cognisant of their commitment to these values.

It is difficult, however, to see such a notion of community morality as anything other than a metaphysical fiction with little or no practical utility.[183] In circumstances when '[t]here are many of us, and we disagree about justice',[184] the very idea of community morality seems extraordinary, due to the sheer impossibility of synthesising the competing interpretations of the values underlying a society's existing constitutional arrangements into a coherent, universally acceptable position. Moreover, when undertaking this task, how could we be assured that a judge (or constitutional theorist) had not, whether deliberately or subconsciously, substituted their own moral or political convictions for those of the community? To root the values of the common law in the will of the people, thus identifying a means by which they could be appreciated by citizens, seems to discount the

---

and Politics (Oxford, Hart Publishing, 2000) 204. See also M Loughlin, *The Idea of Public Law* (Oxford, Oxford University Press, 2003) 114: 'Contemporary public discourse, especially that which appeals to such core values as liberty, equality, and justice, is invariably cast in the language of rights'.

[181] It is also a difficulty which is not cured by the existence of a Bill of Rights, or statutory rights protection of the kind found in the Human Rights Act 1998. While clearly providing a far more accessible menu of rights than is provided by common law constitutionalism, the common law is merely 'supplemented' by such instruments: see, eg Allan, *The Sovereignty of Law* (2013) n 77 above, 323. The literal terms of a Bill of Rights would therefore be *subject* to the fundamental norms of the common law constitution, and potentially susceptible to judicial distortion in the event of inconsistency between the two.

[182] R Dworkin, *Taking Rights Seriously*, 2nd edn (London, Duckworth, 1978) 126.

[183] With customary flair, Griffith, for example, denounced the idea that it might be possible to identify a conception of community morality, in this or any other way, as 'nonsense at the very top of a very high ladder': JAG Griffith, 'The Political Constitution' (1979) 42 *MLR* 1, 11.

[184] J Waldron, *Law and Disagreement* (Oxford, Clarendon Press, 1999) 1.

possibility that our own moral beliefs can taint and distort our interpretation of those held by the community at large. As such, as Christine Sypnowich has noted, the danger is 'that distinguishing true, constitutional morality from erroneous, popular views of morality is a rather arbitrary affair, which has little to do with democracy and much to do with the liberal principles of philosophers'.[185] Rather than offering citizens an insight into the fundamental rights they are afforded at common law, the claim that such rights derive from a conception of the community's morality is a conceit which obscures the very real choices which will be made when a set of supposedly collective values is formulated.

Nevertheless, it is possible that there will be some rights which might be considered to be communally accepted due to their strong precedential force. Such rights may be relatively clearly established because they have been consistently protected in the past by the courts, giving, at the very most, the illusion of being based on some conception of community morality. The problem of imprecision, however, affects even these traditionally acknowledged rights. To take an example, it can be argued that the right to life is fundamental in the UK, and is therefore a part of the common law.[186] Indeed, surely the right to life would be a core component of the common law constitution which is to be protected by the courts from undue legislative interference. The judicial rejection of an Act of Parliament which required the murder of 'all blue-eyed babies', to borrow Sir Leslie Stephen's well-known example, famously cited by Dicey, would seem to be a paradigm case in which it is envisaged that the common law ought to prevail against a truly iniquitous statute.[187] Yet even if it is accepted that the right to life in general should be protected by the common law, because it can be engaged using an absurd hypothetical, its full meaning and implications are still obscure. Does a common law right to life permit abortion? If so, in what particular circumstances? Does a common law right to life mean that an Act of Parliament legalising euthanasia would be unlawful? What view does the common law take of assisted suicide?[188]

---

[185] C Sypnowich, 'Ruling or Overruled? The People, Rights and Democracy' (2007) 27 *OJLS* 757, 762.

[186] The right to life is also used as an example by Richard Ekins to demonstrate the slightly more general point that 'rights adjudication essentially requires political and moral choice in a context of moral disagreement': R Ekins, 'Judicial Supremacy and the Rule of Law' (2003) 119 *LQR* 127, 140–41.

[187] L Stephen, *The Science of Ethics* (London, Smith, Elder & Co, 1882) 143; cited in AV Dicey, *Introduction to the Study of the Law of the Constitution* 8th edn (London, Macmillan, 1915) 79. The 'blue-eyed babies' hypothetical is discussed, and its legal validity rejected, for example, in Allan, *The Sovereignty of Law* (2013) n 77 above, 141–43.

[188] See *R (on the application of Purdy) v Director of Public Prosecutions* [2009] UKHL 45, [2010] 1 AC 345 for a judicial intervention in this area of considerable legal uncertainty which has been much criticised, but deals with a formal, rather than the substantive, issue: see, eg C Gearty, 'Assisted Suicide: The Purdy Case', *The Tablet* (August 2009): www.conorgearty.co.uk/pdfs/Assisted_Suicide_TABLET_august_2009.pdf; J Finnis, 'Invoking the Principle of Legality against the Rule of Law' (2010) 4 *New Zealand Law Review* 601. Addressing in part the substantive issue, see further *R (on the application of Nicklinson) v Ministry of Justice* [2014] UKSC 38, [2014] 3 WLR 200 for a highly complex decision in which, ultimately by a 7–2 majority (although with significant differences within that majority as to the reasons), the Supreme Court held that a declaration of incompatibility under s 4 of the HRA should not be issued with respect to the present legal prohibition of assisted suicide. The substantial disagreement among three distinct blocks of judges in this case—Lords Neuberger, Mance and Wilson;

Common law constitutionalist theory appears to have little or nothing specific to say about complex contemporary moral dilemmas such as these. Yet if such issues were deemed to fall within this theory's scope, the abstract framework of common law constitutionalism would give, in principle, the utmost discretion to the courts to resolve such moral problems through a lens of legality. The imprecision of common law constitutionalism is thus further exaggerated, for not only will the judges be free to decide which rights the common law will recognise—which will inevitably be expressed in general terms to ensure that they remain as uncontentious as possible—but they will also be trusted to determine what the practical political implications of the rights identified as part of its normative nucleus will be. And this imprecision would operate so as to preclude, in practice, citizens from obtaining a coherent understanding of their constitutional entitlements, which could effectively be settled via elite-level discourse, shrouded in mystery.

The imprecision which will be inherent in judicial reasoning about the implications of judicially identified rights cannot be avoided by shifting attention to the second piece of common law constitutionalism's conceptual apparatus—the principle of the rule of law. Indeed, the imprecision of common law constitutionalism is further manifested in its grounding in the rule of law, which would replace the sovereignty of Parliament as the fundamental norm of a common law constitution. Questions as to the content and utility of the rule of law are among the most contested issues in all of legal and political philosophy. This is especially so in relation to 'thick', or substantive, conceptions of the rule of law, which require specific just outcomes to be reached for the ideal to be fully realised. Endicott has maintained that while legal philosophers have 'argued over whether there is any positive virtue in the rule of law', a 'consensus' has been reached about 'the *requirements* of the ideal'.[189] However, such a contention is only plausible, as Goldsworthy has noted, in so far as it relates to 'thin', or formal, conceptions of the rule of law.[190] Indeed, it is difficult to see how there could ever be anything approaching consensus about the content of a substantive conception of the rule of law, the understanding of the principle adopted by common law constitutionalists. For if, as Allan, for example, has suggested, the rule of law requires 'compliance with those conditions under which each person's freedom (or liberty) is secured, consistently with the enjoyment of a similar freedom for everyone', it becomes clear that to fill out this ideal, we are engaging with highly abstract, and contestable, moral and political values.[191] It may be the case, then, as Goldsworthy

Lords Sumption, Clarke, Reed and Hughes; and Lady Hale and Lord Kerr—demonstrates clearly the fundamental difficulties inherent in affording to the courts the responsibility for settling highly contentious moral problems, which would be yet more problematic if structured instead by reference to common law principles.

[189] TAO Endicott, 'The Impossibility of the Rule of Law' (1999) 19 *OJLS* 1, 1.
[190] J Goldsworthy, 'Legislative Sovereignty and the Rule of Law' in T Campbell, KD Ewing and A Tomkins (eds), *Sceptical Essays on Human Rights* (Oxford, Oxford University Press, 2001) 66.
[191] Allan, *The Sovereignty of Law* (2013) n 77 above, 89.

contends, that 'the rule of law is too indeterminate to provide useful guidance' about how governmental power should be structured.[192] But it is certainly the case that basing the theory on a substantive conception of the rule of law exacerbates the imprecision of common law constitutionalism. For if debate about the intrinsic content of the rule of law becomes a proxy for political argumentation, then nothing can be left off the table, and the values which are a function of any particular ideological position can be suggested to require protection on the grounds that they constitute a core element of the ideal of legality.[193] Whether the rule of law guarantees liberty, equality, both, or neither, will undoubtedly therefore remain an open question, as there is no real possibility of a definitive resolution of such fundamentally normative disputes. And again, even the most interested of citizens will find it near impossible to distil from such debates much which can usefully inform their understanding of the limits imposed on legislative power by the notion of legality.

Indeed, the common law constitutionalist reliance on an imprecise substantive conception of the rule of law may in fact be incompatible with the principles which underpin a formal understanding of the rule of law. A number of thin formulations of the rule of law have been advanced which cover much of the same ground.[194] Here, we will focus on Lon Fuller's classic account, for as Kramer—otherwise a positivist critic of the natural lawyer Fuller—has suggested, the rule of law is 'admirably encapsulated in Fuller's eight principles of legality'.[195] Of particular importance to the current discussion are principles two, three, four and seven: that, to comply with the rule of law, legal norms should be published, prospective, understandable and relatively stable.[196] As Waldron has argued, these particular constituent elements of the rule of law are among those intended to contribute to the realisation of a further common goal. This goal is to 'establish law as something predictable, something which individuals can reliably take into account as they go about the planning of their lives'.[197] The rule of law thus places a high value on legal certainty, something which is effectively eschewed by common law constitutionalism. The fundamental rules of the common law constitution are not published, nor promulgated to those subject to them in any way. Nor are these common law rules prospective, for their existence is not revealed in advance of their judicial application. Further, as discussed above, even where it is possible to predict what basic rights may be protected by the common law, their abstract formulation will limit their clarity. It is therefore difficult to see how citizens can hope to understand what the actual practical implications of these rights will be. Finally, the stability of a common law constitution is undermined

---

[192] Goldsworthy, 'Legislative Sovereignty and the Rule of Law' (2001) n 187 above, 78.
[193] For the seminal critique of the politicisation of the rule of law by those who take a substantive approach, see J Raz, 'The Rule of Law and its Virtue' (1977) 93 *LQR* 195.
[194] See, eg RS Summers, 'The Principles of the Rule of Law' (1999) 74 *Notre Dame Law Review* 1691.
[195] MH Kramer, 'On the Moral Status of the Rule of Law' (2004) 63 *CLJ* 65, 65.
[196] LL Fuller, *The Morality of Law* (New Haven CT, Yale University Press, 1969) 49–65, 79–81.
[197] J Waldron, 'The Rule of Law in Contemporary Liberal Theory' (1989) 2 *Ratio Juris* 79, 84.

by the persistent prospect of a sudden, unexpected judicial alteration of the law. It is likely to be hard for most members of society to anticipate when the judges will decide to modify elementary common law norms, since any change will be made unilaterally, with no advance notice given and no consultation carried out. The rhetorical basis for common law constitutionalism is consequently unsound: the imprecision of the theory means that it violates, rather than exemplifies, the ideal of the rule of law.

The innate imprecision of common law constitutionalism provides us with a second reason that this is an unattractive model of governance. In the foregoing discussion, the focus has been on the difficulties that this imprecision creates for citizens, because this shows the theory to be self-defeating. Common law constitutionalism endeavours to protect individual rights, but does so without making the scope and content of those rights either available or discernible in advance of their judicial revelation. These basic common law norms are therefore incapable of constituting a worthwhile guide to behaviour for the citizens within a community. However, it is also important to note that this imprecision will additionally create difficulties for the institutions of government, although this is something which is less likely to be of concern to defenders of common law constitutionalism, given the suspicion of public power which seems intrinsic to this theory. If the courts are to have the final word in relation to the legality of legislation, and yet these putative judicial limits on the content of Acts of Parliament are unspecified, it will be hard for a government to predict whether a proposed policy contravenes the fundamental tenets of the common law. This might induce a cautious, conservative attitude in governments, making them less willing to experiment with more radical or innovative ideas for fear of their legislation being struck down by the courts. Further, this could lead to less efficient governance, with policies which have initially been rejected by the judges having to be redrawn to make them common law compliant. If this cannot be done, due to a lack of resources or judicial intransigence, a government's ability to implement its policy agenda could even be permanently disrupted. Therefore, if the theory were to become generally accepted in the UK, the uncertainty produced by the imprecision of common law constitutionalism would threaten to become a significant practical problem for citizens and the public authorities alike.

Common law constitutionalism purports to be an interpretation of the UK constitution which presents this system of governance in its best possible light. However, the undemocratic nature of the theory, and the imprecision of its content, demonstrate common law constitutionalism to be a normatively unattractive conception of political order. Common law constitutionalism, even when judged on its own terms, must therefore be rejected. But the normative deficiencies of common law constitutionalism also reinforce a further point: the methodology of public law employed by defenders of common law constitutionalism is itself fundamentally objectionable. The imprecision and the undemocratic nature of common law constitutionalism have a common root—the priority which the theory affords to judicial decision-making, which is no longer subordinated to the legislative authority of a sovereign Parliament. To adopt a methodology which takes the legal force of the doctrine of parliamentary sovereignty to be, at least in part, a function of its attractiveness as a fundamental constitutional norm, will not necessarily, of course, produce a constitution in which legislative authority is legally constrained in this way. Indeed, as I argued in Chapter one, the doctrine of parliamentary sovereignty has considerable virtue which would, were such a methodology adopted, be more than sufficient to justify continuing recognition of the legal validity of this norm. Yet, as parliamentary sovereignty is ultimately a legal doctrine, in accepting that it must be normatively justifiable to be legally valid, we in effect shift responsibility for determining the status of Parliament's legislative power, as does common law constitutionalism, to the courts. That the judges may never exercise the power to repudiate the doctrine of parliamentary sovereignty—if they were to be convinced of its continuing constitutional desirability—does not alter the fact that, in collapsing questions of legal validity into those of normative appeal, the potential for the judiciary to do so would exist. In this sense, the very adoption of the methodology favoured by common law constitutionalists would pose a potential threat to the doctrine of parliamentary sovereignty, because it makes the legal content of the constitution contingent upon what the judges understand to be justified. And, for this reason, it is crucial that we appreciate the importance of adopting a methodology of public law scholarship which separates judgements about what the law is, from judgements about what the law ought to be. While we must certainly give consideration to the virtue (or lack thereof) of particular constitutional arrangements, to invite the judiciary to engage with, and resolve, such questions would, ultimately, be to render unintelligible the idea of a constitution founded on legally unlimited legislative power. Not only, therefore, must common law constitutionalism be rejected substantively—on empirical and on normative grounds—but the methodology which its defenders employ must also be rejected.

V. CONCLUSION

The developments in UK constitutional law and practice discussed in this chapter do not pose critical challenges to the doctrine of parliamentary sovereignty. Devolution and the Human Rights Act 1998 were created by law, but do not legally limit the legislative power of the UK Parliament. While these constitutional developments certainly constrain the practical legislative power of Parliament in ways which are significant and complex, these limitations are fundamentally political, and consistent with the doctrine of parliamentary sovereignty. The UK Parliament retains the legal capacity to make or unmake any law whatever, even if its political capability is now further conditioned by new factors. Common law constitutionalism, in contrast, is not consistent with the doctrine of parliamentary sovereignty, but must be rejected as an unsustainable interpretation of UK constitutional arrangements. It is empirically dubious, but, further, even if assessed on its own terms, must be seen to fail. For it presents a distinctly unattractive conception of constitutional order, and in so doing, further demonstrates that a methodology which collapses claims about what the law *is*, into claims about what the law *ought to be*, is fundamentally objectionable. Whether such a method is employed to reach the substantive conclusions defended by common law constitutionalists or not, in making the legal validity of constitutional norms a function of their normative appeal, it gives to the judiciary the ultimate authority to shape a legal constitution which reflects their vision of what is morally or politically justified. Such a conception of constitutional law should be rejected in general on democratic grounds, but also renders incoherent the idea of legislative sovereignty. And whether the legal doctrine of the sovereignty of Parliament is or is not ever eventually displaced in the UK, it should not be done surreptitiously, as a result of such methodological manoeuvring.

Nevertheless, that each of these three challenges to parliamentary sovereignty can be dismissed has not prevented attempts to craft a composite challenge, drawing on, among other things, elements of each to suggest that the cumulative effect on the doctrine is one which is significant.[198] Such claims—which engage broader notions of increasing judicial power and institutional self-confidence, in combination with ideas, both substantive and rhetorical, adopted from common law constitutionalist theory—can be seen to surface most clearly in the crucial modern case on parliamentary sovereignty, *R (Jackson) v Attorney General*.[199] We will consider the decision of the House of Lords in *Jackson*, and its implications, in detail in Chapter five, assessing in particular the extent to which the case represents, as it might appear to, a departure from the clear and long-standing line of precedent which has been discussed in this chapter.[200] Prior to this, however, we must consider a further constitutional development, which might also form part of a composite challenge to the sovereignty of Parliament of the kind which might be thought to emerge in *Jackson*. This is the UK's membership of the European Union. Unlike the challenges considered, and ultimately dismissed, in this chapter, however, there can be no doubt that membership of the European Union, and the constitutional implications thereof, presents potent problems for a Diceyan understanding of the doctrine of parliamentary sovereignty.

---

[198] See, eg Bogdanor, *The New British Constitution* (2009) n 1 above, 284, 283: '[t]he various constitutional reforms discussed in this book all have the effect of in practice limiting the sovereignty of Parliament'; '[i]t remains in form but not in substance'. See also V Bogdanor, 'Imprisoned by a Doctrine: The Modern Defence of Parliamentary Sovereignty' (2012) 32 *OJLS* 179, 183–93.

[199] *R (on the application of Jackson) v Attorney General* [2005] UKHL 56, [2006] 1 AC 262.

[200] See text at nn 119–35.

4

UK Membership of the European Union

I. INTRODUCTION

IN THIS CHAPTER, we consider the first potent challenge to the doctrine of parliamentary sovereignty which stems from modern political and constitutional change in the UK. This is the challenge posed by the UK's membership of the European Union (EU), a supranational 'association of sovereign states'.[1] For, in accordance with the terms of membership of the EU, the national law of EU Member States must take effect subject to EU law, with domestic norms giving way to the extent of any incompatibility between the two.[2] There is thus a clash of two fundamental constitutional principles: the sovereignty of the UK Parliament and the supremacy of EU law. In constitutional practice, a relatively stable relationship appears to have been established in the UK between domestic law and EU norms, yet what is much less clear is how this has been achieved. Has parliamentary sovereignty been reconciled with EU supremacy, and if so, is this a result of a change in our understanding of the doctrine, shifting away from the formulation defended by Dicey? Or is parliamentary sovereignty a constitutional doctrine which has been extinguished by the UK's membership of the EU, out of place and out of time in a 'multi-layered constitution'?[3]

A range of competing theories have been developed responding to these questions. In this chapter, after exploring the nature of the challenge to the sovereignty of Parliament in further detail, we will examine these attempts to explain the domestic constitutional basis of EU law. In particular, will we consider suggestions that a constitutional revolution has occurred, claims that these difficulties can be resolved through techniques of statutory construction, and arguments that the 'continuing' sovereignty of Parliament has been preserved. All of these attempts to conceptualise the constitutional change which has occurred have varying implications for the status of the doctrine of parliamentary sovereignty

---

[1] This is the characterisation of the EU which has been adopted by the German Bundesverfassungsgericht: see, eg F Schorkopf, 'The European Union as An Association of Sovereign States: Karlsruhe's Ruling on the Treaty of Lisbon' (2009) 10 *German Law Journal* 1219.

[2] In accordance with the new terminology put in place by the European Union (Amendment) Act 2008 s 3, which gave effect to the Treaty of Lisbon, throughout this chapter reference will be made to 'EU law' rather than 'EC law', and the 'European Union' rather than the 'European Community'.

[3] See N Bamforth and P Leyland (eds), *Public Law in a Multi-Layered Constitution* (Oxford, Hart Publishing, 2003).

within the UK constitution—some which are not immediately apparent, but will be brought out as each explanation is analysed below. Yet they will all be rejected as unsatisfactory, and instead, I will argue that a manner and form understanding of the sovereignty of Parliament should be adopted to explain the constitutional change which has resulted from the UK's membership of the EU. And in so doing, it will be suggested that—if a manner and form understanding of the doctrine is accepted—the significant legal challenge posed by the supremacy of EU law can be addressed while retaining the sovereignty of Parliament as the fundamental norm of the UK constitution.

II. PARLIAMENTARY SOVEREIGNTY v EU SUPREMACY(?)

The UK formally joined what is now known as the European Union on 1 January 1973. The statute which deals with the relationship between UK law and the various treaties which lay the foundations of EU law is the European Communities Act 1972 (ECA). In accordance with section 2(1) of the ECA, '[a]ll such rights, powers, liabilities, obligations and restrictions from time to time created or arising by or under the Treaties' shall have 'legal effect' and be enforceable in the UK. Further, in addition to this influx of European legal norms, the ECA, by section 2(4), provides that 'any enactment passed or to be passed ... shall be construed and have effect subject to the foregoing provisions of this section'. In other words, the ECA purports to ensure that any domestic legal rule, whether presently existing or a mere future possibility, regardless of its status, will take effect subject to the law of the EU. This reflects, implicitly, the principle of the supremacy of EU law, established by the Court of Justice of the European Union (CJEU) in the seminal case of *Costa*,[4] and subsequently further developed in *Internationale Handelsgesellschaft*[5] and *Simmenthal*.[6] Hidden behind the obscure phrasing and awkward drafting of the ECA, therefore, lay a potentially potent challenge to the traditional Diceyan understanding of the doctrine of parliamentary sovereignty. For, in enacting the ECA, the Parliament of 1972 seemed to have attempted to bind its successor Parliaments. To be legally valid, in accordance with the terms of the ECA, legislation by future Parliaments would have to be compatible with EU law. However, according to the orthodox understanding of UK constitutional theory, this was impermissible, and it eventually fell to the House of Lords in the famous *Factortame* cases to determine, to echo Mitchell,[7] what had happened to the doctrine of parliamentary sovereignty on 1 January 1973.

---

[4] Case 6/64 *Costa v ENEL (Ente Nazionale Energia Elettrica)* [1964] ECR 585, [1964] CMLR 425.

[5] Case 11/70 *Internationale Handelsgesellschaft mbH v Einfuhr- und Vorratsstelle fur Getreide und Futtermittel* [1970] ECR 1125, [1972] CMLR 255.

[6] Case 106/77 *Amministrazione delle Finanze dello Stato v Simmenthal SpA (No 2)* [1978] ECR 629, [1978] 3 CMLR 263.

[7] JDB Mitchell, 'What Happened to the Constitution on 1st January 1973?' (1980) 11 *Cambrian Law Review* 69.

The facts of the *Factortame* litigation are well known. The Merchant Shipping Act 1988 sought to impose new limits on the fishing vessels which could be registered as British. As a result, Factortame was no longer eligible to register its vessels as British, because the majority of the company's directors and shareholders were Spanish, which was not permitted by the new statutory regime. Pending the outcome of a substantive challenge to the Act of 1988, on the grounds that it violated the EEC Treaty, Factortame applied for interim relief to prevent the Secretary of State from enforcing the new registration scheme. In *Factortame (No 1)*,[8] the House of Lords held that as a matter of domestic law, it had no power to suspend the operation of an Act of Parliament, but referred to the CJEU the question of whether EU law required such a remedy to be available. In response to this reference, the CJEU ruled that where a national court considers that the 'sole obstacle which precludes it from granting interim relief is a rule of national law', then the court 'must set aside that rule'.[9] Consequently, the House of Lords granted an interim injunction restraining the Secretary of State from implementing the new registration regime in *Factortame (No 2)*.[10] Notoriously, the only judge who addressed the impact this decision had on the doctrine of parliamentary sovereignty was Lord Bridge, in a passage which is worth quoting in full:

> Some public comments on the decision of the European Court of Justice, affirming the jurisdiction of the courts of member states to override national legislation if necessary to enable interim relief to be granted in protection of rights under Community law, have suggested that this was a novel and dangerous invasion by a Community institution of the sovereignty of the United Kingdom Parliament. But such comments are based on a misconception. If the supremacy within the European Community of Community law over the national law of member states was not always inherent in the E.E.C. Treaty (Cmnd. 5179-II) it was certainly well established in the jurisprudence of the European Court of Justice long before the United Kingdom joined the Community. Thus, whatever limitation of its sovereignty Parliament accepted when it enacted the European Communities Act 1972 was entirely voluntary. Under the terms of the Act of 1972 it has always been clear that it was the duty of a United Kingdom court, when delivering final judgment, to override any rule of national law found to be in conflict with any directly enforceable rule of Community law. Similarly, when decisions of the European Court of Justice have exposed areas of United Kingdom statute law which failed to implement Council directives, Parliament has always loyally accepted the obligation to make appropriate and prompt amendments. Thus there is nothing in any way novel in according supremacy to rules of Community law in those areas to which they apply and to insist that, in the protection of rights under Community law, national courts must not be inhibited by rules of national law from granting interim relief in appropriate cases is no more than a logical recognition of that supremacy.[11]

---

[8] *R v Secretary of State for Transport, ex parte Factortame (No 1)* [1990] 2 AC 85.

[9] Case C-213/89 *R v Secretary of State for Transport, ex parte Factortame* [1990] ECR I-2433, [1990] 3 CMLR 1.

[10] *R v Secretary of State for Transport, ex parte Factortame (No 2)* [1991] 1 AC 603.

[11] ibid 658–59.

There are three important points made by Lord Bridge in justifying the House of Lords' decision to suspend the operation of an Act of Parliament. First, Lord Bridge characterises the restriction on parliamentary sovereignty imposed by EU law as a 'voluntary' one, accepted by Parliament itself. Secondly, Lord Bridge views the ECA 1972 as the source of the court's authority to prevent the relevant provisions of the Merchant Shipping Act 1988 from having legal effect. Thirdly, and most surprisingly, Lord Bridge goes to great lengths to stress that there is 'nothing in any way novel' going on in this case; it is the mere 'logical recognition' of the supremacy of European law. In sum, the judgment is one of arch pragmatism. Lord Bridge avoids having to conceptualise what has happened to the doctrine of parliamentary sovereignty by denying that meaningful change has occurred. Parliament is cast as the author of whatever limited constitutional change might be discerned, with the courts—as ever, in accordance with the traditional role allocated to them by a constitution organised around the concept of parliamentary sovereignty—merely their agent, loyally implementing the instructions contained in statute.

III. A EUROPEAN REVOLUTION?

The House of Lords' striking under-elaboration of this crucial constitutional issue in *Factortame (No 2)* has left the field relatively open for academic work seeking to explain the effect of the supremacy of EU law on the doctrine of parliamentary sovereignty. Perhaps the most notable reaction to *Factortame (No 2)* came from Wade, whose staunch defence of the Diceyan conception of the doctrine was encountered in Chapter two.[12] Wade argued that the decision of the House of Lords confirmed that '[t]he Parliament of 1972 had succeeded in binding the Parliament of 1988 and restricting its sovereignty, something that was supposed to be constitutionally impossible'.[13] This shift away from the traditional understanding of the doctrine of parliamentary sovereignty, now undermined by the recognition that Parliament had been able to bind its successors, was, for Wade, a 'constitutional revolution'.[14] Wade's analysis of the effect of *Factortame (No 2)* is thus a reasonably consistent application of his earlier theoretical account of the basis of legal sovereignty to the problem of the supremacy of EU law: change to parliamentary sovereignty, as the ultimate political fact, is only possible through judicial revolution. Yet even at first glance, this seems open to question. While it is a faithful application of his earlier theory to the circumstances of this particular challenge, one of the deficiencies of Wade's conceptual account of the nature of parliamentary sovereignty appears here to be manifested in practice.

---

[12] See chapter 2 of this volume, pp 75–91.

[13] HWR Wade, 'Sovereignty—Revolution or Evolution?' (1996) 112 *LQR* 568, 568. See also HWR Wade, 'What Has Happened to the Sovereignty of Parliament?' (1991) 107 *LQR* 1, 4.

[14] Wade, 'What Has Happened to the Sovereignty of Parliament?' (1991) ibid, 4.

The counter-intuitive notion to which Wade was committed—that all changes to fundamental constitutional rules must be revolutionary in nature[15]—seems almost to compel him to overstate the impact of EU membership on the UK constitution. As Allison has observed, '[f]or the concept of revolution to be appropriate ... it must refer to something more than important change, for example, to "a fresh start", an overturning of the existing order or a break in continuity of fundamental significance'.[16] On this definition, it seems difficult to conceive of a calculated decision to become a member of the EU, while leaving the essential domestic constitutional architecture of the state unchanged, as a revolution in any meaningful sense.[17] Indeed, perhaps sensitive to the descriptive inaccuracy of this terminology, Wade subsequently qualified his initial reaction, downgrading what had occurred to a 'technical revolution'.[18]

Of greater importance, however, is that Wade's characterisation of this change to the doctrine of parliamentary sovereignty as revolutionary does not sit well with the reasoning of Lord Bridge in *Factortame (No 2)* itself. After all, Lord Bridge made a significant effort to emphasise precisely the opposite point: that the case was in no way novel. Wade was aware of the disjunction between his account and that of Lord Bridge, but did not believe this to dilute the salience of his analysis. For Wade, the House of Lords had merely taken a 'prudential course', turning 'a blind eye to constitutional theory'[19] as a matter of 'necessity'.[20] While it is, of course, neither necessary nor desirable to take everything said by the courts at face value, this does not mean that comments which do not fit with pre-ordained theories ought to be readily disregarded. Rather, although it stretches credulity to believe that Lord Bridge was not fully aware of the obvious alteration of Parliament's legislative authority that *Factortame (No 2)* would finally reveal, some weight must be attached to his insistence that according supremacy to EU law did not require a fundamental restructuring of the foundational concepts of the UK constitution. As I have suggested above, that Wade was led to argue to the contrary is probably due to the latent flaws in his theory of legislative sovereignty itself. Nonetheless, in so far as Wade's account of the state of parliamentary sovereignty post-*Factortame (No 2)* suggests that revolutionary change has occurred, it must be rejected. For, in addition to employing terminology the accuracy of which is questionable in and of itself, Wade's characterisation of the constitutional

---

[15] See chapter 2 of this volume, pp 77–78.

[16] JWF Allison, 'Parliamentary Sovereignty, Europe and the Economy of the Common Law' in M Andenas (ed), *Liber Amicorum in Honour of Lord Slynn of Hadley: Judicial Review in International Perspective* (London, Kluwer Law International, 2000) 184. Allison's reference to 'a fresh start' comes from a letter written by Wade to HLA Hart, in which 'Wade expressly uses the concept of revolution in th[is] sense': 184, fn 49.

[17] For a radically different conception of what might constitute a revolution, see, eg JAG Griffith, 'Why We Need a Revolution' (1969) 40 *Political Quarterly* 383.

[18] Wade, 'Sovereignty—Revolution or Evolution?' (1996) n 13 above, 574.

[19] ibid 575.

[20] Wade, 'What Has Happened to the Sovereignty of Parliament?' (1991) n 13 above, 3, 4.

impact of EU membership is one which radically diverges from the experience of other key actors.

Wade's account does, however, provide a good starting point for an evaluation of the extent of Parliament's legislative power—and therefore the status of the doctrine of parliamentary sovereignty—after *Factortame (No 2)*. Of central importance is Wade's contention that the Parliament of 1972 has successfully bound its successors. If this claim is accepted, in what way have successor Parliaments been so bound? Wade seems to view the ECA as having substantively limited future Parliaments from enacting legislation which is contrary to EU law. This substantive limitation is not, however, absolute, but comes with a caveat. Wade accepts that 'Parliament could indeed repeal the Act of 1972 altogether, take Britain out of the Community and repudiate European law'.[21] Thus, it is only while 'Britain remains in the Community' that 'we are in a regime in which Parliament has bound its successors successfully'.[22] The implication, then, is that on withdrawal from the EU at a hypothetical future date, the traditional understanding of parliamentary sovereignty would be restored.

What is the authority for Wade's proposition that Parliament's power to enact withdrawal legislation has been retained? The ECA is, unsurprisingly, silent on the matter. It might be argued that a full withdrawal statute would not, in any event, be contrary to EU law—particularly after the formal recognition in the Treaty of Lisbon of a right to withdraw[23]—and that such national legislation would not therefore be susceptible to disapplication in accordance with the provisions of the ECA. This is not, however, an argument that could readily have been relied on by Wade. Instead, Wade appears to base his acceptance of the withdrawal caveat on his assessment of contemporary political reality. The real possibility that the UK might have departed from the EU 'if the referendum of 1975 had produced a "No" vote' is cited by Wade in support of his view that, 'at least at this point in time', it would still be open to Parliament to legislate for withdrawal.[24] There can be no doubt that this also remains an accurate assessment of the current political situation. Indeed, for at least as long as discussion of an 'in-out' referendum on membership of the EU endures as a mainstream political issue in the UK, withdrawal is very much a political possibility.[25] The difficulty with Wade's caveat, however, is that on this basis it is potentially transient, for its existence

---

[21] Wade, 'Sovereignty—Revolution or Evolution?' (1996) n 13 above, 570.

[22] ibid 571.

[23] Article 50 Treaty on European Union.

[24] Wade, 'Sovereignty—Revolution or Evolution?' (1996) n 13 above, 570.

[25] See, eg the EU (Referendum) Bill 2013–14, a private members' bill promoted by James Wharton MP, which purports to make provision for a referendum to be held on UK membership of the EU before the end of 2017. While supported by the Conservative Party leadership, the Bill appears unlikely to become law, as it is not supported by the Liberal Democrat members of the coalition government, and therefore not promoted as, or able to benefit from the time available for, government legislation. The holding of an 'in-out' referendum on EU membership before the end of 2017 is to be the basis of a Conservative Party manifesto commitment at the 2015 general election: see, eg 'Tory EU Exit Campaign if No Reform, says Minister', *BBC News Website* (17 May 2014).

seems to be entirely dependent upon his understanding of the current political environment. If our interpretation of the underlying political circumstances were to change—if, for example, in time it became arguable that UK membership of the EU was an enduring phenomenon—it would seem that Wade's substantive limit on Parliament's legislative authority could become absolute.

If Wade's withdrawal caveat, then, is not guaranteed as a matter of legal principle, but merely contingent upon political perceptions, his account must represent a departure from the notion that the UK Parliament is legally sovereign. For the classic position in relation to Parliament's legislative power would seem to be inverted in significant respects: it would be legally limited by EU law, rather than being legally unlimited, with the potential for such limits to be removed conditional upon, rather than regardless of, what is politically conceivable. This may appear to be a statement of the obvious, given the talk of revolutions which pervades Wade's work on this topic. Yet it is a claim which Wade does not actually make explicitly, carefully talking of 'drastic' change to, or 'limitation' or 'concessions' of, sovereignty, but not that it has been repudiated by Parliament.[26] Instead, for Wade, 'the new doctrine makes sovereignty a freely adjustable commodity whenever Parliament chooses to accept some limitation'.[27] But if there is no persistent legal basis for the possibility that such limitations may be removed by Parliament, it seems that this 'new doctrine' is not one of parliamentary sovereignty at all. Instead, it is the use of legally unlimited legislative power to extinguish legally unlimited legislative power.

Given this lack of a persistent legal basis for the possibility of withdrawal from the EU, Wade's position may not actually therefore be far removed from that of a theorist like Mitchell, who believed that the EU Member States had engaged in 'a re-arrangement or pooling of the modes of exercising national sovereignties' to create a 'new legal (and political) order', subjugating domestic constitutional systems.[28] Perhaps this is what Wade intended, with his caveat merely pragmatically recognising that the new constitutional order structuring the UK's relationship with the EU had not, at least yet, acquired complete fixity of character. Indeed, to even call it a caveat might be a misrepresentation of Wade's acknowledgment of the possibility of withdrawal from the EU. It might cohere better with Wade's theoretical work on legislative sovereignty to treat his appreciation of the possibility of withdrawal as little more than the manifestation of his belief that revolutionary political change to basic constitutional norms can never be excluded. If the UK's accession to the EU was effected by non-legal, revolutionary means, causing a shift in basic political facts, a subsequent withdrawal could be similarly characterised as revolutionary. Nonetheless, even if correct, such an interpretation of Wade's analysis still leads to the conclusion that Parliament is no longer legally sovereign, for while a reversion to the pre-EU constitution would remain possible, it would

---

[26] See, eg Wade, 'Sovereignty—Revolution or Evolution?' (1996) n 13 above, 568, 575.
[27] ibid 573.
[28] Mitchell, 'What Happened to the Constitution on 1st January 1973?' (1980) n 7 above, 82.

be achieved, strictly speaking, by revolution, rather than legislation. It is not clear, however, that Wade's analysis of the extent of Parliament's legislative authority post-*Factortame (No 2)* is correct. Instead, I will argue below that we need not join Wade in departing from the legal doctrine of the sovereignty of Parliament in order to explain the constitutional basis of the UK's membership of the EU. And, as a result, it is possible to establish the definitive existence, as a matter of law, of a power of withdrawal from the EU, the force of which is not simply a function of the ongoing political likelihood of such authority being exercised.

Wade's analysis, however, also suffers from an additional deficiency. Since Wade conceived of the ECA as placing substantive limits on Parliament's power to enact legislation, his account cannot incorporate the possibility that an Act of Parliament might be able to take priority over EU law in specific, presumably narrow, instances without membership of the union being repudiated. Suppose that in an exceptional case, a government which had no desire to relinquish the benefits of EU membership by effecting a comprehensive withdrawal determined that it could not, for whatever reason, comply with a particular rule of EU law. Such a government might seek to enact domestic legislation violating EU law which explicitly instructed the courts that this non-compliant Act of Parliament was to have full legal effect, notwithstanding the provisions of the ECA. Such legislation would, of course, be in breach of EU law, but the ascertainment of its domestic legality requires further factors to be considered. Crucially, would national courts really be expected to refuse to accept the unambiguously expressed will of the UK Parliament? In such a case, it seems most likely that the judges' domestic allegiance to Parliament would take precedence over their obligations to the ECJ.[29] Indeed, a compelling argument can be made that this is exactly what the judges ought to do. While it has been well established by the CJEU that the supremacy of EU law is required for the Union to function effectively,[30] the translation of the principle of supremacy into national law must be effected by national law. In the UK, as the House of Lords made clear in *Factortame (No 2)*, the legal force of the principle of the supremacy of EU law derives from the ECA. Yet if Parliament issues a contrary instruction to the courts to that contained in the ECA, the validity of such legislation in the UK would fall to be determined as a matter of UK constitutional law,[31] and the principle of supremacy would have no independent domestic legal force. In such an exceptional case, it would therefore be inappropriate for the UK courts, as matter of principle, to refuse to give effect to legislation enacted by Parliament

---

[29] Support for this view can be found in the well-known judgment of Lord Denning MR in *Macarthy's Ltd v Smith* [1979] ICR 785, 789: 'Thus far I have assumed that our Parliament, whenever it passes legislation, intends to fulfil its obligations under the Treaty. If the time should come when our Parliament deliberately passes an Act—with the intention of repudiating the Treaty or any provision in it—or intentionally of acting inconsistently with it—and says so in express terms—then I should have thought that it would be the duty of our courts to follow the statute of our Parliament'.

[30] Case 6/64 *Costa v ENEL* [1964] ECR 585, [1964] CMLR 425, 456.

[31] For recognition of this point by the Supreme Court in a different context, see *R (HS2 Action Alliance Ltd) v Secretary of State for Transport* [2014] UKSC 3, [2014] 1 WLR 324, [79].

which demonstrated an express intention to contravene EU law. Indeed, given the emphasis placed by Lord Bridge in *Factortame (No 2)* on the 'voluntary' nature of the limitation on Parliament's legislative authority established by the ECA, it seems better to assume that a statutory attempt to circumscribe the domestic effect of EU law, whether generally or in a particular area, could not be judicially ignored. Moreover, from a pragmatic perspective, rather than risk a stand-off with Parliament, it would be prudent for the judges to instead accept such a statute, and leave it to the government, through political negotiation, to deal with the consequences of breaching EU rules. Yet Wade's theory could not accommodate such an eventuality. Instead, in accordance with his analysis of *Factortame (No 2)*, Wade's reading of the ECA would require the courts to reject *any* legislation which violated EU law. The government would then be left with the stark choice of accepting the supremacy of EU law, or withdrawing from the Union. And in so reducing the options available to the judiciary, and by extension, the government, Wade's conception of Parliament's legislative authority post-*Factortame (No 2)* has the potential to create new sites of inter-institutional crisis, adding conflict between Parliament and the courts to conflict between the government and the EU. As such, it seems wrong to imagine that the UK courts would not, or should not, acknowledge the legal validity of an Act of Parliament which explicitly sought to deviate from EU norms in relation to a specific matter, but which did not terminate the UK's membership of the EU. Due to the fact that it does not reflect this constitutional position, Wade's account of the legal status of EU law within the UK must be rejected.

IV. THE CONSTRUCTIONIST ALTERNATIVE

A rival view seeks to avoid the problems that beset Wade's analysis. A constructionist analysis of *Factortame (No 2)* rejects the notion that the primacy of EU norms in the UK has been brought about by revolution. Instead, according to Craig's formulation of this account, 'the courts could, less dramatically, treat section 2(4) of the European Communities Act 1972 as a rule of interpretation to the effect that Parliament is presumed not to intend statutes to override EEC law'.[32] In practice, as Allan has argued, such a rule of interpretation or construction would require 'statutes to be read as compatible with rights arising under European Community law in the absence of express words to the contrary'.[33] Such an approach to the ECA has been said to be preferable to that of Wade in a number of ways. It preserves constitutional continuity, using familiar interpretative techniques to accommodate the domestic supremacy of EU law, rather than requiring the strained supposition of a revolutionary rupture. This seems to

---

[32] PP Craig, 'Sovereignty of the United Kingdom Parliament after *Factortame*' (1991) 11 *Yearbook of European Law* 221, 251.

[33] TRS Allan, 'Parliamentary Sovereignty: Law, Politics and Revolution' (1997) 113 *LQR* 443, 443.

accord well with the understated reaction of the Law Lords to the constitutional change considered in *Factortame (No 2)*. As Allan has suggested, the constructionist explanation leads to the conclusion that in this case 'the House of Lords merely determined what the existing constitutional order required in novel circumstances'.[34] Moreover, the constructionist reading of *Factortame (No 2)* clearly places a less stringent limitation on the legislative power of Parliament. It allows for the possibility that Parliament might wish, in specific circumstances, to produce legislation which is incompatible with, yet prevails over, EU law. On the constructionist analysis, the use of explicit language by Parliament to indicate that a given statute should not be subject to section 2(4) of the ECA would seem to be sufficient to rebut the presumption, which this section creates, that legislation should be read to comply with EU norms. The constructionist approach thus, on its face, seems to respect and sustain the sovereignty of Parliament in a manner that Wade's account does not. However, on closer inspection the constructionist reading of *Factortame (No 2)* actually represents a fundamental challenge to the traditional understanding of parliamentary sovereignty. As Craig has noted, an embrace of the rule of construction proposed above 'serves to preserve the formal veneer of Diceyan orthodoxy while undermining its substance'.[35]

The artificiality of the constructionist analysis of *Factortame (No 2)* is at the root of its problems. There is nothing in the ECA itself which indicates that legislation is to be presumed to be compatible with EU norms *unless express words provide otherwise*. Indeed, the ECA makes no mention of the possibility that explicit language in a subsequent Act of Parliament, indicating the primacy of this later statute, would be sufficient to override the requirements of EU law. Instead, it simply provides that all domestic legal norms are to take effect subject to EU law. What, then, is the authority for the proposition that this is subject to an 'express-words' exception? The issue here is not whether such an exception should or should not be said to exist. As has been argued above, it is a deficiency of Wade's theory that it cannot accommodate this kind of exception, the existence of which is extremely difficult to disregard. Rather, the issue which must be considered here is why the rule of construction which is thought to ensure the supremacy of EU law over Acts of the UK Parliament contains this exception.

According to Allan, a key proponent of the constructionist approach to *Factortame (No 2)*, it is the courts that are responsible for developing the precise content of this rule of construction. For Allan, the doctrine of parliamentary sovereignty is not an absolute barrier to EU law being given domestic primacy: '[e]very other common law rule is subject to such modification and qualification in successive decisions, and there is no reason for treating the rule of obedience to statutes differently'.[36] Crucially, Allan argues, when the judges were called on to decide whether the rule of obedience to statutes had been modified to give

---

[34] ibid 445.
[35] Craig, 'Sovereignty of the United Kingdom Parliament after *Factortame*' (1991) n 32 above, 251.
[36] Allan, 'Parliamentary Sovereignty: Law, Politics and Revolution' (1997) n 33 above, 445.

priority to EU norms, the mere fact that Parliament had legislated to provide for this, by enacting the ECA, was not definitive. Rather, 'exceptions may only be recognised for sufficient reason', and in this instance, a judge's 'belief that Parliament and people had chosen to join ... a supra-national entity, understanding and accepting the legal and political consequences, would clearly be pertinent, if not necessarily conclusive'.[37] In other words, according to Allan, the provisions of the ECA are not enough, taken on their own, to settle the precise nature of the relationship between UK law and EU law. While the provisions of the ECA which attempt to make all national law subject to EU law are certainly important, they cannot condition unilaterally the relationship between these two bodies of legal rules. Instead, the ECA is merely one factor to be taken into account by the courts when they are determining how Acts of Parliament which might appear to violate EU law are to be construed. It is immaterial, then, that ECA makes no reference to Parliament's ability to avoid the requirements of EU law by using explicit language, for the ECA is not the true source of the supremacy of EU law. It is the courts who have, through a rule of construction, given primacy to EU law, and it is the courts who will decide the circumstances in which this primacy may be withdrawn.

An initial difficulty with this aspect of the constructionist account is that it seems to be plainly inconsistent with the reasoning adopted by Lord Bridge in *Factortame (No 2)*. Lord Bridge did not invoke the notion of a judicially established rule of construction to explain the House of Lords' decision to afford supremacy to EU law. On the contrary, Lord Bridge justified the decision in *Factortame (No 2)* on the grounds that Parliament, not the courts, had decided to grant primacy to EU law. The legal cause of this change was the enactment of the ECA, and the courts had a 'duty' to comply with its provisions.[38] This might, however, appear to be deviate from the earlier suggestion of Lord Bridge in *Factortame (No 1)*:

> By virtue of section 2(4) of the Act of 1972 Part II of the Act of 1988 is to be construed and take effect subject to directly enforceable Community rights ... This has precisely the same effect as if a section were incorporated in Part II of the Act of 1988 which in terms enacted that the provisions with respect to registration of British fishing vessels were to be without prejudice to the directly enforceable Community rights of nationals of any member state of the E.E.C.[39]

This characterisation of the effect of the ECA is, however, questionable, because—in addition to the postulation of such a 'hypothetical section' being 'much more than an exercise in construction'[40]—it is contrived to attribute this intention to the Parliament of 1988. Instead, it is the legislation of the earlier Parliament of 1972, and the terms of the ECA itself, which establish the domestic supremacy of

---

[37] ibid 445.
[38] *R v Secretary of State for Transport, ex parte Factortame (No 2)* [1991] 1 AC 603, 659.
[39] *R v Secretary of State for Transport, ex parte Factortame (No 1)* [1990] 2 AC 85, 140.
[40] Wade, 'Sovereignty—Revolution or Evolution?' (1996) n 13 above, 570.

EU law, as was made clear in Lord Bridge's subsequent judgment in *Factortame (No 2)*. Yet even if it were convincing, the claim advanced in *Factortame (No 1)*—which was not repeated by Lord Bridge in *Factortame (No 2)*—provides little support for the constructionist view. For while this speculative analogy as to the effect of section 2(4) may attribute to the wrong Parliament the crucial intention to afford priority to the rules of EU law, the domestic authority of EU law would still appear to be a result of legislative action, rather than any substantive exercise of judicial judgement. It would, admittedly, be an expansive approach to the construction of the Act of 1988 (and indeed, all other Acts of Parliament) to read into it such a provision of profound potential significance. Yet even then, it is clear that the authority to do this would derive from section 2(4) of the ECA, rather than any free-standing judicial jurisdiction to promote the supremacy of EU law. Indeed, the more cogent analysis of Lord Bridge in *Factortame (No 2)* is unequivocal in identifying the ECA as the definitive cause of the domestic supremacy of EU law: as Craig has argued, it is likely this was to ensure that '[i]f … "blame" was to be cast for a loss of sovereignty then this should be laid at the feet of Parliament and not the courts'.[41] Therefore, if the Law Lords in *Factortame (No 2)* presented themselves as being obliged by statute to give priority to EU law, it seems wrong to view this constitutional shift as being somehow judicially crafted.

But even if we cannot take at face value what the judges claimed to be doing in *Factortame (No 2)*, as a constructionist might be led to assert, a more basic problem remains. This problem is that when giving effect to EU law within the UK, the courts have not behaved as if they considered their task to be essentially or exclusively one of reconstructing national law to make it EU-compliant. To reconcile the doctrine of parliamentary sovereignty with the domestic supremacy of EU law, the constructionist account of *Factortame (No 2)* requires the courts to read Acts of Parliament in such a way as to ensure that they cohere with EU norms. Where the courts have a choice between competing interpretations of a statute, some which are compatible with EU law, and some which are not, such a rule of construction would force them to choose from the former category. Indeed, as Lord Oliver observed in *Litster v Forth Dry Dock & Engineering Co Ltd*, a more robust approach to the construction of Acts of Parliament may even be permitted to prevent violations of EU law, allowing 'some departure from the strict and literal application of the words which the legislature has elected to use' where a statute can 'reasonably be construed so as to conform with [EU] obligations'.[42] However, post-*Factortame (No 2)*, where an Act of Parliament is clearly incompatible with the provisions of EU law, the courts will not seek to fashion a contrived interpretation which the actual language used in the statute cannot support. Instead, the courts will make a declaration that the legislation must be

---

[41] Craig, 'Sovereignty of the United Kingdom Parliament after *Factortame*' (1991) n 32 above, 249.
[42] *Litster v Forth Dry Dock & Engineering Co Ltd* [1990] 1 AC 546, 559. See also *Pickstone v Freemans Plc* [1989] AC 66.

disapplied, as, for example, was the effect of the decision of the House of Lords in *R v Secretary of State for Employment, ex parte Equal Opportunities Commission*.[43] The disapplication of primary legislation is patently not an exercise in statutory construction. As Lord Walker noted with great clarity in *Fleming (t/a Bodycraft) v Customs and Excise Commissioners*:

> Disapplication is called for only if there is an inconsistency between national law and EU law. In an attempt to avoid an inconsistency the national court will, if at all possible, interpret the national legislation so as to make it conform to the superior order of EU law ... Sometimes, however, a conforming construction is not possible, and disapplication cannot be avoided. Disapplication of national legislation is an essentially different process from its interpretation so as to conform with EU law. Only in the most formal sense (because of the terms of section 2(4) of the European Communities Act 1972) can disapplication be described as a process of construction.[44]

The constructionist account, therefore, cannot fully explain how domestic prevalence is given to EU law in the UK, for the courts do not merely rely on statutory construction to eliminate any inconsistency between Acts of Parliament and EU norms. The existence of a judicial power to disapply legislation which is incompatible with EU law—plainly apparent in the actual practice of the courts, and crucially distinct from a power of statutory construction—indicates that the constitutional realignment acknowledged in *Factortame (No 2)* cannot simply be attributed to the judicial introduction of a new rule of statutory interpretation.

Further, a constructionist would be unable to justify the very existence of this power to disapply primary legislation while nonetheless maintaining that such an account provides constitutional continuity and preserves, albeit superficially, the sovereignty of Parliament. For if the primacy of EU law stems not from Parliament's enactment of the ECA, but the courts' modification of the rule of obedience to statutes, then the constitutional legitimacy of the power of disapplication must similarly be based on judicial authority. However, if this is the case, then the constructionist account can no longer be 'the easy way out',[45] ensuring the domestic supremacy of EU law while minimising the appearance of change to fundamental constitutional principles. Rather, once it becomes clear that the primacy of EU law cannot have been achieved by statutory construction alone, the challenge posed by this school of thought to parliamentary sovereignty is laid bare. For if the disapplication of Acts of Parliament which violate EU law is justified by nothing more, from a domestic constitutional perspective, than the

---

[43] *R v Secretary of State for Employment, ex parte Equal Opportunities Commission* [1995] 1 AC 1.

[44] *Fleming (t/a Bodycraft) v Customs and Excise Commissioners* [2008] UKHL 2, [2008] 1 WLR 195, [25]. While Lord Walker dissented in part in *Fleming* from the decision of the majority, his discussion of the distinction between disapplication and statutory construction was expository, and was not relevant to the reasons for his dissent. Indeed, as Lord Walker noted, '[i]n these two appeals it is common ground, at least in your Lordships' House, that the national court is concerned with disapplication, not with trying to find a conforming construction': [25]. *Fleming* was thus premised on the fact that there is an 'important distinction' between disapplying and reconstructing a statute: [25].

[45] Wade, 'Sovereignty—Revolution or Evolution?' (1996) n 13 above, 569.

judicial acceptance of such a power, then the UK constitution can no longer be said to be controlled by the principle of parliamentary sovereignty, but by the supremacy of the judiciary, or that of the common law.

V. THE CHALLENGE OF *THOBURN*

The general acceptance of the constructionist interpretation of *Factortame (No 2)* would thus have an immense impact on the contemporary status of the doctrine of parliamentary sovereignty. To see the full constitutional implications of this analysis, the case of *Thoburn v Sunderland City Council*[46] must be examined. For the decision in *Thoburn*, despite the existence of the problems detailed above, appears to offer considerable support to the constructionist understanding of *Factortame (No 2)*, in the elaborate and influential account this case provides of the domestic constitutional basis of EU law.

The critical question for the Administrative Court in *Thoburn* related to the exercise of the power contained in section 2(2) of the ECA, enabling the government, by Order in Council or regulations, to 'make provision ... for the purpose of implementing any Community obligation of the United Kingdom'. By section 2(4), a provision capable of being made in accordance with this power 'includes ... any such provision (of any such extent) as might be made by Act of Parliament'. Section 2(2) thus creates a 'Henry VIII' power, which can be used by the executive to amend existing primary legislation to ensure the compatibility of domestic law with EU law.[47] An exercise of this power was at the heart of *Thoburn*, which crucially concerned the amendment of the Weights and Measures Act 1985 by the Units of Measurement Regulations 1994, the latter having been passed under section 2(2) of the ECA. In its original form, the Weights and Measures Act 1985 had permitted either metric or imperial measurements to be used to quantify goods for the purposes of trade. The amended regime, which was, the court accepted, logically underpinned by the changes made in the 1994 Regulations,[48] required goods to be quantified primarily in metric units. The appellants, having been convicted of various offences under the amended statutory regime, argued that the Weights and Measures Act 1985 *as originally enacted* had impliedly repealed the power contained in section 2(2) of the ECA, passed earlier in 1972, to the extent that this power could be used to make provisions which were inconsistent with the Act of 1985. Therefore, the appellants contended, the enactment of the Weights and Measure Act 1985 precluded the use of the section 2(2) power to create the 1994 Regulations, and thus the purported amendments to the original

---

[46] *Thoburn v Sunderland City Council* [2002] EWHC 195, [2003] QB 151.

[47] See generally NW Barber and AL Young, 'The Rise of Prospective Henry VIII Clauses and their Implications for Sovereignty' [2003] *PL* 112.

[48] As a result, the validity of the 1994 Regulations was the pivotal matter in this case: see *Thoburn v Sunderland City Council* [2002] EWHC 195, [2003] QB 151, [40].

terms of the 1985 legislation would be void. Such an argument, had it been accepted by the court, would have had serious ramifications for all prospective Henry VIII clauses, rendering them 'limited by every subsequent parliamentary statute', and thus, in effect, impossible for Parliament to create.[49] However, Laws LJ, giving the leading judgment of the Administrative Court, rejected the appellants' argument. The Weights and Measures Act 1985 had not impliedly repealed section 2(2) of the ECA because '[g]enerally, there is no *inconsistency* between a provision conferring a Henry VIII power to amend future legislation and the terms of any such future legislation'.[50]

Yet having disposed of the argument at issue in *Thoburn*—reaching a conclusion which was legally sound and largely uncontroversial—Laws LJ did not, however, stop there. Instead, Laws LJ attempted to fill the gap left by the House of Lords in *Factortame (No 2)*, and offer, in Mark Elliott's words, 'for the first time a convincing judicial rationalization of the status of EU law within the UK Constitution'.[51] According to Laws LJ, even when an Act of Parliament is enacted which actually is incompatible with the ECA—as was the Merchant Shipping Act 1988 in the *Factortame* litigation, but not the Weights and Measures Act 1985 at issue in *Thoburn*—the later, inconsistent statute does not repeal by implication the ECA. Instead, the ECA has priority because of its status as a 'constitutional' statute. Building on recent case law in which the courts have discovered, and tried to delineate, a category of fundamental constitutional rights,[52] Laws LJ argued that now '[w]e should recognise a hierarchy of Acts of Parliament: as it were "ordinary" statutes and "constitutional" statutes'.[53] An Act of Parliament is 'constitutional', according to Laws LJ, if it '(a) conditions the legal relationship between citizen and state in some general, overarching manner, or (b) enlarges or diminishes the scope of what we would now regard as fundamental constitutional rights'.[54] This distinction is important, Laws LJ explained, because it allows variation in the circumstances in which different types of statutes are deemed to have been repealed:

> Ordinary statutes may be impliedly repealed. Constitutional statutes may not. For the repeal of a constitutional Act or the abrogation of a fundamental right to be effected

---

[49] Barber and Young, 'The Rise of Prospective Henry VIII Clauses' [2003] n 47 above, 115.

[50] *Thoburn v Sunderland City Council* [2002] EWHC 195, [2003] QB 151, [50].

[51] M Elliott, 'Parliamentary Sovereignty Under Pressure' (2004) 2 *International Journal of Constitutional Law* 545, 551.

[52] See, eg *R v Secretary of State for the Home Department, ex parte Leech (No 2)* [1994] QB 198; *R v Lord Chancellor, ex parte Witham* [1998] QB 575; *R v Secretary of State for the Home Department, ex parte Pierson* [1998] AC 539; *R v Secretary of State for the Home Department, ex parte Simms* [2000] 2 AC 115. These key cases, and the 'principle of legality' which they develop, are considered further in chapter 5 of this volume, pp 206–17.

[53] *Thoburn v Sunderland City Council* [2002] EWHC 195, [2003] QB 151, [62].

[54] ibid [62]. The examples of 'constitutional' statutes cited by Laws LJ along with the ECA are Magna Carta 1297, the Bill of Rights 1689, the Union with Scotland Act 1706, the Representation of the People Acts 1832, 1867, and 1884, the Human Rights Act 1998, the Scotland Act 1998, and the Government of Wales Act 1998.

by statute, the court would apply this test: is it shown that the legislature's *actual*—not imputed, constructive or presumed—intention was to effect the repeal or abrogation? I think the test could only be met by express words in the later statute, or by words so specific that the inference of an actual determination to effect the result contended for was irresistible. The ordinary rule of implied repeal does not satisfy this test. Accordingly, it has no application to constitutional statutes.[55]

The primacy of EU law is therefore due to the designation of the ECA as a 'constitutional' statute which cannot be impliedly repealed by a subsequent incompatible statute, and its effects only avoided where there is evidence of a palpable parliamentary intention to do so. But on what authority can this entirely novel scheme, creating two tiers of parliamentary legislation, be imposed on the UK constitution?[56] This scheme does not, and cannot, derive from Parliament since, Laws LJ asserted, the legislature 'cannot stipulate as to the manner and form of any subsequent legislation', nor can it 'stipulate against implied repeal any more than it can stipulate against express repeal'.[57] Rather, the distinction between 'ordinary' and 'constitutional' statutes is an invention of the 'common law'.[58]

The judgment of Laws LJ in *Thoburn* was plainly an attempt to explain why the courts have, from the *Factortame* litigation onwards, been able to give effect to the domestic primacy of EU law. Laws LJ engineered an elaborate constructionist account of the supremacy of EU law, for he viewed this supremacy as having been established by the judicial creation of 'exceptions to the doctrine of implied repeal, a doctrine which was always the common law's own creature'.[59] This explanation might be thought to improve on the earlier constructionist theory considered above, for it is not based on an artificial interpretation of the terms of the ECA itself. Laws LJ instead contended openly that a judicial alteration of the rules relating to the construction of statutes had been required to insulate the ECA from implied repeal, giving the 1972 Act the degree of fixity necessary to prevail against subsequent contradictory legislation, and thus to ensure the primacy of EU law. For, on this account, without the judicial fashioning of a modification to the doctrine of implied repeal, EU law could not have been bestowed with priority over national legislation in the UK.

It is very difficult, however, to see how this account of the manner in which the domestic supremacy of EU norms is assured can stand with the judgment of Lord Bridge in *Factortame (No 2)*. Lord Bridge gave no indication that the operation of the doctrine of implied repeal in relation to the ECA had been judicially modified. Nor did he argue that this was as a result of the special 'constitutional'

---

[55] ibid [63].

[56] Geoffrey Marshall has, for example, criticised the precise terms of the distinction drawn by Laws LJ as being 'undeniably vague', and having the potential to 'inject an unwelcome element of uncertainty into our public law': G Marshall, 'Metric Measures and Martyrdom by Henry VIII Clause' (2002) 118 *LQR* 493, 495, 496.

[57] *Thoburn v Sunderland City Council* [2002] EWHC 195, [2003] QB 151, [59].

[58] ibid [59]–[60].

[59] ibid [60].

status of this statute in the eyes of the common law. Instead, Lord Bridge viewed the primacy of EU law as flowing from the actions of Parliament. The account put forward by Lord Bridge was clearly underdeveloped. Yet the contention of Laws LJ that there was no conflict between this and his own conclusions, because *Factortame (No 2)* was a case concerned only with the primacy of the '*substantive provisions*' of EU law and not with the '*legal foundation*' on which this primacy was based, is unsustainable.[60] It was exactly the question of the legal foundations of the domestic primacy of EU law that Lord Bridge sought to address in this part of his judgment. That the 'foundation is English law', as Laws LJ maintained, is so general as to entirely cohere with the words of Lord Bridge.[61] However, the two judges fundamentally differ as to the specifics of *how* UK constitutional law has been able to accommodate the substantive supremacy of EU norms. As a result, given the obvious precedential force of the judgment of Lord Bridge in the House of Lords in *Factortame (No 2)*, the authority of the analysis of Laws LJ—offered obiter in *Thoburn* in the Administrative Court, employing a distinction which is at the least unfamiliar to UK constitutional law, and at most fundamentally incompatible with foundational principles—must be significantly diminished.

Moreover, the fiction that a constructionist approach 'preserves the sovereignty of the legislature', reiterated in *Thoburn*, is resoundingly shown to be false on considered analysis of this case and its potential implications.[62] For while Laws LJ believed that Parliament had ultimately retained its legislative sovereignty, notwithstanding the domestic supremacy of EU legal norms, to achieve this result 'the traditional doctrine' had to be 'modified … by the common law, wholly consistent with constitutional principle'.[63] Yet if it is the case that the courts are constitutionally entitled, under the guise of a variation in the common law, to amend unilaterally the conditions by which Parliament's ultimate legislative authority must be exercised, the doctrine of parliamentary sovereignty will have been replaced with one of judicial supremacy. The courts cannot claim to control Parliament's legislative sovereignty without extinguishing it. The judgment of Laws LJ in *Thoburn* thus has implications for the doctrine of parliamentary sovereignty far beyond the relationship between EU law and domestic law. If such judicial reconfiguration of parliamentary sovereignty is constitutionally permissible, then, as Elliott has argued:

> *Thoburn*'s modest modification of the doctrine, namely the disapplication of the principle of implied repeal to 'constitutional statutes', is potentially only a milestone on a much longer journey—which starts with the realization that legislative authority is a function of constitutional law, not a historical fact, and may ultimately arrive at a far more limited concept of law-making power.[64]

---

[60] ibid [66].
[61] ibid [66].
[62] ibid [64].
[63] ibid [59].
[64] Elliott, 'Parliamentary Sovereignty Under Pressure' (2004) n 51 above, 551.

The seemingly endless potential for the judicial limitation of legislative power which *Thoburn* suggests is welcomed by Elliott, who identified the case as marking 'the UK constitution's coming of age'.[65] Yet acceptance of a constructionist explanation for the domestic supremacy of EU law in the UK, and in particular that adopted by Laws LJ in *Thoburn*, must be seen as crucially serving to lay the foundations for common law constitutionalism. Whether such a development would be cause for celebration or concern depends on the normative appeal of common law constitutionalism, and because it is both undemocratic and imprecise, in my view the adoption of such a constitutional structure would be acutely unappealing.[66] Of perhaps greater importance for present purposes, however, is the empirical basis of common law constitutionalism, which was considered in detail in Chapter three, and found to be severely lacking, both historically, and from the perspective of legal precedent.[67] Not only, then, is the authority of *Thoburn* highly questionable in itself, when considered in light of *Factortame (No 2)*, but the common law constitutionalist architecture which the analysis of Laws LJ exploits means the decision is rooted in a disputed conception of the nature of the UK constitution.

It is possible to argue, however, that the strong line of established legal authority which demonstrates the courts' respect for the sovereign legislative authority of Parliament could now be under threat. Indeed, it might be suggested that a shift to common law constitutionalism is at present underway in the contemporary UK constitution—and *Thoburn* may be in the vanguard of this movement, in so far as the explanation of the supremacy of EU law which this case invokes offers the potential for a more comprehensive common law constitutionalism to emerge. However, for *Thoburn* to be even capable of serving such a purpose—setting aside the difficulties generated by its common law constitutionalist underpinning, with respect to the authority for, and the legitimacy of, the propositions invented in this case—it must be able to provide a satisfactory rationalisation of the substantive domestic supremacy of EU law. And, in relation to this point, it has been argued that *Thoburn* suffers from a further fundamental flaw: it misrepresents the nature of implied repeal, and the (non-)application of this doctrine to the ECA. In considering such claims in relation to *Thoburn*, we are provided with a starting point for an alternative approach to explaining the impact of the ECA on the doctrine of parliamentary sovereignty. This is based on the more minimalist notion, which can be defended in a number of ways, that the UK's membership of the EU has been effected as a matter of domestic constitutional law in such a way as to preserve the 'continuing' sovereignty of Parliament.

---

[65] M Elliott, 'Embracing "Constitutional" Legislation: Towards Fundamental Law?' (2003) 54 *Northern Ireland Law Quarterly* 25, 40.
[66] See chapter 3 of this volume, pp 137–49.
[67] ibid pp 131–37.

VI. 'CONTINUING' PARLIAMENTARY SOVEREIGNTY PRESERVED?

Adam Tomkins has argued that the view favoured by Laws LJ, that a common law adjustment of the doctrine of implied repeal has been effected to give domestic priority to EU law, is 'misconceived'.[68] According to Tomkins, the doctrine of implied repeal has a 'narrow application',[69] a view which is shared by Alison Young.[70] Relying on the leading case of *Ellen Street Estates v Minister of Health*,[71] Tomkins argues that '[f]or the court to hold that one statute impliedly repeals another, the two statutes must be "clearly inconsistent" and must each deal with the "same subject matter"'.[72] Applying this to the facts of the *Factortame* litigation, Tomkins maintains that the doctrine of implied repeal was 'irrelevant to the case'.[73] The Merchant Shipping Act 1988 was not incompatible with the ECA because they 'did not deal with the same subject-matter': 'one concerned fishing and the other concerned the legal relationship between the United Kingdom and the European Community. It is frankly preposterous to suggest that there could have been an issue of implied repeal here'.[74] The conclusion of Laws LJ in *Thoburn* that the principle of implied repeal had ceased to operate in relation to constitutional statutes was therefore unjustified—for no question of implied repeal actually arose in *Factortame (No 1)*—while also substantively incorrect as a matter of law. For, as Tomkins contends, 'Acts that deal with constitutional subjects can be impliedly repealed', but 'only by subsequent Acts that deal with the same, constitutional, subjects'.[75] Applying this principle to the ECA, Tomkins suggests:

> If Parliament were to re-legislate on the subject of the relationship between domestic and European Community law, and were to do so in a way that was inconsistent with the terms of the ECA 1972 without expressly repealing the 1972 provisions, then there is no reason why the courts would not hold that the later Act must be construed as having impliedly repealed the 1972 Act.[76]

The ECA thus could in appropriate, albeit 'unlikely', circumstances be impliedly repealed, and the constructionist analysis of Laws LJ, that the primacy of EU law is ensured by the special status at common law of the ECA, must be rejected.[77]

Support for the view that *Thoburn* misrepresents the true nature of the doctrine of implied repeal also comes from Young. Young reaches the same conclusion

---

[68] A Tomkins, *Public Law* (Oxford, Oxford University Press, 2003) 118.
[69] ibid 107.
[70] See AL Young, *Parliamentary Sovereignty and the Human Rights Act* (Oxford, Hart Publishing, 2009) 35–54.
[71] *Ellen Street Estates v Minister of Health* [1934] 1 KB 590.
[72] Tomkins, *Public Law* (2003) n 68 above, 107; quoting the words of Scrutton LJ and Maugham LJ in *Ellen Street Estates v Minister of Health* [1934] 1 KB 590, 595–96, 597.
[73] ibid 119.
[74] ibid 119.
[75] ibid 124.
[76] ibid 124.
[77] ibid 124.

as Tomkins—that no genuine question of implied repeal arose on the facts of *Factortame*—but disposes of *Thoburn* in a different way. Rather than rejecting the observations of Laws LJ outright, Young attempts to reinterpret the *Thoburn* argument about the status of constitutional Acts of Parliament to make it compatible with her overall conception of the doctrine of implied repeal. According to Young, the doctrine of implied repeal will only operate in exceptional circumstances, where statutory interpretation fails to reconcile seemingly inconsistent provisions.[78] Thus, Young maintains, albeit somewhat artificially given the unambiguous language used by Laws LJ, it is better to read *Thoburn* as making the 'more pragmatic claim' that '[a]lthough the doctrine of implied repeal applies in theory to constitutional statutes, it is rare for the doctrine to apply to constitutional statutes in practice'.[79] This is because the 'principles of interpretation that are used to ensure that the doctrine [of implied repeal] applies only where there is a contradiction between two statutory provisions apply even more forcefully when applied to constitutional statutes'.[80] Therefore, according to Young, the ECA had taken priority over the Merchant Shipping Act 1988 in *Factortame (No 1)* not because of a judicial alteration of the doctrine of implied repeal, but because, while seemingly contradictory, the two statutes in question were ultimately reconcilable. The Merchant Shipping Act 1988 was merely 'given its proper meaning in the context of the earlier statute', which 'removed the conflict between the two statutes, meaning in turn that the doctrine of implied repeal did not apply'.[81] According to Young, *Factortame (No 1)* 'involved an application of principles of interpretation and not the doctrine of implied repeal'.[82]

On Young's approach, then, as compared to that of Tomkins, the principle which *Thoburn* purports to establish may be salvageable, rather than fundamentally incorrect. Yet for this to be possible, it must be, in effect, distorted; radically reconstructing the principle from one which provides immunity from implied repeal for constitutional statutes, to one which provides a strong presumption against the implied repeal of constitutional statutes. Young's interpretation of *Thoburn* is nevertheless supported by Goldsworthy,[83] who rejects as 'novel' the claim made by Tomkins that implied repeal only operates in relation to statutes dealing with the same subject-matter.[84] Instead, for Goldsworthy, '[i]mplied repeal is triggered by inconsistency between norms, but if two norms deal with quite different subject-matters, it *may* be possible to interpret them so as to dispel a *prima facie* inconsistency'.[85] Yet if such an approach to implied repeal

---

[78] Young, *Parliamentary Sovereignty and the Human Rights Act* (2009) n 70 above, 36–38, 49.
[79] ibid 41.
[80] ibid 45.
[81] ibid 44.
[82] ibid 44.
[83] J Goldsworthy, *Parliamentary Sovereignty: Contemporary Debates* (Cambridge, Cambridge University Press, 2010) 313–14.
[84] ibid 291.
[85] ibid 293.

is combined with a strong presumption of statutory interpretation 'that some statutes are of such constitutional importance that Parliament is very unlikely to intend to meddle with them indirectly, as a side-effect of provisions dealing primarily with other matters',[86] then the difference in practice with the approach of Tomkins may be minimal. While it may, on this approach, be possible in principle for implied repeal to operate as between the ECA and legislation which concerns a different subject-matter, in practice, a subsequent statute which violates the substantive requirements of EU law (such as, for example, the Merchant Shipping Act 1988 in *Factortame*) should be construed so as *not* to repeal the ECA by implication. For, in light of the strong presumption that Parliament does not intend indirectly to interfere with constitutionally significant pre-existing legislative arrangements, such a statute will not be interpreted so as to evince the intention necessary to repeal by implication the ECA. Therefore, even if the general claim made by Tomkins as to the scope of the doctrine of implied repeal—that it only applies between statutes dealing with the same subject-matter—is not correct, the *Thoburn* analysis of the domestic primacy of EU law still appears to misrepresent the operation of the doctrine of implied repeal. The ECA is simply not immune from the doctrine of implied repeal: it *could* be repealed by implication by a subsequent statute dealing with precisely the same subject-matter,[87] and is *not* repealed by implication by a subsequent statute which violates the substantive requirements of EU law, because such legislation will not be construed so as to evince the intention necessary to effect such a repeal, rather than because the operation of the doctrine has been suspended. On this basis, when the insights of Tomkins, Young and Goldsworthy are combined, it seems clear that *Thoburn*, taken literally, as identifying a common law immunity preventing the implied repeal of constitutional statutes, cannot offer a coherent rationalisation of the domestic supremacy afforded to EU law in the UK constitution.

If the elaborate constructionist analysis of Laws LJ in *Thoburn* is thus inadequate even on its own terms, perhaps this suggests that it is possible to explain the domestic supremacy of EU law without embracing a common law constitutionalist rejection of parliamentary sovereignty. For the internal defects in the *Thoburn* analysis may indicate that an account of the domestic constitutional basis of EU law which does not depart drastically from established foundational principles may be available. Such an approach has been pursued by both Tomkins and Young. While these accounts differ in important ways, as did their critiques of *Thoburn*, both accept a core principle: the primacy which has been constitutionally afforded to EU law has not displaced the notion of legislative sovereignty. Yet while I will suggest that this core principle is correct, in light of the failure of both the revolutionary and the constructionist accounts, there are also difficulties with the specific reasoning employed by both Tomkins and Young. In particular,

---

[86] ibid 313.
[87] Ie a statute concerning the general constitutional basis of EU law in the UK.

both maintain that the supremacy of EU law can be reconciled with a conception of 'continuing' parliamentary sovereignty. In contrast, I will argue that a coherent reconciliation of parliamentary sovereignty and EU supremacy commits us to a reconfigured understanding of the notion of legally unlimited legislative power. In particular, the manner and form theory of parliamentary sovereignty must be embraced.

According to Tomkins 'the doctrine of legislative supremacy remains intact: any rumours pertaining to its death are, as the saying goes, premature'.[88] Two reasons are offered why this is so. First, Tomkins argues, 'it remains the case that under English law nobody has the power to override or set aside a statute'; it is only as a matter of EU law that Acts of Parliament can now be disapplied.[89] For Tomkins, there has been no change to parliamentary sovereignty because it is a doctrine of only one of the 'two legal systems operating in this country'.[90] This argument is, however, problematic. To view UK law and EU law as distinct legal systems operating within a single territory obscures the amalgamation of legal norms which has actually been produced. It seems much better, given the continuing existence of a single, although slightly altered, hierarchy of courts in which arguments about EU and domestic sources can be advanced concurrently, to view EU norms as having been assimilated into the legal system of the UK. But even beyond this, to remain legally sovereign, Parliament must possess a legislative authority which encompasses the norms of any alternative competing legal system that may emerge within its territorial jurisdiction. To characterise EU law as a separate legal system, operating in the UK, in which the doctrine of legislative supremacy is not recognised, does not therefore preserve the sovereignty of Parliament. Rather, the existence of an alternative legal system in which Parliament cannot intervene with impunity is a direct rebuttal of the legislature's claim to possess the power to be the ultimate arbiter of legality in the UK. Even if the EU is a distinct legal system operating within the UK, which is questionable, for Parliament to retain legislative sovereignty it must be a legal system in which Parliament is able to interfere definitively by legal means. When EU norms are recognised as supreme within the UK, this is clearly not the case. Thus, to view EU law as taking domestic effect in the UK as a discrete legal system does not appear to be a fruitful way to defend the continuing existence of the doctrine of parliamentary sovereignty.

The second reason offered by Tomkins to explain the preservation of legislative sovereignty is, however, much more compelling. 'There is nothing in *Factortame*', Tomkins contends, 'to suggest that Parliament cannot make a law that is contrary to Community law'.[91] There might, however, be 'difficulties' in having such a law 'effectively enforced'.[92] Given that the ECA instructs the courts that legislation

---

[88]   Tomkins, *Public Law* (2003) n 68 above, 120.
[89]   ibid 118.
[90]   ibid 118.
[91]   ibid 117.
[92]   ibid 117.

is to take effect subject to EU law, how could Parliament convey an intention to create a statute which was in violation of EU norms, but legally valid nonetheless? Tomkins suggests two ways in which this might be done, both of which have been encountered earlier in this chapter: full withdrawal from the EU and the repeal of the ECA; and the use in a specific statute of a '"notwithstanding" clause'.[93] According to Tomkins, such a 'notwithstanding' clause would provide that 'this Act shall be construed and have effect notwithstanding any provision to the contrary in either (a) the European Communities Act 1972 or (b) Community law'.[94] As I have argued above, in either of these situations—full withdrawal or the invocation of a 'notwithstanding' clause—the acceptance by the domestic courts of an explicit legislative instruction to disregard EU norms would be both likely, and more importantly, legally and constitutionally correct. But it is the implications of this which are most important here. Tomkins takes the existence of these two escape routes from EU supremacy to be evidence that the doctrine of legislative suprem-acy survives in the UK. In a sense, this is true. Parliament does ultimately still pos-sess the means to enact legislation which contradicts EU law. However, what this overlooks is that to make such a claim, an alternative conception of parliamentary sovereignty must be adopted; a conception of parliamentary sovereignty whereby Parliament can lawfully change the procedure for the enactment of valid legisla-tion. For, in enacting the ECA, this is exactly what Parliament has done.

This change of legislative procedure does not relate to the manner in which the ECA itself can be repealed or amended. The ECA can still be repealed or amended by express words in an Act of Parliament, as has been discussed above. Further, it now seems clear that the ECA could also be repealed by implication by a statute which purported to put in place new legal architecture conditioning the relationship between EU law and domestic law, without making any reference to the ECA itself. Parliament might, for example, legislate to provide that EU law would in future have effect in the UK in the same way that the rights protected in the ECHR have effect in the UK according to section 3 and section 4 of the Human Rights Act 1998; that is to say, that legislation should be interpreted to be compatible with EU law so far as it is possible to do so, and if this cannot be done, a declaration of incompatibility should be issued which does not affect the statute's continuing legal validity. Unlikely as it may be to occur, and setting aside the difficulties which would be generated as a matter of EU law (which would obtain in so far as such an alternative regime did not give effect to the supremacy of EU law, which, it seems clear, it would not), there is no principled reason why the domestic courts should refuse to accept the new statutory regime imposed under such circumstances.

If this is the case, the constitutional shift which has occurred to afford domestic primacy to EU norms has not therefore been a common law change *to* the status

[93] ibid 119–20.
[94] ibid 120.

of the ECA, contrary to the *Thoburn* analysis, but a change effected *by* the ECA. The ECA will not be impliedly repealed by a subsequent statute which substantively contradicts EU norms, not because of an alteration of the status of the ECA, but because the subsequent statute will be presumed not to repeal the ECA. Instead, in accordance with section 2(4) of the ECA, the subsequent statute will take effect subject to EU law, and thus be disapplied, unless it expressly provides otherwise. Specifically, this would require such a statute to include the kind of 'notwithstanding' clause outlined above by Tomkins, which explicitly stipulates that it shall not be subject to section 2(4) of the ECA. And this is the crucial constitutional change that has occurred in order to ensure that EU law takes priority over domestic law in the UK. Prior to the enactment of the ECA, Parliament could legislate in relation to subjects within the competence of the EU, such as, to take a now familiar example, the registration of fishing vessels, through the normal legislative process, and repeal by implication prior inconsistent statutory provisions. However, as a result of the enactment of the ECA, if Parliament is successfully to produce legislation which relates to, say, the registration of fishing vessels and which violates EU norms, express words must be used to indicate that this later statute is to have legal priority. In necessitating the addition of this formula, the ECA has changed the manner and form required to produce valid legislation which substantively contradicts EU law.[95]

If it is accepted that the manner and form required to produce valid legislation has been changed by the ECA, the consequences for the traditional understanding of parliamentary sovereignty would be grave, for according to the Diceyan conception of the doctrine, this is something that Parliament simply cannot do. It is thus a conclusion that defenders of Diceyan, or continuing, legislative sovereignty must strenuously avoid. Young acknowledges the force of the argument presented above, while nonetheless offering a 'modest defence' of continuing parliamentary supremacy.[96] In the course of examining the possibility of the interpretive obligation imposed on the courts in section 3(1) of the Human Rights Act 1998 being amended to mirror exactly the more demanding requirements of section 2(4) of the ECA, Young argues that '[a]lthough it may appear as if Parliament needs

---

[95] This conclusion has also been reached by Goldsworthy: see J Goldsworthy, *The Sovereignty of Parliament: History and Philosophy* (Oxford, Oxford University Press, 1999) 15, 244–45; Goldsworthy, *Parliamentary Sovereignty: Contemporary Debates* (2010) n 83 above, 287–98. However, as will be considered below, the basis of my argument that the ECA represents a change to the manner and form for future legislation differs from that of Goldsworthy, in so far as he suggests that this is a consequence of a change to the UK's rule of recognition, a position which I do not accept.

[96] Young, *Parliamentary Sovereignty and the Human Rights Act* (2009) n 70 above, 2. Although Young favours the terminology of 'continuing parliamentary supremacy', this is not to distinguish her understanding of the scope of Parliament's legislative authority from the orthodox position of Dicey, which she also suggests should properly be understood as a theory of supremacy, rather than sovereignty: see 163. See also the more recent discussion of this in AL Young, 'Parliamentary Sovereignty Re-defined' in R Rawlings, P Leyland and AL Young (eds), *Sovereignty and the Law: Domestic, European, and International Perspectives* (Oxford, Oxford University Press, 2013) 71–72, where Young maintains that her account of legislative supremacy does not challenge the 'old' Diceyan view of the doctrine, but provides a 'different justification for its adoption'.

to adopt a specific manner and form to overturn the modified section 3(1), this is not the case'.[97] Instead, what may appear to be a manner and form require-ment—in this case, that created by Young's hypothetical modified section 3(1), but also, therefore, by extension, that ostensibly created by section 2(4) of the ECA, the provision of which it is a direct replica—actually 'stems merely from the scope of the doctrine of implied repeal'.[98] On Young's approach, the requirement that express words must be used to indicate that an Act of Parliament which sub-stantively breaches EU law should nonetheless have full legal effect, regardless of section 2(4) of the ECA, derives from the fact that the operation of the doctrine of implied repeal has been effectively suspended. For, as has been discussed above, according to Young, an Act of Parliament which is substantively incompatible with EU norms does not impliedly repeal the ECA—and thus takes effect in a way which is *compatible* with EU law—because when it is interpreted in the light of section 2(4), the incompatibility with EU law, and thus the conflict between this seemingly 'incompatible' statute and the ECA, will be removed. Yet while the doctrine of implied repeal is, in these circumstances, rendered inapplicable by interpretation, it is not, Young maintains, inapplicable per se. Instead, on Young's approach, the '[i]mplied repeal [of section 2(4)] would also occur if Parliament were to enact legislation expressly stating that it was to take effect notwithstand-ing [EU law]'.[99] The use of express words in a notwithstanding clause is thus not a new requirement of manner and form, but merely the way in which Parliament must demonstrate that it genuinely intends that a substantive statute which con-tradicts EU law should impliedly repeal section 2(4) of the ECA, something which the operation of that section otherwise itself suspends. Parliament can therefore still be considered to possess continuing legislative supremacy, Young contends, for it has not been bound by its successors as to the manner and form required to produce valid legislation. Instead, Parliament can still impliedly repeal provisions like section 2(4) of the ECA, so long as it makes it abundantly clear that this is what it is aiming to do.

This is a powerful attempt to reconcile EU supremacy and the Diceyan concep-tion of parliamentary sovereignty. However, in my view, it cannot be correct that a requirement that express words be used in a statute which substantively violates EU law, to indicate that this legislation is to have full legal effect, contrary to sec-tion 2(4) of the ECA, derives from the scope of the doctrine of implied repeal. This is because if such a provision is included in an Act of Parliament which breaches EU norms, it cannot be considered to be an *implied* repeal of section 2(4) of the ECA. It is true that a statute which violates EU law will not be understood

---

[97] ibid 63.

[98] ibid 63.

[99] ibid, 59–60. Young makes this claim, repeated at 63, in direct relation to her hypothetical 'modified s 3(1)' of a potentially amended Human Rights Act. However, as noted above, given that this modified clause is a precise imitation of s 2(4) of the ECA, it must logically be the case that s 2(4) could be 'impliedly repealed' in the same way.

to repeal the ECA by implication if it does not contain an express indication to the contrary, for it will be presumed that such legislation is not intended to displace such a constitutionally significant pre-existing provision as section 2(4).[100] And that it does not function in these circumstances may be a consequence of the limits of the doctrine of implied repeal. But that the doctrine of implied repeal is not operative in such circumstances does not mean that when such a notwithstanding clause *is* used, the doctrine of implied repeal must be in operation. For if a statute which is substantively incompatible with the requirements of EU law contains a notwithstanding clause which makes express, direct reference to its legal superiority over the ECA, it will not be repealing section 2(4) by implication, but effecting a partial and particular *explicit* repeal of section 2(4). Such a repeal would be partial and particular because it would not entirely repeal section 2(4) of the ECA, but merely render it inapplicable in the future in relation to the specific subject-matter regulated by the statute containing the notwithstanding clause. Additionally, it would self-evidently be an explicit repeal because such a provision would have to make explicit reference to the fact that section 2(4) of the ECA would no longer operate with respect to the subject-matter of the statute.

Nothing short of such a partial and particular explicit repeal would suffice to ensure that a substantive statute would take effect untouched by section 2(4) of the ECA, due to the manner in which this provision operates. As Young notes, section 2(4) of the ECA has been given a special 'disjunctive' reading,[101] so that even where it is impossible for a piece of legislation to be 'construed' to make it compatible with EU norms, it will nonetheless still 'have effect' subject to EU law. The courts will therefore try to interpret the substantive provisions of a domestic statute in such a way as to be compatible with the requirements of EU law. Yet if such an interpretation cannot be achieved, that the statute contains provisions which violate EU law will not, in itself, be sufficient to evince an intention to repeal the ECA by implication, for the courts will presume that—absent an explicit indication to the contrary—no such intention exists. Instead, such a statute would clearly take effect subject to section 2(4), and be disapplied, as was established in the *Factortame* litigation itself.[102] As has been discussed above, the ECA is still susceptible to implied repeal, just not –because of the way section 2(4) is designed, and has been applied—in these circumstances. In relation to a clash between the ECA and a subsequent statute which is both incompatible with EU

---

[100] See text at nn 79–87.

[101] ibid 56.

[102] Incidentally, the actual outcome of the *Factortame* litigation calls into question Young's analysis of the case. The supposed incompatibility between s 2(4) of the ECA and the Merchant Shipping Act 1988 was not resolved, as Young maintains, through the judicial reinterpretation of the 1988 Act. Instead, the 1988 Act was disapplied by the House of Lords, and subsequently replaced by legislation which was compatible with EU law, in the form of the Merchant Shipping (Registration, etc) Act 1993 and the Merchant Shipping (Registration of Ships) Regulations 1993 (SI 1993/3138); see C Turpin and A Tomkins, *British Government and the Constitution*, 6th edn (Cambridge, Cambridge University Press, 2007) 330.

law, and silent as to whether it is intended to be definitively so, there is simply no space, in practice, in which the doctrine of implied repeal can operate. When we appreciate that the courts increasingly seek to limit the operation of the doctrine of implied repeal—holding that the presumption against implied repeal is strong given the high standard of modern legislative drafting,[103] and, in particular, that it is presumed that when legislating Parliament does not intend by implication to repeal existing law[104]—this is unsurprising. The effect of section 2(4) of the ECA, and the legislative action which would be required to violate EU law (short of withdrawal from the Union), must therefore be explained in another way. Section 2(4) must instead be seen as placing an ancillary requirement of manner and form on Parliament, and its successors, to enact valid legislation which is substantively incompatible with EU law. To suggest otherwise—that Parliament must use explicit language to effect an implied repeal—is a contradiction in terms.

VII. JUSTIFYING A MANNER AND FORM UNDERSTANDING OF THE ECA

I have argued above that, in relation to a specific set of circumstances, the ECA has changed the manner and form required to produce valid legislation. Given that this is a significant deviation from constitutional orthodoxy, further justification of this claim is required. The crucial problem with the manner and form reading of the ECA is that it is somewhat artificial. As Geoffrey Marshall has noted, a difficulty with the view I have advocated above 'is that the European Communities Act 1972 does not in terms make any such provision for amending the manner and form of legislation'.[105] The ECA does not overtly stipulate that there is to be a new manner and form for the enactment of valid legislation which is incompatible with EU law, nor does it specify that the novel procedural requirement is that express words must be used to indicate the inapplicability in particular circumstances of section 2(4). But while this is undoubtedly problematic, it is far from a decisive objection to a manner and form understanding of the ECA, for none of the explanations of the relationship between the doctrine of parliamentary sovereignty and EU law considered above derive support from the precise terms of the ECA itself. The ECA is an extremely confusing statute, which seems to have been drafted deliberately to obfuscate its impact on legislative sovereignty. Prior to the passage of the ECA, the Conservative government maintained that it would raise 'no question of any erosion of essential national sovereignty',[106] yet it is unclear how this assertion specifically relates to the status of the doctrine of parliamentary sovereignty. Further, as Danny Nicol has shown, during the promotion of the Bill that would become the ECA, the government failed to offer a consistent

---

[103] *Nwogbe v Nwogbe* [2000] 2 FLR 744, [19].
[104] *Henry Boot Construction (UK) Ltd v Malmaison Hotel (Manchester) Ltd* [2001] QB 388, 405.
[105] Marshall, 'Metric Measures and Martyrdom by Henry VIII Clause' (2002) n 56 above, 500.
[106] *The United Kingdom and the European Communities*, (Cmnd 4715, 1971) [29].

assessment of the impact of EU supremacy on parliamentary sovereignty, with the claims made by different ministers varying between, and even within, the House of Commons and the House of Lords.[107] Such uncertainty would seem to indicate that the silence of the ECA in relation to the doctrine of parliamentary sovereignty does not preclude the adoption of a manner and form understanding of the Act, simply because it is so ambiguous as to preclude very little. While more modern statutes, such as the Human Rights Act and the devolution legislation, contain provisions explicitly detailing how they are to fit into the existing constitutional order, and in particular, specifying how they are to be reconciled with parliamentary sovereignty, the absence of such terms in the ECA seems to be the result of minimalistic drafting designed to defer the comprehensive resolution of the difficult questions encountered above to a later date. While this is regrettable from the perspective of constitutional clarity, it is also understandable that the government of the day lacked the confidence to truly grapple with the implications of the UK's accession to the EU, given that, as Nicol notes, it was 'on virgin territory'.[108] Nonetheless, the ECA's evasion of the issue of legislative sovereignty must leave a manner and form reading of the statute firmly on the table.

The critical issue then is not whether the ECA provides direct textual evidence of an embrace of the manner and form theory of parliamentary sovereignty, but whether the effect of the ECA provides support for such an interpretation. Since the ECA left open the question of its impact on the doctrine of parliamentary sovereignty, the judgment of Lord Bridge in *Factortame (No 2)*, albeit very thin, is the most authoritative explication of the consequences of the domestic primacy of EU law. In my view, a manner and form reading of the ECA is the explanation which most coheres with the reasoning of Lord Bridge.[109] The overriding theme of Lord Bridge's brief excursion into the domain of constitutional principle in *Factortame (No 2)* was of the centrality of Parliament. Parliament, through the enactment of the ECA, was solely responsible for the domestic primacy of EU norms, and any change to its legislative power which had occurred as a result had been accepted voluntarily. The courts, according to Lord Bridge, had merely given effect to the will of the legislature, and there was nothing novel about this. The manner and form understanding of the ECA fits well with the reasoning of Lord Bridge because it, too, treats Parliament as the agent pivotally responsible for this constitutional shift. It is Parliament which has, on this argument, altered the manner and form which must be followed to produce valid legislation which is substantively incompatible with EU norms, and in so doing afforded domestic primacy to EU law.

---

[107] See D Nicol, *EC Membership and the Judicialization of British Politics* (Oxford, Oxford University Press, 2001) 114–16.

[108] ibid 115–16.

[109] This has also been suggested by Paul Craig, although this endorsement of a manner and form understanding of the ECA is relatively tentative: Craig, 'Sovereignty of the United Kingdom Parliament after *Factortame*' (1991) n 32 above, 252.

Indeed, according to a manner and form conception of legislative sovereignty, only Parliament possesses the power to modify the future legislative process. The courts, then, are required to be reactive, not proactive, as Lord Bridge readily appreciated. As a result, while as Nicol has demonstrated, in one sense it is 'highly questionable' whether, as Lord Bridge argued, parliamentarians could have voluntarily opted to give domestic primacy to EU law—given that the ECA's passage through Parliament was afflicted by significant uncertainty in relation to its likely constitutional impact[110]—in another sense a manner and form understanding of parliamentary sovereignty can explain how this *was* a voluntary act of the legislature. Parliament can be said to have accepted the domestic primacy of EU law voluntarily because it was not externally imposed by another institution— whether by the domestic courts, through an alteration of the rules of statutory construction, or by the EU itself, through the CJEU's principle of supremacy—but was established by the legislature through the enactment of the ECA.

Moreover, to conceive of the ECA as effecting a change to the manner and form required to produce legislation which substantively violates EU norms fundamentally preserves the sovereignty of Parliament, since the legislature retains its ultimate power to make or unmake any law. In this way, the change produced by the ECA is not novel, but consistent with fundamental constitutional doctrine. As John Eekelaar has noted, on this 'new' view of parliamentary sovereignty, 'legal acceptance of the re-allocation of legislative competence by section 2(4) of the European Communities Act 1972 for as long as the provision remains in force is implicit in existing constitutional theory, not a departure from it'.[111] An acceptance of this manner and form argument may involve a recalibration of our understanding of the scope of Parliament's legislative authority, but it does not require the laboured supposition of a revolutionary schism, or the surrender of ultimate constitutional authority to the judges. As it maintains both constitutional continuity and the predominance of Parliament, the manner and form interpretation of the effect of the ECA can thus be seen to offer the explanation of the means by which the domestic primacy of EU law has been assured which best fits with Lord Bridge's analysis of this change in *Factortame (No 2)*.

It is from this perspective that one element of Goldsworthy's endorsement of a manner and form interpretation of the effect of section 2(4) of the ECA requires further scrutiny. Goldsworthy's analysis of the ECA provides strong support for a manner and form reading of the ECA: 'Parliament, by enacting section 2(4) of the European Communities Act 1972, and the courts, by the way they have applied that section, have overturned the former assumption that Parliament cannot control the form in which future legislation is enacted'.[112] For Goldsworthy, this is not a limit on the sovereignty of Parliament: instead 'Parliament still retains ultimate legal sovereignty, even though the rules governing its exercise of that sovereignty

---

[110] Nicol, *EC Membership and the Judicialization of British Politics* (2001) n 107 above, 194.
[111] J Eekelaar, 'The Death of Parliamentary Sovereignty—A Comment' (1997) 113 *LQR* 185, 185.
[112] Goldsworthy, *The Sovereignty of Parliament: History and Philosophy* (1999) n 95 above, 244.

have changed'.[113] And although in his later work, Goldsworthy has also suggested that it may instead be possible to explain clashes between the ECA and subsequent legislation which violates EU law using techniques of statutory interpretation, he remains of the view that, if such interpretive explanations were seen to fail, we could still consider Parliament to have 'in effect subjected itself to a mild require-ment as to the form of future legislation, requiring that express words be used to override applicable EC laws'.[114] The difficulty with Goldsworthy's claim that section 2(4) has, in effect, changed the manner and form for future legislation, is what he understands to have caused this change. For Goldsworthy, this change of manner and form is the result of 'a change in official consensus changing the rule of recognition'.[115] This was necessary to enable Parliament to enact legislation changing the manner and form for future legislation because this theory of legally unlimited legislative authority 'has not so far been authoritatively accepted'.[116] And as such, the authority for the claim that the ECA has changed the manner and form for future legislation stems from the fact that this has been 'tacitly agreed' by 'Parliament and the courts'.[117]

Hart's theory of the rule of recognition was encountered in Chapter two, and there I suggested that, while it may be a conceptually useful tool to help us understand the necessarily non-legal basis of a fundamental constitutional norm like the doctrine of parliamentary sovereignty, attempts to engage this notion to explain practical change to the UK constitution may become problematic.[118] This is the first of a number of examples which will be encountered in Part II of this book of the difficulties that may be caused when seeking to explain change to the doctrine of parliamentary sovereignty as change to the rule of recogni-tion.[119] Goldsworthy's use of the rule of recognition in the context of the ECA can be objected to on two grounds. First, it is unnecessary; the notion that the effect of section 2(4) of the ECA is to create a new manner and form for future legislation does not need to be underpinned by a change in official consensus such as to constitute a shift in the UK's rule of recognition. While Goldsworthy is right that the manner and form theory of parliamentary sovereignty is yet to be explicitly accepted in the UK, as I argued in Chapter two, it is an understanding of parliamentary sovereignty which it remains entirely open to us to adopt. As the manner and form theory is a reconfiguration of the idea of legally unlimited legislative authority—rather than an entirely novel constitutional principle—a shift to this understanding of parliamentary sovereignty can be achieved without a change in official consensus. Instead, we are simply developing our view of the

---

[113] ibid 244.
[114] Goldsworthy, *Parliamentary Sovereignty: Contemporary Debates* (2010) n 83 above, 298.
[115] Goldsworthy, *The Sovereignty of Parliament: History and Philosophy* (1999) n 95 above, 244–45.
[116] Goldsworthy, *Parliamentary Sovereignty: Contemporary Debates* (2010) n 83 above, 139.
[117] Goldsworthy, *The Sovereignty of Parliament: History and Philosophy* (1999) n 95 above, 245.
[118] See chapter 2 of this volume, pp 79–83.
[119] See also chapter 5 of this volume, pp 218–22; chapter 6 of this volume, pp 273–75.

implications of a doctrine which is already accepted as the fundamental norm of the UK constitution. The overarching constitutional authority of the doctrine of parliamentary sovereignty is left unchanged by acceptance of the manner and form conception of this notion; rather, the shift is in our understanding of the (extended) scope of the idea of legally unlimited legislative authority, to which we are already collectively committed. Parliament has the legal authority to enact section 2(4) of the ECA, and alter the manner and form for future legislation, because it possesses legislative sovereignty, rather than because of a change in official consensus.

Of course, when there *is* a clear official consensus that such action is within the scope of Parliament's legislative power—as it seems clear that there is, in relation to the enactment of section 2(4) of the ECA—it may seem unimportant whether the authority for the change derives from the fact of Parliament's sovereignty, or from a shift in the rule of recognition. But where there is a lack of any official consensus as to the permissibility of a particular exercise of legislative authority, or even ongoing disputes about the scope of Parliament's law-making power, the distinction will be crucial. For, if change to the sovereignty of Parliament occurs at the level of the rule of recognition, there may simply be no answers until a consensus forms, and a pattern of behaviour is established. However, if we look instead to the legal doctrine of parliamentary sovereignty to resolve, at least initially, questions as to the proper scope of legislative authority, definitive answers reached through the application of existing constitutional principles can at least be more clearly identified and debated. We will see, in Chapters five and six, such difficulties manifested in practice, in debates about the possibility of the judicial limitation of Parliament's legislative sovereignty, and the legal validity of statutory referendum requirements, both of which are much more contested topics than is the (much more clearly established) domestic constitutional status of EU law. Yet the notion that change to the sovereignty of Parliament must proceed on the basis of shifts in extra-legal consensus also presents a further difficulty which is evident even in this context, where the existence of official consensus is not actively in dispute. This relates to the institutions involved in the forming of an official consensus, and is the second ground on which we can object to Goldsworthy's particular manner and form reading of the ECA.

The second difficulty with Goldsworthy's account is that, in suggesting that Parliament's authority to alter the manner and form for future legislation depends on a change in official consensus, which is formed in effect between the legislature and the courts, it affords a prominent, and more active, role to the judiciary in the process of establishing the scope of legislative power. Of course, this is still not a definitive role of the kind attributed to the courts by the constructionist interpretation of the ECA, or of the common law constitutionalism into which such an approach ultimately collapses. Yet it is one which goes beyond seeing the courts as merely *recognising* the implications of the doctrine of parliamentary sovereignty, to one in which the courts play a significant role in *determining* the scope of Parliament's law-making power. While this does not inherently represent a challenge to parliamentary sovereignty[120]—for in contributing to the formation or alteration of a rule of recognition the judiciary would be operating in a non-legal capacity—it may be normatively objectionable to afford to non-democratic actors a potentially decisive role in the development of fundamental constitutional doctrines, especially when it is not necessary to do so. For, as I have argued above, we do not need to ground Parliament's authority to legislate to change the manner and form in a changing official consensus: instead, it can be explained exclusively by reference to the implications of the legal doctrine of parliamentary sovereignty. Moreover, to conceive of the courts as playing this role also jars with the analysis of Lord Bridge in *Factortame (No 2)*, both in so far as it identifies Parliament as the agent of change, with the courts simply reacting to the legislative instructions they have received, and also in the affirmation of constitutional continuity that this represents. The notion that a shift to the manner and form theory of parliamentary sovereignty has been underpinned by a shift in official consensus should therefore be rejected. It is unnecessary to suppose that such a shift must have occurred, and further—in the specific context of the effect of section 2(4) of the ECA—such an account of the basis for this constitutional change does not fit as well with the judicial explanation of their role as a more straightforward manner and form analysis. This is one which simply asserts that the courts have, in relation to the ECA, accepted a legislative instruction from Parliament, the legality of which is sufficiently justified when we adopt a manner and form conception of the doctrine of parliamentary sovereignty.

Finally, in addition to offering the best explanation of actual constitutional practice, there is one further advantage which justifies a manner and form reading of the ECA. The reconciliation of EU supremacy and parliamentary sovereignty which it offers also provides a clear legal rationale, beyond mere realpolitik, for the existence of Parliament's power to violate specific EU norms by including express words in particular statutes, without having to effect a full withdrawal from the EU. To this point, Parliament's retention of such a power has been largely assumed on the basis that in such circumstances it would, and indeed should, be politically necessary for the courts to maintain an ultimate allegiance to the domestic, rather than European, institutions of government. While it seems undeniable that Parliament retains the legislative authority to repeal the ECA outright, and withdraw from the EU, whether it also has, at least as a matter of domestic law, the legal power to simply violate EU law without departing from the Union is less obvious. Yet, if a manner and form conception of parliamentary sovereignty is adopted, a legal basis for the existence of this power can be seen to emerge. On its face, the ECA might appear to place an absolute, substantive limit on Parliament's prospective legislative power, as section 2(4) provides that '*any* enactment passed

---

[120] Although for a contrary view, see the analysis in A Tucker, 'Uncertainty in the Rule of Recognition and in the Doctrine of Parliamentary Sovereignty' (2011) 31 *OJLS* 61, which uses the potential for indeterminacy in a rule of recognition to, in effect, make parliamentary sovereignty a conceptual impossibility.

or to be passed ... shall be construed and have effect' subject to EU law (emphasis added). In accordance with the doctrine of parliamentary sovereignty, of course, absolute limits cannot be placed on the legislative power of Parliament. Yet, when the manner and form theory of the doctrine is adopted, we can view the effect of section 2(4) in a new light. Rather than taking section 2(4) to be a limit on Parliament's ongoing legislative authority, at least while on the statute book, or even rejecting it as entirely ineffective, it must instead be read as merely placing a procedural limitation on the legislature's law-making authority. To take this step, and see that it is necessary to understand section 2(4) of the ECA as offering legal priority to EU law, except where the legislature uses explicit language to indicate the contrary, thus unites the basic intuitive argument in favour of the efficacy of express 'notwithstanding clauses' with a justification founded on legal principle.

This is a legal justification which, crucially, makes the effect of section 2(4) reasonably straightforward to understand and articulate, offsetting the complexity of the language contained in the provision. For in explicitly embracing the manner and form theory we are provided with a conception of legal sovereignty which treats the possibility that Parliament might modify the future law-making process not as an exception, aberration or device deployed simply to evade fundamental tensions, but as an entirely legitimate exercise of legislative authority. That the implicit effect of section 2(4) has been to alter the future legislative process is not, therefore, something that must be suppressed or denied, for, rather than being anomalous, it can be seen as entirely consistent with the broader constitutional framework organised around the doctrine of parliamentary sovereignty. As such, the manner and form theory provides us with the ability to develop a legally coherent account of the domestic constitutional basis of EU law which reconciles parliamentary sovereignty and EU supremacy, while also obtaining a clear picture of the precise extent, and thus the limits, of the reconciliation which has been achieved.

VIII. *THOBURN'S* SHADOW

There is one final issue to consider in this chapter. While I have rejected the revolutionary, constructionist and 'continuing' sovereignty accounts of the domestic constitutional basis of EU law, and sought to defend a manner and form explanation of the effect of the ECA as the best available, debate about the status of EU law in the UK is ongoing. In particular, while I have challenged the constructionist account in general, and the specific manifestation of this approach which was outlined by Laws LJ in *Thoburn*, discussion of this case continues to animate constitutional law in the UK. While I have criticised the sheer novelty of the analysis advanced in *Thoburn*—in particular, the claim that a distinction can be drawn at common law between constitutional and ordinary statutes, the former being immune from the operation of the doctrine of implied repeal—that this case purports to effect a dramatic paradigm shift is most likely the reason it continues to attract significant attention. And regardless of the flaws of the *Thoburn* analysis—the lack of authority possessed by the courts to cultivate a distinction between ordinary and constitutional legislation; the incompatibility with *Factortame (No 2)*; the misrepresentation of the operation of the doctrine of implied repeal—it is possible that sustained interest in the case could lead to it being ultimately endorsed. What, then, has been the judicial reaction to *Thoburn*? Is the account of the domestic constitutional basis of EU law which it offers in the process of becoming authoritative?

The notion that there may exist a category of constitutional statutes which, by that very status, are entitled to some form of special legal recognition has been most explored in the UK in the context of devolution. In *Robinson v Secretary of State for Northern Ireland*[121] the question of the interpretation of the Northern Ireland Act 1998 was in issue, with respect to the consequences of exceeding statutory time-limits for the election of a First Minister and Deputy First Minister by the Northern Ireland Assembly. Lord Bingham, in a majority of three, held this statute was 'in effect a constitution' and was therefore to be 'interpreted generously and purposively'.[122] Yet this principle was used to controversial effect in the House of Lords in *Robinson*, with the dissenting Lord Hutton, in a minority of two, claiming that the approach of the majority was, in effect, using the political objectives of devolution in Northern Ireland to 'alter the meaning' of the statutory words.[123] The question of whether the devolution statutes were constitutional legislation which ought to be interpreted more generously than ordinary legislation was subsequently revisited by the Supreme Court in *Imperial Tobacco Ltd v Lord Advocate*,[124] a challenge to the competence of the Scottish Parliament to enact legislation restricting the display of tobacco products. While this substantive challenge was ultimately rejected, Lord Hope, giving the judgment of the court, moved to address the uncertainty which, post-*Robinson*, had been raised in argument, especially in the Court of Session, as to 'whether a different approach should be taken to the interpretation of the [Scotland Act 1998] from that applicable to other statutes because it was said to be a constitutional instrument'.[125] For Lord Hope, 'the description of the Act as a constitutional statute cannot be taken, in itself, to be a guide to its interpretation. The statute must be interpreted like any other statute'.[126] As such, legislation—whether 'constitutional' or otherwise—should be 'construed according to the ordinary meaning of the words used',[127] with regard had to the purpose of the statute 'if help is needed as to what the words actually mean'.[128] The Supreme Court in *Imperial Tobacco* therefore seems

---

[121] *Robinson v Secretary of State for Northern Ireland* [2002] UKHL 32; [2002] NI 390.
[122] ibid [11].
[123] ibid [61].
[124] *Imperial Tobacco Ltd v Lord Advocate* [2012] UKSC 61; 2013 SC (UKSC) 153.
[125] ibid [10].
[126] ibid [15].
[127] ibid [14].
[128] ibid [15].

to quash the idea that a statute might be designated as constitutional, and attract on that basis an approach to its interpretation which differs from that applicable to other legislation. In this sense, we might see the general idea that there exists a category of constitutional statutes, which obtain from this status some kind of special treatment as compared to ordinary legislation, as one which has failed to gain traction in the period following *Thoburn*.

However, there have also been some recent indications to the contrary from the Supreme Court, which suggest that the basic principle identified in *Thoburn*— that there is a legally significant distinction between constitutional and ordinary legislation—might be acquiring weight. Also in the context of devolution, for example, in *H v Lord Advocate*,[129] Lord Hope suggested that 'the fundamental constitutional nature of the settlement that was achieved by the Scotland Act ... must be held to render it incapable of being altered otherwise than by an express enactment'.[130] It is not at all clear how this fits with the subsequent judgment of the Supreme Court (also delivered by Lord Hope) in *Imperial Tobacco*, for *H v Lord Advocate* was not mentioned in the later case. While, as Perry and Ahmed observe, the comments of Lord Hope in *H v Lord Advocate* are obiter dictum, there is clearly a significant affinity between them and the analysis of Laws LJ in *Thoburn*.[131] Yet *Thoburn* is not cited by Lord Hope in *H v Lord Advocate*, and therefore it is impossible to discern whether he intended to endorse the general principle outlined by Laws LJ—that constitutional legislation is immune to implied repeal—or whether this observation, which is in any event not binding, is limited to the devolution statutes in particular. There is thus considerable inconsistency in this area, with on the one hand 'constitutional' legislation clearly not to be interpreted in a way which differs from ordinary legislation, which contrasts with the limited, and not authoritative, suggestions on the other hand that some such 'constitutional' legislation—whatever that may encompass—*may* not be subject to the doctrine of implied repeal.

The contemporary uncertainty about the existence and implications of a category of constitutional statutes, arising principally in the context of devolution, has also been further exacerbated by a recent decision of the Supreme Court in the context of the topic under direct consideration in this chapter—the constitutional basis of the UK's membership of the EU. In *R (HS2 Action Alliance Ltd) v Secretary of State for Transport*,[132] two challenges were brought using EU law to the government's decision to promote a high-speed rail link ('HS2') between London and various cities in the north of England. It was argued, first, that in accordance with the Strategic Environmental Assessment Directive (SEA),[133] a strategic

---

[129] *H v Lord Advocate* [2012] UKSC 24; [2013] 1 AC 413.

[130] ibid [30].

[131] A Perry and F Ahmed, 'Are Constitutional Statutes "Quasi-Entrenched"?' *UK Constitutional Law Blog* (25 November 2013): www.ukconstitutionallaw.org/blog.

[132] *R (on the application of HS2 Action Alliance Ltd) v Secretary of State for Transport* [2014] UKSC 3, [2014] 1 WLR 324.

[133] Directive 2001/42/EC.

impact assessment ought to have been conducted prior to the government's announcement of its decision in a command paper,[134] and, secondly, that contrary to the Environmental Impact Assessment Directive (EIA),[135] the hybrid Bill procedure, by which Parliament would be asked to provide legal authorisation for the HS2 project, did not provide sufficient opportunities for effective public participation in the decision-making process. Both challenges were rejected by the Supreme Court, with Lords Neuberger and Mance issuing a notable joint judgment (with which all the Justices of the Supreme Court agreed) criticising in strident terms the CJEU for having interpreted both Directives in ways which were contrary to the ordinary meaning of the language used[136] and therefore 'problematic'.[137] Yet while the Supreme Court overtly challenging the interpretative approach of the CJEU raises interesting issues as to the certainty with which the effect of EU law in the UK can be established, and the relationship between the national and European courts,[138] of primary importance in *HS2* were comments made as to the domestic constitutional basis of EU law. For, in relation to the second challenge in particular, it was argued that the EIA should be interpreted in such a way as to require the UK courts to inquire into debates occurring in both Houses of Parliament, and 'to take the step of scrutinising the likely adequacy or otherwise of their procedures and debates'.[139] While the Supreme Court held this interpretation of the EIA was not persuasive, and that there was no indication that the hybrid Bill procedure would be in any way deficient so as to inhibit effective public participation in the decision-making process,[140] the very prospect of such judicial scrutiny of the legislature being potentially required—something which it is perhaps more difficult confidently to dismiss in light of the uncertainty as to how the CJEU might interpret the otherwise clear language contained in the EIA—prompted consideration by the Supreme Court of whether such conduct could ever be envisaged as constitutionally permissible in the UK.

The key difficulty raised by the notion of judicial scrutiny of the legislative process is that it would violate an element of the fundamental principle of parliamentary privilege, by which debates or proceedings in Parliament are not to be impeached or questioned in any court.[141] For Lord Reed, the question potentially raised by this prospect was whether parliamentary privilege 'may have been

---

[134] *High Speed Rail: Investing in Britain's Future—Decisions and Next Steps*, (Cm 8247, 2012).

[135] Directive 2011/92/EU.

[136] *R (HS2 Action Alliance Ltd) v Secretary of State for Transport* [2014] UKSC 3, [2014] 1 WLR 324, [175]–[196].

[137] ibid [158].

[138] See especially, ibid [170]–[174]. See further A Tomkins, 'The Supreme Court's Welcome Attack on the Court of Justice', *British Government and the Constitution: Book Updates and News* (23 January 2014): www.britgovcon.wordpress.com/2014/01/23/the-supreme-courts-welcome-attack-on-the-court-of-justice.

[139] ibid [200].

[140] ibid [98]–[116].

[141] Bill of Rights 1688, Article 9.

implicitly qualified or abrogated by the European Communities Act 1972'.[142] This question, however, 'cannot be resolved simply by applying the doctrine developed by the Court of Justice of the supremacy of EU law, since the application of that doctrine in our law depends upon the [ECA] 1972'.[143] Instead, in the event it were to transpire, 'a conflict between a constitutional principle, such as that embodied in article 9 of the Bill of Rights, and EU law' would have to be 'resolved by our courts as an issue arising under the constitutional law of the United Kingdom'.[144] But what might that resolution be? An answer is suggested by Lords Neuberger and Mance:

> The United Kingdom has no written constitution, but we have a number of constitutional instruments. They include Magna Carta, the Petition of Right 1628, the Bill of Rights and (in Scotland) the Claim of Rights Act 1689, the Act of Settlement 1701 and the Act of Union 1707. The European Communities Act 1972, the Human Rights Act 1998 and the Constitutional Reform Act 2005 may now be added to this list. The common law itself also recognises certain principles as fundamental to the rule of law. It is, putting the point at its lowest, certainly arguable (and it is for United Kingdom law and courts to determine) that there may be fundamental principles, whether contained in other constitutional instruments or recognised at common law, of which Parliament when it enacted the European Communities Act 1972 did not either contemplate or authorise the abrogation.[145]

While no view is expressed by Lords Neuberger and Mance as to whether parliamentary privilege would be classified as such a fundamental principle,[146] what is important here is the broader framework which they purport to establish. The reasoning employed echoes, to a significant extent, that of Laws LJ in *Thoburn*: sources deemed to be of constitutional status are identified, with it then suggested that, on this basis, they might be entitled to some special legal treatment. In *HS2* that special legal treatment is not immunity from implied repeal, as was asserted in *Thoburn*, but immunity from implicit displacement by EU law. While in this respect, the claims made in *HS2* are narrower than those made in *Thoburn*, in an alternative sense they are broader: whereas *Thoburn* was only concerned with constitutional statutes, the vision of UK constitutional order expounded in *HS2* encompasses both legislative instruments and fundamental principles. And the close nexus between the comments of Lords Neuberger and Mance in *HS2* and Laws LJ in *Thoburn* is confirmed in the complementary observations made by the judges in the former case about the analysis developed in the latter; *Thoburn* is described in *HS2* as offering a 'penetrating discussion' which contains '[i]mportant insights into potential issues in this area'.[147]

---

[142] *R (HS2 Action Alliance Ltd) v Secretary of State for Transport* [2014] UKSC 3, [2014] 1 WLR 324, [78].

[143] ibid [79].

[144] ibid [79].

[145] ibid [207].

[146] ibid [208].

[147] ibid [208].

There, are, however, two problems with the suggestions made, which are clearly obiter, in *HS2*. First, while Lord Reed is surely correct to maintain that a clash between a fundamental constitutional principle and EU law would be resolved in accordance with UK constitutional law, it is far from clear that this should not be done by reference to the principle of the supremacy of EU law. The principle of EU supremacy is not one which is alien to UK constitutional law, but instead, one which has domestic effect in UK by virtue of section 2(4) of the ECA. For the notion of the supremacy of EU law is implicit in the instruction which Parliament, via the ECA, has given to the UK courts to give effect to EU law over contrary domestic norms. And while, as has been discussed at length in this chapter, the legislative sovereignty of Parliament—and in particular, the manner and form conception of this doctrine—indicates that this instruction can be revoked, either entirely or in relation to particular issues, this can only be achieved by further legislation. It is, of course, entirely understandable that the UK courts do not want to become embroiled in assessing the calibre of parliamentary debate, and that, indeed, '[t]hese are not matters which are apt for judicial supervision'.[148] However, in questioning the general force of the principle of the supremacy of EU law in the UK, the Supreme Court may be indirectly challenging the sovereignty of Parliament, for it is on this authority that EU law obtains its domestic applicability. That this is the ultimate effect of the judicial questioning of the supremacy principle must be appreciated. The idea that the courts might consider reading limits into ECA—even where their intention is to avoid being engaged in challenges to 'the whole legitimacy of Parliamentary democracy as it presently operates'[149]—should therefore be approached with great caution, for to do so would be to exceed their constitutional authority. And in relation to this specific problem foreshadowed in *HS2*, in the unlikely event it actually arises, alternative solutions can be imagined—in particular, the courts might usefully deploy the concept of non-justiciability to avoid hearing a challenge which could violate parliamentary privilege, and thus focus on the limitations on what can be appropriately dealt with through the judicial process, rather than any supposed limitations on Parliament's legally unlimited legislative power. Alternatively, the worst-case scenario considered in *HS2* might be seen an example of the kind of circumstances in which the power of Parliament to legislate to exclude the application of EU law in relation to particular matters, without repudiating membership of the union—the existence of which has been justified at length in this chapter—could fall to be exercised.

Secondly, the reasoning employed in *HS2*, in common with that seen in *Thoburn*, may contain a broader threat to the doctrine of parliamentary sovereignty. For any legal framework which purports to offer enhanced protection of some kind to sources identified as 'constitutional', whether legislative instruments

---

[148] ibid [109].
[149] ibid [210].

or fundamental principles, must be for the sovereign Parliament to establish, rather than something which can be the subject of a sudden common law discovery. Of course, the scheme here sketched by Lords Neuberger and Mance seems principally to aim to promote the integrity of domestic constitutional fundamentals, and ensure they are not readily overridden by EU law (although, as considered immediately above, it is problematic to conceive of this as a clash between national and EU law, rather than as between national law and the doctrine of UK constitutional law from which EU law derives its domestic authority). Yet how far is it to travel from the claim that Parliament *did not* authorise the abrogation of fundamental constitutional values in this context, to a claim that Parliament *cannot* authorise abrogation of fundamental constitutional values in this, or any other, context? As we have seen in relation to the devolution statutes, it is possible that there could be multiple forms of legal protection for constitutional sources, which, given the fluidity of common law reasoning, could evolve and increase in intensity over time.[150] As such, what might be seen as judicial efforts to constitutionalise the UK constitution,[151] evident in *Thoburn*, and now *HS2*, could eventually, if accepted, leave no place for doctrine of parliamentary sovereignty, to which any such constitutional scheme would otherwise be vulnerable. Consequently, the constitutional order unveiled in *HS2* can be seen as an, admittedly less aggressive, variation of the common law constitutionalist theme. And, as a result, while still tentative and embryonic, the *HS2* scheme can be seen to suffer from the same deficiencies as common law constitutionalism—it is an undemocratic and imprecise basis on which to reorganise the UK's constitutional architecture.

Where does this leave *Thoburn*? Is the account of the domestic constitutional basis of EU law there offered by Laws LJ becoming authoritative, almost by proxy? Significantly, given the obvious sympathy of Lords Neuberger and Mance towards the general approach pursued by Laws LJ, *Thoburn* was not endorsed in *HS2*. We have seen suggestions that *Thoburn* might have identified a principle of broader relevance in *H v Lord Advocate*, but, again, the decision was not explicitly endorsed, with the comments of Lord Hope only obiter dicta, and limited to the context of devolution. There are also real questions about the compatibility of what was suggested obiter in *H v Lord Advocate* with the Supreme Court much more definitively distancing itself from the idea that designation as a constitutional statute might be legally significant elsewhere in the context of devolution, in *Imperial Tobacco*. It might therefore be that the true influence of *Thoburn* is not with respect to its specific explanation of the domestic constitutional basis of EU law, which we have no new reasons to accept as authoritative, and many existing

---

[150] Moreover, as will be discussed in chapter 5, in the context of the devolution, at the same time the courts have been exploring the implications of these statutes being 'constitutional legislation', they have also been establishing common law limits on the law-making competence of the devolved legislatures: see, esp *Axa General Insurance Ltd v Lord Advocate* [2011] UKSC 46, [2012] 1 AC 868.

[151] For a similar description of the effect of *HS2*, but framing an analysis which welcomes the developments which I have criticised, see P Craig, 'Constitutionalising Constitutional Law: HS2' [2014] *PL* 373, 382–92.

reasons not to accept. Instead, the significance of *Thoburn* might be that it has been thematically influential, inspiring increased engagement with reasoning, doctrines and techniques emblematic of common law constitutionalism. Whether *Thoburn* has or has not been a contributing factor in such a shift in judicial tone, it seems clear that such a change in emphasis is occurring; comparing, for example, the lack of confidence of the House of Lords in (barely) addressing issues of first order constitutional principle in *Factortame (No 2)*, with the approach of the Supreme Court in *HS2*, reveals dramatic differences.

To view *Thoburn* in this way, we can see very clearly that *how* we explain the specific issue of concern in this chapter has broader constitutional implications. Some might suggest that to establish precisely the domestic constitutional basis of EU law is, ultimately, an academic matter. As Allan, for example, has maintained, if

[f]or all practical purposes ... the sovereignty of Parliament has been curtailed during continued membership of the European Community ... it is likely to be of little importance, in practice, whether or not we treat this as the consequence merely of a rule of construction of statutes.[152]

If there is broad agreement about the impact that the ECA has had on Parliament's legislative power, and broad agreement about the action that Parliament could take to avoid the effects of the ECA, then does the theoretical basis of the change actually make a difference? Or is it just a case of splitting hairs when maintaining, for example, that a manner and form reading of the ECA is preferable to a constructionist interpretation of the Act?[153] Once it is recognised, however, that the principled foundation for the domestic supremacy of EU law has important implications for the doctrine of parliamentary sovereignty which go well beyond the constitutional relationship between national and European legal norms, it becomes clear that the nature of this foundation must be fully illuminated and understood.

For as *Thoburn* and the subsequent case law that it appears to have informed demonstrate, the impact of the UK's membership of the EU on Parliament's legislative authority has the potential to be used as a springboard for a more extensive challenge to the notion of legal sovereignty. Allan, for example, has argued openly that

[i]f it is possible to recognise limits on the power of Parliament to enact legislation which conflicts with European Community law ... it is equally possible to countenance other limits on parliamentary sovereignty which reflect the demands of constitutional principle.[154]

---

[152] Allan, 'Parliamentary Sovereignty: Law, Politics and Revolution' (1997) n 33 above, 447.

[153] The revolutionary interpretation of the effect of the ECA is set aside here, because it deviates from both the constructionist and the manner and form approach in so far as it (i) posits a break in constitutional continuity, with the exact nature of the constitution post-ECA not being made clear, and seemingly treated as of less significance than the bare fact that such a break has been experienced; and (ii) offers little prescription as to how the effects of the ECA could be, in future, avoided.

[154] Allan, 'Parliamentary Sovereignty: Law, Politics and Revolution' (1997) n 33 above, 448.

Similarly, Craig has noted that

> [a]t the very least it can be said that the fact that the courts have been willing to acknowledge some shift in the traditional picture of sovereignty in the context of the EEC, renders it more likely that they will be willing to accept a limitation of sovereignty in other areas.[155]

If Parliament has sacrificed its legal sovereignty as a result of the UK's accession to the EU, the potential might exist for additional limits to be placed on Parliament's legislative authority. Common law constitutionalist arguments can thus 'piggyback' on the constitutional changes brought about by the UK's membership of the EU in a bid to substantiate their otherwise merely normative contentions. Furthermore—given the significance of the difficulties which the domestic supremacy of EU law ostensibly poses for the sovereignty of Parliament—this could be a key component in a composite challenge to the doctrine, which might draw on a range of inter-secting changes in constitutional law and practice to develop an overall revision-ist narrative, along the lines set out in Chapter three, which rejects the notion of legally unlimited legislative authority in the UK.[156] Both of these techniques, 'piggybacking' and the cultivation of a composite challenge, are exhibited in some of the remarkable judicial claims made in the seminal case of *R (on the application of Jackson) v Attorney General*,[157] which we turn to consider in the next chapter. However, if, as I have argued in this chapter, the doctrine of parliamentary sover-eignty does not have to be abandoned in light of the domestic supremacy of EU law, then such piggybacking, or a composite challenge of which this is the central element, will necessarily be ineffective, and the claims of common law constitu-tionalism must be grounded elsewhere. Indeed, I will argue that, as such, *Jackson* should not be seen as a watershed for the doctrine of parliamentary sovereignty, but rather that it provides further compelling evidence, which can be added to that uncovered in this chapter, of a shift to the manner and form understanding of legally unlimited legislative authority in the contemporary UK constitution.

IX. CONCLUSION

The stable relationship which has been established in UK constitutional practice between EU law and domestic law has not required the doctrine of parliamen-tary sovereignty to be abandoned. Instead, the demands of membership of the EU, and in particular, the domestic supremacy which must be afforded to EU law, have been complied with as a result of the exercise of sovereign legislative authority by the UK Parliament. Further, the conditions under which domestic supremacy has been afforded to EU law—at least, those conditions which obtain

---

[155] Craig, 'Sovereignty of the United Kingdom Parliament after *Factortame*' (1991) n 32 above, 253.
[156] See chapter 3 of this volume, pp 126–49.
[157] *R (on the application of Jackson) v Attorney General* [2005] UKHL 56, [2006] 1 AC 262.

as a matter of UK constitutional law—are compatible with, and indeed, a direct consequence of, the ongoing fact of Parliament's legislative sovereignty. Yet, to be able to make these claims we must move beyond the Diceyan conception of the doctrine. In particular, to justify as a matter of law the existence of Parliament's continuing power not only to enact legislation effecting the UK's withdrawal from the EU, but also to legislate in such a way as to violate specific EU norms while remaining (at least potentially) in the Union, the manner and form theory of parliamentary sovereignty must be adopted. For in enacting section 2(4) of the ECA, Parliament has—in effect—altered the future manner and form for the enactment of legislation which substantively contravenes EU law; to be valid, as a matter of domestic law, such legislation would need explicitly to displace the operation of section 2(4), expressly effecting a partial repeal of this provision of the ECA, which was particular to the subject-matter of the statute in question.

But it is crucial to recognise that a shift away from the Diceyan understanding of the doctrine, and towards the manner and form theory, does not constitute a rejection of parliamentary sovereignty. Instead, it is a constitutional development which fundamentally operates so as to preserve the sovereignty of Parliament, because the manner and form theory is a reconfiguration, and not a repudiation, of the idea of legally unlimited legislative authority. As such, we need not join Barber in accepting that parliamentary sovereignty is now experiencing an 'afterlife', the 'old rule' having been abandoned in *Factortame*, with it impossible now to 'resurrect', even if the ECA were to be repealed.[158] While Barber is of course right to suggest that, as has been considered in detail in this chapter, a significant shift has occurred post-*Factortame*, parliamentary sovereignty is not a monolithic concept which permits of only one (Diceyan) interpretation. Rather, when the challenge which the UK's membership of the EU poses to domestic constitutional orthodoxy is explored, it becomes clear that parliamentary sovereignty persists, yet our understanding of its implications must change.

It might be thought that what is, in section 2(4) of the ECA, ultimately an implicit alteration by Parliament of the manner and form for future legislation is an insufficient basis on which to proclaim a shift in our understanding of parliamentary sovereignty. And this might especially be so, since, as yet, this is an entirely hypothetical characterisation of the action which Parliament would need to take to legislate contrary to EU law, and there are, of course, extremely strong political incentives for this never to be tested. However, as will be seen in the next two chapters, this manner and form reading of the ECA is simply the start of a constitutional pattern which demonstrates a modern shift to this conception of the doctrine of parliamentary sovereignty. And it is a pattern of constitutional behaviour in which Parliament has also exercised its sovereign law-making authority to make explicit changes to the manner and form for future legislation.

---

[158] NW Barber, 'The Afterlife of Parliamentary Sovereignty' (2011) *International Journal of Constitutional Law* 144, 152–53.

5

Jackson

I. INTRODUCTION

I N THIS CHAPTER, we consider the second critical modern challenge to the doctrine of parliamentary sovereignty: that presented by the decision of the House of Lords in the seminal case of *R (Jackson) v Attorney General*.[1] In a sense, however, the *Jackson* case does not present a single challenge to the doctrine of parliamentary sovereignty, but a series of overlapping and interconnected challenges. Three main questions are prompted by the decision of the House of Lords. First, why did the court have jurisdiction in *Jackson* to hear a challenge to the legal validity of an Act of Parliament? Secondly, what are the implications of the decision in *Jackson* as to the legal status of the Parliament Acts 1911 and 1949? Thirdly, what is to be made of the remarkable obiter dicta of Lords Steyn, Hope and Lady Hale, overtly questioning the ongoing force and extent of the doctrine of parliamentary sovereignty in the UK constitution?

In relation to each of these three issues, the sovereignty of Parliament is challenged in a different way. The overall challenge posed by *Jackson* is therefore to navigate through these potential difficulties, with a view to establishing which pose genuine problems for parliamentary sovereignty—and which do not—and further, to consider the implications of those developments which are found to be incompatible with the doctrine. The complexity of this task is only magnified by the varying judicial positions, cutting across these issues, which are articulated in *Jackson*. Consequently, depending on what is emphasised, what is dismissed, and what is glossed over, the case might be thought capable of bearing a catalogue of interpretations. It is therefore very tempting, as Adam Tomkins has argued, to regard *Jackson* simply as a case which 'many of the judges ... wanted to use ... as a vehicle for the expression of a bewildering variety of different views about the past, present and future state of parliamentary sovereignty', in which 'so little was decided'.[2] Nevertheless, that a range of disparate perspectives were expressed regarding a range of disparate issues in *Jackson* does not mean that we must conclude, with Tomkins, that the case 'is authority for not much' other than 'the

---

[1] *R (on the application of Jackson) v Attorney General* [2005] UKHL 56, [2006] 1 AC 262.
[2] See House of Commons European Scrutiny Committee, *The EU Bill and Parliamentary Sovereignty*, HC 633-I (7 December 2010) citing Tomkins' oral evidence at [79].

proposition that we have the right to be concerned about what is going to happen to parliamentary sovereignty in the hands of the courts'.[3] The proposition identified by Tomkins may well be correct, yet it is not the only thing to emerge from *Jackson*. Instead, if we explore the intriguing chaos of this decision of the House of Lords, we can discern that while *Jackson* is not authority for a number of the claims made therein, it is authority for something of real significance.

I will suggest that *Jackson* is further evidence of a shift in constitutional understanding; a second step, following that identified in Chapter four, in the context of membership of the EU, away from the traditional Diceyan conception of the doctrine of parliamentary sovereignty, and towards the manner and form theory. For, in the decision reached as to the status of the Parliament Acts 1911 and 1949, the House of Lords has recognised Parliament's power to enact legislation which explicitly alters the manner and form for future law-making. This, I will argue, is the crucial outcome of *Jackson*, and not, as is often thought, that the decision heralds the coming of common law constitutionalism. Instead, the judicial comments which purport to qualify the legislative sovereignty of Parliament will be rejected, and attempts to exploit these comments in the aftermath of *Jackson*—in particular, in the context of the devolved legislatures in *Axa General Insurance Ltd v Lord Advocate*[4]—also challenged. Ultimately, it will be argued that despite the eye-catching claims to the contrary, the decision in *Jackson* is one which largely reinforces, rather than diminishes, the sovereignty of Parliament, while indicating that the legally unlimited legislative authority allocated by the doctrine must be understood to include, and not exclude, the power to make statutory change to the law-making process.

II. *JACKSON*: TWO DICEYAN DIFFICULTIES

The momentous *Jackson* case concerned a challenge to the legal validity of the Hunting Act 2004. The 2004 Act had been passed without the consent of the House of Lords in accordance with the procedure set out in the Parliament Acts 1911 and 1949. The Parliament Act 1911, by section 2(1), enabled 'any Public Bill (other than a Money Bill or a Bill containing any provision to extend the maximum duration of Parliament beyond five years)' to be presented for royal assent even if rejected in the House of Lords, as long as the draft legislation had been passed in three successive sessions by the House of Commons, over a period of not less than two years. The Parliament Act 1949 further weakened the House of Lords' legislative veto, reducing the number of sessions in which a Bill has to be passed in the Commons to two, and the period of delay to one year. The appellants in *Jackson*, however, argued that the 1949 Act—and also, therefore, the Hunting Act 2004, which had been passed in accordance with the amended and less

---

[3] ibid.
[4] *Axa General Insurance Ltd v Lord Advocate* [2011] UKSC 46, [2012] 1 AC 868.

arduous Parliament Acts procedure—was invalid, because the 1949 Act had itself been enacted using the original 1911 Parliament Act. The 1911 Act, the appellants contended, had created a delegated legislature comprising the House of Commons and Queen, and this subordinate body could not extend the scope of its delegated power by its own enactment. An alteration of the terms of the delegation of power, such as that purportedly effected by the 1949 Act, could only lawfully derive from the body which had made the original delegation: the fully constituted Queen in Parliament. As a result, it was alleged, the 1949 Act, and every statute passed under it, had no legal effect. The House of Lords, however, rejected this argument and upheld the validity of both the Parliament Act 1949 and the Hunting Act 2004. The Parliament Act 1911 had not, the court held, created a new delegated legislature but an alternative method of enacting primary legislation, and the 1949 Act could not therefore be seen as an instance of a delegate extending illegitimately the scope of its own power. Furthermore, since section 2(1) of the 1911 Act did not expressly exclude the use of the Parliament Act process to enact legislation which altered the specific conditions in which this legislative procedure could itself be used, the 1949 Act was not an invalid exercise of this authority.

The decision in *Jackson* creates two initial, and potentially significant, problems for the exponents of an orthodox Diceyan conception of parliamentary sovereignty. First, the fact that the case was heard at all can be seen as a direct challenge to Parliament's legally unlimited power to enact legislation on any subject matter. For a crucial corollary of Parliament's ability to create any law whatsoever is that its Acts cannot be subject to judicial review. As we saw when reviewing the leading case law on the doctrine of parliamentary sovereignty in Chapter three,[5] this fundamental principle of the UK constitution, authoritatively set out in *Edinburgh and Dalkeith Railway Co v Wauchope*[6] and *Lee v Bude and Torrington Junction Railway Co*,[7] was reaffirmed by the House of Lords in *British Railways Board v Pickin*.[8] The crucial statement of constitutional principle, robustly endorsed in *Pickin*, can be seen in the judgment of Lord Morris:

> The question of fundamental importance which arises is whether the court should entertain the proposition that an Act of Parliament can so be assailed in the courts that matters should proceed as though the Act or some part of it had never been passed. I consider that such doctrine would be dangerous and impermissible. It is the function of the courts to administer the laws which Parliament has enacted. In the processes of Parliament there will be much consideration whether a Bill should or should not in one form or another become an enactment. When an enactment is passed there is finality unless and until it is amended or repealed by Parliament. In the courts there may be argument as to the correct interpretation of the enactment: there must be none as to whether it should be on the Statute Book at all.[9]

[5] See chapter 3 of this volume, pp 132–36.
[6] *Edinburgh and Dalkeith Railway Co v Wauchope* (1842) 8 Cl & F 710.
[7] *Lee v Bude and Torrington Junction Railway Co* (1871) LR 6 CP 576.
[8] *British Railways Board v Pickin* [1974] AC 765.
[9] ibid 788–89.

It is initially difficult see how *Jackson*, in which it was argued that *multiple* Acts of Parliament should not be on the statute book,[10] can be reconciled with the strident judgment in *Pickin*. The Attorney General did not contest the propriety of the case being heard, but given what Lord Bingham called the 'strangeness' of 'the exercise which the courts have … been invited to undertake in these proceedings', some of the Law Lords in *Jackson* did attempt to justify their jurisdiction.[11] Lord Bingham distinguished *Pickin* on the basis that it was a case in which the courts were illegitimately asked to 'investigate the internal workings and procedures of Parliament to demonstrate that it had been misled and so had proceeded on a false basis', whereas the appellants in *Jackson* sought to elicit no such judicial intrusion.[12] Instead, *Jackson* was a case in which the courts were merely asked to resolve whether the 1949 Act, and thus those statutes passed under it, were actually 'enacted law'.[13] This, according to Lord Nicholls, required the House of Lords to determine the 'proper interpretation' of section 2(1) of the Parliament Act 1911, a matter which was rightly 'for the courts, not Parliament', regardless of the exceptional constitutional context.[14] The willingness of the court in *Jackson* to engage in more interventionist scrutiny of the legal pedigree of the Parliament Act 1949 could thus be attributed to the absence of a risk of infringing article 9 of the Bill of Rights 1689, which provides that 'proceedings in Parliament ought not to be impeached or questioned in any court'.

What was surely just as important, however, in sustaining the House of Lords' broad interpretation of their jurisdiction in *Jackson* was the fact that the case was effectively a fait accompli. It is so well established in UK public life that the 1949 Act was a legally effective alteration of the Parliament Act legislative procedure that the courts could never have held to the contrary. These inexorable background circumstances were clearly acknowledged by some of the Law Lords. Lord Nicholls noted that 'both Houses of Parliament have unequivocally and repeatedly recognised the validity and effectiveness of the 1949 Act'.[15] Lord Hope went further, arguing that:

> [T]he restrictions on the exercise of the power of the House of Lords that the 1949 Act purported to make have been so widely recognised and relied upon that these restrictions are, today, a political fact. It is no longer open to the courts, if it ever was, to say that the Act was not authorised by s.2(1) of the 1911 Act.[16]

---

[10] Had the argument of the appellants in *Jackson* been accepted, five Acts of Parliament would have been invalid. In addition to the Parliament Act 1949 and the Hunting Act 2004, the War Crimes Act 1991, the European Parliament Elections Act 1999, and the Sexual Offences (Amendment) Act 2000—all also enacted in accordance with the amended Parliament Acts procedure—would also have been legally ineffective.

[11] *R (on the application of Jackson) v Attorney General* [2005] UKHL 56, [2006] 1 AC 262, [27].

[12] ibid [27].

[13] ibid [27].

[14] ibid [51]. The same point was made by Lord Carswell at [169].

[15] ibid [68].

[16] Ibid [128].

The courts could thus afford to allow an unprecedented legal challenge to primary legislation to develop because there was never any danger they would ultimately hold the 1949 Act to be void. However, this casts doubt upon an additional justification for the justiciability of the *Jackson* case advanced by Lord Bingham: that 'a question of law' had been raised 'which cannot, as such, be resolved by Parliament', consequently placing an obligation on the courts to determine the matter in order to satisfy 'the rule of law'.[17] It does not seem right to characterise the issues raised in *Jackson* as unresolved, since for over half a century all the relevant constitutional and political actors had proceeded on the basis that the 1949 Act was a legally valid statute. The ruling of the House of Lords in *Jackson* was not the unavoidable settlement of a constitutional dispute, but simply an affirmation of existing faith.

But while the intervention of the House of Lords in *Jackson* was not therefore necessary, it was also not a particularly worrying incursion into Parliament's sovereign authority. As noted above, the judges in *Jackson* believed their primary task to be ascertaining whether the Parliament Act 1949 was actually a valid statute. The archaic 'enrolled bill' rule, set out in *Edinburgh and Dalkeith Railway Co* by Lord Campbell,[18] and endorsed by Lord Reid in *Pickin*,[19] serves precisely the same function. Of course, the court in *Jackson* could simply have employed a modern version of the enrolled bill test, doing no more than a examining a copy of the 1949 Act printed[20] or published online[21] by Her Majesty's Stationery Office to satisfy itself of the statute's authenticity. Yet while the House of Lords in fact chose to take a more rigorous approach in *Jackson*, it is arguable that this was invited by section 2(1) of the Parliament Act 1911 which, by expressly prohibiting the use of the procedure to enact legislation designed to extend the life of Parliament beyond five years, left it open to the appellants to argue that further implied limits on the power might also exist. Although this argument found favour with the Court of Appeal it was almost entirely rejected in the House of Lords, with Lord Rodger observing that the 1911 Act represented a 'political victory' for the House of Commons which '[t]he courts should not undermine ... by giving the Act an unduly narrow interpretation'.[22] *Jackson*, therefore, does not signal a judicial change of direction, but a change of approach in very specific circumstances. The courts showed a willingness to be more thorough when assessing whether an Act of Parliament had been lawfully created in accordance with a legislative procedure set out in statute, which by its very nature has to specify in writing the conditions under which the procedure will be available for use. While it is feasible that the courts might take a similarly robust approach if called on to examine the validity

---

[17] Ibid [27].

[18] *Edinburgh and Dalkeith Railway Co v Wauchope* (1842) 8 Cl & F 710, 723–25.

[19] *British Railways Board v Pickin* [1974] AC 765, 786–87.

[20] This was the approach taken by Sir Robert Megarry VC in his first instance judgment in *Manuel v Attorney General* [1983] Ch 77, 86–87.

[21] www.legislation.gov.uk.

[22] *R (Jackson) v Attorney General* [2005] UKHL 56, [2006] 1 AC 262, [129].

of Acts produced in accordance with other statutory legislative procedures, such as the Regency Act 1937,[23] *Jackson* should not have an impact on the way the courts approach legislation created via the traditional route. To draw such a distinction may appear arbitrary, yet it is also understandable. For this disparity is a consequence of the judicial recognition in *Jackson* of the fact that—in the limited circumstances in which they exist—statutory conditions relating to the legislative process must be adhered to for valid Acts of Parliament to be enacted. *Jackson* stands as an authority for nothing more than this, and gives the courts no further role in ascertaining the validity of legislation where there are no relevant statutory provisions the interpretation of which can be challenged. And, perhaps most importantly, *Jackson* is very clearly not a precedent which sanctions substantive judicial review of the political merits or constitutional morality of legislation.[24]

The second problem created by the decision of the House of Lords in *Jackson* for defenders of the traditional understanding of parliamentary sovereignty is that the court held that statutes enacted in accordance with the Parliament Acts 1911 and 1949 are *primary* legislation. Based on both the literal wording of the Parliament Acts and the historical mischief that the legislation was designed to remedy, Lord Bingham concluded that the effect of the statutes was to create 'a new way of enacting primary legislation',[25] or what Lord Nicholls called a 'parallel route by which ... any public Bill introduced in the Commons could become law as an Act of Parliament'.[26] The appellants' argument, earlier defended by Wade,[27] that the Parliament Acts had created a delegated legislature which was only therefore capable of producing subordinate legislation was decisively rejected by the Law Lords. Since the legislative procedure set out in the Parliament Acts was designed to augment the ordinary enactment process of the Commons, Lords and Queen acting in concert, the Acts of 1911 and 1949 cannot be said to limit the overall power of Parliament, nor has the legislature 'bound its successors' in any significant sense. However, Parliament has here clearly effected a statutory alteration of the manner and form required to enact valid primary legislation. The regular legislative process cannot therefore, contrary to the analysis of Wade and others defenders of the Diceyan orthodoxy, be a sacrosanct formula which by its very nature is inherently immune to modification by statute. The sheer foundation of Wade's conceptual challenge to Jennings and the manner and form theory

---

[23] On which see generally R Brazier, 'Royal Incapacity and Constitutional Continuity: The Regent and Counsellors of State' (2005) 64 *CLJ* 352. For discussion of the potential effect of s 4(2) of the Regency Act 1937, which limits the power of the Regent to, among other things, assent to bills changing the order of succession to the Crown, see J Jaconelli, 'Regency and Parliamentary Sovereignty' [2002] *PL* 449.

[24] To bring a substantive challenge of this kind to the Hunting Act 2004, following the failure of the arguments in *Jackson*, claims were advanced under the European Convention of Human Rights and EU law in the subsequent case of *R (Countryside Alliance) v Attorney General* [2007] UKHL 52, [2008] 1 AC 719. These substantive lines of challenge were rejected in the House of Lords.

[25] *R (Jackson) v Attorney General* [2005] UKHL 56, [2006] 1 AC 262, [24].

[26] ibid [64].

[27] See chapter 2 of this volume, pp 75–91.

of parliamentary sovereignty, so influential in UK constitutional scholarship, has thus been controverted by the decision of the House of Lords in *Jackson*.[28]

The court did not spell out in full the consequences of this ruling. The implications of *Jackson* may, however, be far-reaching. As Baroness Hale observed:

> If the sovereign Parliament can redefine itself downwards, to remove or modify the requirement for the consent of the Upper House, it may very well be that it can also redefine itself upwards, to require a particular parliamentary majority or a popular referendum for particular types of measure. In each case, the courts would be respecting the will of the sovereign Parliament as constituted when that will had been expressed.[29]

The logic of this analogy seems formidable, and some degree of support for the comments of Baroness Hale can be found in the judgment of Lord Steyn, who appeared to endorse the manner and form theory of legislative sovereignty in his citation of a passage outlining such an approach from Dixon.[30] However, the comments to this effect from Lord Steyn are narrower than those of Baroness Hale, in so far as they are framed by the more limited notion that Parliament can redefine itself for particular legislative purposes:

> [A]part from the traditional method of law making, Parliament acting as ordinarily constituted may functionally redistribute legislative power in different ways. For example, Parliament could for specific purposes provide for a two-thirds majority in the House of Commons and the House of Lords. This would involve a redefinition of Parliament for a specific purpose. Such redefinition could not be disregarded.[31]

Yet the 'constituent elements which make up Parliament: the House of Commons, the House of Lords, and the Monarch', were, according to Lord Steyn, 'static'.[32] As such, if the only statutory change to the legislative process which will be permissible is that to the exercise of power by these three institutions, with the possibility of injecting any external institutional impetus excluded, the conception of legislative sovereignty defended by Lord Steyn cannot be considered to be a full endorsement of the manner and form theory. In any event, however, while Lord Steyn and Baroness Hale were the only two members of the House of Lords to recognise, even tentatively, that further legislative alterations of manner and form would be lawful, it can be argued that in so doing they—and in particular, Baroness Hale—are elucidating the necessary consequences of the court's decision.[33] The

---

[28] See AW Bradley, 'The Sovereignty of the Westminster Parliament and the Abolition of Hunting with Dogs' (2007) *Poteri, Garanzie e Diritti a Sessanta Anni Dalla Constituzione* 235–54, 252–53.

[29] *R (Jackson) v Attorney General* [2005] UKHL 56, [2006] 1 AC 262, [163].

[30] ibid [81]. The passage cited is from O Dixon, 'The Law and the Constitution' (1935) 51 *LQR* 590, 601: 'The very power of constitutional alteration cannot be exercised except in the form and manner which the law for the time being prescribes. Unless the legislature observes that manner and form, its attempt to alter its constitution is void. It may amend or abrogate for the future the law which prescribes that form or that manner. But, in doing so, it must comply with its very requirements'.

[31] ibid [81].

[32] ibid [81].

[33] The judgment which comes closest to denying this is that of Lord Hope, who rejects claims that the 1911 Act has 'redefined' Parliament, and reiterates the orthodox propositions that 'no Parliament

decision of the House of Lords as to the legality of the Parliament Act 1949 is premised fundamentally on the idea that Parliament's sovereign legislative authority includes the power to make changes to the manner and form required to produce valid Acts of Parliament. *Jackson* can therefore be seen to demonstrate judicial acceptance of the legality of an explicit statutory change to the legislative process made by Parliament.[34] And this, in turn, must prompt reconsideration of which conception of the doctrine of parliamentary sovereignty can now be thought to represent orthodox theory in the contemporary UK constitution.

In my view, *Jackson* is a clear sign that a shift to the manner and form conception of parliamentary sovereignty has occurred in the UK constitution. However, the decision of the House of Lords in this case does raise one concern for those who favour the manner and form approach to parliamentary sovereignty. The appellants' contention that the legislative power contained in section 2(1) of the Parliament Act 1911 was subject to implied limits, noted above, was rejected by the House of Lords, but not in its entirety. The Court of Appeal had previously ruled that while the section 2(1) power could be used validly to effect the alterations contained in the 1949 Act, legislation purporting to make more 'significant' constitutional change might be outside the scope of the Parliament Acts.[35] The rather flimsy caveat crafted by the Court of Appeal was criticised by the Law Lords, with Lord Bingham describing it as finding 'no support in the language of the Act, in principle or in the historical record'.[36] A majority of the House of Lords did, however, suggest obiter that the section 2(1) power, in addition to being limited by the express words in the statute—which prevent the Parliament Acts from being used to pass legislation to extend the life of Parliament beyond five years—was also subject to one particular implied limitation. The Parliament Acts could not, according to the majority, be used to pass a statute removing the express limit contained in section 2(1), which would consequently leave the Commons free to extend the maximum duration of Parliament without the consent of the House of Lords. In the words of Lord Nicholls,

> [t]hat express exclusion carries with it, by necessary implication, a like exclusion in respect of legislation aimed at achieving the same result by two steps rather than one. If this were not so the express legislative intention could readily be defeated.[37]

can bind its successors' or 'entrench' an Act against the possibility of repeal: ibid [113]. Yet even this does not amount to a complete denial of the manner and form conception of parliamentary sovereignty, for this theory is not exclusively concerned with entrenchment, and indeed, as will be argued in Part III, use of legislative power to such an end, while legally permitted, may not be justified by the manner and form theory. Moreover, a manner and form reading of *Jackson* is not contingent on accepting that Parliament has here been 'redefined'; indeed, I agree with Lord Hope that such terminology is not 'helpful', because it is a distraction from the broader point established by the decision in *Jackson*: that Parliament has legislated to alter the manner and form for future law-making.

[34] For a similar argument, see HR Zhou, 'Revisiting the "Manner and Form" Theory of Parliamentary Sovereignty' (2013) 129 *LQR* 610, 622–26.

[35] *R (Jackson) v Attorney General* [2005] EWCA Civ 126, [2005] QB 579, [98]–[100].

[36] *R (Jackson) v Attorney General* [2005] UKHL 56, [2006] 1 AC 262, [31].

[37] ibid [59].

The observations of the majority on this point, however, go too far. The Acts of 1911 and 1949 do not evince an 'express legislative intention' to prevent the limitation on the use of the section 2(1) power from being amended or removed by the House of Commons via the Parliament Acts procedure. As Lord Bingham, on this point in the minority, noted, there is 'no basis in the language of section 2(1) or in principle for holding that the parenthesis in that subsection ... are unamendable save with the consent of the Lords'.[38] Had Parliament wished to proscribe the two-step approach, section 2(1) would also have needed to contain a further exclusion clause, prohibiting the enactment under the Parliament Acts of a statute which sought to remove the ban on Bills purporting to extend the life of the legislature beyond five years. If, as I believe *Jackson* indicates, the courts are now prepared to recognise, where relevant, statutory conditions on the use of legislative power, they must only recognise the actual explicit conditions that have been put in place by Parliament, and not implied conditions of their own making. In accordance with the manner and form understanding of legally unlimited law-making authority, only the sovereign Parliament is lawfully empowered to place conditions on the use of its legislative power; the courts cannot. Even those judicial limits ostensibly formulated, as in this case, to protect democracy ultimately achieve the opposite, if the judiciary is elevated illegitimately to a position of constitutional supremacy. The obiter observations of the majority on this point ought therefore to be disregarded, and the view of Lord Bingham preferred.

III. THE COMMON LAW CONSTITUTIONALIST READING OF *JACKSON*

There is, however, an alternative way of understanding the decision of the House of Lords in *Jackson*. According to this interpretation of *Jackson*, the challenges posed by the case to the traditional Diceyan understanding of parliamentary sovereignty are merely symptoms of a broader constitutional transformation. This is not a shift, as I have argued, from one conception of parliamentary sovereignty to another; from the orthodox model of 'continuing' legally unlimited legislative power to the manner and form theory. Instead, the very notion of parliamentary sovereignty is presented as having been subsumed within an emerging common law constitution; a claim that, if accepted, would essentially mark the abandonment of the doctrine. From this alternative perspective, the House of Lords in *Jackson* had little reason to feel apprehensive about entertaining an unprecedented challenge to the validity of an Act of Parliament. Rather, if Parliament is no longer sovereign, the judicial review of legislation becomes something which, both in *Jackson* and in the future, is no longer excluded, and may even become expected.

This is clearly a radical interpretation of *Jackson*, taking the decision of the House of Lords as confirmation of a fundamental reordering of the UK

---

[38] ibid [32]. The majority on this point consisted of Lords Nicholls, Steyn, Hope, Carswell, Brown and Baroness Hale.

constitution. Yet what is most remarkable is that this analysis was developed by a number of judges—primarily Lords Steyn and Hope, with some support from Baroness Hale—in their judgments in the *Jackson* case itself. In an astounding passage, Lord Steyn argued that:

> We do not in the United Kingdom have an uncontrolled constitution as the Attorney General implausibly asserts. In the European context the second *Factortame* decision [1991] 1 AC 603 made that clear. The settlement contained in the Scotland Act 1998 also point[s] to a divided sovereignty. Moreover, the European Convention on Human Rights as incorporated into our law by the Human Rights Act 1998, created a new legal order. One must not assimilate the European Convention on Human Rights with multilateral treaties of the traditional type. Instead it is a legal order in which the United Kingdom assumes obligations to protect fundamental rights, not in relation to other states, but towards all individuals within its jurisdiction. The classic account given by Dicey of the doctrine of the supremacy of Parliament, pure and absolute as it was, can now be seen to be out of place in the modern United Kingdom. Nevertheless, the supremacy of Parliament is still the *general* principle of our constitution. It is a construct of the common law. The judges created this principle. If that is so, it is not unthinkable that circumstances could arise where the courts may have to qualify a principle established on a different hypothesis of constitutionalism. In exceptional circumstances involving an attempt to abolish judicial review or the ordinary role of the courts, the Appellate Committee of the House of Lords or a new Supreme Court may have to consider whether this is [a] constitutional fundamental which even a sovereign Parliament acting at the behest of a complaisant House of Commons cannot abolish.[39]

Lord Hope advanced a similar argument, using modern constitutional developments—in combination with claims as to the potential constitutional fundamentality of the Acts of Union 1707[40]—as a trigger to challenge the contemporary relevance of the doctrine of parliamentary sovereignty:

> Our constitution is dominated by the sovereignty of Parliament. But parliamentary sovereignty is no longer, if it ever was, absolute ... It is no longer right to say that its freedom to legislate admits of no qualification whatever. Step by step, gradually but surely, the English principle of the absolute legislative sovereignty of Parliament which Dicey derived from Coke and Blackstone is being qualified.[41]

---

[39] ibid [102].

[40] ibid [106]. See especially on this point, the comments of Lord President Cooper in *MacCormick v Lord Advocate* 1953 SC 396, 411–13. Such claims that the doctrine of parliamentary sovereignty is 'a distinctively English principle which has no counterpart in Scottish constitutional law' are questionable, both historically and as a statement of contemporary constitutional understanding: see chapter 3 of this volume, n 27. In any event, however, Lord President Cooper explicitly accepted in *MacCormick* that the challenge there advanced was non-justiciable: '[t]his at least is plain, that there is neither precedent nor authority of any kind for the view that the domestic Courts of either Scotland or England have jurisdiction to determine whether a governmental act of the type here in controversy is or is not conform to the provisions of a Treaty, least of all when that Treaty is one under which both Scotland and England ceased to be independent states and merged their identity in an incorporating union'.

[41] ibid [104].

Baroness Hale also displayed some sympathy for the notion that the sovereignty of Parliament has now been qualified—in particular, 'by the European Communities Act 1972 and, in a different way, by the Human Rights Act 1998'—and might be qualified further in the future.[42] It would even be possible, according to Baroness Hale, for the judges to be the authors of such limitations, for '[t]he courts will treat with particular suspicion (and might even reject) any attempt to subvert the rule of law by removing governmental action affecting the rights of the individual from all judicial scrutiny'.[43]

Looking beyond the confused and contradictory rhetoric employed here, with parliamentary sovereignty simultaneously being presented as both enduring and irrelevant, the observations set out above bear all the hallmarks of common law constitutionalism, which was examined, and rejected on both empirical and normative grounds, in Chapter three. In light of this, what weight can be attributed to such bold pronouncements? How authoritative are the claims of three judges in *Jackson* that we have left parliamentary sovereignty behind us, and are now set on a constitutional course which is steadily taking us further away from this doctrine? Initially, it must be noted that these remarks were all made obiter, and thus have no prospective binding effect. Further, they did not attract the support of a majority of the judges in *Jackson* itself. Lord Bingham in particular offered a resolute defence of 'the supremacy of the Crown in Parliament', which he considered to be the 'bedrock of the British constitution'.[44] Subsequently, Lord Bingham has also dismissed the assertions of the doubters in more frank terms extra-judicially, as 'related to no issue raised and no argument advanced in the case, they were based on no authority and were supported by no reasoning'.[45] Two familiar common law constitutionalist claims would need to be substantiated for this radical critique of parliamentary sovereignty to be considered a viable account of the present state of the UK constitution, and thus a credible interpretation of *Jackson*. Parliamentary sovereignty must first be shown to be a doctrine of the common law, and thus susceptible to judicial alteration. Secondly, recent constitutional developments must have demonstrably placed clear legal limitations on the extent of Parliament's legislative authority. However, neither of these complementary conditions has been satisfied.

---

[42] ibid [159].

[43] ibid [159]. However, as Ewing and Tham note, Baroness Hale later played down the possibility of the courts rejecting an Act of Parliament. While giving evidence to the Joint Committee on Human Rights, Baroness Hale described the possibility of the courts possessing a power to strike down Acts of Parliament as 'extremely novel, quite alarming' and noted that the judges 'would hesitate to use it': see KD Ewing and JC Tham, 'The Continuing Futility of the Human Rights Act' [2008] *PL* 668, 682; citing the Joint Committee on Human Rights, *A Bill of Rights for the UK?: Oral and Written Evidence*, HC 150-II (2008) Ev 39.

[44] *Jackson* [2005] UKHL 56, [2006] 1 AC 262, [9]. For explicit rejection of the views of Lords Steyn and Hope, and Baroness Hale, see also Lord Bingham, 'The Rule of Law and the Sovereignty of Parliament', *King's College London Commemoration Oration 2007* (31 October 2007) 22; T Bingham, *The Rule of Law* (London, Penguin, 2011) 166–68.

[45] T Bingham, 'Publication Review: The New British Constitution' (2010) 126 *LQR* 131, 134.

First, the notion that the doctrine of parliamentary sovereignty is a creature of the common law is as oft repeated as it is misleading. As we saw in Chapter three, this claim can be shown to be empirically false from a historical perspective, and from the perspective of legal authority. There are no cases in which the courts crafted the doctrine that gave Parliament legally unlimited legislative authority, or comprehensively explained the nature and rationale of parliamentary sovereignty, because this constitutional fundamental is not a common law construct. Instead, the leading case law on parliamentary sovereignty simply assumes the existence of this legal doctrine.[46] The seemingly unpalatable truth is that the emergence of the doctrine of parliamentary sovereignty in the UK was based on brute fact. The judges did not invent this doctrine; they had no choice but to recognise the constitutional superiority of Parliament, definitively so in the aftermath of the revolution of 1688.[47] Nevertheless, the claim still continues to be perpetuated, even seeping beyond the academic journals, into more mainstream publications.[48] It may be right to say that the work of Jennings contributed to the propagation of this misnomer. While Jennings was under no illusions about the political, rather than judicial, origins of the doctrine, he nevertheless referred to parliamentary sovereignty as a common law rule in order to highlight its susceptibility to statutory modification. However, as I argued in Chapter two, his abiding understanding of parliamentary sovereignty is better reflected in the term adopted by Mitchell to describe the status of the doctrine, that of customary law.[49] The sovereignty of Parliament is a legal doctrine, which was not explicitly created by statute, but this does not mean, as often seems to be assumed, that by a process of elimination it must therefore be a rule of common law.[50] Instead, it is a norm which obtained legal force as a result of its acceptance as law by a broad array of pertinent constitutional actors. It is not a rule of common law conceived by the judges, but a legal norm derived from customary practice. And as the courts did not create this rule, it is not open to them, as seems to be suggested by the minority in *Jackson*, to reinterpret it into oblivion.

The second strand of the common law constitutionalist analysis put forward in *Jackson* must similarly be rejected. The sovereign legislative authority of Parliament has not been qualified by recent momentous constitutional

---

[46] See chapter 3 of this volume, pp 132–36.

[47] See chapter 2 of this volume, pp 64, 66, 78.

[48] See, eg S Sedley, 'On the Move', *London Review of Books*, vol 31 No 19 (8 October 2009) 3, 5: 'It is now widely accepted ... that the doctrine of parliamentary supremacy is itself an artefact of the common law, growing out of the historic compromise between the three limbs of the crown—legislative, judicial and executive—which was reached in the course of the 17th century and has been developed in modern concepts of the rule of law'.

[49] See chapter 2 of this volume, p 100.

[50] For a further example of the tendency to assume that the doctrine of parliamentary sovereignty is a rule of common law, see the controversy over the explanatory notes to the EU Bill 2010–11 prepared by the government, which repeated this flawed claim, and consequently drew criticism from the European Scrutiny Committee; see House of Commons European Scrutiny Committee, *The EU Bill and Parliamentary Sovereignty*, HC 633-I (7 December 2010) [87]–[89].

developments as this minority of judges contended. As I argued in Chapter three, neither the Human Rights Act 1998 (HRA) nor the devolution statutes challenge critically the legal sovereignty of Parliament.[51] These statutes have certainly placed substantial political limits on Parliament's use of its legislative power, but there is nothing new in this. The legislative sovereignty of Parliament does not make it politically omnipotent, only legally unrestrained. The fact that these political limits, unlike many others, have been created by statute still does not mean that they are anything other than merely political limits, which Parliament is lawfully at liberty to disregard. The change brought about by the European Communities Act 1972 (ECA) is more difficult to reconcile with the doctrine of parliamentary sovereignty. However, as was argued in Chapter four, if we embrace a shift from the orthodox Diceyan understanding of the doctrine to the manner and form conception of legally unlimited legislative authority, then it becomes clear that the UK's accession to the EU does not necessitate the renunciation of parliamentary sovereignty. On this view, Parliament retains the power to legislate in violation of EU law, so long as it uses express words to indicate that the contravening statute is to have priority. The effect, therefore, of section 2(4) of the ECA is to change the manner and form required for the production of valid legislation, rather than to make Parliament permanently subject to supreme EU norms.[52] Nor can, as Lord Hope suggested,[53] *Jackson* itself be cited as an instance in which the sovereignty of Parliament has been qualified. In *Jackson*, as discussed above, the courts did not permit a challenge to the merits of the Parliament Act 1949 to be heard. Instead, their primary task was to ensure that the 1949 Act had been legitimately enacted in accordance with the Parliament Act 1911, and was thus a valid statute. This was not a violation of the legislature's legal sovereignty, for the doctrine requires that the courts only give heed to genuine Acts of Parliament, and not defective or counterfeit enactments.

The examples cited in *Jackson* do not therefore prove, even when considered cumulatively, as part of a composite challenge, that the doctrine of parliamentary sovereignty has been qualified. For there is simply no evidence here that absolute, substantive limitations have been placed on Parliament's legislative authority. However, even if this conclusion were wrong, and Parliament had been limited by any of these modern developments—whether independently or cumulatively—it would have been limited by its own hand, because all of these potential modern challenges derive from legislative action. The common law constitutionalist arguments of the kind advanced in *Jackson*, which seek to piggyback on these supposed limitations of parliamentary sovereignty, and consequently to postulate the existence of a judicial power to strike down Acts of Parliament, are thus destined to fail in any event. For even if the developments discussed here did demonstrate that Parliament can absolutely and substantively bind itself, and is therefore no

---

[51] See chapter 3 of this volume, pp 114–26.
[52] See chapter 4 of this volume, pp 173–74.
[53] *R (Jackson) v Attorney General* [2005] UKHL 56, [2006] 1 AC 262, [107].

longer legally sovereign, a claim which I categorically reject, the courts would still not possess the constitutional power to place further limits on Parliament's legislative authority.

There is, therefore, a complete lack of any evidence which can be drawn on to support the common law constitutionalist claims advanced by Lords Steyn, Hope, and Baroness Hale in *Jackson*. Nevertheless, that such claims are entirely without foundation cannot prevent them from being rehearsed. Moreover, in accordance with the common law method, what is initially unsupported by authority or logic may eventually obtain force through persistent exposure. On this basis, it might therefore be thought that the obiter comments in *Jackson* could potentially be located within an existing, and evolving, line of case law concerning the level of protection afforded to fundamental rights and principles recognised by the common law. For this line of authority, while not primarily relied on by the minority in *Jackson*, might be thought to provide some evidence that the doctrine of parliamentary sovereignty could be susceptible to judicial limitation in the future. Indeed, it could be argued that the common law constitutionalist dicta put forward in *Jackson* are actually best viewed as a further significant development in this strand of precedents, which could eventually culminate in the judicial discovery of a power to reject legislation which violates constitutional values deemed to require the protection of the common law.

IV. *JACKSON* AS A DEVELOPMENT OF THE PRINCIPLE OF LEGALITY?

In recent years the courts have begun sporadically to develop a non-exhaustive category of fundamental common law rights, which have been afforded great weight by the judges when engaged in cases before them. This line of cases began with *R v Secretary of State for the Home Department, ex parte Leech (No 2)*,[54] in which the Court of Appeal held that a rule allowing prison officers to examine and stop correspondence between a prisoner and a solicitor, made by the Secretary of State under a wide enabling provision in the Prison Act 1952, was ultra vires. Steyn LJ, giving the judgment of the court, held that a citizen's 'right of unimpeded access to a court' was a 'constitutional right'.[55] While such a basic right could be limited by necessary implication in an Act of Parliament, the court ruled that this would only occur in a 'rare case', and it would 'be an even rarer case in which it could be held that a statute authorised by necessary implication the abolition or limitation of so fundamental a right by subordinate legislation'.[56] *Leech* was followed by *R v Lord Chancellor, ex parte Witham*,[57] in which the Divisional Court held that a general statutory power allowing the Lord Chancellor to set the fees payable for

---

[54] *R v Secretary of State for the Home Department, ex parte Leech (No 2)* [1994] QB 198.
[55] ibid 210.
[56] ibid 212.
[57] *R v Lord Chancellor, ex parte Witham* [1998] QB 575.

access to the courts, contained in the Supreme Court Act 1981, did not empower the making of an Order removing the exemption on the payment of such fees which applied to litigants receiving income support. In his leading judgment, Laws J argued that 'the common law has clearly given special weight to the citizen's right of access to the courts' and had designated it a 'constitutional right'.[58] A right granted constitutional status by the common law 'cannot be abrogated by the state save by specific provision in an Act of Parliament, or by regulations whose vires in main legislation specifically confers the power to abrogate. General words will not suffice'.[59] Indeed, Laws J sought further to expand the scope of protection for such rights, contending that it would be practically impossible for a statute to be sufficiently clear as to limit a constitutional right without doing so in express terms: '[t]he class of cases where it could be done by necessary implication is, I venture to think, a class with no members'.[60]

The doctrine emerging in *Leech* and *Witham* was quickly affirmed and reinforced in two decisions of the House of Lords. In *R v Secretary of State for the Home Department, ex parte Pierson*[61] a majority of the Law Lords held, for differing reasons, that the Home Secretary could not lawfully increase the tariff period of the mandatory life sentence being served by the applicant. Most important for present purposes, however, are the comments of two Law Lords exhibiting an acceptance of the broad thrust of the principles expounded in *Leech* and *Witham*. After surveying a number of authorities, Lord Browne-Wilkinson discerned the following proposition:

> A power conferred by Parliament in general terms is not to be taken to authorise the doing of acts by the donee of the power which adversely affect the legal rights of the citizen or the basic principles on which the law of the United Kingdom is based unless the statute conferring the power makes it clear that such was the intention of Parliament.[62]

Lord Steyn called this the 'principle of legality'.[63] The courts presume that 'Parliament does not legislate in a vacuum', but for 'a European liberal democracy founded on the principles and traditions of the common law'.[64] It is open to Parliament to override these principles and traditions, but the courts will assume that it does not intend to do so unless they are presented with 'a clear and specific provision to the contrary'.[65] Subsequently, in *R v Secretary of State for the Home Department, ex parte Simms*[66] the House of Lords held that prisoners possessed 'a fundamental or basic right' to be visited and interviewed by journalists investigating their cases in order to expose miscarriages of justice, and that

---

[58] ibid 585.
[59] ibid 581.
[60] ibid 586.
[61] *R v Secretary of State for the Home Department, ex parte Pierson* [1998] AC 539.
[62] ibid 575.
[63] ibid 587.
[64] ibid 587.
[65] ibid 587.
[66] *R v Secretary of State for the Home Department, ex parte Simms* [2000] 2 AC 115.

the Home Secretary's blanket ban on such visits—issued under the Prison Rules 1964, established on authority contained in the Prison Act 1952—was therefore unlawful.[67] In reaching this conclusion, Lord Steyn applied the principle of legality set out in *Pierson*, which was supplemented by Lord Hoffmann, who offered his own explanation of the principle, in what has become a highly influential and much cited passage:

> Parliamentary sovereignty means that Parliament can, if it chooses, legislate contrary to fundamental principles of human rights. The Human Rights Act 1998 will not detract from this power. The constraints upon its exercise by Parliament are ultimately political, not legal. But the principle of legality means that Parliament must squarely confront what it is doing and accept the political cost. *Fundamental rights cannot be overridden by general or ambiguous words.* This is because there is too great a risk that the full implications of their unqualified meaning may have passed unnoticed in the democratic process. *In the absence of express language or necessary implication to the contrary, the courts therefore presume that even the most general words were intended to be subject to the basic rights of the individual.* In this way the courts of the United Kingdom, though acknowledging the sovereignty of Parliament, apply principles of constitutionality little different from those which exist in countries where the power of the legislature is expressly limited by a constitutional document (emphasis added).[68]

From this line of cases, culminating in *Simms*, a clear principle emerges. The courts will offer an enhanced level of protection to common law rights that they deem to be of fundamental constitutional importance, and unless Parliament makes it abundantly clear that it intends to authorise the violation of such rights, the judges will assume that both primary and secondary legislation leaves them unscathed.

Is there scope, however, for this line of cases to develop any further? In the future, could the principle of legality go beyond merely protecting constitutional rights from being restricted by implication, and be found to have additional, as yet unrealised applications? In *International Transport Roth GmbH v Secretary of State for the Home Department*[69] Laws LJ offered an obiter assessment of the effect of the *Simms* strand of precedents. As a result of the common law recognition of fundamental constitutional rights, Laws LJ asserted that '[i]n its present state of evolution, the British system may be said to stand at an intermediate stage between parliamentary supremacy and constitutional supremacy'.[70] The unmistakable implication here is that the UK constitution is currently in a state of flux, and further movement away from parliamentary supremacy, in the direction of constitutional supremacy, whatever that might mean, could well be impending. If this is the case, the qualified protection of constitutional rights presently offered

---

[67] ibid 130.

[68] ibid 131.

[69] *International Transport Roth GmbH v Secretary of State for the Home Department* [2002] EWCA Civ 158, [2003] QB 728.

[70] ibid [71].

by the courts in accordance with *Simms* could potentially be expanded, with such rights eventually gaining an absolute, immutable character at common law. Could the possibility of the principle of legality being extended in such a way vindicate the dicta of Lords Steyn, Hope and Baroness Hale in *Jackson*, providing a burgeoning basis for the notion that the courts might ultimately be empowered to reject an Act of Parliament which contravened fundamental tenets of the common law?

In my view, it cannot, for existing authority points to the fact that the *Simms* principle could not coherently be developed along these lines. In *Watkins v Secretary of State for the Home Department*,[71] another case about the examination of a prisoner's legal correspondence by prison officers, two limitations on the scope of the *Simms* principle, which the claimant sought to have transposed onto the law of tort, can be discerned. First, as Lord Rodger observed, 'it is in the sphere of interpretation of statutes that the expression "constitutional right" has tended to be used'.[72] Lord Walker concurred, noting that there was 'a lot of force' in the submission of counsel that 'the notion of core constitutional rights has a part to play in the development of the law, but only in the field of the interpretation of primary legislation ... or in the review of secondary legislation'.[73] The *Simms* principle might thus be seen solely as an interpretive tool, with no application in any other area of law, whether that is the tort of misfeasance in public office, as was contended in *Watkins*, or the rules governing the validity of statutes, established to give effect to the doctrine of parliamentary sovereignty.

Secondly, again in *Watkins*, Lord Rodger argued that:

> Most of the references to 'constitutional rights' are to be found in cases dealing with situations before the Human Rights Act 1998 brought Convention rights into our law. In using the language of 'constitutional rights', the judges were, more or less explicitly, looking for a means of incorporation avant la lettre, of having the common law supply the benefits of incorporation without incorporation. Now that the Human Rights Act 1998 is in place, such heroic efforts are unnecessary: the Convention rights form part of our law and provide a rough equivalent of a written code of constitutional rights, albeit not one tailor-made for this country.[74]

It is therefore also arguable that the fundamental constitutional rights protection offered by the courts in accordance with *Simms* has been supplanted by the enactment of the HRA. The close relationship between common law and European Convention rights was emphasised by the courts at an early stage in the life of the HRA. In *R (Daly) v Secretary of State for the Home Department*[75] Lord Bingham concluded that the application of both common law principles and Article 8(1) of the European Convention on Human Rights (ECHR) led to the same result: a

---

[71] *Watkins v Secretary of State for the Home Department* [2006] UKHL 17, [2006] 2 AC 395.
[72] ibid [61].
[73] ibid [73].
[74] ibid [64].
[75] *R (on the application of Daly) v Secretary of State for the Home Department* [2001] UKHL 26, [2001] 2 AC 532.

policy excluding prisoners from their cells while the cells were searched by prison officers, leaving confidential legal correspondence susceptible to unobserved examination, was unlawful.[76] Nevertheless, while Lord Bingham noted that this would not necessarily be the outcome in every case,[77] with a greater intensity of review often required to ensure compliance with the ECHR,[78] the court in *Daly* certainly did not seem inclined to forsake basic common law rights in favour of an exclusive embrace of the HRA.

However, in the later case of *R (Roberts) v Parole Board*,[79] tension more clearly emerged between the *Simms* presumption that Parliament does not intend to violate constitutional rights by general words, and the reasoning characteristically employed to satisfy the demands of the HRA. In this case, which concerned the legality of the Parole Board utilising special advocates in its hearings, Lords Bingham and Steyn, in the minority, relied on *Simms* to argue that in the absence of express statutory authorisation, the Parole Board lacked the power to adopt a procedure which breached the rules of natural justice.[80] According to Lord Steyn the vires of the Parole Board's 'evisceration of the right to a fair hearing' was the 'primary question' before the court.[81] The majority, however, took an alternative approach and held that the Parole Board's use of special advocates was not necessarily unlawful. Unlike the judges in the minority, Lord Woolf did not treat the legality of the procedure as an absolute matter, and was prepared to give the Board more latitude to 'balance carefully the conflicting interests involved' when setting the procedure to be followed in a particular hearing.[82] In his view, 'non disclosure of information to the prisoner when ... necessary in the public interest' was permissible, both at common law and in accordance with Article 5(4) of the ECHR, so long as there was not a '*fundamental* denial of the prisoner's rights to a fair hearing' (emphasis added).[83] The balancing approach of Lord Woolf, which crucially focused on the weighing of competing interests against one another, and an examination of the degree to which a prisoner's rights could thus be legitimately qualified, seems strongly influenced by the proportionality reasoning adopted under the ECHR[84] and, in this case at least, served to undercut the protection of common law constitutional rights offered by the *Simms*

---

[76] ibid [23].

[77] ibid [23].

[78] See in particular the speech of Lord Steyn, [2001] UKHL 26, [2001] 2 AC 532, [24]–[28], along with the judgment of the European Court of Human Rights in *Smith and Grady v UK* (2000) 29 EHRR 493.

[79] *R (on the application of Roberts) v Parole Board* [2005] UKHL 45, [2005] 2 AC 738.

[80] ibid [23]–[25], [93].

[81] ibid [89].

[82] ibid [82].

[83] ibid [83].

[84] See generally the formulation of proportionality set out by Lord Bingham in *Huang v Secretary of State for the Home Department* [2007] UKHL 11, [2007] 2 AC 167, [19].

principle. Indeed, such was the emphasis on Convention-style balancing,[85] the other members of the majority, Lords Rodger and Carswell, did not even refer to the *Simms* presumption in their judgments. Moreover, *Watkins* itself provided further evidence that the *Simms* approach could be side-lined by the enactment of the HRA. In this case the House of Lords' refusal to extend the application of common law constitutional rights into the law of tort was partly justified on the grounds that, in the words of Lord Bingham, from the creation of the HRA 'it may reasonably be inferred that Parliament intended infringements of the core human (and constitutional) rights protected by the Act to be remedied under it and not by development of parallel remedies'.[86]

More recent authority, however, provides evidence of the general resilience of the common law. Two cases in particular demonstrate an increasing judicial willingness to resolve cases on the basis of common law principle, in preference to exploiting the tools provided by the HRA. First, in *Osborn v Parole Board*,[87] a case concerning the procedures to be followed when determining whether a prisoner could be released or transferred to open-prison conditions, the Supreme Court held that having regard to common law standards of procedural fairness would be sufficient to establish whether oral hearings were required. Lord Reed, giving the judgment of the court, criticised the submissions made on behalf of the appellants for having focused on the ECHR, while paying 'comparatively little attention to domestic administrative law'.[88] While the importance of the HRA was 'unquestionable', for Lord Reed, it did not 'supersede the protection of human rights under the common law or statute, or create a discrete body of law based on the judgments of the European court'.[89] Instead, '[h]uman rights continue to be protected by our domestic law, interpreted and developed in accordance with the Act when appropriate'.[90] It was therefore 'an error in approach ... to suppose that because an issue falls within the ambit of a Convention guarantee, it follows that the legal analysis of the problem should begin and end with the Strasbourg case law'.[91]

Secondly, in *Kennedy v Information Commissioner*[92] a journalist sought to compel the Charity Commission to disclose information it held as a consequence of carrying out statutory inquiries into the affairs of a particular charity. However, section 32(2) of the Freedom of Information Act 2000 (FOIA) made this information exempt absolutely from disclosure. A minority of members of the Supreme Court (Lords Wilson and Carnwath) argued that this absolute ban on disclosure was

---

[85] Lord Carswell in particular adopted a balancing approach quite explicitly: *R (on the application of Roberts) v Parole Board* [2005] UKHL 45, [2005] 2 AC 738, [143]–[144].

[86] *Watkins v Secretary of State for the Home Department* [2006] UKHL 17, [2006] 2 AC 395, [26].

[87] *Osborn v Parole Board* [2013] UKSC 61, [2013] 3 WLR 1020.

[88] ibid [54].

[89] ibid [57].

[90] ibid [57].

[91] ibid [63].

[92] *Kennedy v Information Commissioner* [2014] UKSC 20, [2014] 2 WLR 808.

incompatible with the journalist's right to freedom of expression under Article 10 of the ECHR (which was taken by the minority to include a right to receive official information), and should be 'read down' using the interpretive power contained in section 3 of the HRA. The five-strong majority (Lords Neuberger, Mance, Clarke, Sumption and Toulson), however, took a different view. The FOIA was not an exhaustive scheme for the disclosure of official information,[93] and the Charity Commission could have an additional duty to disclose as a result of its statutory obligations set out in the Charities Act 1993—including those relating to account-ability and transparency—which were to be interpreted in light of the 'common law presumption in favour of openness'.[94] As such, there was no need, as Lord Toulson observed, to use section 3 of the HRA to read the FOIA 'in a manner contrary to Parliament's intention'.[95] Instead, the court could avoid usurping the function of Parliament[96] by ensuring that a refusal to disclose by the Charity Commission was subject to rigorous judicial review, according to which the Commission would need to demonstrate 'some persuasive countervailing considerations to outweigh the strong prima facie case that the information should be disclosed'.[97] Nor was to do so effectively to circumvent the exemption from disclosure created by Parliament in the statutory scheme of the FOIA, for, according to Lord Toulson,

> although the sovereignty of Parliament means that the responsibility of the courts for determining the scope of the open justice principle may be affected by an Act of Parliament, Parliament should not be taken to have legislated so as to limit or control the way in which the court decides such a question unless the language of the statute makes it plain beyond possible doubt that this was Parliament's intention.[98]

And as in *Osborn*, in addition to employing a common law solution in prefer-ence to one offered by the HRA, the majority in the Supreme Court also made explicit comments as to the enduring significance of such domestic norms. For Lord Mance:

> Since the passing of the Human Rights Act 1998, there has too often been a tendency to see the law in areas touched on by the Convention solely in terms of the Convention rights ... But the natural starting point in any dispute is to start with domestic law, and it is certainly not to focus exclusively on the Convention rights, without surveying the wider common law scene.[99]

---

[93] ibid [6].
[94] ibid [47].
[95] ibid [130].
[96] ibid [130].
[97] ibid [56].
[98] ibid [117], quoting *R (Guardian News and Media Ltd) v City of Westminster Magistrates' Court (Article 19 intervening)* [2012] EWCA Civ 420, para 73.
[99] ibid [46].

This sentiment was echoed by Lord Toulson, who observed that '[i]t needs to be emphasised that it was not the purpose of the Human Rights Act that the common law should become an ossuary'.[100]

It may be that this recent resurgence in common law rhetoric,[101] and its exploitation in preference to the remedies offered by the HRA, is a judicial reaction to increased political debate as to the future of statutory rights protection in the UK. As Elliott has suggested, the courts may be attempting to demonstrate that

> if the HRA ceases to cast [a] shadow—by virtue of being repealed at the behest of a future government—the common-law constitutional landscape that is left behind may be remarkably similar to the situation that has obtained during the era of the HRA.[102]

And while such judicial manoeuvring might therefore indicate that the domestic pre-eminence of the common law has not, in general, been ousted by the HRA, nor has the *Simms* 'principle of legality', in particular, been abandoned by the courts, as a number of recent cases demonstrate. For example, in *Secretary of State for the Home Department v GG*[103] the Court of Appeal held that the inclusion in a control order of a requirement that the controlee submit to searches of their person was unlawful. While section 1(3) of the Prevention of Terrorism Act 2005 empowered the Home Secretary to impose by control order 'any obligations that the Secretary of State ... considers necessary' to restrict an individual's involvement in terrorism-related activity, the indicative, non-exhaustive, and yet reasonably extensive list of particular obligations that could be imposed provided in section 1(4) did not expressly include the requirement that a controlee consent to personal searches. Applying *Simms*, Dyson LJ held that this was 'a paradigm case of general words which are neither expressly nor by necessary implication intended to interfere with a person's fundamental rights'.[104] Similarly, in *Ahmed v HM Treasury*[105] the Supreme Court held that section 1(1) of the United Nations Act 1946, which gave the government a broad power to make by Order in Council 'such provision as appears ... necessary or expedient' to enable 'any measures' required to be put in place by a decision of the UN Security Council to be 'effectively applied', did not lawfully empower the creation of Orders which significantly violated fundamental individual rights. Consequently, the Terrorism (United Nations Measures) Order 2006 and the Al-Qaida and Taliban (United Nations Measures) Order 2006, which essentially provided for the freezing of the assets of individuals suspected of being involved in facilitating acts of terrorism,

---

[100] ibid [133].

[101] See also, in the context of the common law 'constitutional principle' of open justice, *A v BBC* [2014] UKSC 25, [2014] 2 WLR 1243, [23]–[27], [40]–[41], esp [55]–[57].

[102] M Elliott, 'Common-Law Constitutionalism and Proportionality in the Supreme Court: Kennedy v The Charity Commission', *Public Law for Everyone Blog* (31 March 2014): publiclawforeveryone.com/2014/03/31/common-law-constitutionalism-and-proportionality-in-the-supreme-court-kennedy-v-the-charity-commission/.

[103] *Secretary of State for the Home Department v GG* [2009] EWCA Civ 786, [2010] QB 585.

[104] ibid [41].

[105] *Ahmed v HM Treasury* [2010] UKSC 2; [2010] 2 AC 534.

without a sufficient appeal process, were both found to be ultra vires. While it is worth noting that the HRA was not applicable in *Ahmed*, as a result of the decision of the House of Lords in *R (Al-Jedda) v Secretary of State for Defence*,[106] the ECHR could have been relied on in *GG*, yet this was unnecessary, as the Court of Appeal was prepared to give priority to arguments based on the common law protection of basic rights.

Finally, in *Al Rawi v Security Service*[107] it was alleged the Security Service had caused or was complicit in the detention abroad of the claimants, who brought actions for damages on the basis of the harm suffered as a result. The Security Service sought to have these civil claims heard using closed material procedures, to prevent the sensitive evidence, on which its defence was largely to be based, from being disclosed in public. However, a majority in the Supreme Court held that, in such circumstances, closed material procedures could not be permitted without 'express parliamentary authorisation'.[108] The 'fundamental common law principle' of open justice[109] was in issue, and this was not to be eroded by development of the common law.[110] As such, as Lord Dyson observed, giving the leading judgment, 'it is not for the courts to extend such a controversial procedure beyond the boundaries which Parliament has chosen to draw for its use thus far'.[111] There was some disagreement among the judges in relation to whether it would *ever* be possible for the courts to allow such a procedure to be used, especially in (hypothetical) exceptional circumstances where to refuse to do so would deny a claimant access to justice.[112] Yet with respect to the situation that was in issue in *Al Rawi*, the principle of legality was exploited by the Supreme Court to limit its own inherent power to control its procedures, rather than to circumscribe the general power afforded by statute to a public official or authority. In this sense, the principle of legality might be seen to have an additional application, operating as a judicial self-denying ordinance, to prevent fundamental common law principles

---

[106] *R (Al-Jedda) v Secretary of State for Defence* [2007] UKHL 58; [2008] 1 AC 332. In *Al-Jedda*, the House of Lords held that it was likely that the European Court of Human Rights in Strasbourg would consider obligations under the UN Charter to take precedence over ECHR obligations as a matter of international law, and as a result, in accordance with the reading of s 21 of the HRA adopted by the court in *R (Quark Fishing Ltd) v Secretary of State for Foreign and Commonwealth Affairs* [2005] UKHL 57; [2006] 1 AC 529, no domestic action for the violation of Convention rights could be brought under the HRA. This is point is discussed in detail by Lord Phillips in *Ahmed*: [2010] UKSC 2; [2010] 2 AC 534, [92]–[99]. The authority of the decision of the House of Lords in *Al-Jedda* is now in question, following the contrary decision of the Grand Chamber of the European Court of Human Rights in *Al-Jedda v United Kingdom* (2011) 53 EHRR 789.

[107] *Al Rawi v Security Service* [2011] UKSC 34; [2012] 1 AC 531.

[108] ibid [77].

[109] ibid [11].

[110] Lord Clarke, the sole dissenting judge as to the result of the case, suggested the contrary: 'I can envisage circumstances in which it might be appropriate to develop the common law by directing that some form of closed material procedure take place': ibid [188].

[111] ibid [47].

[112] Lord Mance and Lady Hale suggested it might be possible to adopt closed material procedures with the consent of the parties: ibid [120]. Lord Phillips suggested such questions should be left open until they actually arose: ibid [196].

from being endangered by the evolution of the common law, which supplements its more familiar function of structuring the interpretation of statutes.

The legitimacy of the *Simms* presumption, and the appropriateness of its application in particular cases, is, of course, a matter for debate. While the courts' desire to rectify significant lapses in natural justice—the abiding undercurrent of this line of cases—is understandable, their subversion of the literal meaning of broad enabling provisions is not uncontroversial, and involves the judges playing off Parliament's intention as embodied in the language of a statute against its 'true' intention. This is a delicate task, and one which has in some cases led to disagreement between the judges. In *R v Secretary of State for the Home Department, ex parte Anufrijeva*,[113] for example, in applying the principle of legality in a case concerning the notification to asylum seekers of the determination of their claims, the dissenting Lord Bingham criticised the majority of the House of Lords for their failure to give effect to 'a clear and unambiguous legislative provision'.[114] Yet in other cases, we see that the opposite criticism has also been advanced. In *Bank Mellat v HM Treasury (No 1)*,[115] for example, the dissenting judgments of Lords Hope, Kerr and Reed criticised the majority of the Supreme Court for undercutting the principle seemingly established in *Al Rawi*—that, as Lord Hope put it, closed material procedures can only be adopted where they have been 'expressly authorised by Parliament'[116]—by locating jurisdiction to hold such a hearing in a general empowering provision. *Bank Mellat* concerned an appeal in which closed evidence had already been adduced in the courts below, on the basis of statutory authority which did not explicitly extend to the Supreme Court. For Lord Neuberger, however, giving the judgment of the majority, the enabling provision establishing the jurisdiction of the Supreme Court to hear appeals contained in section 40(2) of the Constitutional Reform Act 2005 was 'broad' rather than general,[117] and sufficient to permit such procedures, where necessary to do justice.[118] Indeed, the case provides a clear demonstration of the potential for judicial disputes as to what precisely the principle of legality requires of Parliament to permit the violation of fundamental common law rights. For, in contrast with the argument of the minority that express authorisation was necessary to *allow* closed material procedures, Lord Neuberger suggested that, had it been the intention of Parliament to *exclude* appeals on closed evidence to the Supreme Court, legislation to this effect would have been expected.[119] To some extent, therefore, what the principle of legality may require of Parliament can depend on the perspective from which it is approached.

---

[113] *R v Secretary of State for the Home Department, ex parte Anufrijeva* [2003] UKHL 36; [2004] 1 AC 604.
[114] ibid [20].
[115] *Bank Mellat v HM Treasury (No 1)* [2013] UKSC 38; [2013] 4 All ER 495.
[116] ibid [88].
[117] ibid [56].
[118] ibid [44].
[119] ibid [59].

The enactment of the HRA adds a further layer of complexity, as the courts have had to address, albeit somewhat haphazardly, how the common law and statutory mechanisms for rights protection can co-exist. While in the post-HRA era the courts have been willing to continue to use the *Simms* principle to construe legislation, where possible, in such a way as to prevent the infringement of fundamental constitutional rights, Parliament's creation of a statutory scheme of rights protection which explicitly preserves its legal authority to violate basic rights surely fetters the judges from radically expanding the reach of the principle of legality in the future. The recent common law resurgence, while certainly significant, is one which is principally focused on encouraging challenges to first be advanced on common law principles, in order to maintain the currency and integrity of domestic law, rather than because any greater protection is, or might become, available. As is made clear in *Al Rawi* and the minority judgments in *Bank Mellat*, for example, on even the most expansive conception of the principle of legality, there is no doubt that Parliament remains able to legislate to produce results which are incompatible with fundamental common law rights[120]—the dispute instead is about what statutory action is necessary, if desired, to achieve such an objective. The comments of Lord Rodger in *Watkins* may therefore have been premature in promoting the primacy of the remedies provided by the HRA, yet while the principle of legality has certainly not fallen away, nor can it offer any more comprehensive a protection of basic rights, and may indeed offer less than the available statutory mechanisms.

The limited scope of *Simms* seems clear in particular from *Ahmed*. In his judgment in this case, Lord Phillips reiterated that the question of whether the common law can protect fundamental rights is one that arises only in the course of statutory interpretation,[121] although, of course, post-*Al Rawi*, we must additionally now acknowledge that, in limited circumstances, the principle of legality may also potentially be engaged by a sheer need for statutory authorisation where none already exists. Lord Phillips further refused in *Ahmed* to accept that the *Simms* principle allowed the courts to go as far as section 3 of the HRA, and 'depart from the unambiguous meaning the legislation would otherwise bear':[122] 'I do not consider that the principle of legality permits a court to disregard an unambiguous expression of Parliament's intention'.[123] Indeed, Lord Phillips sought to stress that the *Simms* principle does not constitute 'judicial interference with the will of Parliament' but '[o]n the contrary it upholds the supremacy of Parliament'.[124]

It seems quite clear, therefore, that the doctrine of parliamentary sovereignty has not been displaced by the principle of legality, and nor could it coherently

---

[120] Indeed, following the decision in *Al Rawi*, the Justice and Security Act 2013 was enacted providing statutory authorisation for the use of closed material procedures in civil proceedings: ss 6–16.

[121] *Ahmed v HM Treasury* [2010] UKSC 2, [2010] 2 AC 534, [85], [111].

[122] *Ghaidan v Godin-Mendoza* [2004] UKHL 30, [2004] 2 AC 557, [30].

[123] *Ahmed v HM Treasury* [2010] UKSC 2, [2010] 2 AC 534, [117].

[124] ibid [157].

be developed to this end. The *Simms* presumption is merely used by the courts to ensure that Parliament truly authorises official action which may infringe constitutionally significant rights or principles by requiring a clear, although not necessarily explicit, statutory basis to exist for the lawful creation of powers which may be used to this effect. While this may produce some contestable, and even divisive, decisions—as a consequence of the generality of the principle of legality itself—the scope, and thus crucially, the limits of this judicial tool are not a matter which can credibly be disputed. As the response to the Supreme Court's decision in *Ahmed* demonstrates, with the quashed powers to freeze assets being restored by emergency primary[125] and subordinate legislation,[126] Parliament retains the legal authority to legislate contrary to basic common law rights, and there is nothing, other than the controversial minority dicta in *Jackson*, to suggest that this could change in the future. The validity of an Act of Parliament which plainly contravenes fundamental common law rights cannot be judicially impugned, and consequently, the dicta of Lords Steyn, Hope and Baroness Hale in *Jackson* cannot be treated as a natural or logical development of the principle of legality. Instead, such comments must be seen as an aberration.

V. MINIMALIST INTERPRETATIONS OF *JACKSON*

At least on its face, *Jackson* can be seen to provide some support for more than one conception of the foundations of the UK constitution which diverge from the classic Diceyan account of the doctrine of parliamentary sovereignty. As I have argued above, in my view, *Jackson* is an indication that the UK constitution is now based on the manner and form conception of parliamentary sovereignty, rather than an array of fundamental common law principles. However, some have suggested that, despite initial appearances, neither of these two alternatives needs to be embraced. In this section, therefore, we consider potential minimalist interpretations of *Jackson*, which are premised on the notion that the decision of the House of Lords in *Jackson* can be reconciled with an orthodox Diceyan understanding of parliamentary sovereignty. Two such accounts of *Jackson*, which contend, in different ways, that the enduring form of Parliament's legislative power has not been altered, must be addressed.

First, Alison Young, who has defended the orthodox Diceyan conception of the doctrine, has argued that the Parliament Acts can be reconciled with what she

---

[125] Terrorist Asset-Freezing (Temporary Provisions) Act 2010.
[126] Al-Qaida and Taliban (Asset-Freezing) Regulations (SI 2010/1197).

prefers to call 'continuing'[127] parliamentary supremacy.[128] According to Young, the crucial difficulty here for the continuing theory of parliamentary supremacy is that section 2(1) of the Parliaments Act 1911, at least as it was understood by a majority of the House of Lords in *Jackson*, has been 'entrenched'.[129] If, as the majority suggested, section 2(1) contains an implied restriction which absolutely prevents the Parliament Acts from being used to remove the ban on the enactment—by that same statutory legislative process—of legislation which would extend the life of Parliament beyond five years, then, Young maintains, future Parliaments have been bound. For a Parliament wishing to overturn section 2(1) could 'only do so by adopting a specific manner and form—legislation that has the consent of the House of Lords as opposed to legislation passed without its consent'.[130] As I have argued above, I do not find the obiter dicta of the majority on this point persuasive, and therefore doubt whether section 2(1) has indeed bound future Parliaments in the way that Young suggests.[131] Further, in my view, Young adopts an unduly narrow interpretation of the problems caused for the traditional understanding of parliamentary sovereignty by the Parliament Acts and the *Jackson* case. Instead, I have argued that these developments, taken together, clearly establish the much broader proposition that Parliament has the legislative authority to change the manner and form required to enact valid statutes. Nonetheless, Young's attempt to reconcile 'entrenched' manner and form provisions with continuing parliamentary sovereignty must be considered, because her argument could be applied to future manner and form clauses which actually succeed in binding subsequent Parliaments.

Young contends that continuing parliamentary supremacy can be preserved if it is accepted that '[m]odifications of the definition of Parliament or the way in which legislation is passed occur through a change in the rule of recognition'.[132] Such a modification of the rule of recognition could not be effected by Parliament alone, but, as Hart argued, would depend on the change being accepted by those officials engaged in the operation of a system of government.[133] If changes to the manner and form required to enact valid legislation are thus seen to have taken

---

[127] As I argued in chapter 2 of this volume, I do not believe that this terminology is satisfactory, for the dichotomy between 'continuing' and 'self-embracing' parliamentary sovereignty on which it is premised fails to account for all potential conceptions of Parliament's legislative authority, in particular, the manner and form understanding of the doctrine: see pp 81–82.

[128] For discussion of Young's preference for the language of supremacy over sovereignty, see chapter 4 of this volume, p 174. While Young maintains that her account of parliamentary supremacy is compatible with that of Dicey's parliamentary sovereignty, it is not clear that this is ultimately the case: see text at n 144.

[129] AL Young, 'Hunting Sovereignty: *Jackson v Her Majesty's Attorney-General*' [2006] *PL* 187, 194.

[130] ibid 194.

[131] I accept that Parliament is 'bound' by s 2(1) from using the Parliament Acts to extend the life of Parliament beyond five years while the provision remains on the statute book, but do not accept that this explicit limitation contained in s 2(1) cannot itself be removed using the Parliament Acts procedure; see text at n 38.

[132] Young, 'Hunting Sovereignty' [2006] n 129 above, 195.

[133] See HLA Hart, *The Concept of Law*, 2nd edn (Oxford, Oxford University Press, 1994) 113–14.

place at the level of 'political fact'—which is not susceptible to unilateral legislative alteration—Parliament both remains legally incapable of binding itself and its successors, and retains its continuing legislative sovereignty.[134] However, in my view the rule of recognition cannot appropriately be invoked in this way, enabling the remains of the Diceyan theory of parliamentary sovereignty (or supremacy) to be salvaged. Young's attempt to do so thus provides a second example of the difficulties generated when change to the doctrine of parliamentary sovereignty is analysed as change to the rule of recognition.[135] First, it is excessively elaborate to suppose that a particular Act of Parliament which purports to create or amend legal norms is prohibited from having this *legal* effect, but can nevertheless have precisely the effect it fails to have as a matter of law at the level of fundamental *political* fact. This is the jurisprudential equivalent of employing a 'get out of jail free' card. On Young's approach, if change is difficult to conceptualise within an established constitutional system, or leads to an awkward outcome, it can instead be postulated as having occurred at a foundational, non-legal level, avoiding the need for our most elementary constitutional pre-suppositions to be called into question. Young's account thus repudiates the most straightforward explanation of the constitutional change—in this case that the Parliament Acts are statutes which have clear *legal* consequences—in order to protect the orthodox dogma associated with parliamentary sovereignty from revision.

Secondly, it is inherently difficult to prove or disprove whether or not there has been a change in the rule of recognition. What evidence could be produced to demonstrate conclusively that a modification of the rule of recognition has been accepted by the vast majority of officials in the UK? The House of Lords in *Jackson* did not even begin to attempt to carry out an assessment of the views of officials in relation to the status of the Parliament Acts, and it is difficult to see how a court could be thought capable of, or indeed why it might be interested in, undertaking such a task. Where a relatively clear consensus appears to exist—as I suggested it does, in Chapter four, in relation to the legislative authority of Parliament in light of the UK's membership of the EU, and may also be the case with respect to the status of the Parliament Act 1949—the significance of this difficulty may be diminished. Yet having recourse to the rule of recognition to resolve even these disputes—let alone those where the occurrence (or not) of a fundamental change to the established constitutional order is hotly contested—is still extremely unhelpful. For to adopt such an approach essentially means that the propriety of fundamental legal change will no longer be assessed by reference to existing constitutional principles and norms, but by a subjective evaluation of official attitudes, which may readily diverge from the broader commitments of political principle which are reflected in the established governmental structures. To plunge into such uncertain, and potentially unprincipled, territory, should

---

[134] Young, 'Hunting Sovereignty' [2006] n 129 above, 194.
[135] See also chapter 4 of this volume, pp 179–82; chapter 6 of this volume, pp 273–75.

be avoided unless absolutely necessary, rather than encouraged as a means to rationalise challenging constitutional change.

Thirdly, this general uncertainty creates a number of practical problems. How could the precise moment at which an alteration of the rule of recognition occurred be identified? Taking the present example, if, as Young argues, it was not the legal enactment of section 2(1) itself which bound Parliament, when did the legislature become so bound? Did the rule of recognition change in 1911 with the passing of the first Parliament Act, in 1949 when that Act was amended, in 2005 when the *Jackson* case was decided by House of Lords, or some stage in between? Theoretically, the answer is whenever the change was accepted by the officials, but, again, how can this moment be clearly ascertained? The uncertainty produced by characterising such constitutional change as a shift in the rule of recognition, rather than a legal alteration of the manner and form required for the creation of valid legislation, is both undesirable and unnecessary. For while constitutional actors are unsure of the content of the rule of recognition it will be difficult for them to determine the precise requirements of their system's legal validity criteria, potentially leading to doubts about the lawfulness of prospective legislative action. If accepted, the manner and form theory, in contrast, offers greater clarity, with the legislative process definitively modified at the moment that the statute effecting procedural change comes into force.

Further, could statutes purporting to change the manner and form for the enactment of future legislation, such as the Parliament Acts, be effectively repealed if they only have effect at a non-legal, fundamental level? Since, according to Young, Parliament retains its continuing sovereignty, the Acts of 1911 and 1949 must be susceptible to repeal. However, this would have no necessary impact on the content of the rule of recognition, and as such, at the level of political fact Parliament might still be subject to the requirements of a repealed statute. This would be most unsatisfactory, and as a result, as Richard Ekins has argued, it must be the case that the 'contingent status' of the Parliament Act 1949 (that it 'may be amended or repealed at any time') 'is fatal to the claim that it is legally fundamental'.[136] Indeed, in later work Young has herself acknowledged that the significant uncertainty surrounding the practical application of her reading of *Jackson* is problematic: 'it may be difficult in practice to modify the rule of recognition without this also being interpreted as a modification of the theory of parliamentary legislative supremacy, shifting from continuing to self-embracing sovereignty'.[137] Consequently, while this may be a convenient conceptual alternative for defenders of continuing parliamentary sovereignty, to characterise such change as a modification of the rule of recognition is neither the most obvious nor the most logical explanation of such legislative action, and indeed, may

---

[136] R Ekins, 'Acts of Parliament and the Parliament Acts' (2007) 123 *LQR* 91, 111.
[137] AL Young, *Parliamentary Sovereignty and the Human Rights Act* (Oxford, Hart Publishing, 2009) 85.

actually generate a number of practical difficulties which do not beset a more straightforward manner and form account.

Fourthly, such an approach presents one final problem, in that it opens the door to the possibility of the absolute limitation of Parliament. There is nothing to prevent a common law constitutionalist, for example, putting forward the argument that the officials in the UK have now accepted that there are substantive moral limits to Parliament's legislative power that are to be enforced by the judiciary. While it is very unlikely that a change in the rule of recognition could be achieved by academic diktat, given the difficulty in proving or disproving whether or not such a change in the rule of recognition has actually occurred, this has the potential to be a powerful rhetorical claim. And if, as most theorists seem to assume, the courts will be the ultimate arbiters of whether a change in the rule of recognition must be recognised—in practice, if not in principle[138]—the very potential that they might be entitled to accept such a claim is problematic, from a democratic perspective, in itself.[139] Young's attempt to reconcile continuing parliamentary supremacy with the existence of statutory changes to the manner and form required for legislation is therefore ultimately self-defeating. For to invoke the rule of recognition as a relatively routine explanatory tool creates a means by which common law supremacism might indirectly be introduced, which leaves entirely vulnerable the legally unlimited legislative authority which Young, at least ostensibly, seeks to defend.

On Young's analysis, this may be something to be welcomed, rather than regretted. In recent work, for example, Young has suggested that the decision of the Supreme Court in *Axa General Insurance Ltd v Lord Advocate*,[140] which will be discussed in detail below,[141] could be considered an attempt by the courts to initiate a shift in the rule of recognition, which if effective, would place common law limits on the content of Acts of the Scottish Parliament.[142] Yet if judicial attempts to limit the sovereign power of the Westminster Parliament could similarly be rationalised on this basis, it is not at all clear that the conception of 'continuing parliamentary legislative supremacy' which Young defends is still compatible with the 'old' Diceyan understanding of parliamentary sovereignty, as she maintains.[143] Indeed, rather than providing 'a different justification' for the adoption of a Diceyan position,[144] Young's defence of legislative supremacy may instead

---

[138] Although see on this point A Tucker, 'Uncertainty in the Rule of Recognition and in the Doctrine of Parliamentary Sovereignty' (2011) 31 *OJLS* 61, 78–82, 88, exploring in detail the significant role necessarily to be played by the courts in resolving 'uncertainty' where the rule of recognition is 'indeterminate'; such resolution will be based on 'the evaluative judgments of the judiciary'.

[139] See chapter 4 of this volume, pp 181–82.

[140] *Axa General Insurance Ltd v Lord Advocate* [2011] UKSC 46, [2012] 1 AC 868.

[141] See text at nn 181–209.

[142] AL Young, 'Parliamentary Sovereignty Re-defined' in R Rawlings, P Leyland and AL Young (eds), *Sovereignty and the Law: Domestic, European, and International Perspectives* (Oxford, Oxford University Press, 2013) 86.

[143] ibid 72.

[144] ibid 72.

ultimately provide a different route to a common law constitution. For, if judicial claims as to the imposition of common law limits on legislative power are conceived as 'suggestions' to change the content of a rule of recognition, for which they share responsibility with Parliament,[145] a false authority may attach to such notions, making them extremely difficult in practice to rebut. The manner and form understanding of the doctrine of parliamentary sovereignty, in contrast, is unafflicted by this potential difficulty, for it avoids the need regularly to exploit the rule of recognition as a practical explanatory tool, while simultaneously insisting that attempts to place absolute limitations on Parliament's law-making power are constitutionally prohibited. Of course, this certainly does not guarantee that such constitutional prohibitions will never be displaced. However, if such change is ever to occur, it must be debated openly and implemented deliberately, rather than achieved on the basis of elite-level speculation about the 'true' content of a reified, yet ultimately hypothetical, rule of recognition.

A second alternative assessment of the effect of the Parliament Acts, which also seeks to avoid an embrace of manner and form parliamentary sovereignty, is offered by Ekins. Ekins contends that the Parliament Acts 'do not purport to confer authority' to enact legislation, but instead 'are a decision-making procedure that Parliament has adopted to structure its further action'.[146] As Ekins acknowledges, this sounds very similar to the manner and form reading of the Parliament Acts.[147] However, the manner and form interpretation is rejected by Ekins because the Westminster Parliament, unlike those of Commonwealth nations, 'was not constituted by law and the way in which it may act is not prescribed by law. For this reason ... Parliament may not simply amend the legal rules that prescribe when it acts, for no such rules exist'.[148] Instead, the law merely 'recognises Parliament's legislative authority' which is derived from 'custom', and it is left to the three constituent parts of Parliament to determine how their collective authority will be exercised.[149] According to Ekins, the requirement that the Queen, Lords and Commons all assent for Parliament to act is 'not stipulated by law', but based on the fact that '[t]he three branches agree that their joint assent is necessary'.[150] As a result, the Parliament Act 1911 is 'a decision-making procedure that Parliament adopts to enable it to act without joint assent'.[151] For Ekins, Parliament is an institution which 'acts in accordance with its own practice, over which it has control', and thus the Parliament Acts operate 'to extend that practice, supplementing the existing process by which legislators act together'.[152]

---

[145] ibid 86–87.
[146] Ekins, 'Acts of Parliament and the Parliament Acts' (2007) n 136 above, 99, 100.
[147] ibid 100.
[148] ibid 101–2.
[149] ibid 105, 102.
[150] ibid 104.
[151] ibid 106.
[152] ibid 115.

Ekins rejection of the manner and form explanation of the Parliament Acts rests crucially on a distinction between legal norms and customary rules. That the rules setting out how Parliament must act to in order to legislate are based on custom and practice, and not law, is taken by Ekins to mean that these rules are not susceptible to being amended by statute. Although Ekins does acknowledge that it is possible that the structure and composition of Parliament may change over time, the fact that it is 'Parliament' that has the power to legislate is constitutionally fixed: '[f]undamental custom refers us to one institution, which represents the realm and in whom authority vests'.[153] The Parliament Acts have not changed the fact that the Queen, Lords and Commons act in concert to legislate, for the authority to legislate is inherently vested in these three bodies, assembled together in Parliament; nor indeed could the Parliament Acts, or any other statute, have altered this constitutional fundamental. Instead, the Parliament Acts have merely changed the action that is required of the three constituent branches of Parliament for legislation to be successfully enacted, something which constitutionally, being grounded in custom, has always been a matter for Parliament to determine.

The bright line distinction between law and custom upon which this argument is based, however, is suspect. I agree with Ekins that Parliament's legislative authority emerged as a matter of customary practice, and was not a creation of the common law. However, this does not mean that it remains simply a matter of custom, fundamental or otherwise, today. Customary rules can develop into legal norms when they are accepted as generating legal obligations by actors and citizens across the constitutional spectrum. Indeed, this is exactly what happened to constitute the doctrine of parliamentary sovereignty in the UK constitution: what began as customary practice developed into legal doctrine. If this is incorrect, and the rules determining the action required of the Queen, Lords and Commons for the production of valid legislation are merely customary, why would Parliament choose to amend these rules using an Act of Parliament? Surely the three constituent branches of Parliament could simply together agree to change their own practice if, as Ekins contends, they are free to establish in combination the action they must themselves take to exercise their legislative authority and enact a lawful statute. It is, however, extremely doubtful that such an agreement to change parliamentary practice, which could, hypothetically, have been used to attempt to remove the requirement that the assent of the House of Lords be given for a Bill to become an Act of Parliament, would be constitutionally accepted. For as *The Prince's Case* shows, a purported Act of Parliament which is only assented to by the Queen and the Lords, or the Queen and the Commons, will not be recognised as a lawful statute by the courts.[154] That an Act of Parliament was thought to be necessary to create the alternative procedure for the enactment of primary

---

[153] ibid 106.
[154] *The Prince's Case* (1605) 8 Co Rep 1a, 20b.

legislation laid out in the Parliament Acts is a clear indication that rules which may be customary, but are also *legal*, determine how Parliament acts. Such rules, being legal in nature, could not effectively have been displaced or supplemented by the mere agreement of the Queen, Lords and Commons to change their collective practice. Instead, legislation was needed to allow the Queen and Commons to legislate without the House of Lords because the change being made was to the law, rather than to mere custom. Ekins' analysis does not therefore provide a tenable way in which the manner and form conception of parliamentary sovereignty can be avoided. Instead, the enactment of the Parliament Acts, as was accepted by the House of Lords in *Jackson*, must be seen to represent a legislative alteration of the legal rules governing the legislative process. For this to be a coherent and permissible use of the sovereign Parliament's law-making authority, the manner and form theory of legally unlimited legislative power must be adopted.

VI. IMPLICATIONS OF A MANNER AND FORM READING OF *JACKSON*

I have argued in this chapter that *Jackson* must be understood to represent a shift in the UK constitution from the orthodox Diceyan understanding of parliamentary sovereignty, to the manner and form theory of legally unlimited legislative power. But what are the implications of such a reading of *Jackson*? Such is the reticence to embrace this understanding of parliamentary sovereignty—seen, for example, in the efforts explored immediately above which strain to reconcile the decision with the Diceyan orthodoxy—that even scholars who accept that *Jackson* must be understood as a vindication of the manner and form theory have criticised this outcome. Weill, for example, has recognised that *Jackson* is a 'triumph' for the manner and form theory, although does not endorse the decision of the House of Lords.[155] Instead, Weill has argued that the House of Lords could, and indeed should, have rejected the Parliament Act 1949 as invalid,[156] and that as a result of its failure to do so, 'the true outcome of *Jackson* is a further weakening of popular sovereignty'.[157] Yet this claim is based on a highly questionable interpretation of the Parliament Act 1911, which for Weill, must be 'treated as a constitutional document enacted by "We the British People"'.[158] The Parliament Act 1911 is suggested to have received 'popular endorsement', by virtue of the general election held after this legislation had been vetoed by the House of Lords, whereas the Parliament Act 1949 did not.[159] As such, the Parliament Act 1949 was not a

---

[155] R Weill, 'Centennial to the Parliament Act 1911: The Manner and Form Fallacy' [2012] *PL* 105, 110–12.

[156] ibid 123.

[157] Ibid 107.

[158] ibid 106.

[159] ibid 112–19.

valid amendment of the Act of 1911, for this could not be amended 'without the consent of the body that enacted it—the People'.[160]

Such a challenge to the democratic credentials of the decision reached in *Jackson*, and by extension, the manner and form theory employed to reach it, is problematic in a number of respects. First, it depends on a particular understanding of the nature of popular sovereignty, and the cultivation of a false dichotomy between this principle and that of parliamentary sovereignty, which I rejected in Chapter one.[161] Yet even setting this aside, the idea that the adoption of a manner and form analysis of the Parliament Acts in *Jackson* is somehow damaging to the democratic foundations of the UK constitution is difficult to sustain. The second difficulty is with the description of the Parliament Act 1911 as a constitutional document, and the consequences of this designation. Even if the Act of 1911 had been endorsed by the people in any direct or meaningful sense, there is no inherent reason that it would be entitled to any greater legal status as a result. Instead, while 'popular endorsement' of legislation may certainly be politically significant—with the devolution legislation being a prime example—it is not legally relevant to the question of how it is to be amended or repealed. This is not to diminish the importance, in principle, of popular involvement in constitutional decision-making. Rather, it is to recognise that the extent of such direct engagement can nevertheless only be determined by reference to the established constitutional rules in a particular legal system, and not through than vague assertions as to the people's authorship of parliamentary legislation.

Finally, the characterisation of certain institutions as agents of a popular democratic politics in the UK, upon which this critique of *Jackson* and the Parliament Act 1949 crucially depends, can also be disputed. The House of Lords is portrayed as misunderstood rather than undemocratic,[162] putting its veto power, between 1832 and 1911, 'at the service of the People, enabling them to decide on constitutional change'.[163] The fact that in this period the House of Lords was an aristocratic chamber filled with hereditary peers makes claims that it was capable of making a 'fundamental contribution ... to Britain's democracy' impossible to accept.[164] Further, it must also be recalled that the electorate of this era, at whose pleasure the Lords are said to have served, is extremely difficult to equate with 'the People' in any substantive sense, when at no stage in this period were women entitled to vote.[165] At the very least, this is a flawed basis on which the Parliament

---

[160] ibid 119.

[161] See chapter 1 of this volume, pp 48–49.

[162] Weill, 'The Manner and Form Fallacy' [2012] n 155 above, 124.

[163] ibid 116.

[164] ibid 124. See, eg the assessment in D Shell, *The House of Lords* (Oxford, Phillip Allan, 1988) 8: the 'Referendal Theory' was 'a doctrine which emboldened Conservative peers in their opposition to the measures promoted by Liberal governments'. See also WI Jennings, *Parliamentary Reform* (London, Victor Gollancz, 1934) 7: '[w]ith Liberal and Labour Governments in power [the] inefficiency [of Parliament in the last 50 years] has been partly due to the sixty or eighty persons who in fact, if not in theory, form the House of Lords at any given time'.

[165] See chapter 1 of this volume, p 14.

Act 1949, which was explicitly designed to prevent a Labour government with a significant electoral mandate from having its legislative agenda disrupted, or even demolished, by the Conservative dominated House of Lords,[166] can be stigmatised as democratically and constitutionally illegitimate. Indeed, the reverse is true: the Parliament Act 1949 was both democratically justified—in so far as it served further to limit the temporal legislative veto of the hereditary House of Lords—and constitutionally valid—as the House of Lords rightly held in *Jackson*.

In contrast to these claims that the embrace of the manner and form theory in *Jackson* weakens popular sovereignty, I will argue in Chapter seven that, properly understood, this conception of legally unlimited legislative power can actually be used to enhance democratic politics in the UK. For it opens up the possibility that the existing legislative procedure—or, more accurately, procedures, given the status which must be afforded to the Parliament Acts post-*Jackson*—could be altered so as to enable new, more democratic institutions, and indeed the people themselves, to have direct input into the law-making process. Such a way forward seems likely to be far more promising, from a democratic perspective, than that favoured by Weill following *Jackson*, which is to hope that the unelected judges replace the unelected Upper Chamber as the 'the ultimate preserver of constitutional values'.[167] For even if the courts could legitimately establish jurisdiction to exercise the powers claimed over parliamentary legislation by Lords Steyn, Hope and Baroness Hale, and even if such power was to be exercised to vindicate the 'true, lasting, and permanent values of the People',[168] given the fundamental democratic deficiencies of common law constitutionalism,[169] such an arrangement could not be accepted as satisfactory.

Yet, is to attempt to justify the more elaborate use of a legislative power to change the future manner and form to risk overstating the implications of the decision of the House of Lords in *Jackson*? An alternative approach to *Jackson*, while also premised on an acceptance that the case demonstrates that Parliament has the law-making authority to legislate about the legislative process, seeks to limit, quite significantly, the future implications of this outcome. Rather than take the decision of the House of Lords to be a full vindication of the manner and form theory of parliamentary sovereignty—with all that might potentially flow from this, in terms of the expanded lawful scope of Parliament's legislative power—Goldsworthy has argued for a much narrower reading of *Jackson*. On

---

[166] For discussion of the Parliament Act 1949 as a pragmatic measure designed to prevent the disruption of the Labour government's Iron and Steel Bill, see, eg J Tomlinson, *Democratic Socialism and Economic Policy: the Atlee Years, 1945–51* (Cambridge, Cambridge University Press, 1997) 292–93. See also WI Jennings, *The Law and the Constitution*, 5th edn (London, University of London Press, 1959) 191–92: '[t]he insistence on the Conservative party on having a permanent Conservative majority (and what is in fact the same thing) on continuing the hereditary principle, has compelled the other parties so as to reduce the powers of the House of Lords'.

[167] Weill, 'The Manner and Form Fallacy' [2012] n 155 above, 125.

[168] ibid 125.

[169] See chapter 3 of this volume, pp 126–49.

Goldsworthy's account, '[t]he difference between alternative and restrictive procedures is important', and *Jackson* must be understood in this light.[170] An alternative legislative procedure, such as the Parliament Acts, at issue in *Jackson*, will never bind Parliament, and 'does not restrict Parliament's legislative power overall'.[171] In contrast, however, 'Parliament is obligated to follow', and may therefore be bound by, a restrictive procedure.[172] On this basis, Goldsworthy contends, 'Parliament's ability to enact an alternative procedure does not entail that it can enact restrictive procedures. This is because by definition the former cannot, but the latter might, diminish its sovereign power to legislate'.[173] Applying this distinction to the *Jackson* case, Goldsworthy therefore concludes that the comments made as to the possibility of Parliament enacting 'binding restrictive procedures must be classified as *obiter dicta*', leaving 'open' the question of 'whether Parliament can enact mandatory requirements as to procedure or form'.[174]

Goldsworthy's analysis of *Jackson* is a clear and consistent application of his 'procedure and form' model of legislative sovereignty to the issues raised in this case—the legal permissibility of a statutory change to the future legislative process depends crucially on whether 'Parliament's substantive power to change the law ... is diminished or even destroyed'.[175] Alternative procedures will never do this, according to Goldsworthy, whereas restrictive conditions may. As such, to accept the legality of the former tells us nothing about the legality of the latter, for the 'diminishing of substantive power' test is simply not engaged in such circumstances; there is, as Goldsworthy puts it, 'no similarity at all' between these two situations.[176] Yet once we recognise that Goldsworthy's analysis of *Jackson* is located in the wider conceptual framework provided by his procedure and form model, it becomes clear that there is no inherent logic to this rejection of a broader interpretation of the principles operating in *Jackson*. Rather, Goldsworthy's conclusion is a function of the general understanding of legally unlimited legislative authority which he defends. As I argued in Chapter two, there are a number of conceptual difficulties which Goldsworthy's procedure and form conception of parliamentary sovereignty,[177] and one of the most significant difficulties is manifested here, serving, in my view, to undermine his narrower reading of *Jackson*. This difficulty is with the notion that the legal permissibility of statutory changes to the future legislative 'procedure or form' is contingent upon such modifications to the law-making process not serving to diminish Parliament's substantive legislative power. This condition functions to make Parliament's legislative

---

[170] J Goldsworthy, *Parliamentary Sovereignty: Contemporary Debates* (Cambridge, Cambridge University Press, 2010) 176.

[171] ibid 177.

[172] ibid 177.

[173] ibid 179.

[174] ibid 179.

[175] ibid 176.

[176] ibid 178.

[177] See chapter 2 of this volume, pp 97–107.

capacity—the legal scope of its law-making authority—dependent upon an assessment of Parliament's legislative capability—the extent to which it is readily able to legislate in practice. And this is problematic because considerations as to the ease with which Parliament may legislate are not, in principle, relevant to the question of the scope of Parliament's legislative authority, as a matter of law.

In the context of *Jackson*, the challenges which attempts to apply this test in practice generate are clearly evident. Goldsworthy's distinction between alternative and restrictive procedures is based on the claim that the former will never diminish Parliament's substantive legislative power, whereas the latter might. Yet this claim can be contested. If an alternative legislative procedure was created for the enactment of legislation on any subject-matter, which was so easy to exercise that it rendered the traditional legislative process effectively redundant, it would be arguable that Parliament's substantive legislative power *had* been diminished. For example, if Parliament created by statute an 'alternative' law-making process by which the government could present to the monarch for royal assent Bills which could be enacted as primary legislation immediately, concerning any topic, without the assent of either the House of Commons or the House of Lords, this would surely in practice replace the current legislative procedure as the principal means of creating new legislation. For why would a government trouble itself with following the more cumbersome process of obtaining the consent of the Commons and Lords to enact legislation, when it need not do so? While, of course, this is a pretty absurd hypothetical, it is useful to demonstrate the point that it cannot automatically be assumed that alternative legislative procedures will never diminish Parliament's substantive legislative power, simply because they leave the traditional law-making process formally untouched. Indeed, the creation of such an alternative legislative procedure, which served in effect to side-line the two Houses from being involved in the business of enacting statutes, would surely diminish the substantive legislative power of Parliament to a greater extent than even a restrictive procedure which 'subordinated' that power 'to the veto of an external body'.[178]

This point is important in two respects. First, it demonstrates the complexity of applying in practice the 'diminishing of substantive power' test, which rests at the very heart of Goldsworthy's procedure and form model of parliamentary sovereignty. There is considerable scope for disagreement as to what effect any particular change to the legislative process would have on the substantive power of Parliament, and the potential for such contestation would introduce an unwelcome degree of uncertainty into attempts to ascertain the legal scope of Parliament's legislative authority (especially given the role the courts might be expected to play in settling such disputes). Secondly, it shows that it is inappropriate to draw an absolute line on this basis between alternative and restrictive conditions; while it can be accepted that the latter may be more likely to violate

---

[178] Goldsworthy, *Parliamentary Sovereignty: Contemporary Debates* (2010) n 170 above, 176.

the 'diminishing of substantive power' test, it is possible that both may do so. That such a line cannot be drawn is testament to a crucial underlying issue dismissed too readily by Goldsworthy: that there *is* a similarity between alternative and restrictive procedures, in that both alter the way in which legislation is made. We can choose to overlook this essential similarity, or argue that alternative and restrictive procedures should nevertheless be treated differently, but such an argument cannot be based on inherent facts about the complete distinctiveness of the two. Instead, a potential parallel does exist, and the key question is whether we ought to regard a distinction between alternative and restrictive procedures as significant. Goldsworthy's approach does afford significance to this distinction, but it is not clear that it is right to do so, on the basis that an alternative procedure is incapable of diminishing Parliament's substantive legislative power. Instead, while it is in general unlikely that an alternative procedure would violate the requirement that Parliament's substantive legislative power not be diminished, if the test is to be used at all, there is no reason that such procedures should be categorically exempt from having to satisfy it.

However, given the difficulties with the procedure and form model, and the 'diminishing of substantive power' test in general, it is also not clear that this model is one we ought to accept to structure our understanding of the scope of the legally unlimited legislative power of Parliament in any event. And while a distinction between alternative and restrictive procedures is not ultimately justified on Goldsworthy's model, nor is it significant on a manner and form conception of parliamentary sovereignty, which rejects the notion that change to the legislative process will only be lawful in so far as it does not diminish Parliament's substantive law-making power. Instead, in accordance with the manner and form theory, what is important is the procedural nature, rather than any substantive effects, of statutory change to legislative process. From either perspective, therefore, *Jackson* can be seen to offer critical guidance as to the scope of Parliament's sovereign law-making authority, the relevance of which is not diminished or circumscribed by drawing a line between alternative and restrictive procedures. For instead *Jackson* should be viewed as providing crucial recognition of a broad principle which underlies both kinds of statutory action: Parliament's legally unlimited law-making authority encompasses a general power to legislate about the legislative process.

Consequently, *Jackson* does not leave 'open' the question of whether Parliament can enact 'mandatory requirements' as to the future legislative process, but rather the question of whether this power—which does exist—is limited as a matter of law, as Goldsworthy maintains, or not, as the manner and form theory suggests. The House of Lords in *Jackson* showed no indication of accepting that the limit proposed by Goldsworthy—that Parliament's substantive power not be diminished by statutory change to the legislative process—is relevant to the legal scope of Parliament's law-making authority. And while the court did not, of course, settle this in *Jackson*—since no such condition was in issue—the comments of Baroness Hale and Lord Steyn lean instead towards embracing the full manner and form theory, to the extent that this issue is addressed. Ultimately, however, whether Goldsworthy's procedure and form model or the manner and form theory is correct will not be settled by the comments of the judges in *Jackson*, but by whichever provides the better understanding of parliamentary sovereignty. Yet, as the fundamental basis of the decision indicates that one or other must be right, *Jackson* crucially moves us into territory where Parliament's power to legislate to change the legislative process can no longer be denied. As I have argued in Chapter two, in my view, the manner and form theory provides the more coherent account of the parameters of this legislative power. Yet it will ultimately be for the sovereign Parliament to be the leading actor in the determination of this matter, post-*Jackson*. And, as will be considered in Chapter six, in my view, the enactment of European Union Act 2011 now gives a strong indication that the view which Parliament has taken of the scope of its own power is best characterised by the manner and form conception of the doctrine of parliamentary sovereignty.

VII. *JACKSON*'S AFTERMATH: *AXA*

As one of the most significant constitutional cases of the modern era, the multiple questions prompted by *Jackson* have been, and continue to be, debated. While I have argued that the obiter dicta of Lords Steyn, Hope and Baroness Hale questioning the continuing relevance of the doctrine of parliamentary sovereignty are far from the crucial feature of the case, these readily contestable observations have attracted a great deal of subsequent attention. The doctrine of parliamentary sovereignty in general, and the *Jackson* dicta in particular, have been addressed with some frequency by the senior judiciary in extra-judicial lectures and interviews. A split in judicial opinion remains evident, with some judges explicitly recognising the continuing force of the doctrine,[179] while others have defended the sceptical position articulated by a minority of the House of Lords in *Jackson*.[180] Yet this debate has been essentially hypothetical, with the courts having no opportunity of the kind presented by *Jackson* to revisit the question of the UK Parliament's legislative power.

In the aftermath of *Jackson*, however, the matter of whether there can be common law limits on legislative power has been considered by the Supreme Court in the context of devolution. In the important case of *Axa General Insurance Ltd v*

---

[179] See, eg Lord Neuberger, 'Who are the Masters Now?', *Lord Alexander of Weedon Lecture* (6 April 2011); Lord Judge, 'Constitutional Change: Unfinished Business', *University College London* (4 December 2013); Lord Neuberger, 'The British and Europe', *Cambridge Freshfields Annual Law Lecture* (12 February 2014).

[180] See, eg C Coleman, 'A Power Supreme?' *BBC News* (2 August 2010): news.bbc.co.uk/today/hi/today/newsid_8875000/8875944.stm, quoting Lord Phillips: 'If parliament did the inconceivable, we might do the inconceivable as well'; Lord Hope, 'Sovereignty in Question—A View from the Bench', *WG Hart Legal Workshop 2011* (28 June 2011).

Lord Advocate,[181] a challenge was brought to the Damages (Asbestos-related Conditions) (Scotland) Act 2009 on the grounds that it was outside the legislative competence of the Scottish Parliament. Section 29 of the Scotland Act 1998, which establishes the scope of the Scottish Parliament's law-making authority, expressly provides that legislation which is incompatible with the ECHR or EU law will be outside legislative competence. Yet in addition to arguing that the 2009 Act violated the right to peaceful enjoyment of possessions protected by the ECHR,[182] the appellants in *Axa* also sought to argue that section 29 was not exhaustive, and that there were implied common law limits on the legislative power of the Scottish Parliament. The Supreme Court rejected the argument that the 2009 Act was incompatible with the ECHR, and also rejected the suggestion that legislation of the Scottish Parliament was judicially reviewable on the grounds of irrationality, unreasonableness or arbitrariness. Yet, while judicial review was not permitted on these relatively routine common law grounds—because, as Lord Hope argued, it would 'be quite wrong for the judges to substitute their views on these issues for the considered judgement of a democratically elected legislature unless authorised to do so'[183]—such review might be required in 'exceptional circumstances'.[184]

For Lord Hope, this supervisory jurisdiction at common law could exist because its possibility was not excluded by any provision in the Scotland Act 1998.[185] On the basis that the Scottish Parliament is a democratic, but not a sovereign, legislature,[186] Lord Hope argued that in this context the principle of the rule of law—which, reiterating his claim in *Jackson*, was suggested to be the 'ultimate controlling factor on which our constitution is based'—'does not have to compete with the principle of sovereignty'.[187] As a result, the law-making power of the devolved legislature was ultimately subject to constraints imposed by the rule of law:

> We now have in Scotland a government which enjoys a large majority in the Scottish Parliament. Its party dominates the only chamber in that Parliament and the committees by which bills that are in progress are scrutinised. It is not entirely unthinkable that a government which has that power may seek to use it to abolish judicial review or to diminish the role of the courts in protecting the interests of the individual. Whether this is likely to happen is not the point. It is enough that it might conceivably do so. The rule of law requires that the judges must retain the power to insist that legislation of that extreme kind is not law which the courts will recognise.[188]

Lord Reed reached a similar conclusion to Lord Hope, yet employed a slightly different method to do so. Drawing on the principle of legality, as endorsed by the

---

[181] *Axa General Insurance Ltd v Lord Advocate* [2011] UKSC 46, [2012] 1 AC 868.
[182] Art 1, Protocol 1.
[183] *Axa General Insurance Ltd v Lord Advocate* [2011] UKSC 46; [2012] 1 AC 868, [52].
[184] ibid [49], [149].
[185] ibid [47].
[186] ibid [46], [49].
[187] ibid [51].
[188] ibid [51].

House of Lords in *Pierson*[189] and *Simms*,[190] Lord Reed argued that, when enacting the Scotland Act 1998, the UK Parliament 'cannot be taken to have intended to establish a body which was free to abrogate fundamental rights or to violate the rule of law'.[191] As such, while 'it would not be constitutionally appropriate for the courts to review [legislative] decisions on the ground of irrationality',[192] given the political nature of such judgments, the limits on law-making authority contained in section 29 were not exhaustive. Instead, the legislative competence of the Scottish Parliament was subject in addition to implicit common law limits, prohibiting the enactment of legislation which contravened fundamental rights or the rule of law.

The legal status of these comments as to the susceptibility of Acts of the Scottish Parliament to common law review in exceptional circumstances is not entirely clear. It is arguable that, in principle, they are obiter dicta, because, as Lord Reed noted, there was 'no suggestion in the present case that the Scottish Parliament has acted in such a manner'.[193] Yet while no claim was made that the 2009 Act was in violation of the rule of law or fundamental rights, the general question of whether devolved legislation was reviewable on common law grounds, and if so, what those grounds might be, was squarely before the Supreme Court in *Axa*. Moreover, the comments of Lords Hope and Reed on this point were resoundingly endorsed by the other five members of the court, especially Lord Mance, who argued that extremely irrational legislation, such as 'a blatantly discriminatory decision directed at red-headed people', would be open to rejection on common law grounds.[194] As a result, even if the comments of Lords Hope and Reed on this point were technically to be understood as obiter dicta, they are likely to be extremely persuasive in future.

Nevertheless, this argument as to the scope of the legislative power of the Scottish Parliament in particular is highly questionable. Why should section 29 of the Scotland Act 1998 not be viewed as an exhaustive statement of the limits on devolved legislative competence? First, in addition to establishing in the 1998 Act an elaborate delineation of those matters which are reserved and those which are devolved,[195] Parliament has clearly addressed the issue of the protection of rights and fundamental principles. Indeed, section 29 makes it impossible for the Scottish Parliament to legislate incompatibility with the ECHR,[196] which already provides a higher level of rights protection than that applicable to legislation of the UK Parliament in accordance with the HRA. It is therefore at best extremely artificial, and at worst simply misleading, to speculate about what the

---

[189] *R v Secretary of State for the Home Department, ex parte Pierson* [1998] AC 539.
[190] *R v Secretary of State for the Home Department, ex parte Simms* [2000] 2 AC 115.
[191] *Axa General Insurance Ltd v Lord Advocate* [2011] UKSC 46, [2012] 1 AC 868, [153].
[192] ibid [148].
[193] ibid [154].
[194] ibid [97].
[195] Scotland Act 1998 s 28(2)(b), Schedule 5.
[196] ibid s 29(2)(d).

UK Parliament can be 'taken to have intended',[197] when what it did intend is made abundantly clear in the terms of section 29.

Secondly, it is not appropriate to deploy the principle of legality in this context to limit general, yet not ambiguous, statutory language. This was done explicitly by Lord Reed, but is also implicit, to some extent, in the observation of Lord Hope that common law review is not excluded because the Scotland Act 1998 does not so provide.[198] It is hardly reasonable to have expected the UK Parliament to provide expressly in section 29 that the Scottish Parliament should have the power to violate fundamental rights and the rule of law, simply so as to remove entirely the possibility that the courts might develop an additional common law supervisory jurisdiction over devolved legislative competence. But this is effectively what the court is suggesting would have been necessary for section 29 to exhaust the possibility of judicial review in exceptional circumstances. Indeed, this expectation borders on ludicrous when it is recognised that the UK Parliament would essentially have to contradict itself to achieve the entirely legitimate goal of limiting judicial review of devolved legislation to those grounds explicitly specified in the Scotland Act 1998, given the close relationship between ECHR rights—which the Scottish Parliament is legally obliged to respect—and those protected at common law.

Finally, the precision with which this common law jurisdiction to review Acts of the Scottish Parliament has been formulated raises a range of doubts.[199] The notion of exceptional circumstances is extremely vague and barely defined, and the identification of the disputed, fluid notion of the rule of law as the foundation for this authority only serves to amplify, rather than cure, the already conspicuous uncertainty. The difficulty inherent in determining what constitutes an exceptional violation of constitutional principle will make this power remote from ordinary citizens, and inadequate for political decision-makers. Citizens will find it a challenge to determine whether legislation that offends their conception of justice will be similarly received by the judiciary, making a decision to seek judicial review fraught with complexity. Legislators and officials will glean little useful guidance as to how they should properly exercise their power from the underdeveloped premise that flawed legislation may be exceptionally struck down. And with so little which is clear and certain settled in advance, any judicial decision to exercise, or not to exercise, this authority may appear arbitrary to aggrieved parties.[200] Further, there are genuine questions as to the democratic legitimacy of the courts' arrogating to themselves this power, even if it is, in principle, very limited in scope. Yet there can also be no guarantee that this will remain limited to

---

[197] *Axa General Insurance Ltd v Lord Advocate* [2011] UKSC 46; [2012] 1 AC 868, [153].
[198] ibid [47].
[199] See, eg C Himsworth, 'The Supreme Court Reviews the Review of Acts of the Scottish Parliament' [2012] *PL* 205, 210.
[200] See generally M Gordon, 'What is the Point of Exceptional Circumstances Review?', *UK Constitutional Law Association Blog* (18 June 2012): www.ukconstitutionallaw.org/2012/06/18/mike-gordon-what-is-the-point-of-exceptional-circumstances-review.

exceptional circumstances, if the fundamental values which require the protection of the common law simply expand at the whim of the judiciary. In short, the same difficulties which are presented in general by common law constitutionalism are also manifested in relation to this aspect of the judgments of Lords Hope and Reed in *Axa*. The exceptional circumstances review jurisdiction claimed by the Supreme Court can therefore be objected to on the corresponding grounds that it is imprecise and undemocratic.[201]

Yet setting aside temporarily such objections to the decision in *Axa*, does this case also have broader implications for the UK constitution as a whole? In particular, is the decision of the Supreme Court in *Axa* relevant to discussion of the contemporary scope of the legislative power of the UK Parliament? From one perspective, *Axa* is clearly not pertinent to the position of the UK Parliament—the Scottish Parliament exercises devolved legislative power, and that it does not possess legal sovereignty was explicitly cited by Lord Hope as constituting a critical difference between this legislature and the UK Parliament.[202] Further, Lord Hope stated expressly that his judgment in *Axa* did not purport to resolve the clash between the rule of law and parliamentary sovereignty which he considered to have arisen in *Jackson*, and, indeed, recognised that the terms of this relationship are the subject of judicial disagreement.[203] Yet from an alternative perspective, the influence of *Jackson* is acutely apparent in *Axa*. Lord Hope takes his own claims about the rule of law, controversially advanced in *Jackson*, as the seemingly indisputable basis on which exceptional circumstances common law review can be established. The *Jackson* dicta are less obviously relied on in the judgment of Lord Reed, but appear logically to underpin his discussion of what constitutes 'exceptional circumstances', in so far as the scope of this concept is equated with that established in *Jackson*.[204] Moreover, Lord Hope shows no sign of retreating from the claims made in *Jackson* as to the qualified nature of parliamentary sovereignty, and in expanding the reach of the common law to condition concretely the law-making power of the devolved legislatures, creates a foundation from which further escalation can be attempted. For if the rule of law is the ultimate controlling factor in the devolution settlement, can the UK Parliament really be afforded differential treatment in the long term? The democratic legitimacy of the Scottish Parliament is directly discussed and acknowledged in *Axa* by both Lord Hope and Lord Reed, yet still not deemed sufficient to shield absolutely the devolved legislature from the encroachment of the common law. The formal fact of the UK Parliament's sovereignty must therefore be the only thing protecting it from subjection to common law review, yet this might transpire to be a relatively flimsy barrier if the principled democratic arguments which justify this legal

---

[201]   See chapter 3 of this volume, pp 137–49.
[202]   *Axa General Insurance Ltd v Lord Advocate* [2011] UKSC 46, [2012] 1 AC 868, [51]. See also Lord Reed at [138].
[203]   ibid [51], [50].
[204]   See, eg ibid [141], [149].

position have been dismissed by the courts. The UK courts might thus ultimately attempt to use *Axa*, and the subordination of the devolved legislatures at common law which it establishes, as a reason to 'level-up' this protection so as also to extend to the UK Parliament.

However, given the contemporary strength of the doctrine of parliamentary sovereignty in the UK constitution, it is unlikely, for now, that the decision of the Supreme Court in *Axa* will be sufficient to induce such profound change. Moreover, in addition to challenging the correctness of the decision in *Axa* on legal grounds, we might also profitably attempt to assess this decision—and the obiter dicta in *Jackson* which appear to be its inspiration—from a non-legal per-spective. For it might even be debatable whether such claims as those advanced in *Axa*, as to the possibility of common law review of devolved legislation in exceptional circumstances, should even be approached as statements of a legal position. It might be thought better to understand such judicial assertions about exceptional circumstances review as an emanation of inter-institutional politi-cal manoeuvring, rather than a claim about the power of the courts, under the present constitutional order, to reject legislative acts in crisis situations. As public institutions, courts lack a formal outlet through which they can encourage the leg-islature, or the government within it, to take rights, or the rule of law, or democ-racy, seriously. Yet it is possible for the courts to communicate with the other institutions of government through their reported judgments, and a threat to establish a supervisory jurisdiction over legislative functions could be seen to have a similar effect as such encouragement. In light of this, it is perhaps significant that the only specific example of exceptional circumstances offered both in *Axa*[205] and *Jackson*[206] is legislative action designed to oust or abolish the courts' ordinary power of judicial review over administrative action, with the rule of law arguably used here as a conduit to protect the judges' jurisdiction against encroachment by other institutions. A court may purport, therefore, to be developing a jurisdiction to reject legislation in extreme situations, yet we can make sense of such endeav-ours without concluding that this is a power they do in fact possess as a matter of constitutional law.[207]

This approach to such judicial claims would seem to accord with suggestions that *Jackson* was 'a shot across the government's bows', prompted by an (ultimately aborted) attempt in the Asylum and Immigration (Treatment of Claimants) Bill 2004 to oust judicial review of decisions reached in asylum cases.[208] It has also been suggested that *Axa* might be similarly assessed, and treated as something which 'invites ... political restraint'.[209] Yet, if judicial posturing

---

[205] ibid [51].

[206] *R (Jackson) v Attorney General* [2005] UKHL 56; [2006] 1 AC 262, [102].

[207] See Gordon, 'What is the Point of Exceptional Circumstances Review?' (2012) n 200 above.

[208] T Mullen, 'Reflections on *Jackson v Attorney General*: Questioning Sovereignty' (2007) 27 *Legal Studies* 1, 16. On the government's attempted ouster clause, see generally R Rawlings, 'Revenge, Review and Retreat' (2005) 68 *MLR* 378.

[209] M Elliott, 'Holyrood, Westminster and Judicial Review of Legislation' (2012) 71 *CLJ* 9, 11.

about the possibility of exceptional circumstances review is simply a means of re-emphasising the importance of a number of fundamental constitutional values to the other institutions of government, we might question whether such conduct is of any real significance. After all, when it is considered that these fundamental principles must already underpin the existing constitutional settlement, and be embedded to a substantial extent in constitutional practice, the judicial reiteration of their significance may appear to be a rather banal message, even if one delivered in controversial fashion. Further, given the abstract level at which such concepts are necessarily formulated, the invocation of such elementary precepts, devoid of critical detail, will do little to assist with the resolution of the sort of difficult constitutional questions which must be confronted in mundane, as well as exceptional, situations.

The ultimate message of *Axa* may therefore be one as to the relentlessness, but also the superficiality, of common law constitutionalism. The rhetoric of exceptional circumstances review may be both beguiling and expandable, even though strictly lacking in authority and justification. Even if this is now an accurate statement of the legal position in relation to the legislative competence of the Scottish Parliament, and by extension, the other devolved legislatures—a matter which is, in my view, debateable, for the reasons discussed above—the common law review jurisdiction envisaged in *Axa* is nevertheless one which is not applicable to the UK Parliament. *Axa* may demonstrate that some judges are keen to keep alive the possibility that the doctrine of parliamentary sovereignty might eventually be rejected. Yet it is not legally permitted under the terms of the UK constitution for such an event to be judicially accomplished, a matter which neither the obiter dicta in *Jackson*, nor the judgments in *Axa*, are capable of changing. It is important, as a result, to remember what *Jackson* really establishes—and, conversely, what it does not establish—to ensure that the history of the case is not one written by the common law.

VIII. CONCLUSION

Jackson is an extraordinary case, which demands that we consider afresh the nature and scope of the doctrine of parliamentary sovereignty. It exposes a degree of disillusionment with Diceyan dogma; yet given this sentiment is refracted to a range of different ends, we must be discriminating when determining where *Jackson* leaves the contemporary UK constitution. In one sense, *Jackson* signals that there is tangible judicial enthusiasm to engage with, and even attempt to institutionalise, some of the key tenets of common law constitutionalism. It is, however, far from inevitable that the constitution will absorb these ideas. Indeed, the obiter dicta of Lords Steyn, Hope and Baroness Hale, which candidly challenge the present and future force of the doctrine of parliamentary sovereignty, may be the most striking feature of the *Jackson* case, but they are also the most unsatisfactory, and, in substance, of little consequence. Such attempts to engineer a judicial power to strike down legislation are contrary to authority and democratic principle, and must be rejected, like the common law constitutionalist theory from which they emanate. While in *Axa* these ideas have been essentially transposed for use in relation to the devolved legislatures, and demonstrate latent potential to go further, such claims remain both speculative and highly questionable. The doctrine of parliamentary sovereignty simply cannot be displaced by judicial assertion. Even if repeated, suggestions as to the existence of a common law power to reject Acts of the UK Parliament on substantive grounds will remain fundamentally flawed.

Yet to reject the common law constitutionalist reading of *Jackson*—which cannot be salvaged by attempts to view the case as a natural evolution of the interpretive presumption imposed to preserve fundamental common law values by the principle of legality—does not diminish the significance of the decision of the House of Lords. Instead, *Jackson* can be seen to mark a second step in a pattern of fundamental constitutional change: not away from the sovereignty of Parliament, but towards a reconfigured conception of the doctrine. For in holding the Parliament Acts 1911 and 1949 to be lawful statutory alterations of the legislative process, the House of Lords has in my view embraced the manner and form theory of parliamentary sovereignty. The implications of this decision may be debateable. For some they will be narrow, with *Jackson* being only authority for the fact that Parliament may expand the means by which it may enact legislation, as did the Parliament Acts themselves. Yet I have argued for a much broader interpretation of the implications of *Jackson*, on the basis that this is anticipated in the judgments of two of the Law Lords, and, more significantly, because it is justified by the underlying logic of a 'full' manner and form, rather than a more limited procedure and form, understanding of the nature of legally unlimited legislative authority.

Of course, whether this broader interpretation of the implications of *Jackson* is correct must ultimately be settled by future developments. Yet in my view, it is clear that the conceptual coherence of the manner and form theory of parliamentary sovereignty is now being recognised and reflected in UK constitutional practice. In Chapter six we will explore the culmination of this shift in constitutional understanding: the enactment by Parliament of the European Union Act 2011. In addition to the implicit change to manner and form produced, in effect, by the European Communities Act 1972, and the explicit change to manner and form produced by the Parliament Acts—creating, as the House of Lords held in *Jackson*, an alternate means by which legislation can be enacted—we now appear to have a further progression in the use of legislative power to alter the future manner and form. For the European Union Act 2011 also purports to make explicit changes to the manner and form, but does so by establishing procedural conditions with which Parliament is obliged to comply for the valid enactment of future legislation. In the final chapter of Part II, we will evaluate these changes, and seek to determine the effects, and the effectiveness, of the scheme of mandatory referendum requirements that have been imposed by Parliament through the enactment of this legislation.

6

European Union Act 2011

I. INTRODUCTION

IN THE FINAL chapter of Part II, we assess the recently enacted European Union Act 2011 (EUA). This statute, enacted by the Conservative-Liberal Democrat government, is an unprecedented constitutional experiment in the UK. The EUA concerns the relationship between the UK and the European Union (EU), but is considered separately here, rather than as an element of Chapter four, because the crucial issues raised by this statute are not ones generated by the very fact of membership of the EU. Instead, the EUA is significant in relation to the doctrine of parliamentary sovereignty because of the way the legislation seeks to condition the existing relationship between the UK and the EU. Most importantly, the EUA provides that future change to the nature of this relationship—and in particular, in broad terms, change which prompts further powers or competence to be transferred from the UK to the EU—will be legally authorised only where approved by the public, voting in a national referendum. In establishing in detail a series of statutory 'referendum locks', which purport to prevent Parliament legislating to authorise such change to the UK-EU relationship without approval at a referendum, the EUA represents a remarkable use of legally unlimited legislative power. As a result, the implications of the EUA must be analysed as a discrete topic, and accommodated within our understanding of the contemporary state of the doctrine of parliamentary sovereignty in the UK constitution.

I will argue that the EUA is the confirmation of a modern shift to the manner and form conception of parliamentary sovereignty. The enactment of this legislation is the third step in a constitutional pattern mapped in the preceding chapters, which indicates that the manner and form theory is not only conceptually coherent, as I argued in Part I, but now represents the best account available of the current legislative power of the UK Parliament. What is crucial about the EUA, I will suggest, is that it provides clear evidence that Parliament is now operating on the basis that its legally unlimited law-making authority entitles it to enact legislation which explicitly alters the future legislative process. For in enacting the EUA, it is undeniable that this is what Parliament has done, presenting a decisive challenge to the Diceyan orthodoxy associated with the notion that the legislature cannot bind its successors. After outlining the origins and nature of the EUA, three key issues will be considered. First, an issue internal to the EUA: the relationship between the statutory referendum locks contained in the legislation, and section 18, the so-called 'sovereignty clause', which seeks to reaffirm the domestic constitutional basis of EU law. The implications of this sovereignty clause will be examined—in particular, whether it has any impact on the position established in Chapter four—and the suggestion that there could be a contradiction between section 18 and the EUA's scheme of referendum locks rejected. Secondly, the legal effectiveness of the referendum locks will be assessed, with a view to establishing their implications for the future power of Parliament to legislate in relation to the matters covered by the EUA. Thirdly, the constitutional effect of this statutory scheme of referendum locks will be explored, focusing specifically on the status of the doctrine of parliamentary sovereignty following the enactment of the EUA. I will argue that the EUA can only be explained by embracing the manner and form theory, and that consequently, this statute compels us to recognise that a change has occurred to the doctrine of parliamentary sovereignty in the contemporary UK constitution.

II. THE NATURE OF THE EUROPEAN UNION ACT 2011

In its 2010 general election manifesto, the Conservative Party committed to pursue two policies, with respect to the UK's relationship with the EU, which were of significance to the concept of parliamentary sovereignty. First, the Conservatives pledged to 'amend the 1972 European Communities Act [ECA] so that any proposed future Treaty that transferred areas of power, or competences, would be subject to a referendum—a "referendum lock"'.[1] Such a 'referendum lock' would also be introduced, and made applicable to, an attempt to join the European single currency. Secondly, the Conservatives promised, if elected, to 'introduce a United Kingdom Sovereignty Bill to make it clear that ultimate authority stays in this country, in our Parliament'.[2] On the formation following the general election of a new Conservative-Liberal Democrat government, both of these promises were subsequently incorporated into the coalition's *Programme for Government*. The pledge to amend the ECA to subject future transfers of power or competence to 'referendum locks' was to be fully implemented by Prime Minister David Cameron's new government, while the case for the introduction of a Sovereignty Bill was to be further examined.[3] The government's EU Bill, which was introduced in the House of Commons in November 2010, shortly after the general election, eventually incorporated both of these proposals, while also making provision for

---

[1] The Conservative Party, *Invitation to Join the Government of Britain* (2010) 113.
[2] ibid 114.
[3] The Coalition, *Our Programme for Government* (2010) 19.

the ratification, required as a matter of EU law,[4] of changes to the composition of the European Parliament.[5]

The EUA is a technical and complex statute, which introduces a number of varying mechanisms which control a range of potential transfers of an array of powers and competences from the UK to the EU.[6] The statutory referendum locks are the most demanding of these control mechanisms, the key innovation of the EUA, and of greatest importance in relation to the doctrine of parliamentary sovereignty. These referendum locks are part of a broader scheme designed to condition the way in which future governments must obtain legal approval for plans to pass new or further powers or competence to the EU.[7] In addition to the referendum requirements which are applicable to certain categories of such transfers, this scheme requires other kinds of decision to be approved simply by Act of Parliament,[8] or by non-legislative parliamentary approval motions.[9] While some of these alternative control mechanisms clearly also raise issues which are relevant to the circumstances in which Parliament must now exercise its legislative power, in so far as they require specific legislation to authorise the government to take certain action specified in the EUA, they do not challenge classic ideas of legislative sovereignty. For even where, by statute, Acts of Parliament are now required for certain purposes, the enactment of such legislation will be sufficient in itself to make lawful the governmental conduct to which such conditions contained in the EUA apply. In relation to the action which is covered by the EUA's referendum locks, however, difficult questions for the Diceyan account of parliamentary sovereignty are posed. For here, if the requirements of the EUA are taken at face value, an Act of Parliament will no longer, in itself, necessarily be sufficient to authorise certain kinds of governmental conduct. Instead, further conditions must also be satisfied for specified forms of executive action to be considered lawful. These conditions may be requirements as to legislative form—that express provision be made as to certain matters in the legislation—but may also extend well beyond

---

[4] Article 48(4) TEU.

[5] See [2010] OJ C263/1. The key effect of these changes in relation to the UK was to provide for the election of one additional Member of the European Parliament in this country.

[6] The creation of such control mechanisms is not entirely novel; for similar mechanisms in this context, see the European Parliamentary Elections Act 2002 s 12 (providing that treaties increasing the powers of the European Parliament are not to be ratified by the UK unless approved by Act of Parliament) and the European Union (Amendment) Act 2008 ss 5, 6 (providing, respectively, that amendment of the 'founding treaties' is not to be ratified by the UK unless approved by Act of Parliament, and that parliamentary approval is required for a Minister to approve any one of a number of specified decisions made under the EU treaties). The innovation of the EUA is the vastly extended scope of such a scheme of control, and the novel approval mechanisms which it contains.

[7] For an overview of this entire scheme of control, see M Gordon and M Dougan, 'The United Kingdom's European Union Act 2011: "Who Won the Bloody War Anyway?"' (2012) 37 *European Law Review* 3, 10–15.

[8] European Union Act 2011 s 7.

[9] ibid s 10. For provisions which engage approval by parliamentary motion and approval by Act of Parliament, see ss 8 and 9.

this, and require additional procedural steps to be taken, and taken successfully, if legislation is lawfully to authorise specified kinds of governmental action.

The referendum locks are contained in sections 2, 3 and 6 of the EUA. Each of these sections covers a different kind of decision or action relevant to the UK's relationship with the EU, yet the underlying statutory mechanism which establishes how the referendum locks function is essentially, although not entirely, common to all three provisions. Across these three sections, the range of situations in which the EUA may require a referendum to be held to authorise action to be taken in relation to the EU is remarkably broad. The effect of sections 2 and 3 can be considered together, for there are important parallels between these two provisions. Any treaty amending or replacing the existing EU treaties will fall within the ambit of section 2. Similarly, section 3 covers change to the existing EU treaties made using the 'simplified revision procedure' under Article 48(6) of the Treaty on European Union (TEU). Any change to the EU treaties made by either route will, in principle, engage the control mechanisms of the EUA. This does not, however, mean that a referendum will be required in every instance; instead, change to the EU treaties may be exempt from the requirement that a referendum be held in certain circumstances specified by the statute.

The kind of change to the treaties which will attract a referendum under the EUA is set out in section 4. This is a detailed provision, which establishes an extensive list of situations in which it will be necessary for a referendum to be held. These situations, set out in section 4(1), include an extension of the objectives of the EU;[10] the conferral of new, or extension of existing, EU competence (whether that competence is held exclusively by the EU,[11] shared with the Member States,[12] or to support, co-ordinate or supplement the action of Member States[13]); conferring on EU institutions new, or extending existing, power to impose obligations[14] or sanctions on the UK;[15] and changes to voting requirements in relation to specified treaty provisions which would deprive the UK of a veto.[16] And this is simply an indicative, rather than exhaustive, list of the circumstances in which section 4 requires a referendum to be held to authorise change to the EU treaties. The intention of the legislation is clear: to bring nearly any imaginable transfer of power or competence from the UK to the EU within the scope of the EUA's scheme of control. The list of exceptions which section 4 establishes is, in contrast, much more limited: treaty change which would otherwise fall within the scope of this provision, by virtue of satisfying one or more of the conditions set out in sub-section (1), will not do so where it is simply a codification of previous

---

[10] European Union Act 2011 s 4(1)(a).
[11] ibid s 4(1)(b), (c).
[12] ibid s 4(1)(d), (e).
[13] ibid s 4(1)(g), (h).
[14] ibid s 4(1)(i).
[15] ibid s 4(1)(j).
[16] ibid s 4(1)(k).

practice with respect to an existing competence,[17] where the changes concerned do not apply to the UK,[18] or if a treaty merely provides for the accession of a new Member State.[19]

If the change envisaged to the treaties is deemed to fall within the ambit of section 4, both section 2 and section 3 of the EUA require that change to be approved by an Act of Parliament,[20] which must satisfy a common 'referendum condition':[21]

> (2) The referendum condition is that—
>
> (a) the Act providing for the approval of the treaty provides that the provision approving the treaty is not to come into force until a referendum about whether the treaty should be ratified has been held throughout the United Kingdom or, where the treaty also affects Gibraltar, throughout the United Kingdom and Gibraltar,
>
> (b) the referendum has been held, and
>
> (c) the majority of those voting in the referendum are in favour of the ratification of the treaty.[22]

The EUA thus imposes conditions on the Act of Parliament required either to authorise the ratification of a treaty, with respect to section 2, or the approval of a decision under Article 48(6), with respect to section 3. To comply with the terms of the EUA, the approving Act must provide that the authorisation it contains is conditional upon a majority of the electorate voting in favour of the proposed change in a referendum. As a result, in accordance with the terms of the EUA, if a proposed change to the EU treaties is of a kind which attracts a referendum—by virtue of satisfying one or more of the conditions contained in section 4—an Act of Parliament will not provide lawful authorisation for governmental action to confirm that change *unless* the statute makes that authorisation subject to approval at a referendum. An Act of Parliament which purports to authorise such change without the incorporation of a 'referendum condition' would not be legally invalid; rather, it would be legally ineffective, because it would fail to provide lawful authorisation for governmental action confirming a change to the EU treaties. In that sense, taken at face value, the EUA has changed the manner and form for the enactment of legislation which provides lawful authorisation for the government to confirm specified change to the EU treaties. For, unless the approving Act of Parliament incorporates a referendum condition, and that condition is satisfied, such authorisation cannot validly be given.

---

[17] ibid s 4(4)(a).

[18] ibid s 4(4)(b).

[19] ibid s 4(4)(c).

[20] ibid s 2(1)(b); s 3(1)(b).

[21] ibid s 2(1)(c); s 3(1)(c).

[22] ibid s 2(2). A materially identical provision is contained in s 3(2), except that references to 'the treaty' in the above text are there substituted for references to 'the decision', because s 3 pertains to treaty change via the adoption of a decision under the simplified revision procedure contained in Art 48(6) TEU.

But it is not only where a referendum is required that the EUA purports to alter the future legislative manner and form. While this is certainly the most far-reaching change made by the EUA, and will be the focus of discussion in this chapter, it is important to recognise that a manner and form condition is imposed by both section 2 and section 3 even in relation to change which, in principle, falls within their scope, but does not attract a referendum by virtue of section 4. In such circumstances, rather than satisfy the 'referendum condition', the approving Act of Parliament must satisfy the alternative 'exemption condition'.[23] This alternative condition requires that 'the Act providing for the approval of the treaty states that the treaty does not fall within section 4'.[24] Explicit words must therefore be used by an approving Act to establish that it is exempt from the requirement under the EUA that a referendum be held. Moreover, a further alternative exists in relation to treaty change covered by section 3 only. In relation to section 3, an approving Act may, where appropriate, satisfy the 'significance condition' rather than either the referendum or exemption condition. This condition may be satisfied if the change envisaged would fall within section 4 only by virtue of subsection (1)(i) or (j)—broadly, as a result of conferring on an EU institution a new or extended power to impose an obligation or sanction on the UK—but that the effect of such change would be 'not significant' in relation to the UK.[25] To satisfy this 'significance condition' the approving Act must state explicitly that these two criteria have been met. No equivalent provision, allowing for a 'significance condition' to be satisfied exists in relation to section 2.

As a result of the alternative conditions set out in sections 2 and 3 of the EUA, even where the highly demanding referendum condition does not apply, a legislative condition of some kind must still be satisfied by any Act of Parliament which purports to authorise treaty change which falls within the ambit of one of these provisions. In relation to the exemption condition—applicable to both section 2 and section 3—or the significance condition—applicable to section 3 only—this may be relatively easy to do, for it simply requires express language to be used which states that the relevant criteria have been satisfied. Yet this is still significant in principle, because in such circumstances a procedural requirement as to the future legislative form has been imposed by statute, and this must be complied with to enact legislation which validly authorises the governmental action necessary to confirm the relevant change to the UK-EU relationship.

Turning to section 6, the effect of this provision is also to purport to change the future legislative manner and form, but in a slightly more straightforward fashion, at least in terms of the technical statutory mechanism employed. For section 6 of the EUA sets out a series of specific trigger events, which will automatically require approval by Act of Parliament and at a referendum. Most of these trigger events

---

[23]   ibid s 2(1)(c); s 3(1)(c).
[24]   ibid s 2(3). As in relation to the referendum condition, a materially identical provision appears in s 3(3), although again, with references to 'the treaty' substituted for references to 'the decision'.
[25]   ibid s 3(4).

relate to changes, in the context of a wide range of specified substantive provisions of the EU treaties,[26] to EU voting rules—in particular, the adoption of qualified majority voting[27]—or modification of EU legislative procedures—in particular, the application of an ordinary legislature procedure, in place of a special legislative procedure which requires the Council to act unanimously.[28] Yet section 6 further identifies a number of particular decisions which would significantly affect the UK-EU relationship, and which also therefore attract a referendum if they are to be approved in accordance with the EUA. These decisions include joining the euro,[29] participation in a European Public Prosecutor's Office,[30] the removal of border controls under the Schengen Protocol,[31] and the pursuit of a common EU defence under Article 42(2) TEU.[32] With respect to all of the decisions covered by section 6, no assessment of the implications of the change proposed is required against the criteria contained in section 4, and as such, there is no possibility of a referendum being avoided on the grounds of exemption or insignificance. In relation to section 6 decisions, the same referendum condition which operates in relation to section 2 and section 3 applies absolutely, and must be satisfied by the approving Act in order to comply with the EUA.[33] And as such, at face value, section 6 also serves, in the same way as sections 2 and 3 of the EUA, to alter the manner and form for the enactment of legislation which validly confers on the government the legal authority to confirm applicable change to the relationship between the UK and the EU.

If the effect of the EUA can be taken at face value—a matter which is of course controversial, and requires further discussion—the implications of the statute are potentially profound. For the legislation will have succeeded in systemically embedding mandatory referendums into the law-making process, and making the authorisation of certain forms of governmental action by Act of Parliament conditional upon favourable results being achieved in such referendums. Before we consider whether this is indeed the result of the EUA, through an assessment of the legal effectiveness of this scheme of referendum locks, a prior issue must be addressed. Does the content of the EUA reveal an internal contradiction? This potential difficulty is presented when we recognise that the EUA combines this scheme of referendum locks with a further provision of relevance to the doctrine of parliamentary sovereignty: section 18 of the EUA, which was intended to reassert the sovereignty of the UK Parliament, and re-emphasise the contingent status of EU law within the UK constitution. Is a scheme of referendum locks, which purports to limit the power of Parliament to legislate freely on a range of matters,

---

[26] See generally, ibid Schedule 1.
[27] ibid s 6(5)(a), (b)(i), (h), (i).
[28] ibid s 6(5)(b)(ii), (f), (g), (j).
[29] ibid s 6(5)(e).
[30] ibid s 6(3), (5)(c), (d).
[31] ibid s 6(5)(k).
[32] ibid s 6(2).
[33] ibid s 6(1), (4); for the precise terms of the referendum condition, see text at nn 21–22 above.

by appearing to make the lawful authorisation of certain forms of government action conditional on popular approval being obtained at a referendum, ultimately inconsistent with section 18 of the EUA? If so, the EUA might be thought to be a Janus-faced statute, promoting the authority of Parliament at precisely the same time as it limits the legislature's power. We will consider this potential contradiction in the next section.

III. CONTRADICTORY MESSAGES ON SOVEREIGNTY?

The essential argument that the EUA presents, in its referendum locks on the one hand, and section 18 on the other, contradictory messages on sovereignty was reflected in the critique of the (then) EU Bill by the Labour Party, in opposition to the coalition government. At the second reading of the EU Bill in the House of Commons, Yvette Cooper, then Shadow Foreign Secretary, objected in the following terms:

> This Bill is a complete dog's dinner and he knows it, yet the Eurosceptics are salivating nevertheless. The Bill tries to constrain parliamentary sovereignty on the one hand and protect parliamentary sovereignty on the other, using a referendum lock that does one thing and a sovereignty clause that does the opposite—a referendum lock that tries to bind future Parliaments and a sovereignty clause that makes it clear that the Government can do no such thing. It is all in the same Bill, which faces both ways at the same time.[34]

To be able to assess whether such claims about the EUA are correct, however, we must initially examine the nature and effect of section 18.

What began as a proposal for a Sovereignty Bill,[35] and morphed into a plan for a sovereignty clause—which would, according to the then Foreign Secretary, 'place on the statute book this eternal truth: what a sovereign parliament can do, a sovereign parliament can also undo'[36]—ultimately became neither, in section 18 of the EUA. The provision, as ultimately enacted, makes no direct reference to parliamentary sovereignty at all, and opting for the mundane rather than the bombastic, simply reaffirms that the 'status of EU law is dependent on [its] continuing statutory basis':

> Directly applicable or directly effective EU law (that is, the rights, powers, liabilities, obligations, restrictions, remedies and procedures referred to in section 2(1) of the European Communities Act 1972) falls to be recognised and available in law in the United Kingdom only by virtue of that Act or where it is required to be recognised and available in law by virtue of any other Act.[37]

---

[34] *Hansard*, HC Deb Vol 520, col 208 (7 December 2010).
[35] See text at n 3 above.
[36] See, eg 'William Hague outlines plans for UK sovereignty clause in EU Bill', *The Guardian* (6 October 2010): www.guardian.co.uk/politics/2010/oct/06/william-hague-uk-sovereignty-law.
[37] European Union Act 2011 s 18.

As a matter of law, this provision therefore not only changes nothing, but also manages to sidestep most of the difficult questions associated with the domestic constitutional basis of EU law with which we grappled in Chapter four. Given the point reasserted in section 18 is a very familiar one, which could hardly have credibly been doubted before, let alone after, the leading judgment of Lord Bridge in *Factortame (No 2)*,[38] it is questionable whether this provision adds anything to our understanding of the basis of EU law within the UK constitution. Certainly, the key debates as to the nature of the relationship between the supremacy of EU law and the sovereignty of the UK Parliament almost all proceed from the very point which section 18 'clarifies': that the European Communities Act 1972 (ECA) provides the foundation of the domestic constitutional reconciliation which has been achieved. What truly remains contested, however, is whether this is revolutionary or if constitutional continuity has been maintained; whether the constructionist or manner and form understanding of the ECA must be adopted, or whether 'continuing' parliamentary sovereignty has been preserved; and, most significantly, what the limits of any such reconciliation are.

The strong implication of section 18 is that the legal status of EU law in the UK could be removed or altered by change to its domestic statutory basis. But the EUA does not tell us what form of change to that statutory basis would be permitted in accordance with UK constitutional law and principle—in particular section 18 gives no indication as to whether Parliament has the power to legislate expressly to displace the effects of EU law even in relation to a particular subject-matter, without (at least initially) withdrawing from the Union. Accounts of what domestic statutory change might be possible can be sketched, with varying degrees of certainty, by recourse to the different models which seek to account for the effects of the ECA. But argument as to which of these models—revolutionary, constructionist, manner and form, continuing sovereignty—provides the best explanation of the current constitutional position is not advanced by the EUA. Given that, as I have argued in Chapter four, these issues can satisfactorily be resolved by the adoption of a manner and form interpretation of the ECA, this may not ultimately be a great deficiency of the EUA. Yet if section 18 really tells us nothing about the doctrine of parliamentary sovereignty post-*Factortame (No 2)*, it is questionable whether it can be the basis of a message about sovereignty at all, regardless of whether that is one which contradicts the instincts underpinning the creation of a scheme of statutory referendum locks.

It might therefore be tempting to regard section 18 simply as a diverting sideshow from the main innovations of the EUA,[39] rather than the source of a competing vision of sovereignty. Yet perhaps this is to dismiss the rhetorical significance of section 18 too readily. The primary issue which the government sought to address by enacting this provision was the possibility that it might

---

[38] *R v Secretary of State for Transport, ex parte Factortame (No 2)* [1991] 1 AC 603, 658–59.
[39] See Gordon and Dougan, 'Who Won the Bloody War Anyway?' (2012) n 7 above, 7.

become accepted that EU law had acquired some kind of autonomous legal authority in the UK, transcending that which had been afforded by Parliament in the ECA, and therefore not susceptible to displacement by subsequent legislative action.[40] Yet, while there is very little to suggest that such claims stand any chance of being accepted at present,[41] and therefore that the particular premise on which section 18 was included in the EUA is one which has been 'exaggerated',[42] this provision may nevertheless still have some broader salience. For there may be some virtue in a statutory reminder—even if imperfect in form—of the continuing constitutional force of the doctrine of parliamentary sovereignty.[43] Such allusions may not be especially critical in relation to the status of EU law, but perhaps still of latent importance in a domestic climate which is increasingly sceptical of the notion that the UK constitution is founded on a doctrine of legally unlimited legislative power. Moreover, the deficiencies and ambiguity of section 18 do not prevent it from serving this more general function, for to establish that this provision is strictly insignificant, as a matter of law, necessarily requires the recognition, entirely apart from the EUA, of the ongoing, contemporary force of the legislative sovereignty of Parliament. To understand section 18 as irrelevant is, inevitably, to accept that the doctrine of parliamentary sovereignty is not.

It may therefore be possible to conceive of section 18 as transmitting some form of message as to the continuing constitutional importance of the doctrine of parliamentary sovereignty, even if this general indication is not especially enlightening with respect to the status of EU law within the UK constitution. Yet it is not clear that a message of any sort has been fully received by the courts. It is quite remarkable, for example, that section 18 was not cited at any stage in any of the judgments of the Supreme Court in *HS2*,[44] a case in which the domestic constitutional basis of EU law was directly (and controversially[45]) discussed. While this may be explained on the basis that section 18 makes no substantive legal impact, it is still now part of the UK's constitutional scenery, and as such, we cannot proceed past it with barely a glance. Reflection on the terms of section 18 may illuminate little, but it would be a mistake to overlook on this basis its symbolic intent. However, if section 18 is consequently to be understood to broadcast a general legislative endorsement of the doctrine of parliamentary sovereignty, does

---

[40] See the argument to this effect of Eleanor Sharpston QC for Sunderland City Council in *Thoburn v Sunderland City Council* [2002] EWHC 195, [2003] QB 151, 161, which was dismissed by the Divisional Court: [53]–[59], [68]–[70].

[41] That the EU is a creature of the Member States is made clear in the EU treaties. So, for eg, the competence of the EU is limited by the principle of conferral, with all competence not conferred upon the Union remaining with Member States: Art 5 TEU. Further, following the changes made by the Treaty of Lisbon, an explicit right to withdraw from the EU is now recognised: Art 50 TEU.

[42] House of Commons European Scrutiny Committee, *The EU Bill and Parliamentary Sovereignty*, HC 633-I (7 December 2010), [86].

[43] See Gordon and Dougan, 'Who Won the Bloody War Anyway?' (2012) n 7 above, 8.

[44] *R (HS2 Action Alliance Ltd) v Secretary of State for Transport* [2014] UKSC 3, [2014] 1 WLR 324.

[45] See chapter 4 of this volume, pp 185–89.

this have the potential to contradict the EUA's other feature of key constitutional importance: the scheme of referendum locks?

Whether there is a contradiction between the instincts underlying section 18 and the EUA's referendum locks depends crucially on the conception of parliamentary sovereignty adopted. On a Diceyan conception of the doctrine, based on the sweeping assertion that Parliament cannot bind its successors as to the future legislative process, or displace the operation of the doctrine of implied repeal, this is potentially problematic. For the EUA would simultaneously be reasserting the sovereignty of Parliament, in section 18, and purporting to violate the doctrine, in sections 2, 3 and 6. However, while serving potentially to limit Parliament's practical legislative capability, the referendum locks contained in the EUA are not necessarily incompatible with the doctrine of parliamentary sovereignty, if the manner and form theory of legally unlimited law-making authority is adopted. For, as was demonstrated in Chapter two, the manner and form theory is a reconfiguration, and not a rejection, of the notion of parliamentary sovereignty, and the exercise of legislative power to alter the future legislative process can be understood to be a manifestation, rather than a denial, of law-making authority which is legally unlimited.[46]

However, it also cannot readily be assumed that, of the innovations considered for inclusion in the EUA, only the referendum locks pose a problem for the Diceyan conception of parliamentary sovereignty. For the very notion that Parliament could, in principle, legislate in any meaningful way so as to reaffirm the legally unlimited scope of its law-making power also potentially presents a challenge to the orthodox school of thought. Although such difficulties are seemingly evaded in section 18 as actually drafted and subsequently enacted, by assiduously avoiding any mention of 'sovereignty', that such a course of action was even considered raises questions for adherents to the orthodox conception of the doctrine. Of course, this could, and most likely would, have been dismissed by Diceyans as legally ineffectual, yet such a prospect also provokes the broader question of whether, as Wade so influentially argued,[47] Parliament truly is conceptually prohibited from legislating about its legislative power. For if Parliament could reaffirm the scope, or even the nature, of its legislative power by statute, it might be thought much more difficult to sustain claims that it is nevertheless not permitted to legislate to modify the means by which that power is exercised. As a result, even if the EUA had ultimately been drafted so as to emit a much more definitive message on sovereignty with respect to section 18, it is not clear that such a message, being contained in statute, would be one with which defenders of the Diceyan tradition could be genuinely comfortable. On a Diceyan conception of parliamentary sovereignty, the charge that the EUA is internally contradictory might ultimately therefore expose deeper issues as to whether what was envisaged

---

[46] See chapter 2 of this volume, pp 73–74.

[47] HWR Wade, 'The Basis of Legal Sovereignty' (1955) 13 *CLJ* 172; see chapter 2 of this volume, pp 75–91.

for this statute—even if not pursued in full—could be in any respect compatible with the orthodox account of the doctrine.

We can, however, set such concerns aside if a manner and form conception of parliamentary sovereignty is instead embraced. On such an approach, it is potentially coherent for the EUA to introduce a demanding scheme of referendum locks, while concurrently reiterating—albeit in a relatively ineffective way—the constitutional significance of the sovereignty of Parliament. That it is from this perspective that the internal consistency of the 2011 Act can most readily be assured provides further, although not conclusive, evidence that it is appropriate to adopt a manner and form interpretation of the EUA. This is to presume, however, that the EUA's referendum locks are legally effective, and thus in need of evaluation. When the EUA is taken at face value, it strongly appears that this is the case. Yet for this initial judgement to be sustained, we must examine the legal effectiveness of this scheme of referendum locks in more detail.

IV. LEGAL EFFECTIVENESS OF THE REFERENDUM LOCKS

To this point, the nature of the EUA's referendum locks have been outlined, and the question of whether they are compatible with another key feature of the 2011 Act—the reiteration in section 18 that the domestic authority of EU law derives from statute—has been considered. We have seen that, on their face, the EUA's referendum locks purport to alter the manner and form for the enactment of future legislation,[48] an interpretation which is reinforced by the fact that it is from this perspective that the possibility that the Act is internally contradictory can be discounted. But to what extent can these referendum locks be considered legally effective? The answer to this question will of course vary—as did the matter of the EUA's internal coherence, considered above—depending on what conception of the legislative power of Parliament is adopted. Yet in reviewing the competing answers to this question offered by the three leading accounts of the legislative authority of the UK Parliament, we seek to establish which account provides the most credible interpretation of the EUA, both in principle, and with respect to the practical implications of their adoption. And, of course, in addition to enhancing our understanding of the contemporary status of the doctrine of parliamentary sovereignty in the UK constitution on this basis, this inquiry has a further practical motive: to ascertain precisely how constitutional actors might need to approach the EUA's referendum locks, should they be engaged in the future.

---

[48] For a contrary suggestion, see V Bogdanor, 'Imprisoned by a Doctrine: The Modern Defence of Parliamentary Sovereignty' (2012) 32 *OJLS* 179, 189–90, arguing that the EUA's referendum locks constitute a 'substantive limitation upon the powers of Parliament' based on an alteration to 'the rule of recognition'. Yet this seems difficult to sustain, especially when it is also here recognised that 'Parliament can of course repeal the European Union Act at any time'. This may ultimately be a further example of the problematic flexibility of employing the rule of recognition—at which level anything goes—as a routine rationalising device in relation to challenging constitutional change.

First, from an orthodox Diceyan perspective, the question of the legal effectiveness of the referendum locks contained in the EUA permits of a simple answer: they are of no legal effect. On this approach, Parliament cannot bind its successors either substantively, or as to the manner and form for future legislation,[49] and as such, sections, 2, 3 and 6 of the EUA are entirely legally ineffective. Future Parliaments are not obliged to comply with their terms, and may authorise governmental action to confirm the ratification of any treaty, or the approval of any decision, which these provisions purport to cover by simple Act of Parliament. Neither a referendum condition, nor, where applicable, an exemption or significance condition, needs to be satisfied for such authorisation to be lawfully given. Instead, a future authorising Act which makes no reference to any such conditions will be taken to have repealed the EUA's referendum locks by implication. As such, when Parliament comes in future to authorise action which ostensibly falls within the scheme of control established by section 2, 3 or 6 of the EUA, it can simply ignore the requirements of the 2011 Act.

A second alternative approach is provided by the common law constitutionalist understanding of the legislative power of Parliament. Here, however, the answer to our question is more complex. On this account, Parliament may be the supreme legislative institution, but it is not sovereign; instead its power to legislate is legally limited. These limits derive from the principle of the rule of law, which find their expression in the common law, as developed by the judiciary.[50] The permissibility of Parliament legislating to alter the future law-making process must thus be understood within this broader scheme. The legality of such statutory action stems not from an understanding of the nature and implications of legislative sovereignty, but from what the common law ultimately deems acceptable. In the words of Allan, for example, '[t]he relevant questions of manner and form cannot be severed from questions of moral and political substance'.[51] And, on a common law constitutionalist account, it will be for the courts to identify, and to determine, the substantive moral and political questions which any particular attempt to modify the future law-making process might present. In short, whether the referendum locks contained in the EUA will be legally effective will depend on whether they can be justified as a matter of common law. The answer to our specific question must therefore, on the common law constitutionalist approach, be an inconclusive 'maybe': any particular referendum lock engaged by the EUA would need to be judicially assessed in context to establish whether it posited, on substantive moral or political grounds, a condition with which a future Parliament ought to be bound to comply.

The final approach is that offered by the manner and form theory, according to which the legislative sovereignty of Parliament, being legally unlimited,

---

[49] See chapter 2 of this volume, pp 57–59.
[50] See chapter 3 of this volume, pp 126–31.
[51] TRS Allan, *The Sovereignty of Law: Freedom, Constitution, and Common Law* (Oxford, Oxford University Press, 2013) 147.

is understood to include a power to enact legislation which alters the manner and form for valid future law-making.[52] From this perspective, the referendum locks—and indeed, where applicable, the alternative exemption and significance conditions as to future legislative form—contained in sections 2, 3 and 6 of the EUA are legally effective, and must be satisfied if Parliament is to enact valid legislation relating to the matters which fall within their scope. However, this position only obtains while these statutory conditions as to manner or form remain on the statute book. Crucially, the EUA does not purport in any way to entrench these changes to the future legislative procedure, making them removable only in accordance with a particular process. Instead, the legislation is entirely silent on this point, and as such, it can be concluded that Parliament could freely remove the conditions which the EUA imposes by an ordinary Act of Parliament. This is most likely to be done in express terms, yet, in principle, could also be achieved by necessary implication. If, for example, Parliament were to re-legislate on this topic, and create a new statutory scheme of control over decisions which would transfer power or competence from the UK to the EU, but without explicitly repealing that contained in the EUA, to the extent that these two schemes were inconsistent, the more recent would be understood to have displaced the 2011 Act. That the referendum locks contained in the EUA are not entrenched is significant, for it means that while these statutory conditions are legally effective, and must be complied with unless amended, they are not absolute. Instead, the conditions imposed by the EUA are potentially avoidable—entirely lawfully—if a future Parliament sought to free itself from the obligation to adhere to these legislative requirements.

We therefore have a spectrum of divergent responses to the question of the legal effectiveness of the EUA's referendum locks: 'Yes', 'No' and 'Maybe'. To a significant extent, of course, which of these answers we prefer will be a function of which of the three competing accounts of legislative power we favour. And as this book defends a manner and form conception of parliamentary sovereignty, it will be no surprise that, in my view, it is the manner and form account of the EUA which is most compelling. Yet it is the explanatory force of the manner and form theory—in relation to a range of contemporary constitutional developments, culminating in the enactment of the EUA—which provides the fundamental basis for a defence of this account of parliamentary sovereignty. As such, it is in part because the manner and form theory offers the best conceptualisation of the legal effectiveness of the EUA's referendum locks that it is a conception of legislative sovereignty which can be defended in the context of the UK. And that the manner and form theory provides the most credible explanation of the EUA is evident when we see the coherence of adopting such an approach, whereas in comparison, the two alternative accounts are undermined by inherent deficiencies.

---

[52] See chapter 2 of this volume, pp 63–75.

The fundamental difficulty, in principle, for the Diceyan approach to the EUA's referendum locks is this: why would Parliament legislate in a way that could be ignored? This is what the Diceyan analysis ultimately suggests Parliament has done, for the referendum locks are legally ineffective, and can be entirely disregarded in the future. It could be argued that Parliament has simply, in this instance, misunderstood the scope of its legislative authority. Yet given the potential coherence of the manner and form account of the notion of parliamentary sovereignty,[53] is such a conclusion justified? It seems excessively dogmatic simply to insist upon the correctness of the approach to parliamentary sovereignty popularised by Dicey in the face of a clear, and elaborate, indication to the contrary from Parliament. It might, however, be suggested that the present position cannot be established with true clarity until the courts have had the opportunity to consider the effectiveness of what Parliament has purported to do. However, while it is a legal doctrine, the sovereignty of Parliament is a norm which the courts simply recognise, and not a rule the content of which they are entitled to determine. To invite the courts to reject an explicit parliamentary effort to introduce legally binding referendum locks on the basis that the sovereign UK Parliament does not appreciate the nature of its own power is potentially to draw the judges into highly contentious constitutional territory. Such a result would also challenge ideas of legal certainty, and the expectations of constitutional actors which such clear statutory arrangements must surely be understood to generate. When it is considered that in this context, where legal guarantees of referendums are in issue, this would crucially include the expectations of the electorate, such a counterintuitive analysis becomes yet more difficult to substantiate.

In contrast, the fundamental difficulty, in principle, for the common law constitutionalist account of the EUA is this: on what basis are these legislative manner and form conditions subject to review on substantive moral or political grounds? The EUA largely removes the prospect of political discretion being exercised as to whether a referendum is necessary or not, choosing instead to make engagement of these statutory conditions determinable on largely factual grounds.[54] Moreover, even if the courts were ultimately called upon to consider the effectiveness of the EUA's referendum locks, there is no reason at all they should do so on rich substantive grounds. Instead, as in *Jackson*,[55] in which the courts similarly considered the legal effectiveness of the Parliament Act 1949, the judicial exercise to be conducted would not encompass assessment of any moral and political concerns as to the propriety of a specific alteration of the future legislative manner and form. And even if these general difficulties could be set aside, it is far

---

[53] See chapter 2 of this volume, pp 75–108.

[54] For further discussion of this point, and analysis of the appropriateness of this aspect of the scheme, see Gordon and Dougan, 'Who Won the Bloody War Anyway?' (2012) n 7 above, 16–18. The key example of the EUA permitting political discretion to be exercised as to whether a referendum condition ought to apply is in relation to the 'significance' test, which operates in limited circumstances in accordance with s 3(4).

[55] *R (on the application of Jackson) v Attorney General* [2005] UKHL 56, [2006] 1 AC 262.

from apparent what the common law might have to say in this particular context, as to the circumstances in which it is appropriate to obtain further, and direct, democratic legitimation of transfers of power or competence from the UK to the EU. We might readily object to the scheme established by the EUA on a number of substantive grounds, including that the provision made for referendums is too extensive,[56] which will be disruptive to the functioning of the EU,[57] potentially damage the UK's position therein,[58] and might require referendums to be held on highly esoteric matters.[59] Yet these are not issues which could satisfactorily be resolved by judicial intervention. Instead, any such attempts would see the now familiar deficiencies of common law constitutionalism manifested in a new context.[60] The substantive moral and political criteria against which the 'legality' of such referendum conditions would be assessed are too imprecise to be useful, making the prospect of judicial action difficult to predict, and therefore arbitrary in appearance, while also subversive of established constitutional expectations. Further, while competing claims as to what is truly democratic would likely abound in the event of a referendum lock being challenged, it is straightforwardly the case that the courts lack the legitimacy to establish which of these claims is superior on substantive moral or political grounds.

A. Manner and Form Understanding of the European Union Act 2011

The manner and form understanding of the EUA does not suffer from the deficiencies which afflict the alternative models. It neither suggests counter-intuitively that what Parliament has done can be disregarded, nor that the legal effectiveness of the referendum locks is dependent on a judicial understanding of their substantive desirability, once assessed against illusive criteria. Instead, the manner and form theory indicates that we can indeed take what Parliament has purported to do at face value, assessing the legal effectiveness of the referendum locks on that basis. This is, in my view, the most coherent way, in principle, to understand this potentially challenging aspect of the statutory scheme of control

---

[56] See, eg Gordon and Dougan, 'Who Won the Bloody War Anyway?' (2012) n 7 above, 18–23; S Peers, 'European Integration and the European Union Act 2011: an Irresistible Force meets an Immovable Object?' [2013] *PL* 119, 132–34.

[57] See, eg P Craig, 'The European Union Act 2011: Locks, Limits and Legality' (2011) 48 *CML Rev* 1915, 1940–44.

[58] See, eg JEK Murkens, '*The European Union Act 2011: a Failed Statute*' (2012) 3 *Tijdschrift voor Constitutioneel Recht* 396, 405–7.

[59] See, eg Gordon and Dougan, 'Who Won the Bloody War Anyway?' (2012) n 7 above, 27. A referendum would need to be held, to give just one such example, to allow the Council to act by qualified majority, rather than unanimously, when making changes to the list of military products exempt from internal market provisions pursuant to Art 346 TFEU. Even the most committed defender of direct democracy would find a requirement to have recourse to the people in such circumstances difficult even to explain, let alone justify.

[60] See chapter 3 of this volume, pp 137–49.

created by the EUA. Furthermore, it is also an understanding of the EUA which draws considerable support from the attitudes taken to the referendum locks in UK constitutional practice. For the initial evidence overwhelmingly suggests that the manner and form analysis of the EUA, which holds that the referendum locks are legally binding unless or until repealed by Parliament, is one reflected in constitutional practice.

Such an attitude has been apparent since the inception of the EUA.[61] First, the very language of referendum 'locks' indicates that these conditions are intended to have a resolute constraining effect on future decisions,[62] something which is inconsistent with either the notion that they are to have tentative legal effect, pending judicial approval, or the contrasting suggestion they are to be of no legal effect whatsoever. Secondly, an explicit desire to control future behaviour was expressed as the EU Bill progressed through the House of Commons; as the then Foreign Secretary William Hague put it, '[t]he Bill is about the future—let us be clear about that'.[63] Indeed, this is the only intelligible conclusion to be drawn as to the intended effect of the EUA, for the coalition government had already undertaken not to transfer, during in its five-year term in office, such power or competence to the EU which would have engaged a referendum lock pursuant to the EUA.[64] From this perspective, the EUA was necessarily about conditioning the action of *future* governments and Parliaments, because the *present* Parliament would not be asked to provide the kind of authorisation which would have required compliance with a referendum lock.

Thirdly, attempts in the House of Lords to insert into the legislation a 'sunset clause', which would have provided for the scheme of control established by Part I and Schedule 1 of the EUA to expire upon the dissolution of the enacting Parliament, subject to a power to reintroduce this same scheme by order of a Secretary of State in the next parliamentary term,[65] also indicate that the statute is legally effective. The idea that a specific provision would have been necessary to ensure that the scheme of control created by the EUA would lapse at the end of the present parliamentary term demonstrates that, in the absence of such a provision, the legislation would continue to have legal effect. And since such a sunset clause was ultimately rejected by the Commons, and thus not included in the EUA as finally enacted, the present and future legal effectiveness of the scheme of control established by the legislation is difficult to deny. Finally, this conclusion is further

---

[61] See generally Gordon and Dougan, 'Who Won the Bloody War Anyway?' (2012) n 7 above, 24–25.

[62] The terminology of referendum 'locks' was used in both the Conservative Party general election manifesto of 2010, and the coalition's subsequently drafted *Programme for Government*; see text at nn 1–3 above.

[63] *Hansard*, HC Deb Vol 520, col 194 (7 December 2010).

[64] See the Coalition, *Our Programme for Government* (2010) 19. A Written Statement by the Minister for Europe, David Lidington, subsequently confirmed this position: 'there will be no such referendum during this Parliament': *Hansard*, HC Deb Vol 515, col 31WS (13 September 2010).

[65] Amendment 15, Lords Amendments to the European Union Bill (12 July 2011): www.publications. parliament.uk/pa/bills/cbill/2010-2012/0209/12209.1–4.html.

reinforced on consideration of a provision which *is* included in the EUA as finally enacted: the requirement that when authorisation is to be sought to approve action covered by this statutory scheme of control, a statement is laid before Parliament explaining whether the proposed change, in the government's view, falls within section 4 of the EUA.[66] Indeed, that such a statement is laid before Parliament within two months of the proposed treaty change having been agreed is an additional condition which must be satisfied for action to confirm that change to be authorised.[67] While this requirement runs alongside the need for an appropriate authorising Act of Parliament, and is thus not a change to the legislative manner and form which must be followed to produce the necessary approving legislation, that additional practical mechanisms such as this are embedded in the EUA demonstrates clearly that this system of control is structured so as to facilitate compliance with its terms. The statement of reasons to be laid before Parliament supports the process of scrutiny, enabling the legislature to determine whether a government judgement as to whether a referendum, exemption or significance condition is engaged is justified. The existence of such supplementary devices must surely be taken to demonstrate that the EUA's entire system of control is one which has been designed on the premise that it is to be legally effective, and applicable to future Parliaments, rather than something which is not lawful, and can be entirely disregarded.

In response, it might be objected that some support for the Diceyan constitutional orthodoxy was also exhibited as the EU Bill progressed through Parliament. In particular, traditional claims that Parliament is unable to bind its successors were voiced with a degree of frequency,[68] and this mantra was not openly rejected by the government in the course of the Bill being promoted. Indeed, the response of the Foreign Secretary, William Hague, was to equivocate, rather than engage directly with this critique:

> My hon. Friend said that we cannot bind our successors in this respect, but of course that could be said about so many of the laws that we propose, and are proposed under future Governments, which we intend to have long-term effect. If we took that attitude on everything, there would be no point in doing anything or ever getting up in the morning to come to Parliament at all. We are trying to create a long-term and enduring framework, and I believe that we have a very good chance of doing so.[69]

This response thus reaffirms the government's intention to create a statutory framework which is to have future legal effects, yet makes no attempt to reconcile

---

[66]   European Union Act 2011 s 5.

[67]   ibid s 2(1)(a); s 3(1)(a).

[68]   See, eg at second reading in the House of Commons: Douglas Carswell MP, *Hansard*, HC Deb Vol 520, col 201 (7 December 2010); Yvette Cooper MP, *Hansard*, HC Deb Vol 520, col 208 (7 December 2010); Bernard Jenkin MP, *Hansard*, HC Deb Vol 520, col 253 (7 December 2010); Jacob Rees-Moog MP, *Hansard*, HC Deb Vol 520, col 256 (7 December 2010); Chris Heaton-Harris MP, *Hansard*, HC Deb Vol 520, col 261 (7 December 2010).

[69]   *Hansard*, HC Deb Vol 520, col 201 (7 December 2010).

this objective with the Diceyan objection that this is simply not possible. However, although the government's lack of clarity on this point is far from ideal, that such reconciliation was not attempted certainly does not mean it is not possible. Instead, the reiteration of the notion that Parliament cannot bind its successors in this context simply demonstrates the paucity of discussion about the scope of legislative power which is framed using this dogma. For in this respect what is crucial, yet also ambiguous, is what is meant by Parliament 'binding its successors'. The notion may be taken to preclude the enactment of legislation which cannot be reversed by a future Parliament, yet this begs a fundamental question: in what way must legislation be reversible? On the orthodox approach, all legislation must be reversible by necessary implication, yet there is no principled reason that this is required by the idea of legislative sovereignty.[70] However, if this proposition, which is questionable in itself, is understood to prohibit absolutely the enactment of legislation which purports to modify the future legislative process in a way which is legally effective, further incoherence is generated. For while in one sense the EUA *has* bound successor Parliaments—in that they are bound to comply with its terms, while those terms persist unamended—in an alternative sense, the EUA *has not* bound successor Parliaments—in that they can repeal or amend the terms of the EUA by ordinary legislation. The sheer generality of the edict that 'no Parliament can bind its successors' makes it an entirely unsuitable notion around which debates as to the scope of sovereign legislative power can be structured. That this notion featured in parliamentary debates about the EU Bill does not demonstrate that the Diceyan orthodoxy is alive and kicking, because depending on how the claim 'Parliament cannot bind its successors' is understood, it is compatible with a manner and form interpretation of the 2011 Act. The legislature has not, by the EUA, bound its successors absolutely, preventing future legislation on any particular substantive topic, but it has—in a way which is both lawful and compatible with the notion of parliamentary sovereignty—altered the law-making process, with which future Parliaments will be required to comply to enact valid statutes.

This manner and form interpretation of the EUA is bolstered by consideration of early legislative engagements with its terms. Four Acts of Parliament have been enacted in the aftermath of the EUA, all of which provide approval for government action to ratify treaties or confirm decisions which is directly framed by the requirements of the 2011 Act. This basic approach, which is premised on the notions that the EUA is legally effective and that compliance with its terms is required as a matter of law, can be seen, first, in the European Union (Approvals) Act 2013. The 2013 Act by section 1 provides approval, in accordance with section 8 of the EUA, for two decisions taken under Article 352 of the Treaty on the

---

[70] See, eg A Bradley, 'The Sovereignty of Parliament: Form or Substance?' in J Jowell and D Oliver (eds), *The Changing Constitution*, 7th edn (Oxford, Oxford University Press, 2011) 51–52; J Goldsworthy, *Parliamentary Sovereignty: Contemporary Debates* (Cambridge, Cambridge University Press, 2010) 182, 289–90.

Functioning of the European Union (TFEU),[71] and by section 2, further approves a decision covered by section 7(3) of the EUA.[72] And secondly, this approach is evident in the European Union (Approvals) Act 2014, which provides approval, in accordance with section 8 of the EUA, for two further decisions taken pursuant to Article 352 TFEU.[73] Yet while this evidence of the broad approach which Parliament has taken in relation to the requirements of the EUA—one of directly engaging with, and adhering to, its terms—is significant in that in demonstrates the legal effectiveness of the 2011 Act in general, two further examples of legislative action in this context reveal even more.

These two further examples of post-EUA legislative action are the European Union (Approval of Treaty Amendment Decision) Act 2012 and the European Union (Croatian Accession and Irish Protocol) Act 2013. The 2012 Act, by section 1 provides approval, in accordance with section 3 of the EUA, for the European Council decision, taken under Article 48(6) TEU, to amend Article 136 TFEU with regard to a stability mechanism for Member States whose currency is the euro.[74] The 2013 Act, by section 1 provides approval, in accordance with section 2 of the EUA, for the ratification of the treaty concerning the accession of Croatia to the EU.[75] Further, by section 2, the 2013 Act provides approval, in accordance with section 2 of the EUA, for the Protocol on the concerns of the Irish people on the Treaty of Lisbon.[76] But what is most important, for present purposes, about the 2012 and 2013 Acts is the way in which this approval is provided in the legislation; each of the three authorising provisions outlined above explicitly complies with the exemption condition contained in sections 2 and 3 of the EUA. The 2012 Act expressly states that the Article 48(6) decision it approves 'does not fall within section 4 of the European Union Act 2011'.[77] Similarly, the 2013 Act provides explicitly that the treaty it approves 'does not fall within section 4 of the European Union Act 2011',[78] and precisely the same formula is adopted in relation to the Protocol subject to its authorisation.[79] Not only, then, is Parliament engaging with the EUA on the general basis that its terms are legally effective, and compliance

---

[71] The decisions approved are those to adopt the Council Regulation on the electronic publication of the Official Journal (document number 10222/5/11) and to establish a Multiannual Framework for the European Union Agency for Fundamental Rights for 2013–2017 (document number 10449/12).

[72] The decision approved is that taken under Art 17(5) TEU, for the number of members of the European Commission to continue to be equal to the number of Member States (document number EUCO 176/12).

[73] The decisions approved are those to adopt the Council Regulation on the deposit of the historical archives of the institutions at the European University Institute in Florence (document number 6867/13) and the Council Regulation establishing for the period 2014-2020 the programme 'Europe for Citizens' (document number 12557/13).

[74] Decision of 25 March 2011 (2011/199/EU).

[75] Treaty signed at Brussels on 9 December 2011.

[76] Protocol adopted at Brussels on 16 May 2012.

[77] European Union (Approval of Treaty Amendment Decision) Act 2012 s 1(3).

[78] European Union (Croatian Accession and Irish Protocol) Act 2013 s 1(3).

[79] ibid s 2(3).

with them is obligatory, but the legislature has also adhered to the changes to the legislative manner and form established by sections 2 and 3 of the 2011 Act.

Of course, satisfaction of the exemption condition is straightforward: all that is required is for an approving Act to state explicitly that the proposed change does not fall within section 4 of the EUA. Yet that Parliament has felt obliged to comply with the undemanding terms of the exemption condition can be seen as evidence of a broader principle: the legislature accepts that for legislation which falls within the ambit of the section 2, 3 or 6 of the EUA to be validly enacted, the statutory conditions contained therein must be satisfied. And there is no reason why Parliament should depart from this general principle in relation to a statute which *would* fall within the criteria contained in section 4 of the EUA, and thus instead require compliance with the referendum condition.[80] While a referendum condition would certainly be much more challenging to satisfy than the requirement as to legislative form which the exemption condition imposes, from the perspective of the manner and form theory of parliamentary sovereignty, this is immaterial; what matters is that this is a procedural condition, lawfully introduced by Parliament, and as a result, with which compliance is required for the enactment of valid future legislation. And the early evidence of legislative engagement with the EUA strongly suggests that, if approval were sought for government action which would trigger such a requirement under the 2011 Act, it is this manner and form understanding of the legal effectiveness of referendum conditions which Parliament would feel compelled to adopt.[81]

The manner and form interpretation of the EUA can also be supported by subsequent political attitudes to the 2011 Act. One of the most striking consequences of the enactment of the EUA is the manner in which the legal guarantees it purports to introduce have been exploited in political discourse. A crucial case study in this regard is provided by the circumstances in which the UK opted to 'veto' the Treaty on Stability, Coordination and Governance, or 'Fiscal Compact', at the December 2011 European Council meeting in Brussels.[82] The decision of Prime Minister David Cameron to withhold assent to the Fiscal Compact, and

---

[80] Unless, of course, the change falls within the ambit of s 3 of the EUA, and is capable, in the alternative, of satisfying the narrowly defined 'significance condition'.

[81] That the courts also seem to be implicitly accepting the legality of the EUA's referendum locks is apparent from the decision of the Administrative Court in *Wheeler v The Office of the Prime Minister* [2014] EWHC 3815 (Admin). In this case, the court rejected an application for permission to bring judicial review of the proposed decision of the government to give notice, in accordance with the requirements of EU law, of the UK's wish to participate in the European Arrest Warrant scheme. The court rejected an argument that the EUA required a referendum to be held prior to the lawful notification by the government of such an intention, on the grounds that this was not necessary in accordance with the strict terms of s 6 of the 2011 Act; [25]–[40]. In refusing permission to apply for judicial review, the court therefore purported to treat the terms of the EUA as legally valid, ruling that the requirement that a referendum be held would only arise as a matter of law in the circumstances expressly provided for in the 2011 Act.

[82] See generally, M Gordon, 'The United Kingdom and the Fiscal Compact: Past and Future' (2014) 10 *European Constitutional Law Review* 28: S Peers, 'The Stability Treaty: Permanent Austerity or Gesture Politics?' (2012) 8 *European Constitutional Law Review* 404.

thus prevent its terms taking effect as an amendment of the existing EU treaties, had the effect that the changes which were proposed to eurozone economic governance were instead agreed in the form of an inter-governmental treaty between 25 of the 27 Member States, outside the EU's legal architecture. Yet it is difficult to view this veto as a direct result of a desire to avoid triggering a referendum lock contained in the EUA, because none of the proposed changes to economic governance would have fallen within section 4.[83] Indeed, this was to some extent anticipated in advance of the Brussels summit at which the UK veto was wielded, with the Prime Minister stating that as it was not intended to pass power or competence from the UK to the EU, the question of a referendum would be unlikely to arise.[84] Yet the position seemingly adopted by David Cameron in advance of the negotiations—that a referendum would likely be unnecessary—was not, however, unchallenged, both within and without the government. A number of senior Conservatives argued publicly that a referendum might in fact be required to ratify any revising treaty agreed at the Brussels summit. The Work and Pensions Secretary, Iain Duncan Smith, called for a referendum to be held on any 'major treaty change'.[85] The Northern Ireland Secretary, Owen Paterson, said that it was 'inevitable' that a referendum would ultimately need to be held:

> If there was a major fundamental change in our relationship, emerging from the creation of a new bloc, which would be effectively a new country from which we were excluded, then I think inevitably there would be huge pressure for a referendum.[86]

Similarly, the mayor of London, Boris Johnson, argued that it was

> absolutely clear to me that if there is a new treaty of 27 [EU Member States]—if there is a new EU treaty that creates a kind of fiscal union within the eurozone—then we would have absolutely no choice either to veto it or to put it to a referendum.[87]

Such calls for a referendum go beyond the strict legal scope of the EUA, and reveal the political potency of the 2011 Act. For the political rhetoric surrounding the referendum locks has the potential, in practice, to extend the reach of the EUA. The reach and applicability of the Act may be extended in practice if it is accepted that *any* major or fundamental change, either to the EU treaties or the UK's relationship with the EU in general, should be subject to approval at a referendum. This is a strikingly broad proposition, and would cover a range of scenarios which would not otherwise fall within the EUA. When it is noted that the system of

---

[83] One of the crucial reasons for this is the fact that the key changes introduced by the Fiscal Compact would not have been applicable to the UK, as a non-eurozone state, and so if even falling within the ambit of s 4, they would have been exempt in accordance with s 4(4)(b): see Gordon, 'The UK and the Fiscal Compact' (2014) ibid 38–41.

[84] 'Downing Street insists there will be no EU referendum despite Iain Duncan Smith's demands', *The Daily Telegraph* (5 December 2011).

[85] 'Iain Duncan Smith calls for referendum on European "fiscal union"', *The Daily Telegraph* (5 December 2011).

[86] 'Tory minister breaks ranks with Cameron over Europe', *The Guardian* (7 December 2011).

[87] ibid.

referendum locks contained in the 2011 Act is already very extensive,[88] the idea that, in practice, this scheme could become viewed as all-embracing might raise concern. It might be objected that the comments of the senior Conservatives set out above are not statements about the scope, reach or application of the EUA. Instead, it could be argued that they are simply political calls for a referendum to be held. Yet such calls must nevertheless be understood in the context of the EUA. The 2011 Act is the pre-eminent constitutional instrument which establishes the circumstances in which referendums will be required where change is proposed to the UK's relationship with the EU. And the very existence of this legislation has arguably therefore had an important impact on the political environment in which change to the UK-EU relationship is considered, and claims which would have the effect of extending the scope of the EUA are made.

This impact is evident in two senses. First, the existence of the EUA can be seen to have reversed the domestic political presumption that to hold a referendum on changes to the UK-EU relationship will be an exceptional event, rather than an ordinary occurrence. The broad scope of the EUA's referendum locks, which are triggered in an array of circumstances, gives the impression that holding a referendum to approve change to the relationship between the UK and the EU has become the new norm, and we might thus expect calls for referendums to be held, even where not required by the Act, to become regularised. Secondly, the EUA provides a barometer by which the significance of a change to the structure, power or competence of the EU can be measured, and thus offers a comparator which can readily be used to justify calls for referendums beyond the scope of the Act. So, it can be argued, if issue X is covered by the EUA's referendum locks, while issue Y is not, yet is of equivalent (or greater) importance, why should a referendum not also be held in relation to issue Y, even though not required by the EUA? In both of these respects, the 2011 Act can be seen to have contributed significantly to the cultivation of an atmosphere in which it is easier to make and sustain political calls for a referendum to be held, even in circumstances which fall outside the scope of the EUA, while correspondingly making it more difficult for such calls to be convincingly rebutted.

Yet if this assessment of the political impact of the EUA is right, while important to appreciate in itself, it also tells us something about the legal effectiveness of the Act. For if the EUA does have this political potency—in that it appears to make approval at a referendum a routine part of the authorisation of changes to the UK's relationship with the EU, and thus facilitates calls for additional referendums, above and beyond those strictly required by the Act, to be made—it must be founded on recognition of the basic legal force of the legislation. The very possibility of the reach of the EUA being extended, in practice, through political argument presupposes that the Act is legally effective. For if the creation in the EUA of a scheme of referendum locks were a legally ineffective use of Parliament's

---

[88] See Gordon and Dougan, 'Who Won the Bloody War Anyway?' (2012) n 7 above, 18–23.

legislative power, it would be futile to attempt to use parallels with the 2011 Act—whether explicitly or implicitly—to frame arguments for further referendums. If these statutory referendum guarantees are illusory and can be lawfully disregarded, as the Diceyan analysis of parliamentary sovereignty would suggest, it would be nonsensical to consider them to have the potential to be politically extended. Yet the post-EUA political atmosphere shows no sign of debate about whether the referendum locks provided for in the 2011 Act are secure; instead, this seems to be taken for granted, with argument in this context instead focused on whether the legal guarantees which exist ought in some way to be supplemented.[89]

Indeed, this basic political recognition of the legal force of the EUA's referendum locks is also evident in the proposals of the main political parties as to the future of the 2011 Act itself. The Labour party has committed, if elected to government in 2015, to legislate to create a new lock—one which guarantees that a future transfer of power from the UK to the EU will be subject to approval at an 'in/out' referendum on continued membership of the Union.[90] How precisely this new lock would interact with the existing legislative scheme of control is not clear, in particular whether it would replace entirely the EUA as it stands at present, or whether the current locks would persist, and continue to condition future transfers of power or competence to the EU following any initial vote in favour of continued membership. The scope of this new legislative lock is also uncertain: as the Labour leader, Ed Miliband, has indicated that it is 'unlikely' that it would be triggered in the next Parliament,[91] it may that the breadth of the existing scheme of control would need to be narrowed to reduce the possibility of a referendum being prompted on some of the more esoteric matters covered by the EUA. Yet what is certainly clear is that Labour's policy is one premised on the legal effectiveness, in principle, of statutory referendum locks. In this sense, the Labour approach endorses a manner and form interpretation of the EUA, because this logically underpins its policy of legislating to create a new statutory referendum lock. The policy of the Liberal Democrats—to retain the EUA as presently enacted, and have a referendum only if one of the locks therein is triggered by a transfer of power or competence to the EU[92]—is similarly premised on the legal effectiveness of the EUA. And while Conservative policy on EU membership is now dominated by a guarantee to hold an in/out referendum in any event by 2017,[93] whether or not the EUA would be retained following a vote for the UK to

---

[89] See, eg 'Britons are legally entitled to a referendum on Juncker appointment, says George Osborne's father-in-law', *The Daily Telegraph* (2 July 2014). Although the argument made by Lord Howell reported here conflates (flawed) descriptive claims about what the EUA requires with normative claims about what it ought to require, it is a clear example of how the EUA can be deployed to justify assertions which, in effect, would constitute an extension of the strict scope of the legislation.

[90] Ed Miliband MP, Speech at London Business School (12 March 2014): labourlist.org/2014/03/miliband-rules-out-eu-referendum-full-speech-text/.

[91] 'Ed Miliband says in/out referendum on Europe is unlikely', *The Guardian* (11 March 2014).

[92] 'Nick Clegg defeats Lib Dem bid to guarantee EU referendum', *The Guardian* (1 July 2014).

[93] 'David Cameron: in-out referendum on EU by 2017 is cast-iron pledge', *The Guardian* (11 May 2014).

remain in the Union, there can be little doubt that a government led by this party would view the scheme of statutory locks it establishes as legally effective unless or until repealed.[94]

Finally, clear political incentives also attach to the adoption of a manner and form interpretation of the EUA. For if the orthodox Diceyan approach to the 2011 Act is favoured, and the scheme of referendum locks thus deemed legally ineffective, it is possible for them to be entirely disregarded by a future government wishing to approve an ostensibly applicable transfer of power or competence to the EU. Yet to suggest that in such circumstances a referendum requirement can be avoided because it was beyond the legislative authority of Parliament to enact such statutory conditions is a highly problematic political argument. For it would function to deny the effectiveness of seemingly clear legal rights bestowed on citizens by statute. To seek to justify the renunciation of such rights to democratic participation in significant political decision-making on the basis that, as a matter of constitutional doctrine, they were never enforceable to begin with, would be simply unsatisfactory. As such, it would be pragmatic for a future government to accept the manner and form reading of the EUA, and behave as if the referendum locks it establishes are legally effective. Given the locks are not in any way entrenched, the possibility still remains that they can readily be repealed by ordinary Act of Parliament. While this would require a justification for such removal to be more directly advanced, and as such might be less convenient for a government than a more surreptitious approach founded on the idea that these guarantees were inherently ephemeral, it is surely better that these arguments be considered openly, rather than fostering disillusionment among citizens, and giving the impression that constitutional doctrine has been disingenuously exploited. And, of course, such pragmatic concerns as to what can most credibly be justified are also supported by considerations of political and constitutional principle. For to adopt a manner and form interpretation of the EUA also has the advantage of being respectful of legal and democratic values of fundamental importance: on the one hand, the idea that the content of the law should be certain, and its application in practice predictable; and on the other hand, the idea that citizens should be entitled effectively to participate in significant political decision-making.

It might be suggested by defenders of a Diceyan conception of parliamentary sovereignty that such political arguments, whether based on pragmatism, principle, or both, are not determinative of the position as a matter of law. Or, in other words, that even if there are good reasons that future governments and Parliaments ought to adopt a manner and form understanding of the EUA, this does not mean that its referendum locks are legally effective. Instead, the referendum locks may still be legally ineffective, because it is beyond the power of Parliament to legislate to alter the future legislative process, but this does not

---

[94] See, eg David Cameron, 'We need to be clear about the best way of getting what is best for Britain', *The Daily Telegraph* (30 June 2012): 'this Government put in place a referendum lock so that no government can ever again pass powers from Britain to Brussels without first asking the British people'.

prevent political authorities from opting to comply with them for other reasons. Such claims would, however, present an interpretation of constitutional practice which is strained to breaking point, in order to maintain an orthodox conception of legislative authority which is out of place in the contemporary UK constitution. If all indicators point to the fact that the EUA's referendum locks are understood to be legally effective, and, moreover, we can identify good political reasons for the adoption of this approach, it would be contrived to suggest that there is an alternative 'true' legal position which persists apart from, and is obscured by, constitutional practice. Instead, the artificiality of the Diceyan analysis of the EUA demonstrates a more fundamental point: it has been replaced by the manner and form theory of parliamentary sovereignty, which must now be seen to provide the best account of the scope of the legally unlimited legislative authority of the UK Parliament. Clear attitudes as to the position of the law, considerations of political pragmatism, and notions of constitutional value align in this context to demonstrate definitively that the manner and form theory has now been adopted in the contemporary UK constitution.

V. CONSTITUTIONAL EFFECT OF THE EUROPEAN UNION ACT

The key constitutional effect of the EUA is to demonstrate that the manner and form theory now represents the new orthodoxy in relation to the doctrine of parliamentary sovereignty in the UK constitution. The EUA is the third stage in a pattern of constitutional development traced across Part II of this book, and represents the culmination of a modern shift in our understanding of the implications of the idea of legislative sovereignty. The effects and implications of the 2011 Act should not, therefore, be understood in isolation, but located clearly in this contemporary constitutional context. Yet the EUA is nevertheless of great significance, because the enactment therein of a scheme of statutory referendum conditions marks the most decisive and elaborate utilisation of legislative power to alter the future manner and form by the UK Parliament.

There has, of course, been previous legislative engagement with referendums in the UK prior to the enactment of the EUA, but not so directly as to make them a mandatory part of the legislative process. Instead, referendums in the UK have tended to be advisory in nature, at least in formal terms, and held in relation to ad hoc events, such as to establish or extend the devolution settlement,[95] continue membership of the EU,[96] change the voting system for elections to the House of Commons,[97] or in relation to independence for constituent nations of the UK.[98]

---

[95] The referendums held in Scotland in 1979 and 1997; Wales in 1979, 1997 and 2011; Northern Ireland in 1998. See also regional referendums in London in 1998 and the North East of England in 2004.

[96] The national referendum on continuing membership of the EU in 1975.

[97] The national referendum on the alternative voting system in 2011.

[98] The referendums held in Northern Ireland in 1973 and Scotland in 2014.

While such ad hoc referendums must still be authorised by statute, there are also some standing provisions for referendums to be held in certain circumstances, such as in relation to the alteration of local council governance arrangements,[99] changes to local council tax rates,[100] or to adopt neighbourhood development orders or plans.[101] Of greatest constitutional significance, however, is the unique standing provision made in the Northern Ireland Act 1998:

> It is hereby declared that Northern Ireland in its entirety remains part of the United Kingdom and shall not cease to be so without the consent of a majority of the people of Northern Ireland voting in a poll held for the purposes of this section in accordance with Schedule 1.[102]

On the orthodox approach to the doctrine of parliamentary sovereignty, this guarantee can have no legal effect on Parliament's continuing authority to enact legislation granting full independence to Northern Ireland; instead, it might be viewed as a political promise that a referendum will be held before any legislation providing for Northern Irish independence would be passed. And as the provision is expressly framed as a declaration of principle—and one which might in any event be recognised to have a more general authority, quite apart from its inclusion in statute—rather than conceived as a direct change to the future legislative process, such a Diceyan interpretation of the provision has some force. Yet the EUA leaves no such room for ambiguity, in explicitly and deliberately integrating referendum conditions into the future procedure for the enactment of valid legislation. From this more concretely established perspective, we might return to the Northern Ireland Act 1998, and be confident in also adopting a manner and form interpretation of the guarantee contained in section 1(1). For rather than such claims appearing speculative, that this referendum guarantee can also be treated as legally effective—functioning to preclude, as a matter of law, the enactment of valid independence legislation unless its terms have been satisfied—can be firmly recognised in light of the EUA. The 2011 Act, in marking the culmination of a modern shift to the manner and form theory of parliamentary sovereignty,

---

[99] Local Government Act 2000 ss 9M–9N, 27, which makes provision for local referendums to be held on directly elected mayors. A significant number of such referendums have occurred in England, including, most recently, in Salford, Birmingham, Bradford, Bristol, Coventry, Leeds, Manchester, Newcastle, Nottingham, Sheffield, Wakefield, Doncaster and Hartlepool in 2012, Middlesbrough in 2013, and Copeland in 2014.

[100] Localism Act 2011 s 72.

[101] Neighbourhood Planning (Referendums) Regulations 2012 (SI 2012/2031), made pursuant to the Town and Country Planning Act 1990 Schedule 4B and the Planning and Compulsory Purchase Act 2004 s 38A.

[102] Northern Ireland Act 1998 s 1(1). This provision restates a commitment contained in previous legislation concerning devolution of power to Northern Ireland: see, eg the Northern Ireland Constitution Act 1973 s 1 and the Ireland Act 1949 s 1(2), although unlike the Acts of 1998 and 1973, the 1949 Act made departure from the UK conditional upon the consent of the Parliament of Northern Ireland.

now enables prior claims to similar, but less conclusive, effect to be revisited and convincingly confirmed.[103]

Similar considerations also distinguish the EUA from earlier legislative action which, while not engaging referendums to do so, appears to have altered the manner and form required to enact valid future legislation. The Parliament Acts have been considered in detail in Chapter five, and while they must also be understood to represent a clear exercise of legislative power to alter the legislative process—the significance of which is in no way diminished by the claims made as to the constitutional effect, and thus importance, of the EUA in this chapter—such a manner and form account of the 1911 and 1949 Acts could readily be challenged prior to the decision of the House of Lords in *Jackson*.[104] Moreover, even after *Jackson*, if a manner and form analysis of the Parliament Acts is accepted, how far the implications of this extend remains open to debate.[105] A further key example of legislation ostensibly altering the future manner and form, but with respect to which credible doubts can also be identified, is the Statute of Westminster 1931.[106] For some, including Jennings,[107] the requirement in section 4 of the 1931 Act, that an express declaration of Dominion consent be included in Acts of the UK Parliament which were in future to apply in such territories, was a clear example of legislative change to the future manner and form. However, the obiter suggestion of Lord Sankey in *British Coal Corporation v The King*,[108] that Parliament's power 'remains in theory unimpaired'[109] by the 1931 Act—an observation which is, in itself, highly ambiguous[110]—could be understood to provide evidence to the contrary. While in practice, this requirement was complied with by relevant legislation, it was complied with through express recitals of consent in the preambles to the legislation concerned, rather than in the body of such legislation itself.[111]

In *Manuel v Attorney General*,[112] which concerned a challenge to the Canada Act 1982, such recital in a preamble was held by the Court of Appeal to be sufficient to satisfy the express consent requirement, 'if and so far as the conditions of section 4 of the Statute of 1931 had to be complied with'.[113] Yet it is not clear

---

[103] See, eg the general discussion in H Calvert, *Constitutional Law in Northern Ireland: A Study in Regional Government* (London, Stevens, 1968) 23–33.

[104] *R (Jackson) v Attorney General* [2005] UKHL 56, [2006] 1 AC 262.

[105] See chapter 5 of this volume, pp 224–30.

[106] See chapter 2 of this volume, pp 87–89.

[107] See more recently HR Zhou, 'Revisiting the "Manner and Form" Theory of Parliamentary Sovereignty' (2013) 129 *LQR* 610, 629–37.

[108] *British Coal Corporation v The King* [1935] AC 500.

[109] ibid 520.

[110] See chapter 2 of this volume, p 88.

[111] See, eg the preamble to His Majesty's Abdication Act 1936: 'And whereas, following upon the communication to His Dominions of His Majesty's said declaration and desire, the Dominion of Canada pursuant to the provisions of section four of the Statute of Westminster, 1931, has requested and consented to the enactment of this Act, and the Commonwealth of Australia, the Dominion of New Zealand, and the Union of South Africa have assented thereto'.

[112] *Manuel v Attorney General* [1983] Ch 77.

[113] ibid 108.

that this can be taken to provide definitive support for the manner and form theory, in part because of the qualified nature of the decision of the court, but also because the need for certain specific recitals to be contained in a preamble is a potentially brittle foundation on which to sustain broader claims that Parliament may legislate to control the manner or form which the actual terms of future legislation—and not simply the preamble—must satisfy in order to be recognised as valid. Such difficulties are more acute when the constitutional context of the Statute of Westminster is considered; indeed, it is at least arguable that the requirement of Dominion consent referred to in section 4 is simply a reflection of a constitutional principle the authority of which is not dependent on its incorporation in legislation. And as such, it may be the case that the explicit inclusion in a preamble of a Dominion's consent to the enactment of applicable legislation is required by convention, on the basis of fundamental democratic notions of self-determination, rather than by a specific legislative provision contained in the 1931 Act. Such claims are not, in my view, ultimately persuasive, and the legal significance of a statutory provision such as section 4 cannot, on this basis, be discounted. Yet, again, the existence of such credible doubts as to the implications of the Statute of Westminster with respect to the scope of the legislative power of Parliament provides an important counterpoint to the EUA. A manner and form interpretation of the Statute of Westminster may have been the best available, as it also arguably was with respect to the Parliament Acts 1911 and 1949. Yet in relation to the EUA this is, in my view, unquestionably the case. To therefore suggest that the constitutional effect of the EUA is crucial because it confirms the authority of the manner and form theory of parliamentary sovereignty is not to disregard earlier examples of potential salience and significance. Instead, it is to recognise that only now, with the enactment of the EUA's scheme of referendum locks, can we unequivocally maintain that the UK constitution is founded on the manner and form conception of legally unlimited legislative authority.

A. Goldsworthy's Challenge to Referendum Requirements and its Application to the EUA

There is, however, a crucial objection which may be made in response to this conclusion as to the constitutional effect of the EUA. This challenge is posed in the work of Goldsworthy, and concerns an assumption which has underpinned the argument developed throughout this chapter. The key question posed is this: is it actually correct, as has been presumed to this point, to recognise a statutory referendum requirement, in particular, to be a legally permissible alteration of the future legislative process? In suggesting that this assumption is flawed, Goldsworthy is not developing a critique of the manner and form interpretation of the EUA from a Diceyan perspective, since he does not posit that a sovereign Parliament can *never* legislate to alter the future law-making process. Indeed, nor is this necessarily a critique of the account of the legal effectiveness of the EUA's referendum locks which I have developed in this chapter. Instead, this challenge is ultimately to the manner and form theory of legally unlimited legislative authority itself, and is crucially premised on Goldsworthy's competing 'procedure and form' model of parliamentary sovereignty. I sought to challenge a number of aspects of the procedure and form model in earlier chapters of this book, advancing arguments against Goldsworthy's approach both in principle,[114] and with respect to the practical application of the theory to some of the contemporary constitutional developments examined earlier in Part II.[115] Here claims of both kinds must be combined, for in my view Goldsworthy's argument that referendum requirements cannot be considered to be legally permissible changes to the future legislative process should be rejected on conceptual grounds, while the application of this theory to the particular circumstances of the EUA is also problematic.

The fundamental distinction between the procedure and form model of parliamentary sovereignty, and the manner and form theory of such legislative authority, is that while Goldsworthy accepts that a sovereign Parliament has the power to modify the future law-making process, this power is not legally unlimited. Instead, a sovereign Parliament, according to Goldsworthy, is only lawfully permitted to introduce statutory changes to procedure or form which 'do not diminish Parliament's continuing substantive power to legislate'.[116] Applying this general test to the particular circumstances of statutory referendum requirements, Goldsworthy argues:

> Such a requirement goes much further than just requiring Parliament to follow a particular procedure or adopt a particular form in exercising its substantive authority to enact law: by forbidding Parliament to enact law without the approval of an external body—namely, the electorate—it plainly limits its substantive authority.[117]

While accepting that referendum requirements are 'perfectly democratic',[118] Goldsworthy thus suggests that they are just one example of a broader phenomenon, which is inherently incompatible with the doctrine of parliamentary sovereignty because it serves to diminish the substantive legislative power of Parliament: the subjection of legislation to the 'veto' of an external body.[119] In principle, Goldsworthy endorses a 'general rule' that 'a requirement that an external body must assent to legislation cannot be regarded as a legitimate manner and form requirement, because it partially deprives the legislature of its power'.[120] If a referendum requirement were to be treated, in violation of this general rule, as a valid procedural condition, 'then logically, so is a requirement that a private

---

[114] See chapter 2 of this volume, pp 97–107.
[115] See chapter 4 of this volume, pp 179–82; chapter 5 of this volume, pp 226–30.
[116] Goldsworthy, *Parliamentary Sovereignty: Contemporary Debates* (2010) n 70 above, 194.
[117] ibid 138. See also 198–99.
[118] ibid 138.
[119] ibid 199.
[120] ibid 165.

corporation must assent to legislation.[121] For Goldsworthy, the 'absurdity' of affording a legislative veto to a private corporation can be seen to demonstrate the parallel 'impermissibility' of statutory referendum requirements.[122] Yet while referendum requirements cannot, on this basis, be understood to constitute valid legislative procedural conditions, Goldsworthy maintains that they could be imposed by an alternative means: 'a radical change to the customary rule of recognition that underpins Britain's unwritten constitution'.[123]

Goldsworthy's account of the legal (in)validity of statutory referendum requirements can, however, be challenged, in principle, on two grounds. First, it is far from clear that the general rule set out by Goldsworthy—that to require the assent of an external body to the enactment of legislation cannot constitute a legally valid statutory procedural condition—is correct. In large part, this is a function of the overarching difficulties of the 'diminishing of substantive power' test, relied on in Goldsworthy's model to distinguish between those statutory procedural conditions which are legally permissible, and those which are legally impermissible. In particular, as I argued in Chapter two, such a limit on Parliament's legislative authority is neither required by, nor justifiable by reference to, the notion of parliamentary sovereignty, because it engages the idea of 'substantive power' in a sense which is not relevant to the claims made this doctrine. The notion that Parliament possesses legally unlimited legislative authority does not entail that this power should, in practice, be readily exercisable, and a change to the law-making process which makes it more difficult for Parliament to legislate in future does not diminish or extinguish its power to enact law in relation to any relevant subject-matter.[124] The general requirement that legislation concerning a specific topic must also be approved by an external body may make it more difficult to legislate, perhaps even considerably so, but it is still a procedural requirement which does not absolutely prevent Parliament from enacting legislation on that specified topic.

Instead, if Parliament wishes to enact legislation which is subject to such a requirement, it must ensure that the statutory rules it intends to enact are ones which the relevant external body will be content to accept. Parliament is not abandoning the field in such circumstances; instead, it will remain at the heart of the legislative process, debating and scrutinising the detailed provisions of legislation, and determining ultimately what does, or what does not, become incorporated into the terms of the statute. Any such external veto body, in contrast, will have a much more minimal role in the legislative process: the opportunity merely to accept or reject what is presented to it following the deliberation of Parliament. Of course, it would be possible to design a particular external veto 'process' which made it impossible for Parliament to legislate in the future—for example,

---

[121] ibid 165.
[122] ibid 165.
[123] ibid 201. See also 139, 199.
[124] See chapter 2 of this volume, pp 97–107.

by affording that power to a body which became defunct, or was composed of many individual members with the unanimous agreement of all required—at which point we could justifiably view substantive law-making authority to have been destroyed, and such an ostensibly 'procedural' condition to be invalid. Yet to afford a veto to an external body does not inherently produce an effect of this kind, one which is relevant to the continuing existence of the variety of substantive legislative power which is afforded to Parliament by the doctrine of parliamentary sovereignty. And as such, the possibility that external assent requirements could constitute legally valid procedural conditions on future law-making cannot be entirely discounted.

Indeed, this is especially the case when we consider that such a requirement of extra-parliamentary assent already exists in the UK constitution: the royal assent which all legislation must receive, granted by the monarch on ministerial advice. Of course, to describe this as an 'extra-parliamentary' assent requirement, the term 'parliamentary' is used in the literal, rather than the constitutional, sense. For from the constitutional perspective, there is no doubt that it is the composite institution of the Queen-in-Parliament which exercises sovereign legislative authority in the UK. Yet while this legal position is not one established by statute, in the event that the monarch was replaced as head of state in the UK, surely it would be lawful for this power of assent to be passed to a hypothetical President by Act of Parliament. Some might suggest that this would simply constitute a redefinition of what we mean by 'parliamentary' for constitutional purposes—from the sovereignty of the Queen-in-Parliament to that of a President-in-Parliament. Yet such a response is not open to Goldsworthy, for, quite rightly in my view, he rejects such artificial reasoning, in general, as 'formalistic word magic'.[125] Perhaps Goldsworthy's ultimate fall-back would be that such change would need to occur at the level of the rule of recognition, but for reasons discussed already elsewhere, which will be revisited again below in the context of referendum requirements, such claims are themselves problematic. Yet, moreover, in parallel with Goldsworthy's own rejection of the redefinition theory, such an argument might readily be considered a form of conceptual magic, which simply evades what is really going on.

To recognise, in accordance with the manner and form theory, that an external body assent requirement can in principle be understood to constitute a procedural legislative condition, and is therefore potentially a legally valid exercise of sovereign law-making authority, does not, however, mean that to implement such statutory change would be desirable. Indeed, we might in general strongly presume that such procedural conditions ought not to be introduced. At the very least, it seems clear that if an external body were to be afforded such power—which while procedural in nature, is without question of considerable significance—it would need to possess exceptional legitimacy, in some particular regard, for this to be constitutionally or democratically appropriate. We will address such issues, and

---

[125] Goldsworthy, *Parliamentary Sovereignty: Contemporary Debates* (2010) n 70 above, 199.

related considerations, further in Part III of this book, when I will set out a specific normative justification for the manner and form theory,[126] while also exploring some of the ways in which this conception of sovereign legislative power might be appropriately utilised, in accordance with the particular account of its virtue there developed.[127] Yet what is crucial for present purposes is that such concerns about the desirability of deploying external assent requirements, or indeed any legislative procedural conditions, are properly dealt with at this level of justification, rather than at the level of legal validity. Goldsworthy's procedure and form model, in contrast, by associating increased difficulty in legislating with a diminishing of substantive power, takes such matters to go to legal permissibility, rather than to political justification. Yet the notion that Parliament's legislative authority, in principle, is limited by difficulty in legislating in practice is not consistent with the claim, made by the doctrine of parliamentary sovereignty, that its law-making authority is legally unlimited. And on this basis, Goldsworthy's procedure and form model of parliamentary sovereignty should be rejected, both in general, and also as it applies in particular to external body assent requirements.

However, even if this objection to Goldsworthy's general rule concerning external body assent requirements—which rests on flaws which are a function of deeper problems underlying the procedure and form model—is not accepted, a second challenge to his rejection of referendum requirements can be made. This challenge is to the specific reasoning employed by Goldsworthy to locate a requirement as to the assent of the electorate, obtained at a referendum, within the broader generic category of bodies which are 'external' to Parliament. As has been indicated above, Goldsworthy rightly rejects attempts to rationalise referendum requirements as redefining Parliament for certain purposes, considering it to be 'nonsense to say that the electorate can be made part of the parliament that represents it'.[128] Yet this reasoning identifies an important factor which Goldsworthy is prepared to overlook when drawing a parallel between the electorate and any other body which is external to Parliament, even including private corporations. The relationship between the electorate and Parliament is entirely unlike that between Parliament and any other external body. For the electorate is the very source of the legislature's legitimacy: the fact that members of the House of Commons—which has constitutional priority over the unelected House of Lords—are elected by citizens, representative of citizens, and accountable to citizens provides the democratic justification for the exercise by Parliament of legislative authority. Moreover, it is because Parliament is a democratic institution that we can justify allocating to it legislative authority which is subject to no legal limitation, and thus ensuring the constitutional primacy of democracy within the UK constitution.[129]

---

[126] See chapter 7 of this volume, pp 302–17.
[127] See chapter 8 of this volume, pp 330–52.
[128] Goldsworthy, *Parliamentary Sovereignty: Contemporary Debates* (2010) n 70 above, 139.
[129] See chapter 1 of this volume, pp 32–55.

As a result, there are ample reasons to consider a legislative referendum requirement to be a very different kind of procedural condition to an assent requirement
which is afforded to any other body 'external' to Parliament. If Parliament's power
to legislate derives from the electorate, and thus in principle ought to be exercised
in a way which reflects the preferences of citizens, broadly understood, we might
argue that a legislative referendum requirement does not diminish the substantive power of the legislature, even on the understanding of this caveat adopted by
Goldsworthy. Instead, a statutory referendum requirement might be understood
to represent Parliament requesting an affirmation of its general mandate to legislate in relation to some specific issue or issues. To view a referendum requirement as a request for an affirmation of mandate can be seen to institutionalise
considerations which are already, or ought already to be, central to parliamentary
decision-making: ensuring that the legislation which Parliament wishes to enact is
acceptable to a majority of the citizens from whom its authority is generated. On
this understanding, such legislative referendum requirements serve to integrate
into the law-making process mechanisms which reinforce the fundamental democratic principles upon which the UK constitutional settlement is based. And it is
surely more coherent to view such statutory conditions in this way, rather than to
characterise them as giving an 'external' body a power of veto, conjuring the image
that the input of some foreign entity has been illicitly injected into the legislative
process. The preferences of the electorate are already a crucial element of the legislative process, albeit indirectly and politically. For Parliament to exercise statutory authority to make them directly and legally mandatory would formalise this
position, and may make it more difficult to legislate in future. Yet to do so would
reaffirm conditions which already operate in principle in relation to the substantive power of Parliament—here understood as actual power to legislate—rather
than diminish that power. For, while this principle is a crude one, which must be
applied with nuance to the challenging particularity of real world circumstances,
as a matter of democratic theory, practical political power to legislate contrary to
the clearly expressed views of a majority of citizens is not power which Parliament
ought to be understood to possess.[130] As a result, the special nature of a statutory

---

[130] There is often debate, in particular, as to whether Parliament has a moral responsibility to enact
legislation which leads public opinion on certain matters (a prime example being capital punishment),
which might be thought to be grounded in Edmund Burke's famous ideas about representation:
'[y]our representative owes you, not his industry only, but his judgment; and he betrays, instead of
serving you, if he sacrifices it to your opinion': E Burke, *Speech to the Electors of Bristol* (3 November
1774). Yet in complex modern representative democratic systems, the state of public opinion on any
particular matter may not be easy to establish, and, indeed, for any particular MP to discern from the
general fact of their election that they are obliged to take a particular position on a particular issue
which is representative of the views of their constituents will itself require the exercise of judgement.
Such practical difficulties may be reflective of inevitable tensions in the very idea of representation which Burke's simplistic conception does not acknowledge: see, eg H Pitkin, *The Concept of
Representation* (Berkeley CA, University of California Press, 1967); M Brito Viera and D Runciman,
Representation (Cambridge, Polity Press, 2008). The abstract principle set out in the text above is
therefore just that; a democratic ideal which should be understood to frame and inform how we assess
any particular use of parliamentary power, rather than absolutely to determine whether any specific

referendum requirement, by which Parliament seeks direct confirmation from citizens that its general legislative mandate extends to encompass some specified action, means that such conditions must be distinguished from external veto requirements, and can be considered to take effect as legally permissible alterations of the future law-making process.

Statutory referendum requirements can therefore be considered to be permissible changes to the future manner and form for legislating. Goldsworthy's general account of the legal validity of such legislative conditions is in principle inconsistent with the idea that Parliament possesses legally unlimited legislative authority. Instead, the manner and form analysis of referendum requirements should be adopted, according to which such statutory conditions are recognised as fundamentally procedural in nature—and on this basis lawful—with the potential difficulties they might generate, especially with regard to the ease with which legislation may in future be enacted, being confronted instead as (still highly significant) questions of political justification. Further, we must distinguish between referendum requirements and powers of assent or veto given to external bodies; even if the latter were legally impermissible (a contention which can be rejected on a manner and form analysis), a parallel conclusion cannot be reached in relation to the former, given the special nature of such conditions. If the manner and form theory is accepted in preference to Goldsworthy's procedure and form model—as I suggest it should be—it is not strictly necessary to rely on the argument that referendum requirements provide for an affirmation of Parliament's mandate to legislate, in order to establish that such conditions can constitute a lawful exercise of statutory authority. Yet to recognise the special considerations which apply to referendum requirements highlights the difficulties that ensue when the scope of Parliament's legislative authority, as a matter of law, is made contingent upon an assessment of whether its substantive power is diminished. That there exists great scope for genuine debate about such matters provides us with a further reason to favour the approach provided by the manner and form theory, for this offers a less contentious method by which the legal validity of statutory change to the law-making process can be established.

Moreover, adoption of this manner and form approach enables us to by-pass the further unnecessary difficulties which are generated by Goldsworthy's claim that such referendum requirements can only be understood to take effect as changes to the rule of recognition, a position which results from his rejection of the legal permissibility of such statutory change to the future legislative process. We have already encountered a number of problems which present when change to the doctrine of parliamentary sovereignty is rationalised instead as change to the rule of recognition, including questions as to the certainty with which the

---

use of power is justified. It is also, it should be emphasised, distinct from the much broader principle that Parliament should *only* act on the basis of the clearly expressed views of a majority of citizens, a notion which I should not be taken here to endorse.

occurrence of such change can credibly be ascertained,[131] and the propriety of giving the courts a potentially decisive role in establishing the 'new' scope of Parliament's legislative authority.[132] Such issues will again be manifested in this context, in addition to a further difficulty. The threshold for a change in the rule of recognition to be accepted is considerable; a consensus in official attitudes must be evident from their patterns of behaviour.[133] If concerns as to the evidential basis on which a change to the rule of recognition can be identified, and by whom, are set aside, this high threshold for constitutional change is still in itself potentially problematic.

For if certain kinds of constitutional change can only be legally effective as a result of observable, fundamental shifts in the underlying attitudes and conduct of officials—as would be statutory referendum requirements, on Goldsworthy's model—this presents a significant barrier to reform. This is not to deny, of course, that fundamental constitutional change of a variety which can *only* be explained by reference to a shift in the rule of recognition of a legal system may sometimes occur. Yet too hastily to resort to such a rationalisation of challenging, yet not necessarily foundational, constitutional change may have the effect of conceptually embedding conservativism in relation to such matters. This critique has particular force in the context of statutory referendum requirements, which are majoritarian democratic devices. Goldsworthy is understandably concerned about the prospect that 'one political party' might 'use its temporary majority in Parliament to entrench partisan legislation', and suggests that the use of referendums to achieve such a goal must be rejected unless the legislation which is to be entrenched is itself approved at a referendum prior to its enactment.[134] Yet such concerns, I will argue in Chapter seven, are precisely those which should be addressed as matters which go to the political justification for a proposed statutory change to the legislative process. Apprehension about the possibility of contentious legislation being entrenched by referendum requirements is entirely justifiable, yet it is not an adequate basis on which conceptually to prohibit the use of such procedural conditions, as a matter of law, unless the existence of a consensus in their favour can be demonstrated. Referendum requirements themselves do not impose such a high threshold for change, being generally, although of course not inherently, majoritarian decision-making instruments. To therefore contend that Parliament is legally incapable of introducing such procedural legislative requirements, which can instead only be implemented upon satisfaction of a threshold criterion which is considerably greater (and much less transparent) than that to be established by statute, is to inflict a drastic limitation on law-making authority. Such change should not be lightly introduced, but nor should legal theory be used to demand a much higher level of agreement to alter the legislative process either than that

---

[131] See chapter 5 of this volume, pp 218–22.
[132] See chapter 2 of this volume, pp 97–107; chapter 4 of this volume, pp 179–82.
[133] See HLA Hart, *The Concept of Law*, 2nd edn (Oxford, Oxford University Press, 1994) 113–14.
[134] Goldsworthy, *Parliamentary Sovereignty: Contemporary Debates* (2010) n 70 above, 139–40.

which is required to implement other forms of legal or constitutional change, or would be required to satisfy a referendum requirement itself.

With the difficulties of Goldsworthy's general approach to referendum requirements in mind, we turn finally to explore these issues in the context of the specific referendum locks introduced by the EUA. It might be expected, in light of the preceding discussion, that Goldsworthy would definitively reject the argument defended in this chapter, that EUA's scheme of referendum locks are legally valid. And indeed, in written evidence submitted to the European Scrutiny Committee on the (then) EU Bill, Goldsworthy highlighted a fundamental principle derived from this analysis: '[t]o seek to bind future parliaments by prohibiting the enactment of legislation without a referendum first being held is not consistent with the doctrine of parliamentary sovereignty'.[135] Following the enactment of the EUA, however, Goldsworthy's position appears subtly to have altered. First, Goldsworthy argues that in the event of the enactment of subsequent legislation which purported to authorise action covered by the EUA, but which did not adhere to its procedural requirements, the courts would be likely to accept that the 2011 Act had been repealed by implication.[136] Whether this prediction is correct post-*Jackson* is, in my view, far from clear, yet more significant is Goldsworthy's second point. For Goldsworthy notes that, even if the courts did not accept that the EUA could be repealed by implication, it could still be repealed expressly. And as a result, Goldsworthy maintains that the EUA is compatible with his procedure and form model of parliamentary sovereignty:

> According to my theory, a requirement that Parliament must expressly repeal or amend a provision is merely a requirement as to form, and not as to substance ... Thus, a referendum requirement is perfectly consistent with my conception of parliamentary sovereignty, provided that it is not self-entrenched and can therefore be repealed or amended, whether impliedly or expressly, by ordinary legislation.[137]

Goldsworthy thus accepts that the specific scheme of referendum locks contained in the EUA can be regarded as a legally permissible use of sovereign legislative authority, yet he does so on a basis which nevertheless undercuts the broader arguments about the constitutional significance of the 2011 Act which I have sought to defend in this chapter. For if they are to be interpreted merely to constitute a requirement as to future legislative *form*, it becomes much more difficult to maintain that the enactment of the EUA's referendum locks marks a fundamental modern shift to the manner and form theory.

---

[135] House of Commons European Scrutiny Committee, *The EU Bill and Parliamentary Sovereignty: Written Evidence*, HC 633-II (7 December 2010) Ev 31. Goldsworthy qualified this general principle by arguing that such referendum locks could be effective if approved at a prior referendum by the people, yet as this was not a path followed by the drafters of the EUA, it does not need to be considered further here.

[136] J Goldsworthy, 'Parliamentary Sovereignty's Premature Obituary', *UK Constitutional Law Association Blog* (9 March 2012): www.ukconstitutionallaw.org/blog. This line of argument is also apparent in Goldsworthy's earlier written evidence to the European Scrutiny Committee.

[137] ibid.

However, while there can be no doubt that Goldsworthy is correct about the limits of the legal effectiveness of the EUA's referendum locks, which are certainly susceptible to being repealed explicitly by Parliament, it is not clear that the claim that they are compatible with the procedure and form conception of parliamentary sovereignty can be sustained. For in characterising the EUA's statutory scheme as establishing requirements merely as to future legislative form, Goldsworthy focuses exclusively on the circumstances in which a referendum lock can be avoided, but overlooks the implications of a situation in which it is followed. Yet this is problematic when we recall the reason that certain legislative conditions are deemed legally impermissible on the procedure and form model of parliamentary sovereignty: a statutory requirement ostensibly altering the future law-making procedure will not be permitted if it serves to diminish the substantive power of Parliament to legislate. And a referendum requirement will, in particular, not be permitted because it diminishes the substantive power of Parliament by affording a veto on legislation to an external body. As the EUA's referendum locks are not entrenched, Parliament can free itself, by ordinary legislation, of this limit on its substantive power. Yet if Parliament does not do this, perhaps feeling compelled not to repeal these guarantees by the pragmatic or principled political reasons which create non-legal incentives for such compliance,[138] then this limit on its substantive power will persist. That a limit on Parliament's substantive power to legislate can be removed by Parliament does not mean that this limit ceases to operate if it is not removed. Instead, unless or until the EUA's referendum locks are repealed—whether entirely or piecemeal—if circumstances arise in which Parliament must comply with the terms of these legislative requirements, then in those circumstances the legislature's substantive power to enact law is still diminished. For, even if as a matter of law it has 'opted' to do so,[139] Parliament has still subjected its legislative authority to the legally binding veto of an external body.

On this basis, it appears that the procedure and form model leaves Goldsworthy with two options with respect to the EUA's referendum locks. If Goldsworthy's procedure and form model is a conceptually correct statement of the scope of Parliament's legislative authority, the EUA's referendum locks must be rejected, for unless or until repealed, they must be seen, in violation of this theory, to diminish the substantive legislative power of Parliament. Alternatively, if Goldsworthy accepts the legal permissibility of the EUA's referendum locks, the procedure and form model must be rejected. In my view, this second option should be preferred. That the procedure and form theory of parliamentary sovereignty pushes Goldsworthy, with respect to the EUA's referendum locks, towards a conclusion he does not appear to want to draw is further evidence of the difficulties generated by this conception of legislative authority. Collapsing questions as to the legislative capability of Parliament into questions as to the legislative capacity of

---

[138] See text at nn 81–93.
[139] Or, more accurately, Parliament has opted not to free itself from an otherwise binding requirement.

Parliament—or questions as to the scope of its (substantive) practical power to legislate into questions as to the scope of its (substantive) legal authority to legislate—is problematic in principle, but also makes the model contentious to apply in practice, as the example of the EUA clearly demonstrates. And if the courts are potentially to be invited to settle these difficult questions as to the lawful scope of Parliament's legislative power, based on whether or not an ostensibly procedural condition serves to diminish the substantive power of the legislature, such complexity and uncertainty is not desirable.

We should therefore reject the challenge posed by the procedure and form model to the legal permissibility of referendum requirements in general, and the challenge it ought to be understood to pose to the legal effectiveness of the EUA's referendum locks in particular. For a defender of parliamentary sovereignty, it is entirely logical to wish to ensure that the legislature's legal authority is readily exercisable. Yet as I will argue in Chapter seven, there is a way to do this which is more consistent with the notion of legally unlimited legislative power than, and normatively preferable to, Goldsworthy's procedure and form theory. The manner and form interpretation of the EUA which I have set out in this chapter can therefore be seen to survive the objections arising from the procedure and form model, both in terms of the legal effectiveness of this scheme of statutory referendum locks, and with respect to the broader constitutional consequences of the recognition of the legality of these legislative conditions. Goldsworthy's procedure and form model cannot displace the conclusion that the manner and form theory of parliamentary sovereignty is the new orthodoxy in the UK constitution.

VI. CONCLUSION

The substantive content of the EUA can be criticised in many respects. The scope of the scheme of referendum locks which the 2011 Act establishes can be objected to as excessive, prompting potential concerns as to engagement with, and the legitimacy of, direct democratic mechanisms in the UK. Further, it may be questioned why the UK's relationship with the EU has been afforded singular treatment in relation to legal referendum guarantees—if referendums are to be required here, why not also in relation to fundamental domestic political or constitutional issues of comparable importance? Moreover, it is far from clear how firm a position the EUA now occupies on the UK's constitutional landscape. A vote to depart from the EU at a future referendum on membership would render this scheme of referendum locks moot, and the likely status of the Act following a vote to remain in the Union is a matter about which there could be much debate. With respect to the argument defended in this chapter, however, such considerations are largely irrelevant. How constitutional actors engage with the EUA's referendum locks in future will of course continue to be significant, and the longer its legislative terms remain legally enforceable, the greater the body of evidence which will be available to confirm or challenge the interpretation advanced here. Yet in my view, the design of the EUA, the attitudes and reactions to it, and considerations of legal, political and constitutional principle, all clearly indicate that a manner and form understanding of the effectiveness of the Act's scheme of referendum locks should be adopted. Moreover, despite powerful suggestions to the contrary which result from Goldsworthy's alternative procedure and form model of legislative power, and to a lesser extent, suggestions that the section 18 (non-)sovereignty clause indicates the EUA is internally contradictory, we can conclude that the manner and form conception of parliamentary sovereignty now operates in the UK constitution. And since the 2011 Act represents the culmination of a broader pattern of constitutional change traced throughout Part II of this book, even were the EUA to be repealed without a referendum lock ever being triggered, such a conclusion as to the contemporary force of the manner and form theory could still be sustained.[140]

To adopt a manner and form interpretation of the EUA is significant in itself. For it indicates that while the EUA's referendum locks may ultimately be bypassed by future governments and Parliaments, they are not legally ineffective, and must at least, therefore, be engaged with. The political costs of removing statutory guarantees of popular participation in decision-making may be high, yet potentially bearable, depending on how credible a justification for doing so can be developed in the circumstances of any particular case. But in ensuring that these issues must be confronted openly, rather than eluded through claims as to doctrinal irrelevance, a degree of constitutional transparency will at least be achieved. Yet more significant may be the profound potential implications of the change to constitutional orthodoxy in the UK which the EUA marks. Debates as to the scope of the legislative power of Parliament are important to establish the continuing existence (or not) of the doctrine of parliamentary sovereignty in the UK, in light of the challenge posed by a range of modern constitutional developments. But they are not simply important for this reason. Instead, while seeking to explain past and present change, we must also reflect on future possibilities. And if, as I have argued

---

[140] The influence of this modern shift to the manner and form theory is also evident in other contexts. While there has been no attempt to legislate to alter the future law-making process in a way which is equivalent to that seen in the EUA, there is an increasing willingness to view Acts of Parliament as tools which can alter decision-making procedures in other constitutional circumstances. See, eg the (aborted) proposal to require a super-majority vote of 55% in the House of Commons for the dissolution of Parliament in legislation to fix parliamentary terms at five years: The Coalition, *Our Programme for Government* (2010) 26. See also the provision which replaced this, providing for a two-thirds majority vote for an early general election to be held, applicable only in circumstances where the government had not lost the confidence of the House of Commons: Fixed-term Parliaments Act 2011 s 2(1)(b). See further the statutory basis created to give legal force to the requirement that the Royal Charter on press regulation only be amended by a two-thirds majority vote in Parliament: Enterprise and Regulatory Reform Act 2013 s 96, Royal Charter on Self-Regulation of the Press (30 October 2013) [9.4]. Further examples include Labour party proposals to legislate to impose binding fiscal limits on government spending: see 'Ed Balls: Labour will run a budget surplus', *The Guardian* (24 January 2014). And Liberal Democrat proposals to legislate to 'triple lock' pensions following the 2015 general election: 'Lib Dems to pledge "triple lock" law for guaranteed increase of pensions', *The Guardian* (29 June 2014).

in Part II, the manner and form theory now best explains the current scope of the legally unlimited law-making authority of Parliament in the UK constitution, the possibility of using this enhanced legislative power in a range of different situations in the future is opened up.

On this basis, in Part III, we turn to consider two issues. First, in Chapter seven, I set out a general normative justification for the manner and form theory of parliamentary sovereignty. How this theory can be justified has never adequately been explained, but I will suggest that it has a normative value which has not previously been appreciated, once located in a political constitutionalist account of the UK constitution. This normative justification is significant in part because it provides an account through which we can address legitimate concerns as to the potential for Parliament's doubtlessly considerable legal power to be exploited to alter the future legislative process in questionable ways. Yet this normative justification is also significant because it can be developed to inform our understanding of how this hitherto overlooked power might in future be used to particular ends. As such, in Chapter eight, we consider a number of specific examples of how legislative power to modify the manner and form for future legislation might appropriately be utilised by Parliament, potentially with a view to re-invigorating the foundations, or recalibrating the structure, of the UK's political constitution.

Part III

The Virtue and Function of
the Manner and Form Theory

7

A Democratic Justification of the Manner and Form Theory

I. INTRODUCTION

A MODERN SHIFT has occurred in our understanding of the doctrine of parliamentary sovereignty. This shift in the foundations of the UK constitution is to the conception of legally unlimited legislative power set out by the manner and form theory. While able to accommodate the challenges posed by devolution and the Human Rights Act 1998—and survive that posed by the flawed attacks from common law constitutionalism[1]—the orthodox Diceyan understanding of parliamentary sovereignty is incompatible with a number of other contemporary constitutional developments. Instead, a manner and form understanding of parliamentary sovereignty must be embraced if we are to reconcile the doctrine with the legal architecture created to facilitate UK membership of the European Union.[2] Furthermore, the understanding of the Parliament Acts 1911 and 1949 confirmed by the House of Lords in *Jackson*,[3] and the use Parliament has sought to make of its legislative authority in the European Union Act 2011,[4] demonstrate clearly that the manner and form theory provides the best understanding of parliamentary sovereignty as this doctrine is manifested in the contemporary UK constitution. The sovereign UK Parliament must now be understood to possess the legislative authority to enact legally valid legislation which alters the law-making process.

To truly understand the present state and future possibilities of this constitutional norm, however, two further overlapping questions must be addressed in Part III of this book. First, in this chapter, we consider whether this shift in the doctrine of parliamentary sovereignty is in principle justified. Secondly, in the next and final chapter, we address the potential implications of this modern shift to the manner and form theory for the future shape and structure of the UK constitution. As will become apparent, these two issues overlap because when considering the potential future use of the legislative power to alter the manner and form

---

[1] See generally chapter 3 of this volume.
[2] See generally chapter 4 of this volume.
[3] See generally chapter 5 of this volume.
[4] See generally chapter 6 of this volume.

by which legislation is to be enacted, the extent to which, and reasons for which, this conception of parliamentary sovereignty is justified will be highly significant. For the democratic justification of the manner and form theory which will be set out in this chapter—and which is rooted in a political constitutionalist account of the UK constitution—must be understood to condition the circumstances in which the legislative authority to alter the legislative process can legitimately be exercised by Parliament. In this sense, the virtue and (potential) function of the manner and form theory are interrelated: any future legislative change to the legislative process should be conducted in a way which coheres with the underlying justification of this understanding of law-making authority, and in so doing, may also reinforce the democratic foundations of the UK's political constitution to which the doctrine of parliamentary sovereignty affords primacy.

In this chapter, we first consider the need for a normative justification of the manner and form theory, identifying the lack of an adequate existing account. While the work of Jennings does not directly provide us with an explicit explanation of the value of the manner and form theory, I will argue that the initial basis from which one can be developed is nevertheless offered by his views as to the constitutional significance of democracy. From this starting point, we then explore the relationship between democracy, political constitutionalist theory, and the doctrine of parliamentary sovereignty in general. Establishing the nature of the complementary relationship between these notions creates a foundation on which a democratic justification of the manner and form theory can be sketched, and then crucially—once located in a political constitutionalist framework—fully explained and defended. In essence, I will argue that the legal power to alter the future manner and form for law-making can be allocated to the democratic Parliament because, in a range of significant ways, that power will necessarily be conditioned and structured by the operation of the democratic political system in which it is exercised. Finally, the challenge that it is contradictory to justify the manner and form theory on democratic grounds, because this conception of legislative sovereignty inherently expands the powers of the courts to review the legislation of Parliament, will be considered and rejected.

II. THE NEED FOR A NORMATIVE JUSTIFICATION OF THE MANNER AND FORM THEORY

Before examining why a justification of the manner and form theory is necessary, the significance of such normative considerations for a defence of this, or any other, conception of the doctrine of parliamentary sovereignty must be noted. The contemporary constitutional force of the manner and form theory of parliamentary sovereignty is *not* contingent upon this being a normatively attractive understanding of legally unlimited legislative power. Instead, it is the conclusion reached in Part II of this book, that the manner and form theory provides the best explanation of the contemporary scope of the legislative authority of the UK

Parliament, which establishes this conception as the new orthodoxy in relation to the doctrine of parliamentary sovereignty in the UK constitution. For, as was argued in Chapter one, the question of whether Parliament retains its legislative sovereignty—and if so, which understanding of legislative sovereignty best characterises this retained authority—does not collapse into the question of whether Parliament ought to retain its legislative sovereignty.[5] Yet while the normative attractiveness of the manner and form theory is not, therefore, a factor relevant to determination of the present legal scope of Parliament's legislative power, this does not mean it is unimportant. Indeed, the contrary is true; it is of critical importance to seek to assess whether, to what extent, and in what way, prevailing constitutional arrangements and doctrines are justifiable. This is vital if we wish to obtain a fuller understanding of the constitutional architecture and political operation of a state, but also so that the prospect of legal or political change—whether of an evolutionary, reformist or revolutionary character—can be appreciated and evaluated. The normative justification of the manner and form theory developed in this chapter must be understood against this backdrop; it is independent from claims as to the legal authority of this conception of parliamentary sovereignty, and is instead an attempt to explore why the constitutional position which I have suggested now obtains in the UK is one which might be welcomed, rather than received with trepidation.

With the broader purpose of this normative justification established, we turn to the particular need for such an account of the manner and form theory. While sometimes described as the 'new view' of parliamentary sovereignty,[6] the manner and form theory is certainly not a conception of legislative power which has only recently been developed.[7] Yet, although the manner and form theory has for some time been very well established in constitutional discourse, surprisingly little attention has been given to the question of what, if anything, might serve as a normative justification of this approach. There are two key reasons for this. First, the matter of a justification for this theory of parliamentary sovereignty received relatively little attention from the formative manner and form scholars, and in particular, Jennings. As was argued in Chapter two, the political subtext so crucial to Jennings' challenge to Dicey's conception of the rule of law is, in contrast, notable by its absence from their debates as to the scope of the legislative authority of Parliament.[8] Yet it may be one thing to seek to expose values which distort a particular analysis of a constitutional principle or practice, and critique a warped account on that basis—as Jennings arguably did in relation to Dicey's

---

[5] See chapter 1 of this volume, pp 16–21.

[6] See especially RFV Heuston, *Essays In Constitutional Law*, 2nd edn (London, Stevens and Sons, 1964) ch 1. A recent example of the manner and form theory being described as the 'new view' of parliamentary sovereignty is AL Young, 'Parliamentary Sovereignty Re-defined' in R Rawlings, P Leyland and AL Young (eds), *Sovereignty and the Law: Domestic, European, and International Perspectives* (Oxford, Oxford University Press, 2013) 69.

[7] See, eg chapter 2 of this volume, pp 63–68.

[8] See chapter 2 of this volume, pp 59–63.

rule of law[9]—but another thing to seek to justify a competing understanding of such principles or practices. Indeed, such a distinction between 'explanation' and 'justification' appears to have underpinned Jennings' approach, on which these processes were 'different', with explanation being 'the function of constitutional law', and justification a matter of political theory.[10] Jennings employed a 'sociological method' to such explanation, which was 'simply to examine the facts, including the ideas, of any given society.[11] So, while it was important for ideas to be understood as facts, and their implications on practice discerned, they were to be distinguished from those 'subjective theories' which were not grounded in the actual experience of a particular society.[12] It was not appropriate, according to Jennings, for a 'constitutional lawyer … to advocate political principles'; instead, the function of such a scholar was 'to analyse, to find out what are the principles upon which the Constitution, as it exists, is based'.[13]

From this perspective, the contextual methodology employed by Jennings— which contrasted with the ostensibly legalistic, yet ideologically shaped, formalism of Dicey[14]—can be seen only to extend so far. Social and political factors would necessarily be engaged to inform analysis and explanation of the constitution as it existed, yet attempts to justify what was found—drawing on considerations of social, political or, indeed, legal theory or principle—were, in general, not matters for a constitutional lawyer. For the reasons explained above, this limit on the proper functions of a constitutional lawyer is not, in my view, persuasive. Yet whether we accept this limit or not, Jennings' methodological position here does provide a coherent explanation as to why he could engage with Dicey in overtly political terms on the rule of law, yet advanced no general normative justification for the manner and form theory of parliamentary sovereignty. Ideas could be engaged with as facts, and Dicey's reliance on normative principles which were detached from, rather than manifested in, actual practice thus presented a legitimate target for critique. Yet it would not be appropriate for normative principles to be engaged with positively, with consideration of the extent to which prevailing arrangements were justified, if at all, beyond the remit of the constitutional lawyer.

Yet the distinction between explanation and justification adopted by Jennings was not necessarily endorsed by all leading manner and form theorists. And it is from this perspective we can identify a second reason that a normative justification is needed for the manner and form theory: even where an attempt at justification has been made, the result has been unsatisfactory. This is particularly evident in relation to the work of Heuston, the other leading proponent of the

---

[9] See, eg WI Jennings, *The Law and the Constitution*, 5th edn (London, University of London Press, 1959) 316.

[10] ibid 332.

[11] ibid 334.

[12] ibid 332.

[13] ibid 316.

[14] See chapter 2 of this volume, pp 60–61.

manner and form theory. Heuston argued that the 'moral validity' of the idea of legally unlimited legislative authority had been questioned, but the development of a 'new view' of parliamentary sovereignty, 'which has the attraction of being couched in the calm, hard, tightly knit style of the common lawyer rather than in the vague and emotional language of the political scientist', demonstrated that this notion was in fact 'less terrifying than had been thought'.[15] The manner and form theory was, according to Heuston, 'an important development in the history of political thought' for it offered a new way to guard against 'the dangers arising from an abuse of sovereignty'.[16] This 'Anglican solution' would be 'agreeable to many' for it allowed a lawyer to 'subscribe not only to the unlimited power of Parliament, but also to the possibility of legal restraints upon (at least) the mode of user of that power'.[17] Heuston therefore clearly believed that the virtue of the manner and form theory was that it could be used to place procedural limits on the legislative authority of Parliament. The legally unlimited law-making authority constitutionally allocated to the legislature was, for Heuston, a potential hazard in so far as it offered no inherent protection to 'the important but curiously evasive principles of natural justice', and the manner and form conception of parliamentary sovereignty offered the possibility of this power being constrained, at least to some extent.[18] For, according to the manner and form theory, the legislative process could be altered to make it more difficult for Parliament to enact legislation in relation to particular topics judged to be of moral or political significance.

Heuston's justification of the manner and form approach to parliamentary sovereignty has been influential,[19] yet is ultimately unsatisfactory. It bears an underlying similarity to the normative arguments encountered in Part II in favour of a common law constitutionalist interpretation of the UK constitution.[20] Both of these normative accounts are premised on the undesirability of affording to Parliament legally unlimited law-making authority, on the basis of a perceived danger that iniquitous legislation might as a result be enacted. There is, of course, a crucial difference between the 'abuse of sovereignty' justification for the manner and form theory, and common law constitutionalism: on the former it would be Parliament, and on the latter, the courts, responsible for the creation of limits on legislative power. And as a result, the two key arguments advanced against common law constitutionalism in this book—that it is undemocratic to subject the democratic Parliament to limits discovered by the unelected judiciary, which will be

---

[15] Heuston, *Essays In Constitutional Law* (1964) n 6 above, 6.
[16] ibid 30.
[17] ibid 6.
[18] ibid 30.
[19] See, eg this line of reasoning echoed in G Marshall, *Constitutional Theory* (Oxford, Oxford University Press, 1971) 42: the new view offers a means by which 'for the English lawyer or political theorist, sovereignty may be purged of its dangerous absolutism. He can believe both in an ultimate Sovereign and in the possibility of restraint imposed by law upon the way in which legal power is used'.
[20] See chapter 3 of this volume, pp 126–31.

inherently imprecise in nature—do not appear to be applicable to Heuston's defence of the manner and form theory. For while the abuse of sovereignty justification may broadly correlate with the instincts of common law constitutionalism, the manner and form theory does not impose external substantive limits, but simply provides the machinery by which the democratic Parliament may choose to limit itself, and only as to the future legislative procedure. Moreover, as such procedural conditions would be statutory in nature, the charge of imprecision also fails to bite, for any such limitation would necessarily be defined with the degree of certainty which legislation provides, in addition to being promulgated and accessible in advance of its potential application.

Yet for these very reasons, if the critical normative basis for the adoption of the manner and form theory is that the authority of Parliament ought legally to be curbed, support for this conception of parliamentary sovereignty is likely to be ephemeral. For if our normative objective is to curb the abuse of sovereign power, the immunity of the manner and form theory to the key objections to common law constitutionalism is not likely to be viewed as desirable, but disadvantageous to the effective satisfaction of this goal. These limits would be procedural, rather than substantive; fixed, rather than flexible; and introduced at the initiative of Parliament, rather than designed by external actors. There are thus good reasons to imagine that support for the manner and form theory premised on the prospect that it might be used significantly to restrain the legislature would rest upon a rather precarious foundation. Common law constitutionalism, which inherently denies the sovereignty of Parliament, is clearly a far stronger response to anxiety about the potential abuse of legislative power, in that it permits the courts to impose absolute limits on law-making authority, rather than merely enabling Parliament to limit itself and (perhaps) its successors as to matters of procedure. If concerns about abuse of sovereignty are normatively critical, common law constitutionalism would appear to provide a more promising means by which this aim could be pursued than the manner and form theory. And this is especially the case when we appreciate that the contemporary prominence of common law constitutionalism gives it greater credibility than would have attached to the theory at the time Heuston was writing.

It would still, nevertheless, be possible to seek to justify the manner and form theory from the perspective that it might allow the abuse of sovereignty to be prevented. For, setting aside concerns as to whether this would be probable or effective, Parliament could well be encouraged to exercise its legislative power so as to make the achievement of certain substantive outcomes procedurally more demanding.[21] Yet while such an approach to the manner and form theory is not vulnerable to the same normative critique as common law constitutionalism, it must still be regarded as unsatisfactory. To justify the manner and form theory on this basis, and

---

[21] For example, a Bill of Rights might be enacted, but made procedurally difficult to repeal, or include a 'notwithstanding' clause of the kind contained in the Canadian constitution, which requires legislation intended to violate fundamental rights explicitly to specify that those legal guarantees are to be displaced: Constitution Act 1982 s 33.

thus promote the enactment of legislation which constrains, perhaps significantly, the practical legislative power of Parliament would challenge the majoritarian conception of democracy on which the constitutional virtue of the doctrine of parliamentary sovereignty is premised. The majoritarian conception of democracy indicates that authority should attach to the outcomes of democratic decision-making because, in circumstances of pervasive social disagreement about justice, to make decisions by simple majority voting affords respect to the existence of competing views among participants, while giving equal weight to the opinion of each group member in the process of determining a course of collective action.[22] As a result, there should not be substantive limitations on what can be the outcome of a majoritarian democratic decision-making process. But nor should such democratic decision-making be subject to procedural limitations which require outcomes to be reached on super-majoritarian grounds; decisions should be reached on the basis of a simple majority, and higher thresholds cannot legitimately be imposed to make an elevated level of agreement necessary before outcomes can be determined. While the manner and form theory will not permit the imposition of substantive limits on democratic decision-making, it could be used to violate the second proposition which flows from acceptance of the authority of a majoritarian conception of democracy. For it would be legally permissible for the manner and form theory to be used to impose super-majoritarian procedural limits on democratic decision-making. And if a normative starting point is adopted that legislative power, exercised simply on majoritarian grounds, is liable to be abused, then this would very likely be the end to which law-making power to alter the future law-making process would be exercised. On this basis, if legislative authority, exercised and justified on a democratic majoritarian basis, is to be used to restrict such legislative authority, then the account of the virtue of parliamentary sovereignty would collapse under the strain of contradiction. For legislative power would have been exploited to undermine the foundation of the authority of that very same legislative power.

It is this fundamental tension between a justification of the manner and form theory which is premised on its potential to restrict the (ab)use of power, and the primacy of majoritarian democratic decision-making on which the virtue of the doctrine of parliamentary sovereignty is based, that has led many to be cautious of the conception of legally unlimited legislative power defended in this book. Ewing, for example, as part of a broader account of the contradictions in Jennings' work, has suggested that the possibility, generated by the manner and form theory, of

> legal limits on the power of Parliament (and the potential role of the judges to limit the supremacy of Parliament which this implies) contradicts the idea that the people through the electoral system (or otherwise) are the ultimate protectors of the constitution.[23]

---

[22] See chapter 1 of this volume, pp 34–36.
[23] KD Ewing, 'The Law and the Constitution: Manifesto of the Progressive Party' (2004) 67 *MLR* 734, 751.

Similar concerns are expressed by Goldsworthy, who maintains that to recognise Parliament as completely free to limit its legislative authority—on substantive grounds, but also on the 'formal and procedural' grounds which the manner and form theory permits—could 'allow democracy to be subverted'.[24] And such unease is not exclusive to those who are sympathetic to the doctrine of parliamentary sovereignty. Allan, for example, has also expressed apprehension about the 'absurd and unacceptable' potential consequences of a manner and form conception of legislative authority: '[a] Parliament which was strongly influenced by an authoritarian government might seek to entrench all kinds of provision whose vulnerability to repeal (by ordinary majority) it would be important for the courts to preserve on grounds of democratic principle'.[25] Allan's suspicion of the manner and form theory can largely be attributed to his own doctrinal position, a defence of common law constitutionalism founded on the idea that Parliament is not to be trusted with unlimited law-making authority in general, rather than merely positing that power to alter the future legislative process ought to be subject to judicial control. Yet the fact that scepticism about the manner and form theory has such a broad base creates the distinct impression that the normative undesirability of this conception of parliamentary sovereignty should almost be taken for granted.

If such doubts are simply directed to a manner and form theory justified on Heuston's grounds that it may be exploited to prevent the abuse of sovereignty, then we may readily endorse them. For the tension at the core of this justification of the manner and form theory, which would engage majoritarian legislative power to constrain majoritarian legislative power, renders it inconsistent as well as democratically illegitimate. We should not, however, be too quick to presume that Heuston's unsatisfactory account is the *only* justification for the manner and form theory, or that Jennings' earlier unwillingness to explore the normative foundations of this conception of parliamentary sovereignty demonstrates that an alternative is unavailable. Instead, a fresh normative justification for the manner and form conception of legally unlimited legislative power is required. Yet although, for the reasons considered above, Jennings gave no explicit attention to such a project, a starting point for an alternative normative justification of the manner and form theory might nevertheless be traced in his work.

Of particular relevance are Jennings' views on the constitutional significance of democracy, both as a matter of principle, and in practice. In principle, Jennings was clear as to the paramount importance of democracy in the UK constitution: '[i]t is democracy ... that keeps Britain free'.[26] Moreover, the location (and extent) of legislative power was crucially to be established by reference to 'the accepted theory of democracy', which indicated that '[i]f ultimate power is to be

---

[24] J Goldsworthy, *Parliamentary Sovereignty: Contemporary Debates* (Cambridge, Cambridge University Press, 2010) 137.

[25] TRS Allan, 'Parliamentary Sovereignty: Law, Politics and Revolution' (1997) 113 *LQR* 443, 447, 446.

[26] Jennings, *Law and the Constitution*, 5th edn (1959) n 9 above, 24.

vested anywhere, it must be in a representative assembly'.[27] Jennings was, however, conscious of the problems which might stem from the allocation of 'authority transcendent and absolute' to Parliament.[28] Jennings' pioneering study *Parliament* 'was to blaze the trail for public lawyers who want to look beyond the content of the rules and examine the operation of those rules in practice', and demonstrated an acute awareness of the manner in which legislative power was exercised in actuality.[29] 'In substance', Jennings noted, 'Parliament controls legislation as it controls administration, by debating and ultimately approving the policy of the Government'.[30] Consequently, in reality, 'if the Government has a majority in both Houses it can always secure legislation', and the supremacy of Parliament therefore 'places enormous power in the hands of the Government'.[31] Yet Jennings also recognised that this practical position was based on the democratic notion that 'both the Government and the House of Commons derive their authority from the people'.[32] As a result of this democratic character, 'the British parliamentary system can afford strong Governments and does not require constitutional limitations upon parliamentary authority'.[33] For ultimately, Jennings argued, 'the primary protection is the operation of the democratic system, the right of the electorate to choose freely—a right which really means in practice a right to turn out any Government that it does not like'.[34] The importance of democracy in principle was thus reflected in its practical utility. Indeed, for Jennings '[l]egal devices are not and cannot be enough' to prevent oppressive rule.[35] Instead, the accountability of the government to Parliament and the electorate was of principal significance in conditioning the use of legislative power.

It is possible that Jennings ultimately came to lose faith in these ideas, as the tentative conjecture in his later work as to the prospect of a common law power to reject malevolent legislation might be thought to demonstrate.[36] Similarly, the extent of Jennings' commitment to the primacy of democracy, both in constitutional principle and practice, might be questioned in relation to his speculation as to the particular use which might be made of Parliament's power to alter the legislative manner and form. For the two hypothetical examples considered by

---

[27] ibid 316.

[28] WI Jennings, *Parliament*, 2nd edn (Cambridge, Cambridge University Press, 1957) 1. The description of parliamentary power adopted here by Jennings was originally that of Sir Edward Coke: 4 Co Inst 36.

[29] A Tomkins, '"Talking in Fictions": Jennings on Parliament' (2004) 67 *MLR* 772, 785.

[30] Jennings, *Parliament* (1957) n 28 above, 7.

[31] ibid 12.

[32] ibid 8. Jennings certainly recognised, however, that there were flaws in this system, and in a separate publication argued that reform of the House of Commons was necessary to increase its efficiency: WI Jennings, *Parliamentary Reform* (London, Victor Gollancz, 1934). See Tomkins, '"Talking in Fictions": Jennings on Parliament' (2004) n 29 above, 783–85, for discussion of Jennings' proposals, which were mainly 'concerned with ways in which legislative procedure might be improved': 784.

[33] Jennings, *Parliament* (1957) n 28 above, 12.

[34] Jennings, *Law and the Constitution*, 5th edn (1959) n 9 above, 134.

[35] Jennings, *Parliament* (1957) n 28 above, 530.

[36] See chapter 2 of this volume, pp 71–74.

Jennings in the life span of *The Law and the Constitution* were to legislate to prevent the abolition of the House of Lords or the monarchy unless approved by the electorate at a referendum.[37] It is therefore unsurprising that Jennings' support for the manner and form theory has been regarded as 'curious' by Ewing, because the impression given by such examples is that democratic progress 'could be blocked and reactionary institutions protected' on the adoption of this conception of the legislative power of Parliament.[38] Why Jennings chose these particular examples, rather than consider a statutory referendum requirement 'to protect some of the gains of a progressive government, such as the establishment of a national health service, or the public ownership of key levers of economic power, or the abolition of private property', is unclear.[39] As Ewing suggests, it may simply be a consequence of Jennings' appreciation that the 'evolving and enabling constitution can adapt to any need and circumstance'.[40] Yet, alternatively, the conservativism of these examples, serving to protect undemocratic institutions from reform, may correspond with Jennings' hints as to the possibility that the legislative authority of Parliament might ultimately be subject to judicial limitation. And viewed as such, this further evidence might appear to confirm the broader idea of Jennings' loss of faith in the ability of democracy effectively to condition constitutional power.[41]

If this second explanation is correct, and Jennings came to reverse his position as to the ultimate constitutional significance of democracy, and its efficacy in structuring the use of public power, we might discern an alignment between such changed views and Heuston's account of the value of the manner and form theory. And from this perspective, Jennings' views may not appear to provide us with a promising starting point from which to develop an alternative normative justification of the manner and form conception of parliamentary sovereignty. Yet even if this understanding of the overall trajectory of Jennings' constitutional thinking is correct, it does not mean we can disregard his earlier views, regardless of whether he ultimately diluted this position, or even departed from it entirely. And it is on the basis of Jennings' initial ideas as to the importance of democracy in constitutional principle, and the channels of accountability offered by democratic politics in practice, that we might be able to make sense of his acceptance of the manner and form theory, while also beginning to develop a new justification of this conception of legislative sovereignty.

---

[37] For the example of the entrenchment of the House of Lords, see WI Jennings, *Law and the Constitution*, 1st edn (London, University of London Press, 1933) 125. For the example of the entrenchment of the monarchy, see Jennings, *Law and the Constitution*, 5th edn (1959) n 9 above, 161.

[38] Ewing, 'The Law and the Constitution: Manifesto of the Progressive Party' (2004) n 23 above, 742.

[39] ibid 742.

[40] ibid 743. On the theme of the 'evolving and enabling constitution' in Jennings' work see generally 738–40.

[41] ibid 743.

From this starting point, rather than assume that the manner and form theory is inherently about the prevention of certain kinds of legislative action, we must think more broadly about the potential utility of this understanding of law-making power. In particular, the examples provided by both Jennings and Ewing offer too narrow a perspective on what the manner and form theory might be used to achieve. Both focus on the idea that something is to be protected by statute, with the desirability of such action contingent on the substantive value of the object of protection, be it the bastions of the traditional constitution (as for Jennings), or the gains of progressive politics (as for Ewing). Yet if we look 'beyond the stereotypes' of manner and form,[42] and think instead about the virtue which may be inherent in procedures themselves, it becomes clear that the relationship between the manner and form theory and democracy is more complex than can be appreciated merely by consideration of its potential to introduce anti-majoritarian limiting devices. Jennings' recognition of the value of democracy as a matter of constitutional principle, and as a means through which power could be held to account, allows us to re-orientate debate as to the normative appeal of the manner and form theory. This conception of legally unlimited legislative authority must not be seen, and rejected, as inherently undemocratic; instead, the democratic potential of the manner and form theory must be explored. In so doing, a potential compatibility between Jennings' (initial) positions on democracy and on the manner and form theory can be demonstrated. Yet whether the justification which will be developed in this chapter is was one which Jennings' would or would not have accepted—initially, eventually or at all—is ultimately irrelevant to its normative force. For when Jennings' ideas about the significance of democracy are further developed, and rooted in a framework provided by political constitutionalist theory, the foundation of a new democratic justification for the manner and form theory of parliamentary sovereignty can emerge.

III. DEMOCRACY, POLITICAL CONSTITUTIONALISM AND PARLIAMENTARY SOVEREIGNTY

To establish this democratic justification for the manner and form theory, we must first return to consider the relationship between democracy, the doctrine of parliamentary sovereignty and political constitutionalism. The potential for an account of the democratic virtue of parliamentary sovereignty to be reinforced by ideas drawn from political constitutionalism was initially encountered in Chapter one.[43] There, however, while focusing on the doctrine of parliamentary sovereignty in general, political constitutionalist notions were not taken to be essential to the development of an account of the core virtue of this fundamental constitutional norm. Instead, I argued that the virtue of parliamentary sovereignty is

---

[42] Goldsworthy, *Parliamentary Sovereignty: Contemporary Debates* (2010) n 24 above, 186.
[43] See chapter 1 of this volume, pp 32–34.

primarily rooted in democracy, and in particular, a result of the constitutional primacy which the doctrine affords to democratic decision-making. Yet while we do not *need* to engage political constitutionalist theory to establish the value of a doctrine affording legally unlimited legislative power to a democratic Parliament, there is nevertheless an important association between these ideas. We must therefore trace the nature of the connections between political constitutionalism, parliamentary sovereignty and democracy, for in so doing, we will be in a position to explain the particular democratic justification for the manner and form theory.

Modern ideas of political constitutionalism can be seen crucially to derive from the work of John Griffith. In his seminal lecture 'The Political Constitution', Griffith argued that 'conflict is at the heart of modern society', and 'politics is what happens in the continuance or resolution of those conflicts'.[44] Against this backdrop, for Griffith, law was simply 'one means, one process, by which those conflicts are continued or may be temporarily resolved', and '[n]o more than that'.[45] The 'concept of law' was not an inherently 'moral concept'; instead, a law was a 'political act', a statement of 'a power relationship'.[46] This general framework—in which, essentially, 'law is politics carried on by other means'[47]— had specific constitutional consequences: law could not be employed so as to displace the operation of politics. For Griffith:

> The fundamental political objection is this: that law is not and cannot be a substitute for politics. This is a hard truth, perhaps an unpleasant truth. For centuries political philosophers have sought that society in which government is by laws and not by men. It is an unattainable ideal. Written constitutions do not achieve it. Nor do Bills of Rights or any other devices. They merely pass political decisions out of the hands of politicians and into the hands of judges or other persons. To require a supreme court to make certain kinds of political decisions does not make those decisions any less political.[48]

Law could not, therefore, be used to subdue 'potential tyranny'; '[o]nly political control, politically exercised, can supply the remedy'.[49] This meant that 'political decisions should be taken by politicians', who were 'removable', while also responsible and accountable for the exercise of power in ways which were 'real and not fictitious'.[50]

The political constitution is not therefore one which seeks to exclude law. Instead, it serves to emphasise the limits of law as a social instrument, and— recognising that law and politics are inherently interrelated—to establish the necessary priority of politics. Whether the necessary constitutional priority of politics was, for Griffith, simply an empirical truth or also a principled position is open to

---

[44] JAG Griffith, 'The Political Constitution' (1979) 42 *MLR* 1, 2, 20.
[45] ibid 20.
[46] ibid 19.
[47] JAG Griffith, 'The Common Law and the Political Constitution' (2001) 117 *LQR* 42, 59.
[48] Griffith, 'The Political Constitution' (1979) n 44 above, 16.
[49] ibid 16.
[50] ibid 16.

debate. The argument made in 'The Political Constitution' is generally presented as one revealing the world as it is, yet if it is ostensibly a descriptive account, it is also one which reflects 'a preference rooted in principle'.[51] Nevertheless, the principled commitments which are largely latent in Griffith's own work have been made much more explicit in subsequent academic engagement with the notion of the political constitution. As Goldoni and McCorkindale note in introducing a recent collection of such scholarship, a 'normative grounding'[52] for the political constitution has been developed in the work of Tomkins,[53] Bellamy,[54] and Gee and Webber.[55] And it is these efforts overtly to expose the normative underpinnings of Griffith's work which, Goldoni and McCorkindale maintain, have provided 'a full-fledged constitutional *theory* capable of standing as an alternative to the liberal-legal paradigm—a turn, one might say, from the political constitution to political constitutionalism'.[56] Yet just as the political constitution does not seek to exclude law—but instead represents a response to the universal constitutional question of 'how the idea of law within the political constitution (i.e. the constitution of the polity) might best be conceptualized'[57]—political constitutionalism does not need to be conceived as locked in opposition to a legal constitutionalism which seeks to structure and constrain politics.[58] Although these contrasting models may usefully be used as a framing device through which to understand competing constitutional arrangements, or the change to such arrangements,[59]

---

[51] KD Ewing, 'The Resilience of the Political Constitution' (2013) 14 *German Law Journal* 2111, 2116. See also chapter 1 of this volume, n 79.

[52] M Goldoni and C McCorkindale, 'A Note From the Editors: The State of the Political Constitution' (2013) 14 *German Law Journal* 2103, 2109.

[53] A Tomkins, 'In Defence of the Political Constitution' (2002) 22 *OJLS* 157; A Tomkins, *Our Republican Constitution* (Oxford, Hart Publishing, 2005).

[54] R Bellamy, *Political Constitutionalism: A Republican Defence of the Constitutionality of Democracy* (Cambridge, Cambridge University Press, 2007).

[55] G Gee, 'The Political Constitutionalism of JAG Griffith' (2008) 28 *Legal Studies* 20; G Gee and G Webber, 'What Is a Political Constitution?' (2010) 30 *OJLS* 273.

[56] Goldoni and McCorkindale, 'The State of the Political Constitution' (2013) n 52 above, 2104.

[57] M Loughlin, 'Towards a Republican Revival?' (2006) 26 *OJLS* 425, 436.

[58] See, eg T Hickman, 'In Defence of the Legal Constitution' (2005) 55 *University of Toronto Law Journal* 981. The common law constitutionalism which has been discussed at length in this book may be understood to represent a specific variant of 'legal constitutionalism'. This is especially the case with the academic accounts of common law constitutionalism which characterise the common law to be the agent through which the universal values of the rule of law are given expression: see especially TRS Allan, *The Sovereignty of Law: Freedom, Constitution, and Common Law* (Oxford, Oxford University Press, 2013).

[59] For a recent example, see A Le Sueur and J Simson Caird, 'The House of Lords Select Committee on the Constitution' in A Horne, G Drewry and D Oliver (eds), *Parliament and the Law* (Oxford, Hart Publishing, 2013). That legal and political constitutionalism are here together employed as an effective framing device does not mean that we must accept the authors' conclusion that mechanisms which combine law and politics in a new manner can offer a 'third way between these two models of constitutionalism': 283. The intermingling of law and politics is unavoidable in accordance with Griffith's basic framework of the political constitution, and that this is occurring in novel ways does not necessarily indicate that a new model must now be seen to prevail.

this should not be seen to limit the potential for political constitutionalism to be considered apart from legal constitutionalism, 'on its own terms'.[60]

Yet if the constitutional priority of politics is to be more than simply a descriptive account of unavoidable reality, then, and established as the basis for an independent theory of social order, it must obtain its normative force from some further principle. The bare fact that politics is ultimately ascendant over other institutions or social structures which condition human behaviour—which, for example, might be religious, moral, corporate, familial or legal in nature—may be of little normative interest if that politics is of dubious legitimacy. Instead, the nature of the politics in accordance with which power is exercised, and by which power is conditioned, is crucial if its constitutional priority is to be justified. For political constitutionalism, democracy provides that normative force. It is the legitimacy of majoritarian democratic politics, defended in Chapter one, which provides the principled rationale for political constitutionalism. In the absence of an agreed account of what justice requires, a community of political equals must take decisions as to what collective action will be pursued on simple majority grounds.[61] Democratic politics thus provides the means by which constitutional power is to be exercised, and also, at the same time, the conditions on the use of that power: what receives democratic support, in principle, can be achieved; what does not receive democratic support, in principle, cannot be achieved. Griffith was far from a democratic romantic, describing the idea of popular sovereignty as 'nonsense', and arguing that 'the trappings of democracy concealed rather than adorned the body politic'.[62] Yet that Griffith's conception of the political constitution was, ultimately, a democratic one—even if a very thin democratic one—seems apparent in his emphasis on the removability of those in power. While Griffith was more concerned, certainly, with establishing transparency as to the ends of public power, forcing 'governments out of secrecy and into the open', to ensure effective accountability for official action, the ultimate form of accountability he envisaged is surely democratic: those who temporarily govern us are vulnerable to being 'dismissed' (indirectly) if their performance is unsatisfactory.[63] And this is consonant with Griffith's later work, where, in a forceful rebuttal of common law constitutionalism, he became slightly more explicit about the constitutional significance of democratic politics, as means to challenge private corporate power, arguing that '[o]nly democratically elected Governments committed to policies of promoting the public interest can present a challenge to [this] powerful hegemon'.[64]

---

[60] Goldoni and McCorkindale, 'The State of the Political Constitution' (2013) n 52 above, 2105.
[61] See chapter 1 of this volume, pp 35–36.
[62] Griffith, 'The Political Constitution' (1979) n 44 above, 3, 5.
[63] ibid 16, 18. That Griffith is thinking in majoritarian democratic terms, at least in principle, with respect to the taking of political decisions seems evident, for eg, from claims that a law is good 'only in the limited sense that a number of people hold that opinion of it', or his (seeming) implicit acceptance that 'a majority' confers some sort of legitimacy: 19, 20.
[64] Griffith, 'The Common Law and the Political Constitution' (2001) n 47 above, 63.

Much richer accounts of the democratic nature of political constitutionalism can be found in the body of work which more explicitly develops the normative foundations of Griffith's work. Bellamy, for example, has defended 'the constitutionality of "actually existing democracy"', which is 'the claim of actually existing democratic practices to embody constitutional values and to supply mechanisms likely to preserve them'.[65] This account focuses on the capacity of majoritarian democratic politics to establish the freedom of citizens, understood in republican terms as non-domination,[66] while better serving 'the constitutional goods of rights and the rule of law' than is achieved by the introduction of 'less effective and legitimate legal constitutional constraints' on that democratic process.[67] Bellamy's approach is, in effect, to view democratic political constitutionalism as a means by which the broad goals of (liberal) legal constitutionalism may be satisfied: democracy is *not* 'more important than constitutionalism, rights or the rule of law', but 'embodies and upholds these values'.[68] In recognising the value in rights and the rule of law, this moves us considerably on from the position of Griffith, who rejected the former as 'political claims', and the latter, if understood in anything more than formal terms, as 'a fantasy' which can be used 'to throw a protective sanctity around certain legal and political institutions and principles which they wish to preserve at any cost'.[69] Nevertheless, a more modest account of the democratic potential of political constitutionalism might instead be adopted; beyond the minimalism of Griffith's democracy as accountability, but without going so far as seemingly to endorse the objectives of liberal legalist constitutionalism. This may be found in Ewing's suggestion that it is 'a purpose of the political constitution—perhaps greater than the purpose of holding government to account—that it allows for the wishes of citizens to be realized and for these wishes to be translated into law'.[70] This is the '*openness* of the political constitution', which is able 'to provide for popular demands to be met without formal limit', while also sustaining a 'latent transformative potential' by which—in principle—the re-making of social order could be achieved.[71] The capacity of the political constitution to facilitate the democratic empowerment of citizens—both

---

[65] Bellamy, *Political Constitutionalism* (2007) n 54 above, 12, 259.

[66] See generally P Pettit, *Republicanism: A Theory of Freedom and Government* (Oxford, Oxford University Press, 1997); Q Skinner, *Liberty Before Liberalism* (Cambridge, Cambridge University Press, 1998). Goldoni and McCorkindale describe this 'concurrent revival of republican political theory' as 'something of a convenient bed-fellow in the attempt to construct a meaningful alternative to liberal constitutionalism', yet note that it remains an open question whether political constitutionalism must necessarily be grounded in the philosophy of republicanism: Goldoni and McCorkindale, 'The State of the Political Constitution' (2013) n 52 above, 2104. For a powerful critique of Pettit, whose republican theory of government nevertheless ultimately prescribes a similar judicial limitation of democracy to that recommended by legal constitutionalism, see Bellamy, *Political Constitutionalism* (2007) n 54 above, 163–71.

[67] Bellamy, *Political Constitutionalism* (2007) n 54 above, 12.

[68] ibid 260.

[69] Griffith, 'The Political Constitution' (1979) n 44 above, 17–18, 15.

[70] Ewing, 'The Resilience of the Political Constitution' (2013) n 51 above, 2117.

[71] ibid 2117.

through its routine operation and amenability to moments of fundamental change—may thus most profoundly demonstrate the normative force of the theory of political constitutionalism which it inspires.

If political constitutionalism is normatively justified because, and to the extent that, it affords priority to a politics which is democratic in nature, where does the doctrine of parliamentary sovereignty fit in this scheme? As Ewing notes, it is 'frustrating that Griffith makes little reference to this legal principle, for it is difficult to see how a political constitution could operate without it'.[72] Ewing's work, however, fills this gap, outlining the role of the doctrine of legislative sovereignty in the democratic political constitution. For Ewing, 'the legal principle of the sovereignty of Parliament provides both the source of legal authority, and the source of legal restraint of the power of government in a political constitution'.[73] In this sense, it is the 'core legal principle of the political constitution' which underpins the 'political principle that in a democracy there should be no legal limit to the wishes of the people'.[74] On this analysis, the doctrine of parliamentary sovereignty is a fundamental, and highly prominent, legal component of a democratic political constitution. The core virtue of the doctrine—which was described in Chapter one as ensuring the constitutional primacy of democratic decision-making—corresponds with the defining feature of political constitutionalist theory: recognising the priority of (democratic) politics. The doctrine of parliamentary sovereignty is thus the key instrument of democratic political constitutionalism; it is the legal principle which recognises the autonomy of the democratic process, and guarantees the subordination of law to the political results of that process. Moreover, in clearing the field of the possibility of legal limits on law-making authority, it creates a space which politics can, and must, fill. The absence of legal institutional restraints does not leave the exercise of legislative power unfettered; instead, it is conditioned by democratic politics, which—for the political constitutionalist—is in any event likely to be the most effective,[75] as well as the most legitimate, way of structuring the use of public

---

[72] ibid 2118. Griffith's only comment on the doctrine of parliamentary sovereignty in his famous lecture is to deny that it presents a constitutional danger: 'The Political Constitution' (1979) n 44 above, 18.

[73] ibid 2118.

[74] ibid 2118.

[75] For empirical analysis which is critical of the effectiveness with which governmental power can be judicially conditioned and controlled, or the role of courts in promoting social justice, see generally JAG Griffith, *The Politics of the Judiciary*, 5th edn (London, Fontana Press, 1997); GN Rosenberg, *The Hollow Hope: Can Courts Bring About Social Change?* (London, University of Chicago Press, 1991) esp Part 1; KD Ewing and CA Gearty, *Freedom Under Thatcher: Civil Liberties in Modern Britain* (Oxford, Clarendon Press, 1990); KD Ewing and CA Gearty, *The Struggle for Civil Liberties: Political Freedom and the Rule of Law in Britain, 1914–1945* (Oxford, Oxford University Press, 2000); R Hirschl, *Towards Juristocracy: The Origins and Consequences of New Constitutionalism* (Cambridge MA, Harvard University Press, 2004); KD Ewing, *The Bonfire of the Liberties: New Labour, Human Rights and the Rule of Law* (Oxford, Oxford University Press, 2010), which concludes: 'It is thus the supreme irony of the British constitution that liberty and legality would be better served by politics rather than by law; or by power rather than by rights': 284.

authority. The democratic political constitution is thus empowering, but also holds that power to account. The doctrine of parliamentary sovereignty plays an obvious role in enabling the former—as the constitutional source of legislative authority—yet its indirect role in facilitating the latter—by preventing the emergence of absolute legal limits, and thus establishing room for politics—must also be recognised.

We must not, however, overstate the significance of the relationship between democratic political constitutionalism and the doctrine of parliamentary sovereignty for two reasons. First, from a perspective internal to political constitutionalism, we might not wish to be committed to the notion that parliamentary sovereignty is a necessary component of a political constitution. While noting the 'thematic linkages between the idea of political constitutionalism and the doctrine of Parliamentary Sovereignty', Scott has argued that there is 'excessive identification of political constitutionalism with British parliamentary democracy and a lack of consideration for those instantiations of political constitutionalism which are common to all democratic constitutions or are entirely alien to the British system'.[76] This has two potential disadvantages. On one hand, it unduly limits our understanding of the scope and sophistication of political constitutionalism, which 'deserves … more generous consideration' than may be forthcoming if it is understood to be exclusively, or predominantly, associated with the UK's system of parliamentary democracy in particular.[77] And on the other hand, this might endanger the very existence of the political constitutionalist project, if 'the rejection of the specific historical contingencies of the United Kingdom constitution' has been, or comes to be, 'understood as the rejection of the political constitution generally'.[78]

Secondly, while it may go too far to suggest that parliamentary sovereignty is an essential tenet of the political constitution, we should also refrain from viewing the doctrine as necessarily a political constitutionalist doctrine. It is for this reason that, when exploring the virtue of the doctrine of parliamentary sovereignty in general in Chapter one, I did not seek to locate this account of its democratic purpose in a political constitutionalist framework. To accept parliamentary sovereignty as a legal doctrine, or to recognise its democratic virtue, does not entail a commitment to political constitutionalism. And we need not be agnostic as between legal and political constitutionalism, in broad terms, for this to be the case.[79] Indeed, it is entirely possible to accept the legislative sovereignty

---

[76] P Scott, '(Political) Constitutions and (Political) Constitutionalism' (2013) 14 *German Law Journal* 2157, 2169, 2172.

[77] ibid 2172.

[78] ibid 2172.

[79] Dawn Oliver's pragmatic defence of parliamentary sovereignty may represent an example of such agnosticism. Oliver rejects a democratic justification for the doctrine, but advances the pragmatic argument—in a manner reminiscent of political constitutionalism—that there is no need for a dramatic shift to the judicial review of legislation, in part because of the existence of 'elaborate organic systems of intra-governmental and intra-parliamentary constitutional preview': D Oliver, 'Parliament and the Courts: A Pragmatic (or Principled) Defence of the Sovereignty of Parliament' in A Horne, G Drewry and D Oliver (eds), *Parliament and the Law* (Oxford, Hart Publishing, 2013)

of Parliament, and the democratic value of this legal position, from something resembling a legal constitutionalist perspective. For example, Heuston's support for the manner and form theory of parliamentary sovereignty—which, as considered above, was premised on the basis that it offers a potential means by which abuses of power could be prevented—might best be understood in this way.[80]

That acceptance of parliamentary sovereignty may transcend political constitutionalism is further evident on consideration of the modern example of the Human Rights Act 1998 (HRA). The HRA is certainty compatible with parliamentary sovereignty, and may best be understood as placing political limitations on the power of Parliament.[81] Yet when we shift from considering the HRA's compatibility with the sovereignty of Parliament, to the broader question of the Act's compatibility with political constitutionalism—of which this legal doctrine is at most simply one aspect—the relevant considerations become much more complex. For such a judgement cannot be based merely on the ultimate effects of the power given by the HRA to the courts in relation to the legislation of Parliament (to say nothing of the power given for the judicial control of executive action), but must also take account of the broader nature and implications of the new legal mechanisms established by the 1998 Act. For some, the creation of these new processes by which the courts have the duty to assess the compatibility of official or parliamentary action with a body of codified legal rights is consistent with, and has the potential to strengthen, political constitutionalism.[82] For others, the political constitution has been supplemented rather than supplanted, leading to the creation of a 'mixed constitution' engaging both law and politics in an 'increasingly rich constitutional order'.[83] And yet a further position is to regard political constitutionalism as in 'rude health', because the 'infusion of law does not remove so much as compound the politics', and 'opens up' the court room as 'a new arena of political contestation'.[84] Yet the HRA can equally be considered to be transformative, heralding a shift away from the political constitutionalism of old, to a new constitutional legalism. For example, the HRA might be seen to represent the 'cornerstone of the new British constitution', embodying a 'compromise' between the sovereignty of Parliament and the rule of law.[85] Yet an account of the HRA which emphasises its significance as an instrument of legal, rather than political, constitutionalism, does not require the Act's compatibility with parliamentary sovereignty to be denied. While this path has, nonetheless, been followed by

---

n 59 above, 329. Yet in so far as Oliver's account is premised on the need effectively to protect 'constitutionality and the rule of law' it also appears to incorporate elements of legal constitutionalism: 310.

[80] See text at nn 15–18.

[81] See chapter 3 of this volume, pp 120–26.

[82] See, eg R Bellamy, 'Political Constitutionalism and the Human Rights Act' (2011) 9 *International Journal of Constitutional Law* 86.

[83] A Tomkins, 'What's Left of the Political Constitution?' (2013) 14 *German Law Journal* 2275, 2292, 2290.

[84] Ewing, 'The Resilience of the Political Constitution' (2013) n 51 above, 2136.

[85] V Bogdanor, *The New British Constitution* (Oxford, Hart Publishing, 2009) 62, 83.

some,[86] others have argued the legal rights protection offered by the HRA could, in contrast, even be further strengthened without the doctrine of parliamentary sovereignty being displaced.[87] It is not relevant, for present purposes, which of these numerous accounts is correct, or whether the HRA can be reconciled with, or marks the end of, political constitutionalism.[88] Instead, what is significant is that political *and* legal constitutionalist understandings of the HRA can accommodate the Act's compatibility with parliamentary sovereignty.

It would go too far, therefore, to purport to claim parliamentary sovereignty as a doctrine which is exclusively located on political constitutionalist terrain. It is coherent to accept the sovereignty of Parliament, and its resounding democratic credentials, while simultaneously defending a robust and substantive notion of the rule of law, and a statutory scheme of rights protection which permits judicial oversight of the legislature.[89] Nevertheless, while political constitutionalism may not be entitled to capture parliamentary sovereignty, it is, in my view, from this perspective that embracing the doctrine, and its democratic virtue, can best be understood. Political constitutionalism provides the broader framework in which the doctrine of parliamentary sovereignty can most convincingly be located. When viewed as a normative theory which reflects the significance of democratic politics, political constitutionalism requires the cultivation of institutional arrangements which sustain this instinct. And the legal principle of legislative sovereignty, in establishing the primacy of democratic decision-making, provides a compelling foundation on which a political constitution can be structured. The alignment between political principle (democracy) and legal principle (parliamentary sovereignty) is thus reinforced when framed within an overarching constitutional theory (political constitutionalism) to create a consistent, and normatively attractive, constitutional paradigm.

With the nature of the complementary relationship between democracy, political constitutionalism and parliamentary sovereignty now established, we can turn from the general to the specific. For it is by developing these general ideas as to the role of parliamentary sovereignty in a democratic political constitution that a specific democratic justification for the manner and form theory of the doctrine can be explained.

---

[86] See, eg A Kavanagh, *Constitutional Review under the UK Human Rights Act* (Cambridge, Cambridge University Press, 2009).

[87] AL Young, *Parliamentary Sovereignty and the Human Rights Act* (Oxford, Hart Publishing, 2009).

[88] To make any such judgement, of course, a range of additional factors would need to be considered, particularly including the operation and effectiveness political mechanisms for rights scrutiny; see, eg Ewing, *The Bonfire of the Liberties* (2010) n 75 above, 266–75; M Hunt, 'The Joint Committee on Human Rights' in Horne, Drewry and Oliver (eds), *Parliament and the Law* (2013) n 59 above.

[89] The leading extra-judicial statement of such a position is T Bingham, *The Rule of Law* (London, Penguin, 2011).

IV. A DEMOCRATIC JUSTIFICATION OF THE MANNER
AND FORM THEORY

The core virtue of the doctrine of parliamentary sovereignty is establishing the constitutional primacy of democratic decision-making. The theory of political constitutionalism, however, allows us more clearly to understand the implications of this virtue. In preventing the legal limitation of Parliament's law-making authority, the doctrine creates space in which democratic politics can function to condition legislative power. And, when viewed through the lens of political constitutionalism, the significance of the limits and accountability which derive from democratic politics becomes apparent—the conditions are neither inherently trivial nor an afterthought, but a potentially profound and, crucially, legitimate, way to structure legislative power. To rely on non-legal limits to condition legislative authority is, therefore, not merely an unintended consequence of the democratic insistence on the priority of majoritarian decision-making, but a preference which can be justified in its own right. The doctrine of parliamentary sovereignty clears the ground for this to occur, in ensuring that democratic decision-making is not legally limited. But political constitutionalism, completing what is otherwise left implicit, explains why it is not something to be regretted: because democratic politics can, and should, fill this accountability gap.

How do these general considerations apply in the context of the manner and form theory, the specific conception of the idea of parliamentary sovereignty defended in this book? A basic democratic justification of the manner and form theory can develop from a similar starting point to an account of the democratic virtue of parliamentary sovereignty in general. If majoritarian democratic decision-making should not be limited by law in relation to matters of substance, nor should it be limited by law in relation to matters of procedure. In suggesting that the idea of legally unlimited legislative power should be understood to *include* the power to alter the future manner and form for law-making, the manner and form theory offers an expanded account of the scope of parliamentary sovereignty. Parliament may legislate on any substantive matter, as Dicey recognised, but also—by legislation validly enacted in accordance with existing procedural requirements—to modify the law-making process itself. If there is a compelling democratic reason to permit legislation on any substantive matter, this should also be understood to extend to legislation altering the legislative process. For, from this perspective, the democratic legitimacy of legislation does not derive from the content of the norms enacted, but the process by which those norms have been produced. And therefore, if the norms contained in legislation enacted according to a majoritarian democratic process happen to be norms which alter how legislation is in future to be enacted, they are still entitled to benefit from the legitimacy of that process of enactment itself. In short, if legislation which is the result of a democratic decision-making process should be understood to have effect, whether the norms it enacts change the substance of the law, or the process for future law-making, is irrelevant; in either event, the legislation should have legal effect.

This is the basic democratic justification for the manner and form theory. Yet it is liable to elicit a powerful objection. This objection is best captured in the work of Goldsworthy. In rejecting a self-embracing understanding of parliamentary sovereignty,[90] because it would allow Parliament to limit itself in any way at all, Goldsworthy sketches, and responds to, the following challenge:

> It might be thought inconsistent of me, having argued on a previous occasion that it is not unreasonable to trust Parliament with legislative sovereignty, to warn against possible abuses of self-embracing sovereignty. But one of the reasons for entrusting Parliament with ordinary legislative sovereignty is that mistakes and injustices can be corrected by future Parliaments, whereas if full self-embracing sovereignty ... were used to limit their ability to do so, this could become difficult or impossible.[91]

While of course, Goldsworthy is here discussing a self-embracing conception of legislation sovereignty, the general challenge, and response outlined, are still applicable to the manner and form theory. For while the manner and form theory, unlike a self-embracing conception of sovereignty, does not permit the legislative enactment of substantive limits on law-making power, the procedural conditions which it does permit include those which Goldsworthy's procedure and form model would reject, on the basis that they constitute 'substantive limits that are disguised as manner and form requirements'.[92] Indeed, the challenge Goldsworthy here imagines would apply with even greater force in relation to his rejection of more demanding, yet still fundamentally procedural, legislative conditions, the enactment of which is legally permitted by the manner and form theory. For with respect to such procedural conditions, the future statutory correction of legislative mistakes would be made merely more difficult, rather than impossible, and while this is still potentially objectionable, it is less obviously so. In this sense, the strength of Goldsworthy's response to this challenge becomes more significant in relation to the manner and form theory in particular, because a denial of power to create (only) procedural conditions is intrinsically more difficult to justify on the basis that it may be used to constrain Parliament's law-making authority, as the extent of such constraint will necessarily be qualified.

The crucial point made by Goldsworthy, which can be used to challenge a democratic justification of the manner and form theory, is that trust in Parliament to exercise legislative authority is underpinned by the ready possibility that errors can be corrected. The legislative creation of procedural conditions which would inhibit the possibility of statutory correction cannot be permitted, for to trust Parliament with the power to enact law on any substantive matter, we must be

---

[90] The particular account of self-embracing sovereignty challenged here by Goldsworthy is that found in P Oliver, *The Constitution of Independence: The Development of Constitutional Theory in Australia, Canada and New Zealand* (Oxford, Oxford University Press, 2005).

[91] Goldsworthy, *Parliamentary Sovereignty: Contemporary Debates* (2010) n 24 above, 138.

[92] ibid 138. For further discussion of the procedural requirements which are regarded as lawful by the manner and form theory, but legally impermissible by Goldsworthy's procedure and form model, see generally chapter 2 of this volume, pp 97–107; chapter 6 of this volume, pp 267–77.

assured that whatever it does could in future be undone. To allow Parliament to alter the future legislative process is not objectionable in itself, but because, in consequence, it could undermine the basis on which it is trusted to exercise substantive law-making power. An Act of Parliament changing the future law-making process may be just as democratically legitimate, in itself, as an Act of Parliament changing the substance of the law. Yet, there remains a vital difference between these two types of legislation: the existence of a general trust in Parliament to exercise its substantive law-making authority depends upon us withholding power to alter significantly the legislative process. Conversely, if we were to trust Parliament with power to legislate about the legislative process, a general trust in Parliament to exercise legally unlimited substantive power might become unjustifiable. We cannot, therefore, simply extend the justification of legally unlimited legislative power over substantive matters to encompass legally unlimited legislative power over the future law-making process. Different considerations pertain in these different circumstances, and that legislation altering the manner and form is, in essence, as democratically legitimate as legislation altering the law in substance does not provide a sufficient basis to justify the legal permissibility of the former.

With this, we have, in a sense, returned to the Diceyan mantra that 'Parliament cannot bind its successors'. For this very suggestion—that the possibility of the correction of errors justifies our trust in legislative sovereignty—might be seen to provide the principled rationale for the original orthodox rejection of the manner and form theory.[93] Nonetheless, while this provides a potent challenge to the basic democratic justification of the manner and form theory, it is a challenge which can be rejected. For we can contest fundamentally the key idea which underpins this challenge: that while a democratic Parliament can be trusted with legally unlimited substantive legislative power, it cannot similarly be trusted with the authority to alter the future legislative process. It is here that ideas of political constitutionalism, surveyed in the previous section, now become critical. For we must draw on the theory of political constitutionalism to explain why this challenge should be rejected, and how a democratic justification of the manner and form theory can therefore be sustained. Within this political constitutionalist framework, four key concepts will be crucial: trust, reciprocity, commitment, and revolution.

A. Trust

First, political constitutionalist notions of trust can be employed to contest the basis of this challenge to a democratic justification of the manner and form

---

[93] It should be noted that Goldsworthy's procedure and form model is much more nuanced than the Diceyan prohibition on Parliament binding its successors. Yet while there are clear differences between what Goldsworthy and Dicey would deem legally permissible in terms of change to the legislative process, the underlying rationale for what is *not* permitted is arguably the same.

theory. Or, more accurately, it is the political constitutionalist understanding of the *limits* of trust which is significant here. In continuing to accept the legislative sovereignty of the UK Parliament, citizens may appear to place a significant amount of trust in the legislature to exercise that power appropriately. As I argued in Chapter one, it is the fact that Parliament is a democratic institution which makes its possession of this power legitimate. Yet that there is, in principle, a democratic basis for placing trust, understood in a general and abstract sense, in Parliament to possess sovereign legislative authority, must be the start, rather than the end, of our consideration of its power. This much is abundantly clear in political constitutionalist theory, which recognises the need to combine democratic empowerment with democratic accountability. Indeed, as discussed above, it is the importance of such (democratic) accountability through politics which constitutes the primary, near exclusive, focus of the work of Griffith in particular. We must engage in politics to ensure that claims to authority, and its ensuing exercise, are meticulously questioned and persistently challenged; this is the foundation of democratic accountability. Indeed, the necessity of such political action reflects what Poole has suggested is the 'dominant *motif* of Griffith's work: namely, the idea of trust—or, perhaps more accurately, *distrust*—being at the root of all good constitutional thinking'.[94]

While the existence of democratic political authority might, then, appear to be based to some extent on trust between citizens and those exercising power, in political constitutionalism we see the notion of distrust instead emphasised. This can be understood as a consequence of the democratic politics to which political constitutionalism—at least when understood as a normative constitutional theory—seeks to give priority. For trust can be seen to have a 'paradoxical place … within democracy'.[95] In one sense, 'democratic progress is most often sparked by distrust of authorities'.[96] Further, we may see the existence of distrust, in general, as 'essential … to the healthy suspicion of power upon which the vitality of democracy depends'.[97] And, as a result, distrust can be seen as 'democratic and thoughtful, not an anti-democratic outburst of emotion, and is potentially constructive, threatening only to vested political interests'.[98] In another sense, however, while there is 'tension' between trust and democracy, some kinds of trust 'are necessary to its stability, viability and vitality'.[99] Yet even here, in attempting to move away

---

[94] T Poole, 'Tilting at Windmills? Truth and Illusion in "The Political Constitution"' (2007) 70 *MLR* 250, 262. Along similar lines, Poole has more recently suggested that '[t]rust was a *leitmotif* in [Griffith's] work. It was a central theme in his writings on the politics of the judiciary, where his critique can be read as a response to the claim best expressed in Lord Denning's dictum that we need to trust someone, so let it be the judges': T Poole, 'The Elegiac Tradition: Public Law and Memory' [2014] *PL* 68, 76.

[95] ME Warren, 'Democratic Theory and Trust' in ME Warren (ed), *Democracy and Trust* (Cambridge, Cambridge University Press, 1999) 310.

[96] ibid 310.

[97] ibid 310.

[98] V Hart, *Distrust and Democracy* (Cambridge, Cambridge University Press, 1978) xii.

[99] Warren, 'Democratic Theory and Trust' (1999) n 95 above, 313, 310.

from distrust, in the context of politics what 'maintains a background of trust ... is my knowledge that I *could* monitor and challenges authorities ... as well as the *others'* knowledge that I can do so'.[100] As a result, whether democratic politics is framed as being based on distrust of authority, or trust which is assured by the ongoing possibility of scrutiny or challenge, is almost irrelevant. In either case, the political constitutionalist message as to the importance of accountability through scepticism towards authority reverberates strongly. When we speak of (dis)trust in power, therefore, in the context of a democratic political constitutionalist framework, it is in full recognition of the fact that such power must be systemically subject to monitoring and examination.

It is against this backdrop that the question of whether Parliament can be trusted with the legislative power to alter the future manner and form must be confronted. It is crucial to recognise that to permit Parliament to have this legal power is not based on trust which is akin to blind faith. Instead, if a democratic justification of the manner and form theory is advanced, the legislative power to alter the legislative process will necessarily be located in a scheme of democratic political accountability. The democratic justification of the manner and form theory is not, therefore, merely based on the fact that such legislation will be the product of a majoritarian democratic decision-making process. Instead, the political constitutionalist insistence on democratic authority being democratically held to account means that to (dis)trust Parliament with the legal power to alter the future manner and form would simultaneously demand that the exercise of such power be subject to assessment and challenge through the democratic political process. As a result, to argue that it is democratically justified to allocate to Parliament such legislative power is *not* to suggest that the legislature should be absolutely entitled to use that power in any way at all. Instead, while there would be no *legal* limits on Parliament's capacity to use the power imagined by the manner and form theory, there would necessarily be a range of democratic political conditions structuring the exercise of that authority.

This may not directly rebut the powerful challenge to the justification of the manner and form theory at issue in this section. Yet it is nevertheless important that we assess the claim that the manner and form theory can be democratically justified in the proper context. For when this context is made clear, by locating the manner and form theory in a political constitutionalist framework, the gravity of the objection that Parliament should not be trusted with such power is somewhat diminished. It is true that, if the manner and form theory of parliamentary sovereignty is accepted, Parliament could lawfully use its legislative power to alter the law-making process in such a way as to prevent the correction in future of statutory mistakes. Yet this power will not be politically unlimited. Instead, legislative power to alter the manner and form will be conditioned by the operation of democratic politics, and ultimately, Parliament will be accountable to citizens

---

[100] ibid 338.

for the exercise of its law-making authority. In general, the theory of political constitutionalism indicates that such democratic political limits and accountability will, in addition to being the most legitimate, also be the most effective way of conditioning the use of public authority. And when we examine the specific environment in which the legislative power to alter the future manner and form would fall to be exercised, the profound nature of the democratic political limits which could be expected to condition this variety of law-making authority can clearly be seen. As such, when the nature of this democratic political environment is appreciated, it will be possible for us definitively to reject the powerful challenge to the democratic justification for the manner and form theory.

B. Reciprocity

The second concept key to the democratic justification of the manner and form theory is reciprocity. The principle of reciprocity is the notion from which the most profound democratic political limits on the manner and form theory originate. In this context, the idea of reciprocity would primarily operate as between competing political actors; in particular, the main political parties from among which, in a first-past-the-post electoral system which tends to marginalise minority parties,[101] a government will be formed. Bellamy has shown the positive role which competition between parties can play in ensuring 'a balance of power' in a democratic political constitution, 'institutionalising contestation' while also promoting 'inclusion by providing incentives for incumbents to address a wide range of disparate concerns in order to build a broad coalition of supporters'.[102] Such competition between political parties has a further consequence: they have 'an interest in maintaining the rules of the game' because they 'compete over time, anticipating that they will spend periods out of as well as in office'.[103] These general considerations have been explored in the particular context of the obligatory force of constitutional conventions by Jaconelli. The principle of reciprocity, Jaconelli has argued, provides a strong incentive for any particular government to adhere to generally accepted constitutional conventions: 'the party that is in power at the moment respects the constraints that are imposed on it by constitutional conventions in the expectation that the opposition parties, when they attain office, will likewise respect the same constraints'.[104]

The idea of reciprocity between political parties, who have an interest in playing by the rules of the game in anticipation of the fact that their competitors will do the same, can equally be engaged when considering the democratic political

---

[101] See, eg G Lodge and G Gottfried, *Worst of Both Worlds: Why First Past the Post No Longer Works* (London, IPPR, 2011) 4–7.
[102] Bellamy, *Political Constitutionalism* (2007) n 54 above, 230.
[103] ibid 232.
[104] J Jaconelli, 'Do Constitutional Conventions Bind?' (2005) 64 *CLJ* 149, 171.

limits on the legislative power to change the future manner and form. And from this perspective, concern that Parliament might use this expanded legislative power, once recognised, to prevent its 'mistakes' from being subsequently corrected, or its substantive policies from being reversed, can be significantly alleviated. For if one party, while in government, was to encourage Parliament to exercise its legislative power to alter the future manner and form so as to entrench controversial policy decisions, preventing a successor Parliament from reversing those decisions—whether absolutely, or through the imposition of an extremely demanding legislative procedure with respect to certain matters—it would have violated the existing (non-legal) 'rules of the game'. Parliaments in the past have refrained from making such change to the legislative process, and thus it can, at the very least, be seen as an established constitutional expectation—but not a legal duty—that future Parliaments will similarly refrain from so doing. Moreover, this reciprocal obligation to refrain from seeking to use manner and form legislative power to prevent the subsequent reversal of policies by political competitors has a strong principled rationale: it respects the operation of the democratic political system, in which it is legitimate for decisions to be made, and unmade, on the basis of cycling majorities.

   If this notion of reciprocity, underpinned by democratic principle, can be said to operate to condition the legislative power of Parliament as regards the statutory alteration of the law-making process, how might this notion be expressed for convenient use in political practice? We do not need to reinvent the wheel to manufacture a norm which can be used to capture such considerations, for one already exists, and is, moreover, highly prominent in mainstream constitutional discourse. It is the Diceyan notion that 'Parliament cannot bind its successors'. While I have criticised this mantra as inadequately stating the scope of Parliament's legislative power as a matter of *law*, it is entirely serviceable as a notion which captures the state of prevailing *political* practice. If the notion that 'Parliament cannot bind its successors' is therefore repurposed as a fundamental political injunction, rather than simply dismissed as a flawed statement of the legal position, it may be of considerable worth. For while the manner and form theory would accurately represent the extent of Parliament's legislative power as a matter of law—and would therefore permit the enactment of legislation purporting to change the future law-making process—the notion that Parliament cannot bind its successors, now reconfigured as a political norm, could be understood to prevent the use of that power to achieve the undemocratic end of entrenching contentious policies. Indeed, as debates in the House of Commons during the enactment of the European Union Act 2011 amply demonstrate, the norm that 'Parliament cannot bind its successors' is very well established in constitutional practice.[105] Yet if we are freed of the idea that it is a legal rule, it may even be possible to conceive of this as more than a strong political injunction. Instead, we might even come to view

---

[105] See chapter 6 of this volume, p 256.

the notion that 'Parliament cannot bind its successors' as a binding constitutional convention, a position which is supported by the fact that the rule can already be understood to generate the kind of reciprocal obligations which might be seen to underpin the obligatory force of conventional norms in general.

It might be objected that this analysis is disingenuous: the authority of the notion that 'Parliament cannot bind its successors' derives from its recognition as a legal rule, and the fact that it is *on this basis* authoritative cannot therefore be used as the foundation of claims that it is a political or conventional norm. Yet my suggestion here is that, in so far as this has been viewed as a legal norm, derived from the Diceyan account of the doctrine of parliamentary sovereignty, it was wrong to do so. The norm itself overstates the necessary implications of legislative sovereignty, at least when it is taken to prohibit the creation of procedural as well as substantive limits on law-making power.[106] But that it is flawed as a matter of law—as an oversimplification which has now, in any event, been displaced by the modern shift to the manner and form theory of parliamentary sovereignty charted in Part II of this book—does not mean it is constitutionally irrelevant. Instead, rather than being a norm which establishes the scope of Parliament's legislative power, it is a norm which conditions how that power ought to be used. In this narrower sense, the notion that Parliament should not bind its successors is both salient and compelling. That it has been mistakenly treated as a legal norm should not be seen to preclude its proper nature and function from being acknowledged.

It might further be objected that this is a change in form rather than in substance, and is ultimately therefore simply an artificial academic exercise designed to enable the reconciliation of the manner and form theory with the mainstream Diceyan inheritance, while leaving the real world essentially as it is. Yet this is not the case, for in suggesting that Parliament should not—in light of reciprocal political obligations, or even constitutional convention—bind its successors does not exhaust the potential of the legislative power to alter the future legislative process. Indeed, this is far from the case; as we will see in Chapter eight, there are a range of options opened up by acceptance of the manner and form theory which constitute a legislative change to the future law-making process, but *do not* 'bind successor Parliaments' by entrenching controversial policy choices. Indeed, such change to legislative process may be positively democratic in nature and effect. Regardless of whether any further change of this kind is ever actually made to the legislative process, that the manner and form theory opens up the possibility that it can be legitimately considered—rather than discounted as legally impermissible—is, in itself, a crucial element of the democratic justification for this conception of legislative authority.

---

[106] See chapter 2 of this volume, pp 90–91.

C. Commitment

There are thus strong incentives, rooted in the idea of reciprocity between competing political actors, and given constitutional expression in the (non-legal) norm that 'Parliament cannot bind its successors', which function to structure and condition the use of legislative power to alter the future manner and form. As part of a system of democratic political accountability as to the use of power, these notions could be expected significantly to limit the law-making authority of Parliament, and should be understood in particular to preclude the enactment of legislation which seeks to entrench controversial policy decisions, preventing their ready reversal by future actors. Yet while we can therefore anticipate that it would be extremely unlikely for such constitutionally problematic legislation to be enacted, we might also stop to consider whether such concerns—while certainly legitimate—have the potential to be overstated. To do so, the third concept key to explaining a democratic justification for the manner and form theory must be engaged: this is the notion of commitment. The importance of this idea is in establishing a baseline position against which the kind of change to the legislative process which is permitted by the manner and form theory can be measured. For the assumption which seems to underpin the objection that Parliament cannot be trusted with legislative power to modify the law-making process, is that we start from a position where future governments and Parliaments are at all moments free to make whatever policy changes they desire. Yet, of course, this is not the case: as has been acknowledged throughout this book, that Parliament possesses legally unlimited legislative authority does not mean it is omnipotent. Instead, it is subject to a range of fundamental democratic, political, moral and practical limits.[107] We see this demonstrated in famous examples which recur throughout debates about the sovereignty of Parliament, such as the hypothetical statute which mandates the murder of all blue-eyed babies.[108] It may be *legally* possible for such legislation to be enacted, defenders of parliamentary sovereignty argue, but it is not a credible possibility; a democratic legislature simply does not have the practical capability to enact such fundamentally immoral legislation, and in the improbable event that it tried, as will be discussed below, judicial review would certainly not be our remedy.

Yet using absurd examples to frame debate as to the scope of legislative power has the tendency to make such non-legal limits seem ethereal, and reserved for use in only the most extravagant instances. In reality, however, these non-legal limits are largely of a different character: they may vary in strength, but are pervasive, rather than extraordinary. In part, this should be evident from the discussion

---

[107] See chapter 1 of this volume, pp 14–15. As I have used Goldsworthy's work to frame this objection, it should be noted here that I do not mean to suggest that this essential point is one he overlooks; instead, the general fact that Parliament's legislative power is subject to non-legal limits is clearly recognised in his work.

[108] See chapter 3 of this volume, p 145.

above of the conditions in which Parliament can be (dis)trusted with legislative authority; the distinction between distrust and conditional trust in political authority is a marginal one, so long as it is recognised that this power must be subject to rigorous and—crucially, for present purposes—*continuous* democratic political accountability. Yet we must not only focus on 'good' limits—those which are a consequence of democratic politics, and are intended to prevent the exercise of arbitrary governmental power. Instead, we must also recognise the existence of limits which derive from the activity of government itself. Constitutional lawyers concerned with the sovereignty of Parliament can all too easily become preoccupied with the possibility of the use of legislative authority to place eye-catching *constitutional* limits on future law-making power, and disregard the use of legislative authority to place more mundane *political* limits on future law-making power. Yet the use of legislative authority to restrict the freedom for manoeuvre of successive governments and Parliaments is a well-established political strategy. It is here that the concept of commitment becomes significant.

In general, we can see commitment as the taking of action which imposes 'some constraint on future action'.[109] Whether this is done through, for example, a promise or a threat, it is done for a 'purpose': 'to influence someone else's choices'.[110] Effective commitment therefore depends on 'credibility'; the party we seek to influence must develop a 'belief that what is promised or threatened will be carried out'.[111] Making successful commitments poses a special challenge for democratic governments, because this is 'both important and difficult' to achieve when '[p]eriodic free elections make pledges transient'.[112] Ideas of governmental commitment may be especially prevalent in the context of economic policy. The privatisation of national industries presents a particularly important case study. To encourage private investment in newly privatised industries, a government will need to take steps to demonstrate that financial contributions will be secure and profitable. As Levy and Spiller have argued, effective regulation will be required to 'restrain arbitrary administrative action', which in particular necessitates 'substantive restraints on discretionary actions by the regulator, formal or informal restraints on changing the regulatory system, and institutions to enforce the restraints'.[113] This requires 'credible commitment to a regulatory regime', in the absence of which, 'long-term investment will not take place'.[114]

---

[109] TC Schelling, 'Commitment' in P Newman (ed), *The New Palgrave Dictionary of Economics and the Law* (London, Macmillan, 1998) 295. I am grateful to Lindsay Stirton for directing me towards these sources; he should not, of course, be taken to agree with the use I have made of them.

[110] ibid 295.

[111] ibid 297.

[112] ibid 299.

[113] B Levy and PT Spiller, 'A Framework for Resolving the Regulatory Problem' in B Levy and PT Spiller (eds), *Regulations, Institutions and Commitment: A Comparative Study of Telecommunications* (Cambridge, Cambridge University Press, 1996) 1.

[114] ibid 2.

If accepted, such a need for commitment if private investment in industry is to be generated presents particular difficulties in relation to the UK. For the doctrine of legislative sovereignty means that, in principle, the privatisation of an industry could readily be reversed by a future government. Yet while correct as a matter of principle, in practice a broadly effective commitment strategy can still be pursued. In general, as Spiller and Vogelsang have maintained, '[f]ormal and informal institutions (or norms) have evolved to rein in this potential for policy reversals and to restrain government discretion in the regulatory arena'.[115] In the UK, such restraining devices include 'the permanent bureaucracy', the practice of the government promoting 'white papers' to announce, and consult on, proposed shifts in policy, which serves to delay that change, and the 'delegation of substantive powers to regulators'.[116] In the specific context of the privatisation of the telecommunications sector in the UK in the 1980s, the regulatory regime designed was a generally effective guarantor of governmental commitment, in particular through a statutory licensing system—which made licences potentially enforceable through legal action, and difficult to amend against the wishes of the licensee—and the delegation of regulatory power to independent institutions to limit ministerial discretion.[117] Further, a 'diffused ownership structure' was also adopted to try to establish widespread investment in, and broad public support for, the privatisation of British Telecom.[118] These forms of commitment are not absolute, with a statutory regulatory scheme susceptible to amendment, and privatisation, in theory, reversible. Yet such commitment devices, introduced through the exercise of legislative power, make this prospect much more difficult to imagine or achieve. And this difficulty is only magnified we when consider the sheer range of industries which have subsequently been privatised in the UK;[119] the scale of privatisation might arguably be seen to represent a further source of commitment, and certainly provides a further barrier to its reversal.

Against this backdrop, to suggest that the manner and form theory of parliamentary sovereignty must be rejected because it can be exploited to prevent the correction of policy mistakes seems somewhat detached from political reality. For, as the example of privatisation clearly demonstrates, the power effectively to embed even the most controversial policy choices already exists. Where it is believed that governmental commitment to external actors must be demonstrated, as in the context of securing private financial investment in industry, this can be achieved through the regulatory arrangements established by statute. This objection to the manner and form theory is therefore based on a false

---

[115] PT Spiller and I Vogelsang, 'The United Kingdom: A Pacesetter in Regulatory Incentives' in Levy and Spiller (eds), *Regulations, Institutions and Commitment* (1996) n 113 above, 81.

[116] ibid 81–82.

[117] ibid 98, 100–102.

[118] ibid 119, 191–95.

[119] See, eg D Swann, *The Retreat of the State: Deregulation and Privatisation in the UK and US* (London, Harvester Wheatsheaf, 1988).

dichotomy: whether we accept the orthodox or manner and form understanding of legislative sovereignty, it is entirely possible for law-making power to be deliberately used to prevent poor or contested policy choices from being straightforwardly reversed. Admittedly, a manner and form conception of legislative power may offer a government alternative means by which to do this. Yet it is far from clear that legislative power would actually be used explicitly to entrench (in some way) specific contested policy choices, when much the same end can be achieved indirectly, by more flexible, and less controversial means. For to enact, in statute, a regulatory regime which demonstrates commitment, and embeds specific policy decisions, is surely a preferable way for such objectives to be pursued, because it does not require a government to sacrifice the capability to adapt to changing future circumstances. In addition, such a pragmatic approach, by which a government could avoid limiting its own future freedom of action, also coheres with the broader constitutional considerations identified in the previous section. The notion of reciprocity, underpinned by a strong democratic rationale, would, in this context, apply with great political force, and make the entrenchment of controversial policies a highly precarious constitutional path for a government to contemplate following.

The fact that use of the legislative power to alter the manner and form for future law-making so as to entrench contentious policy decisions would, therefore, be arguably unnecessary indicates that we should be reluctant to reject such a conception of parliamentary sovereignty for this reason. For in rejecting the manner and form theory of legislative power we would not simply be preventing the enactment of legislation designed to entrench substantive policies, but also precluding the possibility of any other form of change to the law-making process from being legally effected. To do so in order to proscribe what is already effectively achievable seems especially unwarranted. Yet if concern remains about the potentially undesirable consequences of a shift from the use of regulatory commitment devices, to constitutional prohibitions on the future legislative power of Parliament, this is still an inadequate basis for a wholesale rejection of the manner and form theory. For if the legislative entrenchment of controversial policy decisions would be objectionable—and I accept that in principle it would be—in a democratic political system we should be willing to explain the substantive reasons for this conclusion, and take those substantive reasons as providing the basis for refraining to use law-making authority in this way. Such an approach is more justifiable, from a democratic perspective, than circumventing such political argument by deploying a blanket constitutional prohibition against any change to the legislative process, on the basis that this is what legislative sovereignty inherently requires. We should not become distracted by a desire to prevent the (effectively) unpreventable, and end up preventing more besides. Instead, we must be prepared to confront, rather than bypass, the challenge of delineating what would, and what would not, constitute appropriate use of the legislative power to change the legislative process which is permitted by the manner and form theory.

D. Revolution

The suggestion that the manner and form theory of parliamentary sovereignty ought to be rejected because to do so ensures that we will avoid the possibility of the entrenchment of contentious policies therefore appears to be largely illusory. There are other, already existing ways in which such commitments can be made, which are similarly effective, and arguably more convenient, than entrenchment through statutory procedural conditions. Further, when we acknowledge the absurdity of some of the hypothetical substantive possibilities that we are content to rationalise away to sustain the doctrine of parliamentary sovereignty, that we would, in contrast, completely curtail legislative power to alter the legislative process on such a questionable basis seems even more difficult to defend. If, for example, we are prepared to recognise that Parliament's legally unlimited legislative authority extends to permit, in principle, the lawful enactment of legislation requiring the murder of all blue-eyed babies, to appear more anxious about the possibility of procedural entrenchment seems, at the least, peculiar. The non-legal limits which alleviate either possibility are different, certainly—the objection to the blue-eyed babies statute is fundamentally moral in character, in comparison with the democratic, political and practical considerations which weigh against entrenchment. Yet in both cases these objections would need to be communicated through a common system of democratic political accountability. And as such, the essential manner in which sovereign legislative authority is structured and conditioned will be the same whether that power is to be used to change the substance of the law, or the law-making procedure. In requiring the democratic political system to monitor and challenge the use of legislative power to alter the future manner and form we are not, therefore, asking for anything new, but simply to extend existing accountability mechanisms and processes to encompass a further potential sphere of activity.

What if the system of democratic political accountability fails? There can be no doubt that the UK's system of government is not perfect. While I argued in Chapter one that accounts of Parliament's inadequacy are often overstated, legitimate concerns still exist about its ability effectively to scrutinise legislation promoted by the government. In addition, the strength of the array of external actors, institutions and networks that will be engaged in informing and influencing the legislative process, petitioning and challenging Parliament and the government, will be vital in ensuring the successful operation of a system of democratic political accountability. Yet in this regard, there may be unease about how receptive those who possess law-making authority are to such pressure. An issue of particular importance, which will be considered further in Chapter eight, is whether citizens have become disengaged from the democratic political system, and if present institutional arrangements serve, if not to exacerbate, at least to perpetuate these difficulties. However, while reform of the political system, and indeed of the legislative process itself, may deserve attention, we must be careful not to assume that every bad legislative decision is a result of a failure of democratic accountability.

For democratic decision-making is necessary and legitimate in part because there exists considerable disagreement about what ought to be done in a community. What to us appears to be a 'bad' decision may, therefore, simply be the result of our position being rejected by others, for what they consider to be 'good' reasons. We may regret the fact that this has occurred, and seek to change it, but it is not necessarily indicative of a failing of the democratic political system.

Nevertheless, it is still possible that we may be confronted with a genuinely arbitrary decision, which cannot be justified on democratic grounds. What then? Here, the fourth concept crucial to a democratic justification of the manner and form theory becomes relevant: revolution. If law is simply a social instrument— 'politics carried on by other means'[120]—any particular constitutional system is intrinsically vulnerable to being abandoned, and replaced by an alternative. The idea of revolution is an important aspect of political constitutionalist theory.[121] This concept serves as a reminder of the contingency of constitutional order, with the consequence that if power is exercised in a way which does not accord with the core underlying values of the members of a society, the system itself can be politically reconstituted, and the legal norms within it redrawn. As a result, if non-legal limits do not succeed in adequately conditioning constitutional power, non-legal remedies will always exist. We are, ultimately, no more obliged to accept extreme procedural legislation—for example, a statute purporting to establish, and entrench, a minimal level of income tax—than extreme substantive legislation. Such legislation may, in principle, be lawful, but the norms which we use at any particular moment to determine 'lawfulness' could always, politically, be replaced. Even if a Parliament did succeed in illegitimately binding its successors, it could never do so absolutely.

It might be objected that in suggesting the ineliminable possibility of political revolution to be the ultimate remedy in case of a failure of democratic accountability in this context, I am adopting a similar tactic to one which has been criticised on a number of occasions in Part II of this book: the characterisation of change to the doctrine of parliamentary sovereignty as change to the rule of recognition. It is certainly clear that the conceptual basis of such arguments is essentially identical: law is seen a social construct, the normative force of which depends on established and continuing patterns of belief and behaviour. Yet in objecting to use of the rule of recognition as a relatively routine rationalising device, I have not rejected the legal positivist foundation on which this component of Hart's theory of the nature of law is based.[122] While Hart's essential insight is of profound importance, what I have sought to challenge is the way that the

---

[120] Griffith, 'The Common Law and the Political Constitution' (2001) n 47 above, 59.

[121] See, eg JAG Griffith, 'Why We Need a Revolution' (1969) 40 *Political Quarterly* 383; M Goldoni and C McCorkindale, 'Why We (Still) Need a Revolution' (2013) 14 *German Law Journal* 2197. See also WI Jennings, *Parliamentary Reform* (London, Victor Gollancz, 1934) 13: '[i]f Parliament permits the laws to be warped, there is no remedy but revolution'.

[122] See chapter 2 of this volume, pp 80–83.

rule of recognition has become reified, and used in practice as a conceptual 'get out of jail free card' to explain away problematic constitutional change, or render it compatible with existing doctrinal commitments (whether this is an orthodox understanding of parliamentary sovereignty, or a modified model of legislative authority).[123] For as well as being, in my view, unnecessary, this approach in particular allocates to the courts a significant role in determining the nature and extent of the constitutional change which has occurred. As this is a democratically inappropriate role to be positively afforded to the courts, I adopt here the terminology of 'revolution' rather than that of 'change to the rule of recognition'. For while, in essence, this is essentially a different way of describing the same thing—non-legal change to the fundamental basis of a legal system—it is important to emphasise that there is no *inherent* role for the courts in this process. Such change would ultimately need to be judicially recognised, of course, but this may simply be an incidental function after the fact, rather than actively participating in the process of a constitutional revolution. The terminology of revolution is, moreover, preferable because it stresses that such change would be exceptional, rather than regular. This is not to deny the conceptual possibility that non-revolutionary change to a rule of recognition might occur, but considerations of democratic transparency and certainty strongly militate against understanding constitutional change as being the result of a process which would necessarily be dominated by elite actors. In practice, therefore, we lose little, and gain considerably, by using the language of revolution, rather than that of the rule of recognition, to characterise the inevitable fact that legal norms and powers are ultimately vulnerable to political alteration. In this sense, politics provides a final recourse for citizens in the case of systemic failures to hold constitutional power to account.

A democratic justification for the manner and form theory can, therefore, be sustained. Using the theory of political constitutionalism—and in particular, the concepts of trust, reciprocity, commitment and revolution—we can demonstrate how legislative power to alter the legislative process will necessarily be conditioned and structured through the operation of democratic politics. To (dis)trust Parliament with this power is done on the condition that its exercise will be scrutinised and subject to challenge. Considerations of reciprocity create a normative environment—based on democratic politics, rather than law—which places limits on the use of that power to subvert majoritarian democracy; the repurposed political norm (perhaps even constitutional convention) that 'Parliament cannot bind its successors' provides overt expression of this idea. Concerns about entrenchment can easily be overstated, for the power to use statute to establish strong commitments already exists; to reject on this basis the very possibility of change to the legislative process, which could be democratic in nature, is unwarranted. Finally, as with extreme substantive legislation, extreme procedural

---

[123] See chapter 4 of this volume, pp 179–82; chapter 5 of this volume, pp 218–22; chapter 6 of this volume, pp 273–75.

legislation would always, ultimately, be open to reversal through revolutionary political change.

V. A POTENTIAL CONTRADICTION: PROCESS, POLITICS AND DEMOCRACY … AND THE COURTS?

The most compelling justification for the manner and form theory of parliamentary sovereignty is therefore democratic in nature. For some, however, this might appear strange, perhaps even contradictory. And this might especially be the case when this democratic justification for the manner and form theory must be located in a framework provided by political constitutionalism for it to be fully explained and defended. This potential contradiction is rooted in what the manner and form theory must be understood to add to Dicey's traditional conception of parliamentary sovereignty. A manner and form conception of legally unlimited legislative authority allocates to Parliament the power to alter the future law-making process, in addition to altering any substantive legal norms. This is the maximum sum of legislative power which is compatible with the notion of legislative sovereignty. But in so doing, does the manner and form conception of parliamentary sovereignty necessarily create an increased, and controversial, constitutional role for the judiciary? For on this approach, would judges be required to enforce legal limits on the legislative authority of Parliament? And if so, does this appear to make legislation which is the result of a democratic decision-making process subject to the oversight of an undemocratic institution? In assessing Jennings' support for the manner and form theory, Ewing has suggested that this may well be the case:

> [t]he legal limits on the power of Parliament (and the potential role of the judges to limit the supremacy of Parliament which this implies) contradicts the idea that the people through the electoral system (or otherwise) are the ultimate protectors of the constitution.[124]

The notion of a democratic justification for the manner and form theory—especially one which is supported by claims as to the significance of the political conditioning of constitutional power—may thus be a contradiction in terms, a conception of parliamentary sovereignty which abandons one of the key tenets of the doctrine: that the validity of an Act of Parliament may not be challenged in the courts.

However, a number of considerations demonstrate that the challenge presented by this apparent contradiction is not as powerful as it might first appear. Instead, an acceptance of the manner and form theory would not induce the judicial infringement of the doctrine of parliamentary sovereignty. First, the manner and form theory does not provide the courts with a power to review legislation on

---

[124] Ewing, 'The Law and the Constitution: Manifesto of the Progressive Party' (2004) n 23 above, 751.

substantive grounds. Instead, at the very most, the courts would simply be required to ascertain whether a procedural condition, contained in statute, had been satisfied in the enactment of legislation. Rightly or wrongly, this is something the courts have already done, in *R (Jackson) v Attorney General*.[125] The approach taken in *Jackson* may be more ostensibly interventionist than the enrolled Bill rule—in accordance with which the courts are satisfied of the legal validity of an Act by superficial evidence that it has been duly passed by Parliament—yet the essential objective of the exercise is the same.[126] In both cases, a court is simply discerning whether an Act has been lawfully enacted, in accordance with the legislative procedure applicable at the time. Of course, *Jackson* was a relatively straightforward case, in part because it created a parallel, and less demanding, law-making process, rather than one which made it more difficult for Parliament to enact legislation. Further, there could be no doubt that the Parliament Acts 1911 and 1949, at issue in *Jackson*, altered the legislative process, rather than furtively imposing an absolute substantive limit. Finally, the behaviour of a range of constitutional actors towards this legislation, over a considerable period of time, provided the court with a strong indication that the 1949 Act was broadly understood to be lawful.

A future case may present less benign circumstances. Yet if, to take such an example, the courts were called upon to consider the effect of one of the European Union Act 2011 referendum locks, it would not be inappropriate for them to recognise the legality of these procedural conditions, and hold that future legislation which did not comply with their terms had not been lawfully enacted. To do so would not be to violate the doctrine of parliamentary sovereignty, but to uphold that sovereignty, as understood in accordance with the manner and form theory.

Indeed, such judicial action would not be as extraordinary as it might have sounded to Dicey. For in the contemporary UK constitution, traditional ideas as to the possibility of Acts of Parliament being questioned in the courts have been subtly modified at Parliament's own initiative, although not in such a way as to displace the doctrine of parliamentary sovereignty itself. Acts of Parliament are now subject to review on substantive grounds in relation to their compatibility with EU law and the ECHR, with the courts disapplying legislation which violates the former,[127] or making a declaration of incompatibility where appropriate in relation to the latter.[128] Judicial review on procedural grounds, to establish that legislation has been validly enacted, without considering the merits of the content, seems relatively modest in comparison. Of course, where there is debate about whether legislation which purports to alter the future manner and form has actually placed substantive limitations on successor Parliaments the issue may become much more contentious. Yet the solution offered by the manner and form theory is one which creates limited scope for judicial discretion in such circumstances.

---

[125] *R (on the application of Jackson) v Attorney General* [2005] UKHL 56; [2006] 1 AC 262.
[126] See chapter 5 of this volume, pp 197–98.
[127] See chapter 4 of this volume, pp 162–64.
[128] See chapter 3 of this volume, p 120.

Although the scheme of democratic political conditions considered in detail above would be expected to prevent such cases arising, if the legality of such a statutory requirement did fall to be determined by a court, this would be done by reference to the distinction between procedure and substance alone. As a result, the courts would be required to use essentially objective criteria to make such a decision, with only those limits which—despite being procedural in form— served to make it impossible for Parliament in future to legislate susceptible to being judicially regarded as substantive, and therefore unlawful. Goldsworthy's alternative procedure and form model, in comparison, in requiring courts to make a subjective judgement about whether a seemingly procedural condition has the effect of diminishing the substantive legislative power of Parliament, by making it more difficult to legislate, demands that the courts make far more finely balanced judgements which could readily be contested.[129] Similarly, to conceive of the courts as here playing a role in ascertaining the existence of a shift in a legal system's rule of recognition also provides significant scope for the exercise of judicial discretion,[130] a situation which the manner and form theory—especially when understood in the context of the democratic justification set out in this chapter—clearly avoids.

Secondly, while such judicial power is therefore more tolerable than it might first appear, when understood in context and in comparison to alternative accounts of the role of the courts in such circumstances, it is important that we understand what the alternative would be. If the manner and form theory were not to be accepted, the legal power of Parliament would nonetheless still be limited, albeit in a different way, and arguably to a greater extent. For if the doctrine of parliamentary sovereignty is not understood to permit the legislature to alter the law-making process, Parliament's power will be limited, in the sense that it will not lawfully be able to modify the future manner and form. In potentially providing to the courts an increased, yet still narrow, power to assess the validity of legislation on procedural grounds, we therefore simultaneously open up the possibility of Parliament exercising legislative power in a new sphere. In this sense, to increase the scope of Parliament's legislative power, potentially to a significant extent, we must risk a modest extension of judicial power. Even if not all would accept that this trade-off is worthwhile, it is clear that this is not a transfer of power from Parliament to the courts, or an increase in judicial power at the expense of legislative capability. A shift to the manner and form theory does not, therefore, represent the abandonment of legislative sovereignty; rather, it is an alternative way of characterising relations between Parliament and the courts, which is still shaped by the notion that the former possesses legally unlimited legislative authority.

---

[129] See chapter 2 of this volume, pp 104–07.
[130] See chapter 5 of this volume, pp 218–22.

Finally, while an increase in judicial power as a result of the adoption of the manner and form theory is a possibility which should not unduly concern us, it is, however, far from clear that any such increase in judicial power would necessarily be prompted. For, crucially, even if a case did arise in which the judges were asked to examine the lawfulness of a statutory modification of the legislative process, they would not be required to indulge that request. A lawful statutory alteration of the legislative process need not be justiciable to be accepted and adhered to. The primary responsibility for recognising and abiding by a legislative procedure which had been altered by statute would instead rest with Parliament. If Parliament is further to avail itself of the expanded legislative sovereignty that the manner and form theory offers, both governments and parliamentarians must recognise that, once created, new procedures must be followed for valid legislation in future to be enacted. The courts could thus legitimately take the view that changes to the manner and form for the enactment of future legislation are non-justiciable in general, that it is for the sovereign Parliament to decide whether it is obliged to comply with statutory alterations of the legislative process, and that the remedy for the alleged violation of such provisions must be political rather than legal. Such judicial abstinence would not serve to undermine the effectiveness of statutory change to the legislative process. The authority of such modification of the future manner and form would principally derive from the mere fact of such change having been explicitly written down in an Act of Parliament. The obligatory force of a statutory alteration of the legislative process would thus be inherent in its conspicuous designation as a legal norm. For it would be extremely difficult for the sovereign Parliament to disregard provisions contained in its own legislation. To do so could fundamentally call into question the authority of parliamentary legislation, and even trigger a crisis of faith in the efficacy of Acts of Parliament. Consequently, in this sensitive sphere of constitutional law, the judicial enforcement of statutory change to the legislative process would be of subsidiary importance, with an acceptance of the legally obligatory character of alterations of the manner and form by Parliament, and other pertinent constitutional actors, being decisive in establishing the authority of such provisions.

This was not, of course, the approach taken by the House of Lords in *Jackson*, although it was certainly open to them to follow the spirit of similar denials of jurisdiction found in the line of authority culminating in *Pickin*.[131] On the best understanding of the democratic justification of the manner and form theory, a judicial approach informed by the attitude adopted in *Pickin*, rather than that evident in *Jackson*, offers the most appropriate future direction of travel. However, if, as I have argued in Chapter six, the manner and form theory now represents the new constitutional orthodoxy in the UK, such questions may be largely academic. For if governments and Parliaments continue to proceed on the

---

[131] *British Railways Board v Pickin* [1974] AC 765. See chapter 3 of this volume, pp 133–35; chapter 5 of this volume, pp 196–98.

basis that statutory procedural conditions are legally valid, and binding while in force, then the prospect of a challenge in court may be significantly diminished. Nevertheless, if a case does arise in which a statutory procedural condition has not been complied with, it is unclear whether the courts would even be willing to intercede to reject a purported measure which was not a valid Act of Parliament, something they were not ultimately required to do in *Jackson*. It may well be that such a course of action would be thought too controversial, and if such an exceptional case did occur, a shrewd judiciary might determine that it would not be appropriate for the courts to coerce Parliament to comply with its own modified legislative process. Yet equally, the courts would not be wrong to hold that purported legislation enacted in contravention of an altered manner and form was legally invalid, and, in taking such an approach to ensuring that the measure before them was indeed a genuine Act of Parliament, the judges would not be curtailing illicitly Parliament's sovereign legislative authority. Instead, the doctrine of parliamentary sovereignty indicates that the courts are only to afford legal force to genuine Acts of Parliament, and not to measures which fail to be correctly enacted. If Parliament chooses to exercise its sovereign authority to alter the legislative process by statute, it must at least be prepared for modified procedures to bite in this way. Applying the manner and form theory of parliamentary sovereignty, if the courts were to reject legislation which failed to satisfy an altered legislative process, they would be giving effect to the will of the legislature. Such judicial action would not be required, nor would it necessarily be desirable, but it would be defensible. The claim that the manner and form theory is not justified by its democratic nature, but in fact contradicts such considerations by expanding the constitutional role of the courts, can therefore be rejected.

VI. CONCLUSION

A clear normative justification can be developed to support the manner and form theory, which this book suggests is the conception of the doctrine of parliamentary sovereignty which now prevails in the contemporary UK constitution. This is a democratic justification, which can be fully understood when located in the framework provided by political constitutionalist theory. Rather than prevent absolutely the democratic Parliament from legislating about the future legislative process, we should recognise that this is legally permitted. Yet this does not mean that use of such power will be unfettered; instead, the legislative power to alter the manner and form must be exercised within, and thus structured and conditioned by the operation of, a system of democratic political accountability. When the necessity for, and nature of, such democratic political limits on legislative power are considered, it becomes clear that we need not be ambivalent or anxious about accepting the manner and form theory. Instead, ideas of trust, reciprocity, commitment and revolution indicate that it is possible for this legally unlimited lawmaking power to be effectively conditioned through democratic politics, without necessarily implicating the courts in the enforcement of legislative changes to the legislative process. In this sense, if support for the doctrine of parliamentary sovereignty in general is arguably best understood as reflecting a broader commitment to democratic political constitutionalism, support for the manner and form theory in particular can arguably be best understood as merely an extension of such a commitment. Therefore, just as it is democratic to allocate to Parliament the constitutional authority to legislate about any subject-matter, it is also democratic to allocate to Parliament the constitutional authority to legislate about the law-making process. In either situation, mechanisms of democratic political accountability will condition and control how this power can be used—albeit in different ways, and to different extents, depending on the circumstances—with Parliament ultimately answerable to the electorate for its legislative activity.

To establish a normative justification for the manner and form theory is important if it has now become the new orthodoxy in relation to the doctrine of parliamentary sovereignty in the UK constitution, in part to determine whether this development is to be welcomed or calls for reconsideration. Yet further, given the potentially extensive nature of the power which is afforded to Parliament by this conception of legally unlimited legislative authority, we need to try to understand how it might legitimately be used. That the general allocation to Parliament of legal power to alter the future legislative process is democratically justified in this particular way has direct implications for how that power ought to be exercised. For in addition to indicating how this broad legal authority is to be conditioned and controlled—through channels and mechanisms of democratic political accountability—this specific normative justification also provides substantive guidance as to the contours of, and limits to, this legislative power. If the manner and form theory of parliamentary sovereignty is to be democratically justified, it must not be used in ways which undermine its democratic foundation. Conversely, the fact that it might be used to effect positive democratic constitutional change can further reinforce the justification of the manner and form theory developed in this chapter. As a result, in the final chapter, we turn to consider the potential utility of the manner and form theory, in light of its democratic justification. And in so doing, we will see the crucial interaction between the democratic virtue of the manner and form theory, and the potential functions of this conception of legislative power.

8

The Potential Utility of the Manner and Form Theory

I. INTRODUCTION

THE AIM OF this final chapter is to explore the potential utility of the manner and form theory of parliamentary sovereignty, in light of the democratic justification developed for this conception of legally unlimited legislative authority in Chapter seven. The manner and form theory, I have argued, can be justified on the basis that it allocates expanded legislative power to a democratic institution, which must, and can, be conditioned through democratic politics. Yet this account is not simply a normative justification of an understanding of legislative sovereignty which allocates to Parliament the power to alter, by statute, the future law-making process—an understanding of legislative sovereignty which, I argued in Part II, must now be seen to provide the best explanation of constitutional practice in the contemporary UK constitution. Instead, the democratic justification for the manner and form theory also creates substantive conditions of use which pertain to the exercise of legislative power to modify the law-making process. These substantive conditions of use derive from the notion of democracy itself. In order for the manner and form theory to be democratically justified, the power to alter the legislative process which the theory recognises must be used in a way which reinforces, rather than contradicts, its underlying normative justification. Therefore, when legislating about the legislative process, Parliament must use the power established by the manner and form theory of parliamentary sovereignty in ways which are democratic.

What does this mean? In principle, any legislative change to the future law-making process must be justified politically, rather than legally, by reference to the notion of democracy. This is still a highly abstract guiding principle. It can be narrowed somewhat when it is recalled that a majoritarian conception of democracy has been defended in this book, with a so-called 'constitutional conception' rejected.[1] It is this majoritarian conception of democracy which continues to be relevant to the use of the legislative power recognised by the manner and form theory. When we think about using such power democratically, we therefore refer

---

[1] See chapter 1 of this volume, pp 34–41.

to a procedural conception of collective decision-making, according to which the political equality of citizens is acknowledged and respected by affording each an equal say in determining the future course of communal action. In this sense, decisions are democratic when taken by political equals, on the basis of simple majority voting. A substantive 'constitutional' conception of democracy, in contrast, which privileges certain specific moral or political values, placing them beyond the reach of majoritarian decision-making on the basis that they are democratically fundamental—a category of 'essential' rights and principles about which there will be much disagreement, and which is capable of being understood in a quite expansive way—is not relevant to our present discussion.

Yet even once it is established that it is majoritarian democracy with which we are here concerned, there remains considerable scope for uncertainty. As such, the aim of this chapter will be to explain what I understand the condition of use imposed by the democratic justification of the manner and form theory to require, and to illustrate what Parliament might legitimately attempt to achieve in exercise of this expanded legislative power. First, the context is set for this discussion by briefly exploring the present democratic state of the UK's political constitution. The use of the manner and form theory for democratic purposes will then be considered, providing a broad framework in which more specific examples can subsequently be explored. Three specific types of democratic reform, which would exploit the legislative power recognised by the manner and form theory, will then be set out: reform to the existing legislative institutions; reform to the existing legislative process; and structural reform of the UK's constitutional architecture. Finally, it will be considered whether the pursuit of such possibilities could eventually lead to the displacement of the sovereignty of Parliament as the foundational concept of the UK constitution, and whether, as such, acceptance of the manner and form theory actually has the potential to sow the seeds of the destruction of the doctrine of parliamentary sovereignty.

Given the nature of the argument which will be developed in this chapter, then, two important caveats must be issued at the outset. First, the argument here is not intended to provide a definitive blueprint of how the UK constitution ought to be reformed. Instead, what I aim to do is sketch a number of suggestions which might serve as starting points for further debate, which would be absolutely essential to establish the desirability of the changes here considered. While it will be apparent that I am instinctively sympathetic to much of the reform outlined in this chapter, I do not set out to demonstrate or justify fully the democratic necessity of any of this change. Secondly, the potential options explored in this chapter are not presented as an exhaustive statement of how the legislative power recognised by the manner and form theory might democratically be used. Again, this is simply intended to be a starting point for further discussion, and I am entirely open to the idea that other democratic uses of legislative power to alter the future law-making process might be imagined and justified. While what is presented in this chapter is not, therefore, in any sense a complete vision of where the UK constitution ought to go next, the fact that acceptance of the manner and form theory opens up these possibilities for consideration is itself a key aspect of the democratic virtue of this conception of parliamentary sovereignty. For when the manner and form theory is embraced, debate as to how the legislative process might deliberately be reformed becomes worthwhile, rather than redundant, as excluded by the perpetuation of the Diceyan notion that such change is legally impermissible. Instead, in moving beyond the orthodox Diceyan account of the scope of Parliament's legally unlimited legislative authority, the manner and form theory allows us to expose the traditional legislative process to the political scrutiny upon which a commitment to democratic government rightly insists.

II. THE STATE OF THE UK'S POLITICAL CONSTITUTION

Before we can consider potential change to the UK constitution, we must briefly establish the position from which we start, and in particular, identify the principal deficiencies of our present arrangements. The doctrine of parliamentary sovereignty is an important part of a democratic constitution, in that it operates to establish the primacy of democratic-decision making. Yet as this claim was developed in Chapter one, it was recognised that the existence of the doctrine of parliamentary sovereignty serves, in this sense, essentially as baseline for democratic government. The calibre of any particular system of government depends on a much richer set of considerations than whether a democratic Parliament is constitutionally allocated legally unlimited legislative authority. The doctrine of parliamentary sovereignty is a fundamentally democratic constitutional idea, but one around which a vibrant political culture must nevertheless still be developed. The nature of the broader democratic political system in which Parliament is located, and must function, will therefore be crucial to any attempt to assess the state of the UK's political constitution.

While making an assessment of this sort is, of course, far from straightforward, and to do so comprehensively would be beyond the scope of this chapter, a number of key considerations concerning the contemporary state of the UK constitution can nevertheless be identified. Of particular importance in such a system of representative democracy will be the related issues of how responsive democratic representatives are to the citizens who elect them, and how readily those citizens and other external groups or actors can challenge decisions taken in their name. The importance of these related issues is a reflection of the core ideas of democratic empowerment and accountability discussed in the previous chapter: citizens must be able to influence the actions of those whom they have elected to make decisions on their behalf, while also have the means by which to scrutinise and contest the use which has been made of public power. The formal institutional arrangements established in a constitution will only ever be one part of cultivating an effective and open democratic political culture in which such aspirations might be satisfied, yet they are nevertheless still of significance. And on this basis, we may look to the recent era of constitutional reform experienced in the UK as a starting point from which to analyse the present state of the political constitution.

The modern era of constitutional reform, beginning with the election of the first New Labour government in 1997, and arguably still underway, is one which it is difficult definitively to assess.[2] The broad range of reform instigated has given the constitution a superficial sheen, yet the lack of any particular unifying rationale—perhaps other than a desire to modernise, viewed as an end in itself—makes global evaluation of these fragmented changes challenging to undertake. To seek to craft any coherent, deep or meaningful overarching interpretation of what has occurred may therefore be a largely fruitless endeavour. What may crucially define this era of reform is that it is characterised by its discrete defining features. Some emphasise the significance of measures which have bolstered the power of the courts, such as the Human Rights Act 1998 (HRA) and the creation of the new Supreme Court.[3] Others have suggested the futility of such measures, and that their impact on the constitution has thus been overstated.[4] Freedom of Information (FOI) legislation appears to have produced 'greater transparency and stronger accountability',[5] in addition to prompting the parliamentary expenses scandal,[6] and exposing (in part) attempts by the Prince of Wales to influence government policy.[7] Yet FOI has not been transformative in the UK, in that it 'has not achieved better government decision-making, better public understanding, or greater public participation'.[8] Of greatest significance has been devolution to Scotland, Northern Ireland and Wales, creating new sites of democratic contestation, which are of value in themselves, while also locating responsibility for the exercise of a range of powers more closely to citizens. While the greater scope which has been created for diversity in policy as between the constituent nations of the UK, and the anomalous position of England, has at least the potential to

---

[2] See chapter 3 of this volume, pp 111–13.

[3] See, eg Bogdanor, *The New British Constitution* (2009) n 49 below; R Masterman, *The Separation of Powers in the Contemporary Constitution: Judicial Competence and Independence in the United Kingdom* (Cambridge, Cambridge University Press, 2010).

[4] See, eg KD Ewing, 'The Futility of the Human Rights Act' [2004] *PL* 829; KD Ewing, 'The Futility of the Human Rights Act—A Long Footnote' (2005) 37 *Bracton Law Journal* 41; KD Ewing and JC Tham, 'The Continuing Futility of the Human Rights Act' [2008] *PL* 668; KD Ewing, *The Bonfire of the Liberties: New Labour, Human Rights and the Rule of Law* (Oxford, Oxford University Press, 2010). For the contrary view, see A Lester, 'The Utility of the Human Rights Act: a reply to Keith Ewing' [2005] *PL* 249.

[5] R Hazell, B Worthy and M Glover, *The Impact of the Freedom of Information Act on Central Government in the UK: Does FOI Work?* (Basingstoke, Palgrave Macmillan, 2010) 266.

[6] See, eg P Leyland, 'Freedom of Information and the 2009 Parliamentary Expenses Scandal' [2009] *PL* 675; B Worthy, 'Freedom of Information and Parliament' in A Horne, G Drewry and D Oliver (eds), *Parliament and the Law* (Oxford, Hart Publishing, 2013) 152–57; G Little and D Stopforth, 'The Legislative Origins of the MPs' Expenses Scandal' (2013) 76 *MLR* 83.

[7] See, eg M Gordon, 'Prince Charles' Correspondence Back in Court—Reflections on *R (Evans) v Attorney General*', *UK Constitutional Law Association Blog* (22 July 2013) www.ukconstitutionallaw. org/blog.

[8] Hazell, Worthy, and Glover, *Does FOI Work?* (2010) n 5 above, 266.

generate instability,[9] so far devolution has arguably been, from a legal perspective, 'a success story'.[10] The relatively smooth path to agreement on a legal basis for the 2014 referendum on Scottish independence provides strong evidence that a functional relationship between devolved and central governments can be maintained when even the most fundamentally disputed topics are in issue.[11]

Yet many of the traditional features of the constitution endure, remaining either untouched or merely moderately modified. The House of Lords remains an undemocratic upper chamber, if no longer one dominated by hereditary peers. The voting system for elections to the House of Commons stands apart from the more representative systems used for devolved and European elections,[12] and may be growing increasingly unsuited to a more pluralistic electorate.[13] The head of state remains a hereditary monarch, although succession to the 'modern' crown will no longer be determined by reference to gender, nor will future heirs be disqualified by marrying a Catholic.[14] Some royal prerogative powers have been codified, or in some cases modified, in statute,[15] with a formal account of the 'rules of the game' produced in the form of the Cabinet Manual.[16] Yet the UK government—and within it the Prime Minister in particular[17]—nonetheless retains ample power, and continues to dominate the political system. Although elements of the reformed constitution are still under construction—in particular, the devolution settlement—or under threat of reconstruction—in particular, the HRA—many of the structures and institutions of the pre-reform constitution thus remain resolutely resilient to change.

If we look beyond the change to these formal constitutional arrangements—or the lack of change, depending on the perspective adopted—a number of significant underlying problems persist. The most recent comprehensive audit of UK democracy identified a number of 'core problems'.[18] These included that '[p]ublic

---

[9] J Mitchell, *Devolution in the UK* (Manchester, Manchester University Press, 2009) 225.

[10] A Tomkins, 'Scotland's Choice, Britain's Future' (2014) 130 *LQR* 215, 234.

[11] See generally, ibid 223–30 on the path to a 'lawful referendum'.

[12] See generally *The Governance of Britain—Review of Voting Systems: The Experience of New Voting Systems in the United Kingdom Since 1997* (Cm 7304, 2008).

[13] See, eg J Curtice, 'So What Went Wrong with the Electoral System? The 2010 Election Result and the Debate About Electoral Reform' (2010) 63 *Parliamentary Affairs* 623, 636.

[14] Succession to the Crown Act 2013 ss 1–2.

[15] See, eg Constitutional Reform and Governance Act 2010, placing powers of management over the civil service, and the role of Parliament in treaty ratification, on a statutory footing: ss 1–18, 20–25. For a more fundamental change to the previous position under the royal prerogative, see Fixed-term Parliaments Act 2011, displacing the prerogative power to dissolve Parliament. For further discussion of these issues, see B Thompson and M Gordon, *Cases and Materials on Constitutional and Administrative Law*, 11th edn (Oxford, Oxford University Press, 2014) 163–81.

[16] *The Cabinet Manual: A Guide to Laws, Conventions and Rules on the Operation of Government*, 1st edn (October 2011). For general discussion, see ibid 181–85.

[17] See generally House of Commons Political and Constitutional Reform Committee, *Role and Powers of the Prime Minister*, HC 351 (24 June 2014). This is not, however, simply a contemporary concern; see, eg GW Jones, 'The Prime Minister's Power' (1964) 18 *Parliamentary Affairs* 167.

[18] S Wilks-Heeg, A Blick and S Crone, *How Democratic is the UK? The 2012 Audit* (Liverpool, Democratic Audit, 2012) 9.

faith in democratic institutions is decaying', '[p]olitical inequality is widening rapidly', and 'the influence large corporations and wealthy individuals now wield on the UK political system is unprecedented'.[19] Most concerning of all:

> Almost all available indicators suggest that representative democracy is in long-term, terminal decline, but no viable alternative model of democracy currently exists. All measures of popular engagement with, and attitudes towards, representative democracy show a clear decline over time. Whether we seek to measure it via turnout in elections, membership of political parties, voter identification with political parties, or public faith in the system of government, the pattern is the same. While the same basic trends are found in all established democracies, the UK compares especially poorly on just about every conceivable measure.[20]

Such disenchantment is similarly evident in the most recent British Social Attitudes survey. A clear 'democratic deficit' can be identified, with the existing political system failing to meet many citizens' expectations of what democracy ought to entail.[21] In particular, there is a 'significant democratic deficit' with respect to, among other things, 'the government's ability to … involve citizens sufficiently in decision-making'.[22] Although there is some evidence to suggest that this is not leading to disengagement from the political system—with those reporting the largest deficit with respect to the participatory elements of democracy more likely to be 'critical citizens', and continuing to engage in political activity[23]—the very existence of this gap between expectations and perceived performance in itself gives cause for concern. Further dissatisfaction with the UK political system is evident in a perceived sense of powerlessness, identified in the Hansard Society's most recent audit of political engagement: citizens feel they have 'very little influence on decision-making' locally, but especially nationally, with desire actually to participate outpacing this by a distinct margin.[24] And Parliament, in particular, is seen by only a minority of citizens to be an institution which 'encourages public involvement in politics'.[25]

This presents a rather bleak picture of the present position of the UK's political constitution. That it is one which tends to be exhibited throughout established democratic states does little to assuage the fact that this is a problematic

---

[19] ibid 9–10.

[20] ibid 10.

[21] S Butt and R Fitzgerald, 'Democracy' in A Park, J Curtice and C Bryson (eds), *British Social Attitudes: The 31st Report* (London, NatCen Social Research, 2014) 16.

[22] ibid 13. The data on which this conclusion is based specifically explored views on (i) the extent to which the government explained its decision to voters; and (ii) whether citizens have the final say on the most important issues by referendum.

[23] ibid 15. On 'critical citizens', who 'value democracy as an ideal yet who remain dissatisfied with the performance of their political system, and particularly the core institutions of representative government', see P Norris (ed), *Critical Citizens: Global Support for Democratic Government* (Oxford, Oxford University Press, 1999) 269.

[24] R Fox and M Korris, *Audit of Political Engagement 11: The 2014 Report* (London, Hansard Society, 2014) 28.

[25] ibid 59–60.

state of affairs.[26] Responding to the challenge posed by citizens' contemporary disillusionment is, no doubt, a huge task, given the complex range of factors contributing to this democratic malaise. Any solution will necessarily be political in part, but underlying economic and social dynamics are certain also to be of considerable significance.[27] We must therefore be realistic about the impact that proposals for formal constitutional change may be capable of having on democratic deficiencies, when substantively unequal power relations play a crucial role in conditioning the manner in which the political constitution functions. Nevertheless, while it would be complacent to believe that constitutional reform is a panacea for democratic disenchantment, there remains a responsibility to reassess, and potentially refresh, our constitutional arrangements. That any constitutional solution which might be imagined will not be capable of comprehensively resolving our present democratic difficulties—if indeed such resolution is even possible—does not provide a reason to evade this challenge.

We will shortly consider the way that acceptance of the manner and form theory might enhance our ability to address this profound challenge. Yet while there will be much scope for debate about how precisely this might best be achieved, if democratic disillusionment and decline is the fundamental modern problem for the UK's political constitution, one thing is abundantly clear. A shift to common law constitutionalism is not the solution to the UK's contemporary constitutional affliction. Common law constitutionalism no doubt has grand aspirations, is couched in the agreeable rhetoric of equality, liberty, fairness, and justice, and purports to present us with the holy grail of political philosophy: a system of governance which guarantees just outcomes. But, despite the enticing abstract possibility which it appears to offer, it would be wrong to think that common law constitutionalism stands somehow above the political fray in which the UK's contemporary democratic discomfort is manifested and lamented. For the modern allure of common law constitutionalism is crucially amplified by its presentation as an alternative to the concurrently maligned democratic political process. In both *Jackson* and *Axa*, the high points of contemporary common law constitutionalist reasoning, the envisaged power to reject legislation in exceptional circumstances is sketched as a direct response to arbitrary political action.[28] Subtly, then, a common law constitutionalist analysis thus positions the courts as an institution which is capable of alleviating the potential excesses of an insular, over-powerful ruling elite. Yet the outright repudiation of the doctrine of parliamentary sovereignty which this constitutional philosophy requires, in favour of the venerable values of the common law, is one which must be guarded against.

---

[26] See, eg RJ Dalton, *Democratic Challenges, Democratic Choices: The Erosion of Political Support in Advanced Industrial Democracies* (Oxford, Oxford University Press, 2004).

[27] For discussion of these issues in the US context see, eg LM Bartels, *Unequal Democracy: The Political Economy of the New Gilded Age* (Princeton NJ, Princeton University Press, 2008).

[28] *R (on the application of Jackson) v Attorney General* [2005] UKHL 56; [2006] 1 AC 262, [71], [102], [107], [159]; *Axa General Insurance Ltd v Lord Advocate* [2011] UKSC 46; [2012] 1 AC 868, [49]–[51].

The judicial remedy offered by common law constitutionalism is simply not an appropriate solution to the problems of our political system. We cannot rely on even the most benevolent and enlightened judiciary to fix what are, fundamentally, democratic defects in the UK constitution. As Griffith has argued, '[i]f we are to create a more just and a more free society, we must do it the hard way—without Moses'.[29] The concerted effort needed to improve the condition of the UK's political constitution, as Ewing and Tham suggest, must proceed with 'less loose talk about "rights", and more serious talk about how to create powerful representative institutions'.[30] Common law constitutionalism, in this sense, is not simply a distraction from the genuine work required. Rather, as Bellamy notes, there is a 'real danger' presented by this legalistic alternative: 'tyranny by unrepresentative minorities'.[31] A thriving democratic constitution will not be delivered by even a Herculean judiciary, through their conduit, the common law. For if our democracy requires renewal, to discard the doctrine of parliamentary sovereignty—the core democratic principle of the UK's political constitution—would be utterly perplexing. More and better democratic government is required in the UK. And as such, making the constitution less democratic, a corollary of an acceptance of common law constitutionalism,[32] is surely not what ought to be done. Instead, we can turn to the manner and form theory, to consider the possibilities for democratic political reform which are made available to us by acceptance of this conception of parliamentary sovereignty.

III. USING THE MANNER AND FORM THEORY DEMOCRATICALLY

What does it mean to say that the legislative power to alter the legislative process, recognised by the manner and form theory of parliamentary sovereignty, should be used (and should only be used) democratically? This political limit on the use of such legislative power stems directly from the normative justification for the manner and form theory which was developed in Chapter seven. As a matter of law, it is necessarily the case that the sovereign Parliament may use its power to change the future law-making process in any way at all, for this power is legally unlimited. Nevertheless, for the existence of this expansive legal power to be justified, a strong constitutional condition of use attaches to Parliament's legislative authority to modify the legislative process. As the manner and form theory is justified on democratic grounds—on the basis that it concerns power that must, and can, be conditioned by politics—the legislative authority it recognises should be used in a way which is compatible with the normative basis for its existence.

---

[29] JAG Griffith, 'The Brave New World of Sir John Laws' (2000) 63 *MLR* 159, 165.
[30] Ewing and Tham, 'The Continuing Futility of the Human Rights Act' [2008] n 4 above, 693.
[31] R Bellamy, *Political Constitutionalism: A Republican Defence of the Constitutionality of Democracy* (Cambridge, Cambridge University Press, 2007) 263.
[32] See chapter 3 of this volume, pp 137–49.

Given the doctrine of parliamentary sovereignty in general is a norm which is principally justified on democratic grounds, it might be queried whether this same condition of use must be understood to extend to cover the legislative power of Parliament in general. As a matter of principle, such an extension of this condition of use may well be justifiable, if indeed it is not a necessary consequence of making such a claim in the context of the manner and form theory. In that sense, when Parliament is exercising its substantive power to alter the law, it can credibly be argued that the enactment of undemocratic legislation would not be politically justified. There are two reasons, however, that the political requirement that legislative power be used democratically obtains differently with respect to Parliament's substantive law-making authority in general, than it does in relation to the special additional branch of power recognised by the manner and form theory in particular, and thus is of much less significance in practice.

First, in the context of substantive legislative power—the power to alter substantive legal rules in any way whatsoever—notions of what it means to use that power 'democratically' are likely to be much more varied, given the infinite number of different ends for which that legislative power might be engaged. The notion of democracy would, for example, clearly be engaged in the context of legislation intended to alter voter registration arrangements. Yet clearly, in such a situation, a rich set of practical democratic considerations would necessarily require attention—what is likely to achieve optimal levels of registration, how this might affect turnout, how fraud might be minimised and so on—and the rather minimalistic and abstract majoritarian principle on which the constitutional primacy of democratic decision-making is based will be unlikely to add much to such debates. In that sense, the generality of the political injunction that power should be used democratically may appear essentially rhetorical in the complex circumstances that substantive law-making is liable to present. Secondly, and conversely, in many situations where substantive legislative power is to be exercised to change the law in some way, the notion of democracy will simply be irrelevant. Consideration of reform of deep sea mining legislation, to take an example at random,[33] is unlikely to be animated by debate as to what would be democratic, as opposed to a range of other substantive factors of much greater importance in that particular context.

We might therefore, in principle, suggest that substantive legislation should not be undemocratic in nature, but this is likely either to be either irrelevant or of little practical utility. However, when considering the exercise of the additional power recognised by the manner and form theory, in particular—the legislative power to alter the future law-making process—considerations of democracy will, in contrast, always be relevant, and provide a much more significant guiding principle. For when we are exclusively dealing with questions of legislative procedure, it will be the narrower majoritarian conception of democracy, upon which the

---

[33] See, eg Deep Sea Mining Act 2014.

justification of parliamentary sovereignty is based, which will be directly engaged. In this context, then, the political condition that legislative power should be used democratically becomes much more meaningful, because it serves to focus our attention on a well-defined issue which is of fundamental importance to sustaining the justification for parliamentary sovereignty, rather than appearing to provide—as it does in the context of debate about the use of substantive legislative power—a well-intentioned, but rather intangible gloss on issues which deserve more wide-ranging analysis. The democratic condition of use on legislative power is, therefore, of special importance in the context of the additional law-making authority which is recognised in particular by the manner and form theory.

In the specific context of the exercise of legislative power to alter the future law-making process, then, we are focused on the democratic nature of the procedures used, and the institutions those procedures engage. The legislative authority recognised by the manner and form theory could be used 'democratically' in attempts to pursue a number of (potentially interconnected) goals. These democratic ends might principally include legislating: to remove undemocratic influences, procedures, arrangements or institutions from featuring prominently in the law-making process; and/or—depending on whether we choose to open up new space for this, or simply supplement the existing scheme—to introduce into the legislative process new democratic influences, procedures, arrangements or institutions. A number of specific examples of what this might constitute in the specific context of the UK will be considered in the next section. But in light of the problem of contemporary democratic disillusionment, identified as a key challenge for the UK's political constitution in the previous section, we must note one particular general democratic end that might be pursued using the legislative power recognised by the manner and form theory. This is the potential for the legislative process to be altered so as to enhance existing opportunities, or create further opportunities, for citizens to participate in or influence the legislative process as political equals. Clearly, democratic change to the legislative process of this kind does not provide a comprehensive programme for addressing the democratic disquiet of citizens. Yet reform of the legislative process which does engage citizens more directly in democratic decision-making can at least be seen to offer the potential to challenge some aspects of the political disillusionment which is presently being experienced in the UK.

This is still a rather abstract framework for the democratic use of the legislative power recognised by the manner and form theory. Yet this is inevitable, for even when we narrow our focus to consider the democratic nature of decision-making processes, and the institutions engaged in those processes, from a majoritarian perspective, there will remain scope for debate about what is (or is not) democratic. For example, must all of the institutions engaged in the law-making process be democratic for that process itself to be considered democratic overall? Is a representative democratic process preferable to direct democratic-decision making? In either case, what voting system ought to be used to determine the result we have reached? Such reasonable disagreement is bound to occur, but is not something to be regretted. Instead, a broad commitment to majoritarian democracy requires that we 'rebuild the ship at sea'.[34] No democratic political system will ever be perfect, but will itself be the subject of the very legitimate disagreement which compels the adoption of majoritarian decision-making processes in the first place.[35] The state of the political system must therefore be 'kept under constant review', with such debates 'informed by a culture of democracy, valuing responsible deliberation and political equality'.[36] That the manner and form theory opens up new lines of debate as to the structure of the UK's constitutional architecture is therefore an important part of the democratic virtue of this conception of parliamentary sovereignty. It allows us to take seriously our responsibility to keep the democratic political process under review, and a degree of ambiguity about how the legislative power recognised by the manner and form theory may justifiably be used is thus essential to ensure that such ongoing reappraisals are not improperly constricted.

Crucially, however, while assessment of the use of legislative power to change the future law-making procedure by reference to (majoritarian) democratic principle will be a relatively open process, it will be an exercise in political, rather than legal, justification. From a legal perspective, the validity of legislation altering the future law-making process will be determined simply in accordance with the distinction between matters of procedure and matters of substance. Statutory conditions which are procedural in nature will be lawful, substantive limits on legislative power will not.[37] As a result, broad questions as to the democratic character of procedural legislative conditions are not passed to the courts by the manner and form theory, but instead left to be settled—as is especially appropriate in this context—in the political arena. If this substantive condition of use were a legal requirement, the imprecision with which it is formulated would no doubt be objectionable, on the basis that it created excessive scope for (contestable) judicial judgement to be exercised as to the meaning and demands of democracy. Yet with disputes as to what constitutes a democratic use of legislative power to be

---

[34] Bellamy, *Political Constitutionalism* (2007) n 31 above, 174.

[35] See chapter 1 of this volume, pp 34–41.

[36] J Waldron, 'The Core of the Case Against Judicial Review' (2006) 115 *Yale Law Journal* 1346, 1361–62.

[37] See chapter 2 of this volume, pp 68–75. This, of course, leaves open the question of limits which are procedural, as a matter of form, but make it impossible for legislation in future to be enacted. Such limits ought to be considered as unlawful substantive conditions, in accordance with the manner and form theory. Yet I regard 'impossible in future to legislate' to be a high threshold, and not one which would be met, to take a common example, by a two-thirds super-majority requirement; as explained below, such conditions ought to be dealt with as a matter of political justification, rather than legal validity. Debating what ought to be done in response to unlawful conditions which are procedural in form, but ultimately substantive in effect, should not, however, dominate consideration of the potential utility of the manner and form theory. There is little reason to expect that Parliament would seek to use its power so disingenuously, especially when it will be conditioned by demanding political norms: see chapter 7 of this volume, pp 302–17. As a result, fringe examples of this kind should be regarded as a distraction from the far more important issue of how the manner and form theory might positively be used.

settled politically—as a matter of justification—rather than legally—as a matter of validity—this difficulty does not arise. By drawing this distinction between justification and validity, and locating the assessment of the democratic character of the use of legislative power in the political, rather than the legal, sphere, it is unnecessary to be overly prescriptive about how this condition ought to be understood and implemented. Instead, the democratic benefits of leaving this notion indefinite, and susceptible to development in a number of directions, can be experienced because it is a condition of use which will not fall to be judicially framed and defined, while still nonetheless being capable of structuring constitutionally the use of legislative authority.

In sum, the democratic condition of use is one particular to the special circumstances presented by the additional authority recognised by the manner and form theory—Parliament's legislative power to change the future law-making process. It requires us to focus on the democratic character of the processes by which legislation is created, and the institutions engaged in those processes. It is thus specific enough to provide a meaningful guide to the use of power, while also being sufficiently open to accommodate legitimate, and inevitable, disagreement about how democratic decision-making should be structured. And this balance between specificity and openness can be maintained because the meaning and implications of this constitutional condition of use are to be worked out through the democratic political process itself, rather than framed by legal norms and determined by judicial decision.

Yet while there is ample scope for debate about how legislative power to alter the future law-making process might be used 'democratically', it is equally important to establish what will *not* be justified. In this respect, we can be quite clear in at least some of our conclusions, bearing in mind that the doctrine of parliamentary sovereignty in general, and the manner and form theory in particular, are justified by reference to a majoritarian conception of democracy. For as it is this understanding of democratic principle with which specific exercises of legislative power must be therefore be compatible, we can consequently exclude in particular—at least as a matter of political justification—super-majority requirements. Such conditions will generally stand to be regarded as procedural in nature, and therefore can potentially be considered a lawful use of legislative authority to modify the future law-making process. At a particular threshold, a super-majority condition may cross the boundary from being legitimately considered as procedural in nature, and become substantive in effect. At this point—where a threshold, in effect, served to require an unachievable degree of consensus, or near unanimity, in a society for action to be taken—such a condition would become unlawful, rather than 'merely' unjustified. There is little point in trying to determine where this point lies in the abstract, for it may to some extent be context dependent: an 80 per cent super-majority requirement to enact legislation to extend the life of Parliament beyond five years, for example, might be thought much more tolerable than the same requirement applied to the enactment of legislation approving the government's annual budget. This is not to say that the substantive importance of what is made subject to a super-majority requirement is of crucial importance; but rather that the legality of even high threshold conditions, the procedural nature of which might otherwise be questionable, could go unchallenged over a lengthy period of time, and obtain greater force as a result.

In any event, speculation about where the line should be drawn between super-majority requirements which are authentically procedural in nature, and thus lawful, and those which are only ostensibly so, and thus unlawful, is a hypothetical distraction from the key issue in this context: the creation of *any* super-majority requirement is an unjustified use of the legislative power to alter the future law-making process. A super-majority procedural requirement will be inherently incompatible with the majoritarian conception of democracy on which the justification of the doctrine of parliamentary sovereignty, and in particular, the manner and form theory of legally unlimited power, is premised. Such conditions, even if at what might be thought a more modest two-thirds majority level, present a fundamental challenge to the notion of the political equality of citizens upon which majoritarian democratic government is based.[38] For super-majority conditions violate the requirements that, when making collective decisions, all members of a political community should have 'equal voice and equal decisional authority'.[39] The degree by which they violate these requirements, such as the difference between a 55 per cent super-majority and a 75 per cent super-majority, may be significant in practice, but is irrelevant in principle: any procedural condition which imposes a requirement which exceeds that of a simple majority will, as a result, be undemocratic.

It might be suggested, in reply, that it is possible to justify the imposition of a super-majority decisional threshold as a democratic pre-commitment; the classic analogy used in this regard is to present citizens as Ulysses, seeking to be bound to the mast of their ship, so that they might avoid their society's equivalent of the sirens' call.[40] Yet this analogy does not hold. Where there is disagreement in a community about the nature and importance of the norms or principles which a super-majority requirement is established to protect, this cannot coherently be understood as a rational pre-commitment made in a time of calm and clarity, and designed to prevent rash future action which might threaten abiding fundamental convictions. Instead, it is 'the artificially sustained ascendancy of one view in the polity over other views whilst the complex moral issues between them remain unresolved'.[41] Nor can such constraints be justified as enabling, in the sense that

---

[38] See chapter 1 of this volume, pp 34–36.

[39] Waldron, 'Core of the Case Against Judicial Review' (2006) n 36 above, 1389.

[40] See J Elster, *Ulysses and the Sirens: Studies in Rationality and Irrationality* (Cambridge, Cambridge University Press, 1984). See also J Elster, *Ulysses Unbound: Studies in Rationality, Precommitment, and Constraints* (Cambridge, Cambridge University Press, 2000) 88–96, revising to some extent his prior position.

[41] J Waldron, *Law and Disagreement* (Oxford, Oxford University Press, 1999) 268.

by closing off some lines of action, they make others easier to pursue.[42] For even if it were true that constitutional pre-commitments actually possessed this enabling character—a claim powerfully rebutted by Waldron[43]—then this would merely give us something to balance against their significant limitation of the ability of future generations of citizens to take decisions for themselves as political equals. It would, not, however, make such constraints democratic; as Paine famously argued,

> [e]very age and generation must be as free to act for itself, *in all cases*, as the ages and generations which preceded it. The vanity and presumption of governing beyond the grave, is the most ridiculous and insolent of all tyrannies.[44]

That attempts to defend such super-majority requirements as democratic must be seen to fail means that it cannot be considered justifiable for Parliament to exercise its legislative power to alter the future law-making process so as to impose such procedural conditions. To do so would undermine the democratic foundation on which the general existence of the expanded legislative power recognised by the manner and form theory is based. This being the case, identification of the precise point at which such super-majority requirements cross the line between procedural (in form) and substantive (in limiting effect)—and therefore between lawful and unlawful, as a matter of legal principle—is in practice ultimately insignificant. Since all super-majority requirements are unjustified, from the perspective of democratic political principle, they are also constitutionally illegitimate, and therefore the question of their putative legality ought never to become active. The fact that undemocratic super-majority requirements are to be rejected as an unjustifiable use of legislative authority, however, far from exhausts the possibilities presented to us by the manner and form theory. Instead, we now turn to consider a number of examples of how legislative power to alter the legislative process might be used for positive democratic ends, and in so doing, contribute to a re-invigoration of the UK's political constitution.

IV. MANNER AND FORM AND CONSTITUTIONAL REFORM

The legislative power to modify the future law-making process, allocated to Parliament in accordance with the manner and form theory of parliamentary sovereignty must be exercised to enhance or supplement existing democratic practice. In this sense, use of such power to legislate about the legislative process could constitute a potentially crucial component of any future scheme to reform the UK constitution. As we move into this increasingly subjective territory, it is worth recalling the warning of Jennings, that '[t]he "principles" of constitutional

---

[42] See S Holmes, *Passions and Constraint: On the Theory of Liberal Democracy* (Chicago IL, University of Chicago Press, 1995).
[43] Waldron, *Law and Disagreement* (1999) n 41 above, 275–77.
[44] T Paine, *The Rights of Man* (Mineola NY, Dover Publications, 1999) 9.

lawyers are always a dangerous foundation for the formation of policy'.[45] It might be thought that this danger is less acute when the principle with which we are concerned is democracy, which is hardly the exclusive concern of constitutional lawyers. Nevertheless, the limitations of an academic reform agenda must still be taken seriously; the various uses of legislative power sketched below are simply presented as suggestions potentially deserving of, but certainly requiring, further discussion among all democratic actors. As a result, none of these proposals is intended to be fully developed, as opposed to an initial starting point. And none, it should be emphasised, is in any way suggested to be inherently required by the adoption of the manner and form theory of parliamentary sovereignty. Instead, what I aim to demonstrate is that there are a range of potential ways in which the present legislative process could be altered by statute, and that these options are open to us to pursue—in that they are legally permissible, and democratically justifiable—*according to the terms of our existing constitutional settlement, based on the doctrine of parliamentary sovereignty*. This reform is not legally prohibited, requiring a change in the fundamental norms we accept as underpinning the UK's existing political constitution to occur for it to be plausibly considered. Nor does it require the doctrine of parliamentary sovereignty, and the virtues of a constitutional order based on legally unlimited legislative authority, to be abandoned. Instead, the modern shift to the manner and form conception of parliamentary sovereignty, traced in Part II of this book, provides a clear constitutional foundation for us to think more freely and widely about how the UK's political constitution might be reformed, without supplanting the democratic foundation upon which it is based.

The possibility of democratic constitutional reform to the legislative process will be considered in three broad, but non-exhaustive, categories of change: (i) reform of the existing legislative institutions; (ii) reform of the existing legislative process; and (iii) reform to the structure of the UK constitution. A further category of change to the law-making process, which will not be discussed in detail, is a statutory condition as to the future legislative form, the most obvious example of which is the requirement that express words be used to give effect to some specified policy preference. In refraining from here considering express language requirements in depth, I do not mean to indicate that they are undemocratic or unjustified in character. Indeed, it may well be democratically desirable to insist that some especially controversial forms of legislative action must be expressed with particular clarity to be legally effective, so long as they are still susceptible to being determined on a simple majority basis. Yet the primary reason that requirements of legislative form are of use is that they allow readily rebuttable 'standing commitments' to be made, in relation to subjects deemed to be of special significance, and thus prevent Parliament from contravening key norms or principles by

---

[45] WI Jennings, *The Law and the Constitution*, 5th edn (London, University of London Press, 1959) 317.

'its own inadvertence'.[46] Any democratic benefits of such statutory requirements as to future legislative form therefore accrue essentially incidentally; the primary aim of such conditions is to insist upon a need for certain legislative goals to be achieved in clear and unequivocal terms. While the use of such conditions can still be justified as compatible with the democratic account of the manner and form theory, they are therefore of limited significance—from this particular perspective—when considered as an abstract device, apart from the norms or principles with respect to which they might be employed. The three categories of change which will be considered in this section, in contrast, inherently and directly engage considerations of democratic principle, and thus provide far more interesting and elaborate examples of how legislative power might justifiably be used to alter the future law-making process.

The sheer scope of the reform to the legislative process, and thus to the UK's political constitution itself, which will be shown in principle to be possible when the manner and form theory is accepted thus clearly dispels the notion, rooted in orthodox thinking as to the nature of the doctrine of parliamentary sovereignty, that this fundamental norm somehow serves as a barrier to constitutional change. In no sense, then, are we compelled to conclude that '[w]hatever else may be less than perfect about our current obeisance to parliamentary sovereignty, its real practical deficiency is that it has a chilling effect on constitutional change'.[47] Indeed, rather than view the sovereignty of Parliament as a doctrine which 'obliterates the likelihood of effective mechanisms for constitutional change',[48] we should recognise that this fundamental norm—especially when understood in accordance with the manner and form theory of legally unlimited legislative authority—operates actually to facilitate the consideration of reform(s) to the UK's political constitution. That this can be achieved without the UK morphing into a 'constitutional state based upon a separation of powers', in which the sovereignty of Parliament persists only 'in form, but not in substance',[49] demonstrates that the normative appeal of the manner and form theory, as a matter of democratic principle, is ultimately reinforced by its extensive prospective utility.

---

[46] J Goldsworthy, *Parliamentary Sovereignty: Contemporary Debates* (Cambridge, Cambridge University Press, 2010) 181, 182.

[47] R Gordon, 'Constitutional Change and Parliamentary Sovereignty—The Impossible Dialectic' in M Qvortrup (ed), *The British Constitution: Continuity and Change* (Oxford, Hart Publishing, 2013) 160.

[48] ibid 162.

[49] V Bogdanor, *The New British Constitution* (Oxford, Hart Publishing, 2009) 285, 283. Bogdanor is sympathetic to attempts to cultivate a more 'popular' constitution, yet there is no need to assume that, in so doing, the UK must *also* become a constitutional state: see, eg 306, 310. The manner and form theory of parliamentary sovereignty provides a route to a more popular constitution, without requiring us to abandon the idea of legally unlimited legislative authority.

A. Reform of Existing Legislative Institutions

The first category of democratic change to the legislative process which might be considered in light of our acceptance of the manner and form theory is reform of the existing legislative institutions. There is no reason to treat the existing tripartite Queens-Lords-Commons legislative formula as constitutionally sacrosanct, or assume it is inherently unimprovable. Two obvious options are presented in this category. First, the legislative process might be reformed to remove undemocratic institutions from the legislative process, or limit the extent to which such institutions participate in the law-making process. Most straightforwardly, this could take the form of an alteration of the ordinary legislative process which reduced or eliminated the role played by the Queen or House of Lords. No doubt either suggestion would be a matter for serious, and likely animated, political debate. While the powers of both the monarch and the upper chamber have been significantly curtailed by constitutional convention and statute,[50] for some they remain archaic relics of a pre-democratic age. It may be suggested that the granting of royal assent to legislation is not worth objecting to, given the utter formality of this process in the modern constitution.[51] Similarly, the House of Lords—especially in its present (largely) post-hereditary condition—might be said to play an important role in checking the power of the House of Commons, and bringing expertise to the detailed process of legislative scrutiny.[52] Both of these claims (and others to similar effect which might be imagined) would deserve thorough consideration as part of any political discussion of the merits of such change to the institutions engaged in the process of legislating. But fundamentally, a clear democratic justification exists for removing both the monarch and the House of Lords from the existing legislative process: these institutions are not elected, representative or accountable, and might legitimately have their role in the law-making process eliminated.

This justification would similarly extend to cover further reduction, or indeed clarification, of the role played by either institution in the legislative process. An important example in this respect might be the current requirement of parliamentary procedure that consent be given by the monarch, or in some cases the heir to the throne, before Parliament may consider legislation which might affect their interests.[53] While distinct from the royal assent, which is legally required at the end of the legislative process, the practice of obtaining such consent prior to the consideration of certain categories of legislation may be thought democratically objectionable in principle, or in practice, on the basis that this power will

---

[50] See chapter 1 of this volume, pp 44–45.

[51] See, eg R Brazier, 'Royal Assent to Legislation' (2013) 129 *LQR* 184.

[52] See, eg M Russell, *The Contemporary House of Lords: Westminster Bicameralism Revived* (Oxford, Oxford University Press, 2013).

[53] See, eg House of Commons Political and Constitutional Reform Committee, *The Impact of Queen's and Prince's Consent on the Legislative Process*, HC 784 (26 March 2014).

be exercised on ministerial advice, and therefore in effect, by the government. As a matter of parliamentary procedure, this practice could be dispensed with, or simply more fully illuminated, by non-statutory means, but the potentially contestable nature of such a change might require an Act of Parliament for the necessary clarity to be achieved.[54]

The second option for democratic change in this category would be to introduce new institutions into the legislative process. This would most likely be to take the place of either the Queen or House of Lords, although this would not necessarily be the case. Most obviously, the requirement to assent to legislation could quite straightforwardly be passed to an elected head of state, or an elected upper chamber created in place of the House of Lords. There is much debate about whether such a replacement chamber ought to be entirely or partially elected, whether its functions would need to be altered, and, perhaps most significantly, whether the House of Commons could expect to retain primacy over a reformed substitute for the Lords.[55] But the fact that no universally accepted model might be thought to exist for a revising chamber in a parliamentary democracy does not provide a justification for the continuing failure to replace the House of Lords as presently constituted with something which is democratically defensible.

Yet we might also look to supplement the existing institutions engaged in the legislative process—whether as they are presently composed, or even after some future democratic reform. The direct engagement of citizens, in their entirety, in the legislative process will be considered in the next section. We might also, however, wish to consider proposals for the creation of standing bodies, comprising citizens, and whether there could be a role for such institutions in the legislative process. Such citizens' assemblies, or 'mini-publics',[56] where created, tend to be used in a strictly advisory capacity, often developing proposals in response to a specific mandate, which are then put to the wider community for consideration. Such deliberative institutions have recently been used in Canada, developing proposals for electoral reform in British Columbia in 2004 and Ontario in 2006; to similar ends in the Netherlands in 2006; and in an attempt to rewrite the Icelandic constitution between 2010 and 2012.[57] The composition of the recent

---

[54] This point is discussed ibid [16].

[55] These issues and more were raised in relation to the much criticised, and ultimately abandoned, proposals for reform of the Lords by the coalition government: see, eg Joint Committee on the Draft House of Lords Reform Bill, *Draft House of Lords Reform Bill—Report*, HL Paper 284-I, HC 1313-I (23 April 2012).

[56] See generally, G Smith, *Democratic Innovations: Designing Institutions for Citizen Participation* (Cambridge, Cambridge University Press, 2009) ch 3.

[57] For a brief overview of some of these different processes, see M Gordon, 'Time for a Citizens' Assembly on Lords Reform?', *UK Constitutional Law Association Blog* (17 October 2012): www.ukconstitutionallaw.org/blog; House of Commons Political and Constitutional Reform Committee, *Do We Need a Constitutional Convention for the UK?*, HC 371 (28 March 2013) 10–12; M Gordon, 'Do We Need a Constitutional Convention for the UK?', *Scottish Constitutional Futures Forum Blog* (14 March 2014): www.scottishconstitutionalfutures.org/. On the British Columbia assembly in particular, see generally ME Warren and H Pearse (eds), *Designing Deliberative Democracy: The British Columbia Citizens' Assembly* (Cambridge, Cambridge University Press, 2008).

Constitutional Convention in the Republic of Ireland, held between 2012 and 2014, was structured in a similar way, with two-thirds of its members citizens who were selected at random from the electoral register.[58] We need not, however, assume that such citizens' assemblies can only be used for the ad hoc formulation of constitutional policy proposals. Instead, it would be possible to create standing institutions composed of citizens, and allocate to those institutions a range of tasks, among which might be included some role(s) in the legislative process, in addition to various other potential accountability functions.

The proposal for a 'People's Tribunate' outlined by McCormick, for example, would draw on groups of private citizens, selected at random for one-year-long, financially compensated, non-repeatable terms of office. Such tribunes would be obliged to scrutinise the business of government, but also would have select powers to veto one piece of legislation during a one-year term, or initiate one referendum to be held on a legislative proposal which, if approved, would take effect as law.[59] Such 'extra-electoral practices' may provide a way to 'temper the aristocratic biases of elections',[60] and thus potentially provide a means by which the contemporary democratic disillusionment of citizens could, in part, be addressed. There may, of course, be legitimate questions about the democratic character of institutions designed to cultivate 'broader popular participation',[61] perhaps including the compatibility of such devices with the majoritarian conception of democracy relied upon in this book. Much thought also would need to be given to whether it could be appropriate for such institutions to be allocated powers in relation to the legislative process, or whether bodies composed of randomly selected citizens would be better used to hold those elected to exercise power more comprehensively to account. Yet the fact that the manner and form theory of parliamentary sovereignty creates space in which the merits of such institutions can even be debated—above and beyond the more obvious ways in which we might reform the institutions engaged in law-making—demonstrates the advantages of this conception of legislative authority. For, whether such radical change is thought desirable, at least it now stands to be assessed in terms of its appeal from the perspective of democratic political principle, rather than dismissed as constitutionally impossible.

---

[58] See generally www.constitution.ie/Convention.aspx. The Scottish Constitution Convention, established in 1989, and which produced *Scotland's Parliament, Scotland's Right* (1995), a detailed proposal which formed a basis for devolution, was, in contrast, composed of members of some political parties, religious groups, and civil society organisations, rather than 'ordinary' citizens.

[59] J McCormick, *Machiavellian Democracy* (Cambridge, Cambridge University Press, 2011) 182–87.

[60] ibid 187–88.

[61] ibid 17.

B. Reform of Existing Legislative Process

The second category of democratic change to the legislative process which might be explored is to the process itself. There may in fact only be a rather thin line between supplementing the legislative process through the creation of new democratic institutions, as considered immediately above, and injecting new procedural steps into the law-making procedure. The extent to which the former will overlap with the latter will crucially depend on the role which might be allocated to any new such institutions designed. Yet the key mechanism to be considered in this category is, in my view, best characterised as a change of process, rather than as an institutional supplement to those presently in existence. This democratic mechanism is the referendum. While it has always been possible for Parliament to legislate for ad hoc advisory referendums to be held, the manner and form theory allows this to be taken further, enabling Parliament to make approval by a majority of voters at a referendum a mandatory stage in the legislative process. We have already encountered a clear attempt to exploit this potential in the European Union Act 2011 (EUA).[62] Here, however, our focus is on the democratic advantages and disadvantages of the use of such mandatory referendums more generally. In what circumstances, then, could such an alteration of the future legislative process be of potential value?

The significant logistical inconvenience associated with conducting a referendum in a populous democratic society means that we must think carefully about the circumstances in which it would be appropriate for mandatory legislative referendums to be required. To all but the most zealous of direct democrats or the most engaged of citizens, to alter the legislative process so as to make this requirement a permanent element of our ordinary law-making arrangements would seem plainly inappropriate. Yet a strong democratic argument can be made that, even in a system structured principally by reference to the practices of representative democracy, such as the UK, some decisions are of such overriding importance that they must be made by the people directly.[63] Choices about the essential structure and organisation of the political system might in particular be seen to be of the requisite importance to justify being determined at a referendum. For, as Brazier has argued, '[q]uestions relating to the fundamental structure of the constitution are of a higher order of importance than those in other areas of national policy, and that in itself is a reason for resorting to unusual methods to resolve them'.[64] And, indeed, this notion seems clearly reflected in contemporary UK constitutional practice, with national referendums reserved for issues of

---

[62] See chapter 6 of this volume, pp 240–46.

[63] For consideration of the wide-ranging international experience upon which the UK might draw to inform further engagement with referendums, see especially D Butler and A Ranney (eds), *Referendums Around the World: The Growing Use of Direct Democracy* (Basingstoke, Macmillan, 1994).

[64] R Brazier, *Constitutional Reform: Reshaping the British Political System*, 3rd edn (Oxford, Oxford University Press, 2008) 23.

fundamental importance to the structure of our political system.[65] Nonetheless, the use of such referendums has historically been sporadic, and while there may be an emerging consensus that certain kinds of future change would require direct popular approval—the UK's relationship with the EU being the prime example, to an extent which has even outstripped the terms of the EUA itself[66]—in other contexts matters are less clear cut. At what point does further devolution to one of the UK's constituent nations require a referendum to be held?[67] Would reform of the House of Lords (if it ever eventually comes) be subject to popular approval? Would a referendum be required for the implementation of any new Bill of Rights?

This uncertainty might be abated by statutory referendum requirements. Such provisions would further, if respected, offer a guarantee that the UK constitution would be reformed in accordance with the wishes of citizens as directly expressed in relation to a specified matter, rather than (at most) by implication on the basis of their support for a constituency MP. Such statutory referendum requirements could be enacted in a number of ways. Specific legislative guarantees might be put in place in separate statutory schemes relating to separate substantive matters deemed to be of sufficient significance. The EUA might be seen as the forerunner of such an approach, even if the extensive scope of its requirements means that it might be difficult to describe as a model.[68] An alternative approach would be to enact an overarching legislative scheme designed to make general provision as to the circumstances in which referendums are in future to be required as part of the law-making process. In light of the discussion above, this might most appropriately be attempted in relation to issues of fundamental constitutional significance, whether that admittedly general term is defined in the legislation—perhaps by delineating a number of criteria as to what counts as 'constitutional'[69]—or left deliberately open so as to be determined through subsequent political debate in the context of specific circumstances.

Yet while this is made possible by the manner and form theory, would it be democratically desirable to require even legislation concerning matters of transcendent constitutional importance to be approved at a referendum? A number of challenges may be advanced,[70] but of particular importance are claims that the referendum is a 'conservative device' which serves as 'a block on progress'.[71] If

---

[65] See chapter 6 of this volume, pp 264–65.
[66] See chapter 6 of this volume, pp 259–62.
[67] No such referendum was held prior to the enactment of the Scotland Act 2012, for example.
[68] See chapter 6 of this volume, p 254.
[69] For recognition of this difficulty, and an attempt to identify a non-exhaustive list of examples, see House of Lords Select Committee on the Constitution, *Referendums in the United Kingdom: Report with Evidence*, HL Paper 99 (2010), [71]–[94].
[70] See ibid [36]–[63] for a concise overview. I leave aside the frankly patronising objections that citizens are incapable or uninterested in making such decisions for themselves, for, as Bogdanor notes, 'if well-founded' these are 'objections against the principle of democracy itself': Bogdanor, *The New British Constitution* (2009) n 49 above, 301.
[71] ibid [45].

justified, such concern would only be heightened if the manner and form theory of parliamentary sovereignty were exploited to make referendums a binding element of the legislative process, preventing change from otherwise being effected by a simple Act of Parliament. Yet referendums might additionally be seen to be conservative in that they only allow citizens to affirm or reject proposals put before them by the government. In this sense, referendums may serve as a 'tactical weapon' because, at nearly every stage, their use is firmly 'under the control of the political class'.[72] Accordingly, a mandatory referendum requirement may permit citizens to decide whether or not to sanction a change formally put to them, but it will not enable them directly to contribute to the development of the legislative proposal they are invited to endorse. Moreover, and perhaps most troubling from a democratic perspective, referendums may be highly susceptible to capture by elites, whether political—through control of the power to trigger a referendum at a convenient time, or the framing of a referendum question in a particular manner—or economic—through the domination of single issue campaigns by the use of overpowering financial resources.[73] Combining these three factors, mandatory referendums might be said to offer the worst of all worlds, preventing an elected government from promptly implementing desired reform, failing to offer citizens a tangible role in the legislative process, while enhancing already powerful elites.

Such criticisms demand attention, yet referendums may offer greater promise than this account of their deficiencies suggests. Crucially, as Tierney has argued, such disadvantages may present a 'caricature' of referendums, highlighting deficiencies which similarly obtain in the context of representative democratic practice.[74] Instead, if the conduct of referendums is appropriately regulated, problems of elite manipulation can be confronted,[75] and if the opportunities for deliberation among citizens are appropriately structured, the referendum 'can encourage the fuller engagement of citizens and civil society in democratic processes *within* the broader functioning of representative democracy'.[76] One crucial way in which acceptance of the manner and form theory might be understood to challenge concerns about elite control, is that it enables us to define in advance, in statute,

---

[72] Bogdanor, *The New British Constitution* (2009) n 49 above, 304.

[73] See, especially A Lijphart, *Democracies: Patterns of Majoritarian and Consensus Government in Twenty-One Countries* (London, Yale University Press, 1984) 203: 'most referendums are both controlled and pro hegemonic'. On the financial aspects of elite control, see eg K Gilland Lutz and S Hug (eds), *Financing Referendum Campaigns* (Basingstoke, Palgrave Macmillan, 2009).

[74] S Tierney, *Constitutional Referendums: A Theory and Practice of Republican Deliberation* (Oxford, Oxford University Press, 2013) 128.

[75] ibid ch 4.

[76] ibid 299. Making a similar point as to the potential utility of referendums as a supplement to representative democracy, see also L de Luc, *The Politics of Direct Democracy: Referendums in Global Perspective* (Peterborough, Ontario, Broadview Press, 2003) 190–91; M Qvortrup, *A Comparative Study of Referendums: Government by the People*, 2nd edn (Manchester, Manchester University Press, 2005) 88.

the trigger events which will prompt a referendum to be held.[77] Further, there is no conceptual reason that such trigger events must orientated towards elite action, with citizens merely able to anticipate when they may be required to react to proposals for change. Instead, such statutory trigger events could give citizens the opportunity to be proactive, and initiate a referendum on a particular proposal for legislative change.[78] Such mechanisms for the initiation of legislation may present new challenges beyond those pertaining to referendum requirements which are 'merely' reactive[79]—whether normative or simply technical—yet could potentially be accommodated into the law-making process in exercise of the power recognised by the manner and form theory. Finally, while it is possible to conceive of referendum requirements as blocking instruments, this may well be a matter of perspective; it could equally be argued, in contrast, that if the opinion of the electorate is sought, it is inevitable that in some instances it will take a different view to that of the government in power. Yet this is surely the very point of using referendum requirements at all—to ensure that the seminal change which does occur is only that which has, after direct consideration, been democratically authorised by the electorate.

Perhaps the greatest potential benefit of systematically integrating mandatory referendum requirements into statute would be the impact which might be generated beyond that of legitimising isolated decisions. If at least one aspect of the present democratic malaise in the UK is that the system of government is increasingly dominated by an insular 'political class',[80] the systematic use of mandatory referendum requirements could serve to boost popular engagement with the democratic process.[81] Much would, of course, depend on the particular details of any such statutory mechanisms created, and how great a role was envisaged for citizens in the legislative process. But while the focus here has been on engaging citizens in legislation of constitutional significance, if such engagement with direct democratic decision-making proves fruitful, there is no reason that statutory referendum requirements could not also be considered in relation to other important matters of public policy. Advances in technology may already have reached the stage where citizen engagement in legislative decision-making could become relatively regular, although as Barber has argued, 'unless we are clear about what democracy means to us, and what kind of democracy we envision, technology is as likely to stunt as to enhance the civic polity'.[82] How far

---

[77] On the significance of regulating the power to trigger a referendum, see ibid 289–91.

[78] For an overview of initiatives, see Qvortrup, *A Comparative Study of Referendums*, 2nd edn (2005) n 76 above, 60–61.

[79] Although see generally JG Matsusaka, *For the Many or the Few: The Initiative, Public Policy, and American Democracy* (Chicago IL, University of Chicago Press, 2004), for an empirical analysis which largely rejects claims that initiatives allow special interest groups to dominate.

[80] See generally P Oborne, *The Triumph of the Political Class* (London, Simon & Schuster, 2007).

[81] See, eg Bogdanor, *The New British Constitution* (2009) n 49 above, 304–6; Tierney, *Constitutional Referendums* (2013) n 74 above, 302.

[82] BR Barber, 'Three Scenarios for the Future of Technology and Strong Democracy' (1998) 114 *Political Science Quarterly* 573, 584–85.

down the path of direct democratic legislative decision-making we might wish to travel is thus a matter which itself needs to be the subject of democratic political debate. Yet the context of determining fundamental constitutional issues, at the very least, provides a sphere in which these inclinations can further be explored. As Tierney notes, the 'constitutional referendum is a fixed and growing feature of constitutional politics'.[83] As such, one aspect of responding to this unavoidable contemporary challenge is to consider whether, and if so, how, such democratic mechanisms might be accommodated into the legislative process. And if requiring constitutional legislation consistently to be approved directly and democratically would, over time, encourage citizens to reflect on the basic character of the political process, and give real purpose to such reflections, the potential contribution that mandatory referendums could make to the re-invigoration of democratic politics should not be overlooked.

In considering such reform of the legislative process, so as to incorporate mandatory referendum requirements into the procedure for approving the enactment of constitutionally significant legislation, the issue of entrenchment must finally be addressed. If such mandatory legislative requirements were themselves subject to repeal or amendment only if also approved by citizens voting at a referendum, would the additional limit that this would place on the institutions of government render unstable the conclusion that such statutory mechanisms could, in principle, be democratically justifiable? Such entrenchment of referendum requirements would, in my view, be possible to justify from a democratic perspective. For entrenchment of this sort would not violate the majoritarian principle of decision-making; rather, it would relocate the forum in which a final decision was to be taken on a simple majority basis. Nevertheless, while justifiable, such entrenchment would be far from necessary. While some might argue that this would serve to make such 'mandatory' referendum requirements rather more 'optional', this is not inherently the case. Instead, not to entrench such referendum requirements is to rely on the democratic political system, rather than formal legal guarantees, to ensure that such legislative conditions are adhered to. Moreover, such an approach has the advantage of leaving to Parliament a degree of flexibility if—as is arguably the case with respect to the extensive provision made by the EUA, for example[84]—it is somewhat over-enthusiastic in its early experiments with the legislative power to alter the law-making process, and might, in future, opt to modify some of the more esoteric matters which at present would engage a referendum lock. As a result, while entrenchment of referendum requirements could thus in principle be democratically justifiable, it would be better still—from the same democratic perspective—to avoid such legally binding provisions, and allow politics to determine whether there are any (very limited) circumstances in which it would be appropriate for an otherwise

---

[83] Tierney, *Constitutional Referendums* (2013) n 74 above, 303.
[84] See chapter 6 of this volume, p 254.

mandatory requirement to be more straightforwardly removed. In this way, statute can be seen, and used, as an instrument through which predictable citizen engagement in legislative decision-making might be achieved, without assuming that the constitutional force of such commitments to direct democracy must depend on legal permanence.

C. Structural Constitutional Reform

The final category of democratic reform to be considered in this chapter is change to the very architecture of the UK constitution itself. While much formal constitutional change has occurred in the modern era of reform, the basic structure of the constitution remains fundamentally unchanged.[85] The shift from an uncodified constitution comprising statute, convention, prerogative and common law to a codified formative instrument would indisputably be an immense step. Yet despite the flirtations of *The Governance of Britain*,[86] and the persistent enthusiasm of the Liberal Democrats,[87] a move to codify the UK constitution appears a distant prospect at most.[88] For some this will be a matter for regret, for others less so. But what is perhaps the most interesting aspect of the codification debate, a debate which is for now principally academic, is that it unites a number of what Griffith called 'improbable people'.[89] There are a plethora of reasons for favouring structural change to the UK constitution, many of which are not necessarily complementary, and what motivates the pursuit of such reform will therefore vary as between different advocates. This has the potential to be problematic, as codification is not a uniform process which inherently produces homogeneous results, but one that might be approached differently in different conditions. As Brazier has shown, for example, there are various ways in which—and various extents to which—the UK constitution could be codified,[90] and we need to be clear about the impetus for

---

[85] For a contrary suggestion, see V Bogdanor and S Vogenauer, 'Enacting a British Constitution: Some Problems' [2008] *PL* 38, 38–39: 'It seems that we may have been undergoing a process, unique in the democratic world, with the exception of the Israeli experience, of transforming an uncodified constitution into a codified one, gradually and piecemeal without any sort of consensus on what the end result should be'.

[86] *The Governance of Britain*, Green Paper (Cm 7170, 2007), [211]–[215].

[87] The Liberal Democrats, *For the People, By the People* (Policy Paper No 83, 2007) 5–7.

[88] Some of the preparatory work may have been done, however, in the publication of *The Cabinet Manual* (2011) n 16 above. See also the ongoing work of the House of Commons Political and Constitutional Reform Committee as part of its inquiry *Mapping the Path to Codifying—or not Codifying—the UK's Constitution*, which began in 2010. The PCRC produced a consultation document containing three alternative models for a codified constitution—a constitutional code, a Constitutional Consolidation Act, and a written constitution: see *A New Magna Carta?*, HC 463 (10 July 2014).

[89] JAG Griffith, 'The Political Constitution' (1979) 42 *MLR* 1, 12: 'I do not mean that as people they are improbable. But as radicals'.

[90] Brazier, *Constitutional Reform* (2008) n 64 above, 156–57. See also the work of the PCRC at fn 88 above.

reform if we are to identify whether, and to what extent, such change ought to be pursued. Moreover, if the essential arguments in favour of codification can be isolated, then approaches to recalibrating the structure of the UK constitution which look beyond stereotypical ideas of adopting a written constitution might more readily be developed and evaluated. Acceptance of the manner and form theory, in particular, could offer a different means of effecting significant structural reform to the UK constitution which may appeal to those who would otherwise be proponents of full codification in an overarching written text. Such an approach might, moreover, have the advantage of avoiding the potentially disruptive clash that such structural reorganisation might otherwise cause between the doctrine of parliamentary sovereignty and a codified constitutional instrument, both of which seem to claim—whether explicitly or implicitly—to be constitutionally ultimate.

How, then, could the structure of the UK constitution be recalibrated as a result of embracing the manner and form theory of parliamentary sovereignty? While the traditional understanding of parliamentary sovereignty sees all Acts of Parliament as unavoidably equal, the manner and form approach would allow a distinction to be developed between constitutional and ordinary statutes. We have already encountered this distinction, which was invoked by Laws LJ in an attempt to rationalise the domestic supremacy of EU law in *Thoburn v Sunderland City Council*,[91] and has received considerable attention both in subsequent judicial decisions[92] and the academic literature.[93] While I rejected this explanation of the accommodation of EU law into the UK's constitutional system, it was not because the distinction between constitutional and ordinary statutes is inherently unattractive. Instead, I objected to the foundation on which the distinction was said to be based in *Thoburn*, and the implications of this judicial discovery.[94] For Laws LJ, the distinction between constitutional and ordinary legislation was a construct of the common law,[95] but in addition to being entirely unsupported by authority, this suggestion presents a clear challenge to the doctrine of parliamentary sovereignty. The courts cannot be entitled to alter unilaterally the status of certain statutes by imposing legal conditions upon the manner in which Parliament must exercise its sovereign legislative authority. This is unjustifiable in itself, yet also raises further difficulties if, as *Thoburn* might be understood implicitly to promise by extension, the cultivation of *procedural* common law limits on legislative

---

[91] *Thoburn v Sunderland City Council* [2002] EWHC 195, [2003] QB 151.

[92] See, eg *Robinson v Secretary of State for Northern Ireland* [2002] UKHL 32, [2002] NI 390; *H v Lord Advocate* [2012] UKSC 24, [2013] 1 AC 413; *Imperial Tobacco Ltd v Lord Advocate* [2012] UKSC 61, 2013 SC (UKSC) 153; *R (on the application of HS2 Action Alliance Ltd) v Secretary of State for Transport* [2014] UKSC 3, [2014] 1 WLR 324. See generally chapter 4 of this volume, pp 183–91.

[93] See, eg D Feldman, 'The Nature and Significance of "Constitutional" Legislation' (2013) 129 *LQR* 343; S Dimelow, 'The Interpretation of "Constitutional" Statutes' (2013) 129 *LQR* 498; T Khaitan, '"Constitution" as a Statutory Term' (2013) 129 *LQR* 589; D Feldman, 'Statutory Interpretation and Constitutional Legislation' (2014) 130 *LQR* 473.

[94] See chapter 4 of this volume, pp 164–69.

[95] *Thoburn v Sunderland City Council* [2002] EWHC 195, [2003] QB 151, [60]–[64].

authority now might evolve to permit the creation of *substantive* common law limits on legislative authority in the future. If Parliament, however, chose to legislate to introduce a distinction between constitutional and ordinary legislation, these objections would dissolve.

In such circumstances, Parliament would be able to establish the criteria for constitutional legislation, and also what the legal implications of that status would be. It might be that Parliament would wish merely to make such constitutional legislation subject to an express repeal requirement, as was envisaged in *Thoburn*. Alternatively, however, a different process might be established for the amendment of existing constitutional legislation, or even the creation of new constitutional statutes. To be justifiable, such change to the future legislative process for constitutional legislation would need to be democratic in nature. And as considered in the previous section, one such option might be to make the enactment (or repeal) of constitutional legislation subject to approval at a mandatory referendum. There would, no doubt, be difficulties in defining adequate statutory criteria for the determination of what constitutes a 'constitutional' issue.[96] Yet as in the EUA,[97] a combination of general principles and specific events might be used to cover a range of eventualities, even if any such scheme would be likely in practice to be imperfect to some degree. We might also consider, in this context, a right of legislative initiative for citizens, or whether, if some form of standing citizens' assembly were to be created, if it might play a role in the process of enacting such statutes. Perhaps, in particular, such a body might be engaged as an arbitrator to determine whether statutory criteria as to constitutionality had been satisfied, issuing opinions to this effect of either binding or advisory force. But aside from the benefits which might derive from any specific changes to the process by which such fundamental legislation would in future be enacted, could the deliberate cultivation by Parliament of a distinction between constitutional and ordinary statutes have any intrinsic democratic merit? Could, in other words, such differentiation be democratically valuable in itself?

It might be argued that the key virtue of the development of an identifiably discrete class of constitutional legislation would be the potential for such structural reform to enhance the accessibility to citizens of the UK constitution. It is democratically desirable that, so far as possible, a constitution is accessible to the citizens whose state it structures. The accessibility of constitutional rules is crucial, in a democratic society, to enable citizens to analyse the propriety of governmental action, and hold political actors and institutions to account for the exercise of the power conferred upon them. To be accessible, a constitution should be both readily available and comprehensible: citizens should be able to locate the constitutional norms which govern their polity, and when they find them, be able to understand these rules. It is arguable that the UK constitution fails both of these

---

[96] See especially Feldman, 'The Nature and Significance of "Constitutional" Legislation' (2013) n 93 above, 343–54, 357–58, for discussion of how 'tricky' this can be.

[97] See chapter 6 of this volume, pp 240–46.

requirements of accessibility. The constitution unfolds in a perplexing array of sources, many of which—and perhaps especially the royal prerogative and constitutional conventions—are difficult to trace, let alone understand. Moreover, the interplay between these various different constitutional norms, against a backdrop of often obscure constitutional principles, presents a further challenge to comprehension. Constitutional discourse in the UK might thus appear distinctively elitist to citizens, with knowledge of archaic institutions, unwritten understandings and the circumstances in which there exists a dissonance between the law and practice essential to enable authentic participation. Perhaps it may be objected that all constitutional rules in all jurisdictions will inevitably be inaccessible, regardless of the formal structure in which they are located, because they must be aimed at those actors who are engaged in the day-to-day conduct of government, rather than the public at large. Yet even if this were the case—and it would surely be a matter for great regret if it were—the UK constitution may still be said to present a particularly good example of constitutional inaccessibility, in that even the most basic rules governing the powers of key institutions—the Prime Minister, the Cabinet, the monarch, the Privy Council—are far from readily visible.[98]

Complete codification of the UK constitution in a core legal instrument may appear to offer a solution to this inaccessibility, yet it would be potentially undesirable in a number of ways.[99] The exercise itself would be a complex and potentially divisive undertaking. It may inhibit the prospect of future reform. And while not inherently incompatible with the notion of a legally sovereign Parliament, the adoption of such a codified constitution would, at the very least, be likely to render uncertain the future stability of the doctrine, at a time when its authority is already consistently—if, as I have argued in this book, wrongly—questioned. In light of such uncertainty, the role of the courts under a codified constitution, unless very carefully framed, would thus be liable to expand.[100] In contrast, the existing system, even if inaccessible in some crucial respects, has merits that must still be acknowledged. In particular, as emphasised in Chapter seven, there is considerable value in the use of political norms, expectations and principles to structure and condition governmental behaviour and activity, and, were this even possible, we should be reluctant to see such mechanisms either largely or entirely displaced by the legal regulation of constitutional conduct.[101] If constitutional disputes are to be settled in a way which is accessible to citizens, it is far from clear

---

[98] Perhaps *The Cabinet Manual* (2011) n 16 above, provides some assistance here, but as an executive-focused document, produced (and to be maintained) by the executive itself, we might question whether this is an appropriate or sufficiently accessible source of constitutional rules for citizens. It is certainly not the intention of *The Cabinet Manual* to provide a guide for citizens, as it is 'primarily a guide for those working in government': iv.

[99] For an overview of the issues, see eg Bogdanor and Vogenauer, 'Enacting a British Constitution: Some Problems' [2008] n 85 above; NW Barber, 'Against a Written Constitution' [2008] *PL* 11; J Baker, 'The Unwritten Constitution of the United Kingdom' (2013) 15 *Ecclesiastical Law Journal* 4.

[100] See generally House of Commons Political and Constitutional Reform Committee, *Constitutional Role of the Judiciary if there were a Codified Constitution*, HC 802 (14 May 2014).

[101] See chapter 7 of this volume, pp 293–301.

that the legal arena—in which even greater barriers to citizen engagement and understanding are arguably presented—provides an agreeable solution.

The adoption of a scheme of constitutional legislation, of Parliament's design, might provide scope for us to respond to some of the problems posed by inaccessibility, while avoiding a shift away from the most important elements of the political constitution. The clear identification of statutes which are of constitutional significance, on the basis of their explicit designation as such by Parliament, could make it easier for citizens to retrieve, understand and utilise constitutional rules, a process which is crucial to the healthy functioning of democratic politics. Further, if such a basis for a new constitutional architecture were embraced, Parliament might even be induced or incentivised to augment those constitutional statutes which are presently in existence with additional Acts of Parliament collating and updating constitutional norms. The royal prerogative powers would, in particular, be an obvious candidate to be accommodated within such a statutory scheme. The development of the Basic Laws of Israel might offer an illustration of the kind of approach to reform that this altered constitutional structure could encourage.[102] Parliament would remain central, and could reform the constitution in 'chapters',[103] producing a comprehensible constitutional structure, which could be more accessible to citizens, while also ideally engaging them in the process of reform itself. Yet there would be no requirement for this scheme to be comprehensive, or for all conventional norms and political principles to be legalised. Instead, the designation of certain statutes as constitutional might be thought simply to offer more coherence to the UK's political constitution as presently arranged, without abandoning the basic tenets on which it is already founded. Indeed, if the UK's political system continues to evolve, through devolution, from that of a more traditional unitary state to something resembling a quasi-federal order,[104] a scheme of constitutional legislation—amendable in accordance with statutory referendum requirements—may eventually become required to provide a more settled shape to a transformed polity.

Of course, again, such suggestions for structural constitutional reform would require further and thorough consideration. In this context, as much as any, the real success of such a project would inevitably depend on whether there existed the political will to commit to a significant programme of constitutional reform, substantive as well as structural in nature. Yet, should such political will ever be generated, acceptance of the manner and form theory offers a fresh perspective on our options to shape the UK's future constitutional architecture. And in allowing us to reclaim the idea of constitutional statutes from the courts, this conception of parliamentary sovereignty establishes two key points. First, we need not assume that cultivation of a distinction between ordinary and constitutional legislation,

---

[102] See generally Z Segal, 'A Constitution Without a Constitution: The Israeli Experience and the American Impact' (1992) 21 *Capital University Law Review* 1–62, 19–22.

[103] ibid 20.

[104] See, eg N Walker, 'Beyond the Unitary Conception of the UK Constitution?' [2000] *PL* 384.

whatever this is understood to mean, is a common law project which inherently excludes other political actors, especially Parliament, or citizens in general, from that process. Secondly, we need not assume that in adopting some more formal, accessible constitutional structure for the UK, whether cautiously over time or rapidly if made more urgent by future events, the notion of legally unlimited legislative authority would necessarily be displaced. In both of these ways, this potential approach to changing the structure of the UK constitution, through altering the law-making process for the enactment (or repeal) of constitutional legislation, can be seen as fundamentally democratic in character. In making it available, the manner and form theory thus provides a further way in which the foundations of the UK's political constitution might be refreshed, while avoiding the risk that valuable principles might be lost as part of a shift to a dramatic new constitutional paradigm.

V. THE SEEDS OF DESTRUCTION? LEGALLY UNLIMITED LEGISLATIVE POWER AND PARLIAMENTARY SOVEREIGNTY

There may be legitimate disagreement about the desirability of some, or all, of the examples of democratic reform to the legislative process considered in this chapter. It is nevertheless clear that the adoption of manner and form theory of parliamentary sovereignty creates new possibilities for reforming the UK's political constitution. The legislative institutions or the legislative process may be reformed in a variety of ways which are not exhausted by the initial proposals for democratic change sketched here. Moreover, in changing the legislative process applicable to the enactment (or repeal) of constitutional legislation, structural reform of the UK's constitution might be achieved. Such a scheme has the potential to enhance the (presently lacking) accessibility to citizens of fundamental constitutional norms—which would be of democratic virtue in itself—without the loss of key tenets of the political constitution in an overarching codified legal architecture. Yet the appeal of the manner and form theory is not contingent upon these particular proposals being accepted. Instead, it is enough to recognise the *potential* utility of the manner and form theory, in expanding our ability to think about the possible future(s) of the UK constitution, for the value of this conception of parliamentary sovereignty to become apparent. Most significantly, the change explored in this chapter has, whether considered discretely or collectively, at least the potential further to engage citizens in the legislative process. In an age of significant democratic disillusionment, such innovations—if combined with attempts to engage citizens directly in other crucial political and constitutional activities, such as the holding of elected or non-elected public officials to account—could contribute to an (urgently required) re-invigoration of the UK's political constitution, and therefore deserve serious consideration.

In this final section, the potential implications of the modern shift to the manner and form theory in the contemporary UK constitution, and the possible uses of this power further to alter the future legislative process, will be considered. In particular, a key question is prompted by the opportunities for democratic constitutional reform sketched in this chapter: does the manner and form theory sow the seeds of the destruction of the doctrine of parliamentary sovereignty itself? The difficulty with proposals for Parliament to use its power to invite other actors into the legislative process is that, if heavily exploited, the 'parliamentary' in parliamentary sovereignty may appear strained, if not outright misleading. We cannot, and should not, try to rationalise this difficulty away by resorting to suggestions that Parliament has simply redefined itself. Such artificiality is itself highly misleading,[105] and would, in any event, only serve to suppress the under- lying problem: where can legally unlimited legislative authority be understood to be located in a constitution which supplements representative parliamentary decision-making with regular direct interventions from citizens?

In addressing this potential challenge to parliamentary sovereignty, it is initially worth noting that the circumstances in which this objection could credibly be advanced are, at present, a long way off. Even the frequent use of mandatory statu- tory referendum requirements would not endanger the 'parliamentary' in parlia- mentary sovereignty, for a number of reasons. First, such requirements would be imposed at Parliament's initiative, and if not entrenched—which, as I have sug- gested above, is the approach which can be most readily justified—they could, as a matter of legal principle, and in exceptional political circumstances, be removed at Parliament's initiative. Secondly, if, as would be most likely, such statutory referendum requirements were used in relation to fundamental constitutional legislation only, or matters of general public policy of equivalent significance, they would be exceptional, rather than regular, features of the legislative process. The vast bulk of legislative activity could still rightly be expected to be undertaken by Parliament. Thirdly, a referendum requirement should not be seen as extending a veto to a body external to Parliament. Instead, the electorate is the body from which Parliament derives its legislative power, and we can therefore regard ref- erendum requirements as a request for an affirmation of democratic mandate, rather than a mechanism which diminishes the authority of the legislature.[106]

Nevertheless, in principle it is possible that, in time, with increasing reliance on direct democratic decision-making—perhaps including mechanisms for the enactment of legislation at the initiative of citizens, or integrating standing institutions akin to citizens' assemblies fully into the law-making process—this defence of the primacy of Parliament as the fundamental legislative body would become more difficult to sustain. Yet if this were to become the case in the UK constitution, it might not be a matter for great regret. The democratic virtue of the doctrine of parliamentary sovereignty is that it ensures the primacy of democratic decision-making. Yet, as I suggested in Chapter one, there are two

---

[105] See chapter 6 of this volume, p 270.
[106] See chapter 6 of this volume, pp 271–73.

elements to this claim: (i) that a democratic institution (ii) should possess legally unlimited legislative authority. If our understanding of what constitutes an optimally democratic decision-making institution evolves over time, perhaps as ideas of democratic legitimacy evolve, there is no reason why the 'parliamentary' and the 'sovereignty' in this fundamental constitutional doctrine should not be disaggregated. In other words, if a new democratic institutional focus, or set of legislative arrangements, becomes available, which could be considered more democratic than an elected representative assembly, the constitutional location of legally unlimited legislative power—or (legislative) 'sovereignty'—could legitimately be shifted from its present 'parliamentary' site. Crucially, however, there is no reason to believe that if the 'parliamentary' goes, the 'sovereignty' must go with it. Legislative authority does not need to be vested in a single institution for it to be recognised as legally unlimited. Instead, if that power can be used to legislate about any substantive matter whatever, and it is not subject to legal limits enforced by courts, it can conceptually be considered as a successor to the power possessed at present by the UK Parliament.

Perhaps the difficulty here, however, is that this might *only conceptually* be the case. For if, in practice, law-making power were to be shared among a number of discrete institutions, rather than vested in a single legislature, claims that legislative power was legally unlimited might appear to be a rather artificial technicality. If such power were to be shared among institutions which were engaged in a common process for the enactment of legislation on any topic, this might be less problematic. For if, to draw on our present arrangements for an example, the House of Commons and House of Lords do not agree on a Bill, and it is not enacted, this is a failure of political initiative, rather than a legal limitation on legislative power. The real challenge, however, might be if in disaggregating the 'parliamentary' from the 'sovereignty' in the UK constitution, legislative power were shared between institutions in a different sense. In particular, we might consider the example of the introduction of federal arrangements, with substantive power for certain matters allocated to legislative institutions in each of the separate constituent nations of the UK, and substantive power over other matters allocated to central UK legislative institutions. In such circumstances, it might be possible to suggest, in one sense, that legally unlimited legislative power were vested in the constitutional arrangements as a whole. But, in another sense, difficulties would arise as to the monitoring of the boundaries of competence between competing legislative institutions at the national and federal levels of political activity. And, were the courts asked to enforce these legal boundaries, then legally unlimited legislative power, in the sense we presently experience it in the UK, might simply be superseded.

Such potential difficulties might indicate that we should proceed with care if the question of the disaggregation of the doctrine of parliamentary sovereignty is ever, in future, provoked by shifts in UK constitutional practice. The challenge posed by what might come next could be significant, and while a more democratic set of institutional arrangements for legislative authority may, at some stage, need to be crafted, if law-making power is to be more widely dispersed from the centre, this may place (also democratic) ideas of legislative sovereignty in jeopardy. Yet this would not need to be the case. Instead, we might need to think creatively about how the notion of legally unlimited legislative power which underpins the traditional constitutional foundation of parliamentary sovereignty could be transposed into a new institutional framework. Critical to this process would be recognising the limits of legal restrictions on law-making authority, enforced by courts, and reflecting on how democratic political conditions might instead be used to structure power, even as between competing legislative institutions. Clearly, this would require an elaborate scheme of informal and formal mechanisms to encourage the settlement of institutional disputes through debate, mediation, arbitration and—perhaps ultimately, if compromises could not be achieved—use of direct democratic instruments leaving to citizens the final say on the constitutionality of proposed legislative action.

Such an approach to constitutional design would no doubt pose a significant range of challenges. But the democratic principle that legislative authority should be legally unlimited is one which, in my view, is worth attempting to protect, even if its traditional, and perhaps most natural vessel, the doctrine of parliamentary sovereignty, is eventually overtaken by events. This, I should emphasise, is something that appears a distant prospect, if indeed it is ever to transpire in the UK. It may, moreover, be that the extent to which the UK is already necessarily embedded in inter- and supra-national legal orders that require judicial enforcement of limits on legislative power—in particular the EU—may make this seem unimaginable. If that is the case, the doctrine of parliamentary sovereignty is one which we may need to continue to work to preserve. In this sense, it may be that continued adherence to the language of parliamentary sovereignty is, in itself, as important in maintaining the constitutional primacy of democratic decision-making as the broader principle of legally unlimited legislative authority to which the doctrine serves to give effect. Yet the democratic significance of sustaining this underlying principle, and ensuring that (political) legislative authority is not subject to substantive legal limitations, ultimately defined and imposed by the judiciary, should also not be underestimated. And as a result, it should not be assumed that the only way in which this democratic principle could ever be constitutionally manifested is through a doctrine of legislative sovereignty. How in fact the notion of legally unlimited legislative authority might be secured in an alternative constitutional framework must be a matter for the future, but we would be wrong to embark on such a task convinced of its impossibility. If nothing else, the idea of legally unlimited legislative authority ought to be kept on the menu of future options for constitutional design, so as to provide a corrective against the view that a legalistic constitutional paradigm—in which politics is framed and controlled by law—must inevitably be endorsed.

For now, though, the doctrine of parliamentary sovereignty can be maintained. Understood in accordance with the manner and form theory, this fundamental norm of the UK constitution is capable of providing a solid foundation around which our political constitution could be restructured to greater democratic effect. Some of these potential paths of constitutional reorganisation may be more appealing than others; all, in my view, deserve to be the subject of thorough consideration and debate. Yet the fact that acceptance of the manner and form theory of parliamentary sovereignty has the function of opening up the possibility of these constitutional futures, demonstrates an essential virtue of a constitution founded upon a doctrine of legally unlimited legislative authority. Both in thinking about how we might legislate about the legislative process to re-invigorate the UK's contemporary political constitution, and in the contemplation of our more distant constitutional prospects, such a democratic virtue is one worthy of continued respect.

VI. CONCLUSION

The potential utility of the manner and form theory is significant. The expanded legislative power which this conception of parliamentary sovereignty recognises—the power to legislate to alter the future law-making process—has a range of potential applications. While the scope of this power is extensive as a matter of law, a political condition of use attaches to structure its exercise: to be justified, change to the future manner and form must be democratic in nature. This condition, which derives from the democratic justification of the manner and form theory developed in Chapter seven, serves to focus our attention on change which removes undemocratic influences on the legislative process, or introduces new, more democratic influences into that same process. We have explored three examples of democratic reform to the legislative process which the manner and form theory makes possible, and which might, in part, allow us to respond to the present democratic malaise of the UK's political constitution.

This might, first, include removing undemocratic institutions from the legislative process—such as the monarch or the House of Lords—while introducing new democratic arrangements—perhaps by allocating a role in the law-making process to citizens' assembles. Secondly, this might include the use of mandatory statutory referendum requirements, offering the electorate in its entirety a direct role in the legislative decision-making process in appropriate circumstances. Thirdly, reform to the structure of the UK constitution might be contemplated, cultivating a distinction between constitutional and ordinary legislation, with the former to be enacted or repealed in accordance with some special—and democratic—process. Such structural reform may, moreover, have the advantage of enhancing the accessibility of constitutional rules to citizens, and the coherence of our constitutional arrangements in general, while avoiding a shift away from the democratic political constitution to a codified legal instrument. In presenting us with these new possibilities for constitutional change, by permitting the sovereign Parliament to legislate about the legislative process, the normative appeal of the manner and form theory is further reinforced: it is a conception of parliamentary sovereignty which is democratically justified in principle, while also democratically valuable for constitutional practice.

In the context of the manner and form theory of parliamentary sovereignty, then, the relationship between process, politics and democracy becomes clear. The manner and form theory—in emerging as the best explanation of contemporary constitutional practice in the UK—recognises that Parliament has the lawful power to legislate to change the legislative process. The use of this power to alter the legislative process is conditioned by politics, justified by democracy, and offers the potential to re-invigorate the democratic foundations of the UK's political constitution.

Index